The Sleep of Reason

The Sleep of Reason

EROTIC EXPERIENCE AND SEXUAL ETHICS
IN ANCIENT GREECE AND ROME

Edited by

MARTHA C. NUSSBAUM
AND JUHA SIHVOLA

THE UNIVERSITY OF CHICAGO PRESS
CHICAGO AND LONDON

Martha C. Nussbaum is the Ernst Freund Distinguished Service Professor of Law and Ethics at the University of Chicago. She is the author, most recently, of *Women and Human Development: The Capabilities Approach* and *Upheavals of Thought: The Intelligence of Emotions.* Juha Sihvola is professor of history at the University of Jyväskylä, Finland. He is the author of *Decay, Progress, and the Good Life? Hesiod and Protagoras on the Development of Culture* and the editor of *Ancient Scepticism and the Scepticist Tradition.*

The University of Chicago Press, Chicago 60637
The University of Chicago Press, Ltd., London
© 2002 by The University of Chicago
All rights reserved. Published 2002
Printed in the United States of America

11 10 09 08 07 06 05 04 03 02   1 2 3 4 5
ISBN: 0-226-60914-6 (cloth)
ISBN: 0-226-60915-4 (paper)

Library of Congress Cataloging-in-Publication Data

The sleep of reason : erotic experience and sexual ethics in ancient Greece and Rome / edited by Martha C. Nussbaum and Juha Sihvola.
　　p.　cm.
　Includes bibliographical references and index.
　ISBN 0-226-60914-6 (cloth : alk. paper)—ISBN 0-226-60915-4 (pbk. : alk. paper)
　　1. Sex customs—Greece—History—Congresses.　2. Sex customs—Rome—Congresses.　3. Sexual ethics—Greece—History—Congresses.　4. Sexual ethics—Rome—Congresses.　5. Greece—Civilization—To 146 B.C.—Congresses.　6. Rome—Civilization—Congresses.　I. Nussbaum, Martha Craven, 1947–　II. Sihvola, Juha.
　HQ13 .S54 2002
　306.7'0938—dc21
                                                    2001052755

This book is printed on acid-free paper.

Contents

Acknowledgments

$\mathcal{T}$his volume derives from a conference held at the Finnish Institute at Rome (*Institutum Romanum Finlandiae*) in 1997, itself part of a series of conferences held beginning in 1991, aimed at bringing Finnish scholars in ancient Greek and Roman philosophy into closer contact with scholars from other parts of the world. (All the other conferences have been held at the University of Helsinki.) A conference in 1991 on ancient Greek rhetoric and its philosophical treatment inaugurated the series. It was followed in 1994 by a conference on Hellenistic philosophy of mind, now published as *The Emotions in Hellenistic Philosophy*, edited by Juha Sihvola and Troels Engberg-Pedersen (The Netherlands: Kluwer, 1998). A conference in 1996 on ancient Greek skepticism is now published as *Ancient Scepticism and the Sceptical Tradition*, edited by Juha Sihvola, in the series Acta Philosophica Fennica (Helsinki: Philosophical Society of Finland, 2000). A conference in 2001, at the University of Jyväskylä, addressed the relationship between philosophical theory and political practice. All of the conferences were supported in part by funding from the Academy of Finland, to which we express warm thanks. The Finnish Cultural Foundation also supported our efforts, and we also express warm thanks to them, and to Paavo Hohti.

The conference in Rome was made possible by the gracious hospitality of Paivi Setälä, then director of the Finnish Institute at Rome. We are enormously grateful to her for her enthusiasm for our project, her scholarly participation, and all the arrangements she made to receive an unusually large and diverse group of scholars on the premises of the institute. The institute's beautiful site on the Janiculum, commanding an extraordinary view of the entire city, was an ideal setting for discussion and collegiality. The nearby American Academy at Rome provided lodging for some of the conference participants.

The editors wish to express their warmest thanks to Doug Mitchell, the editor who shaped the volume and encouraged us at every stage; to Neil A. Coffee for his meticulous and judicious reading of the proofs; and to Rick A. Furtak for his excellent work preparing the indices.

Introduction

Martha C. Nussbaum and Juha Sihvola

What desires do you mean?

Those that are awakened in sleep, when the rest of the soul—the rational, gentle, and ruling part—slumbers. Then the beastly and savage part, full of food and drink, casts off sleep and seeks to find a way to gratify itself. You know that there is nothing it won't dare to do at such a time, free of all control by shame or reason. It doesn't shrink from trying to have sex with a mother, as it supposes, or with anyone else at all, whether man, god, or beast. It will commit any foul murder, and there is no food it refuses to eat. In a word, it omits no act of folly or shamelessness.

That's completely true.

On the other hand, I suppose that someone who is healthy and moderate with himself goes to sleep only after having done the following: First, he rouses his rational part and feasts it on fine arguments and speculations; second, he neither starves nor feasts his appetites, so that they will slumber and not disturb his best part with either their pleasure or their pain, but they'll leave it alone, pure and by itself, to look for something—it knows not what—and to try to perceive it, whether it is past, present, or future.

Plato, *Republic* 571C–D

1

This domain of phantasms is no longer the night, the sleep of reason, or the uncertain void that stands before desire, but, on the contrary, wakefulness, untiring attention, zealous erudition, and constant vigilance.

Michel Foucault, "Fantasia of the Library"

$\mathcal{S}$ex eludes rational control, and yet, for that very reason, it is constantly reasoned about. And so it was, intensely, in ancient Greece and Rome. Together with ubiquitous allusion to the ungovernable properties of sexual desire and erotic love went an outpouring of reasoned ethical argument, and often philosophical argument, about the management of desire. Most ancient Greeks and Romans would have agreed, to at least some extent, with Socrates and Glaucon: the appetites are very difficult to manage by reason, and the sexual appetite perhaps most difficult of all. And yet they did not give up, any more than Socrates does. Just as Plato's Socrates proposes an elaborate program of philosophical discipline to control the erotic content of dreams, so in countless ways the Greeks and Romans reasoned ethically about sex, calling philosophy to their aid. From the time of Socrates onward, philosophy of one sort or another was ubiquitous in discussions of sexual ethics, and the philosophers, for their part, were less detached academicians than immersed cultural participants, who took their problems from the culture and hoped to shape the culture in their turn. They proposed arguments about sexual problems, and they also, as does Socrates, proposed practices of self-management that went with the arguments.

Michel Foucault, in the passage we have taken as our second epigraph, speaks of the modern period when he speaks of a constant discourse about sex that exercises constant vigilance and creates a proliferation of categories, shaping not only discourse, but also action and even desire. But as his important writings on Greek and Roman antiquity show, he also believed that this description applied to the Greeks. The classification of pleasures, the obsessive watching over the self, the participation of philosophy in the attempt to turn lawless dreams into good dreams: Foucault was right to see in all of this an enduring preoccupation of the ancient Greek philosophical tradition and of its Roman continuations.

But although sexual ethics is obviously a very important part of the work of the ancient Greek and Roman philosophers, until recently scholars of these philosophical traditions had done little to address this portion of their work and their cultural influence. There were several causes of this omission. First, a dominant Anglo-American conception of what topics were philosophical and what topics were not put sex, and even love and friendship, on the outside of philosophy. In the shadow of logical positivism, all topics concerned with value were suspect. Even ethics and politics could win their place in the curriculum most easily by focusing on the study of ethical and political language. This legacy of the positivist era derived further support from a peculiar British-American prudery that put some topics off limits to the serious academic. These topics included love and friendship, about which it seemed difficult to speak without sentimentality and gush. These topics were thought "womanly," meaning not serious; and so women, if they wanted to be taken seriously, had to avoid them all the more. And the list of forbidden topics included, above all, certain subjects that were not in any case regarded as fit for public discourse in good society.

Although prudish reticence about sex was perfectly general in Anglo-American scholarship of the Victorian and post-Victorian era, the Greeks came in for a disproportionate share of it, because anyone could see that many of their discussions focused on same-sex acts and desire. But same-sex activity, while widely practiced, and publicly recognized by law and penalty, was not one of the things concerning which it was thought fit to speak, especially in the presence of the impressionable young. Typical, in the post-Victorian era (which extended, in classical scholarship, all the way into the 1960s) was the response of Clive and Maurice's tutor, in E. M. Forster's *Maurice*. When the undergraduates reach the part of Plato's *Phaedrus* where same-sex passion is described in moving poetic language, this tutor dryly observes: "Omit: a reference to the unspeakable vice of the Greeks." Many translations, and even some editions of the original texts, followed this advice, omitting sexually explicit material even at the price of conveying a totally misleading impression of the texts and the cultures from which they derived. Lexica and other expert tools of scholarship offered the scholar no assistance in discovering the meaning of erotic images and terms. (It was common to find "unnatural vice" or "a beastly act" listed under quite a few different definienda, with no guidance as to which putatively unnatural or beastly act was designated by the term in question. The student of Catullus who wanted help distinguishing *pedicare* (to play the penetrative role in an anal sex act) from *irrumare* (to play the penetrative role in an oral sex act) would have had none from the dictionary of those days, and this was the situation generally, in both languages. Most bizarre was the behavior of the Loeb Classical Library, a set of facing-page Greek-English and Latin-English translations. When the Greek was sexually explicit, the English on the right-hand page abruptly switched to Latin. And when the Latin was explicit, in the old edition of the poet Martial, the right-hand page switched to *Italian*—as if any foreign tongue at all would protect the young scholar from contact with potentially corrupting material. (These defective editions have now all been replaced.) This situation, of course, made it more or less impossible to do good scholarship on the sexual aspects of literary and philosophical texts.

There is a less obvious further reason why there was no good scholarship on ancient Greek and Roman sexual ethics until recently. To do good scholarship on ancient Greek and Roman philosophy it is necessary to link the writings of the philosophers to their historical and social context. This need is less acute when the topic is logic, mathematics, cosmology, or the philosophy of language, for these are all, in a way, specialized philosophical topics, and the philosophers were not so greatly in conversation with other cultural practitioners when they addressed them. But when the topic is ethics or politics, the need to do interdisciplinary scholarship becomes very great. It is extremely difficult to understand the force and meaning of Plato's and Aristotle's proposals, or even their terminology, without an extensive study of popular morality, difficult though that is to study well. When the topic is sex, the need is perhaps greatest of all, for it is really next to impossible to understand what the philosophers are saying without extensive study of cultural paradigms, of a sort that requires familiarity with history, literature, and visual art. Greek and Roman philosophers talking about sex are likely to be indirect, discrete, and elliptical, so if we look only at what they say, we are likely to miss many insights that a study of the Greek orators, of Aristophanes, and of vase painting will reveal to us, insights that ultimately prove essential to the full decoding of what the philosophers say.

Obvious though this point should have been, it was not taken to heart until very recently. Classics is an interdisciplinary discipline: art history, epigraphy, papyrology, philosophy, philology, literature, history, linguistics, science, gender studies, and no doubt other disciplinary approaches are all in there together, inhabiting the same department or faculty, and one might expect rich interdisciplinary work to flower in such an atmosphere. Sometimes this has happened, but more often each subfield has tended to go its own way, linking itself more to its subject discipline (philosophy, history, art history) than to the work of other students of the same time and place who are their colleagues.

This segmentation of classical scholarship did particular damage to the study of ancient ethical thought, because philosophers were more than usually cut off from their partners in classical scholarship. Ancient historians sometimes belong to a history department, but usually they also belong to the classics department and at least encounter literary scholars at department meetings. The extraordinary revival of first-rate study of the ancient Greek philosophers that began after the Second World War, led by the work of G. E. L. Owen in Britain and Gregory Vlastos in the United States, took place almost entirely within philosophy departments, or, in Oxford, in the philosophy subfaculty. (Cambridge was always an anomaly, since ancient philosophy has always remained in the faculty of classics. This has done some good to interdisciplinary scholarship, and some harm to conversations with other philosophers.) The main concern of Owen, Vlastos, and most of their pupils was to establish that the ancient thinkers had something philosophically interesting to say, and to show what that was. This was, and is, a wonderful way of approaching these thinkers, and it has produced work of lasting importance. But it was insufficient, and it proved particularly narrow in the area of ethics and politics, where knowledge of history and culture is especially crucial. Owen, an extremely knowledgeable classicist and historian of science, did wonderful interdisciplinary work himself in the area of science and mathematics. His work was always informed by close philological scrutiny and by attention to historical context. But he had little interest in ethics, and he did not encourage his pupils to gain the sort of knowledge of ancient history and literature that would be required to approach ethical topics in a subtle contextual manner. Moreover, he had a profound aversion to topics dealing with love or even friendship and mocked them extremely. Sex itself did not appear to him to be a topic of serious academic study. Vlastos was far more interested in these topics, and strongly encouraged his students to pursue them, and yet one may feel even in Vlastos's own work an undue isolation of the philosophical texts from their cultural surroundings.

If the great scholars were too narrow, their pupils were typically more so. In Oxford, the ascendancy of PPE (philosophy, politics, and economics) over greats (a course that combined ancient Greek and Roman history, philosophy, and literature with modern philosophy) as the primary degree course for young philosophers meant that scholars of ancient Greek philosophy who wanted to be taken seriously as philosophers had increasingly to commend the Greeks to peers who had only a glancing acquaintance, if any, with the texts, and almost no acquaintance with their surrounding culture. This exacerbated an already existing tendency to write about Greek philosophy in a detached acontextual way. High-level discussion groups focusing on Greek philosophy almost never sought out the participation of the leading scholars in ancient history and literature who worked on related topics. And the Roman thinkers who seemed hard to study acontextually, and equally hard to commend, as philosophers, to analytic philosophers who were ignorant of ancient cultures, played almost no role in the curriculum.

In the United States, things proceeded in a similar way, but even more extremely. Most American scholars of ancient Greek and Roman philosophy start their study of the languages very late, in college or even in graduate school. This means that they have little time to get the kind of competence that would make it possible for them to read ancient historical and literary authors, or to gain the respect of expert classical scholars in these areas. Teaching, typically, almost entirely within departments of philosophy, they teach almost always from translations and do not get the practice in being a classical scholar that might over time lead them in the direction of new interdisciplinary work. Quite a few expert scholars of ancient Greek philosophy do not know Latin at all, so the study of Roman figures, so important for the topic of sexual ethics, suffers greatly. (Even though, obviously, many Roman thinkers write in Greek, scholars who do not know Latin ought to discourage themselves, and usually do, from pronouncing on such authors when they cannot read the language in which other contemporaries were writing and in which the thinkers themselves probably spoke. Thus, it is unwise to write on Epictetus and Marcus if you cannot read Cicero and Seneca in the original!) Often the leading experts are active as philosophers in other contemporary areas and spend a lot of their time that way, rather than reading ancient history; always they are eager to attract the attention of those who are active in other areas of the philosophical profession. Young scholars have to appeal to philosophers in other areas if they want to get jobs at all. All this shapes, in some ways for the good, but in other ways for the bad, the nature of scholarly work, making philosophical scholars not always the best of commentators on areas that need interdisciplinary cultural understanding to be well studied.

And yet the philosophers have some essential insights to contribute to the study of ancient Greek and Roman sexual ethics. For, as the essays in this volume will show, these two cultures were suffused with argument about sex, much of it deriving from philosophy. Although the nature of that diffusion varies with period and place, from the time of Plato to the second century A.D. it is difficult to study sexual ethics well without understanding the contributions of the philosophers. But understanding the contributions of the philosophers to cultural conversation is not a matter of casually pulling out this or that nugget of insight about sex; usually it requires a much deeper and more extensive study of their arguments, as they discuss sexual matters in the whole context of a philosophical system with elaborate views about mind, emotion, and ethical value. Philosophy is an expert discipline, and training in the analysis of arguments does enable people to go much further with the analysis of Plato and Seneca than they could go starting from literature or cultural history alone. So the absence of the philosophers from a developing scholarly dialogue about sexual ethics has done real damage.

By now, we have all the basic equipment we need to do good interdisciplinary work on ancient Greek and Roman sexual ethics. Foucault's general description of modernity, quoted above, applies with considerable force to the current situation in classical scholarship. The erotic domain is no longer a silent space, the "uncertain void that stands before desire." Erotic life has become a central scholarly preoccupation. Sex acts, sexual desires and fantasies, the ethics of sexual conduct in different times and places—all are now pored over with "wakefulness, untiring attention, zealous erudition, and constant vigilance." This description is true of scholarship on sexuality in almost any area of the humanities and the social sciences. But in no area of scholarly endeavor is this shift more striking than the study of ancient Greece and Rome.

Kenneth Dover's *Greek Homosexuality,* originally published in 1978, inaugurated an era in which honest and meticulous scholarship, unimpeded by prudery or embarrassment, confronted the difficult problems of reconstructing the history of sexual activity and desire. It might have been Dover whom Foucault was describing, for it is hard to imagine a scholar whose work on the previously hidden domain of sexual life is more characterized by wakefulness, untiring attention, zealous erudition, and constant vigilance—and one should surely add to these a somewhat un-Foucauldian virtue that is absolutely central in Dover's canon, the love of truth.

A few years after Dover's magisterial volume appeared, the second and third volumes of Michel Foucault's *History of Sexuality,* building on Dover's pathbreaking historical research, advanced the conceptual sophistication of the enterprise by posing significant questions about the parochialism of the very concepts through which we had investigated the ancient world. Foucault took Dover's analysis one step further: the cultures of Greece and Rome confront us not only with different norms for behavior and desire, but also with different basic concepts and categories. (So much is implicit in Dover's work, but he did not develop this idea explicitly in a general comparative manner.) Foucault argued persuasively, for example, that our own strong binary division between homosexual and heterosexual orientation did not exist in anything like the same form in the ancient Greek world, nor did that world contain the idea that sexuality is an area of special moral anxiety, which at the same time contains the inmost secrets of one's being. Both Dover and Foucault showed how thoroughly the sexual domain is shaped by social norms, and they persuasively argued that these norms affect desire itself, not merely its expression in conduct.

These works have generated a great deal of valuable scholarship, including theoretical work, historical reconstructions, and detailed readings of texts of many different times. Scholars such as David Halperin and the late John J. Winkler have extended Foucault's theoretical contribution with detailed readings of particular texts and issues. Recently Craig Williams's first-rate *Roman Homosexuality* has emerged, a long-awaited companion to Dover's *Greek Homosexuality* on the Roman side and worthy to stand comparison with that classic work. Writings on sexuality have increasingly forged interdisciplinary connections, as literary scholars have become increasingly knowledgeable about the history of art and about political and social history, and as cultural historians increasingly understand literary texts to be part of their domain. (The general shift within history from an exclusive emphasis on political history to a focus on cultural and social history has greatly assisted this development, forging new methodologies and posing new questions.)

Philosophy, however, remains, even today, too far outside the picture. Philosophers, though somewhat more likely than previously to address the literary and cultural surroundings of a philosophical argument, still do so, often, in too cursory a fashion. Meanwhile, literary scholars and historians too rarely connect their work firmly to the arguments of the philosophers — or, when they do, they all too often treat them unphilosophically, lacking interest in the structure of their arguments or the history of an argument within a philosophical tradition. As we have suggested, this lack of connection is the philosophers' fault much of the time, for the unusual self-regard of that profession, combined with the historical and literary ignorance of many of its practitioners, does not make for rewarding interdisciplinary dialogue.

But there are encouraging signs. Particularly important has been the reopening of interest in post-Aristotelian Greek philosophy, spurred by the distinguished series of triennial international Symposia Hellenistica, which have by now brought out a fine series of volumes on major areas of Hellenistic thought, both Greek and Roman. Turning to this philosophical period naturally conduces to interdisciplinarity of approach. For when one deals with the Hellenistic schools and their Roman continuations, it is virtually impossible to pretend that one is dealing with isolated great works and almost necessary to draw connections to a cultural context. And although there is still too much of a tendency to use the Roman texts only as source material from which to reconstruct the positions of the great Greek thinkers (Epicurus, Zeno, Chrysippus), it is difficult not to read the Roman texts, and if one reads them one cannot help seeing their deep rootedness in Roman political and cultural life.

Thus, the turning to Hellenistic philosophy has led to at least some interdisciplinarity on the part of philosophers. One might mention with honor the pathbreaking joint seminar on Roman philosophy taught by philosopher Jonathan Barnes and historian Miriam Griffin at Oxford, which produced the excellent volume *Philosophia Togata* in 1989, and a sequel in 1997. And, more important still, one should mention the successful efforts of Jonathan Barnes and Julia Annas to change the Oxford curriculum to include a Hellenistic paper among the options, something that caused at least some further philosophers to turn their attentions to later Greek and Roman thought. Cambridge, faced with fewer curricular obstacles, has proved a rich breeding place for first-rate work on later Greek philosophy, much of it interdisciplinary in character. Figures such as Myles Burnyeat, Malcolm Schofield, G. E. R. Lloyd, and David Sedley have greatly contributed to the reawakening of attention to history and literature among the philosophers. In London, Richard Sorabji and other younger scholars have pursued a similar program. In the United States, the revival of interest in Hellenistic philosophy has moved more slowly, given the need to focus on authors who can be taught in departmental courses in philosophy and in the "great books" courses that form a staple of undergraduate education, and given the limited linguistic resources of many practitioners. But the increasing presence of good translations of the primary texts, with helpful philosophical commentary, has eased the job of instructors who really would like to teach Sextus Empiricus, or Seneca, or Cicero to their philosophy undergraduates. Teaching them often makes people more likely to write about them, and also to hire younger scholars who write about them. Such an increasing presence of later Greek and even Roman thought in philosophy departments has led, in turn, to an increasing presence of interdisciplinary awareness in the approach to all philosophical texts and issues.

Meticulous cross-disciplinary studies in sexuality, studies that take the historical context of Greek and Roman societies seriously, are also prompted by the fact that ancient Greek norms and arguments traced to ancient philosophers have been used, especially in the United States, in modern sexual controversies concerning, for example, ordinances aimed at protecting gays and lesbians from discrimination. Some opponents of gay rights have tried to justify their arguments with reference to the authority of Western secular philosophical tradition going back to Plato and Aristotle. They have interpreted the Greek philosophers as agreeing with modern conservative Christian views that claim that only conjugal sexual activity is free from the shameful instrumentalization of the body which is necessarily found in homosexual relations and even in masturbation. These kinds of claims have, however, been based on superficial and often misleading readings of Greek texts. Modern sexual controversies cannot of course be decided by appeals to the authority of great philosophers whether or not their arguments are interpreted correctly. We cannot say whether opposition to gay rights is mere prejudice or a legitimate interest simply on the basis of what this or that great historical figure said. Historical studies in ancient philosophers' views of sexual ethics are, however, very important in order to improve our arguments in modern controversies. Seeing that it was possible for the Greeks to think differently of things that many moderns have regarded as natural or even necessary helps us to remove the false sense of inevitability of our own judgments and practices. But this is not all. The Greeks were not just an anthropologically interesting other in relation to us; there were among them excellent philosophers whose texts still show us arguments that our own reason can assess as having great rational power.

Dover's *Greek Homosexuality* showed that first-rate work in the history of sexuality required the joint resources of history, literary study, and philosophy. At the same time, it left much work still to be done. Dover's work did not really extend into the Hellenistic era, a very rich ground for such investigations, nor did he even attempt the description of Roman cultural norms. Even in the periods he did cover, there were many authors and texts that he did not discuss. Furthermore, he was always skeptical of philosophy: as he announces in his recent autobiography, the questions of philosophy seemed to him obvious and not very interesting, so it is not surprising that the part of his book dealing with philosophical texts has struck many readers as in need of supplementation. Foucault was more interested in the philosophers — but not really as arguers. He used Plato, Aristotle, and some later Hellenistic thinkers as sources for the history of culture, rather than as thinkers in their own right. If philosophers far too rarely ask in what ways a philosopher is part of his cultural context, Foucault too rarely asks in what ways a philosopher is a strange outsider in a culture, connected to a specifically philosophical tradition that shapes his response to cultural developments.

Much, then, still remains to be done. Many texts need to be revisited with new questions in mind, and the philosophical debates about sexual ethics need to be further analyzed in a way that is both rigorous and informed by a sense of literary genre and historical context, in dialogue with experts in literary and historical analysis. Sometimes a small nation can provide valuable scholarly paradigms, avoiding the parochialism of the hyper-disciplinary scholarship of larger nations. In Finland, a strong analytically oriented (and therefore largely Anglo-American-oriented) philosophical culture has long coexisted with a small but high-quality classics community. The problems of academic segmentation are certainly not unknown to the Finnish classicists, and there are philologists who avoid all contacts with philosophy and philosophers interested in Plato and Aristotle who have little command of classical Greek. However, the fact that the number of people interested in ancient Greece and Rome is relatively small may also give some advantage to Finnish scholars. People tend to band together — as, for example, in the remarkable project that has led to the translation of major philosophical works of Aristotle into Finnish (now virtually complete), a project that engaged the energies of a remarkable team of scholars from philosophy, classics, and history. Scholars cannot afford to be narrow if they want the field to survive: an expert trained in ancient history may end up writing a commentary on Aristotle's *Analytics* and talking on the radio about Dover's and Foucault's views on sexuality; an expert in medieval logic may write on the *Nicomachean Ethics,* a leading officer of a cultural foundation on the *Rhetoric* and *Poetics,* a lecturer in business ethics may write a scholarly work on the *Topics.* Even though the original intention of the series of Finnish conferences on topics in ancient Greek and Roman philosophy was to encourage younger Finnish scholars by bringing them into contact with leading scholars from abroad, learning has clearly traveled in both directions, as the foreign scholars themselves have learned from the warm interdisciplinary cooperation of the Finnish classical community.

The topic of sexual ethics thus seemed a natural one for a Finnish-American conference to address. This volume grows out of a conference held at the Finnish Institute at Rome in 1997, which brought together leading scholars from Europe and North America for a discussion of ancient Greek and Roman views about erotic experience and sexual ethics. From the beginning we sought a broad interdisciplinary group, and we also sought scholars who could profit from one another's insights to craft their own work in a more sensitive and interdisciplinary way. Since both organizers are, above all, philosophers (though Nussbaum actually got her Ph.D. in classics and Sihvola in history), the decision was made from the beginning to make philosophy central to the discussion but to situate philosophy in a wider cultural conversation. This would be done by the inclusion of classicists from other disciplines, especially those who already conceived of their work in a broad interdisciplinary manner.

The conference aimed to bring together two questions that are too often kept separate: How is erotic experience understood in texts of various different kinds, and what normative ethical judgments and arguments are made about the sexual domain of life? Erotic experience has been a staple of classical scholarship; recent work by scholars such as Dover, Foucault, Winkler, and Halperin has made enormous progress in situating the texts historically and helping us understand the extent to which the erotic eye is a specific cultural artifact, rather than a part of some precultural nature. But studies of sexual ethics (especially within the domain of philosophy) too rarely are informed by the rich and subtle cultural analyses of *erōs* that recent scholarship has brought forth. Studies of erotic experience, on the other hand, are sometimes too little informed by an understanding of the normative arguments of the philosophical traditions. This is especially true of work in Hellenistic and Roman cultures, where the philosophical schools had broad cultural influence. Most politicians, poets, and orators would have been far more intimately acquainted with the arguments of Stoicism and Epicureanism than are, typically, today's historical and literary scholars.

After the conference we commissioned additional chapters by Dover, A. W. Price, and Christopher Faraone, added two further chapters by Halperin (on lesbianism) and Nussbaum (on *erōs* and ethical norms), and asked Samuel Houser and David Leitao for permission to include their already written papers in the collection.

The chapters in the volume are difficult to organize, because almost all of them are in some ways interdisciplinary. Thus, an organization according to primary discipline, which we originally tried, came to seem both misleading and in some ways false to the nature of the enterprise. A chronological organization is not altogether satisfactory, because so many of the chapters range broadly across time, and most deal with more than a single century. An organization according to primary culture (Greece versus Rome) is probably most misleading of all, since so many of the chapters deal with post-Aristotelian Greek philosophy, much of which is reconstructed through Roman texts, and therefore also with Roman texts whose debt to a lost Greek original is often likely but uncertain. Many deal, too, with the authors of the "Second Sophistic," whose work is highly intercultural. One could call Musonius a Roman, and that would not be false, but he is also, as Nussbaum argues, a Platonist and a Stoic (not to mention one who probably wrote in the Greek language). What is interesting is sorting out the contributions of all these elements. So we have finally settled on a (rough) chronological organization as the least misleading; we hope that the reader will be encouraged to pursue the many thematic connections among the essays.

As soon as we announce the chronological principle, we violate it, by beginning with Halperin's "Forgetting Foucault," a general discussion of methodology that cannot be categorized chronologically but that helps to set the scene for the subsequent chapters (almost all of which respond, in various ways, to Dover and Foucault) by reassessing Foucault's legacy and clearing up some pervasive misreadings of Foucault's philosophical contribution. In particular, Halperin addresses some current clichés about sexual acts and sexual actors, arguing that Foucault never held that the Greeks did not distinguish types of sexual actor and going on to give a more nuanced account of what (in Foucault's view, and in Halperin's) is the real difference between the ancient Greek categories and those that obtain in the contemporary world. Although Halperin's chapter has been published elsewhere in the meantime, it was originally presented at the conference and was an integral part of the discussions that ensued. Clearly, getting clear about what Foucault's claims were and what we should make of them is a major part of any recovery of ancient Greek and Roman debates about sexual ethics.

Halperin's chapter is followed by Nussbaum's "*Erōs* and Ethical Norms," a chapter that is both arguably chronologically first, at least in terms of its starting point (beginning with visual art of the early fifth century B.C.E.), and concerned, like Halperin's, with general methodological issues and the reassessment of Foucault's legacy. Nussbaum traces a debate about the ethical status of *erōs* that engages a sequence of philosophers, from Plato through Aristotle and Epicurus to the Greek and Roman Stoics and their Platonist critic Plutarch. The question is whether a passion as violent as *erōs* is said to be can ever be good for the beloved; or, is passionate erotic love compatible with kindness, restraint, and generosity? She argues that the philosophical debate cannot be well understood without seeing the philosophers as participants in a cultural debate. (Indeed, she criticizes her earlier work on Plato for not attending sufficiently to social context.) And she argues that the debate has consequences for our assessment of Foucault's legacy. While Foucault focused on a narrow range of norms (primarily in the area of self-control and self-management) when he examined Greek philosophical texts dealing with sexual pleasure, the tradition actually provides us with a far richer and more interpersonal set of considerations, which, in her view, are rightly regarded as ethically central by the Greek thinkers: norms of kindness, noncruelty, nonegoism, reciprocity. (This chapter was previously published but has been extensively revised.) Recovery of this richer ethical debate helps us to understand what we might possibly have to learn from an engagement with Greek texts and arguments.

Marriage does not take center stage in the philosophical debate about *erōs* and sexual pleasure until we get to Rome. Both Plato and Zeno the Stoic, the leading ancient Greek theorists of sexual pleasure, seem to have been relatively uninterested in the sexuality of women and tend to focus almost all their analysis on pederastic relationships. Even when we are dealing with nonphilosophical materials, writers about Greece of the fifth and fourth centuries have tended to think that sex in marriage is an uninteresting topic, believing that marital sex was generally agreed to be unerotic and primarily reproductive in nature. There is evidence for that view, but there is also unacknowledged evidence for a different view, which suggests a far greater continuity than we might have imagined between the Greek poets and their Roman philosophical and poetic successors. Maarit Kaimio's "Erotic Experience in the Conjugal Bed" breaks new ground in the analysis of Greek views of marital sexuality, arguing that there is actually a great deal of evidence in the tragic poets for the view that both husbands and wives found considerable pleasure in marital sexuality and that deprivation of that sexuality was regarded as a major loss. By a careful study of the range of words associated with the marital bed, she shows that the fifth century had elaborated a complex conception of marital sexuality, thus preparing the way for the much later discussions of that topic (including philosophical discussions) by Hellenistic and Roman authors.

Kaimio's treatment of tragedy insists on the importance of genre and its conventions for good analysis of material in this area. Stephen Halliwell's "Aristophanic Sex: The Erotics of Shamelessness" does the same for Old Comedy. The works of Aristophanes are an invaluable source for any scholar trying to reconstruct the history of ancient Greek sexual customs and norms, and even sexual language. Sexual matters are simply discussed with a frankness that would be impossible in literary or philosophical texts. The comedies have therefore become a mainstay of historical analysis and are used extensively by both Dover and Foucault. Halliwell argues that we cannot analyze Aristophanic sex well unless we focus on the peculiar properties of the genre—in particular, its preoccupation with the flouting of proprieties and with a general shocking shamelessness. Halliwell focuses on *Ecclesiazousae*, a play that has often been brought into philosophical debates because of its similarities to some aspects of Plato's *Republic*. His analysis shows that a good understanding of genre complicates this connection greatly, making it very unwise to draw any straightforward parallels of the sort that are often drawn, and unwise even to make straightforward claims about what Aristophanes recommends. Both Kaimio and Halliwell, in different ways, show what ancient literary genres do and do not offer to the philosophically inclined scholar wishing to pursue the history of debates about sexual ethics. They see the poets as participants, along with the philosophers, in a cultural conversation, but within limits set by the genre within which they work.

In Plato's *Symposium*, the first speaker, Phaedrus, claims that an army composed of *erastēs/erōmenos* pairs would be unusually fine, because each lover would vie to outdo the other in daring and virtuous exploits. This passage has frequently been connected with the famous Sacred Band, an elite Theban corps that apparently was organized on that principle—although scholars differ about whether the reference shows that the *Symposium* was composed before the Sacred Band was a reality (Dover) or once the band was well known (Nussbaum, arguing that the reference coyly exploits the gap between dramatic date and date of composition). Most scholars commenting on the *Symposium*—and on related Stoic texts that make pederastic *erōs* central to civic bonds—have tended to assume that the Sacred Band is a genuine historical corps really organized on an erotic principle. Leitao's "Legend of the Sacred Band" shows how weak the evidence actually is for the historical reality of an elite corps consisting of erotic pairs. He urges the philosophical scholar toward a much more nuanced reading of history, arguing that the band is standardly used for normative purposes, as an emblem of the connection of pederastic *erōs* with freedom from tyranny. For this very reason, we cannot have much confidence in it as history. So what looks like the historical context of a philosophical work may actually be part of the moral philosophy itself.

We now turn (again, since Nussbaum's chapter already discussed the *Symposium* and *Phaedrus*) to Plato, and to Price's "Plato, Zeno, and the Object of Love," which discusses the connection between pederasty and pedagogy in Plato and the Stoics. Addressing himself to the claims of Nussbaum's chapter, Price offers a subtly different reading of Plato's relation to his tradition. He sees the tradition's central problem less as inhibiting violence and promoting kindliness than as reconciling the asymmetry of the partners to a pederastic relationship with the reciprocity and the reciprocal appreciation of character that typifies the ethically best form of love and friendship. He argues that while Plato's *Phaedrus* took this problem very seriously and made some progress in the direction of its solution, by insisting on the *anterōs* (answering *erōs*) of the younger partner, the real breakthrough is made by the Stoics, and in virtue of developments made possible by their philosophy of perception. For the first time it became possible to understand how the bodily form of a younger man might express virtue and make it visible. Price argues, against Nussbaum, that the Stoic solution to the cultural dilemma is successful and admirable, "weav[ing] innovation within tradition" in a constructive way. Philosophical theorizing, he concludes, can both enrich and change life—if it is "quickened as much by collaboration as by resistance from the world of experience."

Aristotle has already been briefly mentioned in the chapters of Nussbaum and Price, and Sihvola now devotes his chapter, "Aristotle on Sex and Love," to the detailed reconstruction of Aristotle's views about *erōs*. This is a notoriously difficult task, because it involves sifting evidence drawn from works of many different types, including, prominently, works on logic in which erotic examples are used en passant to illustrate logical relationships. This task of reconstruction has already been attempted by Price in a justly admired appendix to his *Love and Friendship in Plato and Aristotle*, but Sihvola gives the evidence a more extensive treatment, coming to slightly different conclusions. Like Price, he stresses that the relationship between *erastēs* and *erōmenos* is asymmetrical but contains the potential to develop in the direction of equality and full reciprocity. Unlike Price, he sees Aristotle as in that sense a rather bold cultural innovator. And he insists that Aristotle's *erōs* is more deeply passionate, more intense and exclusive, more connected to vulnerability and risk than previous commentators have understood it to be. The most surprising claim he makes is that this passionate element remains a part of *erōs*, for Aristotle, even after its transformation into a virtuous and reciprocal *philia* is complete.

Not too surprisingly, the chapters so far have focused not only on male-authored texts, but also (Kaimio's and Halliwell's excepted) on texts that say little about Greek women in any way. It is almost impossible to write the history of same-sex sexual relationships between women in Greek antiquity. Sappho's poetry and what exiguous amount can be known about her life have been analyzed again and again from the most wide-ranging viewpoints. But other evidence is so sparse that there has seemed to be nothing much to say. Dover's "Two Women of Samos" argues that one small piece of evidence delivers a great deal of information, if we mine it with all the resources of technical philological and historical scholarship: a fragment of the third-century poet Asclepiades, in the *Greek Anthology*, which attacks two women, apparently for same-sex lovemaking. Looking at every word of the fragment with his customary care, knowledge of genre, and extensive scholarship, and connecting it to other pertinent pieces of evidence (for example, the remark about same-sex female relationships in Plato's *Sympo-*

sium), Dover argues that the poem is strongly hostile to the two women. The question that must then be posed is, Why should same-sex relations between women be attacked while male same-sex relations are strongly favored? Dover argues that one factor is surely the tendency to regard penetration as the essence of *aphrodisia*. Whatever the case, we have reason to see in Greek culture, over several centuries, a striking anxiety and an embarrassed silence about same-sex relations between women.

Dover's chapter was in part inspired by Bernadette Brooten's *Love between Women* (1996). In his second chapter in the volume, "The First Homosexuality," David Halperin engages with Brooten at greater length, arguing that she has failed to notice some important discontinuities between ancient same-sex relations between women and modern lesbianism. It is, he argues, a big mistake even to speak of "ancient lesbianism," as if there were a recognizable thing that we know from our culture that we have now discovered in the past. In a broad discussion of both ancient evidence and the modern origins of our contemporary sexual categories, Halperin applies some of the careful scrutiny of cultural discontinuity that marks his work on male homosexuality to the difficult area of women's relationships. Agreeing with the general line of Dover's argument, but developing the point over a longer period, in relation to a wider range of texts, Halperin concludes that what the ancient Greeks and Romans found disturbing was not sexual contact among women as such, but rather a woman's playing an assertive masculine role, deviating from usual gender categories. The passive recipient of such a woman's attentions could have same-sex relations, and even enjoy them, without incurring social disapproval.

We now move to Rome (which has figured already in parts of Nussbaum's and Price's treatment of Stoic ethics, and in Halperin's analysis of lesbianism). From this point onward, the ethics of marriage become a central focus of the essays. In "Marriage and Sexuality in Republican Rome: A Roman Conjugal Love Story," historian and legal scholar Eva Cantarella focuses on the republic, and on a strange incident in which Cato apparently gave his wife Marcia to his friend Hortensius, so that he could have children — and then took her back after the task had been performed. She argues that this case of "surrogate motherhood" needs to be analyzed against the background of ethical norms of the period, and especially a particular Roman ideal of conjugal sexuality. When so analyzed, it is less bizarre than it initially appears; and the case serves as a lens through which to examine Roman norms.

Musonius Rufus is a little-studied but very important Roman Stoic philosopher. Known in antiquity as "the Roman Socrates," he developed views of female education, marriage, and female virtue that had great influence in antiquity and are still worth studying now. In "The Incomplete Feminism of Musonius Rufus, Platonist, Stoic, and Roman," Nussbaum argues that Musonius cannot be well studied if he is not seen both as a participant in a complex Platonic-Stoic philosophical tradition and as a participant in debates about gender roles in contemporary Rome. She then produces a systematic philosophical analysis (the first in recent scholarship, to her knowledge) of the arguments of two of Musonius's most fascinating works, "That Women Too Should Do Philosophy" and "Should Daughters Get the Same Education as Sons?" along with briefer analyses of several works on marriage and sexuality. Nussbaum argues that Musonius is an odd combination of the progressive and the conservative, in some ways in advance of his culture, in other ways rejecting radical proposals of earlier Stoicism in order to adhere to conventional Roman norms.

Dio Chrysostom is another figure who was highly influential in antiquity but is relatively neglected today. Although he is a quasi philosopher, with strong links to the philosophical tradition, philosophical scholars ignore him. And his views on sexuality have not been systematically studied in a way that brings to bear the insights of recent scholarship on the history of Greek and Roman sexuality. Houser's "Erōs and Aphrodisia in the Works of Dio Chrysostom" is an ambitious and far-reaching study of Dio's views on same-sex relationships, arguing (in a way that corroborates Foucault's general thesis about ancient sexuality) that Dio's ethical worries focus not on same-sex conduct per se, but on indulgence and lack of self-control.

David Konstan's "Enacting Erōs" develops further the themes of his important scholarship on ancient conceptions of philia, or friendship, and on reciprocity and symmetry in erotic relations. Starting from a passage in Lucian's Dialogues of the Gods in which Zeus worries that his terrifying appearance makes him unlovable, Konstan argues that ancient conceptions of erotic love, while often focused on the norm of self-mastery (as Foucault argued), also made room for a different set of norms, focused on symmetry and mutuality. This set of concerns gave rise to a norm of male sexual attractiveness that is very different from the norm of the dominant penetrative male: thus, Dionysus, soft and feminine, is lovable to women in a way that the terrifying Zeus is not. In a wide-ranging discussion moving (chronologically) from Homer and Euripides to Catullus and Lucian, Konstan argues that norms of sexual reciprocity, while especially clearly developed in male-female relations, also make their appearance in the context of pederastic relations.

Simon Goldhill's " Erotic Experience of Looking: Cultural Conflict and the Gaze in Empire Culture" studies philosophical and literary views about erotic gazing in the second century C.E., focusing on novelists Achilles Tatius and Heliodorus, Christian thinkers Clement of Alexandria and Tertullian, and Jewish Platonist Philo. Goldhill argues that Stoic theories of knowledge and perception are broadly influential during this period, and that we cannot understand the theories of erotic gazing produced by these authors without detailed familiarity with the Stoic position. Against this background he traces the moral debate about the "erotic eye," and the connection between vision and (morally assessable) desire.

It has long been acknowledged that one of our significant sources for popular norms and conceptual categories in the area of *erōs* is the papyrological, epigraphical, and archaeological evidence for the use of magical spells in the Greco-Roman world. One of the most influential articles (the title article) in John J. Winkler's *Constraints of Desire* (1990) was devoted to this topic. Christopher Faraone has recently produced a major book, *Ancient Greek Love Magic* (1999) systematically analyzing the magical papyri on this set of issues. In his chapter in the present volume, "Agents and Victims: Constructions of Gender and Desire in Ancient Greek Love Magic," drawing on material that ranges over both cultures and a number of centuries, he develops the insights of the book further, asking what evidence the material on magic gives us about the Greeks' and Romans' understanding of gender categories and of varieties of desire. Against a dominant view that holds that the Greeks believed women to be sexually insatiable and uncontrollable, he argues that, while evidence for that view exists, there is also a good deal of evidence for a contradictory view; that women are self-controlled and interested in *philia*, while men are uncontrolled and focused on intercourse.

The essays come to no single set of conclusions. There are internal differences among them: for example, Price, Nussbaum, and Sihvola all have different views about which thinker best addressed the problem of the selfish character of *erōs*, reconciling pedagogy and pederasty; Kaimio and Faraone appear to have subtle differences concerning wives and what they want. But the common theme of all the essays is complexity, for almost all, in different ways, contend against simple orthodoxies in the depiction of ancient Greek and Roman sexuality, both its norms and its categories, arguing that a more complicated picture ought to be preferred. To an orthodoxy that holds that the Greeks thought a good wife was not interested in sex, Kaimio opposes the poets' complex and often sympathetic portrayals of sexually desiring wives. To a more recent orthodoxy that says that the Greeks recognized only types of act, not types of actor, Halperin opposes a more complex (and, he argues, more correct) reading of Foucault that gives us a more subtle account of the differences between ancient and modern cultures. Against the tendency to use Aristophanes as a straightforward source for popular thought, Halliwell contends that the complexities of genre complicate any such appropriation.

Because the essays focus on the ethical, it is in that area above all that their plea for a complex understanding is most urgent. We find a general agreement (among, for example, Nussbaum, Price, Sihvola, Konstan, and Kaimio) that the ethics of *erōs*, in both Greece and Rome, focused not only on self-mastery but also on reciprocity; that men worried not only about penetrating and displaying their power, but also about being decent and kind, and about being loved for themselves; that women and even younger men felt not only gratitude and acceptance, but also joy and, frequently, sexual desire. What is more, these norms were the subject of debate and conversation — prominently including philosophical conversation — as people understood themselves to have erotic options, and searched for the option that was humanly best. (We should never forget, however, that we have virtually no unmediated access to women's views about all these matters.) In general, the essays see ancient Greco-Roman culture not as a monolith in which rigid norms produce an unvarying series of similar subjects, but, instead, as a scene of searching and arguing, sometimes playful and sometimes deeply serious, in which people, surprised by a new thought, seize the norms tradition gives them and twist them around to a new purpose, or discover a space between the articulated norms in which a newly imagined form of life can flourish — a world in which ideas illuminate the actual, and experience gives its richness to the world of ideas.

Chapter One

FORGETTING FOUCAULT: ACTS, IDENTITIES, AND THE HISTORY OF SEXUALITY

⋙⋘

David M. Halperin

𝒲hen Jean Baudrillard published his infamous pamphlet *Forget Foucault* in March 1977, "Foucault's intellectual power," as Baudrillard recalled ten years later, "was enormous." After all, the reviews of *La volonté de savoir,* the first volume of Michel Foucault's *History of Sexuality* (published the previous November), had only just started to appear. At that time, according to Baudrillard's belated attempt in *Cool Memories* to redeem his gaffe and to justify himself—by portraying his earlier attack on Foucault as having been inspired, improbably, by sentiments of friendship and generosity—Foucault was being "persecuted," allegedly, by "thousands of disciples and . . . sycophants." In such circumstances, Baudrillard virtuously insisted, "to forget him was to do him a service; to adulate him was to do him a disservice." Just how far Baudrillard was willing to go in order to render this sort of unsolicited service to Foucault emerges from another remark of his in the same passage: "Foucault's death. Loss of confidence in his own genius. . . . Leaving the sexual aspects aside, the loss of the immune system is no more than the biological transcription of the other process."[1] Foucault was already washed up by the time he died, in other words, and AIDS was merely the outward and visible sign of his inward, moral and intellectual, decay. Leaving the sexual aspects aside, of course.

(Baudrillard freely voices elsewhere what he carefully suppresses here about "the sexual aspects" of AIDS: the epidemic, he suggests, might be considered "a form of viral catharsis" and "a remedy against total sexual liberation, which is sometimes more dangerous than an epidemic, because the latter always ends. Thus AIDS could be understood as a counterforce against the total elimination of structure and the total unfolding of sexuality." [2] Some such New Age moralism obviously provides the subtext of Baudrillard's vengeful remarks in *Cool Memories* on the death of Foucault.)

Baudrillard's injunction to forget Foucault, which was premature at the time it was issued, has since become superfluous. Not that Foucault is neglected; not that his work is ignored. (Quite the contrary, in fact.) Rather, Foucault's continuing prestige, and the almost ritualistic invocation of his name by academic practitioners of cultural theory, has had the effect of reducing the operative range of his thought to a small set of received ideas, slogans, and bits of jargon that have now become so commonplace and so familiar as to make a more direct engagement with Foucault's texts entirely dispensable. As a result, we are so far from remembering Foucault that there is little point in entertaining the possibility of forgetting him.

Take, for example, the title of a conference, "Bodies and Pleasures in Pre- and Early Modernity," held from 3 to 5 November 1995 at the University of California, Santa Cruz. "Bodies and pleasures," as that famous phrase occurs in the concluding paragraphs of Foucault's *History of Sexuality*, volume 1, does not in fact describe "Foucault's zero-degree definition of the elements in question in the history of sexuality," as the poster for the conference confidently announces. To be sure, the penultimate sentence of *The History of Sexuality*, volume 1, finds Foucault looking forward to the day, some time in the future, when "a different economy [*une autre économie*] of bodies and pleasures" will have replaced the apparatus of sexuality and when, accordingly, it will become difficult to understand "how the ruses of sexuality . . . were able to subject us to that austere monarchy of sex." [3] An incautious reader might take that phrase, "a different economy of bodies and pleasures," to denote a mere rearrangement of otherwise unchanged and unchanging "bodies and pleasures," a minor modification in the formal design of the sexual "economy" alone, consisting in a revised organization of its perennial "elements" (as the conference poster terms them). But such an interpretation of Foucault's meaning, though superficially plausible, is mistaken—and in fact it runs counter to the entire thrust of his larger argument. The change of which Foucault speaks in the next-to-last sentence of *The History of Sexuality*, volume 1, and which he seems fondly to anticipate, involves nothing less than the displacement of the current sexual economy by *a different economy* altogether, an economy that will feature "bodies and pleasures" instead of, or at least in addition to, such familiar and over-worked entities as "sexuality" and "desire." Foucault makes it very clear that bodies and pleasures, in his conception, are not the eternal building blocks of sexual subjectivity or sexual experience; they are not basic, irreducible, or natural "elements" that different human societies rearrange in different pat-terns over time—and that our own society has elaborated into the cultural edifice now known as "sexuality." Rather, "bodies" and "pleasures" refer to two entities that modern sexual discourse and practice include but largely ignore, underplay, or pass quickly over, and that accordingly are relatively undercoded, relatively uninvested by the normalizing apparatus of sexual-ity, especially in comparison to more thoroughly policed and more easily pathologized items such as "sexual desire." (Or so at least it seemed to Fou-cault at the time he was writing, in the wake of the sexual liberation move-ment of the late 1960s and early 1970s, which had exhorted us to liberate our "sexuality" and to unrepress or desublimate our "desire.") For that rea-son, bodies and pleasures represented to Foucault an opportunity for ef-fecting, as he says earlier in the same passage "a tactical reversal of the various mechanisms of sexuality," a means of resistance to the apparatus of sexuality.[4] In particular, the strategy that Foucault favors consists in assert-ing, "against the [various] holds of power, the claims of bodies, pleasures, and knowledges in their multiplicity and their possibility of resistance."[5] The very possibility of pursuing such a body- and pleasure-centered strat-egy of resistance to the apparatus of sexuality disappears, of course, as soon as "bodies" and "pleasures" cease to be understood merely as handy weap-ons against current technologies of normalization and attain instead to the status of transhistorical components of some natural phenomenon or ma-terial substrate underlying "the history of sexuality" itself. Such a notion of "bodies and pleasures," so very familiar and uncontroversial and positivis-tic has it now become, is indeed nothing if not eminently forgettable.

In what follows I propose to explore another aspect of the oblivion that has engulfed Foucault's thinking about sexuality since his death, one particular "forgetting" that has had important consequences for the practice of both the history of sexuality and lesbian/gay studies. I refer to the reception and deployment of Foucault's distinction between the sodomite and the ho-mosexual—a distinction often taken to be synonymous with the distinc-tion between sexual acts and sexual identities. The passage in *The History of Sexuality*, volume 1, in which Foucault makes this fateful distinction is so well known that it might seem unnecessary to quote it, but what that really means, I am contending, is that the passage is in fact so well forgotten that nothing but direct quotation from it will do. Foucault writes,

> As defined by the ancient civil or canonical codes, sodomy was a category of forbidden acts; their author was nothing more than the juridical subject of them. The nineteenth-century homosexual became a personage—a past, a case history and a childhood, a character, a form of life; also a morphology, with an indiscreet anatomy and possibly a mysterious physiology. Nothing in his total being escapes his sexuality. Everywhere in him it is present: underlying all his actions, because it is their insidious and indefinitely active principle; shamelessly inscribed on his face and on his body, because it is a secret that always gives itself away. It is consubstantial with him, less as a habitual sin than as a singular nature. . . . Homosexuality appeared as one of the forms of sexuality when it was transposed from the practice of sodomy onto a kind of interior androgyny, a hermaphroditism of the soul. The sodomite was a renegade [or "backslider"]; the homosexual is now a species.

> [La sodomie—celle des anciens droits civil ou canonique—était un type d'actes interdits; leur auteur n'en était que le sujet juridique. L'homosexuel du xixe siècle est devenu un personnage: un passé, une histoire et une enfance, un caractère, une forme de vie; une morphologie aussi, avec une anatomie indiscrète et peut-être une physiologie mystérieuse. Rien de ce qu'il est au total n'échappe à sa sexualité. Partout en lui, elle est présente: sous-jacente à toutes ses conduites parce qu'elle en est le principe insidieux et indéfiniment actif; inscrite sans pudeur sur son visage et sur son corps parce qu'elle est un secret qui se trahit toujours. Elle lui est consubstantielle, moins comme un péché d'habitude que comme une nature singulière. . . . L'homosexualité est apparue comme une des figures de la sexualité lorsqu'elle a été rabattue de la pratique de la sodomie sur une sorte d'androgynie intérieure, un hermaphrodisme de l'âme. Le sodomite était un relaps, l'homosexuel est maintenant une espèce.][6]

Foucault's formulation is routinely taken to authorize the doctrine that before the nineteenth century the categories or classifications typically employed by European cultures to articulate sexual difference did not distinguish among different kinds of sexual actors but only among different kinds of sexual acts. In the premodern and early modern periods, so the claim goes, sexual behavior did not represent a sign or marker of a person's sexual identity; it did not indicate or express some more generalized or holistic feature of the person, such as that person's subjectivity, disposition, or character. The pattern is clearest, we are told, in the case of deviant sexual acts. Sodomy, for example, was a sinful act that anyone of sufficient depravity might commit; it was not a symptom of a type of personality. To perform the act of sodomy was not to manifest a deviant sexual identity, but merely to be the author of a morally objectionable act.[7] Whence the conclusion that before the modern era sexual deviance could be predicated only of acts, not of persons or identities.

There is a good deal of truth in this received view, and Foucault himself may even have subscribed to a version of it at the time he wrote *The History of Sexuality*, volume 1.[8] Although I am about to argue strenuously against it, I want to be very clear that my aim is to revise it, not to reverse it. I do not want to return us to some unreconstructed or reactionary belief in the universal validity and applicability of modern sexual concepts or to promote an uncritical acceptance of the categories and classifications of sexuality as true descriptors of the basic realities of human erotic life — and, therefore, as unproblematic instruments for the historical analysis of human culture in all times and places. It is certainly not my intention to undermine the principles and practices of the new social history, let alone to recant my previous arguments for the historical and cultural constitution of sexual identity (which have sometimes been misinterpreted as providing support for the view I shall be criticizing here).[9] Least of all do I wish to revive an essentialist faith in the unqualified existence of homosexual and heterosexual persons in Western societies before the modern era. I take it as established that a large-scale transformation of social and personal life took place in Europe as part of the massive cultural reorganization that accompanied the transition from a traditional, hierarchical, status-based society to a modern, individualistic, mass society during the period of industrialization and the rise of a capitalist economy. One symptom of that transformation, as a number of researchers (both before and after Foucault) have pointed out, is that something new happens to the various relations among sexual roles, sexual object-choices, sexual categories, sexual behaviors, and sexual identities in bourgeois Europe between the end of the seventeenth century and the beginning of the twentieth.[10] Sex takes on new social and individual functions, and it assumes a new importance in defining and normalizing the modern self. The conception of the sexual instinct as an autonomous human function without an organ appears for the first time in the nineteenth century, and without it our heavily psychologized model of sexual subjectivity — which knits up desire, its objects, sexual behavior, gender identity, reproductive function, mental health, erotic sensibility, personal style, and degrees of normality or deviance into an individuating, normativizing feature of the personality called "sexuality" or "sexual orientation"— is inconceivable.[11] Sexuality is indeed, as Foucault claimed, a distinctively modern production. Nonetheless, the canonical reading of the famous passage in *The History of Sexuality,* volume 1, and the conclusion conventionally based on it—namely, that before the modern era sexual deviance could be predicated only of acts, not of persons or identities—is, I shall contend, as inattentive to Foucault's text as it is heedless of European history.[12]

Such a misreading of Foucault can be constructed only by setting aside, and then forgetting, the decisive qualifying phrase with which his famous pronouncement opens: "*As defined by the ancient civil or canonical codes,*" Foucault begins, "sodomy was a category of forbidden acts."[13] Foucault, in other words, is making a carefully limited point about the differing styles of disqualification applied to male love by premodern legal definitions of sodomy and by nineteenth-century psychiatric conceptualizations of homosexuality, respectively. The intended effect of his rhetorical extravagance in this passage is to highlight what in particular was new and distinctive about the modern discursive practices that produced the category of "the homosexual." As almost always in *The History of Sexuality,* Foucault is speaking about discursive and institutional practices, not about what people really did in bed or what they thought about it. He is not attempting to describe popular attitudes or private emotions, much less is he presuming to convey what actually went on in the minds of different historical subjects when they had sex. He is making a contrast between the way something called "sodomy" was typically defined by the laws of various European states and municipalities as well as by Christian penitentials and canon law, on the one hand, and the way something called "homosexuality" was typically defined by the writings of nineteenth-century and early-twentieth-century sexologists, on the other.

A glance at the larger context of the much-excerpted passage in *The History of Sexuality,* volume 1, is sufficient to make Foucault's meaning clear. Foucault introduces his account of "the nineteenth-century homosexual" in order to illustrate a more general claim, which he advances in the sentence immediately preceding: the "new persecution of the peripheral sexualities" that occurred in the modern era was accomplished in part through "an *incorporation of perversions* and a new *specification of individuals.*"[14] (Earlier efforts to regulate sexual behavior did not feature such tactics, according to Foucault.) The whole discussion of this distinctively modern method of sexual control is embedded, in turn, within a larger argument about a crucial shift in *the nature of sexual prohibitions* as those prohibitions were constructed in *formal discursive practices,* a shift that occurred between the premodern period and the nineteenth century. Comparing medieval moral and legal codifications of sexual relations with nineteenth-century medical and forensic ones, Foucault contrasts various premodern styles of sexual prohibition, which took the form of specifying rules of conduct, making prescriptions and recommendations, and discriminating between the licit and the illicit, with modern styles of sexual prohibition. These latter-day strategies took the form of establishing norms of self-regulation—not by legislating standards of behavior and punishing deviations from them but rather by constructing new species of individuals, discovering and "implanting" perversions, and thereby elaborating more subtle and insidious means of social control. The ultimate purpose of the comparison is to support Foucault's "historico-theoretical" demonstration that power is not only negative but also positive, not only repressive but also productive.

Foucault is analyzing the different modalities of power at work in premodern and modern codifications of sexual prohibition, which is to say in two historical instances of sexual discourse attached to institutional practices. He carefully isolates the formal discursive systems that he will proceed to discuss from popular moral attitudes and behaviors about which *he will have nothing to say* and that he dismisses from consideration with barely a parenthetical glance: "Up to the end of the eighteenth century, three major explicit codes [*codes*]—*apart from regularities of custom and constraints of opinion*—governed sexual practices: canon law [*droit canonique*], Christian pastoral, and civil law."[15] Foucault goes on to expand this observation in a passage that directly anticipates and lays the groundwork for the famous portrait he will later sketch of the differences between "the sodomy of the old civil and canonical codes" and that novel invention of modern psychiatry, "the nineteenth-century homosexual." Describing the terms in which premodern sexual prohibitions defined the scope of their operation and the nature of their target, he writes, "What was taken into account in the civil and religious jurisdictions alike was a general unlawfulness. Doubtless acts 'contrary to nature' were stamped as especially abominable, but they were perceived simply as an extreme form of acts 'against the law'; they, too, were infringements of decrees—decrees which were just as sacred as those of marriage and which had been established in order to rule the order of things and the plan of beings. Prohibitions bearing on sex were basically of a juridical nature [*de nature juridique*]."[16] This passage prepares the reader to gauge the differences between these "juridical" prohibitions against "acts" "'contrary to nature'" and the nineteenth-century prohibitions against homosexuality, which did not simply criminalize sexual relations between men as illegal but medically disqualified them as pathological and—not content with pathologizing the act—constructed the perpetrator as a deviant form of life, a perverse personality, an anomalous species, thereby producing a new specification of individuals whose true nature would be defined from now on by reference to their abnormal "sexuality." The nineteenth-century disciplining of the subject, though it purported to aim at the eradication of "peripheral sexualities," paradoxically required their consolidation and "implantation" or "incorporation" in individuals, for only by that means could the subject's body itself become so deeply, so minutely invaded and colonized by the agencies of normalization. The discursive construction of the new sexual perversions was therefore a ruse of power, no longer simply prohibiting behavior but now also controlling, regulating, and normalizing embodied subjects. As Foucault sums up his argument, "The implantation of perversions is an instrument-effect: it is through the isolation, intensification, and consolidation of peripheral sexualities that the relations of power to sex and pleasure branched out and multiplied, measured the body and penetrated modes of conduct." [17] Want an example? Take the case of homosexuality. "The sodomy of the old civil and canonical codes was a category of forbidden acts; their author was nothing more than the juridical subject of them. The nineteenth-century homosexual became a personage . . . " So that's how the overall argument works.

Foucault narrowly frames his comparison between sodomy and homosexuality with the purpose of this larger argument in mind. The point-by-point contrast—between legal discourse (*codes* and *droits*) and psychiatric discourse, between juridical subjects and sexual subjects, between laws and norms, between acts contrary to nature and embodied subjects or species of individuals—is ruthlessly schematic. That schematic reduction is in keeping with the general design of the first volume of Foucault's *History*, which merely outlines, in an admittedly preliminary and tentative fashion, the principles intended to guide the remaining five unfinished studies that Foucault projected for his *History* at the time. His schematic opposition between sodomy and homosexuality is first and foremost a discursive analysis, not a social history, let alone an exhaustive one. *It is not an empirical claim about the historical existence or nonexistence of sexually deviant individuals.* It is a claim about the internal logic and systematic functioning of two different discursive styles of sexual disqualification—and, ultimately, it is a heuristic device for foregrounding what is distinctive about modern techniques of social and sexual regulation. As such, it points to a historical development that will need to be properly explored in its own right (as Foucault intended to do in a separate volume), and it dramatizes the larger themes of Foucault's *History:* the historical triumph of normalization over law, the decentralization and dispersion of the mechanisms of regulation, the disciplining of the modern subject, the traversal of sexuality by relations of power, the productivity of power, and the displacement of state coercion by the technical and bureaucratic administration of life ("biopower"). By documenting the existence of both a discursive and a temporal gap between two dissimilar styles of defining, and disqualifying, male same-sex sexual expression, Foucault highlights the historical and political specificity of "sexuality," both as a cultural concept and as a tactical device, and so he contributes to the task of "introducing" the history of sexuality as a possible field of study — and as a radical scholarly and political project. Nothing Foucault says about the differences between those two historically distant, and operationally distinct, discursive strategies for regulating and delegitimating forms of male same-sex sexual contacts prohibits us from inquiring into the connections that premodern people may have made between specific sexual acts and the particular ethos, or sexual style, or sexual subjectivity, of those who performed them.

A more explicit argument to this effect was advanced in the late 1980s by John J. Winkler, in opposition less to Foucault than to what even then were already well-established, conventional, and highly dogmatic misreadings of Foucault. Winkler, a classical scholar, was discussing the ancient Greek and Roman figure of the *kinaidos* or *cinaedus,* a "scare-image" (or phobic construction) of a sexually deviant and gender-deviant male, whose most salient distinguishing feature was a supposedly "feminine" love of being sexually penetrated by other men.[18] "Scholars of recent sex-gender history," Winkler wrote in his 1990 book, *The Constraints of Desire,* "have asserted that pre-modern systems classified not persons but acts and that 'the' homosexual as a person-category is a recent invention." He went on to qualify that assertion as follows: "The *kinaidos,* to be sure, is not a 'homosexual' but neither is he just an ordinary guy who now and then decided to commit a kinaidic act. The conception of a *kinaidos* was of a man socially deviant in his entire being, principally observable in behavior that flagrantly violated or contravened the dominant social definition of masculinity. To this extent, *kinaidos* was a category of person, not just of acts."[19] Ancient

Mediterranean societies, of course, did not exactly have "categories of person," types of blank individuals, in the modern sense, as Winkler himself pointed out. The ancient conception of the *kinaidos*, Winkler explained, depended on indigenous notions of gender. It arose in the context of a belief system in which, first of all, the two genders are conceived as opposite ends of a much-traveled continuum and, second, masculinity is thought to be a difficult accomplishment—one that is achieved only by a constant struggle akin to warfare against enemies both internal and external—and thus requires great fortitude in order to maintain. In a situation where it is so hard, both personally and culturally, to be a man, Winkler observed, "the temptation to desert one's side is very great." The *kinaidos* succumbed to that temptation.

The *kinaidos* could be conceived by the ancients in both universalizing and minoritizing terms—as a potential threat to the masculine identity of every male, that is, and as the disfiguring peculiarity of a small class of deviant individuals.[20] Because ancient Mediterranean discourses of sex and gender featured the notion that "the two sexes are not simply opposite but stand at poles of a continuum which can be traversed," as Winkler pointed out, "'woman' is not only the opposite of a man; she is also a potentially threatening 'internal emigré' of masculine identity."[21] The prospect of losing one's masculine gender status and being reduced to the social ranks of women therefore represented a universal possibility for all men. In such a context, the figure of the *kinaidos* stood as a warning to men of what could happen to them if they gave up the internal struggle to master their desires and surrendered, in womanly fashion, to the lure of pleasure. The clear implication of this warning is that the only thing that prevents men from allowing other men to use them as objects of sexual degradation, the only thing that enables men to resist the temptation to let other men fuck them like whores, is not the nature of their own desires, or their own capacities for sexual enjoyment, but their hard-won masculine ability to withstand the seductive appeal of pleasure-at-any-price. The *kinaidos*, on this view, is not someone who has a different sexual orientation from other men, or who belongs to some autonomous sexual species. Rather, he is someone who represents what *every* man would be like if he were so shameless as to sacrifice his dignity and masculine gender status for the sake of gratifying the most odious and disgraceful, though no doubt voluptuous, bodily appetites. Such a worthless character is so radical and so complete a failure as a man that he could be understood, at least by the ancients, as wholly reversing the internal gender hierarchy that structured and defined normative masculinity for men and that maintained it against manifold temptations to effeminacy. The catastrophic failure of male self-fashioning that the *kinaidos* represented was so complete, in other words, that it could not be imagined as merely confined within the sphere of erotic life or restricted to the occasional performance of disreputable sexual acts: it defined and determined a man's social identity in its totality, and it generated a recognizable social type—namely, the "scare-image" and phobic stereotype of the *kinaidos,* which Winkler so eloquently described.

As the mere existence of the stereotype implies, the ancients were quite capable of conceptualizing the figure of the *kinaidos,* when they so desired, not only in anxiously universalizing terms but also in comfortably minoritizing ones. Although some normal men might acknowledge that the scandalous pleasures to which the *kinaidos* succumbed, and which normal men properly avoided, were universally pleasurable in and of themselves,[22] still the very fact that the *kinaidos* did succumb to such pleasures, whereas normal men did not, contributed to defining his difference and marked out the vast distance that separated the *kinaidos* from normal men. Just as some moderns may think that, whereas anyone *can* get addicted to drugs, only people who have something fundamentally wrong with them actually *do,* so some ancients evidently thought that, although the pleasures of sexual penetration in themselves might be universal, any male who actually pursued them suffered from a specific constitutional defect—namely, a constitutional lack of the masculine capacity to withstand the appeal of pleasure (especially pleasure deemed exceptionally disgraceful or degrading) as well as a constitutional tendency to adopt a specifically feminine attitude of surrender in relations with other men. Hence, the desire to be sexually penetrated by other men, which was the most dramatic and flagrant sign of the *kinaidos*'s constitutional femininity, could be interpreted by the ancients in sharply minoritizing terms as an indication of a physiological anomaly in the *kinaidos* or as the symptom of a moral or mental "disease."[23] Conceived in these terms, the *kinaidos* did not represent the frightening possibility of a failure of nerve on the part of every man, a collapse in the face of the ongoing struggle that all men necessarily waged to maintain and defend their masculinity; he was simply a peculiar, repugnant, and perplexing freak, driven to abandon his sexual and gender identity in pursuit of a pleasure that no one but a woman could possibly enjoy. (And there were even some abominable practices, like fellatio, which a *kinaidos* might relish but no decent woman would so much as contemplate.)

The details in this minoritizing conception of the *kinaidos* have been filled in with great skill and documented at fascinating length by Maud Gleason, most recently in her 1995 book, *Making Men.* "The essential idea here," writes Gleason, corroborating Winkler's emphasis on the gender deviance of the *kinaidos* and calling attention to what she fittingly terms the ancient "semiotics of gender" that produced the *kinaidos* as a visibly deviant kind of being, "is that there exist [according to the axioms of Greek and Roman social life] masculine and feminine 'types' that do not necessarily correspond to the anatomical sex of the person in question."[24] Gleason approaches the figure of the *kinaidos* from an unexpected and original scholarly angle—namely, from a close study of the neglected scientific writings of the ancient physiognomists, experts in the learned technique of deciphering a person's character from his or her appearance. Gleason's analysis of the ancient corpus of physiognomic texts makes clear that the portrait they construct of the figure of the *kinaidos* agrees with the stereotypical features commonly ascribed by the ancients to the general appearance of gender-deviant or "effeminate" men. Like such men, the *kinaidos* could be identified, or so the Greeks thought, by a variety of physical features: weak eyes, knees that knock together, head tilted to the right, hands limply upturned, and hips that either swing from side to side or are held tightly rigid. Latin physiognomy agrees largely with the Greek tradition in its enumeration of the characteristics of the *cinaedus:* "A tilted head, a mincing gait, an enervated voice, a lack of stability in the shoulders, and a feminine way of moving the body." Gleason adds that a *kinaidos* could also be known by certain specific mannerisms: "He shifts his eyes around in sheep-like fashion when he speaks; he touches his fingers to his nose; he compulsively obliterates all traces of spittle he may find—his own or anyone else's—by rubbing it into the dust with his heel; he frequently stops to admire what he considers his own best feature; he smiles furtively while talking; he holds his arms turned outwards; he laughs out loud; and he has an annoying habit of clasping other people by the hand."[25] The *kinaidos*, in short, is considerably more than the juridical subject of deviant sexual acts. To recur to Foucault's terminology, the *kinaidos* represents at the very least a full-blown morphology. As Gleason observes, "Foucault's description of the nineteenth-century homosexual fits the *cinaedus* remarkably well. . . . The *cinaedus* was a 'life-form' all to himself, and his condition was written all over him in signs that could be decoded by those practiced in the art." Gleason hastens to add, however, that "what made [the *cinaedus*] different from normal folk . . . was not simply the fact that his sexual partners included people of the same sex as himself (that, after all, was nothing out of the ordinary), nor was it some kind of psychosexual orientation—a 'sexuality' in the nineteenth-century sense—but rather an inversion or reversal of his gender identity: his abandonment of a 'masculine' role in favor of a 'feminine' one."[26]

Gleason's conclusion has now been massively confirmed by Craig Williams, a specialist in ancient Roman literature, who has undertaken an exhaustive survey of the extant Latin sources. Williams's careful discussion makes it clear that the category of *cinaedus* does not correspond to any type of individual defined by more recent, canonical categories of "sexuality": "when a Roman called a man a *cinaedus*," Williams explains, "he was not ruling out the possibility that the man might play sexual roles other than that of the receptive partner in anal intercourse." Hence,

> the *cinaedus* was not the same thing as a "passive homosexual," since it was neither his expression of sexual desire for other males nor his proclivity for playing the receptive role in anal intercourse that gave him his identity or uniquely defined him as a *cinaedus:* he might engage in sexual practices with women and still be a *cinaedus*, and a man did not automatically become a *cinaedus* simply by being penetrated (victims of rape, for example, would not normally be described as such). A *cinaedus* was, rather, a man who failed to be fully masculine, whose effeminacy showed itself in such symptoms as feminine clothing and mannerisms and a lascivious and oversexed demeanor that was likely to be embodied in a proclivity for playing the receptive role in anal intercourse. *Cinaedi* were, in other words, a prominent subset of the class of effeminate men (*molles*) . . . but hardly identical to that whole class.[27]

Williams goes on to align his own analysis of the *cinaedus* with the tradition of interpretation which extends from Winkler and Gleason to the argument proposed here:

> Likewise I am suggesting that the Roman *cinaedus* was in fact a category of person who was considered "socially deviant," but that his social identity was crucially different from that of the "homosexual," since his desire for persons of his own sex was not a defining or even problematic feature of his makeup as a deviant: his desire to be penetrated was indeed one of his characteristics, but, as we have seen, men called *cinaedi* were also thought capable of being interested in penetrative sexual relations with women. Thus the deviance of the *cinaedus* is ultimately a matter of gender identity rather than sexual identity, in the sense that his predilection for playing the receptive role in penetrative acts was not the single defining feature of his identity but rather a sign of a more fundamental transgression of gender categories.[28]

33

Whatever its superficial resemblances to various contemporary sexual life-forms, the ancient figure of the *cinaedus* or *kinaidos* inhabits a cultural universe of its own.

In fact, the *kinaidos* has not as yet brought us quite into the realm of deviant sexual subjectivity. For whether he was defined in universalizing or minoritizing terms, the *kinaidos* was in any case defined more in terms of gender than in terms of desire. Although he was distinguished from normal men in part by the pleasure he took in being sexually penetrated, his peculiar taste was not sufficient, in and of itself, to individuate him as a sexual subject. Rather, it was *a generic sign of femininity.* Even the *kinaidos*'s desire to play a receptive role in sexual intercourse with other men—which was about as close to manifesting a distinctive sexual orientation as the *kinaidos* ever got—represented to the ancients "merely a symptom of the deeper disorder, his gender deviance," as Williams emphasizes (see n. 18), and so it did not imply a different kind of specifically sexual subjectivity.[29] At once a symptom and a consequence of the *kinaidos*'s categorical reversal of his masculine gender identity, the desire to be sexually penetrated identified the *kinaidos* as womanly in both his gender identity and his sexual desire; beyond that, it did not distinguish him as the bearer of a unique or distinct sexuality. Neither did his lust for bodily pleasure, since—far from being considered a deviant desire, as we have seen—such lust was thought common to all men. Nor was there anything peculiar about the *kinaidos*'s sexual object-choice: as Gleason mentions, it was quite possible in the ancient Mediterranean world for a male to desire and to pursue sexual contact with other males without impugning in the slightest his own masculinity or normative identity as a man—just so long as he played an insertive sexual role, observed all the proper phallocentric protocols in his relations with the objects of his desire, and maintained a normatively masculine style of personal deportment. Unlike the modern homosexual, then, the *kinaidos* was not defined principally by his sexual subjectivity. Even without a sexual subjectivity of his own, however, the *kinaidos*'s betrayal of his masculine gender identity was so spectacular as to brand him a deviant type of person and to inscribe his deviant identity all over his face and body. To put it very schematically, the *kinaidos* represents an instance of deviant sexual morphology without deviant sexual subjectivity.[30]

Let's move on, then, from matters of sexual morphology and gender presentation and take up matters of sexual subjectivity. My chief exhibit in this latter department will be an ancient erotic fable told by Apuleius in the second century and retold by Giovanni Boccaccio in the fourteenth. The two texts have been the subject of a trenchant comparative study by Jonathan Walters in a 1993 issue of *Gender and History*. I have taken Walters's analysis as the basis of my own, and my interpretation closely follows his, although I have a somewhat different set of questions to put to the two texts.[31]

Here, first of all, in bare outline, is the plot of the erotic fable under scrutiny. A man dining out at the home of a friend finds his dinner interrupted when his host detects an adulterous lover concealed in the house by the host's wife, who had not expected her husband to arrive home for dinner, much less with a guest in tow. His meal abruptly terminated, the disappointed guest returns to his own house for dinner ahead of schedule and tells the story to his righteously indignant wife, only to discover that she herself has hidden in his house a young lover of her own. Instead of threatening to kill the youth, however, the husband fucks him and lets him go. The end. This bare summary does little justice to the artistry and wit with which the two stories are told by their respective authors, but the point I wish to make is a historical one, not a literary one. I trust it will emerge from the following comparison.

Apuleius's tale of the baker's wife in book 9 of *The Golden Ass* begins with a description of her lover. He is a boy (*puer*), Apuleius's narrator tells us, still notable for the shiny smoothness of his beardless cheeks, and still delighting and attracting the sexual attention of wayward husbands (*adulteros*) (9.22). According to the erotic postulates of ancient Mediterranean societies, then, there will be nothing out of the ordinary about a normal man finding him sexually desirable. So the first thing to notice is that Apuleius explains the sexual motivation of the wronged husband by reference to erotic qualities inherent in the sexual *object*, not by reference to any distinguishing characteristics of the sexual *subject*—not, in other words, by reference to the husband's own sexual tastes, to his erotic subjectivity. This emphasis on the attractiveness of the boy thereby prepares the way for the ending of the story; it is not necessary for the narrator to invoke any specific sort of erotic inclination, much less a deviant one, on the part of the husband in order to anticipate the *dénouement* of the plot. In fact, as Walters observes, the husband "is not described in any way that marks him out as unusual, let alone reprehensible: he is portrayed as blameless, 'a good man in general and extremely temperate'"; that is in keeping with a story designed, within the larger context of Apuleius's narrative, to illustrate the mischief caused to their husbands by devious, depraved, and adulterous wives.[32]

When the baker discovers the boy, he locks up his wife and takes the boy to bed himself, thereby (as Apuleius's narrator puts it) enjoying "the most gratifying revenge for his ruined marriage." At daybreak he summons two of his slaves and has them hold the boy up while he flogs his buttocks with a rod, leaving the boy "with his white buttocks the worse for their treatment" both by night and by day. The baker then kicks his wife out of the house and prepares to divorce her (9.28).

Boccaccio's tale of Pietro di Vinciolo of Perugia, the tenth story of the fifth day of the *Decameron*, is based directly on Apuleius; its departures from its model are therefore especially telling.[33] Boccaccio's narrator begins further back in time, at the point when Pietro takes a wife "more to beguile others and to abate the general suspect [*la generale oppinion*] in which he was held by all the Perugians, than for any desire [*vaghezza*] of his own" (trans. Payne-Singleton). As Walters remarks, "Boccaccio . . . is at pains to tell us from the beginning that something is wrong with the husband."[34] What Boccaccio marks specifically as deviant about Pietro, or so the foregoing quotation from the *Decameron* implies, is his *desire*.[35] This turns out to refer to his sexual object-choice and to comprehend, in particular, two different aspects of it: first, the customary objects of his sexual desire are young men, not the usual objects of desire for a man, and, second, Pietro (unlike the baker in Apuleius) has no desire for the usual objects of male desire — namely, women. So he has a nonstandard erotic subjectivity, insofar as he both desires the wrong objects and fails to desire the right objects.

Both of these erotic errors are dramatized by the narrative. We are told that his wife's lover is "a youth [*garzone*], who was one of the goodliest and most agreeable of all Perugia," and that when Pietro discovers him, he instantly recognizes him as "one whom he had long pursued for his own lewd ends." Understandably, Pietro "no less rejoiced to have found him than his wife was woeful"; when he confronts her with the lad, "she saw that he was all agog with joy because he held so goodly a stripling [*giovinetto*] by the hand." No wonder that, far from punishing his wife, Pietro hastens to strike an obscene bargain with her to share the young man between them. As for Pietro's sexual indifference to women, we are told that his lusty, red-haired, highly sexed young wife, "who would liefer have had two husbands than one," is frustrated by her husband's inattention and realizes that she will exhaust herself arguing with him before she will change his disposition. Indeed, he has "a mind far more disposed otherwhat than to her" [*molto piú ad altro che a lei l'animo avea disposto*]. At the culmination of the story, Pietro's wife reproaches him for being as desirous of women as "a dog of cudgels" [*cosí vago di noi come il can delle mazze*].[36]

Note that Boccaccio's narrator says nothing to indicate that Pietro is effeminate, or in any way deviant in terms of his personal style or sexual morphology.[37] *You wouldn't know he was a paederast or a sodomite by looking at him.* Nothing about his looks or his behavior gives him away—or gives his wife any advance warning about the nature of his sexual peculiarities. As she says, she had supposed he desired what men typically do desire and should desire when she married him; otherwise, she would never have done so. "He knew I was a woman," she exclaims to herself; "why, then, did he take me to wife, if women were not to his mind [*contro all'animo*]?" Nothing in his morphology made her suspect he harbored deviant desires. And why in any case should we presume that the husband would exhibit signs of effeminacy? He no more resembles the ancient figure of the *kinaidos* than does his literary forebear in Apuleius. Far from displaying a supposedly "feminine" inclination to submit himself to other men to be sexually penetrated by them, the husband in Boccaccio plays a sexually insertive role in intercourse with his wife's lover. That, after all, is the point of the story's punchline: "On the following morning the youth was escorted back to the public square not altogether certain which he had the more been that night, wife or husband"—meaning, obviously, *wife to Pietro* or *husband to Pietro's wife.*[38] What is at issue in Boccaccio's portrait of Pietro di Vinciolo, then, is not gender deviance but sexual deviance.

Finally, in Apuleius's tale the husband's enjoyment of his wife's lover is an incidental component of his revenge and does not express any special or distinctive sexual taste on his part, much less a habitual preference, whereas in Boccaccio's tale the husband is identified as the subject of deviant sexual desires and is only too happy to exploit his wife's infidelity for the purposes of his own pleasure.[39]

A comparison of these two premodern texts indicates that it is possible for sexual acts to be represented in such texts as either *more* or *less* related to sexual dispositions, desires, or subjectivities. Whereas Apuleius's text makes no incriminating association between the baker's sexual enjoyment of the adulterous youth and the baker's character, masculinity, or sexual disposition, Boccaccio's text connects the performance of sodomitical acts with a deviant sexual taste and a deviant sexual subjectivity. In order to update Apuleius's plot it seems to have been necessary for Boccaccio to posit a sodomitical disposition or inclination on the husband's part: he seems to have had no other way of motivating the scandalously witty conclusion of the tale as he had inherited it from Apuleius. Pietro's inclination is not the same thing as a sexual orientation, much less a sexual identity or form of life, to be sure. For one thing, his sexual preference seems contained,

37

compartmentalized, and does not appear to connect to any other feature of his character, such as a sensibility, a set of personal mannerisms, a style of gender presentation, or a psychology.[40] Nonetheless, Pietro's sexual taste for young men represents a notable and perhaps even a defining feature of his life as a sexual subject, as well as a distinctive feature of his life as a social and ethical subject. Pietro may not be a deviant life-form, like the ancient Greek or Roman *kinaidos*—a traitor to his gender whose deviance is visibly inscribed in his personal demeanor—but neither is he nothing more than the juridical subject of a sodomitical act. Rather, his sexual preference for youths is a settled feature of his character and a significant fact about his social identity as a moral and sexual agent.[41]

To sum up, I have tried to suggest that the current doctrine that holds that sexual acts were unconnected to sexual identities before the nineteenth century is mistaken in at least two different respects. First, sexual acts could be interpreted as representative components of an individual's sexual morphology. Second, sexual acts could be interpreted as representative expressions of an individual's sexual subjectivity. A sexual morphology is not the same thing as a sexual subjectivity: the figure of the *kinaidos*, for example, represents an instance of deviant morphology without subjectivity, whereas Boccaccio's Pietro represents an instance of deviant subjectivity without morphology. Thus, morphology and subjectivity, as I have been using those terms, describe two *different* logics according to which sexual acts can be connected to some more generalized feature of an individual's identity. In particular, I have argued that the ancient figure of the *kinaidos* qualifies as an instance of a sexual life-form or morphology, and therefore that the property of *kinaidia* (or being a *kinaidos*) is a property of social beings, not merely of sexual acts. Nonetheless, what defines the *kinaidos* is not a unique or peculiar subjectivity but a shameless appetite for pleasure, which is common to all human beings, along with a deviant gender style, which assimilates him to the cultural definition of woman. By contrast, the sodomitical character of Boccaccio's Pietro di Vinciolo does not express itself through a deviant morphology but through his sexual tastes, preferences, inclinations, or desires—that is, through a deviant subjectivity. Sodomy, in Boccaccio's world, like *kinaidia* in classical antiquity, is a property of social beings, not merely of sexual acts. The relation between the sodomitical act and the subject who performs it is constructed differently in the case of the sodomite from the way that acts and social identities are connected in the case of the *kinaidos*.

Neither the sexual morphology of the *kinaidos* nor the sexual subjectivity of the fourteenth-century Italian sodomite should be understood as a sexual identity, or a sexual orientation in the modern sense—much less as equivalent to the modern formation known as homosexuality. At the very least, modern notions of homosexual identity and homosexual orientation tend to insist on the *conjunction* of sexual morphology and sexual subjectivity: they presume a convergence in the sexual actor of a deviant personal style with a deviant erotic desire.[42] In fact, what historically distinguishes "homosexuality" as a sexual classification is its unprecedented combination of at least three distinct and previously uncorrelated conceptual entities: (1) a psychiatric notion of a perverted or pathological *orientation*, derived from nineteenth-century medicine, which is an essentially *psychological* concept that applies to the inner life of the individual and does not necessarily entail same-sex sexual behavior or desire; (2) a psychoanalytic notion of same-sex *sexual object-choice* or desire, derived from Sigmund Freud and his coworkers, which is a category of erotic intentionality and does not necessarily imply a permanent psychosexual orientation, let alone a pathological or deviant one (since, according to Freud, most normal individuals make an unconscious homosexual *object-choice* at least at some point in their fantasy lives); and (3) a sociological notion of sexually *deviant behavior*, derived from nineteenth- and twentieth-century forensic inquiries into "social problems," which focuses on non-standard sexual practice and does not necessarily refer to erotic psychology or psychosexual orientation (since same-sex sexual behavior is widely distributed in the population, as Kinsey showed, and is not the exclusive property of those with a unique psychology or a homosexual sexual orientation).[43] So, despite their several failures to meet the requirements of the modern definition of the homosexual, both the *kinaidos* and Boccaccio's Pietro, in their quite different and distinctive ways, challenge the orthodox pseudo-Foucauldian doctrine about the supposedly strict separation between sexual acts and sexual identities in European culture before the nineteenth century.

My argument, then, does not refute Foucault's claim about the different ways male same-sex eroticism was constructed by the discourse of "the ancient civil or canonical codes" and by the discourse of nineteenth-century sexology. Nor does it demolish the absolutely indispensable distinction between sexual acts and sexual identities that historians of homosexuality have extracted from Foucault's text (where the term *identity* nowhere occurs) and that, in any case, antedated it by many years.[44] Least of all does it undermine a rigorously historicizing approach to the study of the social and cultural constitution of sexual subjectivity and sexual identity. (Whatever I may be up to in this chapter, a posthumous *rapprochement* with John Boswell is not it.) What my argument does do, I hope, is to encourage us to inquire into the construction of sexual identities before the emergence of sexual orientations, and to do this *without* recurring to modern notions of "sexuality" or sexual orientation and thereby contributing to a kind of antihistoricist backlash. Perhaps we need to supplement our notion of sexual identity with a more refined concept of, say, partial identity, emergent identity, transient identity, semi-identity, incomplete identity, proto-identity, or sub-identity.[45] In any case, my intent is not to reinstall a notion of sexual identity as a historical category so much as to indicate *the multiplicity of possible historical connections between sex and identity,* a multiplicity whose existence has been obscured by the necessary but narrowly focused, totalizing critique of sexual identity as a unitary concept. We need to find ways of asking how different historical cultures fashioned different sorts of links between sexual acts, on the one hand, and sexual tastes, styles, dispositions, characters, gender presentations, and forms of subjectivity, on the other.

It is a matter of considerable irony that Foucault's influential distinction between the discursive construction of the sodomite and the discursive construction of the homosexual, which had originally been intended to open up a domain of historical inquiry, has now become a major obstacle blocking further research into the rudiments of sexual identity formation in premodern and early modern European societies. Foucault himself would surely have been astonished. Not only was he much too good a historian ever to have authorized the incautious and implausible claim that no one had ever had a sexual subjectivity, a sexual morphology, or a sexual identity of any kind before the nineteenth century (even if he painstakingly demonstrated that the conditions necessary for having a *sexuality,* a psychosexual orientation in the modern sense, did not in fact obtain until then). His approach to what he called "the history of the present" was also too searching, too experimental, and too open ended to tolerate converting a heuristic analytic distinction into an ill-founded historical dogma, as his more forgetful epigones have not hesitated to do.

Of course, the chief thing about Foucault that his self-styled disciples forget is that he did not propound a theory of sexuality. That fact about Foucault is the more easily forgotten as Foucault has become, especially in the United States and Britain, the property of academic critical theorists—the property of those, in other words, whose claim to the professional title of "theorist" derives from the reflected status, authority, and "theoretical" credentials of the thinkers they study. As one of those thinkers whose identity as a "theorist" is necessary to ground the secondary and derived "theoretical" status of others, Foucault is required to have a theory. Theories, after all, are what "theorists" are supposed to have.

Now of course Foucault's *History of Sexuality,* volume 1, is theoretical, in the sense that it undertakes a far-reaching critical intervention in the realm of theory. It is, more particularly, an effort to dislodge and to thwart the effects of already established theories—theories that attempt to tell us the truth about sexuality, to produce true accounts of its nature, to specify what sexuality really is, to inquire into sexuality as a positive thing that has a truth that can be told, and to ground authoritative forms of expertise in an objective knowledge of sexuality. Foucault's radical theoretical take on sexuality consists in approaching it from the perspective of the history of discourses, as an element in a larger political-discursive technology: he treats it accordingly not as a positive thing but as an instrumental effect, not as a physical or psychological reality but as a social and political device; he is not trying to describe what sexuality is but to specify what it does and how it works in discursive and institutional practice. That approach to sexuality represents *a theoretical intervention* insofar as it engages with already existing theories of sexuality, but the nature of the engagement remains purely tactical: it is part of a larger strategic effort to effect a thoroughgoing *evasion* of theories of sexuality and to devise various means of circumventing their claims to specify the truth of sexuality—not by attempting to refute those claims directly and to install a new truth in their place but by attempting to expose and to delegitimate the strategies they employ to construct and to authorize their truth claims in the first place. It is this deliberate, ardent, and considered resistance to "theory" that defines Foucault's own practice of theory, his distinctive brand of (theoretical) critique.[46]

To undertake such a theoretical critique, to attempt to reorient our understanding of sexuality by approaching the history of sexuality from the perspective of the history of discourses, is obviously not to offer a new theory of sexuality, much less to try to substitute such a theory for those that already exist. Nor is it an attempt to claim, theoretically, that sexuality *is* discourse, or that it is constituted discursively instead of naturally. It is rather an effort to denaturalize, dematerialize, and derealize sexuality so as to prevent it from serving as the positive grounding for a theory of sexuality, to prevent it from answering to "the functional requirements of a discourse that must produce its truth."[47] It is an attempt to destroy the circuitry that connects sexuality, truth, and power. And thus it is an effort to take sexuality away from the experts and make it available to us as a possible source for a series of scholarly and political counterpractices. *The History of Sexuality*, volume 1, in short, does not contain an original theory of sexuality. If anything, its theoretical originality lies in its refusal of existing theory and its consistent elaboration of a critical antitheory. It offers a model demonstration of how to dismantle theories of sexuality, how to deprive them of their claims to legitimate authority. *The History of Sexuality*, volume 1, is a difficult book to read chiefly because we read it as conveying Foucault's formulation of his theory of sexuality. (There is no easier way to baffle students than by asking them to explain what Foucault's own definition of "sexuality" is: it is the worst sort of trick question.) As a theory of sexuality, however, *The History of Sexuality*, volume 1, is unreadable. That may in fact be its greatest virtue.

For our hankering after a correct theory of sexuality seems scarcely diminished since Foucault's day, least of all among academic practitioners of so-called "queer theory."[48] By juxtaposing to this "theoretical" tendency in queer theory Foucault's own example, by contrasting the queer retheorizing of sexuality with Foucault's strategic undoing of sexual theory, I am not trying to lend aid and comfort to "the enemies of theory" (who would forget not just Foucault but "theory" itself), nor do I mean to contribute to the phobic totalization and homogenization of "theory"—as if there could possibly be any sense in treating theory as a unitary entity that could then be either praised or disparaged. To argue that *The History of Sexuality*, volume 1, contains not a theory but a critical antitheory is not to argue that the book is "anti" theory, against theory, but rather to indicate that its theoretical enterprise, which is the derealization or desubstantialization of sexuality, militates strenuously against the construction or vindication of any theory of sexuality. Moreover, no inquiry into the deficiencies of contemporary work in lesbian and gay studies or the history of sexuality that pretends to be serious can content itself with mere carping at individual scholarly abuses of "theory" (the notion that scholars nowadays have all been corrupted by "theory" is about as plausible as the notion that lesbian and gay academics have seized control of the universities—and probably derives from the same source); rather, it must take up such institutional questions as how many professors with qualifications in "queer theory" are tenured at major universities and are actually guiding the work of graduate students intending and able to pursue scholarly careers in that field.

Nonetheless, I find the doctrinaire theoretical tendencies in "queer theory" and in academic "critical theory" to be strikingly at odds with the anti-dogmatic, critical, and experimental impulses that originally animated a good deal of the work we now consider part of the canon of "theory." Foucault stands out in this context as one of the few canonical theorists whose theoretical work seems calculated to resist theoretical totalization, premature theoretical closure, and thereby to resist the weirdest and most perverse instance of "the resistance to theory": namely, the sort of resistance to theory that expresses itself *through* the now-standard academic practice of so-called critical theory itself.[49] Foucault's refusal of a theory of sexuality resists the complacencies of the increasingly dogmatic and reactionary resistance to theory that misleadingly and all too often answers to the name of "theory." I believe it is our resistance to Foucault's resistance to this resistance to theory, our insistence on transforming Foucault's critical antitheory into a theory of sexuality, that has led us to mistake his discursive analysis for a historical assertion — and that has licensed us, on that basis, to remake his strategic distinction between the sodomite and the homosexual into a conceptual distinction between sexual acts and sexual identities, into a bogus theoretical doctrine, and into a patently false set of historical premises. I also believe it is what has led us to convert his strategic appeal to bodies and pleasures as a means of resistance to the apparatus of sexuality into a theoretical specification of the irreducible elements of sexuality. And it is what has made Foucault's intellectual example increasingly, and quite properly, forgettable. If indeed it is as a theorist of sexuality that we remember Foucault, perhaps Baudrillard was right after all: the greatest service we can do to him, and to ourselves, is to forget him as quickly as possible.

Let me give the last word to Foucault, however. In an early essay on Gustave Flaubert, Foucault described an experience of the fantastic that he believed was new in the nineteenth century, "the discovery of a new imaginative space" in the archives of the library. "This domain of phantasms is no longer the night, the sleep of reason, or the uncertain void that stands before desire, but, on the contrary, wakefulness, untiring attention, zealous erudition, and constant vigilance. Henceforth, the visionary experience arises from the black and white surface of printed signs, from the closed and dusty volume that opens with a flight of forgotten words; fantasies are carefully deployed in the hushed library, with its columns of books, with its titles aligned on shelves to form a tight enclosure, but within confines that also liberate impossible worlds. The imaginary now resides between the book and the lamp. The fantastic is no longer a property of the heart, nor is it found among the incongruities of nature; it evolves from the accuracy of knowledge, and its treasures lie dormant in documents."[50] The history of sexuality, at its best, should serve as a reminder of the one thing that no one who has been touched by Foucault's writing is likely ever to forget: namely, that the space of imaginative fantasy that the nineteenth century discovered in the library is not yet exhausted, and that it may still prove to be productive—both for academic scholarship and for our ongoing processes of personal and cultural self-transformation.

Notes

1. For all of the information and the quotations in this paragraph, I am indebted to David Macey, *The Lives of Michel Foucault* (London: Hutchinson, 1993), esp. 358–60. See, further, Jean Baudrillard, *Cool Memories, I et II: 1980–1990* (Paris: Le Livre de Poche, 1993 [originally published 1987, 1990]) 139–42, esp. 140 ("L'oublier était lui rendre service, l'aduler était le desservir"), and 139 ("Mort de Foucault. Perte de confiance en son propre génie. . . . La perte des systèmes immunitaires, en dehors de tout aspect sexuel, n'est que la transcription biologique de l'autre processus").

For some resumptions of the "forget Foucault" theme, see E. Greblo, "Dimenticare Foucault?" *Aut-Aut,* 242 (March–April 1991): 79–90; and Kate Soper, "Forget Foucault?" *New Formations,* 25 (summer 1995): 21–27.

2. Baudrillard delivers himself of this enlightened opinion in the course of an interview with F. Rötzer, "Virtuelle Katastrophen," *Kunstforum,* January–February 1990, 266: I reproduce here the quotation and citation provided by Douglas Crimp, "Portraits of People with AIDS," in *Cultural Studies,* ed. Lawrence Grossberg, Cary Nelson, and Paula A. Treichler (New York: Routledge, 1992), 117–33 (quotation on 130).

3. Michel Foucault, *The History of Sexuality,* vol. 1, *An Introduction,* trans. Robert Hurley (New York: Vintage, 1980), 159; cf. Michel Foucault, *Histoire de la sexualité,* vol. 1, *La volonté de savoir,* (Paris: Gallimard, 1984 [1976]), 211. Wherever possible, I quote the English text of Foucault's *History of Sexuality,* because it is that text which has influenced Foucault's Anglophone disciples, with whom I am concerned in this essay, but I have altered the published translation whenever necessary to restore Foucault's original emphasis or meaning.

4. Foucault, *The History of Sexuality,* 1:157. See, further, David M. Halperin, *Saint Foucault: Towards a Gay Hagiography* (New York: Oxford University Press, 1995), 92–97.

5. Foucault, *The History of Sexuality,* 1:157 (emended); *La volonté de savoir,* 208.

6. Foucault, *The History of Sexuality,* 1:43 (translation considerably modified); *La volonté de savoir,* 59.

7. This view has now been contested by Mark D. Jordan, *The Invention of Sodomy in Christian Theology* (Chicago: University of Chicago Press, 1997), esp. 42, 44, 163.

8. In a passage that provides the closest textual and historical parallel in Foucault's writings to the famous passage in *The History of Sexuality,* volume 1, Foucault seems to distinguish between sodomy and homosexuality in much the same terms as do those historians of sexuality whose views I am criticizing here. The passage occurs in a book-length transcript of six taped interviews with a young gay man named Thierry Voeltzel that Foucault recorded during the summer of 1976, just as he was completing *The*

History of Sexuality, volume 1, and that he arranged to have published under Voeltzel's name. At one point in the conversation the anonymous interviewer (i.e., Foucault) makes the following observation: "The category of the homosexual was invented lately. It didn't use to exist; what existed was sodomy, that is to say a certain number of sexual practices which, in themselves, were condemned, but the homosexual individual did not exist" [La catégorie de l'homosexuel a été inventée tardivement. Ça n'existait pas, ce qui existait, c'était la sodomie, c'est-à-dire un certain nombre de pratiques sexuelles qui, elles, étaient condamnées, mais l'individu homosexuel n'existait pas]. See Thierry Voeltzel, *Vingt ans et après* (Paris: Grasset, 1978), 33.

In this conversation with Voeltzel, Foucault may sound as if he is saying that once upon a time there were only sexual acts, not sexual actors. (That is how Didier Eribon interprets the passage: see Eribon, *Réflexions sur la question gay* [Paris: Fayard, 1999], 372–442; translated by Michael Lucey as "Michel Foucault's Histories of Sexuality," *GLQ: A Journal of Lesbian and Gay Studies,* 7, no. 1 [2001]: 31–86.) Note, however, that Foucault is simplifying matters for the benefit of his decidedly unacademic interlocutor; that, even so, he stops short of making a formal distinction between acts and identities; and that he never in fact says that before the nineteenth century there were no sexual identities, only sexual acts. What preoccupies him in his exchange with Voeltzel, just as in *The History of Sexuality,* volume 1, is the relatively recent invention of the normalizing "category" of the homosexual, the discursive constitution of a class of deviant individuals as opposed to the mere enumeration of a set of forbidden practices; when he refers to "the homosexual individual," he is referring to the entity constructed by the modern discourses of psychiatry and sexology. It is only lately, Foucault emphasizes in his interview with Voeltzel, that it has become almost impossible simply to pursue the pleasures of homosexual contact, as Voeltzel appears to have done, "just so, when you felt like it, every once in a while, or in phases" [comme ca, quand tu en avais envie, par moments, ou par phases], without being forced to deduce from one's own behavior that one *is* homosexual, without being interpellated by the culpabilizing category of "the homosexual." Voeltzel's narrative therefore reminds Foucault of an earlier historical period when it was possible to *practice* homosexuality without *being* homosexual.

As time went by, and Foucault's thinking about the history of sexuality evolved, he abandoned the contrast between sodomy and homosexuality along with the implicit opposition between practices and persons and came up with new ways of representing the differences between modern and premodern forms of same-sex sexual experience. In 1982, for example, in a review of the French translation of K. J. Dover's 1978 monograph *Greek Homosexuality,* Foucault wrote: "Of course, there will still be some folks disposed to think that, in the final analysis, homosexuality has always existed. . . . To such naive souls Dover gives a good lesson in historical nominalism. [Sexual] relations between two persons of the same sex are one thing. But to love the same sex as oneself, to take one's pleasure in that sex, is quite another thing, it's a whole experience, with its own objects and their meanings, with a specific way of being on the part of the subject and a consciousness which he has of himself. That experience is complex, it is diverse, it takes different forms, it changes" [Bien sûr, on trouvera encore des esprits aimables pour penser qu'en somme l'homosexualité a toujours existé. . . . A de tels naïfs, Dover donne une bonne leçon de nominalisme historique. Le rapport entre deux individus du même sexe est une chose. Mais aimer le même sexe que soi, prendre avec lui un plaisir, c'est autre chose, c'est toute une expérience, avec ses objets et leurs valeurs, avec la manière d'être du sujet et la conscience qu'il a de lui-même. Cette expérience est complexe, elle est diverse, elle change de formes]: Michel Foucault, "Des caresses d'hommes considérées comme un art," *Libération,* 1 June 1982, 27. Here Foucault inveighs against applying to the Greeks an undifferentiated, ahistorical, and transcendental notion of homosexuality defined purely behaviorally, in terms of sexual practice ("sexual relations between two persons of the same sex"), in favor of a more nuanced, contextualized understanding that foregrounds specific, conscious "ways of being" on the part of different historical and sexual subjects. That is very much in keeping with Foucault's emphasis in his famous 1981 interview in *Le gai pied* on homosexuality as a "way of life" (*mode de vie*): Michel Foucault, "De l'amitié comme mode de vie," *Le gai pied,* 25 (April 1981): 38–39; trans. John Johnston in *Foucault Live (Interviews, 1961–1984),* ed. Sylvère Lotringer (New York: Semiotext(e), 1989), 308–12. But now it is not so much a question of opposing "sexual practices" to categories of individuals, as Foucault was inclined to do in 1976; rather, it is a question of systematically defining different historical forms of sexual experience—different ways of being, different sets of relations to others and to oneself, different articulations of pleasure and meaning, different forms of consciousness. The exact terms in which such historical discriminations are to be made, however, remain unspecified. Foucault leaves that practical question of historical analysis and methodology to the individual historian. He is content simply to offer a model of how to proceed in the second and third volumes of his own unfinished *History of Sexuality.*

9. For example, Giulia Sissa, summarizing what she takes to be my position, writes, "before sexuality one does not find homosexuality but only a variety of sexual acts; not an identity, only a freedom of choice"; she bizarrely takes this view to be equivalent to claiming that there is no difference between classical Athens and contemporary San Francisco. See Sissa, "Sexual Bodybuilding: Aeschines against Timarchus," in *Constructions of the Classical Body,* ed. James I. Porter (Ann Arbor: University of Michigan Press, 1999), 147–68 (esp. 147 and 164). My own view is rather more nuanced, and I have tried to be precise in articulating it: "Before the scientific construction of 'sexuality' as a supposedly positive, distinct, and constitutive feature of individual human beings—an autonomous system within the physiological and psychological economy of the human organism—certain kinds of sexual *acts* could be individually evaluated and characterized, *and so could certain sexual tastes or inclinations,* but there was no conceptual apparatus available for identifying a person's fixed and determinate sexual *orientation,* much less for assessing and classifying it" (David M. Halperin, *One Hundred Years of Homosexuality and Other Essays on Greek Love* [New York: Routledge, 1990], 26; emphasis of the central phrase is added). The contrast here is between acts, tastes, and inclinations, on the one hand, and the modern sexological concept of sexual orientation, on the other. For a further refinement of this view, see my article "How to Do the History of Male Homosexuality," *GLQ: A Journal of Lesbian and Gay Studies* 6, no. 1 (2000): 87–124.

10. See, for example, Mary McIntosh, "The Homosexual Role," *Social Problems* 16 (1968/69): 182–92; Randolph Trumbach, "London's Sodomites: Homosexual Behavior and Western Culture in the 18th Century," *Journal of Social History* 11 (1977): 1–33; Richard Sennett, *The Fall of Public Man: On the Social Psychology of Capitalism* (New York: Vintage, 1978); Jeffrey Weeks, *Sex, Politics and Society: The Regulation of Sexuality since*

1800 (London: Longmans, 1981); Arnold I. Davidson, "Sex and the Emergence of Sexuality," *Critical Inquiry,* 14 (1987/88): 16–48; John D'Emilio and Estelle D. Freedman, *Intimate Matters: A History of Sexuality in America* (New York: Harper and Row, 1988); Thomas Laqueur, *Making Sex: Body and Gender from the Greeks to Freud* (Cambridge, Mass.: Harvard University Press, 1990); George Chauncey, *Gay New York: Gender, Urban Culture, and the Making of the Gay Male World, 1890–1940* (New York: Basic Books, 1994); Jonathan Ned Katz, *The Invention of Heterosexuality* (New York: Dutton, 1995); and Carolyn J. Dean, *Sexuality and Modern Western Culture* (New York: Twayne, 1996).

11. See the very careful demonstration of this point by Arnold I. Davidson, "Closing Up the Corpses: Diseases of Sexuality and the Emergence of the Psychiatric Style of Reasoning," in *Meaning and Method: Essays in Honor of Hilary Putnam,* ed. George Boolos (Cambridge: Cambridge University Press, 1990), 295–325.

12. For a similar argument to the same effect, see Ruth Mazo Karras, "Prostitution and the Question of Sexual Identity in Medieval Europe," *Journal of Women's History* 11, no. 2 (1999): 159–77. Karras's article appeared after the original version of "Forgetting Foucault" was published, but Karras arrived at her conclusions independently. Karras's and my approaches have been helpfully compared and assessed by Carla Freccero, "Acts, Identities, and Sexuality's (Pre)Modern Regimes," *Journal of Women's History* 11, no. 2 (1999): 186–92. Karras freely speaks of "sexuality" and "sexual identity" in premodern Europe; "I expect Halperin would disagree with much of what I have said here," she remarks in a rejoinder to Freccero's critique, "but I find his formulations useful nonetheless": see Ruth Mazo Karras, "Response: Identity, Sexuality, and History," *Journal of Women's History* 11, no. 2 (1999): 193–98 (quotation on 198 n. 19). I admit that I find Karras's treatment of the theoretical issues lacking in precision, care, and nuance, and I would not be likely to speak so incautiously about "sexuality" or "sexual identity" in reference to Karras's material, but I welcome her important and persuasive historical argument for the existence of identity categories in European discourses of sex in the medieval period. In that respect, her work is very much in line with the thesis of this essay.

13. Foucault's French text, ironically, allows more scope for misinterpretation than the English-language version, which explicitly emphasizes that the relevant sense of the term *sodomy* in this passage is determined by the formal discursive context of medieval civil and canon law. In Foucault's original formulation, the unambiguous initial phrase "as defined by" does not occur; instead, we find a more offhand reference to "the sodomy of the old civil and canonical codes." Foucault, it seems, did not feel the need to be so careful about instructing his French readers to understand "sodomy" here as a strictly discursive category rather than as a sexual practice or as a cultural representation; instead, it is Foucault's translator who has expanded the original formulation in order to make its meaning clear. As I am concerned with the misreadings of Foucault by scholars who work largely from the published translation of *The History of Sexuality,* volume 1, and as my exegesis of Foucault is facilitated by (without at all depending on) the greater explicitness of the English-language version, I have not hesitated to cite it in my text for the sake of clarity, jettisoning it later, once the interpretative point has been established.

14. Foucault, *The History of Sexuality,* 1:42–43; *La volonté de savoir,* 58–59; italics in original.

15. Foucault, *The History of Sexuality*, 1:37 (translation modified); *La volonté de savoir*, 51; italics added.

16. Foucault, *The History of Sexuality*, 1:38 (translation modified); *La volonté de savoir*, 52–53. Foucault explains, in a sentence that follows the conclusion of the passage quoted here, that "the 'nature' on which [sexual prohibitions] were based was still a kind of law."

17. Foucault, *The History Sexuality*, 1:48; *La volonté de savoir*, 66.

18. A complete and systematic definition of the Latin form of this ancient term has now been provided by Craig A. Williams, *Roman Homosexuality: Ideologies of Masculinity in Classical Antiquity* (New York: Oxford University Press, 1999), 175–78, esp. 175–76: "The word most often used to describe a man who had been anally penetrated was the noun *cinaedus*. But . . . *cinaedus* is not actually anchored in that specific sexual practice. . . . [I]t refers instead to a man who has an identity as gender deviant. In other words, a *cinaedus* is a man who fails to live up to traditional standards of masculine comportment, and one way in which he may do so is by seeking to be penetrated; but that is merely a symptom of a deeper disorder, his gender deviance. Indeed, the word's etymology suggests no direct connection to any sexual practice. Rather, borrowed from Greek *kinaidos* (which may itself have been a borrowing from a language of Asia Minor), it primarily signifies an effeminate dancer who entertained his audiences with a *tympanum* or tambourine in his hand, and adopted a lascivious style, often suggestively wiggling his buttocks in such a way as to suggest anal intercourse. . . . [T]he primary meaning of *cinaedus* never died out; the term never became a dead metaphor." And Williams concludes, "In sum, the word *cinaedus* originally referred to men who were professional dancers of a type associated with the East, dancing with a *tympanum* and seductively wiggling their buttocks in such a way as to suggest anal intercourse. In a transferred sense it came to describe a man who was not a dancer but who displayed the salient characteristics of a *cinaedus* in the strict sense: he was a gender-deviant, a 'non-man' who broke the rules of masculine comportment and whose effeminate disorder might be embodied in the particular symptom of seeking to be penetrated" (178).

19. John J. Winkler, *The Constraints of Desire: The Anthropology of Sex and Gender in Ancient Greece* (New York: Routledge, 1990), 45–46. The formulation is repeated, somewhat less emphatically, by Winkler, "Laying Down the Law: The Oversight of Men's Sexual Behavior in Classical Athens," in *Before Sexuality: The Construction of Erotic Experience in the Ancient Greek World*, ed. David M. Halperin, John J. Winkler, and Froma I. Zeitlin (Princeton, N.J.: Princeton University Press, 1990), 171–209, esp. 176–77.

20. I borrow the distinction between universalizing and minoritizing concepts of (homo)sexual identity from Eve Kosofsky Sedgwick, *Epistemology of the Closet* (Berkeley: University of California Press, 1990), 1, 9, 85–86.

21. Winkler, *The Constraints of Desire*, 50; Winkler, "Laying Down the Law," 182.

22. See, for example, Plato *Gorgias* 494C–E (quoted and discussed by Winkler, *The Constraints of Desire*, 53).

23. For ancient physiological explanations, see pseudo-Aristotle *Problems* 4.26; Phaedrus 4.15 (16). For imputations of mental disease, see Aristotle *Nicomachean Ethics* 7.5.3–4 (1148b26–35); *Priapea* 46.2; Seneca *Natural Questions* 1.16.1–3; Dio Cassius 80.16.1–5; Caelius Aurelianus *On Chronic Diseases* 4.9. Williams, *Roman Homosexuality*,

to whom I owe the foregoing citation from the *Priapea,* also provides additional parallels (Seneca *Letters* 83.20; Juvenal *Satires* 2.17 and 2.50), noting however that "a predilection for various kinds of excessive or disgraceful behavior was capable of being called a disease" by the Romans (he cites a number of compelling instances of such a usage) and therefore "*cinaedi* were not said to be *morbosi* in the way that twentieth-century homosexuals have been pitied or scorned as 'sick'" (181). The medicalizing language, in other words, does not operate in the two cultures in the same way, nor does it give rise to the same kind of disqualification. The point is an important one: the ancient usage is disapproving, but it is not wholly pathologizing.

24. Maud W. Gleason, "The Semiotics of Gender: Physiognomy and Self-Fashioning in the Second Century C.E.," in Halperin, Winkler, and Zeitlin, eds., *Before Sexuality,* 389–415 (quotation on 390), and *Making Men: Sophists and Self-Presentation in Ancient Rome* (Princeton, N.J.: Princeton University Press, 1995), 58.

25. Gleason, *Making Men,* 64; Gleason, "The Semiotics of Gender," 396.

26. Gleason, "The Semiotics of Gender," 411–12. Cf. Halperin, *One Hundred Years of Homosexuality,* 22–24.

27. Williams, *Roman Homosexuality,* 178.

28. Williams, *Roman Homosexuality,* 210–11.

29. Of course, the distinction between gender and sexuality, or between gender identity and sexual object-choice, is artificial, to say the least. Gender identity often is loaded with sexual identity and erotic subjectivity, and in any particular cultural context gender is bound to be quite specifically "subjectified" or "subjectivated." Thus, Williams, *Roman Homosexuality,* 215–18, inquires into the *cinaedus* as a desiring subject. Don Kulick also has warned us against tightly compartmentalizing transgender identity (which is what the *cinaedus* may, in part, embody) as a purely gendered identity, totally independent of matters of erotic desire: see Kulick, *Travesti: Sex, Gender, and Culture among Brazilian Transgendered Prostitutes* (Chicago: University of Chicago Press, 1998), and "Problematic Childhood Sexuality" (paper read at the annual meeting of the American Anthropological Association, Philadelphia, 2–6 December 1999).

30. In an extended series of essays, much discussed and generally well received by professional classicists in the United States and the United Kingdom, Amy Richlin has assailed the historical work of Winkler, myself, and our collaborators (such as Gleason), all of whom she lumps together under the uncomplimentary (not to say phobic) title of "Foucaultians" (see Amy Richlin, review of *One Hundred Years of Homosexuality,* by David Halperin, *Bryn Mawr Classical Review* 2, no. 1 [1991]: 16–18, "Zeus and Metis: Foucault, Feminism, Classics," *Helios* 18, no. 2 [autumn 1991]: 160–80, introduction to *The Garden of Priapus: Sexuality and Aggression in Roman Humor,* rev. ed. [New York: Oxford University Press, 1992], xiii–xxxiii, introduction to *Pornography and Representation in Greece and Rome,* ed. Amy Richlin [New York: Oxford University Press, 1992], xi–xxiii, "Not before Homosexuality: The Materiality of the *Cinaedus* and the Roman Law against Love between Men," *Journal of the History of Sexuality* 3, no. 4 [1992/93], 523–73, "The Ethnographer's Dilemma and the Dream of a Lost Golden Age," in *Feminist Theory and the Classics,* ed. Nancy Sorkin Rabinowitz and Amy Richlin [New York: Routledge, 1993], 272–303, "Towards a History of Body History," in *Inventing Ancient Culture: Historicism, Periodization, and the Ancient World,* ed. Mark Golden

and Peter Toohey [London: Routledge, 1997], 16–35, and "Foucault's *History of Sexuality: A Useful Theory for Women?*" in *Rethinking Sexuality: Foucault and Classical Antiquity,* ed. David H. J. Larmour, Paul Allen Miller, and Charles Platter [Princeton, N.J.: Princeton University Press, 1998], 138–70.) Richlin faults us in particular for approaching the figure of the *kinaidos* from the standpoint of ancient sexual discourses. She prefers to see in that figure a material embodiment of "homosexuality," which she regards as a useful category for analyzing ancient societies—although she concedes that "there was no ancient word for 'homosexual'": Richlin, "Not before Homosexuality," 530; also 571, where Richlin describes her work as employing "a model that uses 'homosexuality' as a category for analyzing ancient societies" (and in the revised introduction to *The Garden of Priapus*, Richlin insists that her approach is distinguished by its "essentialism" and "materialism" [xx]). For a lucid survey of Richlin's equivocations on the issue of whether or not *cinaedi* should be described as "homosexuals," see Williams, *Roman Homosexuality*, 355, n. 319.

Much could be said about the gaps in Richlin's argument, about its simplistic treatment of the interpretative issues, or about its unappetizing but evidently highly palatable combination of an old-fashioned positivism with a more fashionable blend of political and professional opportunism. (Compare, for example, the following two statements by Richlin, both of them made in the revised introduction to *The Garden of Priapus*: "I suggest that Foucault's work on antiquity is so ill-informed that it is not really worth reading" [xxix n. 2], and "Thus *The Garden of Priapus*, though it originated in a different critical space from Foucauldian work, exhibits some similar traits, a true Foucauldian child of its time. . . . I accept wholeheartedly the approach that melds anthropology with history; I define humor as a discourse of power; I view texts as artifacts; I am seeking to piece together social norms by juxtaposing different kinds of evidence that seem to describe different realities, and I am examining what produces those disparities" [xxvii]. In other words: "Everything Foucault said was wrong, and besides I said it first.") Indeed, the ferocity and tenacity of Richlin's polemics have largely succeeded in intimidating and silencing public expressions of disagreement with her. For two exceptions, see Earl Jackson, Jr., review of *Pornography and Representation in Greece and Rome*, ed. Amy Richlin, *Bryn Mawr Classical Review* 3 (1992): 387–96; and Marilyn B. Skinner, "Zeus and Leda: The Sexuality Wars in Contemporary Classical Scholarship," *Thamyris* 3, no. 1 (spring 1996): 103–23.

The point I need to make here about Richlin's critique is that it is doubly ignorant and misinformed—wrong, that is, both about Foucault and about so-called "Foucaultians." In the first case, Richlin claims that in the famous passage from *The History of Sexuality*, volume 1, "Foucault is distinguishing . . . between behavior and essence"; in the second case, she maintains that accounts of sex in antiquity by "Foucaultians" such as Winkler and myself "start from this axiom" ("Not before Homosexuality," 525). In fact, as I have tried to show here, Foucault was not distinguishing between anything so metaphysical as behavior and essence but simply between two different discursive strategies for disqualifying male love. Winkler and Gleason, moreover, far from adhering uncritically to the erroneous reading of Foucault that Richlin herself propounds, explicitly *challenged* the misapplication of such a pseudo-Foucauldian "axiom" to the interpretation of the figure of the *kinaidos*. And in *One Hundred Years of Homosexuality* I made a rigorous distinction between a sexual orientation in the modern sense and the kinds of sexual identity current in the ancient Greek world; the latter, I argued, tended to be determined by a person's gender and social status rather than by a personal psychology. And I was careful to emphasize in a number of passages that it was possible for sexual acts to be linked in various ways with a sexual disposition or sexual subjectivity well before the nineteenth century. (See the passage quoted in n. 9 above. For other examples, see *One Hundred Years of Homosexuality*, 8: "A certain identification of the self with the sexual self began in late antiquity; it was strengthened by the Christian confessional. Only in the high middle ages did certain kinds of sexual acts start to get identified with certain specifically sexual types of person: a 'sodomite' begins to name not merely the person who commits an act of sodomy but one distinguished by a certain type of specifically sexual subjectivity"; 48: the *kinaidos* is a "life-form.") Richlin's "Foucaultians," no less than her Foucault, are the product and projection of her own misreadings. Why her misreadings have been so widely, and so uncritically, acclaimed is another question, an interesting one in its own right, but this is not the place to pursue it.

31. Jonathan Walters, "'No More Than a Boy': The Shifting Construction of Masculinity from Ancient Greece to the Middle Ages," *Gender and History* 5, no. 1 (spring 1993): 20–33.

32. Walters, "'No More Than a Boy,'" 22–23, quoting Apuleius *The Golden Ass* 9.14.

33. See Walters, "'No More Than a Boy,'" 22.

34. Walters, "'No More Than a Boy,'" 24.

35. Walters, "'No More Than a Boy,'" 26: "In Boccaccio's version . . . we find the husband defined wholly in terms of his sexual desire, which marks him as abnormal from the start and indeed sets the plot in motion."

36. Cf. Walters, "'No More Than a Boy,'" 24–25. For the common view in Florentine texts of the period that sodomites "had little erotic interest in women," see Michael Rocke, *Forbidden Friendships: Homosexuality and Male Culture in Renaissance Florence* (New York: Oxford University Press, 1996), 40–41, 123ff., who also provides a useful survey of other literary portraits of sodomites in contemporary Italian *novelle*, many of which correspond in a number of respects to Boccaccio's portrait of Pietro di Vinciolo (123ff. and 295 n. 79). Rocke also points out, however, that many Florentine sources, both literary and judicial, presume that a man with sodomitical desires for boys might equally desire insertive sex with women (124–27).

37. Walters, "'No More Than a Boy,'" 27, also emphasizes this point.

38. See, further, Walters, "'No More Than a Boy,'" 27–28. Whereas the ancient conception of the *kinaidos* foregrounded his effeminacy and passivity, the fourteenth- and fifteenth-century Florentine definitions of "sodomy" and "sodomite" referred only to the "active" or insertive partner in anal intercourse: see Rocke, *Forbidden Friendships*, 14, 110. Cesare Segre, the editor of my text of Boccaccio, gets this point exactly wrong when he says, in a note, that the Perugians regarded Pietro as *un invertito:* Giovanni Boccaccio, *Opere*, ed. Cesare Segre (Milan: Mursia, 1966), 1280. Pietro is a sodomite, but, unlike the *kinaidos*, he is not transgendered, or an invert.

39. An erotic temperament midway between that of Apuleius's baker and Boccaccio's Pietro is represented a century *before* Apuleius in a two-line poem by the Roman poet Martial, *Epigrams* 2.49.

Uxorem nolo Telesinam ducere: quare?
moecha est. sed pueris dat Telesina. volo.

[I don't want to take Telesina for my wife. —Why not?
She's an adulteress. —But Telesina puts out for boys. —I'll take her!]

As Williams, *Roman Homosexuality,* 27, to whom I owe this reference, explains, Martial's joke depends on the background knowledge that a long-standing traditional punishment for adultery in the classical world was anal rape of the male offender. The man imagined in the epigram overcomes his initial reluctance to marry Telesina when it is pointed out to him that her bad character will procure him endless opportunities for enacting a sweet revenge on her youthful partners. Martial's satirical epigram constructs an outlandish scenario in which a man is so fond of insertive anal sex with boys that he is willing to enter into a disgraceful and corrupt marriage merely in order to expand his possibilities for enjoying it. Exaggeration is part of the joke; nonetheless, as Williams—who also cites the passage from Apuleius in this connection—demonstrates with abundant argumentation and evidence, the imaginary husband's preference falls well within the range of acceptable male sexual tastes in Roman culture.

40. Walters, "'No More Than a Boy,'" 26–27, overstates the case, I believe, when he writes, "What we see in Boccaccio's version of the story is one of the earliest portrayals in Western culture of a man defined by his sexuality, which is somehow his most deeply defining characteristic, and which tells 'the truth' about him. We witness here an early form of the constitution and demarcation of the field of sexuality." Cf. Glenn W. Olsen, "St. Anselm and Homosexuality," *Anselm Studies: An Occasional Journal,* vol. 2 (Proceedings of the Fifth International Saint Anselm Conference: St. Anselm and St. Augustine—Episcopi ad Saecula), ed. Joseph C. Schnaubelt et al. (White Plains, N.Y.: Kraus International, 1988), 93–141, esp. 102–103: "If one were to eliminate from Boswell's book [*Christianity, Social Tolerance, and Homosexuality*] all the materials which do not satisfy his definition of 'gay,' one might arguably be left with the truly novel and important observation that, as far as the Middle Ages are concerned, it was about 1100 in certain poems of Marbod of Rennes, and then later in the century in writers like Bernard of Cluny and Walter of Chatillon, and above all in the late twelfth century 'A Debate Between Ganymede and Helen,' that we might see the appearance of a clear erotic preference for one's own sex that, by still being called 'sodomy,' began the expansion of that term into the modern 'homosexuality'" (see also 129–30 n. 61, and 133 n. 87). Olsen puts the point very clearly, and in fact he might have been speaking of Boccaccio's Pietro di Vinciolo, although Boccaccio never uses the term *sodomy* in reference to Pietro. Nonetheless, I would still want to insist that mere sexual object-choice, even the settled and habitual preference for sexual relations with persons of the same sex as oneself, falls short of the definitional requirements of "(homo)sexuality" or "sexual orientation." After all, such exclusive sexual preferences were not unknown in the ancient world: see my partial list of citations in *One Hundred Years of Homosexuality,* 163 n. 53. A "sexuality" in the modern sense would seem to require considerably more than merely same-sex sexual object-choice, more even than conscious erotic preference. In particular, "homosexuality" requires, first of all, that *homosexual object-choice itself* function as a marker of difference, of social and sexual deviance, independent of the gender

identification or sexual role (active or passive) performed or preferred by the individual; second, it requires that homosexual object-choice be connected with a psychology, an inner orientation of the individual, not just an aesthetics or a form of erotic connoisseurship. See *One Hundred Years of Homosexuality,* 24–29, esp. 26–27 with notes; for more recent expansions of that argument, see my essays "Historicizing the Subject of Desire: Sexual Preferences and Erotic Identities in the Pseudo-Lucianic *Erōtes,*" in *Foucault and the Writing of History,* ed. Jan Goldstein (Oxford: Basil Blackwell, 1994), 19–34, 255–61, which documents several instances of same-sex sexual object-choice, and even of conscious erotic preferences for persons of the same sex as oneself, that nonetheless do not satisfy the criteria for homosexuality, and "How to Do the History of Male Homosexuality," which makes the conceptual distinctions in more detail. In the absence of the distinctively modern set of connections linking sexual object-choice, inner orientation, and deviant personality with notions of identity and difference, the substantive category of "homosexuality" dissolves into the descriptive category of "men who have sex with men" (an artifact of AIDS epidemiology, not a sexuality per se), and homosexually active but otherwise non-gay-identified men escape interpellation by the category of "homosexuality."

41. I have chosen to dwell on the figure of Boccaccio's Pietro di Vinciolo not because I believe he is somehow typical or representative of medieval sodomites in general but because he provides the starkest possible contrast with the ancient figure of the *kinaidos:* the latter represents an instance of sexual morphology without sexual subjectivity, or so at least I am contending for the purposes of this argument, whereas Pietro represents an instance of sexual subjectivity without sexual morphology. I do not mean to imply that constructions of the sodomite in premodern Europe *mostly* or even *typically* emphasized sexual subjectivity at the expense of sexual morphology, or that the sodomite was *never* thought to have a peculiar sensibility or style of gender presentation or appearance (on the gradual expansion of the term *sodomy,* see Olsen, "St. Anselm and Homosexuality," 102–3). It is precisely the aim of this chapter to open up such questions for further research.

42. This is not to deny that some lesbians can be conventionally feminine or that some gay men can be conventionally masculine, and that both can pass for straight— some can and some do—but rather to insist that modern concepts and images of homosexuality have never been able to escape being haunted by the specter of gender inversion, gender deviance, or at least some kind of visibly legible difference. For a systematic and brilliant exploration of this issue, see Lee Edelman, *Homographesis: Essays in Gay Literary and Cultural Theory* (New York: Routledge, 1994). See also Sedgwick, *Epistemology of the Closet.*

43. For a further elaboration of this point, see Halperin, "How to Do the History of Male Homosexuality," 107–113, esp. 110.

44. I wish to thank Carolyn Dinshaw for pointing out to me that the term *identity* is absent from Foucault's text.

45. Cf. Alan Sinfield, *Cultural Politics—Queer Reading* (Philadelphia: University of Pennsylvania Press, 1994), 14, noting that premodern histories of homosexuality by social-constructionist historians "tend to discover ambivalent or partial signs of subjectivity; they catch not the absence of the modern subject, but its emergence." He adds,

"I suspect that what we call gay identity has, for a long time, been always in the process of getting constituted." This last remark closes off, rather too glibly, the historiographic and conceptual issues before us.

46. I elaborate further on this point in "The Art of Not Being Governed: Michel Foucault on Critique and Transgression," *boundary 2* (forthcoming).

47. Foucault, *The History of Sexuality*, 1:68.

48. I wish to thank Lee Edelman for discussing the issues in this paragraph with me, for his persistent critiques of this section of my essay, and for supplying me with a number of formulations now contained in it.

A notable exception to this hankering on the part of "queer theorists" for a correct theory of sexuality is Eve Kosofsky Sedgwick, "Queer Performativity: Henry James's *The Art of the Novel*," *GLQ: A Journal of Lesbian and Gay Studies* 1, no. 1 (1993): 1–16, esp. 11: "The thing I *least* want to be heard as offering here is a 'theory of homosexuality.' I have none and I want none." See also Jordan, *The Invention of Sodomy*, 5: "I myself tend to think that we have barely begun to gather [historical] evidence of same-sex desire. We are thus very far from being able to imagine having a finished theory." Statements to this effect in works of so-called queer theory are rather less frequent than one might imagine.

49. For the notion that theory is ultimately "the universal theory of the impossibility of theory" and therefore that "nothing can overcome the resistance to theory since theory is itself this resistance," see Paul de Man, "The Resistance to Theory," in *The Resistance to Theory* (Minneapolis: University of Minnesota Press, 1986), 3–20 (quotations on 19). For a further exploration of these paradoxes, see the scathing remarks of Paul Morrison, "Paul de Man: Resistance and Collaboration," *Representations*, 32 (fall 1990): 50–74.

50. Michel Foucault, "Fantasia of the Library," in *Language, Counter-memory, Practice: Selected Essays and Interviews*, ed. and trans. Donald F. Bouchard (Ithaca, N.Y.: Cornell University Press, 1977), 87–109 (quotation on 90). This passage was originally brought to my attention by James W. Bernauer, *Michel Foucault's Force of Flight: Toward an Ethics for Thought* (Atlantic Highlands, N.J.: Humanities Press International, 1990), 183.

Chapter Two

ERŌS AND ETHICAL NORMS: PHILOSOPHERS
RESPOND TO A CULTURAL DILEMMA

~≈~

Martha C. Nussbaum

I. HANDS UP AND DOWN:
EROS AND NORMATIVE SCRUTINY

*A*n older man stands close to a younger man, who looks up (or, as the case may be, down) at him, often with fond affection. The older man beams beneficently at the young man's beardless face, and with one hand he cups the younger man's chin, in a gesture expressive of tender personal affection. His other hand, however, has other ideas: it fondles the young man's genitals, which are usually exposed. The older man's penis is often erect, the younger man's almost never.[1] The young man sometimes repels the groping hand, but often, too, contentedly allows it.[2]

In this highly conventional and popular ancient Greek image of sexual courtship—named by Sir John Beazley the "up and down position"[3] and found on dozens of vases from the classical period—we see a tension in the Greek concept of *erōs*. To investigate that tension, and the Stoic philosophers' response to it, is my purpose in this chapter. On the one hand, *erōs* is beneficent, showing a tender regard for the young man's personality and his education; on the other hand, it is characterized by strong genital desire, which has the potential for ferocity and blind indifference to the well-being of the beloved. Does the left hand know what the right hand is doing? Or the right the left? The vase images, like some literary texts that I shall later examine, frequently intimate that the two aspects of *erōs* work harmoniously together: the hand that strokes the genitals is just as precise and reverent, just as cautious, as the hand that delicately cups the face. But the Greeks know well that things are not always so. A statue from 470 B.C., the first plate in Dover's *Greek Homosexuality,* shows a Zeus of massive physique carrying off young Ganymede in one squeezing arm, without even a glance at the face; while Zeus strides victoriously ahead, the young man looks down in what seems to be helpless confusion.[4] As the chorus in Sophocles' Antigone observes, addressing Eros, "You take the minds of the just and turn them aside to injustice." Even the gods are not exempt from this madness.[5]

Greek popular morality contained in this way two ideas about *erōs* that proved notoriously difficult to reconcile. On the one hand, *erōs* is seen as a divine gift, connected with illumination and delight for the lover, and with generous educative intentions toward the beloved. On the other hand, *erōs* is a source of madness and distraction, a force that disrupts reasoning and threatens virtue, but if it threatens virtue, it also seems to threaten, inevitably, the good conduct of the lover toward his partner.[6] Nor can we even cleanly separate these two tendencies in *erōs,* for it would appear (according, again, to deeply entrenched popular ideas) that the very madness and distraction in the lover that put virtue at risk are among the sources of his generosity to the beloved. The very passion that threatens virtue may also motivate virtuous actions.

The Greek Stoics are notorious in the philosophical tradition for having held what appear to be contradictory theses about the passions. On the one hand, they hold that all passions (*pathē*) should be not just moderated but even extirpated from human life.[7] On the other hand, they hold that the wise man will be in love, *erasthēsesthai,* will experience *erōs,* with young people of a certain description—both beautiful and apt for virtue.[8] They hold that the wise man's *erōs* will express itself both in sexual conduct and in the education of the young for virtue. Indeed, they hold that the bonds of *erōs* should be basic to the civic fabric of their ideal city.[9] Cicero mocks them for the contradiction, saying scornfully, "What is this 'love of friendship' [*amor amicitiae*]?" (*Tusc.* 4.33), and concluding that Epicurus got it right—erotic love is never a good thing. Plutarch, equally baffled by the Stoic thesis, says that it seems all right to defend a kind of sexualized affection for the young that aims at promoting virtue, but if that is what it is, they had better not call it *erōs,* which we all know to have rather different characteristics (*De communibus notitiis* 1072E).[10]

The Stoic position cannot be well understood in isolation from its cultural context, for it is one in a series of bold philosophical attempts to resolve a cultural tension. Perhaps it succeeds; perhaps it does not. (I shall conclude that Plutarch's critique has much to recommend it.) But we cannot assess the project until we understand the problem it addresses. I shall begin by sketching briefly a picture of the doubleness of *erōs* that we find in much of the nonphilosophical culture of Athens in the fifth and fourth centuries B.C., focusing on evidence from the tragic poets, the orators, and the speeches of Phaedrus and Pausanias in Plato's *Symposium*, which are good sources for certain elements, at least, of the popular thought of the period. I shall then turn to Plato's *Phaedrus*, which first, in the speech of "Lysias," boldly forces the two parts of *erōs* apart, portraying them as not merely in tension but as incompatibles—and then, with Socrates' recantation, even more boldly brings them together, describing a beneficent and generous erotic madness. After briefly discussing Epicurus' take on the problem— since Cicero sees this as the greatest rival to the Stoic account—I shall turn to the Greek Stoics, who define *erōs* as "desire for bodily intercourse" (Andronicus, *SVF* 3.397) as "an attempt to form friendship, inspired by the appearing beauty of young men in their prime" (many sources), and, finally, as "service of the gods directed to the ordering of young and beautiful people" (*SVF* 3.397).

This history is interesting in its own right; but it also has a larger scholarly significance. In his important and profoundly insightful analyses of ancient Greek sexual norms and practices in volumes 2 and 3 of the *History of Sexuality*, Michel Foucault argued that the Greeks do not problematize sexual appetite and activity in the way that Christian and post-Christian cultures commonly do. The sexual appetite is treated as one appetite among the others, and the important consideration, in dealing with all the appetites, is one of self-mastery. The admirable person is one who does not get carried away by any pleasure, but who displays mastery and control of all his pleasures, pleasures of intercourse as well as pleasures of eating and drinking. None of these pleasures is inherently shameful, and all can be managed as elements in a life governed by manly self-control.

Foucault never denied that a complex ethical discourse surrounded all of these appetites, but by focusing on the issue of sexual self-mastery, he did not focus enough, perhaps, on the complex ethical discourse connected with the lover's treatment of the recipient of his sexual attentions. He was in one way importantly correct: the Greeks do regard sex as more like eating and drinking than do many modern cultures, especially those influenced by a connection between sexuality and an idea of original sin. But in another way his assimilation of sex to eating and drinking can mislead us. For the glutton does no harm to food, nor the drunkard to wine. The Greeks knew well that in this sense there is a clear disanalogy among the appetites. Unlike the others, the sexual appetite can be a source of pleasure or displeasure, of kindness or cruelty, of beneficent formation or the blighting of formation, for the young man who is typically imagined as the recipient of the lover's desire. Thus the ethical questions posed in this area became far more complicated than the ethical questions posed in the area of food and drink. What is at stake in sex is not only one's own self-mastery, but also the well-being, happiness, and ethical goodness of another. But if that is so, then one's own ethical goodness is on the line in a double sense. Not only the good of self-mastery, but also the good of being a responsible, decent, kindly social being is on the line. For what one does inevitably has a very profound effect on the being of the other. In other words, sex is doubly, and inevitably, ethical.

As I say, Foucault did not deny this complexity, but he did not draw attention to it either. And other aspects of the thought of Foucault positively lead away from the recognition of the inherently ethical quality of sex. For throughout much of his work Foucault brilliantly drew attention to the tyrannical role of social norms. Norms are generative, for they create the possibility of discourses and even desires that do not exist without them. But they also display the effects of power, and they constrain the activities of those whose desires are made in their image. Whether or not Foucault intended such a reading, many who take their inspiration from Foucault have concluded that norms in the domain of sex are inherently tyrannical and bad. If one were to mingle a certain Foucauldian atmosphere (for it seems better to call it an atmosphere than a reading) with the related view of sexual norms articulated by Gayle Rubin in her important article "Thinking Sex," one would conclude that any division of sexual acts and actors into the good and the bad is bound to be suspect, expressing the desire of power to tyrannize over the powerless. Thus any drawing of ethical lines that separates actors into two categories—any practice of "normalization" (bringing under the scrutiny of norms) in the sexual sphere—is regarded in some quarters as inherently homophobic, or otherwise aimed at the subordination of the powerless. Resistance to all such line drawing is therefore held to be appropriate.

Since the Greeks are a common point of reference in this modern discussion, and since the Greeks are frequently viewed, with loose and mistaken reference to Foucault, as a people who did not moralize about sex (especially same-sex sex) the way we do, it seems important to insist that the Greeks — and, above all, the philosophers (not surprisingly) — were extremely attached to moralizing about sex and indeed thought that it was obvious that such a dangerous passion ought to be hedged around with a wide range of ethical norms. The job of these norms was in fact to define what good sex and bad sex are, with reference both to the ethical character of the desiring lover and to the well-being and ethical character of the beloved. The Greeks did not moralize about sex precisely in the way that modern Americans frequently do; but they did moralize, and they found shocking the very idea that one might not moralize.

I think that some moralizing is a good thing. There are many bad ways of moralizing about sex, and modern American life shows examples of quite a few of them. But one should not conclude from the inadequacy of some particular norms that a norm-free discourse is the best thing. (Is that even a coherent position?) The fact that some norms are based on ignorance, prejudice, primitive shame about the very fact of having a body, and hatred of people who are different does not show us that all norms must be like this and are to be resisted. Indeed, we could hardly avoid using ethical norms in the process of saying what is wrong with such bad norms, and why they should be resisted: they insult people's dignity, they treat them as unequal when they are really equal, or whatever. What each of us has to figure out is, What is the appropriate ethical language to use when we evaluate sexual acts and actors? And we must then also pose the different question, Which of these norms do we wish to translate from the sphere of personal ethics into the public realm of law and politics? Even in that area, one cannot easily take the position that a completely norm-free discourse about sex is either possible or good. A determined Millean, such as I am, who holds that the law has no business interfering with "self-regarding action" (action that affects only the self and other consenting parties), will still seek laws against sexual coercion and various other practices that do harm to non-consenting parties. But most of us will feel the need for a richer menu of ethical norms when assessing conduct in the personal life. Most of us do not want laws penalizing unkindness, or hostility, or egotism; but we criticize these vices in ourselves and in others, and if we have or teach children, we encourage them to do so as well.

Where does this leave us with the Greeks? It means that we should not return to the Greek philosophers, or the culture that surrounded them, in search of a norm-free discourse about the erotic, and certainly not about same-sex acts. Foucault never held out that prospect, nor should we. On the other hand, it does seem reasonable to look to Greek culture for a set of erotic norms that are not colored by a specifically Christian problematization of sex in connection with original sin, or by a presumption, antecedent to scrutiny of the particular case, that all same-sex relationships must be inherently sinful. And this is of philosophical interest, since it is of interest to see what norms emerge as salient when those two prominent ingredients of modern moralizing about sex are subtracted. Norms of kindness, noncruelty, beneficence, lack of coercion, self-control—such norms emerge as independent of the notion of intrinsic sinfulness and organize sexual acts and actors into ethical kinds in a way that may seem less arbitrary and tyrannical, more morally pertinent and worthy, than some of the ways in which we have become accustomed to categorize such acts. Thus, the study of Greek norms may illuminate some of our own best possibilities as we wrestle with a passion that, through all its historical and cultural transmogrifications, remains among the most baffling, dangerous, and magical elements of human life.

II. A Cultural Tension

"Erōs, you who drip longing down upon the eyes, bringing sweet delight to the souls of those against whom you lead your armed assault"—so the chorus of Euripides' *Hippolytus* begins its account of the contradictory properties of erōs.[11] Erōs is beautiful and divine, sent by the gods; it is also fatal, a force of compulsion, stronger than fire or lightning,[12] that can lay waste the mind of the lover and, through that assault, do great and sometimes fatal damage to the object of the love. The chorus goes on to speak of Semele, the object of the erōs of Zeus himself, who was killed in the mythic act of sexual penetration, burnt to death by Zeus's thunderbolt.[13] On the other hand, it is not always this way: erōs can also make the beloved better—even confer immortality. Ganymede, cupbearer to the gods, is evidence of both aspects at once: for his story is one of rape and abduction, and yet its end is glorious. The chorus of Aeschylus' *Suppliant Women*, speaking of the rape of Io by Zeus, which ended her torments and brought her peace and glory, found a memorable phrase to summarize the situation: Zeus, with his rape, "established well-intentioned violence [*eumenē bian ktisas*]."[14]

The dangers of erōs are not confined to same-sex relationships, clearly, although these are thought to be especially powerful sources of erotic temptation.[15] Nor are they confined to the extramarital. It is possible to conceive the passion of erōs for one's own spouse—although this is regarded as an atypical and somewhat ominous phenomenon.[16] The *Antigone* chorus's reflections of the moral dangers of *erōs* have as their occasion Haemon's evident and dangerous passion for his betrothed, which has set him at odds with his father: "You [sc. Eros] have stirred up this strife of kinsmen" (793–94).[17] The normative image of marriage as represented in the wedding formula echoed by Creon immediately before the choral ode eschews the erotic: the wife is given to the husband "for plowing of legitimate children." Or, as Creon says, presumably alluding to that formula, if one woman should prove unavailable, "there are other furrows for his plough" (569). Marriage can avoid the danger of violence and instability by keeping its sexuality free from passion.

One might, of course, stop there: *erōs* simply has those two aspects, the violent and the beneficent, and there is no separating them. But the culture, reasonably enough, regards the copresence of destructiveness and good intentions as a problem to be solved and persistently tries to separate the good intentions from at least the most pernicious of the destructive impulses. Let me briefly examine just four texts that testify to this conceptual (and very practical) struggle: the fragmentary lament of Achilles for the dead Patroclus from Aeschylus' *Myrmidons*, a short passage from Xenophon's *Hiero*, a piece of Aeschines' *Against Timarchus* discussing "just [*dikaios*] *erōs*," and the speeches of Phaedrus and Pausanias from Plato's *Symposium*.

1. Aeschylus famously depicts the relationship between Achilles and Patroclus as an erotic relationship that includes sexual conduct. Whether that is how Homer saw the matter or not (probably not),[18] fifth- and fourth-century Athenians generally interpreted the text this way, in accordance with the popularity of such sexual relationships in their own time.[19] Lamenting Patroclus's death, Achilles, who is cast in the role of the *erastēs* (a fact that Plato's Phaedrus finds peculiar in view of Achilles' surpassing beauty; *Symp.* 180a), exclaims as follows: "And you felt no compunction for [sc. my?] pure reverence of [sc. your?] thighs — Oh, what an ill return you have made for so many kisses." Elsewhere he speaks of his "god-fearing converse with your thighs" (Aesch. frs. 228, 229 Nauck). In other words, he represents the relationship as one that combined sexual passion with reverence, and he expressed this reverence in "converse with your thighs."[20] The audience would understand this as a reference to the established norm of intercrural intercourse — a way of achieving sexual gratification for the *erastēs* that respected the *erōmenos* by not imposing on him the potential shame of penetration. What this brings out more generally is that the state of *erōs* is here envisaged as compatible with generous and even prudent concern for the

well-being of the *erōmenos*—apparently because it is a state characterized by reverence, both toward the gods and toward the young man himself, the two apparently being closely connected. Plato's *Phaedrus*, as we shall see, follows this lead.

2. Xenophon's *Hiero* represents a conversation between the poet Simonides and the tyrant Hiero on the topic of an older man's *erōs* toward young men:[21] "'How do you mean, Hiero? Are you telling me that *erōs* for *paidika* does not grow [*emphuesthai*] in a tyrant [sc. as it does in other people]? How is it then that you are in love with Dailokhos . . . ?' Hiero said . . . 'My passion [*eran*] for Dailokhos is for what human nature perhaps compels us to want from the beautiful, but I have a very strong desire to attain the object of my passion [sc. only] with his love and consent'" (1.31–33).

What is prima facie puzzling to Simonides is, apparently, the restraint of Hiero—who, being a tyrant, could easily have whatever he wants and whomever, without penalty. His restraint makes Simonides wonder whether this tyrant has *erōs* like other people. Hiero answers that he certainly does have *erōs* like other people—indeed, he takes his passion to be a compulsion rooted in human nature. On the other hand, it is combined with a "strong desire" to attain his conquest only with the love and consent of the *erōmenos*. He does not tell us how the two desires, the *erōs* and the "strong desire," are related, but he shows some of the same reverence for the *erōmenos* that Aeschylus's Achilles expressed, and traced to fear of the gods. The compulsion of *erōs* does not necessitate impulsive or violent conduct;[22] whether the passion is managed by external motives coming from a virtuous character or from some reverence internal to *erōs* itself, managed it is, for the beloved's benefit.

3. In the *Against Timarchus* Aeschines, although he attacks the self-prostituting behavior of Timarchus as incompatible with the privileges of citizenship, defends a type of *erōs* in which he says that he himself participates: "For my part, I do not criticize *dikaios erōs*, nor do I assert that those of exceptional good looks have [sc. necessarily] prostituted themselves, nor do I deny that I myself have been *erōtikos* and remain so to this day; I do not deny that I have been involved in contentions and fights which arise from this activity. On the poems which they say I have composed, I admit to the poems, but I deny that they have the character with which my opponents will, by distortion, invest them."[23] Aeschines identifies a type of erotic activity that is "right" or "legitimate"; he associates it with typical marks of passion, such as jealous quarrels and the writing of poetry. "Legitimate *erōs*" does not pay the young for satisfaction, turning them into

prostitutes, nor does it employ violence—Democritus defined "legitimate *erōs*" as "aiming, without *hubris*, at beautiful objects" (B73). Aeschines appears to reserve the name *erōs* for the legitimate variety: being in love with the younger man is associated with fights and romantic transports, but not with coercion or bribery.[24] Once again we have no clear indication of the mechanism by which *erōs*, with all of its violence (which Aeschines acknowledges), generates good deeds. Aeschines speaks of "hard words and blows arising out of this activity"(136), but he appears to be proud of this, thinking of the blows as a manly way of competing for his love against rivals and as imposing no burden on the loved one himself. There may even be, as in Aeschylus, an implicit idea of reverence or respect toward the recipients of the love poems; at any rate, we are to feel a strong contrast between the person in love, who sends his young man fine poetry, and a cruder sort of suitor, who goes out and buys a Timarchus.

4. Two speeches early in Plato's *Symposium* take up the same theme. For Phaedrus there simply is no problem: *erōs* is good through and through, "the cause of extremely great goods for us" (178c). There is no greater good for a young man than a fine *erastēs*, and no greater for an *erastēs* than his *paidika* (178c). For *erōs* consistently inspires good and noble deeds by promoting, more effectively than any other cause, a sense of shame toward base deeds and emulation toward fine deeds (178d). Because of their intense passion for one another, lover and beloved will fight more boldly when each can see the other, and in general display admirable virtue, ashamed at the thought of being seen by the other in any base action. In fact, an army of pairs of lovers would fight more bravely than any other (178e–179a).[25] Love makes even a mediocre person "inspired toward excellence, so that he is similar to the best in nature" (179a). Moreover, lovers are capable of a generosity and altruism that nobody else can touch, going so far as to offer their lives for those they love (179b), something that other relatives and friends are unlikely to do. Phaedrus here mentions Alcestis's offer of her life for her husband, Orpheus's risk of his life to restore his wife, and, finally, Achilles' courageous sacrifice of a peaceful old age through his choice to fight Hector and avenge his *erastēs* Patroclus. (It is noteworthy that according to Phaedrus the *erastēs* and the *erōmenos* have similarly strong motivations for fine conduct;[26] he remarks that the *erastēs* is a "more godlike" figure than the *erōmenos*, since he is divinely inspired, so there is something especially fine in the younger man's devotion to him.)

Two mechanisms, then, are suggested through which strong passion leads to good treatment of its object: the desire to look good before one's love (not to incur shame) and the high estimation of the object, which can lead one to put that object's good before one's own. This high estimation is especially appropriate and efficacious when its object is godlike. Although Phaedrus fails to confront the dangers of violence associated with *erōs*, his psychological observations are promising and will reappear in later solutions.

Pausanias begins and ends with a fundamental point: no action is good or bad per se, but everything depends on the way it is done (181a, 183d). He does acknowledge a doubleness in *erōs*, but he says that there are simply two sorts of erotic conduct, linked with two sorts of people. There are those who love the body only — and these are indeed likely to be bad for those they love, since this love is indiscriminate: "they look only to gratification, neglecting whether it is well done or not" (181b5). Such people are likely to choose both males and females indiscriminately (181b).

The higher type of *erōs* chooses male objects, since it looks to the soul rather than the body. This (and apparently only this) *erōs* is "without share in violence" (181c). Because the soul is the focus, and friendship and education among the goals (as well as pleasure), such lovers choose mature young men whose beard has already begun to grow — on the theory that these people have good judgment, and they are starting a relationship "as if they were going to be together through the whole of their lives and to live together" (181d). They avoid deception and inconstancy (181d), prefer public to secret love (182d), and are willing even to choose relatively ugly youths (*aischious;* 182d), so long as they are noble and excellent. Given the satisfaction of all these conditions, Athenian custom gives the lover great encouragement — to the point of permitting and even praising actions that would appear absurd or bad in anyone else — imploring and supplicating, and oaths, and sleeping on the doorstep, and "being willing to serve in a servitude that no slave ever endured" (183a). Even when they break their promises, there is indulgence (183b).

So all the young man needs to do, in order to receive good treatment, is to test the prospective *erastēs* carefully (184a) and take a good deal of time to look into the man's character. That is what Pausanias says. And yet we wonder whether the problems have really been solved. Pausanias's *erōs* is really *erōs* — it is characterized by distraction, a neglect of everything and everyone else, a willingness to do things usually thought shameful. But if it is this, how do we know that it will not be capable of inconstant and bad behavior to the *erōmenos*? The mention of indulgence for broken promises is particularly ominous. The fact that *erōs* is directed at the soul rather than (primarily) the body offers some reassurance. But we might well feel that Pausanias has not fully come to grips with the danger of the passion, or offered a full psychological argument explaining how his Ouranian love can retain the madness while expecting to avoid its bad consequences.

In short, Athenian culture of the fifth and fourth centuries tries very hard to work out a conception of "legitimate *erōs*" that will recognize the potentially lethal power of the passion but show how that power can be harnessed toward friendship and education. To a great extent this is done by focusing on notions of respect for the soul, reverence for the gods (even for the loved one, or the lover, as inhabited by god), and generous altruism. But there is no stable equilibrium reached here, no point at which the lover does not have to protest a little too much that his intentions are wholly benign. This is because the tradition continues to recognize the passion as a form of madness and continues to hold that "well-intentioned violence" is something of a contradiction in terms.

III. "Lysias": Choosing the Nonlover

Socrates follows Phaedrus outside the city walls, hoping to hear what Phaedrus has been discussing with the famous orator Lysias. The topic, says Phaedrus, will suit Socrates very well indeed (227c), since it was *erōs*. Lysias had written a speech depicting one of the beautiful young men as being propositioned (*peirōmenon;* 227c6)—"but not by a lover [*erastou*]—that was, in fact, the really clever part—for he says that one should give oneself to the person who is not in love, rather than to a person who is" (227c). The speech is introduced, then, as something clever and paradoxical: by playing on the fact that the conventional name for the older party to a male-male sexual relationship is *erastēs*, an agent noun from the verb *eran*, Lysias makes it look like almost a contradiction in terms that one should be asked to give oneself to someone whose mental condition is not characterized as *erōs*. But, as we shall see, the speech is clever precisely because it combines cultural paradox with sound cultural good sense. It presents an argument that is very hard to refute, leading to a conclusion that is strikingly discordant with conventional practice. This may be why it has had such an effect on Phaedrus, whom the *Symposium* has depicted as a rather uncritical enthusiast for *erōs* and a defender of the moral goods that this sort of passion can promote. Socrates, teasing him, implies that he is as if sexually aroused by the speech: "Show me first, my dear fellow, what you are holding in your left hand under your cloak: I bet it's the speech itself (228d).

The speech of "Lysias" has generally received a bad press from its modern commentators. Hackforth condemns the speaker's "coldly prudential calculation," his obliviousness to "romantic sentiment."[27] Charles Griswold says that the speaker is "rather base,"[28] and manipulative in the use he intends to make of the young men. About the related first speech of Socrates, he writes that the speaker's position "condemns passion for the sake of defending reason, but does so in a way that debases man, in whom passion and reason are combined, to the bestial. This is admirably conveyed by the verse that Socrates breaks into"[29]—but of course, that verse ("as wolves love lambs, so *erastai* love a boy"; 241d) depicts the rapacious wolflike conduct of the person in love, not of the Lysianic person-not-in-love. Christopher Rowe calls the speech of "Lysias" "empty, clever, rhetorical and essentially playful," and concludes, "whether the non-lover's position is actually consistent with 'merit' of any sort is another matter."[30] Such arguments may rest on the anachronistic premise that male-male sex acts can be made all right by overwhelming love but are base when we take love away. They may also rest on some rather modern assumptions about the goodness of love, which portray love as glorious and sweet, rather than dangerous and destructive. In any case, I shall argue that this simple condemnation of the speaker is not sustainable if we set the speech in its cultural context, where it is indeed a brilliantly clever response to a young man's dilemma.

One more commentary on the speech must now be introduced before we analyze the speech itself. This is my own earlier analysis. I defended (at least initially) the position of "Lysias" as a very sensible one, using a modern parallel.[31] Imagine, I said, a young woman who has a career in a male-dominated profession where she finds herself surrounded by suitors who are both older and more powerful than she. This young woman, let us imagine, wants both sex and the type of friendship that will be good for her career. Let us suppose (to make the parallel to ancient Athens closer) that the class of available sex partners is limited to the people with whom she must work. The question that faces this woman now is: should she prefer the person who is in love with her, or a person whose attitude is one of balanced friendship? I shall argue that my parallel does in fact help us to get at some of what is attractive about the speech, but that it is less effective, ultimately, than a more direct historical analysis that would show the complexities of what a Greek *erōmenos* would be likely to think and feel. Such an analysis can show us both why the speech seems initially attractive and why, from the very first, it is felt as paradoxical and incomplete.[32]

Throughout, I shall use the conventional terms "lover" and "nonlover" to translate *erōn* and *mē erōn*, for the sake of ease. But it is important to bear in mind that these are rather misleading translations: the Greek distinguishes between the "person who is in love" and the "person who is not in love." Both of these people desire to be the young man's "lover," in the sense of "sexual partner."

The young man is characterized as a typical, good-looking *erōmenos* of good family and good prospects. The speaker assumes that he is interested in the development of his mind and character, in bodily health and strength, in the integrity of his property, in reputation and political advancement, in good relations with his family. It is assumed that he is going to give his sexual favors to somebody: the only question is, to whom? He is now told that his personal aims will be thwarted by a sexual relationship with the passionate lover, and not only not thwarted but considerably advanced by a relationship with the nonlover, if he picks a nonlover who has the right characteristics. The speaker's argument relies on a conception of *erōs* that is deeply embedded in the culture.[33] It leaves some things out, as we shall see, but what it leaves in is familiar. *Erōs* is not defined, but is taken to be a condition of the personality in which an unreasoning "mad" passion, strongly sexual in nature, takes the person over, acquires the force of necessity (231a, 233c), and deprives the person of self-control and deliberation. The object of this passion is the boy's bodily beauty (232e3, 234a); its goal is the lover's sexual satisfaction and pleasure (233e2, 233a), and the satisfaction desired is exclusive (232c). The state is associated with the absence of good reasoning and self-government (231a, d, 233c).

The speaker now argues that a relationship with such a person will have a number of bad consequences for the boy.[34] First of all, he will be associated with a person who is going to neglect his own property and affairs and who will incur the blame and reproach of his friends (231b, 234b), and this cannot be very good for the young man's own advancement. Moreover, such a lover will, by indiscretion, harm the young man's reputation (232a–b) and, by jealousy, cut him off from the other advantageous associations (231c, 232c–d) and make life unpleasant (232c, 233c). Because the lover cares only for the young man's beauty, he will not care for his character or education (232e, 233a–d); by flattery he may even harm his moral development. Moreover, because he never was a friend in the first place he will prove unstable: when his desire ceases he will be off to someone else and his exclusivity now will entail bad treatment then (231 c).

On the other side, we have the nonlover. He too desires the boy's sexual favors, responds to his physical beauty, and hopes to gain sexual pleasure. But his claim to the boy's favor rests on character, rather than passion: he expects to get what he wants "through excellence [*di' aretēn*]" (232d, 234b). His desire has a larger focus than the lover's, for it takes in the boy's character as well as his body (232d). His goal is above all friendly love or *philia*—whose intensity, he points out, can be in its own way as great as that of *erōs* (233c–d). We intensely love members of our family, and will make many sacrifices for them.[35]

This sexual partner, unlike the lover, offers the young man a long-term relationship ("throughout the whole of life" [232a]; "for a long time" [233c5]). Based on something deeper than the evanescence of bodily beauty, the relationship can and will endure. Because it lacks the jealousy and possessiveness of *erōs*, it will not be full of quarrels or cut the young man off from other desirable associations (233c, 232d–e). And it will, throughout, be focused on the improvement of the young man's mind and character (233b etc.).

This speech really is enormously clever, in terms of the cultural tension I have described. Pace Hackforth, Griswold, and Rowe, it says much that is inspired good sense, much that its young target has reason to accept with a Phaedrus-like enthusiasm. For it persuasively drives a wedge between love's madness and its alleged educational benefits. It points out what any Greek young man would have to grant, given the conception of marriage that he grows up with: that *erōs* is not necessary for sexual desire and sexual conduct.[36] It must be emphasized that this would be a completely unremarkable claim, and one with which any Greek youth bent on eventual marriage could be expected to agree.[37] But then, if what the young man wants is an intimate relationship in which he trades his sexual favors for educational benefits,[38] how much better to get it from a nonlover of good character, whose mind is free and clear, whose eye looks beyond beauty to character, and whose gifts will therefore prove enduring. Pausanias suggested that *erōs* itself could take character as its object and become aroused even by relatively ugly youths, so long as they are good and noble (1820). This the Lysianic speaker plausibly doubts, and he has much of the culture behind him when he does so. We do not see pinup art of ugly but noble and intelligent youths. The standard erotic graffito and vase caption is not "So-and-So *gennaios*" (So-and-So is noble), but "So-and-So *kalos*" (So-and-So is beautiful).[39] We all know that *erōs* is hooked on bodily beauty and is a kind of madness born of that beauty. But if *erōs* is narrow in this way, then it is unreliable as a source of generosity and educational assistance. If, furthermore, it is possessive and acquisitive in its aims, it will not wish to deliver such assistance, except as a way of securing sexual favors.

The young man might wonder at this point why he should give himself sexually to anyone at all. Note that Socrates' first, Lysianic, speech omits this positive advice. Here we see clearly the limits of my earlier analysis:[40] for (plausibly enough in modern terms) I imagined the woman in question as having strong sexual desires of her own, and as wishing to gratify those desires as well as desires for friendship and education. The Greek *erōmenos*, as conventionally, normatively imagined, has no such motive. Perhaps he really does, and simply dares not acknowledge it; very likely this was the case for some, if not many, *erōmenoi*, and the speech to some extent may be exploiting a gap between social norm and reality. On the other hand, perhaps he simply believes that it is only by giving the nonlover something precious of his own — and what else has such an inexperienced youth to offer? — that he can reasonably demand such services in return. Whatever his motives, the young man has been given a powerful reason to accept the proposition of the nonlover.

But the audience for this speech would also be aware that something important has been omitted. With the omission of passion and madness, he might sense that "Lysias" has omitted a powerful motive to care for the young man's good. He might begin to ask questions, such as: If the nonlover does not feel exclusive passion for the young man, how do we know that he will focus on giving favors to that young man, rather than to many people? After all, bodily beauty is one part of what he wants, and why, if he is not in love, wouldn't he pursue it in many youths whose character he approves? How do we know that he will not make this same proposition to many people, and dilute his attention and favors accordingly? Moreover, what makes us think that such a person, prudent and in control of himself, will take risks and make sacrifices for the beloved, as people in love are known to do?[41] Doesn't the exclusivity of the passion, and even its mad focus on beauty, have something to do with the readiness of the lover to go to extraordinary lengths to please and help the one he loves? Isn't love, in fact, more generous, and less single-mindedly connected with grasping and possession, than the speech has let on? These reservations are shortly brought to the surface in Socrates' speech, which makes a brilliant proposal for the resolution of the cultural dilemma.

IV. Socrates: Generous Madness

Socrates is ashamed of his own Lysianic speech. He says that this shame has deep cultural roots: "My good Phaedrus, you recognize that the two speeches were quite shameless — both mine just now and the one you read from the book. If anyone should chance to hear them who was noble and gentle in character, someone who either was currently or had been previously in love with another person of similar character, and he heard us saying that lovers conceive great hatreds on the basis of small causes and conduct themselves in a spiteful and harmful way toward their boyfriends, how could he fail to think that he was hearing the speech of people who had been brought up somewhere among sailors, and who had never seen a case of free-and-generous [*eleutheron*] love? Wouldn't he be far from agreeing with our blame of *erōs*?" In other words—and our examination of Aeschines and Pausanias has shown us how plausible Socrates' claim is—there is a conception of *erōs* that is linked to good birth and good character (we would not expect to find it among sailors), according to which *erōs* is itself generous, free from spite and from the wish to harm. The question Socrates must now address is the big cultural question: how can *erōs* be this way, if it is also madness?

Socrates begins by making distinctions. Madness is not a single thing (244a5–6). Some forms of madness may indeed produce harm; some, however, are responsible for very great goods. From this point on, Socrates ignores the harm-producing varieties (which, in fact, he does not explicitly mention—I have supplied that as a way of making sense of his implicit distinction).[42] He certainly does not deny that there may be harm-producing varieties even within madness; he never holds that madness in a lover is sufficient for the good conduct he will describe, and he strongly suggests that it is not. On the other hand, he sets out to describe a variety that is linked with good conduct and generosity, and he will show us that this type is really erotic madness—indeed, that its benefits cannot be had without madness.

Central in Socrates' solution to the cultural problem is an account of how *erōs* can take as its object both bodily beauty and excellence of soul—how, in fact, excellence of soul can manifest itself in the features and shape of the body. "Lysias" had pushed hard here: either the person is focused on character, in which case he is not in love, or he is focused on bodily beauty, in which case he cannot be generous and reliable. Socrates never denies that bodily beauty is extremely important to falling in love; he does not retreat to Pausanias's position that a rather ugly person can still be the object of passion. Sight is absolutely central in his account of falling in love—in fact, desire is imagined as stirred up by particles that stream in from the young man's beauty through the eyes (251c5). What he says, however, is that the "godlike face that represents beauty well and the form of the body" (251a) can itself contain traces or signs of the character, or the god within (252dff.). Some lovers, whose vision of the ideal is faint, will not notice those signs, and will attach themselves to the body alone, seeking reproduction or casual bodily pleasure.[43] But those who have a more vivid memory of the ideal notice its traces in the beloved and seek a beloved in accordance with the characteristics of the soul that they truly admire (251aff.). Whether consciously or not, they search for features that have more than a certain pleasing surface configuration, that express and gesture toward something deeper. Their strongest responses are to the body as illuminated by a soul of a certain type, containing the divine. Love's initial shiver is a shiver of awe (251a), "and then, gazing at him, he reveres him as god, and if he were not afraid of getting a reputation for being mad, he would make sacrifices to his *paidika* as to the image of a god" (251a).

Here we have a crucial step in the resolution of the cultural dilemma. For Socrates has very plausibly described an aspect of the real-life experience of falling in love. He may be wrong to think that people are aroused primarily by admirable moral attributes — rather than, for example, by the other person's similarity to a parent, or by his athletic ability, or something else less high-minded — but he certainly is right to say that the bare, unanimated form of beauty is rarely what arouses desire, if we exclude the crudest sort of promiscuous desire. The "person brought up among sailors" is (if we may disregard the class prejudice that Plato so easily expresses) the person who gets turned on by pinup art, with its generalizable, fungible images and its absence of animation. People of good character, he argues, not implausibly, look for something more than the pinup. (Zeus, says Euripides' chorus,[44] fell in love with Ganymede when he saw him bathing after running a race — so even here excellence, not just a pretty face, was the focus of desire.) Plato's suggestion — not unprecedented, as we have seen, but developed with a new sharpness — is that the real object of love's intensity is the divine.

Socrates' account of the lover's madness makes it perfectly clear that this is really madness, not a tame friendship of the Lysianic kind. Like the Lysianic sort, it involves sexual arousal — this is made unmistakable by the account of what the dark horse wants to do, as well as by the account of the whole response to the boy as being like a tickling and boiling, words by convention strongly associated with sexual arousal (251c).[45] But, unlike the friendship of the nonlover, it is also really a kind of madness and distraction — full of the gadfly's sting of painful longing (*oistrai kai odunatai*; 251d), which cannot permit the lover rest or satisfaction in the absence of the young man's beauty. The joy the lover feels at the sight of the young man is metaphorically described in language suggestive of sexual pleasure and even orgasm: "Seeing him, and channeling desire into herself as through an irrigation trench, the soul releases what had then been pent up, and she takes a respite from her strings and agonies, and reaps right then a pleasure that is the sweetest of all" (251e).

How is this madness made a source of generosity and kindliness? Here we arrive at the heart of Socrates' bold solution. Two motives for good conduct are suggested: reverence and gratitude. Reverence first. Seeing the young man's beauty as not just pinup art, but as something splendid and wonderful, something that contains traces of the divine, the lover is inclined not toward manipulation and use, but toward worship. He does all the things lovers conventionally do—neglecting his relatives and property, sleeping wherever he can be near his love, disdaining reputation—because the loved one is for him a kind of divinity (*sebesthai ton to kallos echonta;* 252a). But this kind of awe actually inhibits greedy sexual aims—the good horse helps to rein in the dark one—and prompts a generous and indeed a self-abnegating treatment of the partner. The second motive is gratitude: "because, in addition to revering the one who has beauty, he finds him the only healer of the greatest pains" (252a). And it is not just that the young man heals the pain that he also causes: he also waters the roots of the lover's wings, helping to restore him to a healthier condition. In less metaphorical language, being in love makes the personality take on a depth and richness that the lover recognizes as good. He understands that the young man is the source of this richness, and he benefits him out of gratitude for this great gift. Finally, as the relationship develops, he recognizes that the loved one is the vehicle of divinity through whom and in whom he follows up the traces of the god he himself reveres; and this epistemological gratitude[46] increases his motives for virtuous conduct. "Thus it comes about that the soul of the lover follows the young man in a condition of awe and reverence" (254e).

So the young man gets a surprise. (What Socrates suggests is that this is a common surprise in real-life love—at least among good people. His own contribution is a new analysis, not the production of a new phenomenon.) He has probably heard bad things about lovers. But as time goes on and their intimacy increases, "the evident good will of the lover strikes and dazzles the *erōmenos,* who sees that all his other *philoi* and associates put together do not contribute even a fraction of the *philia* that the inspired philos does" (255b). He spends time with him, as they touch one another in the gymnasia and other places of association (255b). And then something remarkable happens: he falls love in return, conceiving a desire that is similar to, though weaker than, the desire of the *erastēs* for him (255d). It really is *erōs,* says Socrates, and includes bodily desire—although the young man himself calls it not *erōs* but *philia.* Some such couples make love; the highest contemplative types abstain, holding that sexual activity will distract them from the goods they pursue (256a–e). Although the latter are the best, both types are rewarded by the gods in the afterlife; the indulgent ones recover their wings together "on account of their *erōs*," and live a happy life in the bright heavens wandering around together.[47]

Socrates claims that this is the story of many lovers in his culture—that if we understand correctly the metaphysics behind sexual attraction in good and high-minded people, we shall see that there are good reasons for the cultural connection between love and generosity, love and educational benefits. It is reasonable enough that someone who sees the beloved as containing a god, and who is inspired with mad passion for that god, will behave in a fashion both reverent and generous. Someone who just wants to make love with an attractive body will not behave this way, nor, he holds, will the Lysianic nonlover, operating out of a combination of ordinary friendship with bodily desire. He concludes: "Such and so many, my boy, are the divine gifts that the *philia* of an *erastēs* will give you. But an intimacy with the nonloved, all mixed up with mortal self-possession, retentively dispensing its mortal and niggardly benefits, will give birth in your dear soul to a lack of generosity that is praised by the many as virtue, and will cause it to roll around and beneath the earth for nine thousand years devoid of understanding" (256e–257a).

V. Epicurus Sides with "Lysias"

There are several chapters that should be added to this story before we get to the Stoics. I could talk about the Cynics and the Cyrenaics, and about Aristotle's position, which appears to be indeterminate between that of Pausanias and that of "Lysias."[48] But the most important transitional step, in terms of explaining the later debate, takes place with Epicurus. As I have noted, Cicero sees us as having to choose between Epicurus and the Stoa on the value of *erōs*. Much later, Alexander of Aphrodisias represents the choice in a similar way (*In Arist. Top.* 2.139.21 Wallies). So we should have the Epicurean solution before us as a background to the Stoics, whether they were consciously adverting to it or not. Our task is complex, since we need to confront a possible discrepancy between Epicurus and Lucretius, who is also our primary source for the Epicurean position. I shall be very brief here, since I have treated the material at length elsewhere.[49]

Epicurus himself is unremittingly hostile to *erōs*. He defines it as "an intense desire for intercourse, accompanied by the gadfly's sting and distraction" (*oistrou kai adēmonias;* 483 Usener)—an accurate, if one-sided, account of the cultural understanding—and sternly warns that it is not god sent and that the wise man will never have it (D.L. 10.118). Here, as so frequently elsewhere, he rejects Platonism—perhaps in accordance with his well-known saying "I have spat on the *kalon* and all those who gape at it in an empty fashion" (51 Usener). It seems significant that he refers to the gadfly's sting of longing, which was so prominent a feature of the *Phaedrus's* description of the god-sent madness—in the context of denying that the *erōs* is god sent and that it can be a source of great goods. "For a young person," he advises, "the portion of safety is to guard your youth and ward off those things that pollute everything in accordance with agonizing desires" (*Sent. Vat.* 80). This may have a double meaning: avoid falling in love, and also ward off the mad *erastēs*.

On the other hand, the record is more complex concerning sexual desire and sexual conduct. "Intercourse never helped anyone, and it is lucky if it does not harm" (D.L. 10.118), he wrote in his *Symposium*. A young man who asks for sexual advice is given a related answer: "You tell me that the movement of the flesh has made you excessively preoccupied with achieving sexual intercourse. So long as you do not break any laws, or upset customs that are well designed, or offend any person around you, or harm your health, or waste your property, you may indulge your inclination as you wish. But in fact it is impossible not to run up against one of these obstacles. For sexual intercourse never did any good, and it is lucky if it does no harm" (*Sent. Vat.* 51). On the other hand, "Lysias" recognized all those reasons for avoiding the lover, while telling his young man that sexual intimacy with a nonlover could be the answer. Could Epicurus accept this solution? There are a number of fragments that give indications of positive delight in sex, above all, a famous fragment of the *Peri telous,* or *On the Goal:* "I have no idea what I should consider good, if I take away the pleasures of smell, take away the pleasures of sexual intercourse, take away the pleasures of sound, take away the pleasures of beautiful shapes" (67 Usener).

We must be careful here to distinguish different roles and people. The male recipient of Epicurus's letter is not the *erōmenos* in the speech of "Lysias," for he is imagined as having intense desires for intercourse. He is likely, then, to be a somewhat older male who is thinking about playing the active *erastēs* role with either men or women or both. (Lucr. 4.1053 envisages arousal of the male by both female and young male forms.) So far as I can see, nothing in Epicurus gives us information about the *erōmenos* and the choices about intercourse he ought to make, provided he safely guards himself against (his or another's) "mad" desires. The *erastēs* is permitted sexual expression so long as he contrives to avoid the difficulties that usually attend it—which, thinks Epicurus, it will be difficult, if not impossible, to do. Certainly, he should not take the route of marriage and children, since that will lead to many distractions and impediments.[50] It is striking that Epicurus, in spite of his recognition of the dangers attending intercourse, never takes the Cynic way out by praising masturbation; the fragment from *On the Goal* suggests that *aphrodisia* were still his preference.

Now we must turn to Lucretius, knowing as we do so that we may be diverging from Epicurus.[51] (We have a further difficulty: Latin lacks the clear Greek distinction between *erōs* and *philia*, rendering both by amor.)[52] Lucretius seems to concur in Epicurus's thoroughly negative judgment on *erōs* and "madness." In what appears to be a concerted assault on the views of the *Phaedrus* (or, if not these, then their popular equivalent)[53] he traces many of the harms of *erōs* to the idea that the beloved is divine—and to the related notion that in sexual intercourse the lover will become fused with the divine loved one. Rather than leading to Platonic reverence and generosity, he holds, the divinization of the beloved leads to obsessive jealousy, to an overwhelming desire to incorporate and immobilize, and, through these, to sadistic behavior in lovemaking itself. It leads, as well, to an inability to confront without disgust and disillusionment the evidence of the beloved's everyday bodily reality.[54]

On the other hand, a sexual relationship may avoid the long list of problems attendant on *erōs* if it avoids the overestimation inherent in *erōs* and learns to "yield to human life" (4.1191). In this spirit, Lucretius can recommend marriages (and, possibly, other long-term relationships) based on friendship and character. Like Pausanias, he insists that such relationships do not require outstanding beauty in the partner (4.1278–87); unlike Pausanias, he holds that such relationships at their best are totally lacking in passionate madness. Showing a remarkable interest in women's sexuality, he argues that women do experience sexual pleasure (4.1192–1207); he suggests that this will be recognized by a male only if he does not make his own projects of possession or incorporation the focus of all attention.[55]

In short, Lucretius has defended a position very close to that of "Lysias," though his focus is on the marital relationship rather than on male-male intimacy.[56] (On the other hand, we saw that the position of "Lysias" presupposed and to some extent perhaps modeled itself on an antecedent conception of marriage.) Like "Lysias," he prefers a relationship in which the equivalent of the *erastēs* is not mad, is not in love; he makes many of the same arguments about the connection between love and bad behavior to the equivalent of the *erōmenos*, that is, the woman. The major difference is connected with the shift from the male-male to the male-female relationship: he takes an interest in the woman's sexual satisfaction and (implicitly) urges a woman to prefer the nonlover partly on grounds of her own sexual satisfaction (insofar as she has any choice in the matter—for her own choice is not really discussed in the passage, addressed as it is to a male interlocutor).

VI. FALLING IN LOVE WITH VIRTUE;
OR, TWENTY-EIGHT CANDLES

Do the Stoics side with "Lysias" or with Plato's Socrates? That is, do they banish madness or defend it as productive of very great goods? This is a very difficult question to answer, and we had better begin by simply enumerating some facts that are less controversial.

First of all, it seems fairly clear that for the Stoics the sexual act itself (and whether it is with a man or a woman) is an "indifferent"—that is, something of no positive or negative value in and of itself, but something that can be good if chosen in the right way at the right time, and so on, as virtue would dictate (see Stob. 2.9–11; Sext. Emp. *Pyr.* 1.160, 3.200, 3.245; Origen *c. Cels.* 4.45). This means that they begin from a position on intercourse that is, in effect, that of Pausanias. What we now need to know is, are the motives, aims, and desires conventionally associated with *erōs* among those that can possibly be involved in a virtuous action?

The Stoic wise man is *apathēs:* that is, he experiences none of the *pathē.* The *pathē* are defined by Chrysippus as judgments that involve the ascription of high worth to unstable "external goods," items not fully controlled by the agent's reason and will. All such states are held by Stoics to be bad, both because the value ascriptions are false and because they are attended by bad consequences—weakness, loss of integrity, the propensity to excess.[57] The standard ancient critique of "madness" lies close to these Stoic antipassion arguments, for they do repeatedly insist, like "Lysias," that the person in the grip of any of the *pathē* is in a state in which he is pushed around as if by necessity by his attachments to externals, and in which he cannot reason prudently or soundly. The Stoic doctrine of *erōs* should be understood in the light of this more general doctrine and should, if at all possible, be interpreted in such a way as to render it consistent with that doctrine. (Cicero thinks that this is not possible, but we need not follow him.)

On the other hand, as we have seen, the Greek Stoics strongly approve of *erōs:* "And the wise man will be in love with [*erasthēsesthai*] young men

[young people?] who by their physical form [eidous] display a natural aptitude for excellence, as Zeno says in his *Republic* and Chrysippus in the first
book of his *On Lives*, and Apollodorus in his *Ethics*. They define *erōs* as an
attempt to make a friend[58] due to beauty appearing; and they say that it is
directed not at intercourse but at friendship [lit., it is not of intercourse but
of friendship]. At any rate, they say that Thrasonides, even though he had
the woman he loved [erōmenēn] in his power, kept away from her because
she hated him. So *erōs* is directed at friendship, as Chrysippus also says
in his *On Erōs*; and they say that it is not sent by the gods. And they say
that the prime [hōra] of a young person is the bloom of virtue" (D.L. 7.129 –
30). This account of *erōs* is repeated in many sources, the definition being
given repeatedly and with only slight variation, usually in the form "attempt
to form a friendship on account of the appearing beauty of young men
[people?] in their prime" [epibolē philopoiias dia kallos emphainomenon neōn
kai horaiōn]. Let us now comment on each of the major parts of the Diogenes passage, bringing in other sources as we do so.

1. **Be in love; attempt to form a friendship.** To indicate that the wise
man's being-in-love is not a *pathos*, is not a way of being at the mercy of
some piece of the external world which one has overvalued, the Stoics stress
that it is a deliberately undertaken project: an attempt (*epibolē*)[59] to form a
certain sort of relationship. "They are of the opinion that the wise man will
conduct himself with practical wisdom and dialectically, and sympotically
and erotically" (Stob. 2.65.15 [SVF 3.717]). Just as the wise man will set
himself to drink the right amount but never be overcome by drunkenness,
so too with *erōs:* he will set out to form a good sort of relationship. In the
technical sense of the theory of the passions, where *epithumia* is one of the
four genera of the *pathē*, "Erōs is not *epithumia*" (Stob., passage quoted).[60]

2. **Sexual conduct.** This does not mean that *erōs* will not be attended by
sexual desire (in the Stoic view, a bodily desire like hunger, and not in its
nature a *pathos* or corruption of judgment). When the wise man judges it
appropriate, sexual conduct will follow. As we recall, sexual conduct is an
indifferent—which means that it is virtuous if done by the wise man, with
all of his knowledge of the good. The sexual nature of the wise man's intentions is in fact stressed by the Stoics, who also define *erōs* as a "hunt" or
"chase" (*thēra*) "after a young man [meirakiou] who is undeveloped but naturally endowed for virtue" (Plut. *De communibus notitiis* 1073B). They thus
connect their *erōs* with popular Greek conceptions of the aim of the *erastēs*—
see, for example, Plato *Lysias* 205e–206a and *Symposium* 203d (where *erōs*
is called a *thereutēs deinos* and a plotter about the beautiful).[61] Zeno is credited not only with intense sexual enthusiasm for his young men (Ath. 563e:

see below), but also with theoretical advocacy of intercrural intercourse as a norm of sexual conduct.[62] A speaker in Plutarch reports that Zeno discussed this topic in his *Republic*. Although the speaker himself is a little annoyed at this — he wishes that Zeno had discussed it in a playful after-dinner speech instead — the young men who are his audience are themselves irritated by his irritation, and clearly seem to prefer Zeno's topic. ("This put the young men out of countenance, and they sat in silence": Plut. *Quaest. conv.* 653E.)[63]

We may add that the Stoics apparently do not demand sexual exclusivity in such relationships: "Do not have intercourse with the young man you love in preference to the one you do not (or vice versa), or with a female in preference to a male (or vice versa)" (Sext. Emp. *Math.* 2.190 = *Pyr.* 3.245). While this may simply mean that the wise person will sometimes see good reasons of a particular sort for having intercourse with someone else, it may also mean that sexual exclusivity is more actively discouraged — as indeed some of the texts about the Stoic ideal city appear to suggest. It would appear that avoidance of sexual exclusivity is connected with the prevention of excessively intense attachments that would lead to *pathē*.[64]

3. Young men in their prime. Most versions of the Stoic definition are gender ambiguous: though the "young" is grammatically masculine, the group may include females as well as males. Schofield has argued well that, given the Cynic origins of the Stoic view of sex, and given the Stoic views about female equality, we should understand females to be included alongside males — at least as the younger parties to the relationships but also, if the genders are to be truly equal in the ideal city, as "wise men" who seek youthful beauty.[65] On the other hand, we must grant that Zeno appears to have been much more interested in young men. As Athenaeus writes, "You [sc. Stoics] are oglers of boys, and in this alone emulate the founder of your philosophy Zeno the Phoenician, who never consorted with a woman, but always with boy-friends, as Antigonus of Carystus records in his *Life* of him" (563E; trans. Schofield 1991, 33). The ideal city is built around couples in very much the same manner of the Sacred Band and the imaginary army of Phaedrus's speech in the *Symposium:* the image is that of male-male couples, one member older, one younger, whose mutual loyalty and devotion will give the city strong sources of motivation for virtue (Ath. 561C). Women are certainly not excluded, but they are not the theoretical focus.[66] And the reference to the prime or *hōra* of the beautiful person is especially familiar within the conventions of male-male love.

4. Appearing beauty; the aptitude for excellence. The Stoic definition, like the *Phaedrus*, gives the sight of beauty a central causal role in *erōs*. On the other hand, Stoic texts frequently insist that their kind of *erōs* is "of the soul" rather than "of the body" (see *SVF* 3.721; Ath. 563E: "not bodies but soul"). Further problems come from the fact that they paradoxically insist that young people are actually ugly, since they have not yet become good (Plut. *De communibus notitiis* 1072Eff.). We should solve this problem, I think, by pressing the link with the *Phaedrus:* as in Socrates' conception, so here the outward appearance of a beautiful young person may "display"— as Diogenes in fact says, citing Zeno and Chrysippus—"a natural aptitude for excellence." We cannot tell whether all physical beauty is taken to be the sign of this aptitude, but the Stoics appear to think that it is necessary that some beauty be present—at least if the response to the signs of excellence is to deserve the name of *erōs*. Then the wise man will reason that what he finds so moving is not really the bodily beauty, but the signs of the soul within that make their way into his presence through the body. He can fairly claim that his object is really the soul, not the body, and that the young really are not truly beautiful until they have been educated.[67]

5. *Its goal is not intercourse but friendship.* As we have seen already, intercourse will be available in these erotic relationships, when the virtuous judgment of the wise man chooses it. On the other hand, this is not the goal of the relationship, or what gives it its raison d'être. Diogenes' further explication of the point is revealing. Zeno and Chrysippus, he says, cite the example of Thrasonides, in Menander's *Misoumenos,* who kept away sexually from the young woman he desired because she hated him. The moral of that story is that sex should never be chosen when it cannot be combined with friendship—not that it should never be chosen at all. We can compare the Stoic position with that of a speaker at a philosophy conference who, when asked, "Did you come here in order to eat?" will say, "Of course not. I came here to attend the conference." But this person is highly likely to eat while attending the conference, since she will get hungry—provided she sees no good reason to abstain. The overall goal of the Stoic lover, like that of Pausanias and "Lysias" and the lover in the *Phaedrus,* will, then, be a friendship that improves the character of the young.

6. *Not sent by the gods.* This is puzzling, for in the Stoic universe everything is sent by god. Nor does the plural give us an easy way out (taking the reference to be to popular gods rather that to Zeus)—for Stoics often use the plural in perfectly serious contexts.[68] I am inclined to connect this claim with the denial that *erōs* is madness or passion, for the ordinary conception of "god-sent" *erōs* is closely linked with ideas of madness, transport, and necessity (the ideas "Lysias" pilloried). In other words, we should think of it as a project that is "up to us," not as something that comes upon us sent

from on high. It is always in our power to regulate and even to refuse it. Does this also involve the Stoic in denying the godlike splendor of the loved one's beauty, and the mysterious power of reverence that splendor exerts? It might seem so, but we must reserve our conclusion on this central matter. We could, however, avoid the entire question by adopting the manuscript variant *epimempton*, "blameworthy" (for *theopempton*, "sent by the gods,"), as does Long in the O.C.T.

In order to emphasize their allegiance to the goal of friendship, the Stoics say something surprising about the age of the *erōmenos*. In Athenian convention, the best age is usually understood to be the time between the attainment of full height and the growth of the beard: if we go by modern growth patterns, perhaps fifteen to nineteen, though there is some reason to think that ancient Mediterranean growth patterns were slower.[69] Pausanias had insisted on a relatively high threshold of entry into the *erōmenos* relation: when the beard first starts to grow. His life gave evidence of an unusually high age of exit as well: he and Agathon began their relationship when the latter was eighteen, and it was still going on twelve years later.[70] The Stoics follow this lead. We do not know what they say about the precise age of entry, but their exit age, apparently recommended by Zeno, was found very remarkable by Athenaeus: it was put at twenty-eight.[71] Chrysippus is said to have spoken about the need for the *erōmenos* to shave his chin (564A), and Antigonus of Carystus, in his *Life of Zeno*, stated—probably with mocking intent—that they actually had to shave the rump of the *erōmenos* as well (cited in Ath. 564E). The point of this departure from cultural convention is probably to emphasize that long-term friendship, not momentary bodily delight, is the goal: they will put up even with someone who has become culturally subpar as a sex partner, since they obey in this way the educational requirements of *philia*.[72]

Note that it is very important to the Stoic doctrine that *erōs* so defined should not be reciprocal. For only the wise man can use *erōs* correctly and well; in the hands of the nonwise, such a relation is dangerous. As Seneca says to Lucilius, "You and I, who are still a long way short of being wise men, should not blunder our way into something which is turbulent, uncontrollable, forsworn to another, and cheapened in its own eyes" (*Ep.* 116.4–5).[73] This means, it seems, that the *Phaedrus* doctrine of reciprocal *erōs*, or *anterōs*, must be rejected by the Stoic sage, who must not comport himself in such a manner as to arouse such an intense feeling in the younger partner. This may be a further reason for the Greek Stoics' intense focus on male-male relations, even though their arguments support, in general, male-female equality, for it was the conventional norm that the *eromenōs* would not fall in love in return, though he would certainly have *philia.* However much the *Phaedrus* may depict a known reality, the public norm was otherwise. Females, by contrast, were well known to be very ready to fall in love—in fact, Phaedrus in the *Symposium* compares the wife Alcestis to the *erastēs* in the male-male relationship, despite her younger age, because of the passion she evidently displayed (*Symp.* 179B–D). The education of young women, then, would not so obviously be fostered by an erotic tie, and this may be another reason for Zeno's apparent avoidance of the topic of young women as *erōmenai.*[74]

Perhaps, too, the prohibition of *erōs* for the nonwise explains why things stop at twenty-eight,[75] for the *erōmenos* is now pretty advanced in education and may be able to attempt the transition to the role of wise lover in his own right, a role that is evidently seen as a good one for a Stoic to play, provided that he has become wise.

Now we arrive at the large question: is this really the old *erōs* or isn't it? Is the Stoic wise man "Lysias" or is he Socrates? Cicero clearly thinks that this is the old erotic passion, with all of its dangers, and thinks, therefore, that the Stoics are flatly inconsistent with their doctrine of the *pathē,* inspired, it would seem, by their strong preference for youthful male bodies:

> Let us now turn to the teachers of virtue, the philosophers—who deny that love is directed at intercourse, and in that they take issue with Epicurus, who was not far wrong in my opinion. For what is this "love of friendship"? Why is it that nobody loves an ugly man, or a beautiful old man? For my part I think that this custom was born in the Greek gymnasia, in which this sort of lovemaking is free and permitted. Well, then, did Ennius say: "The beginning of vice is the stripping of bodies among citizens." And even when such loves are modest, as I see they can be, still they bring anxiety, all the more since they supply their own limit and law. Again, not to speak of the love of women, to which nature has permitted a greater freedom, who has any doubt about what the poets mean by the abduction of Ganymede, and who fails to understand the point of Laius's language and what he wants in Euripides' play? What, finally, do the most cultivated men and the greatest poets publish about their own lives in poems and songs? What things Alcaeus, a brave man renowned in his city, writes about the love of young men! Anacreon's whole corpus is love poetry. Above all, Ibycus of Rhegium was ablaze with love, as is clear from his writings. In fact we see that all those loves are based on sexual desire. We philosophers have come forward, with our Plato as authority, whom Dicaearchus reproves,

not unjustly, to attribute authority to love. The Stoics actually both say that the wise man will fall in love, and define love itself as an attempt to form a friendship from the appearance of beauty. But if in the real world there is any such thing without anxiety, longing, care, sighing, let it be—for then it is empty of all sexual desire; and our discourse is about desire. (*Tusc.* 4.70)

Cicero gives the Stoic a stark choice: either sexual desire, in which case we have a full-blown passion, connected with anxiety, longing, and care, or no sexual desire, in which case we have nothing to worry about. He reproves Plato as the origin of the Stoic doctrine, but he seems unwilling to consider seriously either of the alternatives that Plato's *Phaedrus* offers us: either the nonlover "Lysias," who has sexual desire without anxiety or jealousy because he lacks the madness of *erōs*, or the lover described by Socrates, who has sexual desire without anxiety or jealousy ("using neither spite nor ungenerous hostility toward his *paidika*"; *Phdr.* 253a) precisely because he has a particular species of erotic madness, one that sets him on the road to reverence and generosity. His criticism is useless without further argument to show why neither of these precisely described alternatives is available as a psychological reality. Moreover, it would appear to be in bad faith, given that Cicero, as much as any fifth-century Athenian, accepts a conception of marriage according to which it should contain sexual conduct, therefore of necessity sexual desire, without containing *erōs*. So he knew very well the possibility that he denies, when male-male love enters the picture.

We turn now to Plutarch, who has a different criticism to make. It is that if the Stoics lack all pathos as they understand it, then we should not really let them call their state *erōs:* "Nobody would stop the enthusiasm of the wise for young men [people?], given that there is no pathos in it, if it is called a 'chase' or 'making friends'—but they wouldn't let them call it *erōs.*"[76] In other words, according to the common conception of *erōs*, it contains elements—presumably of "mad" transport, of longing, of intense need for an ungoverned external object—that make it in its very nature a pathos as the Stoics understand that term. Either the wise man is just chasing after young men whom he views as potential friends with an eye to virtue and education (with sex included where appropriate)—in other words, he is "Lysias"—or else he is really needy vis-à-vis, and intensely focused on, that one person, in which case his state is *erōs* according to the common conception, but then he is not a Stoic.

Is Plutarch right? What, we now ask, is the wise man's love like? We should try, at least initially, to imagine it in a way that is consistent with

Stoic doctrine of the *pathē*. The wise man, then, falls in love with a beautiful young man (let us say), whose physical forms show signs of the promising soul within. The beauty is crucial in inspiring the love—in this way *erōs* is distinct, it would seem, from Roman Stoic ideas of marital affection.[77] Since he is wise, this love is consistent with perfect virtue. This means that it is not characterized by a mistaken overestimation of the importance of its object, vis-à-vis the wise man's own *eudaimonia*. The wise man can certainly have boundless respect and friendship for the humanity of his partner; but he should never think of his partner as an absolutely essential element in his own flourishing. He must at all times keep up the Stoic practice of *praemeditatio malorum:* that is, he must rehearse to himself all the disasters that can befall the young man, or the relationship, or himself, reminding himself that such things are sometimes the will of Zeus. When a disaster does arrive, he must not feel distress or pain—he must tell himself that this was, all along, Zeus's will. So long as things are going well, he can move toward the gratification of his pleasures under the guidance of *boulēsis*, or rational wish, and he can attempt to avoid bad consequences under the guidance of *eulabeia*, or prudent caution.[78] Finally, he can find joy in the relationship—not, however, the "cheerful joy" that the Stoics denounce, but the "solid," reliable joy that is defined as *eulogos eparsis*, rational uplift.[79]

In effect, the central object of the wise man's good affective attitudes is always his own virtue and will, seen as sufficient for good life. He will act for the sake of others as the Stoic doctrine of the social *oikeiōsis* recommends, remembering that his own virtue and reason are just part of the rationality of the universe as a whole, and that the interests of others are, in the universal scheme of things, on a par with his own. In benefiting others he does not treat them as merely instrumental to his own projects; he may respect and benefit them for their own sake. On the other hand, his view must be that no concrete human relationship, no form of action toward another concrete human being, is necessary for his *eudaimonia*. All his actions, including his other-regarding actions, will be selected with a view to his own rational perfection, and this will dictate the way in which the interests of others are permitted to count for him. The young man, then, will be seen as a valuable occasion offered by the world for the exercise of social virtue—as one of the rational beings in the universe toward whom that virtue is appropriately exercised. His role is thus somewhat like the role of property, or money, or political office, which also provide occasions for the exercise of virtue—although, given that he is a rational human being, he will merit a respect and concern that these things do not. At the end of each day (if he follows the practice recommended by Seneca *De ira* 3.36),[80] the wise man will go over his actions, asking himself whether he has been too concerned with an external object, too reliant on the things of chance. Since he is fully wise, the answer will be no.[81]

How, then, can he really be in love? We can certainly see how such a man could "chase" after attractive sexual partners within the constraints imposed by virtue, in much the same way that he would chase after a good meal. (If we return to my example, the philosopher who goes somewhere to attend a conference will not skip the conference to eat, but in the breaks he may well "chase" after a good meal, and genuinely enjoy it.) [82] We can also understand how such a man could be a really good friend to his young partner, fostering his development toward virtue in a measured and balanced manner. (He would not feel obliged to foster the development of all young men equally, since he would remember that the Stoics perform their duties where life has stationed them, and it is rational to give our near and dear a greater measure of our time and concern.) What we have a hard time imagining is that this man would ever do the things standardly associated with *erōs*—sighs and longing, sleepless nights outside the loved one's door, extravagant gifts, the disregard of other duties, the disregard of property, the disregard of life itself. We know well that he will not do what Aeschylus's Achilles did, mourning the death of Patroclus with haunting erotic memories of thighs and kisses.

What has become of reverence and gratitude, the two key Platonic mechanisms for turning madness into virtue? The Stoic wise man will have no more reverence for his boyfriend than for any other human being who is making progress. He will have, in fact, less reverence for him than he has for himself, for the wise—not the unwise—are "godlike" (D.L. 7.119). He would not feel Plato's "shudder" of religious awe at the sight of that well-adjusted young brow and that ear open for the logos. As for gratitude, certainly the young man contributes nothing to one who is already complete, beyond a theater for the operations of his virtue. But the whole world is that.

All this, the Stoics will say, is an advantage of their sort of *erōs*. All this, Plutarch plausibly says, is a reason for not calling it *erōs* at all.

Plutarch has not tried to enter very deeply into the spirit of Stoic *erōs*. He does not try to see how similar, in many respects, the wise man's benevolent actions will be to the actions of the conventional *erastēs* without, it is claimed, including the usual risks of jealousy, possessiveness, and insensitivity to the young man's true needs. Nor does he try to imagine the Stoic lover's attitude in a sympathetic light. One can indeed see something fine and awe inspiring in the spiritual intensity of a person whose first devotion is to the universe as a whole, and to rationality as a whole; and one can see great attractions in being the boyfriend or girlfriend of such a person, whose vision of humanity and of the universe would indeed lift one beyond oneself, and beyond the narrow obsessions of a passion in which one is oneself turned into a divinity. In this sense, the Stoic lover is not "Lysias," for the nonlover of "Lysias," though he did make a claim based on *aretē*, offered no clear picture of a vision or understanding of the world toward which he would intend to lead his beloved. He has Stoic *apatheia* without Stoic physics, and that can indeed seem a cramped and stingy sort of union. The Stoic, by contrast, offers an understanding of life so awe inspiring in itself that it claims to transcend the merely personal; inhabiting it, both lovers will feel reverence and awe for the logos, and that, they claim, is more exhilarating than feeling it for one another. Indeed, they can claim in one way, and with good reason, to be fulfilling the spirit of Socrates' teaching in the *Phaedrus:* for their partnership, like that of Socrates' lovers, is above all partnership toward knowledge and truth, and its joy is the joy of that illumination.

On the other hand, Socrates contends that these benefits require madness and the surrender of self-sufficiency, before an object whom one deeply needs and whose absence one desperately minds. It requires both longing and gratitude. All this the Stoics are committed to denying. And in this sense what they recommend is crucially unlike *erōs*. It is beautiful and it is splendid—but Plutarch is basically right, it is not *erōs* according to the common conception, even when we make allowances for their desire to improve on the common. In leaving madness out, they have made too radical a break. The Stoics may offer much beyond "Lysias," but they are certainly not the inspired Socrates. Unable to accept that Socrates' solution because it is too "mad," too full of longing and passivity, they return to a position that is in some important respects, though not in all, that of "Lysias" and Epicurus. They use the name of *erōs* because they are physically aroused by their partners' beauty and want to have sex with them. So far so plausible. But by leaving out need, reverence, and gratitude they have left out some of the value of the old *erōs*, no matter what wonderful educational experiences they offer instead. The relationship goes well beyond that proposed by "Lysias," but it has, in the end, a similar gap at its heart. Could such a love really do for the city what Plato thinks *erōs* will do, linking citizens through bonds of selfless devotion? Or will it, as Plato asked, "breed in the dear soul a stinginess that is praised by the many as virtue?" (*Phdr.* 256e–257a).

To put it another way, isn't the Stoic wise man all too like Plato's man brought up among sailors, who had "never seen an example of free and generous love"?

The mysterious beauty of *erōs*, in the common conception, was the beauty of a deep opening in oneself, a surrendering of boundaries toward surprising incursions of influence from the world. This Plato's Socrates preserves, with its sting of madness and his liquids flowing in as through an irrigation trench — connecting this surrender, plausibly and powerfully, with the goods of generosity and altruism. The Stoic self is determined at the outset to close all such openings, to stop up all the holes through which such liquids might enter, to be a house carefully sealed against the elements. Stoics cannot have this solid joy, I argue, and have all the goods of *erōs* too.

VII. Ancient and Modern Norms

One of the claims of this essay has been that we must study the ancient Greek philosophical debates about *erōs* in their historical context. Thus, I have criticized my earlier treatment of the *Phaedrus* for its all too easy transportation of Plato's example into a modern context, which neglected, I now argue, some norms and problems peculiar to that context, neglecting in the process some of the more interesting contributions of the dialogue. On the other hand, my prefatory remarks in section 1 suggest that precise historical attention to the Greek ethical debate might possibly still make a contribution to our modern reflections about the erotic and the ethical. It is now time to connect these two claims.

One way of connecting the two claims should by now be obvious: when the Greek thinkers are studied in their own context, and not simply as projections of modern norms, our thought is freed from certain specifically modern prejudices and assumptions about what issues and categories are most salient. This is itself a contribution to our thinking. Thus, as Foucault so well put it, they free our thought so that it can think itself differently. We see that it is possible, even in the context of same-sex relationships, to focus on ethical issues other than "the morality of homosexual conduct" as a long Christian tradition has tended to define that issue, namely, as an issue about same-sex inclination and conduct, as to whether these are immoral just on account of their same-sex nature. The Greek debate shows us, further, that when one ceases to take that particular ethical focus one does not ipso facto become a raving beast deaf to all ethical questions (a stereotype on the American Right). Nor need one react to these stereotypes by becoming a subversive parodic countercultural resister of all norms. One may become, in fact, a sensitive ethical human being who does not happen to have a particular set of characteristic American obsessions. Indeed, what should strike us with great force about the Greek debate is its highly refined ethical character, its persistent focus on dividing ethical actions and actors from unethical actions and actors — in a way that does not single out same-sex desire and conduct for particular blame. Insofar as there is blame, it attaches to bodily excess, to overweening, to exploitation, to lack of generosity, to deception — all issues that arise in both the same-sex and the opposite-sex context.

But the texts, I believe, do not simply free us; they also give us some worthy paradigms to follow. For even though our culture is in many respects different from the culture of the Greeks, we still have on our hands the central problem of this debate: whether or not the powerful erotic passions of human beings can be made harmonious with the virtue of the lover and the well-being of the beloved. When we fall in love, we do terrible things to one another. And the debate I have traced, if it leaves the right answer in doubt, seems to pose the right questions: about generosity and restraint, about kindness and education, about the proper balance between passion and the other concerns of a life.

Even the answers put forward by the philosophers deserve our most serious scrutiny. It is very tempting to think that the Stoics may be correct. We should love only within the strict constraints of a vigilant moral idealism. The Stoics make a valuable contribution to our thinking when they attempt the conjuring trick of keeping *erōs* alive, and whole, inside morality.

Is it just a trick? Or does it work? Each of us must judge. For those who reject it, Plato's *Phaedrus* offers us yet another possibility: an *erōs* that is more genuinely a passion, more closely connected to other passions and vulnerabilities and to a genuinely reciprocal exchange of passion and benefit. Perhaps even that ideal is too refined, too high-mindedly moral and intellectual, to satisfy us (or Plutarch) as an image of what real human love can offer at its best. Maybe, then, even that ideal moralizes love so relentlessly that it loses the surprise and the radiance that we associate with that passion. Again, each of us must judge. What seems irrefutable, however, is the proposition put forward by all the philosophers I have considered: that it is only coarse and callous people who see sex as extraethical (whether they do so by focusing on reproduction or on pleasure). In people of good character, sex is a matter for ethical judgment, indeed, for a lifelong process of ethical self-scrutiny. For justice is in our lives, and sex is in our lives. If we care about both, we cannot but anxiously seek to bring them closer together.

Notes

This chapter appeared in an earlier form under the title "Erōs and the Wise: the Stoic Response to a Cultural Dilemma," in *Oxford Studies in Ancient Philosophy* 13 (1995): 231–67, and also in *The Emotions in Hellenistic Philosophy*, ed. J. Sihvola and T. Engberg-Pedersen (The Netherlands: Kluwer, 1998), 271–304. The present version contains both revisions and additions (sections I and VII are essentially new). My analysis is closely connected to my account of the Stoic passions in Nussbaum 1994b, chaps. 10–12, and to Nussbaum 1994a, appendix 4 of which is coauthored by Kenneth Dover and me. But the chapter also returns to the topic of chaps. 6 and 7 of Nussbaum 1986, in the belief that the analysis given there was insufficiently grounded in the historical and cultural context of Plato's thought. On Stoicism, I have learnt much from Brad Inwood's unpublished manuscript "Why Do Fools Fall in Love?" and, of course, from Schofield 1991. For comments on earlier versions, I am grateful to Victor Caston, Kenneth Dover, Troels Engberg-Pedersen, Christopher Gill, Brad Inwood, Malcolm Schofield, and Richard Sorabji.

1. Dover 1989. Dover initially claimed that there are no examples of erections for the younger partner, but in his second edition he grants that one vase may well depict such an erection: see p. 204, where he insists that this vase "remains, however, exceptional."

2. There are many variants—for some, see the illustrations in Dover 1989. The younger partner is most frequently of mature height, though sometimes shorter; often he is taller and more solidly muscled than the older. The upper hand sometimes touches shoulder or neck rather than face, and sometimes it simply reaches toward the face rather than touching it. On the age of the younger partner see text below, and Nussbaum 1994a.

3. Dover 1989, 94–95, referring to Beazley 1947, 199; Dover calls the position "the most characteristic configuration of homosexual courtship in vase-painting" (94) and describes many variants.

4. It is difficult, however, to interpret facial expressions on semiarchaic statues, given the narrow range of stereotypes that seem to have been in use.

5. Soph. *Ant.* 781ff., esp. 787ff.: "and not one of the immortal gods can escape you, not one among human beings, who live for a day; and the one who has you is mad. You even take the minds of the just and turn them aside into injustice." On Zeus's abduction of Ganymede see Soph. fr. 320 Nauck: Ganymede's thighs "set Zeus aflame"; for other literary accounts see Dover 1989, 197. For other examples of gods gripped by *erōs* see Dover 1989, 197ff., focusing especially on Pindar's account of Pelops and Poseidon in *Ol.* 1: "Pindar's gods are too refined to digest anything but ambrosia, but never so insensitive that their genitals cannot be aroused" (198).

6. On love and madness, an excellent discussion focusing on later evidence is Winkler 1990.

7. For some evidence on this point see *SVF* 2.443–55. See my discussion in Nussbaum 1994b.

8. See, e.g., *SVF* 3.650–53, to be discussed below.

9. For a comprehensive discussion of the evidence see Schofield 1991, 57ff.

10. Plutarch's position is not that sexual desire and conduct are inherently at odds with education for virtue. He seems to admit that there could be an educative relationship that included sexual desire and sexual conduct—he just holds that if it lacks *pathos* it should not be called *erōs:* see below.

11. Eur. *Hipp.* 525ff.

12. Ibid., 530–31.

13. Ibid., 555ff.: "O holy wall of Thebes, o mouth of Dirce, you could speak along with me of the way in which Cypris advances. For, arranging a marriage for the bearer of Bacchus, son of Zeus, by means of the flaming thunderbolt, she put her to bed with a bloody fate."

14. Aesch. *Supp.* 1067. (Possibly the *eumenē* is predicative: "established violence as well intentioned.") Zeus's touch "with a healing hand" is *eumenēs*, kindly or well intentioned, because it releases her from the torments and wanderings she has endured. Invoking Io's story, the suppliant women here pray to Zeus for deliverance from bad marriages and for the distribution of power to women (*kai kratos nemoi gunaixin;* 1068–69). The author of the *Prometheus Bound* records the legend that the impregnation of Io was caused by the calm touch of a hand, apparently without any further physical act: *epaphōn atarbei cheiri kai thigōn monon,* "caressing her with an unimpassioned hand and merely touching her" (849). The question of rape is thus pushed to the background.

15. Dover 1989, 60ff.

16. On Herodotus's story of Candaules, who fell in love with his wife, see the good discussion in Halperin 1989.

17. See the good discussion of the ode in Winnington-Ingram 1980, 92–99.

18. See the discussion in Dover 1989, 53, 197; and also Halperin 1990, 86–87.

19. On this see Dover 1989, 53, 197, referring to Aeschin. 1.142 (who holds that the relationship was not explicitly described by Homer because a cultivated audience would find it self-explanatory) and Pl. *Symp.* 180a4–7, where Phaedrus criticizes Aeschylus's judgment that Achilles was the *erastēs*.

20. See Dover 1989, 197.

21. See Dover 1989, 61. I follow his translation (and therefore system of transliteration). Note that the younger man's "love" is, as we might expect, *philia* and not *erōs*.

22. See the discussion of *anankē* in Dover 1989, 61–62.

23. Aeschin. *In Tim.* 136; see Dover 1989, 43ff. (his translation).

24. See Dover 1989, 43ff., arguing that *dikaios erōs* should be understood not as a subspecies of *erōs* but as the only genuine type of *erōs*.

25. On the reference to the Theban Sacred Band, see my discussion in Nussbaum 1994a. And see now Leitao's chapter in this volume.

26. In these examples Alcestis is treated as an *erastēs* (*dia ton erōta;* 179c), as is Orpheus.

27. Hackforth 1952, 31.

28. Griswold 1986, 48. Other peculiarities in Griswold's account of the speech of "Lysias" are his description of the nonlover as having "mastered his eros" (45) (no, he never had it), and its erroneous claim that "the speaker says nothing about his own personal qualities" (46), whereas he twice mentions his *aretē*.

29. Griswold 1986, 69.

30. Rowe 1986, 144, 146. Rowe oddly states that "the speaker implicitly claims not only that he is not in love with the boy, but that he does not desire him physically either; it is to be a purely businesslike transaction" (145). But of course the speaker does allude, however discreetly, to his desire: "You know how matters are with me" (230e6), and "with an eye not to the present pleasure, but also to the benefit which is to come" (233b6–c1), where the "also" implies that pleasure is at least a part of what is envisaged. It is perfectly clear that the *charizesthai* that is under discussion implies sexual conduct, and Rowe himself grants this ("but he wants to sleep with him"; 145). So why does Rowe deny sexual desire to the nonlover, and how does he envisage this wanting-to-sleep-with-him, in the absence of desire? In short, if the older man does not desire the younger, what is the speech all about, and why does he make it?

31. Nussbaum 1986, 207–8. I go on to argue that ultimately this initially plausible position is found unsatisfactory—for good reasons; I shall not take issue with that part of my analysis, though I shall add some new points.

32. Nussbaum 1986, by contrast, suggests that the first two speeches are heard as plausible until Socrates actually criticizes them.

33. A critical discussion that brings this out well is that by Ferrari (1987, 50ff., 88ff.). See also 90ff., where he gives an attractive account of the prudent self-interest of the typical *erōmenos*.

34. As Ferrari points out (1987, 89ff.), the speech does not altogether deny that there may also be good consequences; it focuses on the fact of the ambivalence of *erōs*, which is itself seen to be a bad thing from the boy's point of view. The claim is that he can have the good consequences without the ambivalence.

35. Ferrari (1987) seems to me to neglect this claim (and its plausibility) when he calls the relationship promised by the nonlover "business-like" (51).

36. As Kenneth Dover points out to me, this statement would still be true if the words "Greek" and "given . . . with" were deleted!

37. We may remark, too, that the writers who insist that the position of "Lysias" is base because it leaves out romantic passion do not apply this judgment consistently, condemning the ancient Greek norm of marriage. "Lysias" in effect is reconstituting the male-male relation along marriage-like lines.

38. I do not mean to suggest that the young man is selling himself for a reward—something that would be socially unacceptable—but he is expected, still, to make a prudent calculation of costs (disadvantages) and benefits, as we can see from Pausanias's speech.

39. See Dover 1989, 111–14. Note that *kalos* here means "physically beautiful," not "noble." Dover does note exceptions to this general tendency, however. Archaic graffiti on rocks on the island of Thera include praises of youths for being *agathos* and even *aristos;* a fragment of Callimachus around four centuries later refers to a graffito that praises a youth for being *sophos* (see Dover 1989, 113).

40. And in general, the analysis fails to explain why the speech both allures and shocks.

41. See Phaedrus's speech, above.

42. It is implicit because the harm-producing varieties have been prominently recognized before, because the recognition of "divine" *mania* does implicitly distinguish this variety from a merely mortal variety, and because the later discussion of rhetoric explicitly recognizes the duality in madness; see 265a: one sort of madness results from human diseases, one from divine causes.

43. Pl. *Phdr.* 250e. I analyze this difficult passage in detail in Nussbaum 1994a, arguing that its criticism includes both those who focus on reproduction and those who seek casual bodily pleasure alone in male-male relations. (As Pausanias pointed out, these will often be the same people: for those who go for the body rather than the soul are indifferent between women and males — *Symp.* 181b). It appears to be a working assumption of the speech that the only reason for turning to women is reproductive.

44. Eur. *Tro.* 821 ff.

45. See Dover 1989, 162–65. I have also profited from an unpublished paper by Malcolm Pettingill on this topic. On the theme of reciprocity in Socrates' speech as a whole, see the excellent analysis in Halperin 1986.

46. Gratitude, I note, will be termed a *pathos* in Hellenistic arguments and linked to anger, both requiring the ascription of high importance to an unstable "external good," and both being ways in which a person with such an attachment responds to the attempts of others to foster or harm it. Plato's lover's gratitude, similarly, seems to involve an acknowledgment of deep need: in the absence of the beloved he suffers great pain.

47. For a close analysis of the dialogue's attitude to sexual conduct, including the views expressed in this passage, see Nussbaum 1994a.

48. On Aristotle see Nussbaum 1994a.

49. Nussbaum 1994b, chap. 5.

50. For the difficulties of reconstructing Epicurus's position here, given the textual corruption in a crucial passage in Diogenes Laertius, see Nussbaum 1994b, 152–53.

51. On the other hand, the later tradition is likely to view them as one. It is impossible to tell to what extent Cicero and other thinkers who contrast Epicureans and Stoics have formed their picture of the Epicurean tradition on the basis of Lucretius's poem.

52. Of course *amicitia* (or the odd Lucretian variant *amicities*) will also be used for *philia* in some cases.

53. For discussion of the theme of the divine mistress in poetry of Lucretius's time and later, see Nussbaum 1994b, chap. 5.

54. On all this see Nussbaum 1994b, chap. 5.

55. In the sick relationships he criticizes, the aim of incorporation leads to a frenzied biting and grasping, which not only ignores the object's pleasure but also deliberately inflicts pain; for analysis of this material, and the related material on female pleasure, see Nussbaum 1994b, chap. 5.

56. Lucr. 4.1053 makes it clear that the relationship could be a male-male relationship; that is just not what the poet-speaker finds most interesting — perhaps because it would be unlikely to illustrate his theme of mutual pleasure.

57. Here I am giving the barest summary of Nussbaum 1994b, chap. 10. For all relevant texts and an attempt to interpret them, see that chapter.

58. *Philopoiia*, and "friendship" below renders *philia*. Although these translations are very imperfect, they are chosen to mark the distinction between *erōs* and *philia*. From the presence of the word *philia* one may conclude that what is envisaged is a relationship involving some sort of reciprocity or mutuality; one may not infer that it is weak in affect nor, indeed, on the other hand, that it contains affect of any kind (since *philia* may exist between family members who do not know one another).

59. See the excellent discussion of the term by Schofield (1991, 29 n. 14), who points out that Cic. *Tusc.* 4.72 renders it by *conatus*. The definition of *epibolē* in Stob. 2.87.18 as "an impulse [*hormē*] before an impulse" is well explained by Schofield as growing from the idea that before one can be motivated to do something one must make it one's project, set oneself to do it.

60. See Schofield 1991, 29–30.

61. Cited in this connection by Schofield (1991, 29 n. 13). Of course Diotima will go on to offer a novel account of the best goal for this chase, so the presence of "chase" language would not by itself establish that the Stoics saw sexual conduct as one part of the permissible goal.

62. See Dover 1989 and Nussbaum 1994a (with further references) on the connection between this norm and interest in the well-being of the *erōmenos*.

63. Schofield, after producing the evidence on sexual conduct's "indifferent" status and on Zeno's interest in intercrural intercourse, which I have also produced, suggests without argument that "Zenonian love proper" was "of course a sublimated Platonic form of love." Schofield offers us no reason to prefer this conclusion, and by linking Zeno closely with the Cynics he gives us yet further reason not to prefer it — for Cynics were not in the least given to sublimation. Brad Inwood, "Why Do Fools Fall in Love?" (unpublished manuscript), argues, convincingly I think, that the Stoic position is similar to that of Pausanias: where sexual conduct is concerned, all the difference is made by the mode of execution and the disposition of the agent.

64. See, e.g., D.L. 7.131: "among the wise, women should be in common, in such a way that any man at all may have sexual relations with any woman at all . . . and that we should love all children equally in a paternal manner and that the jealousies arising from adultery will be removed." We might compare Lucr. 4.1065–66, where the advice to be promiscuous is a therapeutic strategy to break the hold of obsessive love.

65. Schofield 1991, 43–46. He argues that Zeno accepts Plato's proposals on female equality but rejects his conclusion that bonds of family devotion should replace erotic bonds as the "cement of society."

66. See also the Zeno passage cited in the next note, where praise of the manly bloom of the young male is juxtaposed with some very derogatory remarks about women.

67. My solution is thus similar to that of Schofield 1991, appendix B, 112–14, although he does not make the connection with the *Phaedrus*. In appendix C Schofield cites a striking extract from Zeno preserved in Clement of Alexandria, in which the appearance of such a young man is described: "Let his face be unclouded, his brow not relaxed, his eyes neither gaping nor drooping, his neck not slouching down, his limbs not slack, but tensed up like tuned strings, his ear alert for the logos. Let his attitudes and his movement give no hope to the wanton. Let proper shame and manliness

flower upon him, but away with the stimulation of perfume-shops and goldsmiths and wool shops, and the rest of the shops, where women spend the whole day dressed up like courtesans, as if they were sitting in a brothel" (my translation).

68. E.g., D.L. 7, which defines the religious duties of good people to "the gods" (repeatedly); the wise are experts in matters relating to "the gods."

69. See my discussion in Nussbaum 1994a, with references.

70. See Dover 1989, 84.

71. Ath. 563E, addressing the Stoics, qua followers of Zeno: "you who say that we should continue with those we are in love with until they are twenty-eight years old."

72. On the other hand, if the shaving referred to in a joke really took place (which we should doubt), this would suggest a desire to prolong the delight of youthful appearance.

73. This is the topic of an excellent discussion in Inwood, "Why Do Fools Fall in Love."

74. Athenaeus remarks, not apropos of the Stoic view but in the same context, that the Spartans treated girls like *paidika* before marriages.

75. Strictly speaking, of course, the evidence does not state that they stop then; on the other hand, given Antigonus's mocking purpose, if the Stoics had urged continuation to an even later age, we might have expected him to mention it.

76. See Schofield 1991, 30, whose translation I generally follow.

77. On Stoic marriage see especially the fragments of Seneca's *De matrimonio*, ed. Hense. One fragment tells the story of a man who fell passionately in love with his own wife. Seneca remarks: "It does not matter from what decent cause one goes mad. That's why Sextus used to say, 'That man is an adulterer who loves his wife too passionately.'" (The entire fragment is translated in Nussbaum 1994b, 473 n. 48.) Seneca draws the conclusion that a good Stoic husband will love "by judgment" (*iudicio*), not by passion, and will be self-controlled about intercourse—avoiding, for example, the time during his wife's pregnancy, when damage to the fetus was thought to be possible.

78. On the *eupatheiai* see SVF 3.431–42.

79. See SVF 3.432, and the discussion of the two sorts of joy in Sen. *Ep.* 23.

80. I do not mean to suggest that we can trace this practice back to the original Greek Stoics; Seneca says he got it from his teacher Sextius, who was eclectic and influenced by Pythagoreanism.

81. Notice that something very similar will be true of the wise man's attitude to his own children: he may focus intensely on his own because that is where his station has placed him, but he may not care about them in such a way that he will feel grief at a child's death. Cicero tells the exemplary story of a father who, informed of his child's death, said, "I was already aware that I had begotten a mortal" (*Tusc.* 3.30).

82. The parallel is of course faulty, since the "chase" of the Stoic wise man is not purely recreational, but is tied in with his virtuous activity as an educator of the young.

References

Beazley, J. D. 1947. "Some Attic Vases in the Cyprus Museum." *Proceedings of the British Academy* 33:195–244.

Dover, K. J. 1989. *Greek Homosexuality.* 2d ed. Cambridge, Mass.: Harvard University Press.

Ferrari, G. R. F. 1987. *Listening to the Cicadas: A Study of Plato's Phaedrus.* Cambridge: Cambridge University Press.

Griswold, C. 1986. *Self-Knowledge in Plato's Phaedrus.* New Haven, Conn.: Yale University Press.

Hackforth, R. 1952. *Plato: Phaedrus.* Cambridge: Cambridge University Press.

Halperin, D. 1986. "Plato and Erotic Reciprocity." *Classical Antiquity* 5:60–80.

Halperin, D. 1989. "Plato and the Metaphysics of Desire." *Proceedings of the Boston Area Colloquium for Ancient Philosophy* 5:27–52.

Halperin, D. 1990. "Heroes and Their Pals." In *One Hundred Years of Homosexuality and Other Essays on Greek Love.* London: Routledge.

Nussbaum, M. C. 1986. *The Fragility of Goodness: Luck and Ethics in Greek Tragedy and Philosophy.* Cambridge: Cambridge University Press.

Nussbaum, M. C. 1994a. "Platonic Love and Colorado Law: The Relevance of Ancient Greek Norms to Modern Sexual Controversies." *Virginia Law Review* 80:1515–1651. A shorter version appears in *The Greeks and Us*, ed. R. B. Louden and P. Schollmeier (Chicago: University of Chicago Press, 1996), and also in M. C. Nussbaum, *Sex and Social Justice* (New York: Oxford University Press, 1999). All page references here are to the longer version.

Nussbaum, M. C. 1994b. *The Therapy of Desire: Theory and Practice in Hellenistic Ethics.* Princeton, N.J.: Princeton University Press.

Rowe, C. 1986. *Plato: Phaedrus.* Warminster: Aris and Phillips.

Schofield, M. 1991. *The Stoic Idea of the City.* Cambridge: Cambridge University Press. Reissued, with a new foreword by Martha Nussbaum, Chicago: University of Chicago Press, 1999.

Winkler, J. J. 1990. "The Constraints of Desire: Erotic Magical Spells." In *The Constraints of Desire: The Anthropology of Sex and Gender in Ancient Greece.* London: Routledge.

Winnington-Ingram, R. P. 1980. *Sophocles: An Interpretation.* Cambridge: Cambridge University Press.

Chapter Three

Erotic Experience in the Conjugal Bed:
Good Wives in Greek Tragedy

✄

Maarit Kaimio

$\mathcal{L}$ast year, the speaker of the Finnish Parliament, Riitta Uosukainen, published a book which created a sensation in the country.[1] It was not the political content of her published speeches which attracted the main attention of the public, but one of the imaginary letters addressed to different people with which she enlivened the book. This particular letter was addressed to her husband, and in it she told how greatly she had again yesterday enjoyed their lovemaking on their waterbed. "Oh what a splash from the screwing!"[2] The reaction of the public was overwhelming. Some were indignant, thinking that such disclosures were beneath the dignity of the Parliament; the majority were delighted at the sincerity and boldness of the speaker. The funny thing was that this was considered news at all. Really, it should have been no surprise to anybody that a middle-aged married couple enjoyed sex together.

Something similar can be seen in the attitude toward conjugal sex in Greek literature and especially, I contend, in modern studies of Greek literature. The power of Cypris is universally celebrated in Greek poetry, sometimes as the source of great enjoyment, but more often as an enslaving, inescapable force, bringing more pain than pleasure and frequently disaster and destruction. The tone of the erotic encounter is largely dictated by the genre of poetry: sensuous, bittersweet, or vehement in lyric and elegiac poetry, piquant and lustful in iambics, exuberant, satisfying, and obscene in

95

comedy, and uncontrollable, violent, and destructive in tragedy. The authors are all male, except in lyric; there is, however, a similarity in the general tone in the erotic descriptions of Sappho and, say, Ibycus and Anacreon. The subjects of the feelings described are mostly presented as not quite young, often even rather old; they are male or female in lyric, mostly male in elegiacs, iambics, and comedy, and female in tragedy. The objects of desire may be of either sex; often they are clearly younger than the subject. Thus, certain conventions of genre play a great part in the representation of desire in Greek poetry; naturally, they reflect the attitudes and conventions of the social context, but they do not exhaust the possibilities of erotic experience in the society in question. One example is my theme, erotic experience in the conjugal bed. This is certainly not a prominent theme in Greek poetry, but neither is it nonexistent. It has been ignored more by modern commentators on Greek poetry than it was by the Greek poets themselves.

The reasons for the subdued existence of erotic experience in the conjugal bed in Greek poetry are obvious: for one thing, a satisfying marital sex life does not offer the tremors, tensions, and triumphs preferred in the erotic experiences in poetry, and any description of the details of the sexual act itself is mostly out of the question in the society of ancient Greece, as far as the legal wife is concerned. In Athens especially, the good reputation of the wife was essential to the stability of the household [oikos] and as the words given to Pericles by Thucydides (2.45.2) witness, the best wife was the one least spoken of. This silence does not, however, tell anything of the existence or nonexistence of marital sex in Athens, or of the satisfaction or dissatisfaction felt by the partners. The subject was simply not discussed in public.

There is no doubt about male dominance in Athenian society. In sexual matters, the men had several accepted options: they could satisfy their desire with male lovers, hetairas, or female slaves as well as with their wives. The women were allowed no sexual experiences with men before marriage, and the marriage was an affair of exchange between two households, where the possible sexual attraction of the girl toward her future husband was not a matter of consequence. The ideal marriage in upper-class classical Athens, as presented in literature, is the picture drawn by Xenophon of Ischomachus and his much younger bride. The nearest he comes to discussing the sex life of the married couple is the passage where Ischomachus advises his wife to abstain from using makeup, since both husband and wife are more worthy of love as bodily companions if they approach each other in as healthy and natural a state as possible (Oec. 10.5–8).

Modern studies of Greek literature and society have especially emphasized the Greek male view of women as belonging to the untamed, animal world, subject to strong desires, morally weak, and thus to be subjected to careful surveillance and firm dominion.[3] On the other hand, the equation of marriage and death has been brought forward.[4] Marriage is represented as both a physically and mentally painful experience for the girl; the loss of maidenhood and the paternal home is compared to a death in the context of the marriage, which is conceived of as an initiation ritual leading to the new status of wife and mother.[5] These two views of woman — one as heavily susceptible to animal lust, the other as totally ignorant of sexual matters until initiated ("stabbed to death") by the husband — seem rather contradictory but are both explicable in the light of the male view presented by Greek literature. The mutual love of husband and wife, with emphasis on a kind of equality, although always retaining the dominant position of the man, becomes a subject discussed in literature only in late Hellenistic or early Roman times, as for instance by Plutarch and Musonius Rufus. The sexual symmetry of mutual love is especially prominent in the Greek idealistic novel, as demonstrated by David Konstan, who also emphasizes the novelty of this kind of description of a sexual relationship in Greek literature.[6]

As regards Greek drama, Konstan points out that in Greek comedy, girl citizens are never represented as the subjects of erotic desire, and even young wives express only a conjugal loyalty based on duty, not desire.[7] In tragedy, he sees eros figuring as an adulterous motive, destructive to wedlock; he is, however, inclined to underrate the sexual side of the heroines, attributing, for instance, Medea's revenge more to a heroic indignation over a violation of oaths than to sexual passion, and seeing throughout Euripides' *Helen* conjugal loyalty, not passionate love.[8] Thus, the married life of a female heroine tends to become desexualized. Other critics have stressed more the sexual motivation of the female characters in tragedy, but then female sexuality tends to be generalized as destructive.[9] According to Simon Goldhill, "in the classical period, it is hard to find a narrative of female desire that does not end in disaster."[10] How, then, are we going to find any erotic experiences connected with good wives in Greek drama?

I shall take another look at some well-known good wives in tragedy — mainly Deianeira, Alcestis, Euadne, and Helen — and argue that the Greek language used to describe their married life is strongly suggestive of sexual activity and even erotic enjoyment. Disasters may follow, but they are not always straightforward results of female desire. I shall begin with examining the usage and semantic connotations of the words for "bed" in tragedy and continue with interpreting some particular passages, with special attention to the accompanying imagery.

"Bed" is a very prominent word in many tragedies dealing with the relationships between men and women.[11] There are three main words used in tragedy, εὐνή, λέκτρον/λέκτρα and λέχος / λέχη. All of them are mainly poetic words and thus dignified in tone.[12] Εὐνή and λέχος especially have a strong poetic tradition in early Greek epic; λέκτρον is slightly less common in epic. The usages of these words in epic are well analyzed in *Lexikon des frühgriechischen Epos*.[13] A difference is seen in that εὐνή is also used of the resting place or nest of animals, while the derivatives of the verb λέχομαι are used only of men and gods. In the original meaning of the words there is also a difference in that εὐνή refers to a ready-made bed with mattress and bedclothes, while λέχος and λέκτρον originally refer to the frame of the bed. All three words can be used in early epic in connection with lying, sitting, or sleeping on a bed, but remarkably often they denote either the concrete piece of furniture as the place for sexual activity, as, for example, in *Odyssey* 10.347—Κίρκης ἐπέβην περικαλλέος εὐνῆς [I went up to Circe's beautiful bed],"—or the sexual act itself, as, for example, in the formula ἐμίγη(ν) φιλότητι καὶ εὐνῇ [(I) lay (with . . .) in love and intercourse] (*Il.* 3.445, *Od.* 23.219). The sexual activity can be marital as well as extramarital.

In tragedy, the words for "bed" are occasionally used to denote the place of resting or sleeping, or specifically the sickbed or the grave, but in the great majority of cases they have sexual connotations. They are nearly synonymous and often used in combination with each other for fullness of expression;[14] very rarely are they used together with clearly differentiated meanings, as in Euripides *Phoenician Women* 946, where Haemon is ruled out as a possible candidate for sacrifice: κεἰ μὴ γὰρ εὐνῆς ἥψατ', ἀλλ' ἔχει λέχος [for although he has not touched the (marriage) bed, he has a spoken bride].[15] More often, they seem to be interchangeable. Euripides, for instance, uses all three words in the choral passage of *Medea* 635ff., where the chorus prays for temperance, σωφροσύνη: they hope that Cypris will not turn their passion toward extramarital relationships (ἑτέροις ἐπὶ λέκτροις), but will safeguard marriage without strife (ἀπτολέμους δ' εὐνὰς), keeping a vigilant eye over the sexual life of women (λέχη γυναικῶν). Each of the words used appears in tragedy in all the senses given by my paraphrase.

Compared with words in the epic usage, the words in tragedy are even more frequently used as *nomina actionis*, denoting sexual activity or sexual relationships; they also frequently acquire the meaning of a distinctly institutionalized sexual relationship, that is, marriage, as, for instance, in Euripides *Ion* 977, where Creusa, when exhorted to kill her husband by the old servant, replies that she is inhibited from doing so: αἰδούμεθ' εὐνὰς τὰς τόθ' ἡνίκ' ἐσθλὸς ἦν [because I respect our marriage of those days when he was true]. "Bed" in tragic diction is also frequently used of the partner in marriage, the wife—a usage not found in early epic—as, for example, in Euripides *Iphigenia at Aulis* 1355: τὴν ἐμὴν μέλλουσαν εὐνὴν μὴ κτανεῖν, [(I said) that they should not kill my future wife]; and Euripides *Orestes* 1080: σὺ δ' ἄλλο λέκτρον παιδοποίησαι λαβών [take someone else for your wife to beget children]. But the bed need not be marital; even without such additions as δόλιος, "treacherous," or ἀλλότριος, "belonging to another," "bed" can clearly mean an extramarital sexual life, as in Aeschylus *Agamemnon* 1447, where Clytemnestra exults that the death of Cassandra adds extra spice to her sexual life: ἐμοὶ δ' ἐπήγαγεν / εὐνῆς παροψώνημα τῆς ἐμῆς χλιδῇ; or when in Euripides *Hippolytus* 495 the nurse retorts that she would not suggest this course to Phaedra merely "for the sake of sexual pleasure" [οὐκ ἄν ποτ' εὐνῆς οὕνεχ' ἡδονῆς τε σῆς]. It can also refer to a person's sexual life in general, as when Medea's motivation is discussed in Euripides *Medea* 265ff.: ὅταν δ' ἐς εὐνὴν ἠδικημένη κυρῇ, / οὐκ ἔστιν ἄλλη φρὴν μιαιφονωτέρα [when a woman is slighted in her sexual relationship, there is no mind more vindictive]. It has been argued that Medea is mainly enraged because of the breaking of vows or because of the situation of helplessness into which she is driven by Jason's new marriage, but although these facts certainly add to her distress, I, for one, think that Jason hits the nail on the head when he answers (*Med.* 568ff.), "you would not say so, if you would not feel sore because of sex" [εἴ σε μὴ κνίζοι λέχος]; "since you women go so far that if your sex life is satisfactory [ὀρθουμένης εὐνῆς], you think you are perfectly happy, but when something untoward happens to your sexual relationship [ἐς λέχος], you turn the best and most beautiful to a hateful thing." Jason's interpretation of Medea's motives is made quite clear in the end, when he sums her behavior up as follows (*Med.* 1336ff.): "after you had been married to me and had born children to me, you destroyed them because of sex [εὐνῆς ἕκατι καὶ λέχους]—no Greek woman would have done that."

What has this to do with the good wives of Greek tragedy? I wish to emphasize that the vocabulary which in Greek tragedy is constantly used of marriage and marriage-like relationships such as concubinates, as well as of irregular sexual relationships, is strongly permeated by the idea of the bed as the place for sexual activity. By the constant use of these words, even good wives are presented as sexual creatures. Certainly it is commonplace in Greek tragedy to wish that Eros and Aphrodite should strike a virtuous woman only in moderation. However, this should not be read as meaning that the woman should not enjoy her sexual life too much—as is often implied in modern criticism of Greek tragedy—but as a warning not to cross the line between morality and immorality in her actions. In her prayer to Cypris, Helen expresses this very clearly—"If you would be moderate [με-τρία], you would be the sweetest of gods [ἡδίστη]"—and as instances of immoderation she mentions deceitful erotic relationships, swindling tricks, and deadly love potions (Eur. *Hel.* 1102ff.). She does not refer to sexual enjoyment as such as immoderation, as is shown by the use of the superlative ἡδίστη, "sweetest, most enjoyable." A good wife is true to her husband—that goes without saying—but she is also loving and sexually active. In tragedy, such things are generally seen as good days gone, as, for instance, when the chorus of Aeschylus's *Persians* describes the grief of young wives when they hear of the Persian defeat (541ff.): αἱ δ' ἁβρόγοοι Περσίδες ἀνδρῶν / ποθέουσαι ἰδεῖν ἀρτιζυγίαν, / λέκτρων εὐνὰς ἁβροχίτωνας, / χλιδανῆς ἥβης τέρψιν, ἀφεῖσαι, / πενθοῦσι γόοις ἀκορεστοτάτοις [and the Persian wives, indulging in soft wailing through longing to behold their late-wedded lords, abandon the daintily wrought coverlets of their couches, wherein their delicate youth had its joyance, and mourn with complainings that know no satiety].[16] The overpowering sorrow corresponds to the former luxurious lifestyle of the Persian wives, while such words as ποθέω, ἥβη, and τέρψις ("to desire," "youth," "pleasure") combined with λέκτρον and εὐνή make the erotic enjoyment clear. Similarly, Euripides describes in a choral song the happy night of a young Trojan couple a moment before the sack of Troy (*Hec.* 914ff.): it is the moment of sweet slumber [ὕπνος ἡδὺς], the husband is already lying in the bedchamber [ἐν θαλάμοις], the wife is doing her evening toilet before going to bed [ἐπιδέμνιος ὡς πέσοιμ' ἐς εὐνάν]. The words are suggestive of the erotic aspects of the bed, and in fact (with a slight irreverence for strict logic, if one follows the exact words and thinks that the alarm of attack came when the wife was still sitting at the mirror), she says that she left her dear bed [λέχη δὲ φίλια] in her nightdress to rush out. These wives are not Greek, it is true, but their eroticism is not presented in any way as un-Greek; in the case of the Persian wives, it is the luxury of the bed that is un-Greek, not the love for the husband. Nor is the disaster of war in any way connected with their sexuality, although the latter is used to point out the contrast between the happiness of the past and the cruelty of the present.

In the occurrences of "bed" in a sexual sense in tragedy, the word is often connected with a genitive (or possessive pronoun) denoting one of the partners in the sexual relationship.[17] The person named may be male or female. For example, in Euripides *Helen* 391 Menelaus says that Atreus sired him "from Aerope's bed" [Ἀερόπης λέκτρων ἄπο], and and in 1093 Hera is addressed as "you who lie in Zeus's bed" [ἣ Δίοισιν ἐν λέκτροις πίτνεις].

Both men and women can speak of "my bed." In this connection, one might ask what actually were the sleeping arrangements of Athenian husbands and wives. Although the audience of the Athenian theater naturally realized that the imaginary world of tragic heroes was not identical with their own, they must have applied the words they heard in the theater to their own experiences. Did husbands and wives sleep together or in separate bedrooms? Did they share the same bed habitually, or only for sexual intercourse? Such questions have only recently been asked.[18] The archaeological evidence does not give clear answers—most of the beds were made of perishable material,[19] and in most cases the upper story of the house, where the bedrooms are supposed to have been, has not been preserved.[20] The literary evidence does not give a coherent picture. The distinction of male and female space in the house is frequently emphasized, but as Michael Jameson has argued, it is possible that it was essentially conceptual and behavioral.[21] In any case, the sleeping arrangements of the master of the house and his wife certainly need not be identical with those of slaves of both sexes and other members of the family. We have also no reason to suppose that the sleeping habits of husband and wife were really uniform in Athens: a newlywed couple might sleep in the same room and bed, while an older couple might not, and the care of infants brought its own problems.[22] However, there are many allusions in literature indicating that it was common for a married couple to sleep together in the same room.[23] As for the use of the—presumably rather narrow—beds as a "single" or "double" bed, we have no clear evidence from Athens. In the epic tradition, there is the famous bed of Odysseus, built by himself around the trunk of a growing olive tree, whom no one else, except one trusted female servant, had ever seen. This bed is described by Penelope as "our bed" (εὐνῆς ἡμετέρης; *Od.* 23.226)—a rare expression indeed. However, although it is taken for granted that Odysseus and Penelope slept together on this magnificent bed in the early days of their marriage, it is clear that Penelope did not use it while Odysseus was away: she slept upstairs in the women's quarters (*Od.* 4.787ff., 17.101ff., 19.594ff.).

In tragedy, the expressions giving the owner of the bed naturally do not refer to the piece of furniture as such, be it "double" or "single," in separate quarters or in a room shared by man and wife, but to the person as a sexual creature, having the power of decision—within the limits set by the society—over his or her sexual behavior. There are, however, two connections where there is a clear difference between the sexes as to the usage of "my bed." First, only a man uses "bed" as a term denoting his sexual partner, usually his wife, as in Euripides *Electra* 1036ff.: "when . . . the husband sins forsaking the bed he has in the house [τἄνδον παρώσας λέκτρα], the wife wants to imitate her husband by taking a lover." Similarly, the noun ἄλοχος, "bed-fellow," is used only of the wife.[24] The only example where "bed" is very near to the meaning "my husband" is Euripides *Andromache* 932ff., where Hermione says that bad women corrupted her with their talking: "Do you allow that wretched captive slave woman to share your bed (husband)? By the goddess, if she were in my house and took advantage of my bed, she would no longer see the daylight." The point in Hermione's speech is that these women are morally depraved and have exercised a bad influence upon her, and so their manner of speaking is probably meant to be reproachable, too—the women speak of the sexual side of their marriage too much as a man would speak.[25]

The second difference lies in the use of phrases "save my bed" and "shame my bed." Only a woman has a bed to save for her husband (see, e.g., Eur. *IA* 1202f.); the phrase is not used of a man. A man can shame a woman with his bed (Eur. *El.* 44), a man can shame another man's bed (Eur. *Hipp.* 944), a man can shame a woman's bed (Eur. *Med.* 1354), a woman can shame her bed with lovers (Eur. *Hipp.* 408), but a man cannot shame his own bed. In these usages we clearly see the sexual ethics current in patriarchal Athens: the woman is the bed of the man—her position in the society is to be a wife and mother; and it is the duty of the woman to be faithful to her husband. Similar obligations are not imposed on the husband, although men may be willing to make promises of monogamy to honor their wives (as Theseus in Eur. *Hipp.* 860 and Admetus in Eur. *Alc.* 328ff.) and wronged women may accuse their men of deceit (as Creusa in Eur. *Ion* 880). The good wives of tragedy generally accept this rule of things, as Deianeira expressly states (Soph. *Trach.* 436ff.). Curiously enough, it is the paragon of a good wife, Alcestis, who does not accept it. I will come to this later.

The good wives of tragedy accept their identity as the bed. It is, however, not merely a denial of the self, symbolized by a silent strangling in the depths of the *thalamos*, the marriage chamber, which many of them choose at last. Nicole Loraux emphasizes this view, characterizing their lives as "a life that finds its meaning outside the self and is fulfilled only in the institutions of marriage and maternity, which tie women to the world and lives of men;"[26] according to her, the only way tragedy grants them the exercise of their freedom is to kill themselves. There is, I think, more in the identity of these women than Loraux allows—at least a little more selfishness, freedom, and even capacity for pleasure.

The good wives of tragedy are proud of their "bedworthiness." One could say that they have wholeheartedly adapted themselves to the sexual ethics of their patriarchal society and as such are typical idealized heroines created by male authors. But we should not deny them an identity of their own based on such ethics. In Euripides' *Helen*, where the heroine lives in chastity in Egypt while the Greeks fight over her phantom in Troy, the whole play is centered on the question of who will be in possession of Helen's bed, or better, to whom she will give the possession of her bed. Already in the prologue of the play, her bed seems to acquire a life of its own. "Paris came to Sparta in order to possess my bed" (29f.), but Hera "threw to the winds my bed with Alexander" (32), who "thought he had me—a shallow thought, because he had not" (36f.). She came to Proteus in Egypt, "in order that I could keep my bed untouched for Menelaus" (47f.). She is cursed by all "since they think I have deceived my husband" (54f.). Hermes has prophesied that she will once more live in Sparta with her husband, "so that I would not prepare my bed for anybody else" (59). As long as Proteus lived, she was safe from marriage, but now his son Theoclymenus "hunts to marry me" (63). "But I honor my husband of bygone days and lie as suppliant here at the tomb of Proteus, praying that he would save my bed for my husband, so that even if my name has a bad reputation in Greece, my body would not cause shame to me here" (63ff.). Even if she is a plaything in the hands of gods, she retains the dominion of her bed; she makes the final choice whether to succumb to her new suitor or not, and she is proud of her decision. This opportunity to exercise her own will is given already by Homer to Penelope, with frequent allusions to her—either genuine or faked—determination to marry one of the suitors. Of course, from the point of view of the audience, it is not a real choice—everybody knows that Penelope must wait for Odysseus. In Helen's case, the heroine is rewarded with a happy ending; this is not exceptional in tragedy, although not common either. For instance, in Euripides' *Andromeda* the heroine apparently fell in love with her rescuer Perseus and stood determinedly beside him, opposing her parents, without a disastrous end.[27] Naturally, however, tragedy likes to present good wives as "faithful unto death." In Euripides' *Alcestis*, the free decision of the wife—who is ready to die in place of her husband—is especially poignant. She expressly points out that she had other options: it would have been possible for her to continue living, to acquire another husband after Admetus—"I could have had any Thessalian man I wanted"—and to live in affluence and power (*Alc.* 284ff.). But in spite of the opportunity to go on enjoying her youth, she chose to die for Admetus, because she did not want to live without him (287ff.). She is also very proud of her decision, convinced of her moral superiority to all other women

(306, 324f.). So is Euadne in Euripides' *Suppliant Women*, who jumps onto the pyre of her husband, in firm opposition to her father's pleas, certain of her exemplarity (Eur. *Supp.* 1050ff.).

Even in those cases where the women exercise their own free will only insofar as they are free to kill themselves, we should not see the marriage bed, which usually is linked with the death scene, only as a sign of a life finding its meaning outside the self. It is of course true that the bed symbolizes the husband and the marriage, but it also symbolizes the sexual life of the woman and thus a significant part of the self of the woman. Iocasta's pain on her marriage bed in Sophocles' *King Oedipus* (1241ff.) is a case apart from the others: the incestuous sexual relationship with her own son marks with its horror all her reminiscences of the marriage bed, whether with the father or with the son. In more normal relationships, the bed recalls the satisfying sexual life before the catastrophe.

When Deianeira enters her house for the last time, she first, crying, takes her leave of the household altars, the familiar domestic utensils, and her domestic staff—all important parts of her daily life (Soph. *Trach.* 904ff.). Then she goes into the *thalamos* of Heracles, the intimate scene of their married life.[28] It is a significant detail that she not only rushes to the bed, but first carries bedclothes to the bed and makes it up (915ff.).[29] A woman bent on taking her life would not do this merely in order to sit on soft cushions when plunging the sword into herself. Preparing a bed is a deeply significant action for a woman: making a bed for a child is an expression of her care and protection, making a bed for a guest, of her generosity and capability as the mistress of the house, while making a bed for a man is an anticipation of sexual meeting. So, Deianeira prepares Heracles' bed as if she would once more meet her husband there, and then takes her leave of it with hot tears: ὡς ἔμ' οὔποτε / δέξεσθ' ἔτ' ἐν κοίταισι ταῖσδ' εὐνάτριαν [for you shall never more welcome me as the companion of the bed on this couch] (921f.). It is impossible to render in translation the rich variety of the Greek words for bed, bedclothes, and lying in this context.[30] They are there to stress the importance of the sexual side of Deianeira's marriage, which is now over for her forever. True, her marriage to Heracles has been no easy one—she deplores the long intervals between the visits of her husband to her bed (31ff.), is consumed by anxiety over his labors (28ff., 37ff., 141ff.), and has to bear the frequent lovers of her husband (438ff., 459ff., 543f.). However, her worst fear is that she would be deprived of the best of men (176f.).[31] In an adult woman's life, fear and joy are inseparably intertwined, as she explains to the young women of the chorus (141ff.): "Doubtless ye must have heard of my distress, and therefore come; but how my heart is racked ye cannot know—pray God ye ne'er may know it by suffering! Like to us, the tender plant is reared and nurtured in some garden close; nor heat, nor rain, nor any breath of air vexes it, but unruffled, unperturbed, it buds and blossoms in sequestered bliss; so fare we till the maid is called a wife and finds her married portion in the night—dread terror for her husband or her child."[32] The literary tradition of the passage describing the sheltered existence of unmarried girls (144–47) has been well analyzed, for example, by P. E. Easterling and T. C. W. Stinton,[33] and it is clear that it has affinities with the *locus amoenus* and *Nymphengarten* topoi of ancient literature.[34] The erotic aspects of these topoi have frequently been noted. But I would like to point out the peculiar use of the erotic aspect in this passage. Deianeira draws a sharp distinction between the inexperienced (ἄπειρος) girls and her own situation as a grown-up married woman: only when they are called women (or wives), and no longer virgins, can they understand her pains and troubles. In their sheltered lives, they know nothing about heat, heavy rain, or violent winds. All these are well-known poetic images for the power of love.[35] In their sheltered, paradise-like existence the girls do not feel the heat, the rain, or the storm wind, but like young plants, they need light, moisture, and air[36]—and the literary tradition of *locus amoenus* hints at the slumbering eroticism. But when they become women, all these forces burst on them full blast, both in their positive sense as sexual enjoyment and negative sense as pain and worry—which in Deianeira's case gains the upper hand. The same idea is contained in line 147, which usually is understood as "in joyful existence, they exult in their untroubled life," with ἡδοναῖς taken as a kind of modal dative.[37] I suggest taking ἡδοναῖς ἄμοχθον together, as the Greek word order and the rhythm of the sentence suggests: the girls live a life "untroubled by (sexual) pleasures". ἡδονή is certainly a word suggesting the sensual pleasures of adulthood rather than the carefree joys of childhood. The dative, instead of being a rather loose solitary word expressing accompanying circumstances, can be taken as an instrumental dative, commonly used with the verb μοχθέω and not unnatural with the negative adjective ἄμοχθος, as the frequent use of ἄμικτος and ἀκήρατος, "unmixed with something," with the dative shows.[38] The oxymoron "untroubled by pleasures" suits perfectly Deianeira's situation: the pleasure of being married to Heracles, the best of men, brings to her endless trouble.

It has been said that Deianeira, the ever-frightened little bride who turned her face away when her suitors fought for her, does not understand the power of her own sexuality and is thus led to the disastrous deed of using the love philter given by the centaur.[39] I think Deianeira understands her sexuality very well after more than twenty years of marriage to Heracles, as well as that of her husband. Her words about the sickness (νόσος) caused by Eros, to which they all are subjected, are no mere idle talk (438ff., 543ff.). When the truth about Iole, the beautiful captive girl Heracles is bringing home with him, is brought home to Deianeira, it is the sexual side of her marriage about which she is worried. She expresses this with the very concrete image of two women embraced under one blanket (539f.: καὶ νῦν δύ' οὖσαι μίμνομεν μιᾶς ὑπὸ / χλαίνης ὑπαγκάλισμα) and the fear of the blooming youth winning over her withering middle age, so that Heracles shall be called her husband, but Iole's man (550f.: μὴ πόσις μὲν Ἡρακλῆς / ἐμὸς καλῆται, τῆς νεωτέρας δ' ἀνήρ). She is unbelievably naive in her blunder of believing in the centaur's sincerity, but otherwise she is very realistic in sexual matters. As for Heracles, his total disregard for both his wife's and his son's feelings is one of the most disturbing features of this play. His coldness is contrasted by the empathy felt by his son, when he has learned the truth. This contrast is emphasized by the surprisingly erotic wording used of Hyllus embracing his dead mother (938f.): ἀμφιπίπτων στόμασιν . . . πλευρόθεν / πλευρὰν παρεὶς ἔκειτο [he embraced her, kissing her, lying side by side by her].[40]

The bed is central to Alcestis's death scene, too, although she does not die on it. A servant describes Alcestis's behavior in the house on her dying day as astonishing (157). What she means by "astonishing" is probably the composure she shows at first in her attire, her movements, her words, and even in her complexion—and perhaps she refers also to the sudden change of all this. It is the bed in the thalamos which triggers this change. On the bed, she cries, remembers the first sexual union with her husband on it, and takes her leave of it. "I do not hate you" she says (179)—not a very glowing confession of love, but, considering the situation, expressing a positive attitude toward her husband. What is remarkable considering the continuation of the plot is that in her final words she takes for granted that another woman will take her place on the bed, "not better than I, but surely happier" (181f.). This thought leads her to a complete change of behavior: she flings herself onto the bed, kisses it, and wets it with her tears, and when she rises to go away, she rushes back several times to the bed. It is made quite clear that what breaks Alcestis's iron composure in the face of death is the thought of another woman in her husband's bed.

Later, in her final conversation with Admetus, she deftly prevents this danger by asking a small favor in return for the price of her life—that he would never marry again (299ff.). She bases her arguments solely on the good of her children—a stepmother would probably cause difficulties for them. Although in Greek tragedy the development of a person's thoughts and the process of the change of mind are generally not fully explained, and we see instead a person speaking and acting in one way in one scene and in another in the next, in this case there is a clear indication of how Alcestis comes to the decision to make this request. Immediately after the description of her frantic behavior on the bed, the servant mentions how the children clung to their mother and cried, and how she turned to take them in her arms and addressed them for the last time. It is thus made quite understandable that when she has conjured into her mind the hateful thought of a new wife in her husband's bed, she uses her children as an excuse to prevent this from happening. An appeal based on her love of her husband and on her wish to keep him sexually all to herself even after her death would not have been possible for a virtuous wife; an appeal for the good of the children finds universal approval and in the emotional atmosphere of the moment, an easily given promise by the husband. However, this is an outrageous thing for Alcestis to do. In her subtle and virtuous way, she takes a step as novel and bold as Medea, who kills her children to revenge herself upon her husband, or Deianeira, who resorts to a love philter to win back her husband's sexual favors. It was certainly not the normal practice in Greek society that a widowed man did not marry again, and it was surely not considered proper that the wife would take steps to prevent it. We can see many references to the moral principle that even if it was not considered proper for the husband to bring shame to his wife by compromising her position as the mistress of the house, it was not proper for the wife to show annoyance at the husband's other sexual relationships. Thus, we can say that Alcestis, even though she is considered the paragon of wifely virtues, in fact does not accept the male-centered morality of her environment—because of the bed.

In the discussion of my two last examples of good wives, Euadne and Helen, I shall pay particular attention to erotic imagery. A few introductory remarks are necessary. The realm of sexual life in Greek is, as in other languages, an endless source of imaginative vocabulary and figurative speech. It is made an especially fruitful field for witticisms in Greek comedy, as the detailed studies of Jean Taillardat and especially Jeffrey Henderson show.[41] In more serious poetry, such as lyric and tragedy, there are certain topoi of erotic imagery which return in various guises—the force of love as fire or wind or sickness, for instance, the flowery meadow as virginity about to be plucked, the rain as the cause of the fecundity of the earth, and so on. The figurative expressions may be quite concrete and yet retain the elevated tone required by the genre. A wonderful example of this kind of imagery is already found in Homer, where the description of the union of Zeus and

Hera, although it is veiled in a golden cloud, is strongly suggestive of sexual detail.[42] Other famous examples are the speech of Aphrodite in honor of cosmic love in Aeschylus's *Danaids*, where all gifts of nature nurturing humanity are born from the moisture of the marriage of Heaven and Earth.[43] As is clear from the wording of the fragment, it is marriage and conjugal union which is celebrated with this imagery, and in this connection one should note the emphasis on reciprocity and the erotic enjoyment of the female partner (lines 20f. ἐρᾷ μὲν ἁγνὸς οὐρανὸς τρῶσαι χθόνα, / ἔρως δὲ γαῖαν λαμβάνει γάμου τυχεῖν [the holy heaven desires to wound the earth, and the earth is possessed by the desire to accept the marriage]). Erotic imagery of a different tone, but equally suggestive in sexual detail, is found in Clytemnestra's speech over Agamemnon's dead body (Aesch. *Ag.* 1389–92).[44] The erotic insinuations of this passage have been well analyzed by J. L. Moles,[45] who points out that it is a hideous perversion of the traditional motif of the joyful sexual reunion of the long-separated husband and wife, the prime example of which is of course *Odyssey* 23 (232ff., 254f., 295f.). Elizabeth Craik has in two recent articles[46] argued that especially in the later plays of Euripides, a rapprochement between tragedy and comedy can also be seen in the use of sexual imagery, pointing out that it was the same audience which attended both tragedy and comedy in the same festival, and thus the audience would react in the same way to the same verbal stimuli.[47] She emphasizes that such stimuli should be sought in dramas which explicitly deal with erotic subjects, and a pointer to the sexual innuendo of the words can be seen in the dense occurrence of sexually suggestive words in a sexually significant context. It is hard to draw the line between obvious, probable, and possible innuendos of this kind—if there is a line to draw—and I could not be sure of all of her examples any more than of all my examples below. But I agree with her in that "tragedy is more specific about sex than has commonly been supposed"[48]—as is obvious from my discussion so far.

In the case of Euadne, the sexual imagery is so blatant that nobody can fail to recognize it.[49] She begins her lyric song (Eur. *Supp.* 990ff.) with a reference to her wedding ceremony, and in the obvious parallelism of wedding torches and the funeral pyre of her husband announces her intention to be consumed by the fire of her passion (1006f., 1019ff., 1027ff.). Especially clear is the sexual tone in 1019ff., σῶμά τ' αἴθοπι φλογμῷ / πόσει συμμείξασα φίλον / χρῶτα χρωὶ πέλας θεμένα [I join with my loving body to my husband in the burning flame, pressing my skin tight into his][50] and in her final, iambic words to her father in 1070f., καὶ δὴ παρεῖται σῶμα—σοὶ μὲν οὐ φίλον, / ἡμῖν δὲ καὶ τῷ συμπυρουμένῳ πόσει [and now I give up my body—it is no pleasure to you, but it is to me and to my husband, who burns together with me.]

In Euripides' *Helen*, the whole theme of the play is erotic, and there are many passages where sexual innuendos can be seen. Elizabeth Craik has pointed out some possibilities.[51] I shall discuss the opening lines of the play, the recognition duet, and the second stasimon in its context.

The play opens with Helen's prologue, where she explains her surprising situation (Eur. *Hel.* 1ff.): Νείλου μὲν αἵδε καλλιπάρθενοι ῥοαί, / ὃς ἀντὶ δίας ψακάδος Αἰγύπτου πέδον / λευκῆς τακείσης χιόνος ὑγραίνει γύας [These be the Nile's fair-flowing virgin-streams, who, fed with white snow melting, not with rain from heaven, waters Egypt's lowland fields].[52] The meaning of the Nile as καλλιπάρθενος has exercised the ingenuity of commentators.[53] I agree with R. Kannicht that the interpretation of the humanist scholars, "formosis nymphis decorus" [fair with its beautiful nymphs], gives the best sense, without further specification of river nymphs or Nereids. But I do not agree with A. M. Dale when she remarks (ad loc.): "Perhaps Euripides did not think very closely about it." I believe Euripides thought very closely indeed when he wrote these beautiful first lines of this drama, which shimmer between seriousness and playfulness, between the tragic tones of war and warm eroticism. These three lines paint a landscape of a fruitful earth well watered with moisture. The sensuous fecundity calls immediately to mind the literary tradition of the happy union of heaven and earth, of which I cited examples above. The commentators have duly pointed out the interest Euripides took in the favorite geographical topic of his day, the sources of the Nile,[54] but I think that another motive behind these words is the idea of a fertile landscape not moistened by rain from heaven—an image of ready sexuality, but yet in a state of virginity. In a playful way, καλλιπάρθενος mirrors the state of Helen herself: she is not a πάρθενος, but she lives the life of a beautiful virgin, yet ready for—and threatened by—sex. If you start looking for words with sexual innuendo, there is no end of them in this passage—what with the different words for moisture (ῥοαί, ψακάδος, ὑγραίνει) and field or furrow (πέδον, γύας) or the verb τήκομαι (τακείσης) with its frequent erotic use in poetry. The geographically minded part of the audience might be enthusiastic about this reference to the sources of the Nile, but at least part of the audience might be alert to the beautifully sensuous, sexually provocative, and slightly comic subtones of the verses.

As is obvious from my presentation so far, I strongly object to David Konstan's view of Euripides' *Helen* as a tragedy which does not represent eros as a significant motif. "It is conjugal loyalty, not passionate love, that is stressed throughout the *Helen,*" he writes.[55] I think Helen gives a far more erotic impression than mere conjugal loyalty. Her first encounter with Menelaus begins with her frantic flight to the tomb, while Menelaus tries to block her way; the scene has erotic notes, as Craik has pointed out (543–44: πῶλος . . . κῶλον; 548: δέμας δείξασα),[56] and Helen feels she is hunted again (545). The first recognition scene is a tragicomic variation of conventional scenes,[57] since Menelaus refuses to believe his eyes, and Helen is forced to conclude that "although I found you, I shall not have you as my husband" (592). It also plays with the archetype of all Greek homecoming scenes, the meeting of Odysseus and Penelope, in that now it is the husband who is slow to yield to the wife.[58] Even in the recognition duet (625ff.), it is Helen who is much more emotional; this is reflected in the meter, too, in that Menelaus mostly has iambic lines, and Helen lyrics.[59] Helen's words are ecstatic and erotic, while Menelaus is contented mostly with expressions like "so do I." I think that Helen's first lines have been interpreted by the commentators too matter-of-factly:[60] It is hard to believe that ἐν μακρᾷ φλογὶ φαεσφόρῳ (629) would mean simply "after a long time,"[61] thus echoing chiastically "the long time" from 625f. In addition to this meaning, the "light-bringing flame" surely refers to the joyful conclusion of the waiting. Such words as τέρψις, ἀσμένα, and περί τ' ἐπέτασα χέρα φίλιον give additional warmth to the usual formulae of recognition scenes (such as ἔχω σε χερσί, ἔλαβον, "I have you, I hold you in my arms"), while the frequent *anadiploseis* strengthen the emotional vibrations. There are further erotic insinuations in Helen's lines: περὶ δὲ γυῖα χέρας ἔβαλον ἡδονάν, ὦ πόσις, ὡς λάβω [I embrace you, so that I could enjoy you, o husband] (634f.), the reference to their wedding procession (639f.), and the wish to make the best of the opportunity now they have at last come together, to which Menelaus replies that, indeed, he would wish for the same (645ff.).[62]

At 1288ff., leading to the second stasimon, they really let go. They have obtained from Theoclymenus all the promises needed for the accomplishment of their escape and, as the first step, are going to retire to the palace to get the promised bath and new clothes for Menelaus. Theoclymenus is still with them, and so they speak with words full of double entendres. "You must love your present husband, and leave the one who is no more," says Menelaus. "If I come safely back to Greece, I shall put a stop to your former bad reputation, if you will be such a wife for your bedfellow as you should be." "That will happen," answers Helen. "My husband shall never reproach me. You will be near and know that. But now, poor man, come inside, get a bath and change your clothes. I shall not be slow to render you my good services. For you will be more generously inclined to do what is good to my dearest Menelaus, if you find me such as is due to you."[63]

What do you think they do, once they are inside and Menelaus takes off his clothes? Can there be any doubt after these words, in this situation, when they have found each other after seventeen years of war and wanderings and have good hopes of a successful escape, but cannot as yet be sure of their future? At this moment, Euripides lets the chorus sing the song of Demeter's frantic search for her daughter. This song has long been a sore spot for the commentators; it used to be considered a prime example of Euripidean *embolima*, which have next to nothing to do with their immediate dramatic context.[64] Recent research has been more understanding. The similarity of Helen's situation to those of both Demeter and Persephone has been noted,[65] and the relief and joy brought to Demeter by the intervention of Aphrodite and the Graces with their music and dance has been seen as an indication of the good hopes of rescue.[66] I would like to call attention to the description of the effect of Demeter's sorrow upon the earth, the dwindling of the fertility of fields, animals, and people, the drying up of all the springs of water (1325–37), and to the role of Aphrodite in the accomplishment of the return to joy (1346–52). The joyful aspect of sexuality as the trigger for Demeter's change of mind is firmly rooted in the myth, whether it is brought up by Aphrodite, Iambe, or Baubo.[67] In this drama, the favorable intervention by Aphrodite at the command of Zeus is especially appropriate, as the recent troubles of Menelaus have been caused by the anger of Aphrodite, and, as Theonoe knows, the conflict between the wishes of Aphrodite and Hera must be solved by Zeus this very day (878ff.). Moreover, the song is suggestive of ecstatic music in both its first and last strophes,[68] with its references to hectic movements and loud instruments (1301–2, 1308–9, 1362–65). The song is notable in its syncretism, the elements of the cult of Demeter mingling with that of the Great Mother and Dionysus, in whose worship wild, rousing music played an important part.[69] It is very probable that the words of the song were sung to a rhythm and mode suggesting wild excitement to the audience, and coming after the introductory conversation of Menelaus and Helen, the effect could be explicitly that of the excitement of sexual union.[70]

After the choral song, Helen enters saying that everything is all right in the house (1369)—a somewhat surprising opening in a tragedy, where the audience is accustomed to get alarming news from the palace, especially after joyful choral songs. First, Helen attributes this to the fact that Theonoe has not told her brother that Menelaus is alive and present. This is a bit surprising, too: nobody has had any reason to doubt that she would tell, since she had very firmly promised not to do so (998ff.). Perhaps Euripides wishes to emphasize this because Theonoe expressly said before that to tell her brother would be the option favored by Cypris, who was bent on destroying Menelaus (887–88). Now, through the previous song we have the impression that Cypris, at the exhortation of Zeus, has turned positive (1339ff.), and Helen's mention of Theonoe's cooperation confirms this. Then Helen says how well her husband has seized his opportunity: Menelaus is described in all the glory of a soldier in armor, with spear and shield (1374–82). This is of course motivated by the coming events—Menelaus must indeed fight in the faked funeral ship—but could it have sexual connotations as well? δόρυ and ὅπλα (which occurs twice) are very commonly used as sexual imagery. Be that as it may, Menelaus's sudden reincarnation as a hoplite hero after his wretched rags of a shipwrecked man brings him forward—first through Helen's report, then in visual form—as a truly manly figure for the first time in this play. Then, Helen mentions her own activity inside, how she gave him new clothes and how she washed him: καὶ λουτροῖς χρόα / ἔδωκα, χρόνια νίπτρα ποταμίας δρόσου [and I bathed his body, giving a long-awaited wash with the pure water of the river] (1383f.). Again, words with sensuous connotations—the mention of skin, the longed-for bath, the moisture, and the overall intimation of the ritual of nuptial bath. At this moment, Helen abruptly stops, since Theoclymenus appears, "thinking that he is just about to marry me." Silence! she calls to herself, and hopes the chorus will keep quiet too. So we do not hear anything more about what happened inside. ("Oh what a splash from the screwing!")

I hope that my discussion has shown that eros in tragedy is not only a destructive force leading to adultery, but also a powerful force inside the marriage. The so-called good wives of tragedy are by no means asexual creatures, yielding to the demands of the marriage bed out of a sense of conjugal duty, but filled with desire toward their husbands. They fulfill the dream of the Athenian man of a loving, erotic, but scrupulously faithful wife, even to the point of being ready to die for or because of her husband. Because we are dealing with tragedy, even the extremely good wives are led to extreme actions, often—but not always—disastrous to them and their family. Deianeira, true to her name, destroys her man; Euadne brings sorrow to her father through her devotion to her husband; Alcestis demands unnatural fidelity from her husband—and in the fairy-tale ending of the drama, is saved from death because her husband all but breaks his promise. The resourceful, erotic Helen—a clear forerunner of the heroines of the romantic novel—is intriguing in her chastity, so foreign to her traditional figure in literature.

This idealized, but still slightly disturbing picture of the good tragic wife is in harmony with the male view prevailing in Greek literature of women as full of untamed sexual drive. It must be said, however, that the male authors of tragedy paint in their dramas a many-sided picture of the sexuality of women, and it may be that this reflects, although in the extreme tone typical of tragedies, the normal life of Athenian married couples, where marital sex was an important factor—also for the wife.

Notes

1. R. Uosukainen, *Liehuva liekinvarsi* (Helsinki: WSOY, 1996).

2. Author's translation.

3. See, e.g., S. Pomeroy, *Goddesses, Whores, Wives, and Slaves: Women in Classical Antiquity* (New York: Schocken Books, 1975), 8f., 96ff.; J. Gould, "Law, Custom and Myth: Aspects of the Social Position of Women in Classical Athens," *Journal of Hellenic Studies* 100 (1980): 55ff.; and E. Cantarella, *Pandora's Daughters: The Role and Status of Women in Greek and Roman Antiquity* (Baltimore and London: Johns Hopkins University Press, 1987; originally published in Italian, 1981), 28ff. Cf. the surveys of research by J. Blok, "Sexual Asymmetry: A Historiographical Essay"; and H. S. Versnel, "Wife and Helpmate: Women of Ancient Athens in Anthropological Perspective," in *Sexual Asymmetry: Studies in Ancient Society,* ed. J. Blok and P. Mason (Amsterdam: Gieben, 1987), 1–57, 59–86.

4. R. Seaford, "Wedding Ritual and Textual Criticism in Sophocles' 'Women of Trachis,'" *Hermes* 114 (1986): 56–59; idem, "The Tragic Wedding," *Journal of Hellenic Studies* 107 (1987): 106–30.

5. Seaford, "Wedding Ritual," 53f.; idem, "The Tragic Wedding," 106, 113; C. Calame, *The Poetics of Eros in Ancient Greece* (Princeton, N.J.: Princeton University Press, 1999; originally published in Italian, 1992), 116–29.

6. D. Konstan, *Sexual Symmetry: Love in the Ancient Novel and Related Genres* (Princeton, N.J.: Princeton University Press, 1994).

7. Konstan, *Sexual Symmetry,* 143, 145f.

8. Ibid. 176f.

9. See, e.g., N. S. Rabinowitz, "Tragedy and the Politics of Confinement," in *Pornography and Representation in Greece,* ed. A. Richlin (New York: Oxford University Press, 1992), 36–52; Calame, *The Poetics of Eros,* 141–50.

10. S. Goldhill, *Foucault's Virginity: Ancient Erotic Fiction and the History of Sexuality* (Cambridge: Cambridge University Press, 1995), 149.

11. Eva Cantarella points this out when discussing Euripides: "'bed' is the key word in Euripidean tragedy to express how the poet and his audience conceive the

man-woman relationship" (Cantarella, *Pandora's Daughters*, 68). She continues with a discussion of *Andromache*, which play, however, is not a good example of the connotations of the bed in Euripides, since in this tragedy, the main issue is, quite exceptionally, the infertility of the wife, not the sexual relationship as such. On "bed" in melic poetry, see Calame, *The Poetics of Eros*, 34f.

12. εὐνή is used in prose, too, often of the lairs of animals (e.g., Xen. *Mem.* 3.11.8, *Cyn.* 5.9.1) but also of the beds used by men for sleeping (e.g., Hippoc. *Mul.* 145.13, 177.4; the phrase ἐξ εὐνῆς = "on waking up" appears in Ar. *Vesp.* 552 and *Av.* 1286).

13. The use of εὐνή is analyzed by R. Führer; λέκτρον and λέχος by G. C. Wakker. See also S. Laser, "Das Bett bei Homer und im älteren Epos," in *Archaeologia Homerica*, ed. H.-G. Buchholz (Göttingen: Vandenhoeck & Ruprecht, 1968), vol. 3, P, 1–15.

14. As in λέκτρων εὐναί (Aesch. *Pers.* 543; Eur. *HF* 798); see E. Bruhn in *Sophokles*, ed. F. W. Schneidewin and A. Nauck, vol. 8, *Anhang* (Berlin: Weidmannsche Buchhandlung, 1899), 118, §205, par. IV.

15. The texts of the tragedies are quoted, unless stated otherwise, from the Oxford Classical Texts (Oxford: Clarendon Press): Aeschylus, ed. D. Page (1972); Sophocles, ed. H. Lloyd-Jones and N. G. Wilson (1990); and Euripides, vols. 1–3, ed. J. Diggle (1984, 1981, 1994). *Pho.* 944–46 are deleted by Diggle.

16. *Aeschylus*, vol. 2, trans. H. W. Smyth, Loeb Classical Library (London: William Heinemann; Cambridge, Mass.: Harvard University Press, 1926).

17. This is also typical of the use of εὐνή in early epic; see *Lexikon des frühgriechischen Epos*, s.v. 3bα. It may be noted that the relationships "in bed" are almost exclusively heterosexual; I have found only one instance of homosexual love—the reference to Ganymede, "the dear pet of Zeus's bed" [Διὸς λέκτρων τρύφημα φίλον] (Eur. *IA* 1049f.).

18. For instance, Gisela Richter does not raise the question of sleeping arrangements at all in her thorough discussion of Greek beds in G. M. A. Richter and A. W. Barker, *Ancient Furniture: A History of Greek, Etruscan and Roman Furniture* (New York: Oxford University Press, 1926). Along with the interest in women's lives and in the use of space in Greek society, this question has come up: e.g., Eva Keuls, *The Reign of Phallus: Sexual Politics in Ancient Athens* (New York: Harper and Row, 1985), argues (212) that because of the narrowness of Greek beds, men and women used the same bed only for intercourse, while Michael Jameson, "Private Space and the Greek City," in *The Greek City: From Homer to Alexander*, ed. O. Murray and S. Price (Oxford and New York: Clarendon Press, 1990) maintains that a bedroom for the married couple was probably normal, referring to Theophr. *Char.* 13.8, 18.4–5, 19.5 (192 n. 20), without taking a stand on the question of joint or separate beds; Sarah Pomeroy discusses the problem in more detail in *Xenophon Oeconomicus: A Social and Historical Commentary* (Oxford: Clarendon Press, 1994), 292–93, 295, remarking that "after the night spent in the bridal chamber, sleeping arrangements seem to have altered so that man and wife slept apart," with reference to Pl. *Leg.* 808a and *Lys.* 1.9–12. The passage of Plato, however, points out the duty of both man and wife to wake up before their servants and does not imply anything about their sleeping arrangements; for Lysias, see n. 22 below. But Pomeroy also emphasizes that Xenophon's Ischomachus and his wife are often together in bed, citing *Oec.* 10.8 (293).

19. See Richter, *Ancient Furniture*, 54–72. An exception is the stone platforms for wooden κλῖναι of the men's dining room, *andron*.

20. S. Walker, "Women and Housing in Classical Greece: The Archaeological Evidence," in *Images of Women in Antiquity*, ed. A. Cameron and A. Kuhrt (London and Canberra: Croom Helm, 1983), 81–91; W. Hoepfner and E.-L. Schwandner, *Haus und Stadt im klassischen Griechenland* (Munich: Deutscher Kunstverlag, 1986) suggest that the bedchamber, *thalamos*, and the women's quarters, *gynaikonitis*, were generally located upstairs (264); see also M. H. Jameson, "Domestic Space in the Greek City-State," in *Domestic Architecture and the Use of Space*, ed. S. Kent (Cambridge: Cambridge University Press, 1990), 92–113.

21. Jameson, "Private Space and the Greek City," 192. For the differences of scholarly opinion concerning the *gynaikonitis* in Athens, see Pomeroy, *Xenophon Oeconomicus*, 295 n. 220.

22. Cf. Ar. *Thesm.* 477ff., where a couple married for three days sleep together (and then the wife sneaks out to her lover, pretending to go to the privy); Ar. *Nub.* 1ff., where the old Strepsiades sleeps in the same room with his grown-up son and his slave. Lys. 1.9ff. is a good example of the flexibility of sleeping arrangements: the speaker — a gullible cuckold — says that they used to have the women's quarters upstairs and the men's quarters downstairs, but after a baby was born, they switched rooms, so that the wife did not have to descend the stairs (with the baby) when she had to wash the baby. This does not, however, mean that the wife slept permanently with the baby and the female slaves at first upstairs and later downstairs; the continuation of the story makes it quite clear that the new arrangement, as meant by the husband, was that he slept together with his wife upstairs, while the servants slept downstairs with the baby. In this situation, the wife developed the new habit of apparently starting the night with her husband and then moving to sleep downstairs to suckle the child (and meet her lover). Such was the choreography on the night when the speaker came unexpectedly from his estate to town: the married couple was sleeping together upstairs, until the servant downstairs made the baby cry on purpose, and the husband forced his wife to go down, where her lover was waiting.

23. Cf. the examples from Theophr. *Char.*, Xen. *Oec.*, Ar. *Thesm.*, and Lys. 1 cited in notes 18 and 22.

24. Cf. Eur. *Alc.* 165f.; Arist. *Pol.* 1253b mentions πόσις καὶ ἄλοχος as the partners of marriage.

25. In Soph. *Ant.* 573 the meaning is different, although Creon's tone is exasperated when he says to Antigone ἄγαν γε λυπεῖς καὶ σὺ καὶ τὸ σὸν λέχος. Here, λέχος does not mean "your man" — it is not Haemon himself who irritates Creon but "you and (the continuous talking of) your marriage vex me overmuch."

26. N. Loraux, *Tragic Ways of Killing a Woman* (Cambridge, Mass., and London: Harvard University Press, 1987; originally published in French, 1985), 23.

27. For possible reconstructions of the plot, see T. B. L. Webster, *The Tragedies of Euripides* (London: Methuen, 1967), 192ff.

28. Strictly speaking, this is not the scene of their wedding night, although Deianeira speaks as if it were (920: ὦ λέχη τε καὶ νυμφεῖ' ἐμά [o my bed and my wedding]),

since they are living not at home, but in Trachis in a friend's house since the murder of Iphitus by Heracles (38ff.).

29. This action probably conveyed to the audience that Deianeira did not use this bed and bedroom during Heracles' fifteen-month absence; cf. the sleeping habits of Penelope during Odysseus's absence (described above). This impression is strengthened by the expression τὸν Ἡράκλειον θάλαμον [Heracles' bedroom] (913).

30. δεμνίοις (915), στρωτὰ . . . φάρη (916), ἐν μέσοισιν εὐνατηρίοις (918), λέχη τε καὶ νυμφεῖ' ἐμά (920), ἐν κοίταισι ταῖσδ' εὐνάτριαν (922).

31. The emphasis on marital sex is pointed out by D. Wender, "The Will of the Beast: Sexual Imagery in the Trachiniae," *Ramus* 3 (1974): 13. However, she sees Deianeira's sex life in a totally negative light: in her death scene "she reenacts all the threatened rapes by monsters, and all those times when Heracles hurt her 'in her heart.'"

32. πεπυσμένη μέν, ὡς ἀπεικάσαι, πάρει / πάθημα τοὐμόν· ὡς δ' ἐγὼ θυμοφθορῶ / μήτ' ἐκμάθοις παθοῦσα, νῦν δ' ἄπειρος εἶ. / τὸ γὰρ νεάζον ἐν τοιοῖσδε βόσκεται / χώροισιν αὑτοῦ, καί νιν οὐ θάλπος θεοῦ, / οὐδ' ὄμβρος, οὐδὲ πνευμάτων οὐδὲν κλονεῖ, / ἀλλ' ἡδοναῖς ἄμοχθον ἐξαίρει βίον / ἐς τοῦθ', ἕως τις ἀντὶ παρθένου γυνὴ / κληθῇ, λάβῃ τ' ἐν νυκτὶ φροντίδων μέρος, / ἤτοι πρὸς ἀνδρὸς ἢ τέκνων φοβουμένη (Soph. *Trach.* 141ff.). Translation by F. Starr, *Sophocles*, Loeb Classical Library (Cambridge, Mass.: Harvard University Press; London: William Heinemann, 1913).

33. P. E. Easterling, *Sophocles: Trachiniae* (Cambridge: Cambridge University Press, 1982), ad loc.; T. W. C. Stinton, "Heracles' Homecoming and Related Topics," *Papers of the Liverpool Latin Seminar* 5 (Liverpool: Francis Cairns, 1985): 410–12.

34. Cf. H. Thesleff, "Man and *locus amoenus* in Early Greek Poetry," in *Gnomosyne: Menschliches Denken und Handeln in der frühgriechischen Literatur: Festschrift für Walter Marg zum 70. Geburtstag*, ed. G. Kurz, D. Mueller, and W. Nicolai (Munich: Beck, 1981), 31–45; and R. Merkelbach, "Sappho und ihr Kreis," *Philologus* 101 (1957): 25–29.

35. θάλπος θεοῦ refers to the sun but could also suggest the heat of another god, Aphrodite; cf. Alcman 59a: "Eros . . . warms my heart"; Sappho 48: "you cooled my heart which was burning with desire"; and Ibycus 286.10–11: "the scorching madness from Cypris." For ὄμβρος, cf. Aesch. *TrGF* (= *Tragicorum Graecorum Fragmenta*, 1–4, ed. B. Snell, R. Kannicht, and S. Radt [Munich: Vandenhoeck & Ruprecht, 1971–85]) fr. 44, 3–4: "the rain, falling from the amorous heaven, impregnates the earth." For the violent winds of Eros, see Sappho 47: "Eros shook my heart like a wind"; and Ibycus 286, 9–10: "the Thracian north wind rushing from Cypris." See also Calame, *The Poetics of Eros*, 14–17.

36. Cf. Catullus 62.39ff., "ut flos in saeptis secretus nascitur hortis—quam mulcent aurae, firmat sol, educat imber," which probably reflects the tradition of Greek wedding song. On meadows and gardens, see Calame, *The Poetics of Eros*, 153–74.

37. Cf. Easterling, ad loc.: "Probably dative of attendant circumstances, in the midst of pleasures."

38. ἄμοχθος appears elsewhere in Soph. *TrGF* fr. 410, Eur. *TGF* (= *Tragicorum Graecorum Fragmenta*, ed. A. Nauck [1899; reprint, Hildesheim: Georg Olms Verlagsbuchhandlung, 1964]) fr. 240, and Pind. *Nem.* 10.30, but without further determination. ἄμικτος with dative is common: cf. LSJ, s.v.; cf. Eur. *Hipp.* 1113: ἀκήρατον ἄλγεσι θυμόν [heart not knowing (= unmixed) with pain]; and Eur. *HF* 1314: οὐδεὶς δὲ

θνητῶν ταῖς τύχαις ἀκήρατος [no mortal lives without calamity]. It might be expected that ἄμοχθος would be used with separative genitive, but, in fact, we find that both separative genitive and instrumental dative are used with similar adjectives: cf. the examples given above and Eur. *Hipp.* 949: ἀκήρατος; Eur. *IA* 982: ἄνοσος; Eur. *Bacch.* 491: οὐκ ἀγύμναστος, all with genitive; but Eur. *Hel.* 533: οὐδ' ἀγύμναστον; Eur. *TGF* fr. 344: οὐκ ἀγύμναστος, with dative.

39. Cf. C. Segal, *Tragedy and Civilization: An Interpretation of Sophocles* (Cambridge, Mass., and London: Harvard University Press, 1981), 64f., 77f.

40. Cf. Heracles' words about his relationship with Iole in Soph. *Trach.* 1225–26: μηδ' ἄλλος ἀνδρῶν τοῖς ἐμοῖς πλευροῖς ὁμοῦ / κλιθεῖσαν αὐτὴν ἀντὶ σοῦ λάβοι ποτέ [that no other man than you would ever have the woman who has lain by my side].

41. J. Taillardat, *Les images d'Aristophane: Études de langue et de style* (Paris: Les Belles Lettres, 1962); J. Henderson, *The Maculate Muse: Obscene Language in Attic Comedy*, 2d ed. (New Haven, Conn., and London: Yale University Press, 1991).

42. *Il.* 14.346–51: ἦ ῥα, καὶ ἀγκὰς ἔμαρπτε Κρόνου παῖς ἣν παράκοιτιν· / τοῖσι δ' ὑπὸ χθὼν δῖα φύεν νεοθηλέα ποίην, / λωτόν θ' ἑρσήεντα ἰδὲ κρόκον ἠδ' ὑάκινθον, / πυκνὸν καὶ μαλακόν, ὃς ἀπὸ χθονὸς ὑψόσ' ἔεργε. / τῷ ἔνι λεξάσθην, ἐπὶ δὲ νεφέλην ἕσσαντο / καλὴν χρυσείην· στιλπναὶ δ' ἀπέπιπτον ἔερσαι. [At this he took his wife in his embrace, and under them earth flowered delicate grass and clover wet with dew; then crocuses and solid beds of tender hyacinth came crowding upward from the ground. On these the two lay down and drew around them purest vapour of golden cloud; the droplets fell away in sunlight sparkling]. Translation by R. Fitzgerald, *Homer: The Iliad* (Oxford: Oxford University Press, 1984). See R. Janko, *The Iliad: A Commentary* (Cambridge: Cambridge University Press, 1992), vol. 4, ad 346–53.

43. Aesch. *TrGF* fr. 44: ἐρᾷ μὲν ἁγνὸς οὐρανὸς τρῶσαι χθόνα, / ἔρως δὲ γαῖαν λαμβάνει γάμου τυχεῖν· / ὄμβρος δ' ἀπ' εὐνάεντος οὐρανοῦ πεσὼν / ἔκυσε γαῖαν· ἡ δὲ τίκτεται βροτοῖς / μήλων τε βοσκὰς καὶ βίον Δημήτριον, / δένδρων τ' ὀπώραν· ἐκ νοτίζοντος γάμου / τελεῖθ' ὅσ' ἔστι· τῶν δ' ἐγὼ παραίτιος [The holy heaven yearns to wound the earth, and yearning layeth hold on the earth to join in wedlock; the rain, fallen from the amorous heaven, impregnates the earth, and it bringeth forth for mankind the food of flocks and herds and Demeter's gifts; and from that moist marriage-rite the woods put on their bloom. Of all these things I am the cause]. Translation by H. W. Smyth, *Aeschylus*, vol. 2, fr. 25. The text of lines 25–26 given by the MSS of Athenaeus 13.600b is faulty; the translation quoted above is based on Hermann's conjecture, δενδρῶτις ὥρα δ' ἐκ νοτίζοντος γάμου / τέλειός ἐστι, while the text of *TrGF* quoted above employs the conjecture by Diels, "and the fruit of trees. From the moist marriage-rite everything is brought to fulfilment."

44. Aesch. *Ag.* 1389ff.: κἀκφυσιῶν ὀξεῖαν αἵματος σφαγὴν / βάλλει μ' ἐρεμνῇ ψακάδι φοινίας δρόσου, / χαίρουσαν οὐδὲν ἧσσον ἢ διοσδότῳ / γάνει σπορητὸς κάλυκος ἐν λοχεύμασιν [So did he fall and quickly breathed away his life, and spouting out a sharp jet of blood he struck me with a dark shower of gory dew, while I rejoiced no less than the crop rejoices in the Zeus-given moisture at the birth of the bud]. Translation by H. Lloyd-Jones in *Aeschylus: Oresteia* (London: Duckworth, 1982).

45. J. L. Moles, "A Neglected Aspect of *Agamemnon* 1389–92," *Liverpool Classical Monthly* 4, no. 9 (1979): 179–89.

46. E. Craik, "Sexual Imagery and Innuendo in *Troades,*" in *Euripides, Women and Sexuality,* ed. A. Powell (London and New York: Routledge, 1990), 1–15, and "Tragic Love, Comic Sex?" in *Tragedy, Comedy and the Polis,* ed. A. H. Sommerstein, S. Halliwell, J. Henderson, and B. Zimmermann (Bari: Levante editori, 1993), 253–262. In the former article, Craik discusses the frequent use of the vocabulary of ships and oars as sexual imagery, and in the latter mainly Euripides' *Hippolytus,* with some references to *Helen.*

47. Craik, "Tragic Love, Comic Sex?" 262.

48. Craik, "Tragic Love, Comic Sex?" 254.

49. See, e.g., C. Collard, *Euripides: Supplices* (Groningen: Bouma's Boekhuis Publishers, 1975), 2:355, 358, 367, 370, 381.

50. I adopt the reading φίλον of the MS and the interpunction as in Collard, *Euripides* (see Collard, ad loc.). J. Diggle in his text (Oxford, 1981) adopts φίλῳ, suggested by Wecklein. Collard (ibid.) points out that φίλον means here more than ἐμόν, "my"—"the adjective here retains the deeper connotation it often carries in overtly sexual contexts."

51. Craik, "Tragic Love, Comic Sex?" 261f.

52. Translation by A. S. Way, *Euripides,* vol. 1, Loeb Classical Library (London: William Heinemann; Cambridge, Mass.: Harvard University Press, 1912).

53. E.g., as meaning that the Nile has no tributaries mingling their waters with it, or as a reference to the Nile delta. See A. M. Dale, *Euripides: Helen* (Oxford: Clarendon Press, 1967); and R. Kannicht, *Euripides: Helena* (Heidelberg: Carl Winter Universitätsverlag, 1969), ad loc.

54. Kannicht, *Euripides,* 2:16, points out that the theory that the Nile had its origin in melting snows is a topos of tragedy from Aeschylus onwards, citing Aesch. *Supp.* 559, *TrGF* fr. 300, Soph. *TrGF* fr. 882, and Eur. *TGF* fr. 228.

55. Konstan, *Sexual Symmetry,* 177.

56. Craik, "Tragic Love, Comic Sex?" 261.

57. See M. Kaimio, *Physical Contact in Greek Tragedy: A Study of Stage Conventions* (Helsinki: Academia Scientiarum Fennica, 1988), 36f.

58. The implications of the similarity and dissimilarity of Penelope and Euripides' Helen are discussed by I. E. Holmberg, "Euripides' Helen: Most Noble and Most Chaste," *American Journal of Philology* 116 (1995): 19–42.

59. See Kannicht, *Euripides,* 2:175f.; and Dale, *Euripides,* 106.

60. Eur. *Hel.* 625ff.: ὦ φίλτατ' ἀνδρῶν Μενέλεως, ὁ μὲν χρόνος / παλαιός, ἡ δὲ τέρψις ἀρτίως πάρα. / ἔλαβον ἀσμένα πόσιν ἐμόν, φίλαι, / περί τ' ἐπέτασα χέρα φίλιον ἐν μακρᾷ / φλογὶ φαεσφόρῳ [O Menelaus, best beloved, the time was long, but even now the joy is here! Friends, friends, with rapture my lord have I found, and with arms of love have I clasped him round; and the goal of the sun's long race is with brightness crowned]. Translation by A. S. Way, *Euripides.*

61. As it is interpreted by Dale, *Euripides,* 107f., and Kannicht, *Euripides,* 2:184.

62. The erotic *sous-entendu* of lines 644–47 is pointed out by A. P. Burnett, *Catastrophe Survived: Euripides' Plays of Mixed Reversal* (Oxford: Clarendon Press, 1971), 85. Burnett would give lines 644–45 to Menelaus and 646–47 to Helen.

63. Eur. *Hel.* 1288ff.: Με. τὸν παρόντα μὲν / στέργειν πόσιν χρή, τὸν δὲ μηκέτ' ὄντ' ἐᾶν·—ἦν δ' Ἑλλάδ' ἔλθω καὶ τύχω σωτηρίας, / παύσω ψόγου σε τοῦ πρίν, ἢν γυνὴ γένῃ / οἵαν γενέσθαι χρή σε σῷ ξυνευνέτῃ. / Ελ. ἔσται τάδ'· οὐδὲ μέμψεται πόσις ποτὲ / ἡμῖν· σὺ δ' αὐτὸς ἐγγὺς ὢν εἴσῃ τάδε. / ἀλλ', ὦ τάλας, ἔσελθε καὶ λουτρῶν τύχε / ἐσθῆτά τ' ἐξάλλαξον. οὐκ ἐς ἀμβολὰς / εὐεργετήσω σ'· εὐμενέστερον γὰρ ἂν / τῷ φιλτάτῳ μοι Μενέλεῳ τὰ πρόσφορα / δρῷης ἄν, ἡμῶν τυγχάνων οἵων σε χρή.

64. See the discussion of different interpretations by Kannicht, *Euripides*, 2:327ff.

65. E.g., by C. Wolff, "On Euripides' *Helen*," *Harvard Studies in Classical Philology* 77 (1973): 70ff.; and D. M. Juffras, "Helen and Other Victims in Euripides' *Helen*," *Hermes* 121 (1993): 45–57, who emphasizes that Helen may be compared to a whole class of innocent and unwilling victims.

66. These hopes are realized when the chorus, after the messenger's speech giving the story of the escape, sings as the third stasimon a propemptic hymn wishing them a good journey to Greece. See, e.g., A. N. Pippin, "Euripides' *Helen*: A Comedy of Ideas," *Classical Philology* 55 (1960): 156; G. Zuntz, "On Euripides' *Helen*: Theology and Irony," *Entretiens Fondation Hardt* 6 (Geneva, 1960): 199–241; A. Podlecki, "The Basic Seriousness of Euripides' *Helen*," *Transactions of the American Philological Association* 101 (1970): 411ff.; C. Segal, "The Two Worlds of Euripides' *Helen*," *Transactions of the American Philological Association* 102 (1971): 595ff.; and Wolff, "On Euripides' *Helen*," 70ff.

67. Iambe in *Hymn. Hom. Dem.* 2.202f.; Baubo in *Hymn. Orph.* fr. 52.

68. The textual difficulties of the last strophe (lines 1354–55 and 1366–67) make the exact interpretation of its meaning impossible.

69. For the syncretism of the ode, see Kannicht, *Euripides*, 2:328–33. For music, cf. W. Burkert, *Greek Religion* (Cambridge, Mass.: Harvard University Press, 1985), 178; and M. L. West, *Ancient Greek Music* (Oxford: Clarendon Press, 1992), 180f.

70. Strong suggestiveness of sexual union can be heard in a few examples of modern Western symphonic music. I call attention to the second movement of Jean Sibelius's *Kullervo Symphony*, where after an opening dialogue between Kullervo and his (unknown) sister, an orchestral part accompanies their intercourse, after which the singers continue in a dialogue revealing their identities; another example is Richard Wagner's *Liebestod* in *Tristan und Isolde*. I do not suggest an identical effect in Euripides' *Helen*; we do not know anything of the descriptive powers of Greek music. We do know, however, that the different modes of Greek music possessed different, very suggestive emotive powers which were considered to have even ethical significance; thus, the effect of this wildly ecstatic song sung in this particular context could be, mutatis mutandis, something comparable to the modern examples mentioned.

Chapter Four

ARISTOPHANIC SEX:
THE EROTICS OF SHAMELESSNESS

❧

Stephen Halliwell

𝒯he uncouth old protagonist of Aristophanes' *Acharnians* marks his achievement of a personal peace with the Spartans, and hence his return to his countryside deme, by celebrating a private, miniaturized version of the Rural Dionysia. The only part of the festival he is able to enact before being interrupted by the hostile chorus of Acharnian charcoal burners is a phallic procession and song—the very thing Aristotle designates in the *Poetics* (4.1449a10–15) as the cultural forerunner of comic drama itself. Dicaeopolis treats himself and his family as a surrogate deme, just as he will later become, in fulfillment of his name, a surrogate or symbolic city. Assuming the organizing role of a demarch or local magistrate, he enlists the services of his daughter as a basket carrier, of Xanthias and another slave as carriers of the phallic pole, and of his wife as a spectator. He completes the procession himself as the solo singer (probably in lieu of a chorus) of the phallic song (*to phallikon*, 261) in buoyant iambic rhythm.[1]

The song is addressed to Phales, the personified phallus. He is invoked with a cascade of vocatives—a kind of comic aretalogy, conveying Dicaeopolis's exuberant acclamation of the god's attributes:

> Φαλῆς, ἑταῖρε Βακχίου,
> ξύγκωμε, νυκτοπεριπλάνη-
> τε, μοιχέ, παιδεραστά, . . . (263–65)

Phales, companion of Bacchus,
Fellow-komast, nocturnal wanderer,
Marriage defiler, lover of boys, . . .

The opening of this ode is indebted to an older tradition of iambic/
comic parody: so much is suggested, at any rate, by the affinities with Hipponax fragment 3a West, where Hermes is addressed as "Hermes dog stran-
gler, Maionian Candaules, companion [*hetaire*] of thieves."[2] As with this
fragment of Hipponax, Dicaeopolis's vocatives include the perversely ad-
miring adaptation of what would ordinarily be an abusive term, that is,
moichos, "adulterer" or "marriage defiler."[3] Dicaeopolis characterizes Phales as a rampant hedonist whose combined indulgence in alcohol and sex
takes place in a nocturnal setting that intimates both decadence and illicit-
ness; the *komos* (or revel) in which he participates with his divine *hetairos*,
Dionysus himself, is no orderly celebration but an immersion in promiscuous phallic gratification. Moreover, the connection between *komos* and
symposium evokes a world of specifically urban and aristocratic debauchery,[4] an ethos far removed from that of the uncultivated countryman Dicaeopolis himself, who has already told us he "hates the city" (33). Indeed,
when Dicaeopolis goes on to communicate his own sexual fantasies to the
phallic god, they belong to a very different social milieu, that of the farmer
who finds a neighbor's young slave girl stealing wood from his land, bundles
her to the ground, and rapes her on the spot. The imagined use of force on
the slave girl is accentuated by the rhythmically and phonically powerful sequence of four verbs, the first three of which are metaphors from wrestling:[5]

μέσην λαβόντ', ἄραντα, κατα-
βαλόντα καταγιγαρτίσαι (275–76)

To seize her round the waist, to lift her up, to
Hurl her to the ground and—squeeze her grape pip out!

Although one can use the term "rape" here only in a nonlegal sense, it is
probable that Dicaeopolis's treatment of the Thracian slave would (if exe-
cuted in reality) be an illegal act, and evidently a gross provocation against
his neighbor.[6] In its naively "agricultural" style, the fantasy forms a piquant
counterpart to Phales' nocturnal excesses. It is therefore misleading of Jeffrey Henderson to speak in this context of "frolic[ing] and hav[ing] sex out
in the fields," of "fornicat[ing] naturally," of "playful [*sic*] sexual aggressive-
ness," and of "wholesome sex."[7] These phrases sentimentalize the comic

bluntness of Dicaeopolis's phallic impulses, as does Kenneth Reckford's judgment that the song is "innocuous" and "only slightly indecent."[8] Part of the rough pungency of Dicaeopolis's song lies in the way it runs together nostalgia for the countryside with a coarseness of sexual imagination and feeling. This blending of ingredients is caught by the unique word *kata-gigartisai* (only quoted by later scholars), to squeeze out a grape pip — or perhaps "crush out" would be better, given that the verb duplicates the *kata-* prefix of the preceding wrestling term, *kataballein*. Dicaeopolis allows the making of wine (or the enjoyment of grapes — the difference is insignificant for the thrust of the humor) to merge in his sensory imagination with a violent act of copulation. But why should this count as any more "wholesome" than the stupor of the nocturnal adulterer? Are we, as putative Athenian males, and as most modern critics take for granted, invited to *savor* and "sympathize" with Dicaeopolis's lust? Or might we, with an element of superiority, regard it as comic precisely in virtue of its blatant, raw surrender to the unfettered urges of the id? Should we (Athenians), in short, laugh *with* or *at* Dicaeopolis? And how far are these alternatives complicated by the fact that Dicaeopolis is filling a "ritual" role, that of the phallic chorus within a Dionysiac festival? Perhaps the position of the protagonist is intrinsically ambivalent in the psychological responses which it invites or allows. As I shall shortly stress, the Dionysiac occasion of the play's own performance sanctions the imaginative suspension of normal standards of shame, but the suspension is not wholly unthinking, and the mind of a spectator might waver between appreciation for Dicaeopolis's earthy sex drive and a sense of the ludicrous grossness of a character whose erotic ideal is the lecherous sexual "wrestling" of a young slave girl.[9] There are far-reaching though inaccessible problems here, both historical and psychological, about the kind of pleasure provided by Old Comedy.

If one wants to say, as I do, that the phallic song in *Acharnians* serves as a kind of metaphorical enactment of Aristophanic comedy's own nature, we have to be prepared to allow that proposition a rather complex force. It is important, but not sufficient, to grasp the appropriateness of a phallic song for a genre in which the visible phallus was probably the almost invariable accoutrement of male characters — a sign of comic masculinity whose presence marked a perpetual scope for indecency.[10] It is important too, if we are alert to the song's status as a microcosm of its genre, to notice the cluster of associations between four motifs: first, the idea of a drunken *komos* (comedy's own cultural namesake); second, the pursuit of uninhibited, even illegal sensuality (comic pleasures tend typically towards the hybristic); third, the celebration of *release* from the serious pressures of life ("escaping from troubles and war" [269–70]—something of a cliché in Aristophanes); and, finally, mocking disparagement of the city's officialdom (here represented by the military leader, Lamachus [270]). There is a rank shamelessness about all this, a brazen kicking over of restraints, which, whatever its relationship to the actual phallic songs that took place in the ceremonials of the Rural and other Dionysia, aptly instantiates the Dionysiac spirit that animates Old Comedy as a whole. But the symbolization of comedy in Dicaeopolis's phallic song brings with it teasing paradoxes too. The comic protagonist relishes the thought of unrestricted sexual license: adultery for Phales' urban phallus, rural rape for his own. But he voices these sentiments in a ritual performance in which his own *oikos*, his own wife and daughter, participate.[11] That fact about the fictional scenario mirrors the larger cultural circumstance that the audience of Old Comedy itself is encouraged, at some level, to enjoy sexual shamelessness (as well as other kinds of behavior subversive of public morality) as part of an experience which takes place within an elaborate framework of civically organized religious celebration. It must have been this aspect of phallic celebrations, in an earlier but ritually cognate context, which struck Heraclitus, to judge by his remark that "if it were not Dionysus in whose honor they process and chant a song to genitals [*aidoia*, lit. "shameful parts"], their behavior would have been most shameful."[12]

A tension of this kind, arising from a religiously and civically sanctioned suspension of the norms of shame, is partly constitutive of Old Comedy in general and can be seen specifically at work in the phallic song of *Acharnians*. The tension heightens an ambiguity about Dicaeopolis's own (sexual) identity, between the disarmingly frank libido of an uncultured, alienated rustic and the liberated vitality of a Dionysiac worshiper. If we accept my suggestion that the song be seen, on one level, as a kind of metaphor or symbol for the genre in which it occurs, this ambiguity infects the (sexual) pleasure of comedy itself. As I have indicated, the song juxtaposes the komastic, quasi-aristocratic rampages of the insatiable Phales with the literally down-to-earth sexuality of the protagonist himself. It is as if Dicaeopolis, in his persona as old, decrepit *agroikos*, cannot quite imagine himself in the world of the degenerate *komos*. For him, the violent deflowering of a neighbor's slave girl is a suitably countrified equivalent to the enjoyment of other men's wives and sons which he projects onto the phallic god himself. At the same time, this is Dicaeopolis's very own song, and as the celebrant of the comic phallus he has to be in some sense identified with all the pleasures which it envisages: he does, after all, end his song by inviting Phales to drink with him (277). Moreover, later sections of *Acharnians* will spoil any neat sociology of Athenian sexual behavior that we might have hoped to construct from the contrasting phallic activities in the song. Something akin to Phales' debauchery is actually the subject of Dicaeopolis's complaints at one point in the play, in his (parodic) account of the antecedents of the war with Sparta (523–29). There, the supposed theft of a Megarian prostitute, Simaetha, by "young men drunk on kottabos" (i.e. symposiasts) evokes a realm of scandalously komastic misdemeanors similar in bent to the epithets of the personified phallic god. Yet by the end of *Acharnians* Dicaeopolis's own triumphant, inebriated return from the archon's feast and drinking contest at the Anthesteria, with a couple of girls whom he instructs to massage his erect phallus (1216–21),[13] will apparently assimilate the comic hero after all into a world of urban dissipation where sexual pleasures can become a form of conspicuous consumption.

On further consideration, however, I think we can see that the conclusion of *Acharnians* underlines rather than resolves the paradox which surfaced in the protagonist's earlier phallic song. There is something obtrusively incongruous about Dicaeopolis's swaggering return from the archon's feast with two sexually compliant dancing girls: this is a sexual consummation enjoyed by a character who is, from one point of view, grotesquely implausible for the role. The theater audience of *Acharnians* sees the same old rustic, decrepit character they saw at the start—a man, on his own admission (1–2), accustomed to being starved of pleasures. But by the end of the play his phallus has become activated in a way which cuts across the distinction between urban *komos* and rural rape. That crossing of boundaries is paradigmatic of the comic phallus, paralleled, for example, by Philocleon's theft of the pipe girl from the symposium in *Wasps* (and Philocleon, like Dicaeopolis, engages in a sort of one-man *komos*). And to appreciate this feature of the genre calls for recognition of the disparities and deformities characteristically mediated by Aristophanes' treatment of sex.

Old Comedy, to adapt Heraclitus's point, is a kind of institutionalized shamelessness. That, as I have suggested, is the prime respect in which the phallic song in *Acharnians* encapsulates and embodies a central element in comedy's own cultural formation. The phallic costume normal for male characters in the genre, together with the exaggerated features that could be built into distorted masks and the actors' padded belly and buttocks, served as visible reminders of comedy's generic interest in flouting the restraints of shame and decency in both word and action.[14] Shamelessness and ugliness easily become entwined in Greek notions of *to aischron*, and this evaluative association has extensive implications for the sexuality (as well as other aspects) of Aristophanic comedy.[15] Two prominent features of the genre can be summarily cited in support of this claim. The first is that sexual rewards for male characters in Aristophanes fall almost entirely to figures (Dicaeopolis in *Acharnians*, Demos in *Knights*, Philocleon in *Wasps*, Trygaeus in *Peace*, Peisetaerus in *Birds*) who are markedly implausible candidates for this role in virtue of age (advanced), social standing (low), and material or psychological profile (crude, often disgruntled, generally lacking in urban(e) elegance). The second is that female sexuality in Aristophanes is predominantly characterized by divergence from, and sometimes the flagrant transgression of, ideal *sōphrosunē*, "self-discipline." On both scores, and in stark contrast to the gradual romanticization of the comic genre in the middle and later fourth century, Old Comedy gives negligible space to the sexual success of characters who are either young or in their prime and displays the very reverse of an inclination to dramatize situations in which we are left with a sense of harmonious fit between the agents and the objects of sexual desire. It offers, with scarce exceptions, a grotesquely paradoxical erotics within which the disadvantages of "ugliness" are transformed into the supremacy of shamelessness. Even in *Lysistrata*, Aristophanes' most sentimental comedy, where marital reunion is the final outcome of the plot, the sexual fruition of the heroine's plan is essentially expressed in the scene where Reconciliation—instructed by Lysistrata, at one point, to take the men by the phallus (1119)—is turned into an object of anatomically explicit lust on the part of both Athenian and Spartan males (1112–88). In the similarly comic-allegorical cases of Theoria ("Festivity") and Opora ("Harvest"), brought back to earth by Trygaeus in *Peace*, the carnality which the naked female figures both embody and arouse is emphatically associated with the world of prostitutes.[16] Something similar is in play with Reconciliation: her body, open for public inspection in a way no respectable Athenian wife's could possibly be, represents less of a lofty ideal (whatever Lysistrata herself may *say*) than the shamelessness of Aristophanic sex incarnate.

But shamelessness—the comic violation of norms of public decency and inhibition prevalent in Athenian culture—functions in numerous ways, many of which cannot be closely addressed in this chapter. In *Knights*, the sausage seller's quasi-prostitutional availability becomes a qualification (as well as a perverted metaphor) for political success, and this is part of the play's larger satirical confusion between the world of "backstreet" Athenian low-life and the exploitative degradation of its democratic politics.[17] In *Clouds*, on the other hand, shamelessness stands for a cultural corruption so pervasive that the entire theater audience is explicitly tarred with the epithet "wide-arsed" (*euruprōktos*), here referring literally to the anatomical punishment of adulterers and by extension to sexual debauchery in general

(1085ff.). In *Birds*, differently again, sexual immodesty becomes a motif linking men, gods, and birds, and it ultimately underwrites the protagonist's achievement of a sexual victory over Zeus himself.[18] In *Thesmophoriazusae*, the rupture of the norms of shame is brought about by a recurrent confusion of masculine and feminine identities that connects the kinsman of Euripides with the poet Agathon and the figure of Cleisthenes, and the transvestite dimension of this theme foregrounds comedy's own theatrical manipulation of masks, phallus, and other devices of costuming for its representation of male and female bodies. In *Frogs*, sexual shamelessness appropriately finds its center in none other than the god Dionysus, who at one point imagines himself masturbating while watching his own slave's coition with a prostitute (542–48): the conjunction of slaves and prostitutes is a common topic in Aristophanes, and it occurs elsewhere in *Frogs* itself in the debasement of Euripides' Muse to the status of a versatile whore (1306ff.).

Even this range of examples can give only a superficial idea of the scope of what I mean by the shamelessness which typifies much Aristophanic sex. To get a richer idea of the comic erotics of his work, we need detailed consideration of a particular case. I therefore want to devote the rest of this chapter to the long section of *Ecclesiazusae* (almost exactly a fifth of the play) in which the ramifications of Praxagora's sexual communism are explored. Although this scene has received a good deal of attention, my own interpretation of it will diverge sharply from the existing consensus.

Complications and puzzles about Praxagora's scheme of sexual communism confront us from its first announcement at 613ff. The scheme has not been anticipated at all before this point in the play, a lack of preparation rather typical of Aristophanic plot making. This gives the dramatic moment a kind of improvisatory quality which puts severe constraints on the sort of sense we can expect to make of the new idea. Praxagora's proposal of sexual communism is prompted by a reference to male sexual desire which *buys* itself satisfaction (611–12). It is not exactly obvious whether Blepyrus's question envisages a context of prostitution or a case of seduction through gifts.[19] But the implication of automatic and immediate gratification for payment can hardly escape association with the former, and this increases the ironic resonance of Praxagora's use of the verb "sit" at 617 (*kathedountai*, "the ugly women will sit alongside the proud"), since *kathezomai* or *kathēmai* was the mot juste for the trade of cheaper sexual professionals.[20] Prima facie, the reference to childbearing at 615 (cf. 635ff.) might seem to keep the scheme within the realms of relations between citizen males and females, but this is not decisive:[21] after all, if marriage and the family are to be abolished (though, with characteristic insouciance, Aristophanes will treat Praxagora and Blepyrus as still married in the final scene: 1126, 1137; cf. 727), what place will remain for the distinction between legitimate and illegitimate offspring? What we have here, then, is an incipient blurring of sociosexual categories that foreshadows the more extensive uncertainty and fluidity which I shall soon try to demonstrate in the second half of the play.

Against the background of that suggestion, it is useful to pose a question that most interpreters overlook. Is Praxagora really abolishing the practice of prostitution, or turning it into a kind of civic duty for everyone—everyone, at any rate, capable of being an object of desire (i.e., in the play's terms, everyone other than the irredeemably "ugly")? If prostitution entails making oneself available for others' sexual pleasure in pursuit of one's own gain, is not Praxagora's system a recipe for a kind of compulsory, if back-to-front, prostitution? When she returns to the sexual issue at the conclusion of the agon (693ff.), Praxagora pictures the new state of affairs in terms which decidedly evoke prostitution by streetwalkers near, say, the city gates or down at the Piraeus.[22] The combined images of women soliciting openly in the sidestreets (*kata tas diodous*, 693), and explicitly in competition with one another, carry suggestive connotations to which we shall need to return. The effect is similar to the picture projected by Theophrastus's malicious slanderer (*kakologos*), when he says of certain women: "they snatch passersby off the street; this house of theirs has its legs in the air . . . ; they copulate in the street like dogs."[23] A little later Praxagora does speak directly of abolishing prostitution (718–24).[24] But her explanation, that she wants the citizen women to have the young men for themselves, highlights two ironic implications of her sexual blueprint: first, it posits a situation in which the former citizen wives will in some sense take the place of prostitutes; second, it envisages that these same women will have a general appetite for sexual partners and will not want competition from (slave) prostitutes. Both implications help to prepare the ground for what will transpire, with some grotesque modifications, to be a notable species of Aristophanic paradox. Praxagora's relationship to prostitution will turn out to be somewhat analogous to, say, Peisetaerus's relationship to urban life—an escape that ultimately converts itself into a reconfigured version of the sorts of things from which it was supposedly taking flight.

Despite its initial formulation from a male point of view (614–15), Praxagora's sexual communism is ostensibly designed, in its equal treatment of the sexes, to involve a wider degree of "sharing," *koinōnia*, than is the case with her economic measures (where, notoriously, she arranges for men to be the principal beneficiaries, while women cater for their needs in ways which bear close resemblance to the previously prevailing patterns of gender subordination [599–600, 654]). There is, anyhow, a basic incommensurability between the two halves of the program, the economic and the sexual, even though in both cases Praxagora is, in a sense, abolishing property rights (whether the property is one's land, say, or one's own body). Whereas wealth can, in principle, be redistributed so as to satisfy some criterion of equality, sexual gratification would need to be turned into a kind of measurable commodity in order to become susceptible to such organization. But this is impossible, at the very least on the current scenario, since Praxagora's plan is predicated upon personal differences (beauty versus ugliness) which generate discrepant patterns of sexual desire: beautiful people desire other beautiful people, but are repelled by the ugly, who nonetheless themselves have desire for sex with the beautiful. So, at any rate, runs the schematically reductive logic of the play. That asymmetry is the key to Aristophanes' outré presentation of sexual communism, because it necessarily produces the consequence that while the beautiful must pay for their sexual entitlements (supposing they can ever reach them) with sexual obligations, the ugly will, it seems, have unqualified rights to be gratified by others. Of course, from this and other points of view, the absurd implications of the scheme ramify unresolvably, way beyond the possibilities of prediction or calculation. The whole conception raises numerous potential questions to which it has no intention of supplying answers. Above all, the play contains no hint as to how a calculus of sexual obligations and entitlements could ever be constructed: for example, how many ugly people must a beautiful person satisfy before (s)he is entitled to some sexual satisfaction of (her) his own? That is a symptomatically Aristophanic exercise of the comic poet's privileged irrationality, and perhaps a satirical exposure of the unfulfillable contradictions of utopianism. But the most important entailment for my immediate purposes is that Praxagora's would-be "democratic" plan (631) amounts to an inverted erotics of appearances that opens up the supposed certainty of success to the sexually shameless.[25] And that, I have already contended, is a quintessential constituent of Aristophanic sex.

The sex scene (as I shall call it for convenience) at *Ecclesiazusae* 877ff. illustrates this point in a very intricate way. A revealing but neglected way of approaching this episode is to take account of certain possibilities, available within Praxagora's scheme, which Aristophanes chooses *not* to dramatize. Two things are conspicuous by their absence. The first is the spectacle, actually envisaged at 628–34, of beautiful citizen women being compelled to submit to ugly men — one permutation, in other words, of the "compulsory prostitution" which I suggested that we can think of Praxagora's new regime as requiring.[26] The second omission is the sight of beautiful Athenian "wives" (as they formerly were) actively seeking sexual pleasure with males of their choice, but without the previously obtaining stigma of adultery, a concept which has no application under the new conditions. It may in general be unproductive to ask why a comic poet has declined certain dramatic options, but there is real point in doing so in this instance, partly because of the expectations which were aroused by the original formulation of sexual communism. One suggestion at least merits consideration. While Old Comedy, including the earlier parts of *Ecclesiazusae* itself, repeatedly extracts humor from the idea of Athenian women's penchant for adultery, anything like a concrete realization of the theme on stage, even with fictional characters, seems to have been unattractive to the poets.[27] We are here in territory where the potential comic rewards of inviting the male citizen psyche to imagine a familiar stereotype translated into graphic detail might be outweighed by the risk of touching too uncomfortable a source of anxiety.[28] If so, it will not be surprising that Aristophanes has avoided dramatizing a still more subversive notion integral to Praxagora's scheme: the wholesale, promiscuous sexual availability of Athenian women. And that will serve as a cautionary reminder that there are some limits to the shamelessness which Old Comedy asks its audience to enjoy contemplating.

Whether or not such an explanation makes sufficient sense in terms of the always contorted engagement between Aristophanic humor and the cultural psychology of classical Athenians, it remains striking that the sex scene in *Ecclesiazusae* occludes some of the most significant implications of Praxagora's sexual communism as expounded earlier in the play. This goes hand in hand with another feature of the scene that I have already touched on and now wish to elaborate more fully, its extensive blurring of the social-cum-sexual identity of the women involved. In looking at the traces of this blurring, I shall concentrate on the earlier part of the scene, involving the first hag and the young girl. On any reading, it is here that the keynote for the scene as a whole is struck; what comes later, with the two further hags, simply stretches the comic material to further extremes.[29] Now, most interpreters carry into this scene a straightforward assumption that these women, both the hags and the girl, are supposed to have citizen status, that is, to be *gunaikes astai* of the class qualified, under actual Athenian conditions, to produce legitimate citizen offspring for Athenian husbands. But I stressed earlier that the question put by Blepyrus (at 611–12) which prompted Praxagora's description of her system seems to depict an ambiguous situation, open to interpretation as either prostitution or seduction by gifts. I would now add that there is in fact no explicit or exclusive reference to citizen women at 611–34,[30] though that passage ostensibly anticipates a state of affairs involving them. That formulation is not pedantic but a way of drawing attention to a factor that, particularly in performance, contributes to a characteristically Aristophanic looseness and fluidity of dramatic impression. It is a matter, I maintain, of noticing how the comic imagination operative at 613ff. starts to allow the possibilities of fantasy to float free from the categories and distinctions of social reality, and in the process to complicate the identities of the comic agents concerned. And what starts unobtrusively in that first passage, as perhaps no more than an inchoate vagueness in the sweep of the plan, becomes a more overt effect of category blurring—indeed, something much more spicily paradoxical—in the situation pictured at 693ff., where, as I earlier stressed, the evocation of a street of prostitution ought to be unmistakable.

The confusion of categories and identities is a hallmark of Aristophanic comedy. His plays construct fantasy worlds in which, to name only a few salient instances, it is possible for an Athenian rustic to become a private "city" in his own right, a sausage seller to become leader of the people (at the same time as a "new slave" in a household), a peasant to become a quasi-Euripidean hero, an old man to become both a bird and a god, or a citizen wife to become a military general and organizer of a political coup. Yet this overwhelming fact about the playwright's work has not prevented scholars from interpreting the setting and personnel of the sex scene in *Ecclesiazusae* with a narrowness that obscures a large part of its comic impetus. In particular, the status of the women concerned has been settled to the satisfaction of most interpreters by a simple reference back to Praxagora's original conception of her new law, even though that conception itself, as I have shown, was full of ambiguities.[31] The thesis I want to develop, by contrast, is that in the sex scene Aristophanes conjures up a distorted sexual demimonde whose grotesque features make impossible (and comically undesirable) any direct correlation with the previously obtaining status categories of Athenian women to which Praxagora's plan was, we may think, "supposed" to apply. The one essential link with the original scheme is the application of the law that obliges the beautiful to gratify the ugly before (if ever) they can satisfy their own libido—a kind of hyper-*isonomia* ("equality before the law"). However, Aristophanes eschews the option of exploring the consequences of sexual communism for Praxagora and other wives like her. Instead, he creates a thick dramatic texture of erotic squalor within which the comically exaggerated contrasts between young and old, beautiful and ugly, passionate and lustful cancel out much of the point of trying to read the scene consistently in relation to the social types who occupied the earlier parts of the play. Where we are accustomed as critics to speaking of the "consequences" of Praxagora's program, it would be truer to the dynamics of the work to talk of abrupt discontinuities which lend the plot its paradigmatically Aristophanic unpredictability. From a play which started with wives making their way secretly out of their houses, we have passed through an announcement of sexual communism purporting to guarantee sexual pleasure for all, have been warned (at 693ff.) of the prospects of what sounds like a new and inverted form of prostitution, and finally reach, in the sex scene itself, a ludicrously disordered demimonde in which the houses of the stage set have become houses of disrepute — *oikiai* become *oikēmata*, if you like.[32] Against the background of this transposition in ambience and ethos, it is naive to insist, as the consensus of modern scholarship does, on literalist consistency in the sociosexual terms of Praxagora's regime.

Two groups of details in particular invite the audience, from early on in the sex scene, to interpret the setting as a demimonde in which the issue of citizen status, together with its sexual implications, is obscured (not to say dispensed with) by reductive concentration on comically intensified factors of age, physical appearance, and degrees of lewdness. One is the mise-en-scène in a street where women (one of whom at least, the first hag, is dressed in sexually provocative style) are waiting for male clients.[33] Observe the hag's opening question, whose plural ("Why aren't *the men* here?" [877]) owes less to the nature of Praxagora's project than to the implied mentality of a sexual professional: why else expect a plurality of Athenian men to come to *this* particular place? This clearly bears out Praxagora's imagined scenario of women preying on men "in the side streets" at 693ff. and evokes a "red-light district" of the sort salaciously alluded to by Theophrastus's malicious slanderer, cited earlier, and vividly depicted in a long fragment of Xenarchus (fr. 4 *PCG*), poet of Middle Comedy, describing the rich variety of prostitutes on display at the brothels.[34] Beyond the level of general affinity, Aristophanes' scene specifically if hyperbolically matches a notion that appears in both these other passages and was no doubt a piece of popular cynicism — the idea that women in such districts are sexually predatory enough to "snatch" or "drag" men off the streets.[35] In this connection, we need to catch a nuance carried by the verbs *parakuptein* at 884 and 924, *diakuptein* at 930, and *ekkuptein* at 1052, all of which can describe the sly or surreptitious action of "peeping" out of a door or window. They characterize forms of behavior thought potentially scandalous for respectable females but suitable for women seeking to attract the attention of men or to entice male clients.[36] This overtone of prostitution or commercial sex at *Ecclesiazusae* 877ff. is reinforced by the motif of rivalry between the women, especially between the first hag and the girl, a rivalry which does not strictly make sense within the new sexual rules. Tellingly, it is the *girl* who voices this rivalry at 885–87, in terms which suit competition between two prostitutes over a particular "patch": "you thought I wouldn't be here to stop you picking all the grapes for yourself and attracting someone by your singing." Commentators have failed to notice that this nuance is implied by the indefinite pronoun (*tina*, "someone") at 886 (echoing the hag's use in 881), as well as by the girl's threat to "sing a rival song" (*antasomai* [887]). Why should the girl worry whether just *anyone* might be lured in by the woman next door, and why think of singing a *rival* song, unless we are to consider her as in some degree participating in a game of quasi-commercialized sex?

I shall come back shortly to this motif of rivalry, as well as to the issue of the girl's own status, but the reference to singing brings us to the second dimension of the scene which makes it evocative of a context in which the women comport themselves like sexual professionals. The first hag, already humming to herself when she comes out (880), thinks of singing as part of her strategy of sexual attraction. That it is an "Ionic" song she decides to sing (883) confirms what we might anyhow have guessed, that this marks the repertoire of a practiced eroticist, whatever precise label we might want to put on the class of women of which she forms a hideous specimen. When the song begins (893), it turns out to be an exercise in sleazy "cabaret" mode, advertising the sexual expertise of "riper" women[37] and denigrating her younger rival with catty obscenities. What we are offered here must be a disfigured version of the singing and related accomplishments of certain courtesans.[38] In the course of the exchange of songs between the women, the hag makes two points which underscore the sexual ethos of a demimonde: at 897–99 she sings of being more faithful than a younger rival to "whatever lover I'm with," a phrase which makes richest sense if we think of her as at any rate aspiring to be some kind of *hetaira*,[39] and at 918–20 she accuses the girl of being the kind of whore who supplies a service in fellatio.[40] These details are of a piece with the larger components of the setting already discussed—the "brothel district" background and the "cabaret" singing—and buttress the overall effect of an ambience of "professional" sex, comically transplanted from a commercial to a would-be utopian framework.

It might be objected, however, that even if the persona of the first hag, and therefore of her later counterparts, mixes features redolent of a prostitute and/or cheap *hetaira*, rather than a (former) citizen wife, surely the girl next door represents something less crude—an innocent young Athenian, who wants only her own true lover. I question whether this sentimental view, adopted by virtually all interpreters, is right.[41] I have already commented on the way the girl speaks and sings in a spirit of sexual rivalry with the first hag, as though she were not exactly averse to soliciting men herself. Nonetheless, she is evidently waiting for a man who means something special to her—her "companion" (*hetairos*), as she calls him (912), for whom she admits to feeling an intensely sexual desire and longing (*erōs* and *pothos* [954–57]). But this in itself tells us little; it is compatible with more than one hypothesis about the girl's status; and in fact it may actually tilt the balance away from the impression that she is a citizen daughter—a type of female character rarely given a voice, still less an erotic voice, in Attic comedy.[42] Another possible clue to her status is the reference to her mother's absence at 913–14. The significance of this is elusive, but I am inclined to doubt whether it is meant to be taken as a marker of citizen background.[43] On the contrary, it lends itself to interpretation as a euphemistic sign of a situation in which an older *hetaira* is "grooming" her daughter for a sexual profession. One documented instance of a mother-daughter pair of *hetairai* is that of Theodote and her mother in Xenophon's *Memorabilia*, and other alleged cases of mother-daughter collaboration in the provision of sexual services appear in Apollodorus's account of the career of Neaira.[44] Even if this interpretation of *Ecclesiazusae* 913–14 remains optional, there is little incentive to treat the lines as a hint of citizen status.

But above all, the eroticism of the matching songs at 952–68, where the girl pines for her lover and the lover sings from the doorstep in *paraclausithyron* fashion (that is, serenading outside a locked door), is so patently and sentimentally stylized as to make the supposition of a parodic relationship to an existing song type irresistible and, by the same token, to rule out any obvious link with the circumstances of an Athenian citizen daughter. There have been several attempts to diagnose the character of this duet. Maurice Bowra, that connoisseur of the erotic, suggested an indebtedness to popular song, but his argument has been criticized by others.[45] Though I cannot pursue the point in detail here, I think the most likely area of affinity, if we can safely extrapolate back from later evidence, is with the "low-life" scenes of subliterary mime, for this seems to have been a genre of performance in which both the lovelorn young girl and the lecherously ravenous older woman have an appropriate place.[46] Finally, it is telling that the young man twice refers to the girl as *tēn kalēn*, "the pretty one," first at 947 and later at 1080: this locution has a nuance of anonymity which suits an ambience other than that of an adolescent or premarital relationship between two Athenians of citizen class.

It is unnecessary to fit together the various details I have mentioned into a completely coherent reading of the girl's social-cum-sexual status, and likewise with that of the hags. What we need here is not a sociologically

plausible hypothesis to connect their behavior to the possibilities of contemporary Athens,[47] any more than we would look for such a hypothesis to
make sense of, say, Dicaeopolis's private market in *Acharnians* or the infil-
tration of the Thesmophoria by Euripides' disguised kinsman. What matters
is to acknowledge that Aristophanes has taken the theme of sexual communism as the cue for a virtually self-contained episode[48] whose comic energy
is only tenuously related to Praxagora's original conception of the "sharing,"
koinōnia, of desire. The force of this contention can be (very briefly) brought
out by a double contrast with *Lysistrata.* In *Lysistrata* the "striptease" scene
between Myrrhine and Cinesias does maintain the thread of the heroine's
plan, the logic of the sex strike; and it correspondingly keeps in view the
heroine's control of the situation: Myrrhine carries out Lysistrata's instructions, and Cinesias's frustration contributes consequentially to the men's
capitulation. But in *Ecclesiazusae* it is a notorious fact that Praxagora herself
is written out of the play after her departure at 727. I suggest that we need
to place this point in a perspective which incorporates the material I have
been examining, especially the playwright's decision to convert his sexual
theme into an opportunity for a mode of humor which leaves behind the
possibilities of participation by a character like Praxagora herself. In short,
the relentless shamelessness to which Aristophanes reduces the story of sexual communism leads him to discard altogether the type of female characters on which the earlier parts of the play were based. It matters far less,
therefore, what assumptions we make about the notional social status of the
women involved in the sex scene than that we recognize how Aristophanes'
imagination has taken us into a world where the Athenians' sociosexual
codes of shame have been thoroughly routed by female libido pushed to
comically repulsive extremes.

The approach I have taken to the sex scene in *Ecclesiazusae* makes it
much harder than many readings of the play have acknowledged to find an
intelligible subtext to the "consequences" of Praxagora's scheme of sexual
communism. There have been a number of interpretations of the play which
discern in its later scenes a critique of the heroine's communistic utopia
and its presuppositions about human nature.[49] But the only assumption
about human nature which the sex scene really exploits is, for comic purposes at least, a very simple one, namely, that sexual desire is an experience
common to the "beautiful" and the "ugly," yet highly asymmetrical in its
operations vis-à-vis those same simplified categories. Hence the need, originally perceived by Praxagora, to build a principle of compulsory sexual
services, cutting across the alignments of desire, into the workings of sexual
communism. The sex scene does in a very basic sense illustrate the new law

of sexual entitlements and obligations. Yet it does so with a disorientatingly selective twist, ignoring in particular, as I remarked earlier, the sexual accessibility of attractive women who used to be Athenian wives (like Praxagora herself) to the attentions of ugly old men.[50] From my point of view, this leaves us with an aptly paradoxical conclusion. If I am right, the sex scene in *Ecclesiazusae* unfolds a demimonde scenario which is perhaps the ultimate, the most grotesque manifestation of the Aristophanic impulse to translate sexual subjects into exhibitions of shamelessness. But it is at the same time a scene which thereby allows itself the large privilege of imaginative evasion. We cannot even begin to ask what such shamelessness means for the woman who opened the play by hinting at the secrets of female eroticism.

In one respect the sex scene might seem to be the reverse of the phallic song in *Acharnians* from which I started. Where the latter is a fantasy of the phallus triumphant, the former depicts a sort of failure of the phallus: the only male character in the scene is balked in his own desires and forced to submit to the lust of the most ghastly of the hags, a submission psychologically equivalent, for him, to death (1107–11). In part this contrast reflects a wider inequality, noted earlier, in the sexual fortunes of young and old in Aristophanes. But beyond that, my juxtaposition of these two scenes lends support to the idea that wherever we find ourselves on the spectrum of sexual possibilities in Aristophanes (and the plays employ, somewhere or other, just about every configuration of desire between male and female, old and young, free and slave),[51] the dominant dynamic in his treatment of the subject is the obtrusive breaching of the city's publicly endorsed norms of decency and restraint in both the pursuit and fulfillment of desires. The disruption or contradiction of these norms is what I have denoted by the category of "shamelessness." For Aristophanes and his audience the comic phallus, in all its various conditions, was itself the symbol of what, on the basis of Heraclitus fragment 15, I earlier called the "institutionalized shamelessness" of the genre, a point we glimpse in the well-known passage in *Clouds* where the parabatic voice of the poet makes (ironic) claims for the quasi-female modesty (he uses the adjective *sōphrōn*, 537) of his play and contrasts it with the stock humor of the "thick, red-tipped dangling leather phallus, there to make the boys laugh" (539–40). What could be less indicative of *sōphrosunē*, of self-discipline and inhibition, than an ostentatious phallus? Yet its presence, attached to most if not all male characters in the genre, and characteristically accompanied by the padded enlargement of other anatomical regions (a theatrical device used for female figures too), is a visible sign of comedy's reduction of sexuality to a level of immodesty that is ludicrous rather than truly threatening. But for this to be so, the audience of comedy must be to some extent complicit in the shamelessness of the performance:[52] able to enjoy it, as Plato acutely perceived (*Republic* 10.606c), only by suspending its own evaluative norms, its own standards of shame. To say this is not to offer a determinate answer to my earlier question, "Should we (Athenians) laugh *with* or *at* Dicaeopolis?" (or any other sexual agent in the comic city), but to register that the pleasure of comedy cannot be understood outside the frameworks of cultural psychology. So far as Aristophanic sex is concerned, this makes it apt to conclude that the erotics of comedy should count as a special case of Dionysiac voyeurism.

Notes

1. Michael Silk, "Aristophanes as a Lyric Poet," in *Aristophanes: Essays in Interpretation,* ed. J. Henderson (Cambridge, 1980), 99–151, at 131–33, gives a stimulating reading of the ode's vigor, though he exaggerates its "universal" appeal and fails to reckon sufficiently with the possibility that the audience is invited to view Dicaeopolis's high spirits with a degree of amused detachment. D. Whitehead, *The Demes of Attica* (Princeton, N.J., 1986), 212–22, gives a survey of what is known about the Rural Dionysia. E. Csapo, "Riding the Phallus for Dionysus," *Phoenix* 51 (1997): 253–95, is a wideranging but perhaps overpsychologized study of one kind of phallic ritual in Greek religion.

2. The vocative *hetaire,* "companion," is a feature of traditional hymnic style: see, e.g., *Hymn. Hom. Hermes* 290, 436.

3. C. Patterson, *The Family in Greek History* (Cambridge, Mass., 1998), 121–25, gives one recent view of the scope of the term *moichos.*

4. *Clouds* 1073–75 juxtaposes boys and women in a list with strong symposiac coloring; interestingly, thoughts of adultery soon follow (1076, 1079ff.). Arist. *Soph. El.* 167b9–11 attests a popular association between adultery and nocturnal wandering, though not (apparently) in a komastic context.

5. Cf., e.g., *Eccl.* 260–61. J. Taillardat, *Les images d'Aristophane* (Paris, 1965), 335–37, discusses wrestling imagery in Aristophanes, but he omits the passages from *Acharnians* and *Ecclesiazusae.*

6. The combination of [Xen.] *Ath. Pol.* 1.10, Dem. 21.48, Aeschin. 1.15, and [Dem.] 53.16 suggests (though not unproblematically) that while striking another's slave would in general be unlawful, it could be done with impunity when dealing with a slave caught stealing from one's property. But even if that is so, it is hard to believe that rape was allowed in these circumstances: the action Dicaeopolis envisages would surely count as some sort of assault, perhaps even hybris (despite the difficulties involved in applying this concept to the treatment of slaves: cf. N. Fisher, *Hybris* [Warminster, 1992], 58–60). Hybris is of more general importance for the understanding of Aristophanic protagonists than has been commonly realized. Silk, "Aristophanes as a Lyric Poet," 132–33, while acknowledging (if somewhat coyly) the sexual violence of

the song, seems to miss the point in stating that the girl's servile status "allows [Dicae-opolis] to get away with it." Sexual punishment of a female slave by her own master is a different matter: *Wasps* 768–69 and *Birds* 1253 allude to this possibility.

7. J. Henderson, *The Maculate Muse* (New Haven, Conn., 1975; reprint, with ad-denda, New York, 1991), 59–60: p. 59 contains a series of other misleading statements about sex in the first part of *Acharnians*. A. Bowie, *Aristophanes: Myth, Ritual and Comedy* (Cambridge, 1993), 26, apparently endorsing Henderson's reading of sex in *Acharnians*, reproduces the latter's euphemization of the phallic song by speaking of Dicaeopolis "sing[ing] lyrically of catching a pretty slave-girl stealing."

8. K. Reckford, *Aristophanes' Old-and-New Comedy* (Chapel Hill, N.C., 1987), 457.

9. Plato's suggestion, in *Republic* 10.606c, that the experience of comedy lures the audience into enjoying things they would be ashamed of outside the theater, is highly pertinent here. But for the parallelism with the preceding argument about tragedy (stressed at 606c2) to hold, we need something corresponding to the idea that the mind tells itself that "these are *other people*'s experiences it is watching, and there is nothing shameful for itself" (606b1–2) in enjoying them. This would imply that at least some spectators of comedy do not identify fully with the dramatic agents whose behavior gives them pleasure.

10. Cf. L. M. Stone, *Costume in Aristophanic Comedy* (New York, 1981), 72ff.

11. That particular paradox is anticipated, before the phallic song begins, at 254–56, where Dicaeopolis's anticipation of his daughter's marriage is entirely scurrilous in tone. Lines 259–60 might also be designed to give scope for visual obscenity in rela-tion to the daughter. L. K. Taaffe, *Aristophanes and Women* (London, 1993), 26–27, thinks Dicaeopolis's organization of the procession makes him comparable to the di-rector of a comedy.

12. Heraclitus B15 DK: for a helpful reading of some of the fragment's significance see C. H. Kahn, *The Art and Thought of Heraclitus* (Cambridge, 1979), 264–66. The idea that a religious context can justify or validate *aischrologia*, shameful speech, is found also in both Plato and Aristotle: see S. Halliwell, "Comic Satire and Freedom of Speech in Classical Athens," *Journal of Hellenic Studies* 111 (1991): 67–69.

13. The display of Dicaeopolis's rejuvenated phallus, anticipated at 1147–49, finds generic parallels at *Knights* 1384–95, *Wasps* 1341ff., *Peace* 1351 (cf. 859–67), and *Birds* 1253–56.

14. We can to some extent gauge the impression of Old Comic costuming from the fourth-century south Italian vases (so-called *phlyax* vases), some of which appear to illustrate reperformances of Old Comedies in Magna Graecia. See esp. O. Taplin, *Comic Angels* (Oxford, 1993), with illustrations.

15. Cf. Reckford, *Aristophanes' Old-and-New Comedy*, 59–60. Aristotle's definition of comedy, *Poetics* 4.1449a32–34, focuses on the shameful/ugly (*aischron*), though Aristotle had doubts about the extent to which Old Comedy took the principle: see S. Halliwell, *Aristotle's Poetics* (London, 1986; reprint, 1998), 273–74.

16. *Peace* 847–50 allows the idea that Theoria and Opora were "prostitutes" on Olympus; a sequence of sexual-anatomical jokes follow, up to 909; the slave takes Theoria for a prostitute again at 873–74, and we see his phallus aroused by the sight of the women (879–80). In theatrical terms, we should imagine Theoria, Opora,

Reconciliation, and other similar figures (even Basileia at the end of *Birds*) not as "really" beautiful (I speculate that beauty was always deliberately "disfigured" by the conventions of masking and padding in Old Comedy), but as grotesquely enlarged symbols of female anatomy as perceived through the eyes of "shameless" male libido.

17. Particularly important are *Knights* 427–28, 721, 878–80, 1242, where the idea of anal availability is used to link (and blur) the worlds of political apprenticeship (for the relevant comic-sexual topos cf. *Clouds* 1089, 1093–94, and *Eccl.* 102–4, 112–13) and cheap male prostitution. *Knights* 638–42 is quite different: the bizarre suggestion of J. Davidson, *Courtesans and Fish-Cakes* (London, 1997), 273 (cf. 172), that the sausage seller here "gets buggered. . . . in the courts" (the scene is in fact inside the Boule!), is a total misconstrual of the text.

18. In *Birds* the old men initially fantazise salaciously about sexual liberty (137–42, cf. 669), male gods are thought of as habitual adulterers (556–60), birds are gifts which win sexual gratification for the lovers of boys (705–7), birds' wings are promoted as equipment for adulterers (793–96), and Peisetaerus, satyr-like, threatens Iris herself with rape (1253–56).

19. The term *meirax* seems to be purely a marker of an age range (cf. 696, 1138), and could apply equally to a young prostitute or citizen daughter. A. H. Sommerstein, *Aristophanes Ecclesiazusae* (Warminster, 1998), at 611, suggests Blepyrus is thinking of a *hetaira* but that Praxagora anticipates citizen status for such women too under the new regime; yet having apparently anticipated a blurring of sexual and civic statuses, Sommerstein later ignores the point (his note on 877–1111 appears discrepant); cf. n. 31 below.

20. Probably as a result of the use of *kathezomai* and *kathēmai* for tradesmen's activity, these verbs can be used of prostitutes plying their trade, a point disregarded by the commentators on *Eccl.* 617: see Aeschin. 1.74, 120, Pl. *Chrm.* 163b7–8 (where the connection with low commerce is explicit), [Dem.] 59.67 (ditto), and Isae. 6.19; there may already be an allusion to this usage at Semon. fr. 7.90–91. The idea of women sitting *alongside* one another at *Eccl.* 617 reinforces the evocation of a bordello setting (cf. the row of prostitutes at Xenarchus fr. 4.4–6 *PCG*, and Eubulus frs. 67.4, 82.3). It is even conceivable that there are overtones of a prostitute's style of allure at Ar. *Lys.* 149; cf. Ischomachus's warning to his wife that women who wear cosmetics and "sit around" (*aei kathēmenai*) invite comparison with prostitutes of some sort (euphemistically called "women who adorn themselves and deceive").

21. *Paidopoiein*, "to bear children," is not unequivocal: while the verb (normally in the middle voice with female subjects) sometimes implies the production of (supposedly) citizen offspring (e.g., [Dem.] 59.17, Aeschin. 2.177), it need not do so (cf. [Dem.] 59.122, where the point is properly spelled out).

22. For prostitution at the city gates, see Ar. *Knights* 1400–1402 (with 1242–47 for homosexual prostitution in the same area); in the brothels of Piraeus, see Ar. *Peace* 165, Isae. 6.19, and Aeschin. 1.40, with D. Halperin, *One Hundred Years of Homosexuality* (London, 1990), 183 n. 29, R. Garland, *The Piraeus* (London, 1987), 214.

23. Theophr. *Char.* 28.3. Although Ussher, *Aristophanes Ecclesiazusae*, 175, cites this parallel, his note misses its implications: cf. n. 31 below. Ussher, *The Characters of Theophrastus* (London, 1960), 241, accepts that Theophrastus's slanderer is depicting a particular house as a brothel.

24. Contrary to Ussher, *Aristophanes Ecclesiazusae*, 176, on 718–20, the point about slaves at 721 must be *additional* (as *kai . . . ge* suggests) to the general point about *pornai* at 718–19; but 721 is nonetheless best taken as a reference to slave-prostitutes (compare the use of *hupharpazein*, "snatch," with *sunharpazein* in Theophr. *Char.* 28.3, cited in n. 23). For a different attribution of lines see Sommerstein, *Aristophanes Ecclesiazusae*, on 719–20, though his text, 98, has a change of speaker missing at 721.

25. This is diametrically opposed to the sexual communism of Plato *Republic* 5, where the scheme aims to harness sexual attraction to the eugenic enhancement of the group. On the vexed relationship between *Ecclesiazusae* and *Republic* 5 see S. Halliwell, *Plato Republic 5* (Warminster, 1993), 224–25, with further references; and Sommerstein, *Aristophanes Ecclesiazusae*, 13–18.

26. Praxagora does not of course *purport* to be establishing a new form of prostitution; thus, the verb *charizesthai*, "gratify" (629), is commonly used of granting a lover's desire for sexual intercourse. The prostitutional dimension of her scheme is, so to speak, comically inadvertent; compare the satirical irony of *Wealth* 153–59. "Prostitution is not easily defined": K. J. Dover, "Classical Greek Attitudes to Sexual Behaviour," *Arethusa* 6 (1973): 68.

27. J. Henderson, *Three Plays by Aristophanes* (New York, 1996), 27, makes the same point. No wife in Aristophanes *admits* to adultery; the closest thing—and it is not very close—is perhaps the innuendo of *Lys.* 107.

28. This conjecture implies nothing about the actual incidence of adultery in Athens, on which see J. Roy, "An Alternative Sexual Morality for Classical Athens," *Greece and Rome* 44 (1997): 11–22.

29. Later parts of the scene make more of certain themes, such as the symbolism of death and the underworld; but they are not my concern here.

30. On *paidopoiein*, "to bear children," at 615 cf. n. 21 above.

31. Ussher, *Aristophanes Ecclesiazusae*, xxxii n. 1, cites some older scholars (though the reference to Dale is incorrect) who regarded the women as having the status of courtesans or prostitutes. Ussher's denial ignores the range of details discussed in my text. Likewise with other curt denials, such as T. Gelzer, *RE* Suppl. Band. xii (1971), col. 1497. M. Vetta, *Aristofane: Le Donne all'Assemblea* (Milan, 1989), 234, compromises a little, speaking of "la trasformazione cortigianesca delle donne libere" but denying that the women are prostitutes. K. J. Dover, *Aristophanic Comedy* (Berkeley, 1972), 192, speaks of "members of humble citizen families," but there is nothing in the scene to support this line (though cf. nn. 43, 47 below); Sommerstein, *Aristophanes Ecclesiazusae*, on 877–1111, similarly speaks of a "submerged class of citizen women," while acknowledging their *hetaira*-like behavior (cf. n. 19 above). Henderson, *The Maculate Muse*, 103, 106 n. 61, sees traces of the "whore" and *hetaira* in the behavior of the women; but Henderson, *Three Plays by Aristophanes*, 150, abandons this position, now taking the women to be "widows or spinsters" (cf. the same author's "Older Women in Attic Old Comedy," *Transactions of the American Philological Association* 117 [1987]: 105–29, at 118, referring to the "merry widow" type). H.-G. Nesselrath, *Die Attische Mittlere Komödie* (Berlin, 1990), 319 n. 95, is doubtful whether the females in this scene are to be regarded as *hetairai*. Bowie, *Aristophanes*, 266, thinks age (and its implications for female freedom) the key factor, but he ignores the indications of a demimonde, as does Taaffe, *Aristophanes and Women*, 123–28. N. Slater, "Waiting in the Wings: Aristophanes'

Ecclesiazusae," Arion 5, no. 1 (1997): 115, refers back to Praxagora's abolition of prostitution, but that would be decisive only if "documentary" consistency and the avoidance of category confusion were traits of Aristophanes' work, which is the reverse of the truth.

32. *Oikēma* denoted a building, perhaps sometimes an individual room or booth, used by prostitutes (female or male): see, e.g., Pl. *Chrm.* 163b7–8 (with n. 20 above), Xen. *Mem.* 2.2.4, Aeschin. 1.74, Isae. 6.19, Dinarchus 1.23.

33. Apart from her heavy make-up and diaphanous dress (878–79; see Ussher, *Aristophanes Ecclesiazusae*, ad loc., for a possible association with prostitutes), the first hag may have visible pudenda: see the obscene gesture (exact nature uncertain) at 890, and the girl's gibe at 904, though neither is decisive evidence for the intended costuming. As regards the vexed and much-discussed issues of staging, I take the first hag to be outside a door at 877ff., and the girl at a window at 884.

34. Xenarchus fr. 4.9 *PCG* refers to older alongside younger prostitutes (cf. n. 20 above). Although the sex scene in *Ecclesiazusae* is hideously exaggerated in this respect, there is no doubt that some Athenians may have had a taste for older prostitutes: see Halperin, *One Hundred Years of Homosexuality,* 89–90, with illustrations.

35. Theophr. *Char.* 28.3, Xenarchus fr. 4.13 *PCG*; cf. esp. Ar. *Eccl.* 1020. At Xen. *Mem.* 2.2.4, Socrates speaks hyperbolically of the streets "being full" of prostitution. There is a reference to open streetwalking by prostitutes in the Solonian law attested at Lys. 10.19, [Dem.] 59.67, and Plut. *Sol.* 23.1.

36. *ekkuptein* and *parakuptein* are close to synonymous: Athenian husbands do not want their wives to be caught doing either at the house-door (Ar. *Thesm.* 790, 797–99); and the suspicion or hope of sexual availability mentioned in the second of those references is underlined at *Peace* 979–85. A more oblique consideration is that compounds of *kuptein* lend themselves to glimpses of normally hidden parts of the anatomy: see, e.g., *Frogs* 238, 413, and *Thesm.* 1187b.

37. For this (comic) idea of ripeness cf. Taillardat, *Les images d'Aristophane,* 50, §51, adding Archil. fr. 196A.26 West, where *pepeira* means (sexually) "*over*-ripe."

38. Davidson, *Courtesans and Fish-Cakes,* 93, makes two pertinent suggestions: one, that the scene may be a parody of an erotic show (but he overlooks the relevance of mime: cf. n. 46 below); the other, that there is a likely connection with traditions of singing and wit on the part of *hetairai.* Cf. *Frogs* 1301, 1327–28 for other comic references to the songs of sexual professionals.

39. Cf. the end of the play, 1161–62, where "bad *hetairai*" are said always to remember only the last man they had. The hag's reference to "my lover Epigenes" at 931 also implies a *hetaira*-like status, or, at any rate, the delusion of one; cf. the young man's gibe at 994.

40. I follow the attributions of Ussher, *Aristophanes Ecclesiazusae*, but if 920 is given *to* the girl, as by Vetta, *Aristofane,* 110, the obscenity in her mouth would be a further consideration against her supposed innocence. Cf. the dancing girl stolen from the symposium by Philocleon at *Wasps* 1341ff., where the implication of 1346 is that fellatio would have been unpleasant or demeaning for the woman; cf. the contemptuous use of *laikastria* at *Ach.* 529, 537, and the slave's expectation at *Peace* 855 (with the reference to prostitutes at 849). M. Kilmer, *Greek Erotica* (London, 1993), 114–17,

claims that certain images in Greek vase painting support the inference that fellatio could be regarded as an act undertaken without pleasure, and sometimes only on compulsion, by women. If this is right, it would presumably go along with a view that fellatio was not to be expected from *hetairai* of higher pretensions. But *Lys.* 17 may allude to fellatio in marriage.

41. The girl's supposed citizen status has rarely if ever been questioned: see, e.g., A. H. Sommerstein, "Aristophanes and the Demon Poverty," *Classical Quarterly* 34 (1984): 314–33, at 320 n. 39: "an unmarried citizen girl"; likewise D. MacDowell, *Aristophanes and Athens* (Oxford, 1995), 320: "a girl of citizen birth (not a prostitute or courtesan)." Henderson, *Three Plays by Aristophanes*, 26, at any rate implies a problem: "the horny citizen girl in *Assemblywomen* is a striking anomaly in all of extant comedy." His reference to the absence of the girl's "parents" [*sic*] on 150 is misleading.

42. Cf. in particular the girl's use of *philos* at 953: David Konstan suggests to me that elsewhere such usage is always confined to *hetairai* among female characters in comedy.

43. K. J. Dover, *Greek Homosexuality* (London, 1978), 149–50, treats this as a sign that the girl's family background is poor, thus making chaperoning difficult; cf. n. 31 above.

44. See Xen. *Mem.* 3.11.4, where the implication (tactfully understated) is that the mother retains some supervision of Theodote's life as a *hetaira;* and [Dem.] 59.18–20 (on Neaira and the other "daughters" of Nicarete, where the relationship is, allegedly, adoptive), ibid. 67 (on Neaira and her daughter Phano). Plots involving a young woman under the control of an older, in a household without males, become common in New Comedy: see V. J. Rosivach, *When a Young Man Falls in Love* (London, 1998), 51–75.

45. M. Bowra, "A Love-Duet," *American Journal of Philology* 79 (1958): 376–91 (reprinted in *On Greek Margins* [Oxford, 1970], 149–63). For criticism see S. D. Olson, "The 'Love Duet' in Aristophanes' *Ecclesiazusae*," *Classical Quarterly* 38 (1988): 328–30; and L. P. E. Parker, *The Songs of Aristophanes* (Oxford, 1997), 546 (the latter rather doctrinaire in her view that Aristophanes would not have reproduced popular song types too closely); but the popular song hypothesis is given qualified approval by C. Kugelmeier, *Reflexe früher und zeitgenössicher Lyrik in der Alten attischen Komödie* (Stuttgart, 1996) 144–49. Sommerstein, *Aristophanes Ecclesiazusae*, on 952–75, points out the incongruities of the song on the lips of "a citizen maiden," but does not requestion the latter as a premise.

46. See esp. *PLond. Lit.* 50 for the girl in love, and *POxy.* 413 verso, cols. 1–3: there are short summaries of these and other mimes in I. C. Cunningham, *Herodas: Mimiambi* (Oxford, 1971), 8–10, and texts in the appendix to the same author's Teubner edition of *Herodas Mimiambi* (Leipzig, 1987), 36ff.

47. This is not to deny that the sex scene may trade, at some level of awareness, on a sense of grey areas of Athenian society in which citizen women, for economic or other reasons, might be involved in commercial sex: cf. [Dem.] 59.113 for a forensic orator's (hyperbolic) allusion to such possibilities.

48. Sommerstein, *Aristophanes Ecclesiazusae*, 21, makes the interesting observation that this is the only scene in extant Greek comedy "whose entire cast is peculiar to it and includes no character appearing elsewhere."

49. See esp. S. Said, *"L'assemblée des femmes: Les femmes, l'économie et la politique,"* *Les Cahiers de Fontenay* 17 (1979): 33–69, who appears to find in the play's gradual erosion of Praxagora's utopian promises a rather dark comment on human nature.

50. This and other omissions make it very hard to follow Henderson, *Three Plays by Aristophanes*, 235 n. 104, in supposing that the new sexual regime is designed to "appeal to ordinary men" in Aristophanes' audience. What is appealing to the "ordinary" male psyche about the triumph of grotesque, old females?

51. The main exception is probably female homoeroticism (just hinted at in *Lys.* 79–92?), on which see Dover's contribution to this volume.

52. Ar. *Clouds* 1096–1104 exploits this point for local comic effect.

Chapter Five

THE LEGEND OF THE SACRED BAND

🙚🙚

David Leitao

This chapter aims to take a fresh look at the tradition of the Theban Sacred Band, a fourth-century-B.C.E. military unit that legend suggests was composed entirely of lovers and their beloveds. Scholars have tended to take our sources for this tradition at face value,[1] but if we read these texts with greater sensitivity to their rhetorical strategies, we will discover that the historicity of an erotic Sacred Band rests on the most precarious of foundations. But my goal in problematizing the truthfulness of this tradition is not ultimately to offer decisive proof that Thebes never had an erotically constituted fighting force (although I believe they probably did not), but rather to redirect our attention to the discursive conditions that made it possible for an erotic Sacred Band, based on however small a kernel of historical truth, to take its first steps onto the scene of history.

A BAND OF LOVERS AND BELOVEDS

The Sacred Band (ἱερὸς λόχος in Greek)[2] is described as an elite Theban military force of three hundred men that remained undefeated for about forty years in the middle of the fourth century B.C.E. The band was credited with victories over much larger Spartan forces at Tegyra in 375 and again at Leuctra in 371 and was eventually annihilated by the forces of Philip at

Chaeronea in 338.[3] A few scholars have detected references to the Sacred Band that fall outside this period. Some point to a passage in Diodorus that describes a special Theban force of three hundred composed of "charioteers and footmen" [ἡνίοχοι καὶ παραβάται][4] that fought at the front of the line at the Battle of Delium in 424: these were probably originally pairs of men who fought from chariots in the Homeric fashion, although in 424 they were clearly fighting as hoplites.[5] Others have pointed to a third-century epigram by Phaedimus in which Apollo of Schoenus (a village near Thebes) is asked to "direct an arrow of Eros at these youths [ἠίθεοι] in order that they defend their fatherland, emboldened by the friendship of young men [φιλό-τατι κούρων]" (Anth. Pal. 13.22.4–6).[6] Neither passage, however, mentions the Sacred Band by name, and the poem by Phaedimus may be alluding to the tradition of an earlier Sacred Band or even be invoking a more generic topos about the role of eros in binding a fighting force together (more in "Utopian Philosophy" below).

Our primary focus in this chapter is the tradition that the Sacred Band was composed of pairs of lovers and their beloveds, and it will be useful, before we begin to examine the sources for this tradition, to consider just what this means. It surely does not mean simply that pederastic affairs were permitted to intrude on army life at Thebes, as such intrusions were apparently not uncommon in Greek armies. We hear, for example, of Greek soldiers on campaign quarreling over paidika or pursuing boys who happened to be in camp or in a village nearby.[7] Occasionally paidika are described as being present during battle itself, but when our sources are specific about what they are doing there it often turns out that they are not actively engaged in fighting. Xenophon's account of the Spartan general Anaxibius and his beloved at Cremaste in 389 B.C.E. is illustrative. Anaxibius and twelve Spartan harmosts are said to have "died fighting" [μαχόμενος ἀποθνήσκει and μαχόμενοι συναπέθανον, respectively], whereas Anaxibius's beloved, whose fate is described between that of Anaxibius and the harmosts, is said merely to have "remained by [Anaxibius's] side" [αὐτῷ παρέμεινε] (Hell. 4.8.39). Xenophon does not say that the boy was a regular in the army,[8] nor would we expect him to be: boys who were still young enough to be eromenoi were generally not old enough to be part of the muster.[9] The boy's presence in some such cases may perhaps be explained by a desire on his part to witness the battle.[10] So while there are a number of texts that mention the presence of paidika on campaign, they point to nothing more than a sporadic and ad hoc practice and suggest that in many cases, at least, the youth was present not as a regular hoplite, but for other reasons.[11] There was also another way in which the institution of pederasty manifested itself in the army, and that was through the presence of former lovers and beloveds in the same unit. This was doubtless the case of Alcibiades and Socrates on campaign at Potidaea (432) and later Delium (424), and Plato hints at the salutary effect the presence of each had on the other.[12] But our sources for the Sacred Band describe a phenomenon quite different from these ordinary pederastic intrusions on army life: (1) the Theban Sacred Band seems to have been composed *exclusively* of pairs of lovers and beloveds,[13] and (2) these pairs were presumably involved in an active and ongoing relationship of an intense emotional, if not sexual, nature.[14] A Sacred Band so constituted would have been radical indeed.

Even for Thebes. Classical Thebes was known for its local pederastic customs. Plutarch tells us that lovers presented their beloveds with suits of armor when the latter were inscribed on the citizen rolls, and Aristotle records that lovers and beloveds swore oaths at the tomb of Iolaus.[15] But while these ethnographic details are not inconsistent with the existence of an erotically constituted military band, neither do they entail such an institution. The presentation of armor obviously marked the beloved's passage from boyhood to manhood and thus, quite likely, the *end* of the pederastic tie, as did a similar custom reported for classical Crete; the oath reported by Aristotle, possibly a citizenship oath, may have taken place on the same occasion.[16] Indeed, Theban gift giving and oath swearing were perfectly compatible with the pederastic norms of other Greek cities, especially Sparta and the cities of Crete, where pederastic practices were more thoroughly institutionalized. An army of lovers and beloveds would have been a different story.

THE SOURCES FOR THE SACRED BAND

The texts that explicitly mention an erotic Sacred Band are surprisingly few and late and are all of questionable historical value. Plutarch himself, who is the author of our fullest account of the origin and exploits of the Sacred Band, suggests that of those writers who wrote about the Sacred Band, only a minority (ἔνιοι, "some"; *Pel.* 18.2) claimed that it was erotically constituted. And his view is to some extent reflected in the texts that survive: there are eleven texts by nine different authors that refer explicitly to a Theban Sacred Band,[17] and six mention an erotic composition. Moreover, there is a clear genre distinction between those texts that mention an erotic Sacred Band and those that mention a nonerotic battalion. The latter all derive from a pro-Boeotian historiographical tradition that originated in the second half of the fourth century B.C.E. Plutarch's *Life of Pelopidas* (except chapters 18–19, see more in this section below) draws on Callisthenes, and the reference at *Life of Alexander* 9.2 may as well; Diodorus is based for the most part on Ephorus, but many scholars have argued that the passage in which Diodorus mentions the Sacred Band by name (the so-called elegy of Pelopidas) comes directly from Callisthenes; Cornelius Nepos is dependent on either Callisthenes or Ephorus; and Dinarchus mentions the Sacred Band in a speech delivered in 323, very likely under the influence of Callisthenes' *Hellenica* or Ephorus's *Historia*, both of which had been published only a few years before.[18] All five sources for the nonerotic tradition, then, can be traced back to the pro-Boeotian histories of Callisthenes and Ephorus.

The six texts that mention an erotic Sacred Band—Hieronymus of Rhodes, Dio Chrysostom, Plutarch (*Pel.* 18–19), Polyaenus, Maximus of Tyre, and Athenaeus—are what we might call "moralistic" texts, and most of these seem to draw on a tradition of writing about *eros* that goes back to the early fourth century. We may start with chapters 18 and 19 of Plutarch's *Pelopidas*, our most extensive source for the Sacred Band. Although Plutarch's main source for the *Life of Pelopidas* as a whole seems to be Callisthenes, it has been shown that his digression on the Sacred Band (chaps. 18–19), introduced ominously by "as they say" [ὥς φασι], actually derives from a work on *eros*.[19] The evidence is worth considering briefly. Two of the anecdotes in the digression turn up also in Plutarch's *Amatorius*.[20] Another anecdote—this one about the bravery of a Theban lover on the battlefield—is told of a Cretan in Aelian's *De Natura Animalium* (4.1), in a passage in which Aelian discusses the erotic protocols of partridges and Cretans. Finally, Plutarch attempts to explain the sacredness of the Sacred Band by referring to Plato's designation of the lover as an *entheos philos*, "divinely inspired friend." This exact phrase turns up in the *Phaedrus* (255b), where Plato claims that neither relatives nor friends can offer the true friendship that a "divinely inspired friend" can. But the term *entheos* also turns up twice in the speech of Phaedrus in the *Symposium* (179a, 180b), the first of these in the context of proposing to create a city or army out of pairs of lovers and their beloveds. This is almost certainly the Platonic passage Plutarch here has in mind, and it is not the only probable allusion to Plato's *Symposium* in this digression.[21] Plutarch's knowledge of the erotic tradition of the Sacred Band, then, appears not to derive from local Boeotian historians, as some have argued, or even from Callisthenes or Ephorus, but from a tradition of writing about *eros* that goes all the way back to Plato.[22]

The other five texts that describe an erotic Sacred Band exhibit similar generic affiliations. The eighteenth *dissertatio* of Maximus of Tyre is a defense of Socrates' vision of chaste pederastic love. Hieronymus of Rhodes, who in fragment 34 describes the historical role played by pederastic couples in resisting tyranny, derives his examples, according to Wehrli, from an earlier work on *eros*.[23] This certainly is the origin of Athenaeus 561c–562a, which is an extended discussion of the role of Eros as promoter of civic and military cohesion. The twenty-second oration of Dio Chrysostom is a discussion of how the philosopher would manage the state, and the philosophical Epaminondas is cited for stationing lovers beside beloveds "in order that they . . . be witnesses of each other's bravery and cowardice" (22.2). The effects of shame on the warrior's comportment was a theme taken up already by Plato in the *Symposium,* and there are hints here also of the *Republic* written by the Stoic Zeno, who appears to have advocated binding citizens to each other through bonds of *philia* created by *eros* (more in "Utopian Philosophy" below). Polyaenus, finally, the second-century-C.E. strategical writer, might seem to be the exception, but as we shall see shortly, his source for the Sacred Band is probably ultimately a utopian philosophical text.

But it is not only the erotic element of the tradition that we ought to view with caution: there is evidence that even the historiographical texts, which mention a nonerotic Sacred Band, have greatly exaggerated the role played by the Sacred Band in the key battles of Tegyra, Leuctra, and Chaeronea. The Battle of Tegyra (375 B.C.E.), for instance, the first great victory of the new Theban army over a much larger Spartan adversary, is considerably embellished by Callisthenes. Ephorus, whose account is preserved by Diodorus, describes a victory of five hundred Theban picked troops (ἐπίλεκτοι ἄνδρες) over twice as many Spartans (Diod. 15.37.1). In Callisthenes' account, as it is preserved by Plutarch, the Thebans overcome odds in excess of four to one: three hundred members of the Sacred Band and a few cavalry defeat an enemy that "far exceeded them in number" [ὑπερβάλλοντας πλήθει], a number we know Callisthenes put at fourteen hundred Spartans.[24] And credit for the victory belongs to Pelopidas and his Sacred Band alone. Ephorus's account differs from Callisthenes' in four significant respects. First, the picked men are not referred to as the Sacred Band. Second, the number of these picked troops is five hundred, not three hundred, the conventional number given in most of the sources that mention the Sacred Band by name. Third, the battle is not identified geographically with the village of Tegyra, but with Orchomenus, the larger city nearby, where the defeated Spartan army was based. Fourth, Pelopidas is not even mentioned, let alone credited with the victory.[25] The conclusion is obvious: Callisthenes' version exaggerates the magnitude of the victory in the interest of Theban panegyric and exaggerates, if not invents, the role of Pelopidas and the

Sacred Band.[26] We need not doubt that a special corps of picked troops fought for the Thebans at Tegyra: many Greek armies in the fifth and fourth centuries employed crack forces. But there is reason to wonder whether it was the Sacred Band under the leadership of Pelopidas.

Accounts of the Battle of Leuctra also show signs of tinkering. There are four major accounts of the battle—Callisthenes, Ephorus, Xenophon, and Pausanias—but only one attributes a role to Pelopidas and mentions the Sacred Band by name, and once again that is Callisthenes.[27] Ephorus, as epitomized in Diodorus, credits the entire success at Leuctra to Epaminondas's "oblique phalanx formation" and the resulting engagement of a single wing, which he had manned by "picking out the best men from the whole army" [ἐκλεξάμενος . . . ἐξ ἁπάσης τῆς δυνάμεως τοὺς ἀρίστους] (15.55.2). Is this a reference to the Sacred Band? Possibly. And yet, once again, the Sacred Band is not mentioned by name; no specific number of "picked troops" is given; they appear to be "picked" for this specific occasion; and they have nothing to do with Pelopidas. Xenophon's silence on the presence of the Sacred Band (and on the tactical innovations Ephorus and others attributed to Epaminondas) is more compelling still: some scholars have cried foul, alleging that Xenophon was anti-Theban and sought any opportunity to diminish the accomplishments of the Theban hegemony, but recently Victor Hanson has demonstrated, decisively in my mind, that Xenophon's account is accurate and sensitive to the tactical realities of fourth-century warfare, and that the accounts of Ephorus and Callisthenes, two men whose grasp of military affairs was ridiculed in antiquity, aimed to embellish the achievements of Epaminondas and Pelopidas, respectively.[28] It seems clear that Pelopidas and the Sacred Band do not appear in the accounts of Xenophon and Pausanias for the same reason that they are absent from the fourth-century account of Ephorus: the Sacred Band was not thought to have played any (special) role at Leuctra.

Evidence for the role of the Sacred Band at the Battle of Chaeronea is perhaps the most tenuous of all, as the tradition is recorded by Plutarch alone, at *Pelopidas* 18.5 and at *Alexander* 9.2, both notices introduced by a qualifying "it is said" [λέγεται]. A comparison between the account of Plutarch and that of Diodorus, our fullest source for the battle, is revealing. Both accounts describe a battle that pitted Philip against Athenians on the right side of the Macedonian line, and Alexander against Thebans on the left side of the line. And both credit the young Alexander with a decisive move, Diodorus claiming that he was the first to break the continuity of the enemy line (16.86.3), Plutarch that he was the first to break the ranks of the Sacred Band (*Alex.* 9.2). It is tempting to see this as an attempt by Plutarch's

ultimate (pro-Alexandrian) source to embellish this youthful victory of Alexander's by characterizing it as a victory over not just any Thebans, but the
most impressive fighting force Thebes was ever known to have fielded. While
Plutarch, himself a native of Chaeronea, would doubtless have had access
to local sources for the battle of 338, he seems clearly to draw here, once
again, on fourth-century sources. And Callisthenes of Olynthus, whom Plutarch cites by name at *Alexander* 27.4, 33.1, and 33.10 and at *Pelopidas* 17.2,
who seems unique in his presentation simultaneously of a pro-Theban and
pro-Alexandrian perspective, and who, as we have seen already, is intimately
associated with the early tradition of the Sacred Band, is a good candidate.[29] Interestingly, it is on the basis of these brief notices in Plutarch on
the presence of the Sacred Band at Chaeronea that a number of modern
scholars have supposed that the Lion Monument discovered at Chaeronea
at the beginning of the twentieth century marks the burial site of the Sacred
Band and that the skeletons of 254 men found buried within the enclosure
of the monument are their bodies.[30] But the inference seems hardly justified when Plutarch, our only source for the presence of the Sacred Band at
Chaeronea and himself a native of the town, does not mention the monument, and Pausanias, who saw it and presumably reports local tradition,
states only that it marks the burial site of "the Thebans who died in the
struggle against Philip."[31]

Plutarch is our most important conduit for the tradition of the Sacred
Band, and yet even he seems to hesitate to vouch for the historicity of a
specifically erotic band. In his *Amatorius*, for example, where he lists several
examples in which *eros* promotes military valor, he fails to mention the Sacred Band by name or even, it seems, allude to it. He does mention four
other examples of military *eros* at Thebes: (1) the practice whereby Theban
lovers presented suits of armor to their beloveds when the latter were inscribed onto the citizen rolls, (2) the customary oaths sworn by Theban
lovers and their beloveds at the tomb of Iolaus, (3) Epaminondas's two beloveds and his death on the battlefield near one of them, and (4) the Theban Pammenes' playful criticism of Homer for failing to station lovers beside beloveds and Pammenes' subsequent change in the order of the battle
line (ἤλλαξε δὲ καὶ μετέθηκε τάξιν τῶν ὁπλιτῶν). All four traditions are
perfectly consistent with the erotic tradition of the Sacred Band, and yet
none necessarily entails the existence of a Sacred Band composed exclusively of lovers and beloveds. The Pammenes anecdote comes closest, but
we cannot be sure that Pammenes' new formation was erotic (the emphasis in Plutarch's three versions of the anecdote is always the humorous criticism of Homer), and even if it was, there is no indication that the change

was anything more than an ad hoc formation for a particular occasion. Moreover, when Plutarch mentions the Pammenes anecdote at *Quaestiones Conviviales* 618cd, he credits Epaminondas [32] with the actual change in battle formation (whatever it was) and then proceeds to use it to make a playful argument about banquet seating. That Plutarch in the *Amatorius* does not mention the name of Thebes's erotic army or its early leaders Gorgidas and Pelopidas is a bit puzzling and makes us suspect that even for Plutarch the legend of the Sacred Band was most at home in the panegyric tradition surrounding Pelopidas.

And yet even when it comes time to present his panegyric history in the *Life of Pelopidas*, Plutarch finds it necessary to distance himself from the erotic tradition of the Sacred Band by recourse to an unusual number of qualifiers: [33] ὥς φασι ("as they say"; 8.1) introduces the entire digression on the Sacred Band, ἔνιοι δέ φασιν ("some say"; 18.1) introduces the minority tradition that it was erotically constituted, λέγεται ("it is said"; 18.4) introduces an erotic version of the myth of Iolaus and Heracles, εἰκός ("it is probable"; 18.4) introduces his dubious Platonic etymology of the name of the Sacred Band, and λέγεται ("it is said"; 18.5) introduces the claim that the Sacred Band remained undefeated until Chaeronea and the anecdote about Philip on the battlefield. Indeed, such qualifiers seem almost to be part of the tradition itself. Already Dinarchus, our earliest reference to the Sacred Band (and a nonerotic one), presents the legend of the Sacred Band as "stories" [*logoi*] told by his "elders" [*presbuteroi*] and further qualifies his reference to Pelopidas's leadership of the band with "as they say" [ὥς φασιν] (1.72–73). Likewise, Dio Chrysostom introduces his mention of an erotic Sacred Band with λέγεται (22.2). Plutarch, for his part, seems willing to report the traditions associated with the Sacred Band in his moralizing biography of Pelopidas but simultaneously maintains his distance from them, especially the tradition about its erotic composition.

We have noticed two interesting things about the texts that refer explicitly to a Theban Sacred Band. First, the role of the band at Tegyra, Leuctra, and Chaeronea seems to have been picked up in just one strand of Greek historical writing about the Theban hegemony, a strand that seems to go back to Callisthenes of Olynthus. It is pointless to speculate about why Callisthenes might have insisted on a special role for the Sacred Band, when the accounts of Xenophon, Ephorus, and Pausanias were silent: it might have been a desire, as Fuscagni and Sordi have argued, to fashion Pelopidas into a Greek prototype for Philip II, whose panhellenic foreign policy to some extent followed in the footsteps of Pelopidas and Epaminondas. [34] It seems that legends frequently grew up about special military bands: sometimes nonexistent bands were invented, as Thucydides alleges happened in the case of Sparta's so-called Pitanate *lochos* (1.20.3),[35] and sometimes the activities of actual bands were embellished. Callisthenes' account of the Sacred Band was, at the very least, an embellished account. Second, we noticed that among those sources that do mention a Theban Sacred Band, it is only in what we might call the more moralistic texts — Hieronymus of Rhodes, Dio Chrysostom, Plutarch (*Pel.* 18–19), Polyaenus, Maximus of Tyre, and Athenaeus — that we hear of the band's erotic composition. The silence of historiography and related genres cannot be explained in terms of genre incompatibility. The historians routinely describe the composition of Greek armies where the composition is noteworthy and do not eschew the erotic when this plays a significant role in historical developments: Xenophon in the *Hellenica*, to take an example we have already discussed, is not at all reticent about mentioning the presence of *paidika* in army life and on the battlefield.[36] The failure of the erotic Sacred Band to make it into the historical tradition leads one to suspect that it was not considered "historical" by writers who were most concerned with that sort of "truth".

Plato and Xenophon

With these doubts about the later tradition of the Sacred Band in mind, let us turn now to two important earlier texts in which some scholars have detected allusions to an erotic Sacred Band: the *Symposia* of Plato and Xenophon. Plato's Phaedrus caps his discussion of the civic benefits of *eros* with what must have struck his auditors as a novel proposal: "If it could be contrived that a city or an army be formed of lovers and beloveds, there is no way that men could establish their city on a better footing than they would by avoiding all disgrace and by striving to outdo each other in honor. Why such men fighting together, even if few in number, would defeat practically the whole world" (Pl. *Symp.* 178e–179a). Xenophon's Socrates, as if replying to Plato's Phaedrus, argues that sexual relationships between men and boys do *not* provide a context for the performance of brave deeds: "And yet Pausanias, lover of the poet Agathon, has said, in defending those who wallow in lack of self-control [*akrasia*], that an army composed of lovers and beloveds would be especially strong. For he said he thought that these men would be especially ashamed to abandon one another, a remarkable thing to say, that men accustomed to ignore criticism and to behave shamelessly [ἀναισχυντεῖν] toward each other [sc. sexually] would be ashamed [αἰσχυνοῦνται] to commit a shameful act [αἰσχρόν τι] [sc. in battle]. And he used to bring forth as evidence the fact that the Thebans and Eleans have come to these conclusions [ταῦτα ἐγνωκότες]: he said that they arrange their *paidika* beside themselves in battle even though they are sleeping with them" (Xen. *Symp.* 8.32–34). Dover thought that the relative chronology of these two texts and their possible relation to historical developments at Thebes was crucial. He dated Plato's *Symposium* on internal grounds to after 385 and observed that the first activities that tradition ascribes to the Sacred Band can be dated to 375. Detecting an explicit allusion to an erotic Sacred Band in Xenophon, but not in Plato, he judged that Xenophon's *Symposium* must postdate Plato's, and that the Sacred Band must have been founded at some time between the publication dates of the two works.[37] But this argument, which has been remarkably influential, suffers from two serious weaknesses. First, Plato's failure to mention Thebes in connection with Phaedrus's fantasy of a city or army of lovers and beloveds need not imply that the Sacred Band was not yet in existence: it is quite possible that he consciously avoided mentioning a new Sacred Band by name in order to maintain the fiction of his dramatic date of 416, confident that his sophisticated reader would still "get" the allusion to contemporary Theban practice. Second, and more important, Dover's relative dating of the two texts and the foundation of the Sacred Band depends on his assumption that Xenophon's *Symposium* constitutes good evidence for the existence of an erotic army at Thebes. We have already seen that the later tradition of an erotic Sacred Band rests on shaky foundations; any doubts about the evidentiary value of this passage would threaten to render Dover's chronological argument circular.[38]

So what does the passage from Xenophon tell us about the military practices of the Thebans? We should keep in mind, first of all, that this passage does not refer to the Sacred Band by name. Furthermore, whatever it is that the Thebans and Eleans do, it is represented as being different—at least quantitatively and possibly also qualitatively—from a fighting force (στράτευμα) composed exclusively of lovers and beloveds: the military practices of the Thebans and Eleans are offered as an *analogy* to justify attempting what Pausanias presents as a utopian experiment (cf. ἂν γένοιτο). Why propose creating a an army of lovers and beloveds if that very thing already exists? Now let us consider the way that Socrates represents Pausanias's claim about the Thebans and Eleans: they station beside themselves youths with whom they are *currently* sleeping.[39] The presence of *paidika* on campaign, as we have seen, is not unknown: in the *Hellenica*, Xenophon described the death of the Spartan commander Anaxibius near his beloved, and here in Xenophon's *Symposium*, just after the passage quoted above, Socrates implies that Spartan lovers were sometimes stationed near their

beloveds when he states that Spartan youths fight bravely "even among foreigners and whenever they are not stationed in the same place as their lover"
[καὶ μετὰ ξένων κἂν μὴ ἐν τῇ αὐτῇ [πόλει] ταχθῶσι τῷ ἐραστῇ] (Xen. Symp.
8.35).[40] What Socrates considers noteworthy about the Thebans and Eleans,
in contrast to the Spartans, is that they pursue a distinctly carnal interest in
their beloveds (8.34–35): men in all three cities—Thebes, Elis, and Sparta
—are represented as sometimes stationing themselves near their beloveds,
but the Thebans and Eleans do this "even though they are sleeping with
them [συγκαθεύδοντας γοῦν]."

It is the carnality of Theban and Elean pederasty that Pausanias finds
useful in his attempt to justify his utopian proposal for creating a fighting
force of carnal lovers and beloveds. His argument is indeed just one in a series of arguments that apologists for conventional pederasty have advanced
to justify their carnal desires, and Socrates is prepared to combat them one
by one through a combination of peremptory denial and rational argument.[41] In response to the argument that Ganymede was the catamite of
Zeus, Socrates insists that Zeus loved Ganymede not for his body, but for
his mind (psychē), and brings forth as proof both an etymology of Ganymede's name ("taking pleasure [ganu-] in the mind [mēd-]") and the claim
that Ganymede was the only one of Zeus's loves who was made immortal
(Xen. Symp. 8.29–30). And he attacks the argument that Achilles and Patroclus and other heroic pairs were conventional pederastic couples[42] by
denying that Homer made Patroclus a paidika and arguing that it is perverse
to think that heroes would be motivated to perform great deeds because
they slept with each other (συγκαθεύδειν, the same word that was used of
the carnal interests of the Thebans and Eleans) (8.31).

Socrates adopts a similar approach to Pausanias's claims about eros and
military valor. He begins by emphasizing the physicality of the love that
Pausanias advocates—thus, Pausanias himself is described as an "apologist
[ἀπολογούμενος] for those who wallow in lack of self-control [akrasia]"
(8.32)—and proceeds to use this prejudicial characterization to attack Pausanias's general argument about the salutary effect of shame in motivating
battlefield bravery in lover and beloved: it is impossible, Socrates argues, to
believe that men so devoted to shameless conduct in the bedroom would
avoid shameless conduct on the battlefield in the presence of their paidika
(8.33). Socrates' argument, then, seizes on the carnality of Pausanias's lovers
in arms ("even though they are sleeping with them"), not the wisdom of
ranging lovers and paidika side by side in battle. Socrates then turns to Pausanias's claims about the military practices of the Thebans and Eleans. He
first suggests that the Thebans and Eleans are not relevant to their discussion

of Athenian *eros*, since those peoples are subject to a very different morality: carnal pederasty is "customary [νόμιμα] for them, blameworthy [ἐπονείδιστα] among us" (8.34). In Plato's *Symposium*, the erotic otherness of the Thebans and Eleans was invoked by none other than Pausanias as a way to justify the "complicated" [ποικίλος] approach of the Athenians (Pl. *Symp.* 182a); in Xenophon, Socrates deliciously turns a version of the same argument against Pausanias himself. Socrates' second assault on Pausanias's Theban and Elean "evidence" is to suggest that, far from promoting military valor, their practice seems to indicate that lovers in these cities do not trust their *paidika* to behave virtuously; Spartan youths, by contrast, do not need to be stationed beside their lovers in order to fight bravely (Xen. *Symp.* 8.34–35). Rather than deny the truth of Pausanias's so-called evidence from Thebes and Elis, Socrates essentially stipulates to it (with a distancing "he said") for the sake of argument and then proceeds to attack Pausanias's position on moralistic grounds.

Pausanias's reference to Elis alongside Thebes is another clue that the primary function of this "evidence" is to deliver rhetorical punch. For while there is an elaborate later tradition about an erotic battalion at Thebes, there is not a single piece of evidence that corroborates Pausanias's claim about the Elean military.[43] This "Elis" is not a place about which Pausanias has authentic knowledge, and neither, in this context, is "Thebes." The pair "Thebes and Elis" functioned as a symbol of sexual permissiveness within Athenian debates about pederasty, just as "Sparta" frequently functioned as a symbol of sexual self-restraint. Xenophon, in his *Constitution of the Lacedaemonians*, uses the Boeotians and Eleans as foils for the purely platonic friendships between Spartan men and boys: here the Boeotians are imagined as having intercourse with boys as "married" pairs (συζυγέντες ὁμιλοῦσιν) and the Eleans as obtaining physical gratification from boys in exchange for gifts (2.12–13). It is interesting that here, where Xenophon speaks in his own name, he makes no mention of erotic *military* customs for either Thebes or Elis. Plato in the *Symposium* deploys "Boeotians" and "Eleans" in a very similar way, there as foils for the "moral problematization" characteristic of Athenian and Spartan pederasty (Pl. *Symp.* 182b). When one refers to "Thebes and Elis" in Athenian discussions of *paiderastia*, one is not invoking authentic knowledge of these places, but rather an ethnographic, cultural "knowledge".[44] One can no more believe that Thebans and Eleans were completely lacking in sexual self-control than that the Spartans never got past first base (pace Xenophon) or that more than a handful of Athenians ruined sex with "moral problematization" (pace Plato). For the Athenians, whose stage was graced by the likes of Laius and Oedipus, "Thebes" in particular represented an erotic "other."[45]

It is tempting to suggest that Socrates has chosen to focus on an apologetic argument about the military practices of the Thebans and Eleans (rather than, say, an apologetic argument about the tyrant slayers at Athens) because Thebes and Elis were such easy targets for his attack on sexual relationships between men and boys. The real Pausanias might well have made the arguments Socrates attributes to him. But the similarity between Pausanias's general claim about the salutary effects of erotic *taxis* and that articulated by Phaedrus in Plato's *Symposium* suggest that the fantasy was in the public domain, and that different authors might attribute the sentiment to different speakers for rhetorical effect. And it is not difficult to guess at Xenophon's motivation in attributing the idea to Pausanias, whom he introduces as "the lover of the poet Agathon": the relationship between Pausanias and Agathon was notorious not only for continuing long after Agathon became a man, but also for remaining an unabashedly sexual one.[46]

So what is the status of Pausanias's claim about the military practices of the Thebans and Eleans? I would argue that it has about the same status as the argument that Homer's Achilles and Patroclus were lovers. Both are the fantasies of an apologist for conventional pederasty. Although there were some who believed that Achilles and Patroclus were indeed lovers (they could look to Aeschylus for support), many others felt that this was a misreading of Homer. So too the argument about the erotic military customs of the Thebans and Eleans. I suspect that someone had given an erotic interpretation to some actual feature of Theban military life, and that this conscious eroticization came to be repeated, by some still as fantasy and by others now as fact. Was there a Theban institution ripe for reimagining along erotic lines? One possibility is the custom whereby Theban lovers presented their beloveds with suits of armor when the latter came of age. Another possibility is the elite pairs of "charioteers and footmen" that Diodorus tells us fought at Delium. We have "pairs of men" in an elite band at Thebes, the home of Laius and of carnal excess: the inference that these pairs were erotic was easily made.[47]

But not everyone accepted this fanciful erotic interpretation of Theban military customs. Xenophon was surely one. Xenophon was a military expert and can be expected to have had good information about the military organizations of other states. Not only does Xenophon not speak in his own name in the *Symposium*,[48] but when he does speak in propria persona in the *Hellenica*, for instance, he has nothing to say about an erotic Theban army.

This in spite of the fact that he devotes countless pages in the *Hellenica* to the activities of the Theban military during the years from 375 until 362, years that the Sacred Band was supposedly active, sometimes giving great detail about the constitution of the battle line. Alleged anti-Theban bias is probably, as we have seen, a red herring: Ephorus's pro-Theban account also does not mention any Sacred Band, much less an erotic one. Xenophon's Socrates might stipulate to Pausanias's "evidence" of erotic military traditions in Thebes and Elis in order to make out an argument against carnal love. But this is not a tradition Xenophon the military historian puts any stock in.

There is even less reason to suppose that Plato is alluding to an erotic Sacred Band. Arguments that Plato does, through Phaedrus, allude to an erotic Sacred Band have always depended ultimately on the reliability of the Sacred Band tradition as a whole and of Xenophon's "evidence" for it in particular. But with that tradition in doubt and with no explicit reference in Phaedrus's speech to Thebes or Boeotia, it seems far wiser to look elsewhere for a context for Phaedrus's proposal. In fact, the notion that the presence of one's beloved brings the best out of a man was something of a topos in fourth-century Athenian moral discourse. Xenophon himself speaks approvingly of the general concept in his treatise *On Hunting* (12.20), and Plato makes use of the idea in a more political context in book 5 of the *Republic*, where Socrates proposes that men who distinguish themselves in battle (ἀριστεύσαντα) be given the privilege of kissing and being kissed by anyone they wish from among the boys and lads who accompany them on campaign (ὑπὸ τῶν συστρατευομένων μειρακίων τε καὶ παίδων) (468bc). The scenario envisioned here is a bit different from the one envisioned in the *Symposia* of Plato and Xenophon, for *eros* is imagined to motivate valiant behavior in the adult lover alone. The presence of boys and lads on campaign (συστρατευομένων) in this fanciful passage from the *Republic* does not, of course, mean that *paides* and *meirakia* served in the Athenian or any other fourth-century army, unless we are prepared to accept Plato's reference to women on campaign (*Rep.* 471d) as a reflection of reality. Plato here, and in Phaedrus's speech in the *Symposium*, thinks of the army as a model of the polis as a whole, an equation that was not uncommon in Greek utopian thought.[49]

This brings us to another observation about Phaedrus's proposal in Plato's *Symposium*: it is distinctly utopian in form. It is an example of a generic argument attested in Herodotus, Thucydides, and elsewhere in Plato that takes the form "if state X were governed according to principle Y, it would be the strongest and most unified in the world."[50] In the next section, we shall consider how this utopian form of argument became attached to notions about the salutary effects of *eros*, but first I would like to return briefly to the testimony of Polyaenus. We might be inclined to trust the author of a work called *Stratēgēmata* [Military stratagems] when he tells us that the Sacred Band was composed of pairs of lovers and beloveds. But consider the language he employs: "The band was three hundred lovers and beloveds. Because they loved each other, they would [ἂν] never flee, but would either die on behalf of each other or would defeat the enemy" (2.5.1). The lack of historical specificity in this report is foreign to the practice of Polyaenus, who generally provides straightforward battle narratives, including in his numerous anecdotes about Leuctra and Chaeronea.[51] It is the potential optative, really, that gives him away: this passage, which poses as a quasi-historical anecdote, is really just a reframing of Phaedrus's utopian vision, except that whereas the Thebans were originally brought forth (e.g., by Xenophon's Pausanias) as fanciful evidence to support such a utopian proposal, the Theban Sacred Band has now come to embody it.[52]

UTOPIAN PHILOSOPHY AND THE SACRED BAND

If the legend of the Sacred Band acquired much of its character from the panegyric history of Callisthenes and his local Boeotian sources, it seems to have acquired its erotic content from one remarkably influential strand of fourth-century political philosophy. There are hints of the role philosophy would play in the shaping of Theban history already in Pausanias's clever use of "evidence" about Thebes and Elis, but the full effects of this philosophical intervention are not felt until somewhat later and are discernable by us first in the third-century Peripatetic philosopher Hieronymus of Rhodes.

Hieronymus placed the Sacred Band at the head of a list of examples in which *paiderastia* helped to bring down tyranny (fr. 34 Wehrli).[53] What does the Sacred Band have to do with the toppling of tyrannies? Maximus of Tyre, in his digression on Thebes's "sacred band of love," explains: just as Harmodius and Aristogeiton liberated Athens from the Pisistratids, so Epaminondas "liberated Thebes from Spartan rule through an erotic stratagem" (18.2). It is not clear whether Maximus is thinking here of Tegyra and Leuctra, battles that led to the expulsion of the Spartans from Boeotia, or possibly to the liberation of the Cadmea from the Spartan garrison in 379, a success that was more widely credited to another famous stratagem, this one involving beardless youths dressed as women.[54] What is important is that certain activities of the Sacred Band in the 370s had become refashioned as examples of resistance to tyranny. Hieronymus's reference to the role of the philosophical Epaminondas suggests that he too was thinking, at least in part, of the Sacred Band's liberation of Boeotia from Spartan rule in the 370s. But he may also have had in mind another tyrannical adversary. For one of the other examples Hieronymus gave of pederastic couples who resisted tyranny was the pair Chariton and Melanippus, who attempted to assassinate Phalaris, the sixth-century tyrant of Acragas; when their plan was foiled, they so impressed Phalaris with their bravery under torture that he released the two with praise. This story is interesting because a structurally similar tale is told by Plutarch in connection with the Sacred Band: so moved was Philip at the sight of the fallen bodies of three hundred lovers and beloveds at Chaeronea that he declared, "May those who think these men did or suffered anything disgraceful perish miserably!" (*Pel.* 18.5).[55] Philip here is presented as a sort of tyrant figure who, like the Sicilian tyrant Phalaris, is moved by the sight of men and youths joined together in love for each other and for freedom. It is tempting to think that Hieronymus had in mind also this stand of the Sacred Band against Philip at Chaeronea when he ranked the Sacred Band first in a list of lovers who resisted tyranny.

Hieronymus's views about the political advantages of pederastic love have a respectable philosophical pedigree. The idea that men bound to one another by love are the staunchest defenders of liberty was articulated in the fourth century by Heraclides Ponticus (fr. 65 Wehrli) and Phanias (frs. 14–16 Wehrli), and even earlier, and perhaps first, by Plato in the *Symposium*, where he has Pausanias argue that tyrants are hostile to the institution of pederasty because they cannot tolerate the free thinking of men bound by love, and that it was because of their love for each other that Harmodius and Aristogeiton brought down the tyranny at Athens (*Symp.* 182bc).[56] Tyrants were, of course, just as well known for being pederasts themselves (and abusive ones at that)[57] as they were for being hostile to the institution of pederasty. But it is Pausanias's *opposition* between pederasty and tyranny that becomes influential on later erotic discourse[58] and on the development of the legend of the Sacred Band in particular.

The legend of the Sacred Band has some affinity, then, with philosophical discussions about the role of pederasty in Greek political life, although it is not yet clear why men and youths bound in love were believed to be uniquely qualified to resist tyranny, or why Plato's Phaedrus might want to create a whole "city or army" of such pairs. The answer to this question is to be found in a tradition of utopian speculation about the best way to constitute the polis, and there are traces of this utopian tradition in some of the texts that describe an erotic Sacred Band. Let us return to the anecdote about Pammenes' critique of Homeric *taxis*. In the *Life of Pelopidas*, Plutarch reports that Pammenes rebuked Nestor for drawing up battle lines by tribe and phratry rather than by pairs of lovers and beloveds, claiming that it was common knowledge that men would abandon their family members in a moment of danger, but a lover would never abandon his beloved or vice versa. In the *Quaestiones Conviviales*, Plutarch repeats Pammenes' critique and there describes the result of erotic *taxis* as a phalanx that "breathes together as one" [σύμπνους] and "is bound together organically" [ἔμψυχον ἔχουσα δεσμόν].[59]

Embedded in this humorous anecdote is what appears to be a serious political argument: the relationship between lover and beloved affords a better context for the citizen to benefit his polis than the relationship between family members. The contrast between kinship and erotic relationships turns up also in the speech of Plato's Phaedrus, and there, as we have seen, the argument is more broadly political, articulated so as to justify creation of a "city or army" [πόλιν . . . ἢ στρατόπεδον] (*Symp.* 178e–179a) of lovers and beloveds. Indeed, in this context, "army" is nothing more than a designation of the "city" in its defensive mode. Now these comments of Pammenes and Phaedrus take the form of empirical observations about human nature—that the presence of a lover generates a greater sense of shame than the presence of a family member—and they recall the more general doctrine attributed to Socrates by Aeschines of Sphettus that *eros* can stimulate one to cultivate virtue.[60] But the explicit contrast with kinship ties also recalls the argument put forth by many utopian thinkers in the fourth century that the state is most unified when the social bonds between citizens trump the blood bonds between kin.[61] And indeed, unity is central to Pammenes' vision: to organize an army along erotic lines is not only to promote valiant behavior in individuals (through the operation of shame), but also to promote cohesion (cf. σύμπνους; ἔμψυχον δεσμόν) throughout the army as a whole. If Pammenes suggested that *eros* could promote unity within an army, Zeno of Citium, in his *Republic*, argued that *eros* could play this role in the state more generally. Zeno, like Plato, proposed to abolish the family,[62] presumably in order to destroy the parochial ties of kinship, which were so destructive to civic unity. And one metaphor he chose to describe the social bond between citizens that would take the place of kinship was the erotic bond between lover and beloved, a bond uniquely capable of promoting *homonoia* (political unity) within the city.[63] It is probably an earlier version of this sort of grand utopian argument that Plato's Phaedrus is alluding to when he proposes to create a "city or army" of lovers and beloveds.

The general notion of *eros* as a force that binds citizens together appears to be old and widespread. Aphrodite was often worshiped in Greek cities as a deity concerned with civic unity,[64] a function she inherited from her Near Eastern counterpart Ishtar, who was as much a civic and martial goddess as a goddess of love. Where Aphrodite was concerned with the city as a whole, she was given epithets like *Pandēmos* (Of all the people), *Agoraia* (Of the people in assembly), and *Hēgemonē tou Dēmou* (Leader of the people), and etiological myths for these cults are frequently linked to important political moments in a city's history, such as synoecism or the adoption of a new constitution. But she was also, in a number of cities, the patron of magistrates and in this capacity is thought to have promoted unity amongst magistrates as well as amity between the magistrates and the people.[65] One sometimes sees Eros, too, as a god concerned with civic unity more generally. For example, on Samos, the festival of Eros was called the Eleutheria (Festival of freedom); in Thespiae, the most important civic festival was the Erotidia (Festival of Eros); and the Athenians sacrificed to Eros alongside Athena during the Panathenaea, Athens's annual festival of civic renewal.[66] It is in this capacity as promoter of civic cohesion, I think, that Eros was worshiped in specifically military contexts. Athenaeus tells us that the Spartans, for instance, "sacrifice to Eros before the troops are drawn up for battle, on the grounds that their safety and victory depend on the friendship of those who are drawn up [ἐν τῇ τῶν παραταττομένων φιλίᾳ]" (561e), and he describes a similar custom for the Cretans. But his third example of Eros's capacity to promote military cohesion, the Theban Sacred Band, is anomalous: the Theban soldiers, according to Athenaeus, are differentiated hierarchically according to sexual role (lovers and beloveds), whereas the Spartans appear to be social equals; and the Thebans are bound together in *eros* (erotic passion), while the Spartans, he states quite clearly, are united in *philia* (friendship). Athenaeus's juxtaposition of these two rather different phenomena hints that the legend of an erotic Sacred Band may have originated as an exaggeration of the custom of some cities (e.g., Sparta and the cities of Crete) to sacrifice to Eros in order to promote *philia* among their men in arms.

In view of this broader sense of *eros* as a force that brings people together, it is perhaps not surprising that philosophers sometimes described the bond between citizens in terms not only of *philia*, but even of *eros*. For example, Aristotle, in a discussion of the importance of *philia* as a unifying force within the state, critiques the celebrated speech of Aristophanes in Plato's *Symposium* as a political argument. In Aristotle's view, Aristophanes' call for a merging (συμφῦναι) of lover and beloved goes too far: the result is not unity, but obliteration (*Pol.* 1262b8–18). The kind of *philia* that promotes civic unity is one that recognizes the autonomy and individual identity of each citizen. What is interesting for our purposes is that Aristotle can view Aristophanes' argument about *eros* as, in part, an argument about how the polis should be constituted.[67]

What is puzzling is that the *eros* that Plato's Phaedrus and Zeno speak of is not just *eros* as a generic force of social cohesion, but a distinctly pederastic *eros*. And pederastic *eros* is not at all an obvious metaphor to describe the political bonds between citizens. Given the hierarchical nature of the pederastic relationship, the metaphor was well suited to describe the replication of the citizen body from generation to generation: indeed, it appears that pederasty was sometimes promoted, especially among the well born, as a form of "displaced fathering" and recruitment of the political elite.[68] Pederasty might also be an appropriate metaphor to describe the harmonious political relations between generations: Plutarch, in fact, suggests that the Theban lawgiver instituted pederasty in order to balance the impetuosity of youth with the grace and deliberative capacity of maturity (*Pel.* 19.2). But the hierarchical bond between lover and beloved would seem to be far less suited to describe the relations between citizens of the same rank and age.[69] How did this specifically pederastic vision of a city of lovers and beloveds develop from the more general notion of *eros* as a force that animates the *philia* between citizens and between soldiers? Schofield has argued that Zeno's city of love was inspired by the prominent role that institutionalized pederasty was believed to have played in the Spartan system,[70] and one wonders whether an idealized image of Sparta does not also lurk behind the proposal made by Plato's Phaedrus to create a city or army of lovers and beloveds. The pederastic bond, then, may have been chosen as a metaphor for civic cohesion not because of the hierarchical nature of the bond, but in spite of it: what was important was that pederasty of a highly institutional type was Spartan and thus thought to be a key ingredient behind Spartan military success. Another source of this specifically pederastic civic metaphor might be the figure of Socrates, who was known to have described his entire philosophical approach as fundamentally "erotic." It is tempting to see in the notion of a city of lovers and beloveds an elite Socratic society composed of well-born men and youths who do not merely philosophize about what is just for the city, but actually implement it. Such an elite society may well be reflected in Plato's society of guardians, whose bravest fighters (φύλακες, or "guards") will be rewarded with kisses from the most beautiful youths, and in Zeno's society of sages, who "will fall in love with [ἐρασθήσεσθαι] youths who reveal through their appearance a natural propensity for virtue" (D.L. 7.129).

The utopian proposal for a city (or army) of lovers and beloveds, whatever the ultimate philosophical origin, appears to have been made in the name of political unity, and it is unity that enabled a city to counter the threats of enemies abroad and tyrants at home. This connection between pederastic *eros* and political freedom is made explicit by Zeno: "Eros was a god who promoted friendship [*philia*], freedom [*eleuthēria*], and also unity [*homonoia*]" and "helped to promote the safety [*sotēria*] of the state" (Ath. 561c). Zeno's terminology is as much political as it is militaristic: while *sotēria* refers most directly to success against external threats, *eleuthēria* can designate "freedom" from tyranny as well as from external domination.[71] This complex of ideas, which we see articulated so clearly in Zeno, is implicit already in the sympotic speeches of Plato's Phaedrus and Pausanias and supplies the larger philosophical context in which to understand Pammenes' speculation about the sources of military (and civic) cohesion and the Sacred Band's deployment of such cohesion against tyrants.

The legend of the Sacred Band seems to have begun in the early fourth century as a fanciful real-world analogy that initially supported and ultimately replaced a utopian proposal to build a city or army on the ennobling bond between lover and beloved. The citizens of this ideal polis would be unified and conspicuous in their love of liberty, and it was perhaps this idea that gave the Theban Sacred Band a history. For although an actual Sacred Band—if there even was one—must have fought many battles from 375 to 338, the tradition of the Sacred Band focused on just three battles in which the man-loving Thebans fought tyrants on Boeotian soil: Tegyra and Leuctra, where the Thebans toppled the Spartan hegemony and restored freedom to Boeotia and Greece, and Chaeronea, where they fell bravely to the tyrannical Philip, who brought Greek liberty to an end. Tegyra and Leuctra had probably already been fashioned into stands against tyranny in Callisthenes' *Hellenica,* and possibly already in the obscure Boeotian chroniclers on whom Callisthenes is supposed to have drawn, and Chaeronea, Thebes's answer to the heroic stand of Leonidas and the three hundred Spartans at Thermopylae, may have come to be understood in similar terms. But it was not until this panegyric history became attached to the erotic political philosophy of men like Plato, Xenophon's Pausanias, and Zeno of Citium that the legend of the Sacred Band acquired its distinctive erotic dimension.

Notes

Thanks are due to Benjamin Acosta-Hughes, Kathryn Morgan, Thomas Hubbard, and Martha Nussbaum, who each commented extensively on an earlier version of the argument presented here. An oral version was presented in February 1999 at the University of Chicago and benefited from the keen questions of many of those in attendance.

1. See, e.g., Dover 1965; Buffière 1980, 95–101; Sergent 1986, 44–52; DeVoto 1992; and Ogden 1996, 111–15. Buck 1994, 110–11, for one, is skeptical.

2. The origin of the name, mentioned first in Dinarchus 1.73, is obscure. In Homer, the epithet ἱερός is used of an army (στρατός, *Od.* 24.81) and of small groups of guards (*Il.* 10.56, 24.681), and there the word probably retains its more archaic meaning of "strong" or perhaps "endowed with (divinely-inspired) strength" (see Chantraine 1968–80, s.v. ἱερός). It may be significant that the phrase ἱερὸς στρατός in Hom. *Od.* 24.81 was used to describe the Achaean army when it buried Achilles, Patroclus, and Antilochus, all three associated later with pederastic love. See also Plut. *Amat.* 760c, where lovers who defend their beloveds against the clutches of tyrants are said to defend them "as though defending holy [ἱεροῖς] and inviolable shrines."

3. Tegyra: Plut. *Pel.* 16.2, 19.3; cf. Diod. 15.81.2. Leuctra: Dinarchus 1.72; Cornelius Nepos *Pel.* 4.2; Plut. *Pel.* 20.4; Diod. 15.81.2; Dio Chrys. 22.2; Maximus of Tyre 18.2. Chaeronea: Plut. *Pel.* 18.5, *Alex.* 19.2.

4. All translations of Greek and Latin texts are the author's.

5. Anderson 1970, 158–9 and 311–12 nn. 35–36; Buck 1994, 110–11; Ogden 1996, 114–15. Like this force of three hundred at Delium, the Sacred Band was also supposed to have fought in front, spread out across the length of the army, until Pelopidas detached them from the rest of the army and constituted them as a self-standing unit (Plut. *Pel.* 19.3). Interestingly, Thucydides' account of the Battle of Delium (4.89–101) makes no mention of this force.

6. Buffière 1980, 100; Ogden 1996, 113.

7. Quarreling: Xen. *An.* 5.8.4. Pursuing boys: Xen. *An.* 4.6.1–3, 7.4.7–8, *Hell.* 5.4.57; Polyaenus 5.3.4; cf. Xen. *An.* 4.1.14, *Ages.* 5.4–5.

8. Cartledge 1981, 32 n. 32, has questioned whether he was even a Spartan.

9. Cf. Ael. 4.1, who describes an adolescent (*meirakion*) beloved as "not yet called to arms because of his age" [καλούμενον δὲ δι' ἡλικίαν ἐς ὅπλα μηδέπω]. See also Ogden 1996, 109. Plut. *Lyc.* 18.4, which describes Spartan lovers being penalized when their beloveds are heard to cry "while fighting" [ἐν τῷ μάχεσθαι], is most likely a reference to mock battles in which boys in the *agela* engaged (see Plut. *Lyc.* 16.5, 17.2).

10. This was clearly the case with the *paidika* of Cleomachus of Chalcis during the Lelantine War: "He asked his *eromenos*, who was present, whether he was going to watch the battle" (Plut. *Amat.* 760ef).

11. Many other cases are ambiguous. Asopichus, once the *eromenos* of Epaminondas, is said to have died beside him at Mantineia (Plut. *Amat.* 761d), but there is no evidence that the two were still actively beloved and lover. Likewise, the Spartan Archidamus lamented the death of his beloved Kleonymus, who died at Leuctra (Xen. *Hell.* 5.4.33), but we do not know that Archidamus was even present at the battle, nor can

we assume that they were still sexually involved. A legend from Megara says that the hero Diocles protected his beloved in battle, before perishing himself (Scholia ad Theocr. 12.27–33), but here too it is not clear that the beloved was actually armed, and the myth is, in any event, designed to play up the erotic aspects of the cult of Diocles at Megara. See also Plut. *Amat.* 761c; Ael. *NA* 4.1.

12. At Potidaea, Socrates saved the wounded Alcibiades, "not wishing to abandon him" (Pl. *Symp.* 220e). At Delium, Alcibiades, on horseback, vowed not to abandon Socrates and Laches, who were on foot (221a). Plato makes it clear that the joint military service took place *after* Alcibiades' attempted seduction of Socrates (see 219e: ταῦτά [Alcibiades' attempted seduction] τε γάρ μοι ἅπαντα προυγεγόνει, καὶ μετὰ ταῦτα στρατεία ἡμῖν εἰς Ποτείδαιαν ἐγένετο κοινὴ καὶ συνεσιτοῦμεν ἐκεῖ.).

13. See, e.g., Polyaenus 2.5.1: "the band was composed of three hundred lovers and beloveds" [ὁ λόχος ἦν ἐρασταὶ καὶ ἐρώμενοι τριακόσιοι]; Plut. *Pel.* 18.1: "this force was created out of lovers and beloveds" [ἐξ ἐραστῶν καὶ ἐρωμένων γενέσθαι τὸ σύστημα τοῦτο].

14. Greeks of the classical period seem generally not to have used the terms *erastes* (lover) and *eromenos* (beloved) of a relationship that had ceased to be sexual. See, e.g., Thuc. 1.132.5 (reference to the former beloved of the Spartan king Pausanias as παιδικά ποτε ὢν αὐτοῦ); Aeschin. 1.155–57 (contrast between men who were *eromenoi* in the past and youths who are *eromenoi* at the present).

15. Suits of armor: Plut. *Amat.* 761b. Oaths: Arist. fr. 97 Rose; Plut. *Amat.* 761de.

16. Ritual presentation of armor in Crete: Ephorus *FGrH* 70 F 149 = Strab. 10.4.21. Oaths: in the cities of Hellenistic Crete, citizenship oaths marked a boy's graduation from his military training in the *agela* (herd) system (see, e.g., *Inscriptiones Creticae* 1.19.1, 2.5.24).

17. Dinarchus 1.72–73; Hieronymus of Rhodes fr. 34 Wehrli = Ath. 602ab; Cornelius Nepos *Pel.* 4.2; Diod. 15.81.2; Dio Chrys. 22.2; Plut. *Pel.* 17.2, 20.2, 23.2; Plut. *Pel.* 18–19, which, as we shall see, draws on a different source than the passages from the *Pelopidas* just cited and must therefore be treated as an independent reference to the Sacred Band; Plut. *Alex.* 9.2; Polyaenus 2.5.1; Maximus of Tyre 18.2; Ath. 561f. On possible references in Plat. *Symp.* 178e–179b and Xen. *Symp.* 8.34, see "Plato and Xenophon" below. I leave out Plut. *Amat.* 761b, which alludes vaguely to an erotic battle formation implemented by the Theban Pammenes; Anna Comnena *Alexias* 7.7.1–3, which mistakenly attributes a *hieros lochos* (without any claims about its composition) to the Spartans; and Hesychius s.v. *hieros lochos*, which does not identify the band as Theban (he could as well be referring to the Carthaginian *hieros lochos* mentioned at Diod. 16.80.4, 20.10.6, 20.11.1, 20.12.3, 20.12.7).

18. Plutarch: Westlake 1939; Georgiadou 1997, 19–24; cf. *Alex.* 27.4, 33.1, 33.10, which draw on Callisthenes' *Praxeis Alexandrou*. Diodorus: Westlake 1939, 11, 16–17. Nepos: Westlake 1939, 11–12; Georgiadou 1997, 38–39. Dinarchus: Shrimpton 1971, 313–14, 317.

19. Jacoby 1919, 1697; Westlake 1939, 13.

20. They are Pammenes' famous rebuke of Homer for not arranging lovers beside their beloveds, which is mentioned yet again in Plut. *Quaest. conv.* 618b–d, and Aristotle's reference to lovers swearing oaths around the tomb of Iolaus, which Ross has assigned to Aristotle's *Erotikos* as fr. 2.

21. E.g., the notion that lovers and beloveds are ashamed to behave in a cowardly way in the presence of each other (*Pel.* 18.2–3 beside Pl. *Symp.* 178d, 179a; see also Xen. *Symp.* 8.33, *Cyn.* 12.20). It is interesting that in the *Symposium* passage, Phaedrus justifies his proposal for a city or army of lovers and beloveds by observing that lovers are much more loyal to their beloveds than relatives or friends, a sentiment very similar to that of the passage from the *Phaedrus,* in which the full expression *entheos philos* is employed: it is quite possible that Plutarch, who is probably quoting from memory, has conflated these two Platonic references to the lover as *entheos* (*Phaedrus* 255b and *Symp.* 179a).

22. Pace Dover 1965, 11–12. On this tradition of erotic writing, see Schofield 1991, 28; Parker 1992, 100–101; Kahn 1994.

23. Hieronymus of Rhodes fr. 34 Wehrli and commentary ad loc. The fragment may even have come from Hieronymus's *Symposium,* although Wehrli assigns it to the *Historika Hypomnēmata* [Historical anecdotes].

24. Plut. *Pel.* 17.2 = Callisthenes *FGrH* 124 F 18. See esp. Sordi 1989, 124–25.

25. Diodorus's mention of Tegyra, Pelopidas, and the Sacred Band at 15.81 seems clearly to come from a different source, undoubtedly Callisthenes. See Sordi 1989, 124.

26. Jacoby ad *FGrH* 125 F 18; Sordi 1989, 124–25. For a general discussion of the topography and strategy of the battle, see Buckler 1995.

27. Callisthenes ap. Cornelius Nepos *Pel.* 4.2. Nepos's linking of Pelopidas and the *delectus manus* with the victory at Leuctra suggests that Nepos here followed Callisthenes rather than Ephorus.

28. Hanson 1988. On the low esteem of Ephorus and Callisthenes as military historians, see Polyb. 12.17–22, 12.25f.3–4. Bibliography on Xenophon's alleged anti-Theban bias and on the alleged superiority of later accounts of the Battle of Leuctra may be found in Hanson 1988, 191 n. 3.

29. If Callisthenes did discuss the role of the Sacred Band at Chaeronea, it would not have been in the *Hellenica,* whose account ended in 356 with the beginning of the third Sacred War, but in the *Praxeis Alexandrou* [Exploits of Alexander].

30. See, e.g., Pritchett 1958, 310–11; Parke 1970.

31. Hammond 1938, 216–18, suggests that the monument marked the burial of the Macedonians, rather than the Thebans, as Pausanias claimed, and indeed Pausanias himself may be combating such a view at 9.40.7, when he insists that Philip was not accustomed to setting up trophies.

32. Four different founders are identified by the sources: Pammenes (if Plut. *Amat.* 761b is in fact a reference to the Sacred Band); Gorgidas (Plut. *Pel.* 19.3; Polyaenus 2.5.1); Pelopidas (Plut. *Pel.* 19.3 suggests he reorganized it as a separate battalion); and Epaminondas (Dio Chrys. 22.2; Plut. *Quaest. conv.* 618cd; Maximus of Tyre 18.2), to whom there was a tendency later to attribute all Theban innovations (see Hanson 1988, 192–99, 204–5).

33. Cf. Jacoby 1919, 1697; Georgiadou 1997, 154; pace Dover 1965, 12; Sergent 1986, 47. On this linguistic distancing strategy, see Pauw 1980, 90–91; Hammond 1993, 6–8, 11, 17, etc. See also the λέγεται at Plut. *Alex.* 9.2, which introduces the claim that Alexander was the first to defeat the Sacred Band.

34. Fuscagni 1975; Sordi 1989, 123–28.

35. On the Pitanate *lochos*, see Kelly 1981.

36. For other examples from the historians, see Thuc. 1.132.5; 6.53–61; Xen. *Hell.* 4.8.39, 5.4.56–7, *An.* 5.8.4, 7.4.8 and generally Hindley 1994; Theopompus *FGrH* 115 F 247 = Ath. 604f–605a.

37. Dover 1965, 9–16. Thesleff 1978 argues that Xenophon wrote in two stages: part of his *Symposium* was completed before Plato wrote, part of it (especially book 8, from which our passage derives) was written after, and indeed in response to, Plato.

38. There is one additional piece of evidence for the relative chronology of these texts and that is Ath. 216ef, which seems to draw on a work called "Reply to the Partisan of Socrates" [Πρὸς τὸν φιλοσωκράτην] by the Hellenistic literary critic Herodicus of Babylon. Herodicus/Athenaeus assumes that Xenophon's portrait of Pausanias is based on Plato's portrait of him: because Plato's Pausanias did not say the things that Xenophon attributed to him in his *Symposium*, Herodicus/Athenaeus assumes that they either occurred in a different version of Plato's *Symposium* or were invented by Xenophon. What is interesting is that Herodicus/Athenaeus assumes that these two passages are in dialogue with one another and reflective of debates within the Socratic circle; this excerpt from Herodicus does not mention the possibility that these passages refer to some independent historical reality.

39. Hence the force of the present participle συγκαθεύδοντας.

40. See Dover 1989, 192. Lange's bracketing of πόλει has been accepted by Marchant in the Oxford text.

41. See Hindley 1999, 91–98, who contrasts the chasteness that Socrates advocates in this speech with the less rigid view toward male love advocated by Xenophon himself and by Socrates elsewhere in the Xenophontic corpus.

42. This argument was apparently also made in the defense of Timarchus (Aeschin. 1.133); in that case, Aeschines responded not, like Xenophon's Socrates, by denying that the relationship between Achilles and Patroclus was erotic (even as he acknowledges Homer's silence on the matter), but by stressing instead the nobility of their love, which stands in stark contrast to the mercenary liaisons of Timarchus (1.141–50).

43. Xen. *Hell.* 7.4.13, 16, 31 describes an elite Elean force of three hundred but gives no hint of any erotic composition. The supposed male beauty contest at Elis, whose winner received a shield (Ath. 609f), is irrelevant, pace Buffière 1980, 89–91; Sergent 1986, 139–41.

44. Cf. Maximus of Tyre 20.8; 39.5.

45. In virtue of the border it shared with Athens, Thebes was probably the original "other" within Athenian social discourse. See generally Zeitlin 1990.

46. Dover 1989, 84, 144.

47. Cf. also the force of "many young men and the best older men" that Epaminondas and Gorgidas, two men credited with organizing the Sacred Band, assembled to expel the Spartans from Thebes in 379 (Plut. *Pel.* 12.2).

48. The epitomizer of Athenaeus even suggests that he put the proposal for an erotic battalion into Socrates' mouth "jokingly" [γελοίως]. Ath. *Epitome* vol. 2.1 p. 81 Peppink.

49. See Ferguson 1975, 24–25, 58; Sordi 1973, 83–85.

50. Dover 1965, 14–15, citing Hdt. 5.3.1, Thuc. 2.97.6, Pl. *Rep.* 471cd, *Menex.* 100a.

51. Polyaenus's actual anecdotes about the Theban army at Leuctra (2.3.2–3) and Chaeronea (4.3.2–3) make no mention of the Sacred Band, much less an erotic Sacred Band.

52. Onasander, another strategical writer, states the principle of erotic *taxis* as a present general condition (*Stratēgikos* 24), presenting it as a general principle for generals to bear in mind, not as an anecdote associated with a specific historical army.

53. Wehrli prints the entire list at Ath. 602ab as reflecting the thought of Hieronymus.

54. On the tyrannical associations of the oligarchic junta installed by the Spartans, see Plut. *Pel.* 6.1, 7.2, 9.2, and generally Leitao 1999, 249–50, 254–58, 263–64.

55. The terminology here is interesting: ποιεῖν καὶ πάσχειν can refer to military conduct ("fighting and being killed"), but also to sexual roles ("being active and being passive," which would normatively refer to *erastes* and *eromenos*, respectively).

56. Thuc. 6.54–9, in order to combat the argument that Harmodius and Aristogeiton were motivated by political reasons, claimed that the assassination was precipitated instead by an insult that grew out of an erotic rivalry. But Thucydides' focus on the erotic background of the case is still a far cry from Pausanias's quite original claim that the erotic *was* the political.

57. Tyrants (and other bullies) as abusive pederasts: Hipparchus (Plut. *Amat.* 760bc; cf. Thuc. 6.54; Maximus of Tyre 18.2); Periander of Ambracia (Arist. *Pol.* 5.10.1311a39–41; Plut. *Amat.* 766ef; Maximus of Tyre 18.1); Archias of Corinth (Alexander Aetolus fr. 3.7–10 Powell = Parth. 14; Diod. bk. 8 fr. 10; Plut. *Amatoriae Narrationes* 772ef; Maximus of Tyre 18.1); and Phalaris of Acragas (Plut. *Amat.* 760bc; Hieronymus of Rhodes fr. 34 Wehrli = Ath. 602ab). Cf. also Plut. *Narr. Am.* 773e–774d on the pederastic abuses of the Spartan harmost in Oreos, avenged (along with other Spartan sexual crimes) by the Thebans at Leuctra.

58. The opposition between tyranny and *eros* becomes associated, by the time of Athenaeus (602cd), even with the figure of Polycrates of Samos, a tyrant represented in earlier tradition as a consummate *paiderastēs*.

59. Cf. also *Amat.* 761b. When Plutarch tells us at *Pel.* 18.2 that Pammenes made this rebuke "in jest" [μετὰ παιδιᾶς], I think he is referring only to Pammenes' playfulness in framing his comment as a rebuke of Nestor, and does not mean to undercut the seriousness of his argument.

60. Kahn 1994, 101–3.

61. See Ar. *Eccl.* 635–7; Pl. *Rep.* 460cd, 461c–e.

62. I.e., by having women and children held in common: Schofield 1991, 12, 25–26.

63. Ath. 561c = *SVF* I.61; Schofield 1991, 22–56.

64. Sokolowski 1964; Croiset and Salviat 1966; Burkert 1985, 155.

65. Sokolowski 1964.

66. Samos: Ath. 561f–562a. Thespiae: Plut. *Amat.* 748f.; Paus. 9.31.3; Ath. 561e. Athens: Ath. 561de; Burkert 1985, 232.

67. Cf. also Pericles' famous exhortation to his fellow citizens to become "lovers [*erastai*] of the city" (Thuc. 2.43.1). Here, the erotic metaphor works a bit differently,

with *eros* describing the bond between citizen and the state rather than the bond between citizens. Nevertheless, its function is the same: Pericles' *eros* is the ultimate symbol of his vision of a city in which private interest is wholly subordinated to public interest.

68. See Cartledge 1981, 22, 28–29.

69. Halperin 1990, 95–104, argues that the egalitarianism that was at the heart of Athenian democratic ideology was underwritten by the inviolability of the male citizen's body. To describe the social bond between two citizens in pederastic terms would necessarily be to subordinate one of them socially and sexually.

70. Schofield 1991, 35–41. See also Pl. *Leg.* 636bc, 836bc.

71. See Schofield 1991, 48–56.

References

Anderson, J. 1970. *Military Theory and Practice in the Age of Xenophon.* Berkeley.

Buck, J. 1994. *Boiotia and the Boiotian League, 423–371 B.C.* Edmonton.

Buckler, J. 1995. "The Battle of Tegyra, 375 B.C." *Boeotia Antiqua* 5:43–58.

Buffière, F. 1980. *Eros adolescent: La pédérastie dans la Grèce antique.* Paris.

Burkert, W. 1985. *Greek Religion, Archaic and Classical.* Translated by J. Raffan. Cambridge, Mass.

Cartledge, P. 1981. "The Politics of Spartan Pederasty." *Proceedings of the Cambridge Philological Society,* n.s., 27:17–36.

Chantraine, P. 1968–80. *Dictionnaire étymologique de la langue grecque.* Paris.

Croiset, F., and F. Salviat. 1966. "Aphrodite gardienne des magistrats: Gynéconomes de Thasos et polémarques de Thèbes." *Bulletin de Correspondance Hellénique* 90: 460–71.

DeVoto, J. 1992. "The Theban Sacred Band." *Ancient World* 23:3–19.

Dover, K. 1965. "The Date of Plato's *Symposium.*" *Phronesis* 10:2–20.

———. 1989. *Greek Homosexuality.* 2d ed. Cambridge, Mass.

Ferguson, J. 1975. *Utopias of the Classical World.* Ithaca, N.Y.

Fuscagni, S. 1975. "Callistene di Olinto e la 'Vita di Pelopida' di Plutarco." In *Storiografia e propaganda,* edited by M. Sordi, 31–55. Milan.

Georgiadou, A. 1997. *Plutarch's Pelopidas: A Historical and Philological Commentary.* Stuttgart.

Halperin, D. 1990. *One Hundred Years of Homosexuality, and Other Essays on Greek Love.* London.

Hammond, N. 1938. "The Two Battles of Chaeronea (338 B.C. and 86 B.C.)." *Klio* 13: 186–218.

———. 1993. *Sources for Alexander the Great.* Cambridge.

Hanson, V. 1988. "Epameinondas, the Battle of Leuktra (371 B.C.), and the 'Revolution' in Greek Battle Tactics." *Classical Antiquity* 7:190–207.

Hindley, C. 1994. "*Eros* and Military Command in Xenophon." *Classical Quarterly* 44: 347–66.

————. 1999. "Xenophon on Male Love." *Classical Quarterly* 49:74–99.

Jacoby, F. 1919. "Kallisthenes." In *Paulys Real Encyclopädie*, 10:1674–1726. Stuttgart.

Kahn, C. 1994. "Aeschines on Socratic Eros." In *The Socratic Movement*, edited by P. Vander Waerdt, 87–106. Ithaca, N.Y.

Kelly, D. 1981. "Thucydides and Herodotus on the Pitanate Lochos." *Greek, Roman and Byzantine Studies* 22:31–38.

Leitao, D. 1999. "Solon on the Beach: Some Pragmatic Functions of the *Limen* in Initiatory Myth and Ritual." In *Rites of Passage in Ancient Greece: Literature, Religion, Society*, edited by M. Padilla, 247–77. Lewisburg, Pa.

Ogden, D. 1996. "Homosexuality and Warfare in Ancient Greece." In *Battle in Antiquity*, edited by A. Lloyd, 107–68. London.

Parke, H. 1970. "Sacred Band." In *Oxford Classical Dictionary*, 2d ed., edited by N. Hammond and H. Scullard, 943. Oxford.

Parker, H. 1992. "Love's Body Anatomized: The Ancient Erotic Handbooks and the Rhetoric of Sexuality." In *Pornography and Representation*, edited by A. Richlin, 90–111. Berkeley.

Pauw, D. 1980. "Impersonal Expressions and Unidentified Spokesmen in Greek and Roman Historiography and Biography." *Acta Classica* 23:83–95.

Pritchett, W. 1958. "Observations on Chaeronea." *American Journal of Archaeology* 62:307–11.

Schofield, M. 1991. *The Stoic Idea of the City*. Cambridge.

Sergent, B. 1986. *L'homosexualité initiatique dans l'Europe ancienne*. Paris.

Shrimpton, G. 1971. "The Theban Supremacy in Fourth-Century Literature." *Phoenix* 25:310–18.

Sokolowski, F. 1964. "Aphrodite as Guardian of Greek Magistrates." *Harvard Theological Review* 57:1–8.

Sordi, M. 1973. "La restaurazione della lega beotica nel 379–8 A.C." *Athenaeum* 51:79–91.

————. 1989. "Pelopida da Tegira a Leuttra." In *Boiotika. Vorträge vom 5. Internationalen Böotien Kolloquium zu Ehren von Professor Dr. Siegfried Lauffer*, edited by H. Beister and J. Buckler, 123–30. Munich.

Thesleff, H. 1978. "The Interrelation and Date of the *Symposia* of Plato and Xenophon." *Bulletin of the Institute of Classical Studies* 25:155–70.

Westlake, H. 1939. "The Sources of Plutarch's *Pelopidas*." *Classical Quarterly* 33:11–22.

Zeitlin, F. 1990. "Thebes: Theater of Self and Society in Athenian Drama." In *Nothing to Do with Dionysos?* edited by J. Winkler and F. Zeitlin, 130–67. Princeton, N.J.

Chapter Six

PLATO, ZENO, AND THE OBJECT OF LOVE

≈

A. W. Price

1

*O*ne Greek term for a lover of boys was *philomeirax*.[1] Out of it, Athenaeus teasily coined *philosophomeirakiskos* (*Deipnosophistae* 13.572B), roughly "pedophilosopher." Such as it was, the term might have been applied to the founders both of the Academy and of the Stoa. For Plato, the first unmarried man in Europe (as Jasper Griffin informally dubs him), there is recurrent internal evidence. Gregory Vlastos was not forgetting much when he wrote, "In every passage I can recall which depicts or alludes to the power of sexual desire the context is homosexual" (1981, 25).[2] For Zeno, there is the assertion by Antigonus of Carystus, not a sympathetic biographer but a contemporary one, that he was exclusively attracted to boys (Athenaeus, *SVF* 1.58.35–36 = *Deipnosophistae* 13.563E).[3] Neither had any cause to be ashamed: at least in the classical period, it was perfectly possible to attach a penchant for pederasty to the pretensions of a moralist. Both could appeal to a long tradition, in many Greek cities, that made pederasty a mode of education (see Dover 1978, 202–3). Among dramatic poets, Euripides wrote that *erōs* was the chief primer of wisdom and virtue (Athenaeus *Deipnosophistae* 13.561A = fr. 897 N²), Alexis that no tutor was more attentive (fr. 290 Kassel-Austin). Outside the utopias that they invented, which feature educational equality between the sexes, Plato and Zeno had impartial reason to privilege the pederast as pedagogue.

What then most animates their accounts is the difficulties they faced in relating the educative to the erotic satisfactorily. Aristotle adduced the morals of the marketplace and expected trouble: "Recriminations are common in *philiai* [partnerships in friendship, pleasure, or commerce] not in the same direction, and it is not easy to see what is just; for it is hard to measure different directions by this one unit. We find this in the case of lovers; for the one seeks the other as pleasant to pass his life with, while the latter seeks the other at times as useful. When the love is over, one changes as the other changes, and then they calculate the quid pro quo" (*Eudemian Ethics* 7.10.1243b14–20). Within the framework of Aristotle's theory, this is a mixed *philia*, of pleasure on one side and of utility on the other (cf. *Nicomachean Ethics* 9.1.1164a7–8). It is uncertain whether he is being cynical and empirical (denying that lovers are really friends), or abstract and schematizing (abstracting love from friendship). In either case, he imputes a problem of commensurability, of how to find a common metric for things that differ in kind. What makes this acute, within his picture, is that these relationships, unlike any that we classify as friendship, are self-serving on both sides (see *Nicomachean Ethics* 8.3): since both parties are in it for what they can get out, and not (like benefactors) for what they can put in, each insists on a fair return. Even if the incommensurabilities could be resolved, the high-minded apologist must object that the lover's intentions are being assigned the wrong structure: educating the boy becomes a price that the lover is willing to pay, an accidental means to his end and not part of his goal. Instead of recruiting *erōs* as the handmaid of philosophy, this relegates philosophy to the service of a love worthy not of free men, but of sailors (cf. Plato *Phaedrus* 243c7–8).

No doubt a more generous view could be rescued out of Aristotle's cynicism or schematism. Take a more ambivalent passage: "[Lover and beloved] do not take pleasure in the same things, but the one in seeing the other and the other in receiving attentions from the lover; and when the bloom of youth passes the friendship sometimes passes too (for the one finds no pleasure in the sight of the other, and the other gets no attentions from the first). Yet many are constant, if familiarity has led them to love each other's characters, these being alike" (*Nicomachean Ethics* 8.4.1157a6–12). Here is a concession to break the fetters of a context again depreciatory of the *philiai* of pleasure and utility. Out of enjoyment and exploitation of the bloom of youth, by lover and beloved respectively, may emerge a reciprocal appreciation of character that transforms the relationship, infusing it with the mutual concern (essential to what we count as friendship) that Aristotle associates only with the *philia* of character.[4] So long as the loved one retains his physical and mental immaturity, he may offer the lover his body, as the lover offers him his mind, out of an equal generosity.[5] This surely merits no moral complaint, but should it satisfy Plato and Zeno? Plausibly not, for *erōs* is thereby morally accommodated, but not itself fully moralized. Education comes in, not indeed as a mercenary quid pro quo, and yet as an expression of friendship collateral to any fulfillment of *erōs*. Indeed, the structure of the friendship still excludes that the exercise of *erōs* should itself be educative.

The difficulty can be generalized. The pederast is in search of a boy with a beautiful body, the pedagogue of a boy (or girl) with a promising mind. One and the same person may happen to be both, and a pederast who is also a pedagogue may have reason (mercenary or generous) to take him as his object in both roles; but his erotic and educative projects may come together *only* in their object.[6] Plato and Zeno had to attempt accounts that made a unity of the two projects. Plato offers no real solution, I think, in his *Symposium*; he shows equal insight and ingenuity in the *Phaedrus*; but the breakthrough—made possible only by theoretical developments—is evidenced in the fragments of the early Stoa.[7]

2

In Plato's *Symposium*, Socrates pretends to report from a priestess Diotima an account of love that subsumes its teleology within that of desire in general. Generic *erōs* is identified with desire meant Socratically, both in its full generality and as all directed finally towards the subject's happiness (*eudaimonia*), that is, towards his possession of good things (204d4–205a3). It is further argued that, desiring to possess good things always, he desires immortality together with the good (206a9–207a4). Specific *erōs* can then be defined as the desire to achieve that double goal through "generation in the beautiful" (206e5). One would presume that immortality demands not generation but personal survival; to which it is opposed that, even within a single human life, generation *is* survival. Physical survival is the piecemeal replacement of an old body by a new one, through its "hair and flesh and bones and blood"; mental survival (by which is meant the survival of a mentality) involves the replacement of old mental states by new ones that replicate their content (207d7–208a7). Hence the propagation of one life into another, physical or mental, is equally survival of a kind. It is in pursuit of this that men hope to beget physical offspring on women, and mental offspring on boys (208e1–209c4).

This account places pedagogy at the center of pederasty. (Indeed, it has a void to fill; for nothing whatever is said about sexual relations outside the cycle of generation.) It is true that vices may be as readily inculcated as virtues—indeed, more readily, if it is easier to become bad than good. Diotima gives no explicit examples of corruption; but she cites the impact of poets and lawgivers (209c7–e4), which Plato believed to be pernicious. However, Socrates holds that someone who obtains what is not really good is not obtaining what he really wants (*Gorgias* 468d5–7); hence, success does not bring him happiness. There follows an exposition of philosophical love in the famous ascent passage (210a4–212b7). Though it needs arguing (see Price 1997, 257–60), I believe that the teleology of "generation in beauty" is still present, with a focus now set less upon the fact of propagation than upon its content, which develops through the stages of the ascent. If this is a correct reading, personal pedagogy remains at the heart of the lover's project.

Yet why should mental fecundity connect with physical beauty, or indeed with *erōs* in its common acceptation? Presumably even the young Socrates, whom Diotima is supposed to have been instructing, was not an object of beauty; nor is she said to have been in love with him. (Her role was rather that of the shadowy mentor whose continuing presence throughout the ascent is lightly indicated.) And Homer and Lycurgus are cited to confirm the superiority of mental to physical progeny (209c7–e4) although their procreation was not erotic. Plato recurrently touches on the problem, but he rather lulls the reader into disregarding it than resolves it himself. He has Diotima exploit the connotations of *kalos* (which are wider than those of "beautiful"), arguing thus: "Wisdom is actually one of the most beautiful things, and Love is love in relation to what is beautiful, so that Love is necessarily a philosopher" (204b2–4). He has her repeatedly associate procreation with beauty (206c4–d2, 209a8–b7, c2–3)—though, as she trades on an ambiguity between begetting and bringing to birth, she risks implying that midwives need to be beautiful as wives do (an implausibility that will not be present when Socrates portrays himself as a midwife; *Theaetetus* 148e6–151d3). Within the lesser mysteries, the stimulus to mental propagation is a beautiful mind in a beautiful body (209b4–7). Within the greater mysteries, a modest physical requirement remains: "He must consider beauty in souls more valuable than beauty in the body, so that, if someone who is decent in his soul has even a little bloom, this suffices for his loving and caring for him" (210b6 – c1).[8] Yet why should Diotima demand even that? In order, one may suspect, to preserve the common connotations of *erōs* even after the logic of her account has dispensed with them.

No doubt there are things to be said in extenuation. Oddly, physical beauty may be more apropos through the ascent than it is to the mental fecundity of the lesser mysteries. As the complacent educators of 209, whether lovers, poets, or lawgivers, are already pregnant in what they wish to propagate, one would suppose that they require mental receptacles but not physical stimuli. The emerging philosopher of 210 is only one step ahead of the boy to whom he communicates his progress (consider the recurrent *logoi*; 210a8, c1, d5); so he continues to be in need of inspiration. To him beauty is one, even if beauties are various and of varying value; thus it is fitting for him (*harmotton*, 206d2), although he is to focus upon mental beauty, to remain perceptive of physical beauty also. And if the boy looks beautiful, his appearance can be a continuing reminder of that ideal Beauty which the lover can only, according to Platonic teaching elsewhere, be *re*discovering through recollection. And yet, if an impression of physical beauty is marginally helpful to philosophy, but really irrelevant to the practices and motivations of erotic pedagogy (understood as an attempt to survive through propagating one's own mentality), the unity of philosophical *erōs* remains elusive.

3

The phenomenology of *erōs* is more richly explored within Socrates' second speech in the *Phaedrus*. Socrates offers this to Phaedrus in order "to wash out the bitter taste" (243d4 – 5) of two speeches critical of *erōs*, one written by Lysias and read out by Phaedrus, and another that he has improvised to better it. He approaches his conclusion with a word of depreciation: "This, dear god of love, is offered and paid to you as the finest and best palinode of which I am capable, especially given that it was forced to use somewhat poetical language because of Phaedrus" (257a3 – 6). The reader has to use his own judgment about what to take seriously, and how seriously to take it (cf. Price 1989, 72 n. 24.). He will certainly take absolutely straight the best proof of the immortality of the soul that Plato ever devised, presented here by Socrates with a concision more Aristotelian than poetic (245c5 – 246a2). Elsewhere, he will be uncertain, hesitant to take fantasy literally, but reluctant either to dismiss the theses it clothes or to try to discard their clothing.

About the relation of pederasty to philosophy, Socrates rather teases than instructs us. The man who is at once an *erastēs* of boys and a *philos* of wisdom (*paiderastēsantos meta philosophias*, 249a2) is promised a rapid return to the Platonic heaven; and Socrates ends with a prayer that Phaedrus may henceforth devote his life at once to *erōs* and to philosophy (*pros erōta meta philosophōn logōn*, 257b6). Quite how the "pedophilosopher" is of a piece is never made explicit. Indeed, despite the programmatic demands that prefaced Socrates' first speech (237b7–d3), and a later claim that his second speech has met them (265d5–7), that "right-hand" *erōs* which is both mad and god-sent (266a2–b1) is never actually defined, nor its intentionality determined. Nothing is said that contradicts the characterization of *erōs* in the *Symposium* as directed towards "generation in the beautiful" (*Symposium* 206e5), and a later passage conceives the goal of rhetoric in closely related terms (*Phaedrus* 276e4–277a4). Yet there is at least a shift of attention, away from the prolongation of a family tree, physical or mental, to the mutual loyalty of the nuclear couple. Without a definition, we cannot expect to identify the relation between pedagogy and pederasty with any rigor; yet Plato must intend to present it as internal and not accidental.

Socrates starts his palinode by distinguishing *erōs* as a species of god-sent madness, and by describing the nature of the soul, and its way of life before incarnation. All souls, human and divine, are essentially immortal, and naturally winged and feathered; for a soul to become incarnate is for it to break its wings and lose its feathers, so that it falls to earth and into a body. The proper study of souls is Forms, "his closeness to which gives a god his divinity" (249c6). Each god is pictured as leading a procession of souls its own way to the summit of heaven, from whence the Forms come into view: "Many and blessed are the paths to be seen along which the happy race of gods turns within the heavens, each of them performing what belongs to him; and after them follows anyone who wishes and is able to do so, for jealousy is excluded from the divine chorus" (247a4–7). Abstracting from the imagery, we may draw two striking implications: first, that investigation of the Forms is naturally a concerted activity; secondly, that Forms may properly be investigated in different ways by different mentalities. (However, it is not conceived that different mentalities may cooperate; this will turn out to be decisive for erotic object choice.)

Once a soul has fallen to earth, its task is to return to heaven through the aid of recollection. Only souls that have seen something of the Forms can be incarnated as men; for men are linguistic animals, and grasping general terms involves recollecting Forms (249b5–c2). That is an early exercise of recollection, in which only a Platonist will detect anything transcendent.

A more disorienting experience is open only to a few: when a soul recently initiated and still uncorrupted sees "a godlike face or some form of body which imitates beauty well" (251a2–3), the Form of Beauty somehow becomes apparent to it. Socrates is uncertain how to capture this. Of Wisdom, which is not so apparent, he says both that it is not seen by sight, and that it does not allow any "such clear image of itself to reach our sight" (250d3–6). The first contrast might suggest that Beauty is seen directly, the second that is seen indirectly but clearly. He concludes, somewhat indefinitely, that Beauty is "most manifest and most lovely" (d7–e1). Presumably what he wishes to capture is that the Form only becomes apparent in dependence upon a physical image, but that this opens, and does not obstruct, experiential access to the Form. Socrates' uncertainty mirrors the lover's own confusion: he reverences the boy "as a god," and, if he did not fear to seem crazy, would sacrifice to him "as to a statue and a god"—though the boy is neither, and nothing could be both. Somehow, the Form appears as both immanent and transcendent. Other Forms are not thus apparent to experience: Wisdom offers no image to sight (250d4–6), and, like Justice and Temperance, can only be apprehended through "dulled organs" (b1–5), that is, presumably, not in perceptual experience but in rational abstraction. We may speak of "quasi-perceiving" Beauty, or (see Price 1989, 76–78) of perceiving it "in" or "through" the boy.

What is the effect of this paradoxical experience? Here we meet some apparent vacillation. Socrates first speaks as if a sight of Beauty is love at first sight: "Few souls are left who have sufficient memory [that is, of the Forms]; and these, when they see some likeness of the things there, are driven out of their wits with amazement and lose control of themselves" (250a5–7). Yet later he speaks of a search and selection according to mental congeniality. Of the original followers of Zeus, "each selects his love from the ranks of the beautiful according to his disposition" (252d5–6); more fully, they "seek" for a natural leader and philosopher (*zētousi*), "scrutinize" him (*skopousi*), and "fall in love" with him if they "find" him to be suitable (*heurontes erasthōsi*; e1–4). Similarly, followers of Hera "seek" to "find" someone regal (253b1–2). In short, followers of any god "seek" that their boy should be naturally like him (b3–4). If so, succumbing to *erōs* presupposes an act of selection.

What are the effects of falling in love? Here there are two sources of variety: different gods, who inspire different ideals, and different parts of the soul. In the famous allegory of soul as chariot, reason is the charioteer, and spirit and appetite the two horses, good and bad. Too little is said to give independent life to spirit (though cf. Price 1995, 78–9), but the passage fully and vividly describes how reason's perception provokes appetite's desire (253e5–254a7). What concerns us here is how pederasty becomes pedagogy. In its own manner, even appetite operates through persuasion, conscripting reason to act as a go-between: it "compels" the charioteer to "remind" the boy of the pleasures of making love (254a5–7). When it is being true to its own nature, reason has its own passivities and activities, of which the reader has somehow to make a unity. Passively, the lover finds that seeing the boy (though not remembering him) stimulates the regrowth of his soul's feathers (251b1–252a1); reciprocally, the boy experiences the same as he sees his own reflection in his lover's eyes (255b7–d6). Actively, the lover tries to fashion the boy on the model of their god (252e4–5, 253a6–c2), thereby, in Aristotelian terms, developing his potentiality into actuality; at the same time, perhaps with the help of a guide (indicated as lightly as in the *Symposium*; 252e6), but certainly through the inspiration of the boy, he is developing his own mentality (252e5–253a6). How all this comes together is not made plain. The soul's wings remind us of Cupid's, but roughly symbolize its cognitive capacities (which Plato takes, of course, to be morally motivating as well as intellectually enabling). It cannot be that the lovers regain the use of their wings just through gazing on each other: the stream of beauty that is pictured as entering the lover's eyes may open the outlets of his feathers (251d1–3), but broken wings (248b3) require not just relaxants but physiotherapy. We can anyway presume that the *égoisme* of Platonic dialectic is *à deux*: for Plato (see Price 1989, 91), *Lernen* (learning) is *Lehren* (teaching). If either lover is to reascend to the Platonic heaven, each must regain his mental powers through exercising them with the other (and so sharing the same plumage; 256e1).[9]

Quite how we relate imagery to reality is crucial to how we take Socrates to be connecting pederasty and pedagogy. I interpret him as follows. A man's first susceptible sight of a beautiful face alerts him consciously to his future as a lover of beautiful boys, unconsciously to his past as a beholder of Beauty itself. On a Platonist reading of his implicit purposes, he then looks out for a boy *through* whom he can quasi-perceive Beauty, and *with* whom he can share his style of conceiving it and other Forms. When he finds one, he opens his eyes to the stream of beauty and so enters freely upon a *vita nuova* in which love inspires him to acquire and transmit new habits and practices (252e7–253b1). Since his seeing the boy is his quasi-perceiving the Form, which not only yields delight, but inspires discourse in some mode characteristic of him, and the boy has been selected (in effect) as someone who is able to apprehend the Forms in just that mode, erotic experience and educational activity are two aspects, passive and active, respectively, of a single project.[10]

What has prompted me to set out more fully than before both a problem and a solution is, however, a different solution. In an eloquent and illuminating essay, Martha Nussbaum has found in the *Phaedrus* a tighter tie between visible beauty and mental congeniality. Let me quote a few sentences (1995: 248–49): "Central in Socrates' solution to the cultural problem [of how a state of madness can be beneficent] is an account of how *erōs* can take as its object both bodily beauty and excellence of soul—how, in fact, excellence of soul can manifest itself in the features and shape of the body. . . . Sight is absolutely central in his account of falling in love. . . . However, the 'godlike face that represents beauty well and the form of the body' (251a2–3) can itself contain traces or signs of the character, or the god within" (252d1ff.). As a solution to the cultural problem, this may be welcomed. As an interpretation of Plato, it has to be scrutinized. Let me first concede some details that become felicitous on Nussbaum's reading (with doubts in parentheses).

Slight vacuity becomes acuity if the "godlike face that represents beauty well" is indeed a face that reflects the beautiful mentality of a god. (Yet there is no suggestion of that within the immediate context.) Instead of a double focus within Socrates' imagery, whereby the lover is at once compelled "to gaze intensely on the god . . . grasping him through memory" (253a1–3), and to look at Beauty through the boy's face, we can take him instead to be seeing both Form and god through the face.[11] (Yet if gazing on this god reduces to attending to the Forms in the manner that he symbolizes, the double focus belongs rather to Socrates' imagery than to his meaning.) If he is perceiving the god through the boy, it is still clearer why he would sacrifice to the boy "as to a statue and a god" (251a6) and ascribes to the boy what he derives from the god (253a3–6). (Yet the lover as described in 251a would seem to have in mind no god in particular.)

In a way, it also suits Nussbaum well that it should be the charioteer (that is, reason or cognition) who sees "the erotic vision" (*to erōtikon omma;* 253e5), for it can only be reason that discriminates qualities of character.[12] Indeed, it suits her nicely if *omma* here specifically means the eyes (see de Vries 1969, ad loc.); for, as Athenaeus quotes from some lost Aristotle, it is there that "modesty dwells" (*Deipnosophistae* 13.564B = fr. 96 R³). It may suit her less well that the charioteer's perception is said to excite the horses, good and bad, appetite as well as spirit; for this surely suggests that its object (like that of the sexually stimulating perceptions of 250e) is physical beauty. No doubt it is possible, if rather Victorian, to be sexually stimulated by moral merits (rather as Genet's characters are by moral defects); but it is implausible that that is what Socrates has in mind. However, there is an alternative: perhaps the bad horse both selects and distorts what it receives from the charioteer, so that it registers the vision of a "godlike face" (251a2) impelling a gaze as the impression of an attractive one inviting an ogle.[13] Indeed, we need to suppose this even if we hold that "godlike" indicates only a transcendent mode of visual beauty; for (as is clear from the contrast, albeit between persons and not parts of a person, that is drawn within 250e1–251a7) it is the materiality and not the ideality of beauty that enkindles copulatory desire.[14]

Elsewhere, Plato shows an implicit awareness that a state of mind may become visually manifest. A phenomenon that almost becomes a *topos* is the blush. Hippothales blushes when asked about the younger boy Lysis (*Lysis* 204b5, c3–4, d4), and again, from pleasure, when Socrates has pretended to prove that love must be reciprocated (222b2)—a phenomenon that makes it easy for Socrates to detect who is in love (204b8–c2). Hippocrates blushes as he talks to Socrates, as day is dawning, about his youthful aspirations (*Protagoras* 312a2). Charmides blushes, and so looks by a befitting bashfulness all the more beautiful, when Socrates asks him a flattering question (*Charmides* 158c5). Less congruously, the grown-up Thrasymachus blushes when he senses that he is losing the argument (*Republic* 1.350d3). If we can read Plato as accommodating such phenomena theoretically, so much the better for his fidelity to his own experience.

And yet, though I have no singly decisive objection, I am not persuaded to read the *Phaedrus* along these lines. Nussbaum is free to read Socrates' talk of the lover's "selection" (252d6) less literally, and awkwardly, than I have. But I think that the awkwardness is motivated. I take it to arise because Socrates wishes both to acknowledge the relevance of the beloved's character to the lover's object choice at 252c3ff. and to retain his earlier explanation of the unique power of physical beauty at 250b1–e1. There, as I noted, he emphasized a distinction: Justice and the rest we apprehend dimly, grasping their images with "dulled" organs (b1–5), presumably not perceptual ones; Beauty alone we perceive vividly, somehow *seeing* it by means of images in or through which it becomes apparent to experience. If it were implicit in the later passage, what is certainly not explicit, that the boy's character is perceptually apparent to the man, that would surely cloud the contrast.[15]

A less local obstacle is constituted by Plato's general views about the limits of perception. In the *Theaetetus*, he has Socrates insist—to reexpress the point in Aristotle's jargon — that only the "proper" objects of some particular sense or other are objects of perception (184d7–185a3); hence, color can be seen, as sound can be heard, but "being and nonbeing, likeness and unlikeness, same and different" (185c9–10) cannot be perceived, and can only be apprehended through the "calculations" (*analogismata*; 186c3) of "the soul itself" (b7–8). The same is said not only of "being," but of "utility" (c3), which is a value (if not a moral one).[16] Now it is already true on my reading that the *Phaedrus* is extending the limits of perception (how seriously on Plato's part is an open question), for the Beauty that is seen in or through a complexion is of a different category from color. Yet we can read this as a tipsy epicycle upon the sobrieties of the *Theaetetus*. Even if the Form of Beauty is not exclusively a Form of physical beauty, physical beauty of the kind that Socrates has in mind has to be *seen* to be believed (unless with the aid of the visual imagination), and his claim in 250d is precisely that quasi-perceiving Beauty is a mode of perceiving physical beauty. So long as he is not raising any sophisticated questions about the relation of perception to cognition, he may well allow himself to entertain the thought that Beauty is a transcendent object of *sight*.

I have acknowledged that Plato was implicitly familiar with the physical as expressive of the mental in the phenomenon of the blush; the question is whether he accommodates it theoretically. Perhaps he might have done so, despite his dualism of mind and body.[17] (After all, we have seen that he allows one Form, if only that of Beauty, to be quasi-perceived despite his usual dichotomy between an intelligible world of Forms and a visible world of material things.) And yet it seems that, within his way of thinking, mental and physical beauty are contrasted or juxtaposed, never blended as they become in the experience of someone who sees a mind in a body. In the *Charmides*, Charmides is said to have a beautiful face, also body, also mind (154d1–e7). Each is to be detected in turn: the face at once, the body if it is stripped of its clothes, the mind if it is stripped, metaphorically, in discussion. In the *Symposium*, as we saw, the lover begins by appreciating physical beauty; he then ascends to mental beauty, and values it more highly, so that now just a little beauty of body will suffice for him (210a4–c1). There is no suggestion that a mind can lend beauty to an otherwise mediocre body — just as there is no suggestion, later on, that it detracts from Alcibiades' beauty of form (*eumorphia*) that he lacks the "altogether different" beauty which he ascribes to Socrates (218e2–3). The closest relations that Plato, when theorizing, allows between body and mind are agreement and harmony (*Republic* 3.402d1–4; cf. *Timaeus* 87d4–8); those are still relations that hold between different and separate things.

His personal paradigm remains Socrates, precisely because he had an unusually ugly body to contrast with an unusually beautiful mind; Alcibiades likens him to little statues containing figures of the gods inside (*Symposium* 215a6–b3). Socrates' relation to his body vividly exemplifies the general predicament of the incarnate soul, trapped like an oyster in its shell (*Phaedrus* 250c6). A shell, like a mask, obscures, and does not express, what lies within.

I conclude that Socrates' second speech in Plato's *Phaedrus* is sensitive to questions about the relations of pederasty to pedagogy, and of beauty to educability. We may well feel that its inventions are elaborate but not ideal, and that Nussbaum is alert to a phenomenon that philosophy should recognize. But for a solution along her lines, and a theoretical framework to accommodate it, we must proceed to the Stoics.

4

If we move directly from Plato's *Phaedrus* to the *Stoicorum Veterum Fragmenta* (as Johannes von Arnim was invaluably to collect them), we enter a new world.[18] In place of a living organism, as it were, with head and feet (cf. *Phaedrus* 264c2–5), we have the scattered bones of a fragmentary skeleton. In a way, the accidents of transmission may have been apt: Stoic dogmas may lend themselves better to doxographic compilation than Platonic fantasy and irony. And what little we retain includes what Socrates' second speech failed to supply: a definition. Yet we have a delicate task to perform: making the most of fragments, while bearing in mind that it is fragments that we are making the most of.

I have suggested that a restrictive idea of perception made Plato theoretically blind, however personally sensitive, to the visible presence of minds in bodies. If all that can strictly be perceived are the "proper" objects of each sense, there must be a gulf set between perception and thought. Aristotle was to insist (*De Anima* 2.6) that we perceive not only proper objects, but "common" objects (such as shape and movement), plainly apparent to more than one sense, and also "incidental" objects (such as man, and even son of Diares), not plainly apparent to sense at all. He has good arguments against assigning incidental objects not to perception but to inference: for instance, the sun appears one foot across, but is not believed (nor, therefore, inferred) to be so (3.3.428b3–4). About the workings of incidental perception he is less explicit. Plausibly it involves the cooperation of *phantasia* in its role as imagination. In interesting cases where perception is evaluative, it must also involve pleasure or pain: "To feel pleasure or pain is to act with the perceptive mean towards what is good or bad as such" (3.7.431a10–11). Such perception becomes crucial in the *Nicomachean Ethics*: it is by perception, not reason, that we detect not only whether bread has been baked as it should (3.3.1113a1), but whether a deviation from the mean is blameworthy (2.9.1109b20–23). Even the lower animals can perceive incidental objects: the lion perceives that the ox is near by its lowing (3.10.1118a20–21). Yet rational subjects must have a richer repertory which exploits the possession of concepts. Aristotle makes room for this when he tells us that *both* parts of the human soul, rational *and* irrational, are peculiar to human beings (*EE* 2.1.1219b37–38). However, it is only implicitly that he allows concepts to affect perceptions. A conception to do justice to this central part of our perceptual experience (vivid to us in the example, made famous by Wittgenstein, of the image that really *looks* different according as we see it as a duck or as a rabbit) had still to become explicit.

With Aristotle, we have full evidence of a fragmentary view; with the Stoics, we have what looks like fragmentary evidence of a full view. Aristotle marks a crucial transition between Plato and the Stoics, but these took a decisive further step when they proposed that *all* the impressions of rational animals are rational (Diogenes Laertius, *SVF* 2.24.21–22 = LS 39A6 = *Vitae Philosophorum* 7.51). Every operation of the adult human mind is distinctively human, and different from those of the lower animals. In their relation to the commanding faculty or control center (*hēgemonikon*), the senses are likened to the tentacles of an octopus (Aëtius, *SVF* 2.227.25–27 = LS 53H2–3); the image conveys that even our perceptions are applications of concepts. It is not implied that our perceptions are beliefs, for these additionally involve the element of consent (*sunkatathesis*). Cicero reports an illustration by Zeno: he "would spread out the fingers of one hand and display its open palm, saying 'An impression is like this.' Next he clenched his fingers a little and said, 'Assent is like this'" (Cicero, *SVF* 1.19.34–36 = LS 41A2–3 = *Academica* 2.145). Further, beliefs are verbal, while perceptual impressions are verbalizable.[19] In thought, we articulate the concepts that are already active within our perceptions.

This new (or newly explicit) conception had the corollary that there is no clear a priori limit to the concepts that may infuse perception. Cicero (LS 39C1–2 = *Academica* 2.21) lists first "white," "sweet," "fragrant," and "bitter" (which Aristotle would take to label proper objects of perception), but also "melodious" (which is surely more complex), and then "horse" and "dog" (which label incidental objects). Plutarch tells us that Chrysippus (who became head of the Stoa thirty years after Zeno's death) went further in his book *On the End* (*Peri Telous*): we can even perceive good and bad (*SVF* 3.85 = *De Stoicorum Repugnantiis* 1042E–F, 1062C). More precisely, Plutarch has Chrysippus claim that we can perceive goods and evils (including theft and adultery, courage and cowardice), and "the good," but his meaning was presumably that we can perceive things *as* good or evil, either generically or specifically. And Cicero is explicit: our eyes "recognize" (*cognoscunt*) virtues and vices (*De Natura Deorum* 2.145).

No doubt Chrysippus introduced refinements.[20] Yet we can be sure that both the conception and the corollary go back to the founder, Zeno, for we read that Cleanthes said that Zeno claimed that character was cognizable (*kataleptos*) from appearance (*SVF* 1.204 = D.L. 7.173).[21] This conveys that he admitted not only impressions of moral character, but cognitively reliable ones.[22] Doubtless it was by such an impression that Cleanthes once detected a pathic by his sneeze (*SVF* 1.618 = D.L. 7.173).[23] Clement of Alexandria preserves from Zeno, probably verbatim, a sketch of "a beautiful and properly loveable image of a young man" (*SVF* 1.246; see Schofield 1991, 115–18): "Let his countenance be pure; his brow not relaxed; his eye not wide open nor half-closed; his neck not thrown back, nor the limbs of his body relaxed, but keyed up like strings under tension; his ear cocked for the *logos;* and his bearing and movement giving no hope to the licentious. Let modesty and a manly look flower upon him." Despite Malcolm Schofield's suggestion ("Zeno is urging young men to *aim for* a particular sort of physical bearing"; 1991, 117), I take this not to be a lesson in deportment addressed to a would-be Stoic *erōmenos* (not that Zeno was unwilling to give one, cf. *SVF* 1.245 = D.L. 7.22), but a lesson in erotic object choice addressed to a potential *erastēs* supposed to be making an inspection and selection (somewhat like a horse trader). Once the lesson is learned, much time should be saved: external scrutiny can take the place of intimate acquaintance.

The corrupt lover might misapply the lesson for his own purposes. The Stoics no more *define* a neutral genus of *erōs* than they do of good and bad emotions (*eupatheiai* and *pathē*); but, in the manner of moralists, they make certain broad contrasts. *Erōs* is spoken of in two senses (Stobaeus, *SVF* 3.180.23–24; cf. scholium, *SVF* 3.181.24). Bad *erōs* is desire (*epithumia;* Stobaeus, *SVF* 3.180.33–34); its object is the body (scholium, *SVF* 3.181.24); its goal is sexual intercourse (*SVF* 3.180.19 = D.L. 7.130). Good *erōs* is for the soul (scholium, *SVF* 3.181.24); its goal is friendship (*philia; SVF* 3.718 = D.L. 7.130). More precisely, we have several citations, with some abbreviation, of what seems to have become the school definition of, I take it, good *erōs* (the *erōs* that deserves its name). I quote from Stobaeus:

"*erōs* is a resolve to make friends, on account of beauty being manifested, with youths in bloom" (*SVF* 3.650; see Schofield 1991, 29). Let us stay with this formulation.[24]

My phrase "being manifested" renders the term *emphainomenon*. This participle (or occasionally the variant "manifestation," *emphasis*) is recurrent, and evidently carefully chosen. We miss that fact, and permit good *erōs* too simple a cause, if, with Schofield, we translate simply "apparent." The verb *emphainō* is often used literally to mean "reflect."[25] It is also used derivatively of displaying or revealing character.[26] It so functions within a dictum ascribed to Zeno's *Republic* that would seem to anticipate the definition: "The wise man will love those youths who by their appearance manifest (*emphainontōn*) a natural endowment for virtue" (*SVF* 1.248 = D.L. 7.130). Beauty that is "manifested" is beauty of mind and heart made apparent in outward appearance.[27] Thus, the term is fit to capture the paradox, now accommodated within theory, of a beauty that is not *visual* and yet becomes *visible*.[28]

An associated phrase is *anthos aretēs* (the flower of virtue), identified by two of our sources, Plutarch (*Amatorius* 767B) and Diogenes Laertius (7.130 = *SVF* 3.718), with "bloom" (*hōra*) as a stimulus to *erōs*. Schofield is skeptical, commenting as follows (1991: 114): "This is evidently an attempt to make sense of '[youths] in bloom' in [the definition]. The attempt obviously does not work. On Zeno's story, the youthful object of the sage's love is not yet virtuous — not yet in full flower — but merely naturally endowed for virtue. Moreover, if I am right, [the definition] aims at an account of love which is ethically neutral in any case." He thus supposes that the identification of "bloom" with "the flower of virtue" is an apologist's gloss upon the school definition of *erōs* that carries no authority. This seems doubly speculative: first, neither author evidently uses "flower of virtue" to *make sense* of "youths in bloom"; secondly, if others did, they may have been Stoics. Whether original or imported, does the identification work? I have noted two main grounds against taking the definition to be ethically neutral: the simple contrast that is drawn between a good love set on friendship and a bad one set on sexual intercourse, and the inapplicability of the phrase "on account of beauty being manifested" to a love inspired by visual beauty.[29] If the definition is morally loaded, the identification of "bloom" with "flower of virtue" applies only to the object worthy of love (*axioerastos*) that a good love (*spoudaios erōs*) finds it fit to befriend (Stobaeus, *SVF* 3.180.25–27). It is of such a person that Zeno wrote (if Clement is quoting him), "Let modesty and a manly look flower upon him" (*epantheitō; SVF* 1.58.29–30). So the metaphor of moral "flowering" most likely goes back to Zeno himself;

yet is it still a fatal objection that the flower of *virtue* can only be the possession of a sage, not of a youth?[30] We have to attend to the various senses of *anthos* (which relate much like those of the Latin *flos*). Literally, it denotes *flower* or *blossom*, which any apple-grower would distinguish sharply from *fruit* (*karpos*).[31] The term then took on the figurative meaning of "flower of youth" (cf. Proust's *jeunes filles en fleur*), still in distinction from maturity. Thus, in Plato's *Symposium*, the *anthos* of the body (183e3) is not its physical prime or *akmē* (which Aristotle thinks is reached at thirty; *Rhetoric* 2.14.1390b9–10), but its visual peak (which for males is at adolescence). Finally, the term could be used figuratively in nonphysical and nonerotic contexts in which the contrast with fruit was lost. Thus, the phrase *anthos aretēs* is indeed ambiguous: in an erotic context it may well mean "the blossom of virtue," while in other contexts it would rather signify "the ripeness of virtue."[32] It is possible that, in withholding the phrase from moral promise in order to reserve it for moral perfection, Schofield is reenacting a Stoic disagreement, verbal or real. Diogenes Laertius informs us, in a miscellaneous context (but shortly, though not immediately, after a remark about friendship), that Zeno called beauty "the flower of temperance," while others called temperance "the flower of beauty" (*SVF* 1.330 = D.L. 7.23).[33] We cannot recover the context of either claim or know whether they shared one. I am tempted to suspect a play on words: Zeno may have meant that youthful beauty was the *blossom* of temperance, others that temperance was the *acme* of mature beauty. If they thought themselves at odds (which the passage leaves open), they were speaking at cross purposes.

Quite apart from the *bloom*, difficulties attach to the *beauty* that is manifested, as Plutarch sets out succinctly: "The young are ugly, since they are common and stupid, and the wise are beautiful; and yet none of these who are beautiful is either loved or worth loving. And this is not yet the strange part, which is that those who were in love with the ugly cease loving them when they become beautiful" (*SVF* 3.181.5–9 = *De Communibus Notitiis* 1073A; cf. *Stoicos Absurdiora Poetis Dicere* 1058A). Part of his argument may be expanded as follows: the Stoics hold that virtue and vice are all or nothing, and that there is nothing in between them;[34] so vice must be predicable, without a scintilla of virtue, of even the most promising of the morally immature; now vice is presumably as visible as virtue; how then can they attract the love of a sage? To this much of his criticism there may be a ready answer. The Stoics acknowledged the existence of "progressors" (*prokoptontes*), unwise until the moment of enlightenment; and they surely must have recognized that, though these do not count as being virtuous *at all* (since virtue does not come in degrees), yet their transitional state is commendable in the young, and should be perceptible with pleasure. Indeed, Plutarch is consistent only in always controverting the Stoics: he argues from their own premises *both* (in order to embarrass their definition of *erōs*) that a promising boy could no more manifest beauty than a wicked man (*SVF* 3.181.9–13 = *De Communibus Notitiis* 1073B), *and also* (in order to question their preference for pederasty) that girls and boys may equally "make a manifestation of a natural endowment for virtue" (*Amat.* 767B). A sentence of Cicero may reflect the compromises of a later age, but ends pertinently: "Since life is passed not in the company of men who are perfect and truly wise, but of those who do very well if they show likenesses of virtue, I think it must be understood that no one should be entirely neglected in whom any mark of virtue is evident" (LS 66D = *De Officiis* 1.46). It is plausible to suppose that a mark of virtue (*"significatio virtutis"*) may be perceptibly and agreeably present in a progressor, especially a precocious one, even though virtue is as yet absent. Which is surely confirmed by the passage, probably of Zeno's, already quoted from Clement (*SVF* 1.246).[35]

Yet saying that only parries Plutarch's point, for a paradox remains. We read in Stobaeus (*SVF* 3.630) that the good man is "lovely" (*epaphroditos*, Latin *venustus*)—which is only a variation on the commonplace that he (and he alone) is beautiful (*SVF* 3.591, 594, 597–99);[36] and yet, as Sextus Empiricus observes, no one falls in love with old men (*SVF* 3.97.35 = *Adversus Mathematicos* 7.239).[37] Even if a youth can be visibly progressing, and so beautiful *in a way*, why should he be a *better* object of a moralized *erōs* than a man who is morally mature (and so at least middle-aged)? And why should he *cease* to be an object of *erōs* once he has achieved maturity (and middle age) himself?[38] Presumably the Stoics did not intend a definitional full stop, whereby "a resolve to make friends on account of beauty being manifested" *counts as erōs* when and only when it happens to take a youth as its object; rather, the bloom and the beauty must *connect*. So the thought has to be that the "flower of virtue" has a double parentage: the virtue that it visibly promises, and the visual bloom that it permeates. Plutarch cites Ariston (more likely Zeno's pupil than the Peripatetic) as saying that a pure and orderly character can shine through (become *diaphanēs*) in outward bloom and charm (*hōra* and *charis* of *morphē*), just as a properly made shoe shows the natural shapeliness of a foot (*SVF* 1.390 = *Amat.* 766F). If we take Ariston at his word, the visual and the moral beauty of a young progressor do not *coexist;* instead, they become one (rather as the shape of the shoe *is* the shape of the foot). And the visual bloom becomes indeed the *blossom*, and not just (say) the *bud*, of virtue: the beauty of virtue is *beautifully* prefigured. The phrase *anthos aretēs* is thus pregnant, and not out of place; it contains in germ the heart of my argument. We must suppose that the Stoics conceived of visual and visible beauties as uniting, within the person of a promising adolescent, in a blend that is only apparent to the man who is at once an actual sage and a potential lover. In the terms of a Ciceronian contrast, *flos aetatis* (flower of youth) can be infused with *spes virtutis* (promise of virtue). If there is a mystery here in the chemistry of eyes and heart, it may be one that is not invented but revealed.

The definition of a good *erōs* that I have been discussing is inexplicit about its manner of operation. The dictum of Zeno's that I cited (*SVF* 1.248 = D.L. 7.129) says expressly that what is manifested by the boy's appearance is "a natural endowment for virtue." A related characterization that we meet in Plutarch is close to Zeno but introduces the metaphor of the chase (*thēra*): "Love is a sort of chase after a lad who is undeveloped but naturally endowed for virtue" (*SVF* 3.181.14–15 = *De Communibus Notitiis* 1073B). The term "chase" may sound predatory to us; but hunting was a common Greek metaphor for courtship (see Dover 1978, 87–88), and Plutarch pairs it with "making friends" (1073C). That it becomes the lover's task to *develop* the boy's potential is already a natural corollary of the requirement that he have that potential if he is to inspire *erōs*. Arius Didymus makes the corollary explicit when he defines the science of love as "knowledge of the chase after naturally endowed youths, [a knowledge] which is directed toward turning them to living in accordance with virtue" (Stobaeus, *SVF* 3.180.30–31).

The charm of such activity is easy to conceive: in enhancing the qualities that attract him, the lover is at once indulging and increasing his enjoyment of them. Yet we can see the advantage of a deep explanation of his motivation of the kind that Plato offered in his *Symposium*. A theory that derived erotic love from a primal need to procreate could easily rationalize why the *erōmenos* must be immature (if not why he should be more than coincidentally attractive): he has to be receptive of a new mentality.[39] As it is, keeping to the evidence we have, we can only suppose that the Stoics take over from *erōs* as commonly conceived and experienced that the *erōmenos* must be "in bloom," and introduce the desire to educate not as a cause but as a corollary of *erōs* as they define it. Yet we can confirm the corollary by relating it to their understanding of the explicit goal of *erōs* within the definition, which is making friends. They ascribe to sages a monopoly not only of beauty, but of friendship: "They say that friendship exists only among the virtuous, on account of their similarity" (*SVF* 3.161.15–16 = LS 67P = D.L. 7.124). Consequently, the definition connects twice with pedagogy: loving a promising youth, the man *can* educate him; desiring his friendship, he *must* do so. A good *erōs* must take views as long as those of a bad *erōs* are short; for the friendship can be achieved only *after* the pedagogy has succeeded, and so only in the Indian summer, if not in the aftermath, of the erotic relationship. However, this may preecho the eventual friendship before it overlaps with it. If, as I suggested, the Stoics were willing to apply to progressors a conception of moral beauty in the bud, they may also have allowed that a foretaste of friendship can unite the wise and the wise-to-be in a shared anticipation of the full friendship that is to be achieved once the boy's nature has become second nature. To allow that is to predicate of the budding friendship—call it *prōtophilia*—significant features of friendship itself.[40] Like Aristotle, the Stoics conceive of this as mutual benefit, not in the manner of a quid pro quo, but with the thought that to benefit a friend is *eo ipso* to benefit oneself: "All goods are common to the virtuous, and all that is bad to the inferior; therefore, a man who benefits someone also benefits himself, and one who does harm also harms himself" (Stobaeus, *SVF* 3.626 = LS 60P). A mature friendship is a sharing of virtue: Seneca assures Lucilius that good men are mutually helpful, exercising one another's virtues and maintaining wisdom in her position (*Epistulae Morales* 109.1). A pederastic relationship that makes a person virtuous and wise cannot be equally reciprocal, but the benefit that it bestows is greater, and equally shared. Whereas, according to Seneca (*Epistulae Morales* 9.15), a sage does not *need* friends in order to live happily, a progressor may well need a mentor in order to become happy. And, for his part, the lover can hardly find a better way of practicing his actual qualities than in realizing the qualities of a person who will owe to him not only their friendship, but his capacity for friendship. His education will be at once an exercise of *prōtophilia* and a preparation for friendship proper. Much as in Plato, the pedagogic project combines the private urgency of *erōs* with the public value of doing good.

5

To a large extent, the Stoic definition of *erōs* is the key to their conception. Yet in one respect the pedagogic demands derivative from a demanding conception of friendship appear to have made a curious and concrete difference to their practice in disregard of the definition. We read that, harping on the theme "One must love not bodies but the soul," they prescribed retaining an *erōmenos* until the age of twenty-eight (Athenaeus, *SVF* 1.247 = *Deipnosophistae* 13.563E). That it was praiseworthy to sacrifice a little bloom for a little more maturity was not a new idea. Plato's Pausanias, who contrasted noble with vulgar love in a manner anticipatory of the Stoics, had distinguished lovers who "do not love boys so much as those who are already beginning to be intelligent, and this occurs around the time when the beard is growing" (*Symposium* 181d1–3). That preference still respected the convention that it was high time for an *erōmenos* to switch to being an *erastēs* when adolescent down had finally made way for the adult beard. According to the Hippocratic tradition, most famously set out in an elegy of Solon's (27) which divides a man's life into hebdomads (periods of seven years), that allowed just seven years, from fourteen to twenty-one, for a youth to play the role of an *erōmenos* without any suspicion of unmanliness on either side. Clearly, reality was more variable. At the start of Plato's *Protagoras*, a friend teases Socrates for still "hunting" after Alcibiades when he was a *man*, "with his beard already coming" (309a1–5); and yet, if Plato is careful and C. C. W. Taylor correct (1991 ad loc.), Alcibiades was then just seventeen. In taking precisely twenty-eight as the terminus, the Stoics were of course falling in with conventional hebdomadology;[41] but in envisaging *erōmenoi* well into their twenties they were breaking with a tradition alive within their own definition. On the other hand, we have no evidence that they also preferred a later starting point. How may they have rationalized a terminus a quo certainly not before fourteen, and a terminus ad quem as late as twenty-eight?

A scholiast ascribes to Zeno (but also to Aristotle and the Pythagorean Alcmaeon) this gloss upon the age of fourteen: "Then perfect *logos* is displayed" (*SVF* 1.149). The grammatical interests of the Stoics make it natural to suppose that "perfect *logos*" in their mouths meant in part a full mastery of syntax. We can also cite Aëtius, who has them hold that by fourteen there exists a conception of good and evil (*SVF* 2.764). Taking these together, we can infer that an adolescent boy was accepted as a potential participant in ethical dialogue. Why twenty-eight? It may be pertinent that Solon placed within the fourth hebdomad, from twenty-one to twenty-eight, the peak in a man's strength, "by which men indicate virtue" (27.7–8).[42] At least according to Aristotle (*History of Animals* 7.1.582a29), twenty-one itself was a little early: at that age men, unlike women, have still to grow. Materialists about the mind, the Stoics found physical fitness more than a *sign* of a sound character. When we read in Stobaeus: "Just as strength of body is adequate tension (*tonos*) in the sinews, so strength of soul is adequate tension in deciding and acting or refraining" (*SVF* 3.68.29–31), we must remember that tension was *at once* physical and mental. Hence they will naturally have supposed that a man's twenties were a crucial period of moral maturing just in virtue of human biology. However, their main reason is likely to have been grounded within ethics: their ambitious and "all-

or-nothing" conception of what it is to be virtuous demanded more time for ethical progression.

And yet the upshot was problematic. I have argued that the Stoics could reconcile moralistic ideal with erotic reality through a fusion of visual and visible beauties, of *flos aetatis* and *spes virtutis*. But a bearded young man in his twenties would have lost the bloom that transmuted mental promise into bodily blossom. So in linking pederasty to pedagogy, while raising the leaving age to match an exigent conception of what it was to be educated, the Stoics risked extending their conception of *erōs* well beyond the "youths in bloom" of their definition, in a manner that either etiolated *erōs* or enjoined erotic eccentricity. Plutarch anyway accuses them of the first, complaining, "Nobody would stop the enthusiasm of the wise for the young, given that there is no passion [*pathos*] in it, if it is called 'a chase' or 'making friends'—but they wouldn't let them call it 'love'" (*De Communibus Notitiis* 1073C). There may be some terminological trouble here. The Stoics defined *pathē* as species of false belief, and so could have nothing of them; the sage's loves must have counted as *eupatheiai*, emotions that escaped illusion and anxiety by valuing intentions and deprecating contingencies, and so achieved elation without agitation. Hence, their alternative to passion was not impassibility. However, Plutarch has a concrete ground of complaint in the extended age range for an *erōmenos:* in Greek eyes, a decently masculine *erōs* that admitted *men* as its objects risked being *erōs* only in name.

It may be that the Stoic answer was to stress a distinction. What Athenaeus has in mind is not a man who falls for a beard, but an established *erastēs* who *retains* his *erōmenos* even past his visual prime. It is even possible (though not likely within such a context as he offers) that what is envisaged is that the *erōmenos* be retained not *as* an *erōmenos*, but so as to become a friend. (If he was simply discarded before becoming virtuous and eligible for friendship, the goal of *erōs*—which was friendship—would never be achieved.) If the Stoics did intend the relationship to remain erotically charged, they may have been sensitive to a feature of human attachment overlooked by the later Greek *topos* (see Tarán 1985) that the arrival of a beard put an *erōmenos* out of court. No more erotically than personally do we reassess one another every day. (Love is not love which alters when it alteration finds.) If Stoic eyes could see a mental future in an adolescent face, they could surely see a physical past in an adult one; and then they could enjoy perceiving mental beauties in physical features reminiscent of recent visual charms. (Here the conceptual theory of perception can do further work.) This could constitute the psychological truth lying behind an anecdote in Plutarch: Euripides is said to have exclaimed, as he kissed an Agathon who was already growing (or had already grown) a beard, "Of all those who are beautiful even the autumn is beautiful" (*Amat.* 770C)— though Plutarch himself endorses that only for Alcibiades "and a few others" (*Alcibiades* 1.5).

Athenaeus raises the different possibility of a recourse to technology when, apparently echoing early satire aimed at the Stoa, he accuses the Stoics of taking their *erōmenoi* around with shaven chins (*Deipnosophistae* 13.564F, cf. 563D–E). This was at least a conceivable solution: Dio Chrysostom describes how those who first tried shaving their beards found that their faces became "pretty and boyish beyond their years when rid of that down" (*Orationes* 33.63.7–8). Aristophanes already mocked Agathon for practising a close shave (*Thesmophoriazousae* 191–92); a smooth cheek may have helped him to retain, well into adulthood, lovers (perhaps including Pausanias) less willing to make allowances than Euripides. And yet one might well dismiss Athenaeus's charge as scurrilous if two considerations did not give one pause. First, the early Stoics inherited a Cynic preference for impropriety. It has not been relevant here to draw attention to their conscious unconventionalities; but if Zeno could raise Plutarch's hackles (*SVF* 1.252 = *Quaestiones Conviviales* 653E) by finding space in his *Republic*, rather than in some *Symposium*, for his "intercruralities" (*diamērismous*, presumably candid and unceremonious discussion of intercrural copulation), he may not have disdained to resolve our problem in a similarly down-to-earth way.[43] Secondly, Athenaeus cites names: he has Chrysippus observe, presumably without disapproval, that shaving the beard increased under Alexander (*Deipnosophistae* 13.564F–565A); he also has Antigonus of Carystus accuse the Stoics of leading their *erōmenoi* around "with shaven chins and posteriors" (565F)—which is more likely a vulgar parody (much in the manner of comedy, always imputing anality) than an invention out of nothing.

Be that as it may: it is not our task to extricate the Stoics from embarrassments of their own making. Relevant here is rather that we have evidence that the awkwardness that has arisen is not the mirage of a misinterpretation, but a reality that raised eyebrows at the time. The Stoics were concerned both to change men's lives and to respect common experience (*sōzein tēn sunētheian*; Plutarch *De Communibus Notitiis* 1063D). They strove to weave innovation within tradition, not demanding of the *erastēs* a totally new sensibility, but rather reconceiving the conventional bloom of the *erōmenos* in a way permitted by their philosophy of perception and prescribed by their moralization of *erōs*. It is remarkable how far they succeeded.

6

A modern liberal philosopher who looks back at such attempts to define a distinctively philosophical love is likely to feel that they were all misconceived. Proust somewhere remarks, "There is no such thing as a good choice in love, for in love all choice is bad." A philosopher may find his loves touched by his philosophy (and vice versa), but hardly in ways that he would wish to have planned. Love, like life, is something that happens. Isaiah Berlin understood that when, toward the end of his life, he wrote this for the Chinese: "'Where is the song before it is sung?' Where indeed? 'Nowhere' is the answer—one creates the song by singing it, by composing it. So, too, life is created by those who live it, step by step" (Ignatieff 1998, 295). What we may be readiest to admire in Plato and the Stoics is a sensitivity to reality that illumines their ingenuity in theory—a sensitivity richly displayed in all we have of Plato, and economically evidenced in what little we have of Zeno. These are theorizers who are always making things up, but in ways that are quickened as much by collaboration as by resistance from the world of experience. Even as they urge a change of life, they open our eyes to the intricacies and amenities of the actual lives that are the only lives we know we can lead.

Notes

1. The Greek terms for lover and beloved within a pederastic relationship were *erastēs* and *erōmenos*, respectively. I shall frequently use the term "boy" for the *erōmenos*, and occasionally the term "man" for the *erastēs*, without intending any precise implications about their absolute or relative ages. As I briefly discuss later, convention prescribed for an *erōmenos* any age between fourteen and twenty-one—which overlaps with Martha Nussbaum's slightly sanitizing suggestion of "the age of a modern college undergraduate" (1994, 1551).

2. Two exceptions to prove the rule are *Republic* 5.468b12–c4, and *Laws* 8.836a7. Sir Kenneth Dover is circumspect but hardly dissentient: "We must leave open the possibility that [Plato's] own homosexual emotion was abnormally intense and his heterosexual response abnormally deficient" (1978, 12).

3. Malcolm Schofield cites a third-century Cynic poem which identifies "Zenonian love" with a form of homosexuality (1991, 45 n. 39). On my modes of reference to sources for the early Stoics, see n. 18 below.

4. Aristotle concedes causal cross-currents: beauty alone may provoke only a desire for pleasure; but an athlete who is both beautiful and brave may inspire goodwill in response to *both* qualities (*Nicomachean Ethics* 9.5.1167a18–21).

5. I once suggested (1989, 249), in connection with another passage (*Nicomachean Ethics* 7.5.1148b28–34), that Aristotle has a quasi-medical concern to keep pederasty to "looking rather than loving," as Plato had put it (*Laws* 8.837c4–5). I should have noted that, as his anxiety attaches to *habituation* to sexual passivity *from boyhood*, no blanket proscription of sexual relations is in question. Further, I may well have been wrong to set aside the discussion of anal intercourse in the pseudo-Aristotelian *Problemata* (4.26); for Aristotle's own *History of Animals* (7.581b12–21) connects a need of surveillance of young adolescents, male and female, with a special concern about the dilation of certain "passages." His own predilections may have been, or become, connubial; but he says nothing that begins to tell against intercrural intercourse that is not too frequent with a boy who is not too young. I fully accept correction on this point by Nussbaum (1994, 1591–92).

6. Schofield raises a slightly different question: "On Plato's premises, there is no reason why someone who exhibits the physical beauty which provokes the philosopher's desire must also be someone likely to develop into a morally admirable person" (1991, 31); he nicely labels this "the Alcibiades problem." It is pertinent to the Stoics, but less apt to Plato: in the *Symposium*, the lover on his way to becoming a philosopher may well switch objects as he ascends from physical to mental beauty (210a4–c2); in the *Phaedrus*, he selects someone congenial to love from the ranks of the beautiful (252d5–6).

7. Here I follow Schofield (1991, 32) and Nussbaum (1995, 258–59) on the Stoics, and diverge from Nussbaum (1995, 248–49) on Plato—for she finds the breakthrough already present in the *Phaedrus*. Each is a parent of this essay (*patēr tou logou; Symposium* 177d5), though I shall sometimes bite the hand that feeds me. In quotations from Plato, I keep fairly close to C. J. Rowe's translations of the *Symposium* and *Phaedrus* (1998, 1986).

8. Translators vary between permitting an *erōmenos* who has *little* bloom or *a little* bloom—a tiny but telling difference. I take *kan smikron* (*Symposium* 210b8) to indicate the second. If so, Socrates is demanding a little physical appeal (if not much), and not just supposing idly that any boy is physically appealing to a degree. In either case he is not far from Pausanias, who commended loving the noblest and best "even if they are plainer than others" (182d7).

9. It is true that the term *homopteros* itself only ascribes a similar nature, and not a common growth, to the lovers' plumage. Yet one may compare Aristotle *Nicomachean Ethics* 8.4.1157a10–12 (quoted earlier), where, in a related context, *homoētheis ontes* ("being alike in character") ascribes to lovers who remain faithful an affinity that they realize together (see Price 1989, 247–48).

10. Of course compare the recurrent connection between attending to an object, and communicating about it through *logoi*, in the ascent passage of the *Symposium*. What is lacking there is the complication of differing cognitive mentalities.

11. Thus, de Vries comments ad loc., "The 'image' of the god is meant, which is present in the beloved" (1969, 162).

12. The tripartite psychology of the *Phaedrus* is in some ways simplified (Price 1995, 77–78), and I doubt whether it is really a good question which part of the tripartite soul is the subject of all or some perceiving (ibid., 70–71). However, if we *are* to

identify some part as the subject of the erotic perception, we have to opt for reason, for the perception is also recollection of a Form.

13. Compare how, in the *Republic* (8.561d2), the democratic man, though a creature of appetite, takes on a dilettantish taste for philosophy that presumably derives by way of depravement from the philosopher's passion for truth. (See Price 1995, 62–63.)

14. The interpretation of *Phaedrus* 250e is disputed (see Nussbaum 1994, 1575–78). I still incline to think that it deprecates heterosexual intercourse as animal, and homosexual intercourse as not even that (Price 1989, 230). It is then all the more striking that Socrates is later indulgent to the occasional but continuing lapses of a spirited man and boy (256b7–e2). Presumably what redeems these lovers is that, unlike those of 250e who know no better, they are ambivalent (c6–7). If Plato means what Socrates says, he is not distant from a thesis of the Stoics (see n. 43 below): it is all right for lovers to indulge each other sexually so long as this is marginal to their relationship. However, Plato's conflictual psychology must make him more anxious: he would rather say not that it is alright, but that it need not be fatal. Though he lacks any doctrine of Original Sin, he would agree when Peter Geach writes (albeit with Christian qualifications), "A plunge into sex is of its nature a plunge into a strong current running the wrong way" (1977, 146).

15. Thus, it tells against Nussbaum that what is said to deliver the lover from evil by reminding him of the Form of Temperance is not the sight of a temperate face, but a vision of the Form of Beauty, associated in his memory with the Form of Temperance, that is inspired by the "flashing" of a face seen close up (*Phaedrus* 254b4–7). (For "flashing" as an erotic visual phenomenon, cf. the parallels that de Vries cites ad loc. from the *Palatine Anthology*.)

16. We may well be surprised by the implication that shape cannot be seen. This can hardly be an oversight, when the *Republic* had admitted that the same size and shape may *look* different at different distances or in different media (10.602c7–12). Plato may be supposing that *visual* shape can be *seen* as *tactile* shape can be *felt*, and that "shape" is equivocal between different modalities of shape (see Bostock 1988, 115). This would not seem to help Nussbaum, for there is no visual modality of moral character (as there may well be of beauty).

17. This needs heavy qualification in any case, not least because Plato does not conceive of the body as a *machine* for living; see, on the *Phaedo*, Price (1995, 36–37).

18. In my references to *Stoicorum Veterum Fragmenta* (= *SVF*), a pair of numbers signifies volume and section, a trio of numbers volume, page, and line. I also refer, where possible, to Long and Sedley (1987) (= LS). I generally add the original references for passages cited in *SVF* or LS when the author's works are widely available. I make use, where possible, of translations in LS or Schofield (1991). Inwood and Gerson (1997, 203–32) usefully translate what is believed to be the Stoic part of Arius Didymus's *Epitome of Ethics* as preserved in Stobaeus's *Eclogae*—though different ways of giving references make it impossible to collate their version directly with *SVF* or LS (and their understanding of Stoic *erōs* is very different from mine).

19. On whether perceptual impressions are verbalizable without residue, compare Frede (1987, 161–62) and Striker (1996, 84–85).

20. It may have been to match this complexity that Chrysippus preferred to call

impressions not "imprints," but "alterations" or "modifications" (*SVF* 2.55 = LS 39A3 = D.L. 7.50); see Frede (1987, 167).

21. *SVF* 1.204 also cites Aëtius as having the Stoics say that the wise man was "cognizable from his appearance evidentially (*tekmēriōdōs*)," which suggests not the evident, but the evidenced. Cf. Galen, *De Placitis Hippocratis et Platonis* 170.23–25 Lacey: the location of the *hēgemonikon* eludes us "because there is no clear perception, nor any evidence (*tekmērion*) from which one could infer it." I take Aëtius to be missing the point that I am pressing.

22. On "cognitive impression" (*phantasia katalēptikē*), see LS 1.250–52, Frede (1999).

23. For later evidence that I shall not cite elsewhere, see Philo, *SVF* 3.592; Marcus Aurelius *Ad Se Ipsum* 3.2 (and texts cited ad loc. by Farquharson 1944). Evidence for Greek acceptance that character could be inferred from physiognomy goes back well before the Stoics (e.g., Plato, *Phaedrus* 253d3–e4; Aristotle, *Analytica Priora* 2.27); their philosophical innovation, I am suggesting, was in explicitly making character not inferable but perceptible.

24. An incidental obscurity within the definition is the term *epibolē*: I render it as "resolve," Inwood and Gerson as "effort," Schofield as "attempt" (after Cicero's *conatus; SVF* 3.652 = *Tusculan Disputations* 4.72). Arius Didymus records that an *epibolē* is a "preliminary impulse" (*hormē pro hormēs*; Stobaeus, *SVF* 3.41.30)—which means what? The easiest suggestion would seem to be this: conceiving the project of making a friend (cf. *hē epibolē tēs historias*, "my historical project"; Polybius *Historiae* 1.4.2) precedes willing particular actions towards realizing it; this relates it closely (if imprecisely) to *orousis*, of which we are sparely told that it is "a movement of the mind towards something future" (Stobaeus, *SVF* 3.40.13). Schofield (1991, 29–30 n. 14) is ingenious: despite his translation, he takes the preliminary impulse to be not an attempt, but an impulse to an attempt (here, the attempt to make a friend), called "preliminary" on the ground that trying is prior in realization, if not in conception, to succeeding. However, we read that only a mental act of "reservation" (roughly, qualifying an impulse by a *Deo volente*) insulates an *epibolē* from the danger of frustration (Stobaeus, *SVF* 3.564); but an impulse to try is not vulnerable to external contingency in the manner of an impulse to succeed. Brad Inwood (1997, 64 n. 25) cites an oral suggestion by Richard Sorabji which is ingenious too: the preliminary impulse is toward the goal, variably good or bad (ethical or sexual), of the motive *behind* the desire to make a friend. However, it is essential to Sorabji, as it is not to Schofield, to take the definition as ethically neutral. One consideration that tells against that, as will become clearer, is the Stoic conception of friendship.

25. It is so used of colors in a mirror (Plato *Timaeus* 71b8), of letters in mirrors or in water (*Republic* 3.402b6), of the Milky Way in water (Aristotle *Meteorologica* 1.8.345b26), as parallel to an echo (*Analytica Posteriora* 2.15.98a27), and of light in the bronze bowl of a lamp (Xenophon *Symposium* 7.4).

26. It is so used of character apparent on the face (pseudo-Aristotle *Physiognomica* 2.806a30), of virtue apparent in a boy's appearance (Plutarch *Alcibiades* 4.1—doubtless a Stoic reminiscence), and of character more apparent in speech than on the face (*Cato Major* 7.2).

27. Thus the Stoic lover escapes a Biblical *either/or:* "For the Lord seeth not as man seeth : for man looketh on the outward appearance, but the Lord looketh on the heart" (*I Samuel* 16.7).

28. The paradox is further disarmed by the Stoics' materialist view of the mind, which took every virtue to be a body and even an animal (*SVF* 3.305–7). A modern materialist obsessed by brain states might still have problems, but Clement alludes to a visible tension or *tonos* (*SVF* 1.58.27). The concept of tension was central to the Stoics' psychophysiology of virtue.

29. Indicative too, though less reliable (since there may be some telescoping), are contexts in Stobaeus. Arius Didymus continues after the definition I quoted (Stobaeus, *SVF* 3.650), "This is why the sage will also be expert in love, and will love those worthy of love, i.e., those well born and naturally endowed," which surely implies (even if it does not entail) that it is good *erōs* that is being defined. And elsewhere he associates the definition with a denial that *erōs* is either desire or "for any common thing" (*SVF* 3.180.33–35). When he immediately precedes that by saying that "loving itself," *to eran auto*, is an "indifferent," since it may on occasion happen to common people too (32–33), he evidently means love as a determinable, which, unlike *erōs* proper, is an abstraction without a nature, and neither good nor bad. It is true that Diogenes Laertius appears to use the Stoic definition of *erōs* to capture a species of desire (7.113 = *SVF* 3.96.28–29); but Schofield finds the passage "evidently lacunose" (1991, 31 n. 17).

30. I presume that Schofield would contrast the virtue that distinguishes the wise (and can be called "the natural perfection of a rational being qua rational"; *SVF* 3.19.27–28 = D.L. 7.94) from the modesty (or sense of shame, *aidōs*) that becomes the young (cf. Plato *Charmides* 158c5–6), and contend that a youth can display the flower of modesty but not of virtue. In fact, the Stoics take *aidōs* to be equivocal: it may signify either "fear (*phobos*) at the expectation of blame," which is "the finest passion" or *pathos* (Nemesius, *SVF* 3.101.34), or "caution (*eulabeia*) against correct blame," which as a species of good emotion or *eupatheia* (Andronicus, *SVF* 3.105.40) must presuppose right reason. Neither sense seems precisely pertinent here, but perhaps even a respectable young man may have an expectation of blame *conditional* upon his acting as any young man may be tempted to act.

31. Thus their colors are sharply contrasted in pseudo-Aristotle *De Coloribus* 5.796b6ff.

32. So Apollonius of Tyana (first century A.D.) called madness "the flower of irascibility" (Stob. *Ecl.* 3.549.12 W)—just as an Elizabethan writer was to call matrimony "the Flower of Friendship" (Tilney, *Brief and Pleasant Discourse of Duties in Marriage* 1568, A 8). However, this does not fit the only other occurrence of *anthos aretēs* that I have retrieved from the *Thesaurus Linguae Graecae* data bank: Theodoret writes (in the fourth century A.D.) that a heart parched by a dearth of *logos* lacks the power to "put forth the flower of virtue" (Migne, *PG* 80, 1677B). Here the botanical metaphor is alive, though there is no contrast between flower and fruit. Nor was there when Democritus called temperance "the flower of old age" (68 B 294 DK).

33. This involves an emendation, to *sōphrosunē* from *phōnē* ("voice," which indeed makes no sense).

34. They compared those who are drowning though close to the surface, or blind

though about to recover their sight (Cicero, *SVF* 3.530 = *De Finibus* 3.48; Plutarch, *SVF* 3.539 = LS 61T = *De Communibus Notitiis* 1063A–B); also a stick that is straight or crooked (*SVF* 3.536 = LS 61I1 = D.L. 7.127). We must remember that, for the Stoics, to be vicious is not to be wicked, but to lack the unified ethical knowledge that constitutes virtue and yields all the virtues, and of any unitary body of knowledge it is plausible to say that a man either has it, or does not have it.

35. See also Seneca (LS 60E5 = *Epistulae Morales* 120.8): "Virtues and vices, as you know, border on one another, and a likeness of what is right pertains to those who are also depraved and base." Here his point of view is critical; a different context might permit an element of appreciation.

36. Thus, the Stoics proposed earnestly what Socrates used to pose playfully (cf. *Theaetetus* 185e3–5; Xenophon *Symposium* 5). *epaphroditos* suggests but need not signify sexual attractiveness (cf. Hindley 1999, 93–95).

37. Whence the force of the paradox whereby Socrates keeps becoming rather the *erōmenos* than the *erastēs* of Alcibiades and others (Plato, *Symposium* 219e3–5, 222a8–b4).

38. There is also a paradox at the other end. Young boys do not count as virtuous or vicious—there *tertium datur*—until they have acquired *logos* (Alexander of Aphrodisias, *SVF* 3.143.28–32). When they do (at around fourteen), the best of them become at once visibly vicious and worthy of love. But we have already addressed that.

39. Daniel Babut (1963, 61) briskly explains the immaturity as a presupposition of the educative project (citing Stobaeus, *SVF* 3.180.30–31). In the absence of Plato's analogies between intellectual and sexual procreation, this deeroticizes *erōs*, demoting the central Stoic definitions and characterizations to become corollaries, more or less plausible, of a pedagogic vocation. Such streamlining fits a preconception of the Stoics, but I believe that an interpretation sensitive to the evidence must be less Bauhaus and more baroque.

40. When Plutarch writes that *erōs*, attaching itself to a soul young and well endowed, brings it through friendship to virtue (*Amat.* 750D), he must have what I am calling *prōtophilia* in mind. So must Arius Didymus when he counts anyone worthy to be loved (*axioerastos*) as worthy to be befriended (*axiophilētos*) also (Stobaeus, *SVF* 3.180.25–26).

41. So was Aristotle when he placed prime of mind at "around forty-nine" (*Rhetoric* 2.14.1390b10–11). Contrary to a suggestion by the Oxford translator ad loc., this signifies not his own age at the time of writing (let alone, as Roland Hall once put to me, an Aristotelian joke), but seven times seven, the close of the seventh hebdomad, in which Solon placed a man's mental and verbal prime (27.13–14).

42. Alternatively, "by which men complete virtue" (depending on whether one emends from *mnēmata* to *sēmata* or *peirata*). See the pseudo-Hippocratic *De Hebdomadibus* (5.24–5 R), which places in the fourth hebdomad a "growth of the whole body," i.e., presumably, in breadth as well as in height.

43. I have risked giving a priggish impression of Zeno by focusing upon his account of *erōs*, which is indeed moralistic, and neglecting his sexual permissiveness. Within the Stoic scheme of values, pederastic lovemaking was an "indifferent" (Sextus,

SVF 1.249 = *Pyrrhoneae Hypotyposes* 3.200); perhaps for Zeno it was a "preferred indifferent" (cf. Stobaeus, *SVF* 3.128 = LS 58E). Epiphanius testifies that he would have men make love to their boyfriends "without hindrance" (*SVF* 1.253); and yet Zeno implies that this falls outside the projects that make up a good *erōs* when he also tells us, according to Sextus, not to discriminate between boyfriends and others in making love (*SVF* 1.250 = *Hypotyp.* 3.245). Thus, lovemaking is central to a bad *erōs*, and tangential to a good one. The lovemaking that has its place within the life of the wise is not an expression of *erōs*, even when the parties to it happen to be *erastēs* and *erōmenos*.

References

Babut, D. 1963. "Les Stoïciens et l'amour." *Revue des Etudes Grecques* 76:55–63.

Bostock, D. 1988. *Plato's Theaetetus.* Oxford: Clarendon Press.

de Vries, G. J. 1969. *A Commentary on the Phaedrus of Plato.* Amsterdam: Adolf M. Hakkert.

Dover, K. 1978. *Greek Homosexuality.* London: Duckworth.

Farquharson, A. S. L. 1944. *The Meditations of the Emperor Marcus Antoninus.* 2 vols. Oxford: Clarendon Press.

Frede, M. 1987. "Stoics and Skeptics on Clear and Distinct Impressions." In *Essays in Greek Philosophy.* Oxford: Clarendon Press.

———. 1999. "Stoic Epistemology." In *The Cambridge History of Hellenistic Philosophy,* ed. K. Algra, J. Barnes, J. Mansfeld, and M. Schofield. Cambridge: Cambridge University Press.

Geach, P. 1977. *The Virtues.* Cambridge: Cambridge University Press.

Hindley, C. 1999. "Xenophon on Male Love." *Classical Quarterly* 49:74–99.

Ignatieff, M. 1998. *Isaiah Berlin: A Life.* London: Chatto and Windus.

Inwood, B. 1997. "Why Do Fools Fall in Love?" In *Aristotle and After,* ed. R. Sorabji. London: Institute of Classical Studies.

Inwood, B., and L. P. Gerson. 1997. *Hellenistic Philosophy.* 2d ed. Indianapolis: Hackett.

Long, A. A., and D. N. Sedley. 1987. *The Hellenistic Philosophers.* 2 vols. Cambridge: Cambridge University Press.

Nussbaum, M. C. 1994. "Platonic Love and Colorado Law: The Relevance of Ancient Greek Norms to Modern Sexual Controversies." *Virginia Law Review* 80:1515–1651.

———. 1995. "Eros and the Wise: The Stoic Response to a Cultural Dilemma." *Oxford Studies in Ancient Philosophy* 13:231–67.

Price, A. W. 1989. *Love and Friendship in Plato and Aristotle.* Oxford: Clarendon Press.

———. 1995. *Mental Conflict.* London: Routledge.

———. 1997. "Afterword" to reprint of *Love and Friendship.* Oxford: Clarendon Press.

Rowe, C. J. 1986. *Plato: Phaedrus.* Warminster: Aris and Phillips.

———. 1998. *Plato: Symposium.* Warminster: Aris and Phillips.

Schofield, M. 1991. *The Stoic Idea of the City.* Cambridge: Cambridge University Press.

Striker, G. 1996. "Epicurus on the Truth of Sense Impressions." In *Essays on Hellenistic Epistemology and Ethics.* Cambridge: Cambridge University Press.

Tarán, S. L. 1985. "*Eisi triches:* An Erotic Motif in the Greek Anthology." *Journal of Hellenic Studies* 105:90–107.

Taylor, C. C. W. 1991. *Plato: Protagoras.* Rev. ed. Oxford: Clarendon Press.

Vlastos, G. 1981. "The Individual as Object of Love in Plato." In *Platonic Studies.* 2d ed. Princeton, N.J.: Princeton University Press.

Chapter Seven

ARISTOTLE ON SEX AND LOVE

Juha Sihvola

"If then every lover in virtue of his love [erōs] would prefer A, i.e., that the beloved would be such as to grant him favors [houtōs echein hōste chari-zesthai] without, however, actually granting them (for which C stands), to the beloved's granting his favors (for which D stands) without being such as to grant them (for which B stands), it is clear that A, i.e., being of such a nature, is preferable to granting the favors. To receive affection [phileisthai] in virtue of love [kata ton erōta] is thus preferable to sexual intercourse [sun-ousia]. Love then is more related to affection than to intercourse. If it is most related to this, then this is its goal. Intercourse then either is not an end at all or is an end for the sake of receiving affection. The same goes for other appetites and arts, too" (Arist. An. Pr. 2.22.68a40–b7).[1] This passage is not taken from any ancient treatise on the psychology or ethics of erotic love. It is an illustrative example used by Aristotle in the Prior Analytics in his brief and not-too-sophisticated discussion of the logic of preference. The point is just to demonstrate how one can infer which is the preferable of two goods if one knows which is preferable of two combinations each consist-ing of a preferred and a nonpreferred member of two pairs of opposite al-ternatives. Aristotle uses a wide variety of examples in his logical works, and it is by no means clear to what extent they reflect his own view of their contents. Often it is obvious that their function is merely hypothetical in making a logical point and their contents are quite irrelevant from the viewpoint of the philosophical issues at stake. However, if one looks at Aristotle's *Rhetoric*, it is remarkable how much the accounts of popular reputable ethical beliefs which an orator needs to know in order to persuade his audience actually rely on doctrines and terminology developed either by Aristotle himself or by the philosophers in the Academy.[2] The same seems to be true of logical treatises, too. One needs of course to be cautious in using the rhetorical and logical treatises to reconstruct Aristotelian doctrines, but they certainly should not to be ignored or overlooked.

The *Prior Analytics* passage I quoted is important since it is one of the very few passages in Aristotle's works where the psychological structure of erotic love is explicitly analyzed. The passage distinguishes two aspects in erotic love, one a desire directed to sexual intercourse, and the other a desire directed to receiving friendly affection. It is the latter desire that defines the goal and focus of erotic love, whereas intercourse is said to be either not a goal at all or a goal subordinate to the more valuable goal of friendly love. In this passage, there is no implication whatsoever that intercourse is somehow morally problematic or dangerous. The affectionate desire is supposed to lead to intercourse under normal conditions. Intercourse itself is thought to be a good thing that one is normally supposed to desire and pursue, even though it is a lesser good which does not as such constitute the ultimate goal of love.

Even though the dangers and anxieties involved in love are not conspicuous in this passage, it seems clear that the distinctions made in it are connected to the characteristic Greek ways of seeing a tension or conflict between the different aspects of *erōs*. The Greek philosophical discussion on the nature of love was very much structured around this conflict in classical and Hellenistic times. Various philosophically interesting solutions were suggested by the Platonists, the Epicureans, and the Stoics. It is useful to begin by sketching the conceptual field of the Greek discussion of erotic love in order to see how Aristotle fits in.[3]

I

To put it in a rather simplistic and sketchy way, the cultural dilemma inherent in the Greek views of *erōs* is the following: how is it possible that the very same powerful desire and affection which is capable of producing pleasure and delight in its subject and generating well-wishing intentions toward its object, ultimately aiming at his or her moral improvement, is also capable of generating mad passion that disrupts the reason and virtue of its subject and is in its violent obsession quite indifferent as to the well-being of its object? The recognition of the erotic dilemma obviously leads to explorations of possible solutions. Can the two aspects of *erōs* be distinguished in practice, is any sort of reconciliation possible between them, or is it possible to exclude the dangerous and destructive impulses from one's erotic experiences without simultaneously destroying the benevolent intentions, too?

Several different solutions to the erotic dilemma are suggested in classical and Hellenistic popular texts and philosophical treatises. Some of them recommend erotic etiquette, the following of which is supposed to avoid the unintended destructive implications of sexual desire and conduct, for example, by preferring intercrural to anal intercourse and so saving the beloved from the shame of penetration. Some consider it sufficient to avoid such by-products of sex as prostitution and violence, whereas phenomena like jealous quarrels and romantic seductions are regarded as essentially belonging to the game of love and being enjoyed without noteworthy danger or moral harm. Some texts suggest that if erotic desire is focused on the character of the beloved rather than his body, all of its positive ingredients can be retained while its undesired consequences can still be avoided. So they recommend affectionate love, which is directed to the soul of the beloved, rather than pure bodily sex. Some philosophical solutions understand the relation between affection and sex just the other way around. It is passionate love and affection which are represented as potentially dangerous and preferably avoided by the so called Lysianic speech in Plato's *Phaedrus* and Epicurus, while, at the same time, sexual conduct in itself and the desire for it are considered rather unproblematic. The Stoics accept both sex and affection with certain qualifications. Sexual conduct is in itself indifferent but acceptable when pursued with the appropriate state of knowledge and character. Affectionate love, or *erōs*, is also even experienced by the ideally wise person of the Stoic ethical theory, but presumably it has to be a domesticated version of conventional *erōs*. It has to be purified of its dangerously passionate elements in order to be consistent with the Stoic ideal of *apatheia*. Finally, there is the quite exceptional praise of passionate love in the Socratic speech of the *Phaedrus*: here it is suggested that the element of madness itself motivates the goodwill and generosity of the lover toward the beloved. So passionate love is seen as an indispensable source of moral value, not despite but just because of the uncompromising passion involved.

II

The exploration of Aristotle's texts does not, at least at the first sight, seem to be too promising a task in this context. The meagerness of the material related to erotic love in the extant Aristotelian treatises is an undeniable and in some ways almost astonishing fact. However, Aristotle wrote several treatises on human psychology in general and ethics in particular. These treatises contain extremely profound and perceptive analyses of pleasures, desires, emotions, and affections—virtues of character understood as appropriate dispositions related to different emotions. Two whole books in the *Nicomachean Ethics* and one book in the *Eudemian Ethics*, in all about sixty pages of Greek text, are dedicated exclusively to the notion of *philia*, which broadly refers to all different relationships involving reciprocal benevolence and is translated as friendship or love depending on the preference of the commentator. Even here references to the erotic aspects of those relationships are few and far between. Even Aristotle's biological studies provide little help, although they pay much attention to the sexual behavior of animals and, for example, classify the different methods of intercourse meticulously.[4] However, the psychological dynamics and ethical problems of erotic desire are not in focus in Aristotle's biology.[5]

Aristotle's silence or at least taciturnity on erotic issues certainly calls for an explanation. Different answers have been suggested by earlier commentators. I shall here mention and comment on three possible solutions.

1. It has been suggested that Aristotle's reasons were personal: perhaps he was just not interested in the topic or did not consider it important enough for a philosophical exploration. In the aristocratic culture of fourth-century Athens, an erotic culture which favored relationships that included sexual conduct between older and younger males was at the height of its popularity, and it was these types of relationships that were thought to be especially powerful and at the same time ethically problematic sources of erotic passion. Perhaps Aristotle, who came from the Macedonian periphery, did not feel any personal attraction to the curious habits and practices of the metropolitan aristocracy. Perhaps he was quite satisfied with heterosexual relationships, which were not considered by him or contemporary popular writers to call for any special philosophical attention.

These kinds of explanations from personal history are unsatisfactory for many reasons. First, quite apart from the extent of our familiarity with the details of Aristotle's life, extrapolations from personal preferences and experiences to philosophical views are a risky business indeed. Second, since the analysis of the prevailing reputable views was such an essential part of

Aristotle's philosophizing, especially in his ethics, one would expect him to pay attention to prevailing sexual practices and their social consequences, whatever his personal preferences. Third, we do not have much reliable material on which to base an account of Aristotle's personal sexual life. And fourth, the scarce biographical information on Aristotle's life which is preserved for us by doxographers does not at all support claims of his indifference to erotics.

Even though the biographical material on Aristotle is notoriously unreliable, it is still worthwhile to look at those remarks that have some relevance to his attitudes on erotics.[6]

First, the biographical material does not suggest that Aristotle was not interested in passionate sexual relations or that he was an outsider to pederastic culture. Diogenes Laertius mentions a story (5.3) according to which Aristotle had been a pederastic beloved of Hermias, the tyrant of Atarneus and also a former student of the Academy, who had invited Aristotle to stay at his court after he had left the Academy at the time of Plato's death. The story is not accepted as historically accurate even by Diogenes, and it is generally rejected by commentators as a mischievous attempt to ridicule Aristotle. It probably dates from an anti-Macedonian pamphlet written by a sophist from Isocrates' school, Theocritus of Chios, of whom Diogenes also cites a scornful epigram that may also contain a hint of a pederastic relation between Hermias and Aristotle. Theocritus wrote, "To Hermias the eunuch, although he was a slave of Eubulus, an empty monument was dedicated by empty-witted Aristotle, who on account of the incontinent nature of the belly chose to live at the mouth of the muddy river, Bosborus, rather than at the Academy" (D.L. 5.11).

But although the scornful tone of these remarks is obvious, I am not sure whether this is a sufficient reason to infer that the reference to a pederastic relation between the tyrant and the philosopher is simply false, although such an inference might be encouraged by later views of pederasty as an unspeakable vice.

Much more interesting than the vague hints of pederasty are the stories of Aristotle's relations with his wife Pythias and the slave woman Herpyllis with whom he lived after his wife's death. Pythias was a relative of the tyrant Hermias, most probably a niece and a stepdaughter (Strabo 13.1.37), whose marriage to Aristotle might well, as Diogenes says, referring to a book of Demetrius of Magnesia, have been used by the tyrant as a means to strengthen his ties with the philosopher and secure his loyalty.[7] Diogenes also mentions Aristippus's book *On the Luxury of the Ancients*, according to which Pythias was originally a concubine (*pallakis*) of Hermias (5.4). This claim again has been interpreted by modern commentators as being derived from anti-Aristotelian defamatory writings. What is interesting to us is that the same source, which Diogenes apparently by mistake names as Aristippus, also suggests that Aristotle fell in love (*erasthēnai*) with Pythias and was so exceedingly delighted (*huperchairōn*) by the tyrant's consent to their marriage that he sacrificed to his wife in the same way as the Athenians used to do to Demeter in Eleusis and that he composed a paean to Hermias. Other sources cited by bishop Eusebius (*Praep. Evang.* 15.2) suggest that the reason for the exceptional sacrifice was not delight but the deep grief Aristotle felt after his beloved wife's early death. Be that as may, there seems to be some historical reality behind these stories, as Aristotle's paean to Hermias is preserved by Diogenes, and its exceptionality is further underlined by the claim that it later gave rise to a charge of impiety against the Stagirite. In any case, it is interesting that these stories ascribe to Aristotle a very powerful, even exceptional emotion of affectionate love for his own spouse.

Aristotle's strong affectionate ties to his wife are also reflected in his will, in which he asks to be buried together with the bones of Pythias, in accordance with her own instructions (D.L. 5.16).[8] In his will, he also praises the affectionate (*spoudaia*) care which he had received from his concubine Herpyllis, the mother of his son Nicomachus (D.L. 5.13), although it is only at this time that he posthumously releases her from the status of a legal slave. Seen against the normative descriptions of married life in classical times, Aristotle's attitude to the important women in his life seems to have been rather exceptional.[9] According to a standard view, reflected in several classical texts, marriage was first of all understood as a means for producing legitimate children. Even though Maarit Kaimio has convincingly shown that there are many more traces of positively evaluated erotics in marriage at least from the female viewpoint, even in the literature of classical Athens,[10] it is not misleading to say that it was often thought that pleasure, passion, and even companionship should rather be sought in other types of sexual relationships. So if any conclusion at all can be drawn from the fragmented and questionable information on Aristotle's life, it would be that one would expect at least above-average interest in the psychology and ethics of erotic love.

2. There have also been suggestions that there was nothing particularly exceptional in the scarceness of Aristotle's comments on erotic love.[11] One should perhaps rather see Plato's enthusiastic praises of divine *erōs* in

the *Symposium* and the *Phaedrus* as exceptions, not Aristotle's moderate and commonsensical attitude. Plato connected his erotic vision to transcendental metaphysical concerns that Aristotle did not share or did not consider worthwhile to pursue in his treatises. If erotic love is viewed from the viewpoint of the actual Athenian social practices that are analyzed in Aristotle's ethical treatises without mixing in idealistic metaphysics, the rather peripheral position given to it should perhaps not be seen as so unusual. So a comparison between Plato and Aristotle would not seem to do justice to the latter.

This line of argument is, however, not quite convincing. Plato was by no means the only classical author who was interested in erotics; in fact, the tensions and problems of love were explored by many writers, philosophers and nonphilosophers alike, independently of particular metaphysical concerns. And certainly Epicurean and Stoic philosophers regarded sexual and erotic desires as worthy of lengthy discussions without metaphysical concerns or with rather different concerns from those of Plato.

3. There is yet another possible explanation. Perhaps Aristotle's relative silence on *erōs* is purely accidental. In the list of his works given by Diogenes Laertius (5.22–27) we can find at least three titles which could have provided us with the missing analyses of erotic desire. Among titles that probably refer to early works in dialogue form we find both *Eroticus* and *Symposium*, both said to have consisted of just one book. Later in the catalog, there is mention of *Theses on Love* (*Theseis erōtikai*), consisting of four books, the title of which might refer to a collection of material based on the cooperative researches by the members of the Lyceum.

The suggestion that Aristotle's lost writings may have included even extensive analyses of erotic love could perhaps get some support from a comparison with what we know about his writings on the emotions in general. The nature and value of the emotions are discussed rather extensively even in the extant Aristotelian works. The most systematic analysis is presented in the *Rhetoric*, which is structured to serve the needs of a political orator and which by definition cannot include philosophical and scientific analyses based on first principles. A good case can, however, be made for a claim that the account of the emotions does not and cannot just report popular views but is based on Aristotle's own considered analyses on the subject, to a remarkable extent based on his background at the Academy.[12] It is possible and not unlikely that Aristotle also wrote a more scientific and systematic treatise on the psychology of emotion. Here too Diogenes' list provides a couple of titles which could have included the long-lost Aristotelian theory of the emotions: *On Being or Having Been Affected* (*Peri tou paschein ē peponthenai*), *On the Emotions* (*Peri pathōn*) or *On Anger* (*Peri orgēs*), and *Affections* (*Pathē*), each in one book. Even though our case may be weakened by the fact that each of the titles in Diogenes referring to *pathē* consists of just one book, to the length of which no lower limit can be defined, we can reasonably assume that Aristotle also worked on central themes of moral psychology in those treatises that are not preserved for us. These might well even have included more extensive analyses of erotic love than do the *Rhetoric* and other extant treatises.

III

Without taking any definitive stand on these points, it seems clear that the reconstruction of Aristotle's view of sexual and erotic love is a worthwhile task whether or not the emerging picture can be understood as an outline of the contents of Aristotle's lost writings on *erōs*. In fact there have been some attempts to sketch a consistent picture of Aristotelian *erōs* on the basis of the scattered remarks of the philosopher. Anthony Price and Martha Nussbaum, for example, have tried to relate Aristotle to the framework constituted by Greek popular norms and philosophical views of love.[13] According to Price, Aristotle's attitudes to sex, as well as his moral views in general, were relatively close to standard Greek popular morality. He compares the view he reconstructs on the basis of Aristotle's comments to Pausanias's speech in the *Symposium*, in which the concentration on the soul of the beloved rather than his body is assumed to ensure that the potential bad consequences of erotic passion can be avoided. Nussbaum agrees with Price and also sees similarities between Aristotle and the Stoic conception of *erōs*.

In the following, I shall argue that while these resemblances between Aristotle and the popular and the Stoic views cannot be denied, his conception is not so standard for at least two reasons. First, the Aristotelian notion of *erōs* offers at least implicitly more prospects for heterosexual love than classical popular morality in general. Second, because Aristotle does not wish the passionate element of *erōs* to be domesticated even in its development to the highest form of friendship, virtue friendship, it should be seen as more congenial to the Socratic speech in the *Phaedrus* than the Lysianic one.

IV

In his discussion of the virtue of temperance, Aristotle, following common usage, refers to sexual pleasure by the term *ta aphrodisia* (*Eth. Nic.* 3.10.1118a32; *Eth. Eud.* 3.2.1230b27), "the pleasures of Aphrodite." In accordance with Platonic tradition, pleasure produced by sexual activities and corresponding appetite directed to it are understood as being structurally analogous to the pleasures of eating and drinking and the appetites of hunger and thirst. These three are the basic appetites (*epithumiai*) that are common to all animals, humans and nonhumans alike (*Eth. Nic.* 3.10.1118a23–25). Human appetites are a broad class of pleasure-directed desires, most of which are, however, unavailable to other animals because they do not derive any pleasure from corresponding sensations, that is, those of sight, hearing, and smell. The common appetites are directed to the pleasures of taste and touch, and strictly speaking primarily to the latter, since Aristotle claims in the *Eudemian Ethics* that animals are not attracted by those pleasures of taste that are sensed by the tip of the tongue, but only by those that are sensed by the throat, the sensation of which seems more like touch than taste, anyway (*Eth. Eud.* 3.2.1231a13–15). It is only these three basic appetites with which the virtue of moderation is concerned. The structural analogy between the appetites of hunger, thirst, and sex is that they are all related to the bodily processes of replenishment and dissolution (*Rh.* 1.11.1369b33–35; cf. Pl. *Phlb.*) An appetite is initiated by a pain produced by dissolution, and it is directed to a pleasure produced by corresponding replenishment, and these pains and pleasures are perceived first of all by the senses of touch and taste.

Basic appetites are according to Aristotle natural (*phusikai*), which means that everybody experiences them if he or she is without food, drink, or even sexual intercourse (*eunē*) [14]—if one is, as Homer says, young and vigorous (*Eth. Nic.* 3.11.1118b8–12). Whereas Plato thought that appetites, desires, and emotions connected to the body are by their essential nature unreliable and misleading, Aristotle seems to lack all this anxiety almost completely. It is just the other way round; he thought that humans are innately disposed to develop correct forms of emotional and desiderative response in situations calling for the virtues of character such as courage, justice, and moderation. The term "natural virtue" refers to these innate dispositions, which are possible for both children and nonhuman animals (*Eth. Nic.* 6.13.1144b3–17; cf. *Eth. Nic.* 3.8.1116a23–b9; *Eth. Eud.* 3.1.1229a21–30; 3.7.1234a24–30).[15]

The appetites of hunger, thirst, and the desire for sex are, however, morally problematic, mainly for two reasons. First, although human beings have an innate inclination toward virtue with respect to them, without the guidance of reason they are likely to develop in harmful directions. Second, because these appetites are directed to those pleasures that we share with other animals (*Eth. Nic.* 3.10.1118a23–25), misguided use of them appears slavish and bestial. Excess especially in appetites that concern the most universal of senses is justly reproached, according to Aristotle, "because it does not belong to us as human beings but as animals" (*Eth. Nic.* 3.10.1118b2–4). Aristotle emphasizes that the virtue of moderation is a mean between two extremes, just like all other virtues of character. This means that it is perfectly possible to diverge from virtue in the directions of both excess and deficiency. However, by their nature, human beings are much more inclined toward having too much than too little of bodily appetites. "Mistaking on the side of deficiency as regards pleasure, and taking less than the proper amount of delight in them, does not occur often; such insensitivity is not human." says Aristotle (*Eth. Nic.* 3.11.1119a6–7) If a person did not find any food, drink, or sexual activity pleasant and worthy of pursuing, he would be far from being a human being. This type is so rare that there is not even a special name for it (*Eth. Nic.* 3.11.1119a7–11).

V

The discussions concerning the virtue of temperance in the *Nicomachean* and the *Eudemian Ethics* make it quite clear that Aristotle did not see erotic appetite directed to sexual conduct in itself as implying particularly difficult moral problems. It is a natural desire which every healthy human being is disposed to feel, at least before becoming too old and weak. Its excess is a vice but so is the lack of sensitivity related to it. If Aristotle's attitude to sexual appetite so far seems to be rather straightforward, the same appears to be true of its interpretation, but only so far.

However, there are two details which few commentators have noted. First, in the *Eudemian Ethics*, Aristotle seems to notice that aphrodisiac pleasures cannot quite be put in the same line with the pleasures of eating and drinking. Even though touch and perhaps also taste are important senses in sexual pleasures, there is more to them. The virtue of temperance is usually not at all concerned with the pleasures of beautiful things and the pain of ugly things. Sexual appetite is, however, as is noted by Aristotle here (*Eth. Eud.* 3.2.1230b26), an obvious exception: it is of course the sight of erotically arousing objects which not only initiates the appetite but is also often sufficient to give pleasure. Aristotle thus recognizes that erotic appetite is even at this most basic level a much more complicated and sophisticated desire than hunger and thirst.

Second, one standard way of distinguishing ancient Greek sexual ethics from later conceptions is by assuming that the Greeks were not primarily concerned with the different types of sexual conduct and its objects and the classification of these into permitted and forbidden forms. What appears to be more important is the state of knowledge and character on the basis of which sexual activities are pursued. Controlling and modifying the intensity of one's desires and recognizing the requirements of the situation are supposed to be more important than the identity of a particular act or its object.[16] It is, however, noteworthy that Aristotle characterizes the temperate person as not taking any pleasure in those things which the intemperate person likes most but, quite the contrary, actively disliking them, and in general finding no pleasure in wrong things (*Eth. Nic.* 3.11.1119a12–14), and, correspondingly, he characterizes the intemperate person as delighting in things that should not be enjoyed but hated, or if delighting in things that should be enjoyed, then delighting more than is appropriate and more than most people do (*Eth. Nic.* 3.11.1118b25–27). Even though Aristotle is positive that sexual appetite is in itself a natural and acceptable desire, these characterizations strongly suggest that there are cases where the moral error is indeed more related to the object of love—that is, such things being enjoyed which should not be enjoyed at all or such things not being enjoyed which should be enjoyed by the virtuous person—rather than the intensity of desire or the state of character from which the desire in question arises. We shall see that this point has some importance for our understanding of how Aristotle defined the most problematic areas in sexual ethics.

VI

I shall now expand on these two points by looking at other passages in which Aristotle refers to erotic love. I shall first argue that erotic appetite indeed has a much more complicated nature than hunger and thirst, to which it is often compared. The *Prior Analytics* passage I quoted at the beginning is perhaps the clearest example of distinguishing intercourse and affection as the two aims of erotic desire, of which the former is and should be at least in some cases subordinated to the latter. This distinction gets some support from a couple of passages in the *Topics*. Aristotle remarks that love (*erōs*) cannot simply be defined as the appetite for intercourse (*epithumia sunou-*

sias) since the one who is more intensely in love does not—necessarily—feel a more intense appetite for intercourse, although they should both have become more intense simultaneously, had they been the same thing (4.7.146a7–12). A somewhat similar point is also made in another passage in the *Topics*, however, this time concerning the notion of *philein:* Aristotle says that the word has to be homonymous, since when used of a frame of mind it has hatred as its contrary, whereas when used of a physical activity it does not admit of a contrary (1.15.106b2–4).

Although one might doubt the reliability of the examples given in the logical works, where they might merely have been used hypothetically or in order to illustrate popular views without serious commitment, the double-aspect view of *erōs* clearly fits well with Aristotle's remarks in ethical treatises. For example, in the three following brief passages we can see that the more complicated nature of *erōs* in comparison with hunger and thirst seems to be based on its origin in the visual response to bodily beauty.

> Goodwill seems to be the beginning of friendship, just as love [*to eran*] arises in virtue of the pleasure of the eye, for no one falls in love without first being delighted by the form of the beloved, although the one who is merely charmed by the beloved's outward appearance is not really in love; only such a person is in love who longs for the beloved when absent [*aponta pothē*] and desires his or her presence [*parousias epithumē*]. (*Eth. Nic.* 9.5.1167a3–8)

> For lovers the sight of the beloved is the thing they love most and they prefer this sensation to others because the existence and the origin of love are most of all due to it, and so likewise friends too find it most choiceworthy to live together. (*Eth. Nic.* 9.12.1171b29–33)

> Lovers are delighted when they are able to talk or write about their loved ones or do any little thing that has to do with them. When they are remembering all such things, it seems to them that they are actually able to perceive the loved ones. It is the beginning of all love that we are delighted not only when the loved ones are present but also when we remember them in their absence. (*Rh.* 1.11.1370b19–25)

Mental acts of imagination through memories and expectations are essential to all kinds of pleasures and corresponding appetites, including hunger and thirst (see *Rh.* 1.10–11), but in erotic desire it is the visuality that emerges as the salient feature. The vision of a beautiful body generates erotic appetite, but it is also possible for this vision to develop into an enjoyment of the beauty in the beloved's soul (*Pol.* 1.5.1254b38–1255a1). Therefore, an erotic lover does not merely seek satisfaction of his desire for intercourse, but also seeing his beloved and the return of affection. Even though erotic love is not typically a relation between equals, a certain kind of mutuality is certainly assumed.

These two aspects of erotic love, desire for intercourse and desire for affection, have been interpreted in terms of the Platonic tripartition of the soul: desire for intercourse is an appetite (*epithumia*), whereas desire for affection belongs to the class of spirited desires (*thumos*).[17] Aristotle sometimes criticizes the Platonic division of the soul as well as other attempts to distinguish separate parts in the soul (*De An.* 3.9.433a22–b7), but he also himself accepts and explicitly follows the division of desires into three kinds: rational (*boulēsis*), spirited (*thumos*), and appetitive desire (*epithumia*).[18] The difference between the two types of nonrational desires is the following: appetite is inherently directed to seeing and reaching for things as pleasant independently of the evaluations of reason, whereas spirited desire sees and reaches for things as beautiful or noble (*kalon*). Unlike pleasure reached for by appetites, this beauty or nobility is a version of the good evaluated and reached for by reason. Spirited desire is thus distinguished from appetite by its sharing of an evaluative outlook with reason and so being able to understand and follow reason's commands.[19] One passage on the basis of which it is possible to argue for locating affection involved in erotic love within spirited desires is found in the *Topics:* if the spirited faculty is the seat of anger and if hatred follows anger, hatred too must be located in the spirited faculty, and if this is true, the contrary of hatred, which is affection, must also be located in the spirited faculty (*Top.* 2.7.113a35–b3).[20]

It is certainly helpful to distinguish intercourse and affection as the two aspects of Aristotelian *erōs* and see a kind of expansive process in the development of affective love. Still, one should be cautious in interpreting it in terms of the Platonic tripartition. The *Topics* passage mentioned above is purely dialectical. It is possible to reconstruct the argument for the spirited location of affection on the basis of it, but in fact Aristotle's intention is to give advice for the dialectician who is arguing *against* one of the premises of this argument. What Aristotle actually says is that if one wants to deny that hatred follows anger, this is possible if one is successful in arguing that affection is in the *appetitive*, not the spirited faculty. Nothing about Aristotle's own commitment to the rival versions of tripartite psychologies can be derived from this particular example.

It is also clear that, in Aristotle's view, an erotic desire for sexual conduct can be expanded to a desire for mutual affection between oneself and the beloved conceived as a beautiful and pleasant person. His psychology, however, seems to allow this to happen under the category of appetitive desire. Both Aristotle's remarks in his discussion of temperance in his ethical works and the lengthy analysis in the *Rhetoric* 1.11 make it clear that appetites are a broad category under which those which concern the pleasures we have in common with other animals are only a subclass. This can be seen from the distinction between nonrational appetites (*epithumiai alogoi*) and appetites associated with reason (*epithumiai meta logou*) in the *Rhetoric* (1.11.1370a18–19). Nonrational appetites include all natural appetites that are activated spontaneously through psychophysical changes or perceptions of objects related to them. These include hunger, thirst, and the appetite for sexual intercourse, but also other appetites connected with sensations of smell, hearing, and sight. Appetites associated with reason are more conditioned by culture and, as a result, involve certain types of beliefs.

What is important is that Aristotle did indeed outline a kind of expansive process in the development of erotic love. Love begins from the sight of a beautiful person, but a perception of bodily beauty expands into a perception of more abstract qualities of the beloved such as the beauty of his or her character. In a parallel way, the desire for intercourse develops into a desire for receiving affection, which constitutes the proper goal and sense of an erotic relationship. The erotic relationship as such is classified by Aristotle under the categories of the less valuable friendships, that is, one based on utility, and especially one based on pleasure. There is a danger of dissolution in friendships based on erotic attraction if the qualities which motivate the relationship disappear (e.g., if the pederastic beloved grows too old). However, Aristotle also sees an emergence of the best kind of friendship, that based on virtue, from erotic love in which the partners have developed affinity and affection as well as reciprocal concern and respect between themselves. Having concluded that Aristotle clearly recognized the potential of passionate erotic love in the development of human virtue and happiness, let me now move on to the other point I raised above, the point concerning the moral problems related to sexual relations.

VII

I shall focus on four areas that Aristotle regarded as potentially problematic in sexual relations. These are (1) marriage, (2) incest, (3) dispositional passivity, and (4) the inequality of partners.

1. Marriage. In the light of our sources, Aristotle's own attitude to married life seems to have been somewhat exceptional in comparison to popular morality in classical times. His emotional devotion to his wife does not have too many parallels in classical literature. Aristotle notoriously regarded women as intellectually inferior to men and incapable of controlling their own lives and of participating in public and political life. However, his description of marriage sees the prospects of the husband-wife relationship as much broader than just producing legitimate children:

> Friendship appears to belong to husband and wife by nature. Human beings are by their nature even more inclined to form couples than they are political, insofar as the household is more primary and more necessary than the polis, and producing offspring is more common to animals. For other animals, community extends only so far, but human beings do not live together only in order to produce offspring, but also for the sake of things belonging to life. The division of functions begins immediately, and those of man and woman are different. They assist each other when each gives what is proper to him or her for the common good. For this reason there seems to be both pleasure and utility in this kind of friendship. But it can be based on virtue if each partner is good. Both of them have their own virtues and are capable of delighting in them. Children appear to be a bond of union, and therefore the childless marriages are more easily dissolved, for children are a common good for both parents, and what is common holds them together. (*Eth. Nic.* 8.12.1162a16–34)

Even though the relationship is unequal, the virtue of each partner enables the highest type of friendship to develop between husband and wife. The tendency to form lasting couples, which is regarded by Aristotle as most unusual among animals (*Eth. Eud.* 7.10.1242a22–26), provides a basis for what is supposedly the most fundamental social institution among human beings. Family life is not just for producing offspring, it is also for activities of life performed together for the common good as well as for mutual affection and delight.[21]

It is striking that Aristotle does not seem to have anything to say about the sexual life in marriage. There is no mention of marriage in the discussion of the virtue of temperance and the management of basic appetites. Aristotle refers several times to the wrongfulness of violating marriage or adultery (*moicheia*). However, one should be careful about what is at stake here. *Moicheia* means violating the rights of other husbands to their wives and possibly the rights of fathers to their daughters. It does not cover all extramarital relations: it is a *moicheia* to sleep with one's neighbor's wife, but to go to a prostitute or engage in sexual conduct with a pederastic beloved is not. On the basis of Aristotle's remarks on the topic it is quite obvious that he understood the moral problem of adultery in this way, completely agreeing with popular Greek norms. When Aristotle remarks that sleeping with a married woman, while knowing who she is, is unjust even under the influence of passion (*Eth. Nic.* 5.6.1134a19–22), he obviously implies that it is not unjust without this knowledge. The same point can be seen in the remark that men dispute the charge by admitting intercourse but denying adultery on the grounds of ignorance or compulsion (*Eth. Eud.* 2.3.1221b23–25). A good husband cannot be blamed if he believes he has had sex with a prostitute in good faith, even though she in reality happened to be the neighbor's wife. Having extramarital intercourse is adultery only on the condition that it is knowingly performed with a certain type of woman.

It is also worthwhile to notice that *erōs* is mentioned neither in the context of marriage nor in the remarks about adultery. So if the latter seem to permit certain types of extramarital relationships with other women, we cannot infer that they would be cases of erotic love. On the other hand, the fact that *erōs* is not mentioned in the context of marriage does not preclude the possibility that Aristotle could have allowed it some role at least in some cases of married sex.

So we may conclude that Aristotle's views of the relation between sex and marriage do not radically diverge from prevalent popular morality, although he has figured the relation between husband and wife in a much more broadminded way than most of his contemporaries we know of. Marriage does not present particularly acute problems for the proper management of sexual desire, and there even seems to be place for *erōs* between husband and wife. However, the marriage rights of other husbands and fathers define certain types of sexual acts that are regarded as forbidden and reproached.

2. Incest. In the *Politics*, Aristotle criticizes Plato's prescriptions for the ideal state. He also makes a point about sexual relations between fathers and sons and between brothers: "It is strange that one [i.e., Plato] who makes sons common only debars intercourse between lovers but does not prohibit erotic love or other practices which are quite inappropriate between father and son or between brothers, because even erotic love in itself is quite inappropriate in these cases. It is also strange that he does not prevent intercourse for no other reason than the too-powerful nature of pleasure involved, but he does not think it makes any difference if the partners are father and son in the one case and brothers in the other" (*Pol.* 2.4.1262a33–39).

For some strange reason this passage has sometimes been presented among those in which Aristotle has been said to condemn same-sex relationships, although it should be clear, especially in comparison with the criticized passages in the *Republic*, that Aristotle's point is almost the opposite. Plato actually suggests that in the ideal state the lover should only kiss and touch the beloved as a father would a son, because otherwise uncontrolled erotic appetite would lead to disastrous consequences (Pl. *Rep.* 403b–c). While it is not clear that Aristotle's criticism against what Plato really said is particularly fair, its obvious point is that the prohibition of intercourse between the lover and the beloved is hypocritical when the real danger in the Platonic abolition of the family is incest. Aristotle's view seems to be that intercourse between the lover and the beloved is not as such dangerous at all, but erotic love between partners who are too closely related is, even if it does not lead to actual sexual conduct. The fact that incest was seen as morally problematic does not call for any particular explanation in Greek culture, even though it is remarkable that Plato and Aristotle mention erotic relations only between fathers and sons. Father-daughter incest is not mentioned at all.

3. Habitual passivity. So far I have avoided distinguishing between heterosexual and same-sex relationships, partially because one of my intentions has been to show that most of what Aristotle says about sexual desire and erotic love can be applied to both types without the distinction being particularly important. In fact, Aristotle says relatively little about same-sex relationships, practically nothing about sex between women, and makes only scattered remarks about sex between men. In the *Politics*, there are apart from the passage quoted above, which in my view does not primarily deal with same-sex relationships, a brief remark about the Celts, who are said to openly favor intercourse between males (2.9.1269b24–25), and two references to same-sex sexual conduct among warlike peoples in general (2.9.1269b28) and among the Cretans in particular (2.10.1272a22–25).[22] No moral stand whatsoever is taken in any of these passages.

Now we finally come to the famous passage at *Nicomachean Ethics* 7.5, the interpretation of which has proved to be central in recent legal controversies about the status of same-sex relationships (1148b15–1149a4). I shall not present a full critical discussion of it, first, because I have little original to add to what has already been said by others, and second, because I do not find it very important from the viewpoint of sexual ethics. Briefly speaking, Aristotle's point is here to classify certain activities which are not naturally pleasurable but become such because of sickness, habit, or innate deformities, and which, for that very reason, are *not* morally reproachable. These activities extend from cannibalism and cutting the stomachs of pregnant women to rather harmless-sounding habits like biting one's nails or eating coal and earth. Among the latter, there is something which is in an unfortunate way expressed enigmatically: *hē tōn aphrodisiōn tois arresin* (1148b28), according to the most plausible interpretation, the disposition of men toward passivity in sexual conduct. Even though Aristotle's expressions are vague, the passage seems to say that it is especially this disposition that is produced by habits having their origins in violent treatment — presumably sexual abuse — in childhood. The passage does not by any means include any moral condemnation of same-sex relations or even habitual passivity; the latter is something that is produced by unhappy conditions in one's childhood, for which one cannot oneself be blamed. Of course Aristotle's point can still be interpreted as a part of marginalizing strategy which marks off certain type of behavior, whatever it is, as deviant.[23]

Just as an afterthought, I would tentatively like to suggest an interpretation of the phrase that would even more radically diverge from traditional translations. If we reject the idea that the dative *tois arresin* refers to the object of aphrodisiac desires and presume instead that it refers to their subject, why should we necessarily see any reference in this passage to either any passive role in sexual conduct or even any kind of same-sex relationship? If the literal meaning of the phrase is "the something of male aphrodisia." There might still be some extra work for our imagination to fill in the missing word. What about just plainly excess of sexual appetite in males, which is not morally reproachable if it is produced by childhood abuse?

4. Inequality of partners. Several passages both in the *Eudemian* and the *Nicomachean Ethics* point to problems that arise from the asymmetry between the lover and the beloved in erotic relationships. Aristotle remarks that it is often the cause of strife that the readiness of each partner does not have the same source even though they assume their relationship to be based on some sort of equality (*Eth. Eud.* 7.3.1238b32–39). Another passage refers to recriminations in love affairs which are based on the fact that the motive of affection is different in each partner: the one might seek the other as a pleasant person, while the latter seeks the other for his utility. This leads to strife because the former wishes the latter to share his life, while the latter needs the former only at times (*Eth. Eud.* 7.10.1243b15–20). Such combinations of pleasure friendship and utility friendship are also said to be transient because of the dissimilarity between the partners, whereas the best kind of friendship, based on character and virtue, is enduring (*Eth. Nic.* 9.1.1164a2–13). The combination of pleasure and utility are not the only possible motives for the lover and the beloved. Aristotle also mentions in connection with lovers a friendship of utility between contraries, which he sees as particularly unpromising basis for a lasting relationship, and a friendship where the parties seek different pleasures from each other. Even the latter is not likely to endure, but it is still preferable to any utility friendship, and it is this type of love affair that is presented by Aristotle as a potential source of a lasting friendship of character (*Eth. Nic.* 8.4.1157a3–12).

Love relations in these passages are described in terms which clearly imply that pederastic relationships between males are assumed to be in question. However, there are few such elements that could not also appear in descriptions of heterosexual love affairs. This confirms the point I have already made that the gender of the partners almost nowhere figures prominently in Aristotle's remarks about sexual love.

VIII

Now it is time for some tentative conclusions. The picture I have outlined here has been scooped out of bits and pieces, and it is still only a report of a work in progress, but I hope that a rather consistent view has begun to emerge. Aristotle's appreciation of erotic love is mainly positive, although he also points to several potential moral problems in sexual relationships. It is remarkable that he did see so little difference between same-sex and heterosexual relationships. Both of them are understood as asymmetrical, in accordance with classical popular morality, but Aristotle also saw a possibility for a development toward the most perfect form of friendship, that based on virtue, in both of them, here diverging from conventional norms of his time.

For the very last, I have saved one precious piece of supporting evidence for my claim that Aristotle would rather side with Socrates than Lysias in the *Phaedrus*. In the *Nicomachean Ethics* 9.10, Aristotle recognizes the intensity and exclusivity of erotic love: "It does not seem to be possible to be really good friends with many people, for the same reason that it is impossible to be in love (*eran*) with several people. Love is a kind of excess of friendship (*huperbolē philias*), and this is directed to just one person, and similarly one can be a very good friend of only a few" (1171a10–13).

This exclusive passion is quite different from the cool, detached, and domesticated *erōs* of the Stoics. At least if we think that the passionate aspect of *erōs* does remain as such even in its transformation into virtue friendship—and I see no reason why we should not think it does—Aristotelian *erōs* implies taking risks and accepting one's vulnerability before the contingencies of the outside world to an extent which no Stoic would accept as rational.

Notes

1. All translations are mine.

2. On the discussion concerning the reliability of the *Rhetoric* in revealing Aristotle's own doctrines, especially his views of the psychology of emotion, see, e.g., John M. Cooper, "Ethical-Political Theory in Aristotle's *Rhetoric,*" in *Aristotle's "Rhetoric": Philosophical Essays*, ed. David J. Furley and Alexander Nehamas (Princeton, N.J.: Princeton University Press, 1994), 193–210; Stephen Halliwell, "Popular Morality, Philosophical Ethics, and the *Rhetoric,*" in Furley and Nehamas, *Aristotle's "Rhetoric",*, 211–30; and Gisela Striker, "Emotions in Context: Aristotle's Treatment of the Passions in the *Rhetoric* and His Moral Psychology," in *Essays on Aristotle's Rhetoric*, ed. Amélie Oksenberg Rorty (Berkeley: University of California Press, 1996), 286–302. All these articles agree that the psychology of emotions is indeed a special case: in order to be persuasive and direct the emotions of his hearers, it is not sufficient for an orator to know what the hearers *think* of the emotions; the orator must know what the emotions actually *are* and how they work.

3. The ambiguity of Greek *erōs* has been analyzed, e.g., in K. J. Dover, *Greek Homosexuality*, 2d ed. (London: Duckworth, 1989); A. W. Price, *Love and Friendship in Plato and Aristotle* (Oxford: Oxford University Press,1989); J. J. Winkler, *The Constraints of Desire: The Anthropology of Sex and Gender in Ancient Greece* (New York: Routledge, 1990); David Halperin, *One Hundred Years of Homosexuality and Other Essays on Greek Love* (London: Routledge 1990); Martha C. Nussbaum, "Platonic Love and Colorado Law: The Relevance of Ancient Greek Norms to Modern Sexual Controversies," *Virginia Law Review* 80 (1994): 1515–1651; and Martha C. Nussbaum, "Eros and the Wise: The Stoic Response to a Cultural Dilemma," *Oxford Studies in Ancient Philosophy* 13 (1995): 231–67.

4. See, esp., the *Generation of Animals*.

5. On the question of sex in Aristotle's biology, see Daryl McGowan Tress, "The Metaphysical Science of Aristotle's *Generation of Animals* and Its Feminist Critics," *Review of Metaphysics* 49 (1992): 307–41; and Marguerite Deslauriers, "Sex and Essence in Aristotle's *Metaphysics* and Biology," in *Feminist Interpretations of Aristotle*, ed. Cynthia A. Freeland (University Park, Pa.: Pennsylvania State University Press, 1998), 138–67.

6. On Aristotle's life and sources concerning it, see Ingemar Düring, *Aristotle in the Ancient Biographical Material*, Studia Graeca et Latina Gothoburgensia no. 5 (Göteborg: Årskrift Universitetet Acta, 1957); and W. K. C. Guthrie, *A History of Greek Phi-*

losophy, vol. 6, *Aristotle: An Encounter* (Cambridge: Cambridge University Press, 1981), 18–45.

7. There is also another tradition according to which Pythias was Hermias's sister, whom Aristotle only married after the tyrant's murder.

8. The general consensus of scholars accepts Aristotle's will as reported by Diogenes as authentic.

9. A somewhat remote parallel can be found in Herodotus's story of Candaules, who is also said to have fallen in love with his own wife (Herod. 1.8–12). See David Halperin, "Plato and the Metaphysics of Desire," *Proceedings of the Boston Area Colloquium in Ancient Philosophy* 5 (1989): 27–52.

10. Maarit Kaimio, "Erotic Experience in the Conjugal Bed: Good Wives in Greek Tragedy," in this volume.

11. See, e.g., Price, *Love and Friendship,* 236.

12. See n. 2 above. There is great deal of recent work on Aristotle's view of the emotions. See Simo Knuuttila and Juha Sihvola, "How the Philosophical Analysis of Emotions Was Introduced," in *The Emotions in Hellenistic Philosophy,* ed. Juha Sihvola and Troels Engberg-Pedersen (Dordrecht: Kluwer 1998); and Juha Sihvola, "Emotional Animals: Do Aristotelian Emotions Require Beliefs?" *Apeiron* 29 (1996): 105–44, and the literature mentioned in them.

13. Price, *Love and Friendship,* 236–49; Martha C. Nussbaum, "Platonic Love and Colorado Law,": esp. 1581–93.

14. The word *eunē* means literally marriage bed but is very often a euphemism for sexual intercourse in general. The context makes it quite clear that it is the figurative and not the literal meaning which is intended here.

15. Aristotle's remarks on natural virtue are unfortunately brief and fragmented, and the notion remains somewhat vague. It gains some importance in later Hellenistic discussions among the Peripatetics and other schools. See the excellent analyses by Stephen A. White, "Aristotle on Natural and Perfect Virtue," in *Proceedings of the Boston Area Colloquium in Ancient Philosophy,* vol. 8, ed. John Cleary (Lanham, Md.: University of America Press), and "Moral Menageries: Eudemus and Peripatetic Naturalism" (paper read at the Budapest conference on Eudemus, June 1997). Cf. Juha Sihvola, "Eudemus, Animals, and the Emotions: A Comment on Stephen White" (paper read at the Budapest conference on Eudemus, June 1997).

16. See esp. Michel Foucault, *Histoire de la sexualité,* vol. 2, *L'usage des plaisirs* (Paris: Gallimard, 1984).

17. Price, *Love and Friendship,* 236–37.

18. This division is explicitly stated in many places in the Aristotelian corpus: *Eth. Eud.* 2.7.1223a26–27, 2.10.1225b24–26; [*Mag. Mor.*] 1.12.1187b36–37; *De An.* 2.3.414b2, 3.9.432b3–10; *De motu animalium* 6.700b19–22; *Rh.* 1.10.1369a1–4; *Pol.* 7.15.1334b17–25; *Top.* 4.5.126a6–13.

19. On Platonic tripartition and its application by Aristotle, see John M. Cooper, "Reason, Moral Virtue, and Moral Value," in *Rationality in Greek Thought,* ed. Michael Frede and Gisela Striker (New York: Oxford University Press, 1996). Cf. Sihvola, "Emotional Animals," 123–31.

20. See Price, *Love and Friendship*, 237.

21. On Aristotle's description of marriage, see Price, *Love and Friendship*, 167–73; and Stephen Salkever, *Finding the Mean* (Princeton, N.J.: Princeton University Press, 1990).

22. Nussbaum, "Platonic Love and Colorado Law," 1587, interprets the last passage as speaking about single-sex residence rather same-sex sexual conduct, because she does not regard the idea of mandatory male-male intercourse as plausible. However, the crucial and ambiguous phrase *pros tous arrenas homilia* also appears in the passage on warlike peoples in general, where it clearly refers to sexual conduct. It would be strange if the meaning were different in two such closely related passages.

23. See David Halperin, "Forgetting Foucault: Acts, Identities, and the History of Sexuality," in this volume.

Chapter Eight

TWO WOMEN OF SAMOS

Kenneth Dover

Anthologia Palatina (AP) 5.207 (Asclepiades 7) is an epigram in which the Samian poet Asclepiades (early third century B.C.E.) attacks two women thus:

> αἱ Σάμιαι Βιττὼ καὶ Νάννιον εἰς Ἀφροδίτης
> φοιτᾶν τοῖς αὐτῆς οὐκ ἐθέλουσι νόμοις,
> εἰς δ' ἕτερ' αὐτομολοῦσιν ἃ μὴ καλά. δέσποτι Κύπρι,
> μίσει τὰς κοίτης τῆς παρὰ σοὶ φυγάδας.

A strictly literal translation is "The Samians [fem.] Bitto and Nannion are not willing to frequent/attend [the school/house/camp] of Aphrodite in accordance with the rules of [the goddess] herself, but desert to other things which [are] not good. Mistress Kypris [= Aphrodite], abhor those fugitives/exiles from the going-to-bed in your company!"

We do not know whether Bitto and Nannion are the real names of real people known to the poet, or fictitious names for real people, or the names of wholly fictitious characters. Bitto is the name of a woman named with her patronymic on a Samian tomb (*Griechische Vers-Inschriften*, vol. 1 [*GVI*], 1734) contemporary with Asclepiades; it occurs also, a little earlier, among a small set of names on an Attic inscription (*Inscriptiones Graecae*, edition minor, vols. 2–3 [*IG* ii²], 8931; a dedication?), and about 100 B.C.E. in an

222

epitaph from Chios (*GVI* 474) commemorating Bitto and Phainis, wool spinners from Cos, "poor old women" but πρῶται γένος "foremost in their sex/kind/calling" (cf. LSJ, s.v. γένος, IV and V). From the early fifth century B.C.E. onward, many women called Nannion are known to us, including a Νάννιον Σαμία on an Attic dedication of about 360 B.C.E. (*IG* ii² 10229). Some were hetairai, including one mentioned by Hyperides (fr. 141 Kenyon, before 322 B.C.E.), the subject of a comedy by Eubulus, a contemporary of Hyperides.

φοιτᾶν with a genitive strongly suggests "attend [the school] of" rather than simply "visit [the house] of"; compare Aristophanes *Knights* 1235: ἐφοίτας ἐς τίνος διδασκάλου, "what teacher's [school] did you attend?" There is a passage of Aristophanes' *Clouds* in which "attendance" on a teacher and "desertion" to a rival teacher both occur. The dispute is between Right and Wrong over which of them shall educate the young man Pheidippides. The chorus, setting up the contest, says (935–38): "You [Right] expound the teaching you gave the men of old, and you [Wrong] the new education, so that when he [Pheidippides] has heard you both disputing, he may make his choice and go [φοίτᾳ] [to the school he chooses]." At the end of the dispute Wrong, having shocked Right by nonchalantly saying "Well, what's wrong with being εὐρύπρωκτος?" "wide assed," namely, from habitual subjection to sodomy, then compels him to admit that most of the audience are "wide assed." Right cries despairingly (1102–4) "You buggers! . . . I'm getting out and deserting to you [ἐξαυτομολῶ πρὸς ὑμᾶς]!"

The notion of Aphrodite's "school" implies that just as a poet is "taught" by the Muses (Solon fr. 13.51) and skill in weaving is imparted by Athena (e.g., Hesiod *Works and Days* 64), so the sexual skills desirable in a hetaira —which may, in the present context, beg the question (see below)—are imparted by Aphrodite.

The activities to which Bitto and Nannion have "deserted" are stigmatized as μὴ καλά, which the Budé editors of *AP* volume 5 translate "sans beauté"; so too Brooten (1996, 42): "not beautiful." Certainly, when human beings, animals, trees, buildings, and so on—that is to say, spatiotemporal continua—are called καλός, the reference is to their visual beauty, but in its application to behavior the process which led eventually to its becoming the most general term of approbation in Greek began with Homer; in *Iliad* 6.326 Hector condemns Paris's "skulking" as οὐ καλά. Notable examples from much nearer the time of Asclepiades are Euripides *Bacchae* 1040 ("it is οὐ καλόν to rejoice over the accomplishment of ills"), Plato *Symposium* 185A ("that for money he would submit to anything at anyone's hands, and that is οὐ καλόν"), and Menander fr. 272 ("when you don't know, it is καλόν to learn from those who do") (cf. Dover 1974, 69–73). The judgment in such cases is plainly moral; and in any case it would be surprising to find other people's sexual activity evaluated in terms of its visual appeal to a third party.

At this point there is a linguistic detail requiring scrutiny. Ambiguity is often inherent in relative clauses; English can usually avoid it by punctuation, but punctuation in a Greek text is a matter of modern editorial decision. Unpunctuated, "they turn to other things which are disgraceful" could mean (A) "they turn to other things, and/but those things are disgraceful" or (B) they turn to other things, [namely] those things which are disgraceful." Gow and Page rightly observe that the negative μή is generic ("A. excuses himself from envisaging the particular perversity to which the pair is addicted"). Like many distinctions in Greek, the difference between the negatives οὐ and μή in relative clauses is not always as sharp as the rule suggests (Stahl 1907, 770), but interpretation B has high probability on its side. If Asclepiades had wished to use the specific negative οὐ, there was no metrical obstacle, for he could have said αὐτομολοῦσι, τὰ δ' οὐ καλά or (using the "epic" relative ὅς τε, common in his younger contemporary Callimachus, e.g., in *Hymn to Artemis* 16, 141) αὐτομολοῦσιν, ἅ τ' οὐ καλά. As it is, he seems to be attributing to Bitto and Nannion a liking for "deviance" in general. That squares with the fact that whereas in Anacreon fr. 358 Lesbos is almost certainly associated with what we call "lesbianism," in Aristophanes *Wasps* 1346 λεσβίζειν, "treat in the lesbian way," unquestionably denotes something which a woman can do to a man, and in Pherecrates fr. 159 "Lesbian women" are assumed to be λαικάστριαι, "*fellatrices*," "cock-suckers" (cf. Theopompus Comicus fr. 36, treating the inhabitants of Lesbos as the "inventors" of fellatio).

But what, specifically, did Bitto and Nannion do to merit condemnation for "deserting" Aphrodite? Since the Greeks took it for granted that a man's lust was normally and naturally aroused by the beauty of young people of either sex, there was no word in the classical language for "male homosexual"; but there does appear to have been one for "female homosexual." Plato in his *Symposium* introduces "Aristophanes" as a character and puts into his mouth a view of sexual love which is radically different from Plato's own view and explicitly rejected later in the work (205E; cf. 212C). "Aristophanes" tells a fantastic fable, according to which every human being was originally double, male-male or male-female or female-female, until those beings were all cleft in two by Zeus. Proceeding as if each one of us alive now were an immediate product of that brutal separation, and showing the reckless disregard for genetic realities which is so characteristic of fables (cf. Dover 1966), he explains sexual love as a search, on the part of every individual for his or her "other half." Whether we are heterosexual or homosexual depends on which of the original three kinds (γένη) we are "from." Thus, women who are from an original female-female are αἱ ἑταιρίστριαι (191E).

This word does not occur elsewhere in what we have of classical literature, but it is important to notice the definite article: "*the* ἑταιρίστριαι," not (e.g.) "and these we might call ἑταιρίστριαι"; Plato assumes we know the word. A feminine noun in -ίστρια implies the existence of a masculine noun in -ιστής—for example, κιθαριστής, "(male) lyre-player," and κιθαρίστρια, "(female) lyre-player," θεριστής, "(male) reaper," θερίστρια, "(female) reaper," and many others. The male ἑταιριστής happens not to occur in extant classical literature, but in Pollux (the Atticist's Roget) it is classified (6.188) with words for "womanizer," denoting a man with a strong appetite for hetairai, who are nearer to "mistresses" than (except in the utterances of stern moralists, jealous rivals, or political adversaries) to prostitutes. On that analogy ἑταιρίστρια might be expected to denote a woman who seeks "specialist" hetairai catering for female clients. Bitto and Nannion may, for all we know, have been such specialists, but the fact that there are two of them points very strongly to their being a bonded lesbian pair.

Though working in a genre of which the salient features are elegance, originality, and wit, rather than the forthright moralizing of archaic elegy, Asclepiades adopts a standpoint of remarkable hostility toward lesbians. The appeal to Aphrodite to "abhor" Bitto and Nannion is strong language, given that the suffering inflicted by Greek deities on those who offend them is often atrocious. But why should Aphrodite abhor lesbians? She was not a goddess "of" heterosexuality, but a goddess whose province was genital friction, ἀφροδίσια, a word frequently referring to such friction between males. Plato's "Athenian" in *Laws* 836C uses it with that reference; so too Xenophon *Hiero* 1.29 speaks of "ἀφροδίσια with boys," and in his *Oeconomicus* 12.13f., as in Plato *Phaedrus* 254A, it is plain that male homosexual friction is meant. In *AP* 5.54 (Dioscorides 7) a distinction is drawn between "child-begetting Kypris" and "male-boy Kypris," the latter (i.e., anal penetration) being recommended for husband and wife when the wife is heavily pregnant. *AP* 12.261 (Asclepiades 20) praises a girl, Dorkion by name, who is φιλέφηβος, "fond of young men in the eighteen-to-twenty age range" and "knows how to implant the swift arrows of Kypris" by dressing "like a tender boy."

A conceit that male homosexuality is the special province of the god Eros, the personification of love in the sense which that word bears in our expressions "fall in love" and "be in love" rather than in that of Aphrodite, appears in *AP* 12.86 (Meleager 18), where the poet is torn between the "mad-for-women flame" kindled in him by Aphrodite and the "male desire" instilled by Eros, and he declares that the goddess herself will say "the cheeky lad is the winner." Yet θῆλυς, "female," is an acceptable attribute of ἔρως, as we see from *AP* 12.17 (Asclepiades 37), where "male fires"—compare the "male fire" of *AP* 5.6 (Callimachus 11)—prevail over "female ἔρως" because desire for a male is "sharper" than for a female by as much as a male is stronger than a female. In Greek poetry, and especially in the epigrammatists, the relation between Aphrodite and Eros is variable: mother and son, or mistress and servant, or partners in action on their victims. It is noticeable that Aphrodite is the more prominent of the two in connection with prostitutes and hetairai; "purchased Aphrodite" is enjoyed by the clients of the famous Lais in *AP* 7.218 (Antipater of Sidon 23), three old whores who are "pirate-ships of Aphrodite" are the subject of *AP* 5.161 (Asclepiades 40), and both *AP* 5.158 (Asclepiades 4) and 5.203 (id. 6) are presented as dedications by hetairai (cf. "Simonides" 1, *AP* 5.159).

Why, then, should lesbians be denigrated when male homosexuality is so favored? As observed by Halperin (1990, 35), Winkler (1990, 39), and Brooten (1996, 241 n. 75, 325), there was a strong tendency in the ancient world to regard *penetration* of a "passive" person by an "active" person as the essence of ἀφροδίσια. In addition, the fact that lesbians exist is threatening to men; it amounts to a devaluation of the penis. The patently lesbian character of some poems of Sappho did not damage her reputation as a poet, but in the classical period admiration for her art seems to have coexisted with something like a "conspiracy of silence" about any sexual orientation which resembled hers. Extant vases from the mid–sixth century B.C.E. onward provide us with hundreds of representations of males, very often with erections, attempting to seduce younger males by caressing their faces and genitals (and sometimes succeeding in the attempt), but so far we have only two vases in which a woman touches the genitals of another woman: see Kilmer (1993, R207) and Brooten (1996, figs. 2–3). Apart from the fable told by "Aristophanes" in the *Symposium* Plato mentions lesbianism only once: in *Laws* 636C, where the pleasure of sexual intercourse between "the female and the male nature, joining in procreation," is "granted by nature," but that of "males with males or females with females" is παρὰ φύσιν ("contrary to nature" or "going beyond nature"), attributable to "lack of self-control [in the pursuit] of pleasure." Plato certainly did not regard the *desire* for homosexual friction as "unnatural"—that is obvious from *Phaedrus* and *Symposium*, to say nothing of the reaction of his Socrates to the beauty of young Charmides in *Charmides* 155CD (Dover 1989, 155), but Plato would have been the last person to imagine that we have any kind of right to do what we desire. The "lack of self-control" to which he refers is not all that different in implication from Herodotus's statement (1.135) that the Persians adopted from other cultures "luxuries of all kinds" (εὐπα-θείας παντοδαπάς), "including sexual intercourse with boys, which they learned from the Greeks."

But the most important indication that lesbianism was one "luxury" which Greek males from the mid–sixth century B.C.E. onward were unable to tolerate is the total absence of any reference to it in Aristophanic comedy. As modern readers, we have the impression that in that genre *any* aspect of sex (or excretion) can be exploited, in the coarsest language, for humorous purposes. Yet precisely when we might expect references to lesbianism, it is missing: in *Lysistrata,* in which the women (except Lysistrata herself) are as frustrated sexually as the men; in *Women at the Thesmophoria,* which contains a long speech (466–519) full of jokes about the "misdeeds" of women; and in *Women in Assembly,* a fantasy about the transfer of all power, including (hetero)sexual initiative, to the women of Athens. It is hard to resist the conclusion that lesbianism was a topic which aroused such anxiety in a male audience that the comic poets were unable to treat it humorously. The same can be said, incidentally, of menstruation; but perhaps the most striking analogy is the absence from comedy of even the faintest allusion to the great plague of 430 B.C.E., which killed a third of the population of Athens—only five years before the first surviving play of Aristophanes, and in a decade represented by many historians' and commentators' citations from lost comedies. At the very beginning of the fifth century B.C.E. the tragic poet Phrynichus was heavily fined for putting on a play, *The Fall of Miletus,* which "reminded the Athenians of their own misfortunes" (Herodotus 6.21.2). Perhaps for Greek men, women who loved other women were a persistent "misfortune."

As normally happens with any hypothesis about Greek literature, confirmation or refutation hangs upon evidence of which the existence is known but the nature, so far, is not. In the period from the mid–fifth century B.C.E. to the mid–fourth there were at least five comedies, by different authors, entitled *Sappho.* One of them is represented by a twenty-one-verse passage and a single word, one by a four-verse passage, one by a two-verse passage, and the remaining two by a single word each. Better acquaintance with them would do much to clarify the attitude of classical Athens to lesbianism.

References

AP. Anthologia Palatina ("The Greek Anthology"). Each reference to *AP* in this chapter is followed in parentheses by the appropriate reference to A. S. F. Gow and D. L. Page, eds., *Hellenistic Epigrams*, 2 vols. (Cambridge, 1965).

Brooten, Bernadette. *Love between Women*. Chicago, 1996.

Dover, K. J. "Aristophanes' Speech in Plato's *Symposium*." *Journal of Hellenic Studies* 86 (1966): 41–50.

———. *Greek Homosexuality*. London, 1978; rev. ed., Cambridge, Mass., 1989.

———. *Greek Popular Morality in the Time of Plato and Aristotle*. Oxford, 1974; republished, New York, 1994.

GVI. Peek, Werner, ed. *Griechische Vers-Inschriften*. Vol. 1. Berlin, 1955.

Halperin, David J., *One Hundred Years of Homosexuality*, New York, 1990

IG ii². Kirchner, J., ed. *Inscriptiones Graecae*. Editio minor. Vols. 2–3. Berlin, 1913–1940; republished, Chicago, 1974.

Kilmer, Martin. *Greek Erotica*. London, 1993.

Stahl, J. M. *Kritisch-historische Syntax des griechischen Verbums der klassischen Zeit*. Heidelberg, 1907.

Winkler, John J. *The Constraints of Desire*. New York, 1990.

Chapter Nine

THE FIRST HOMOSEXUALITY?

David M. Halperin

$\mathcal{T}$he history and vicissitudes of the term "lesbian," its gradual emergence as the name of a concept or category of erotic experience, dramatize both the challenges and the rewards of work in the history of sexuality. For "lesbian" is at once a very old word and a very new word. It dates back not only to ancient Greece, but to the preclassical period of Greek civilization. And yet it belongs very much to the modern sciences of sexual orientation, to gay liberation and second-wave feminism, to the jargon of contemporary identity politics.

"Lesbianism" has often appeared to be a kind of afterthought, a supplement to "homosexuality" (which, like all gender-neutral terms, tends to refer more particularly to males than to females). And yet some recent scholarship has suggested that the category of female same-sex love was constituted earlier than the modern category of homosexuality and may even have been its precursor. The difficulties presented to the historian of sexuality by the multiple temporalities of "lesbianism" are therefore exemplary: they pose basic questions about the ontology of the sexual, about the very nature and mode of being of "sexuality," about the historicity of the modern sexual subject. They also point to a number of methodological problems of considerable and wide-ranging interest: how to distinguish language from experience, categories of thought from forms of subjectivity, continuities from discontinuities in the historiography of sex and gender.[1] In short, any attempt to write the history of lesbianism is bound to raise a series of issues whose complexity and suggestiveness indicate how much we have yet to learn from the nascent project of the history of sexuality, and how broad an intellectual engagement will be necessary in order to learn it.

So just how old is "lesbian"? The word itself is originally the adjectival form of the Greek place-name Lesbos, which refers to a large island in the Aegean Sea six miles off the northwest coast of Asia Minor, probably settled by Aeolian Greeks in the tenth century B.C.[2] That island was the birthplace and home of Sappho, who composed lyric poems in Greek towards the end of the seventh century B.C. and the beginning of the sixth. Many of her poems express love and desire for women and girls. Sappho's work was greatly admired in the male literary culture of classical antiquity, and sufficient numbers of her poems survived by the third century B.C. to fill nine books, although they have come down to us (with one possible exception) only in fragments. Nonetheless, Sappho's poetry and her fame have proved sufficiently powerful to impart to the adjective "lesbian" its now-familiar sexual meaning. "Lesbian" is in that sense by far the most ancient term in our current lexicon of sexuality.

But "lesbian" is also very new. Consider the following scene in *Antic Hay*, a novel by Aldous Huxley published in 1923. Toward the end of the narrative, a young critic, escaping the abuse of one of his friends, whose art exhibition he has snidely reviewed, and avoiding another friend, whose wife he has unknowingly seduced, takes refuge in the home of a society lady, arriving just as she and another guest are embarked on the second course of a long and indolent lunch. The lady greets him rapturously, invites him to join her and her guest at table, and begs him to tell them "all about" his "Lesbian experiences." Which he proceeds to do, launching into an account of his adventures "among the Isles of Greece," as the novelist coyly puts it.[3] The obvious referent of this playful language is heterosexual dalliance. Huxley appears to be invoking the archaic association of the word "Lesbian" with female sexual abandon in order to refer to his character's amorous pursuit of various women. The usage is admittedly precious, by the standards of the day, even arcane. But it is not impossible. Less than eighty years ago, a cultivated social observer could portray a party at which the term "Lesbian" gets thrown about in civilized banter and applied not only to heterosexual love affairs but to the *male* participant in them without causing the slightest puzzlement or consternation. No such idiom exists today. Sometime between 1923 and the present, then, the word "lesbian" came to mean one thing and one thing only. Despite the antiquity of the term, the mutation of the word "lesbian" into a standard designation for "female homosexual" is a very recent development.

In fact, the transformation of "lesbian" into the proper name of a particular sexual orientation, into a conceptual shorthand for "female homosexual," took a very long time. Neither the island nor the people of Lesbos are associated with "lesbianism" in our sense of the term before the second century A.D. (A possible exception is Anacreon, fr. 358 Page, in the later sixth century B.C., but since scholars dispute both the text itself and its interpretation in terms of this very question—whether or not the mention of Lesbos in this poetic fragment should be understood as a reference to female homosexuality—Anacreon's verses cannot be adduced as evidence either for or against such an association.) In other words, it took nearly a thousand years for a definite link to be made between Lesbos and "lesbianism." The women of Lesbos acquired very early a reputation for sensuality, even licentiousness, but same-sex desire did not initially contribute to it. From at least the fifth century B.C., if not before, the sexual act associated with "lesbianism" in antiquity was fellatio. The Greek verb *lesbiazein*, which is attested for the first time in the classical period, meant "to give head."

The early history of the figure of Sappho herself also defeats modern expectations. It took six centuries for Sappho's same-sex erotic attachments to attract recorded comment. The celebration of the beauty of women by women was at least to some degree conventional in the Greek lyric tradition. In fact, the earliest attestation of female homoerotic desire in a piece of Greek literature occurs in the work of a male author—namely, the late-seventh-century Spartan poet Alcman, who wrote choral odes to be performed (apparently) by a cohort of unmarried girls. In the fragmentary remains of these poems, individual maidens extol the beauty and allure of those whom they especially admire among their leaders and age-mates, and they mention their favorites by name (frr. 1, 3). Far from being a transgression of the laws of desire or of male authority, such same-sex female erotic expressions were scripted for these girls by a male writer. Sappho, too, was greatly esteemed by male readers, who, initially at least, do not seem to have regarded her love poetry as irregular or anomalous. At the same time, her expressions of passion for women were not taken to indicate a rejection of men. On the contrary, Sappho was represented in classical Athenian comedies of the fifth and fourth centuries B.C. as the lover of various men, sometimes even as a prostitute. A red-figure Attic hydria, attributed to the Polygnotus Group, from about 440 B.C. portrays Sappho in what may be a female homoerotic setting (Beazley, *ARV*[2] 1060, #145). But—and this is a fact as curious as it is overlooked—no extant ancient writer of the classical period found the homoeroticism of Sappho's poetry sufficiently remarkable to mention it. So either Sappho's early readers and auditors saw nothing homoerotic in her poems or they saw nothing remarkable in Sappho's homoeroticism. Neither of those alternatives seems very satisfactory to us, or even very plausible, but this interpretative difficulty ought to force us to consider a new set of questions about what the ancients counted as sex and sexuality, how they understood different erotic practices and identities, and how they distinguished different sexual subjects—questions to which I will return briefly at the conclusion of this essay. In any case, the first writers to touch on the question of Sappho's erotic deviance, so far as we know, were the Roman poets of the late first century B.C. and early first century A.D. (Horace *Odes* 2.13.24–25; Ovid *Heroides* 15.15–19, *Tristia* 2.365).[4]

From that period onwards, Sappho and Lesbos could be associated at times with certain aspects of female same-sex love and desire, with certain female same-sex sexual practices, and with certain forms of female sex and gender deviance. In addition to being portrayed as an exemplary poetess, a passionate lover of men, and a whore, Sappho could now qualify as a "tribade." This term, an ancient Greek word borrowed by Roman writers and first attested in Latin in the first century A.D. (Phaedrus 4.15 [16].1, Seneca the Elder *Controversiae* 1.2.23), was originally understood in antiquity to signify a phallic woman, a hypermasculine or butch woman, and/or a woman who sought sexual pleasure by rubbing her genitals against those of other women. The identification of Sappho as a tribade therefore led to the word "Lesbian" being *applied* to acts or persons we might qualify as "lesbian" today, although neither the referents of that term nor its meaning were identical to those of the modern word "lesbian." Thus, in Lucian's second-century-A.D. *Dialogues of the Courtesans*, a character remarks, "they say there are women like that in Lesbos, with faces like men, who are unwilling to let men do it to them,[5] and instead consort with women, as though they themselves were men" (5.2). As Alan Cameron points out, "The Lucian passage proves that the women of Lesbos enjoyed a reputation for same-sex inclination by the Roman period, but *that is not quite the same as using the word Lesbian to mean that.*"[6] In fact, what Lucian refers to would be more accurately described as "tribadism," not "lesbianism,"[7] insofar as the speaker fully conflates female same-sex desire with gender deviance or sexual role reversal, and the focus of the passage appears to be women *who assume a masculine identity, appearance, and sexual style in their relations with other women,* rather than women who desire women, or the women whom they desire. It is not exactly the "homosexuality" of the "women like that in Lesbos" that attracts particular comment, then, but their striking departure from a whole set of social norms governing feminine comportment—norms that conflate gender identity, self-presentation, personal style, erotic inclination, and sexual practice.

By the early tenth century, a Byzantine bishop of Caesarea by the name of Arethas could include the plural noun *Lesbiai* ("Lesbians"), along with "tribades" and other Greek words for female sexual deviants, in a gloss on a text by the second-century Christian writer Clement of Alexandria. But that, once again, is not the same thing as defining *Lesbia* as "lesbian" or "female homosexual," and in any case Arethas himself did not have much understanding of the ancient terminology or its meaning.[8] Similar confusions persisted throughout the medieval period, in which a variety of terms for referring to female-female sex existed, though male sexual practices tended to generate the models for understanding female same-sex relations.

A vocabulary for describing sexual relations between women was gradually consolidated, first in France and then in England, from the sixteenth through the eighteenth centuries. But "lesbian" was not initially the term of choice to designate female same-sex eroticism. "Tribade" and its derivatives came to be the words most commonly used to refer to women who had sex with women, especially in medical or anatomical texts, though also in poetry, moral philosophy, and other learned discourses, from at least 1566 onward.[9] Although early modern authors first employed "tribade" when speaking about those ancient women who had already been labeled "tribades" in classical texts,[10] the word soon achieved a more contemporary application. But it remained closely tied to specific sexual practices or anatomical features, and it continued to signify a masculine woman, a phallic woman, or a woman who performed genital rubbing with other women. Even when, in the latter part of the sixteenth century, the French libertine writer Pierre de Bourdeille—better known as the Abbé de Brantôme—devoted part of a chapter of the work later called *Les dames galantes* to a survey of women who had sex with women, and spoke in generic terms of "ces amours femenines [*sic*]," he still organized his discussion not around a category of female homoeroticism per se but around a more particularized topic (namely, did a married woman who made love with another woman thereby commit adultery and cuckold her husband?), and he remained focused on a specific number of traditional commonplaces pertaining to women who sexually desired other women (such as masculine identification, sex-role reversal, hermaphroditism, the use of dildos, and the impossibility of competing with men).[11]

Brantôme also makes substantive use of the adjective "lesbian," speaking startlingly on two occasions of "force telles dames et lesbiennes" and "ces lesbiennes."[12] But the context of his usage ties the word closely to its proper meaning as a place name. In the first passage, the reference to the "many such ladies and lesbians in divers places and regions" follows immediately upon a direct quotation from Lucian about "women like that in Lesbos" and so continues the geographical allusion; in the second passage, Brantôme observes that some of "these lesbians" do not give up sexual relations with men, "even Sappho who was their mistress": here, the speedy mention of Sappho, whose connection to Lesbos and its "lesbian Ladies" Brantôme had duly invoked at the outset of his discussion, serves to reassert the topographical force of the word's meaning. "Lesbian" in this period, then, remained largely a proper name, a place-name, a geographical designation—though, as Brantôme's usage indicates, a name strongly associated with sexual relations between women and often embedded in discourses pertaining to female same-sex erotic practices.[13] For example, a 1646 libertine poem in French by François de Maynard, preoccupied with female finger fucking, is entitled, in discreet Latin, "Tribades seu Lesbia" ("Tribades, or Lesbia" ["Matters Lesbian"?]). In *The Toast*, a mock epic poem by William King published in 1732, the geographical reference shades into the sexual: "What if *Sappho* was so naught?/ I'll deny, that thou art taught/ How to pair the Female Doves,/ How to practice *Lesbian* Loves." The expanded 1736 edition of the poem refers to "Tribades or Lesbians," thereby demonstrating that "'Lesbian' could be used both as an adjective and as a noun" in English in the early eighteenth century,[14] though not that it had as yet fully become the name of a sexual rather than a topographical entity. By the end of the eighteenth century in France and England, however, "Sappho," "Sapphic," "Sapphist," "Lesbos," and "Lesbian" had become virtually interchangeable with "tribade" and its derivatives. But even though "Lesbian" could be *applied* to love between women in the early modern period, it is probably not until the latter part of the nineteenth century that the word acquired an autonomous meaning, becoming almost a technical term, a proper name for a particular kind of erotic practice or sexual orientation. And that meaning did not become dominant or exclusive until the latter part of the twentieth century, as we have seen. Even among lesbians, especially of the less educated classes, the words "gay" and "queer" continued to be current until the onset of second-wave feminism and the triumph of lesbian feminism in the late 1960s and early 1970s.

The historiographic issues raised by the multiple temporalities of "lesbian," as a word, a sexual classification, and a category of erotic experience, emerge with particular clarity from a close reading of Bernadette Brooten's 1996 book, *Love between Women*, a study of female homoeroticism in classical antiquity and the early Christian Church.[15] At certain moments in the book, Brooten emphasizes the gaps that separate ancient sexual discourses from our own. At other moments, she insists on the correspondences between ancient and modern sexual subjects, arguing for the existence in the ancient world of sexual orientations that we would recognize and define as lesbian or homosexual today. The task that Brooten sets herself of surveying all the evidence for how the ancients and early Christians understood erotic relations between women has the effect, perhaps unintended, of dramatizing the historical, theoretical, and interpretative problems that historians of sexuality, and of homosexuality in particular, confront constantly in their daily practice and that endow the history of (homo)sexuality with its considerable theoretical and historiographical interest.

Brooten writes from a lesbian-feminist perspective. Her book is a testimony of the extent to which contemporary political engagements can open up a series of scholarly questions and lead to a new understanding of even very distant historical phenomena. At the same time, the book's focus on what Brooten calls "ancient lesbians" (17) and its invocation of the lesbian category to describe the historical phenomena it studies provides a test of both the benefits and the limits of applying contemporary sexual categories to premodern human subjects. It obliges its readers, especially those of us who are classicists, historians of sexuality, queer theorists, or all three at once, to reexamine our ways of understanding the relations of continuity and discontinuity between ancient and modern societies, between premodern and modern sexual categories, and between male and female homosexualities. It thereby provokes a reconsideration of the some of the basic conceptual issues surrounding the very definition of the lesbian category as well as the practice of lesbian historiography and the history of (homo)sexuality more generally.

Such a reconsideration is long overdue, but there is nothing astonishing about the fact that we have had to wait so long for an impetus to undertake it. Ancient references to female homosexuality and homoeroticism are not especially numerous, but they are widely scattered. A great many of them occur in the sorts of texts that classicists rarely read, perhaps because they rarely possess the specialized technical competence necessary in order to interpret them. I am referring here to texts that belong to the corpus of obscure, largely neglected, technical, and now-defunct ancient disciplines, such as astrology, magic, dream analysis, physiognomy, and medicine. Many of these texts have not been edited for more than a century, and some have never been translated. The scholarship on them is arcane, of widely varying date and reliability, and, for the most part, not written in English. All of these factors have doubtless contributed to discouraging scholars from attempting to write a history of lesbianism in the ancient world, above and beyond the theoretical, methodological, and historiographic complexities involved in the task of writing the history of an erotic identity at once so old and so new.

It is all the more fortunate that Bernadette Brooten, in the course of a book-length effort to reinterpret the notoriously obscure passage in Paul's Letter to the Romans condemning same-sex sexual practices, has gone to the trouble of assembling, for the first time in the history of classical scholarship, nearly all the ancient Greek and Latin sources that bear on the topic of female homosexuality in classical antiquity.[16] Brooten supplements this material with a consideration of ancient Jewish sources and a brief survey of visual representations. She makes all this primary and secondary material available to English-speaking readers and situates it in its original social and discursive context so as to enable them to assess the evidence independently and to draw their own conclusions from it. Her book will be a necessary point of reference for all future investigations of the topic. At the same time, her methods and conclusions are debatable. What makes Brooten's treatment of the ancient material open to criticism is precisely the way she goes about grappling with the conundrum of the oldness or the newness of lesbianism as a sexual category and experience. I would like to see this conundrum resolved by means of a different strategy from the one Brooten employs, but I must acknowledge that any such effort will have to begin by an extended confrontation with Brooten's work. And so that is what I shall undertake in the remainder of this essay. Although I shall have a number of criticisms, often quite sharp, to make of Brooten's readings of the ancient texts, my aim in making them is to further the project of rethinking lesbian history which Brooten's own work has already so powerfully advanced.

Brooten emphasizes from the outset of her study that the sexual conventions and categories of ancient Greek and Roman civilization were very different from modern ones. She argues, more specifically, that the ancients tended to conceptualize sexual relations in terms of a hierarchy of so-called active and passive sexual roles; by comparison, the sameness or difference of the sexes of the individuals engaged in any particular sexual act was, in and of itself, of minor significance to them. Brooten puts this point as follows in the introduction to her book: "Roman-period writers presented as normative those sexual relations that represent a human social hierarchy. They saw every sexual pairing as including one active and one passive partner, regardless of gender, although culturally they correlated gender with these categories. . . . The most fundamental category for expressing this hierarchy was active/passive—a category even more fundamental than gender for these writers" (2). It was the *comparative* lack of salience of the relation of gender-difference or -sameness between the sexual partners that explains in part why the modern meaning of "lesbian" is hard to document in texts from Greek and Roman antiquity. The basic point could be articulated more precisely by saying that the ancients "evaluated sexual acts according to the degree to which such acts either violated or conformed to norms of conduct deemed appropriate to individual sexual actors by reason of their gender, age, and social status" and that those norms presupposed a strict correlation of superordinate and subordinate social status with "active" and "passive" sexual roles. The most salient *erotic* distinction made by the ancients rested not on a physical typology of anatomical sexes (male vs. female) or even on gender differences (man vs. woman) but on the social articulation of power (superordinate vs. subordinate social identity).[17] The result was a social/conceptual/erotic grid that aligned masculinity, activity, penetration, and dominance along one axis and femininity, passivity, being penetrated, and submission along another. Those two axes corresponded to, but could function independently of, gender differences.

Brooten's analysis of ancient sexual discourses returns to this point a number of times. For example, she observes that for the ancient astrologers "the fundamental division is not between males and females, nor between heterosexual and homosexual, but rather between active and passive" (126–27) and that for Ptolemy in particular "activeness and passiveness are more fundamental than biological maleness and femaleness" (128)—although she quite correctly points out that a passive male is regarded differently from an active female.

At the same time, Brooten tends to treat the ancients' distinctive preoccupation with the relations between sexual role and social status as an idiosyncratic cultural idiom within which the ancients were nonetheless quite able to express their attitudes to "lesbianism" and to "sexuality" more generally, as if these modern categories also prevailed in antiquity and were not made inapplicable by the ancients' habit of classifying erotic actors in terms of sexual role, social status, and gender identity. Again and again Brooten draws upon her considerable expertise in decoding the cultural languages of ancient Mediterranean societies in order to translate the perceptions of

Greek and Roman writers into the supposedly timeless terms that we currently use today in order to refer to different "kinds" of "sexuality." In effect, then, Brooten treats ancient sexual discourses as though they provide a transparent medium through which the learned interpreter can discern the outlines of the fundamental and universal realities of sexual life. For example, at the beginning of her book, Brooten says that "a strict distinction between active and passive sexual roles . . . shaped the way that people viewed female homoeroticism," as if "female homoeroticism" were a *thing*—a single, stable object, that can be *viewed* from different perspectives—rather than a social and discursive production in its own right, a culturally constituted category of both erotic arousal and social organization.

Implicit in Brooten's way of thinking and writing is the presumption that we, nowadays, are more or less in possession of the facts of life when it comes to sex. We "know" that there is such a thing as human sexuality; we "know" that sexual orientation is one of the basic categories of human experience. Brooten never explicitly argues that such presumptions are correct, or that our current psychological or behavioral models of sexuality are in fact valid. She may actually not believe they are.[18] But her rhetoric has the effect of anchoring modern sexual categories in some transhistorical reality by implying that our understanding of sexuality was shared by the ancients. The opening sentences of her book, for example, insist that "people from various walks of life" in the ancient world "acknowledged that women could have *sexual contact* with women," "knew . . . about *sexual relations* between women," and had "a heightened awareness of *female homoeroticism*" (1; my italics). Later, Brooten speaks of "the awareness of *sexual love* between women on the part of male authors" in antiquity (16; my italics again). These four assertions are all, in their own way, indisputable, thanks in large part to Brooten's own research: numbers of ancient texts cited by Brooten bear out her claim that some women in the ancient Greco-Roman world had erotic and sexual relationships with one another, and that numbers of male authors were aware of it. That is a crucially important, and long-overdue, scholarly achievement. Nonetheless, Brooten's fourfold description of what the ancients "knew," although couched in language that strives admirably to be neutral, descriptive, objective, and not culturally loaded, betrays in the unwitting equivalence it constructs between "sexual contact," "sexual relations," "homoeroticism," and "sexual love" the force of the pressure exerted on Brooten's thought by modern sexual concepts.

For "sexual contact" is a behavioral term, which evokes the sexological and sociological language of the Kinsey reports, whereas "sexual relations" is a euphemism for intercourse drawn from the lexicon of the various forensic disciplines, and "homoeroticism" is a coinage of nineteenth-century psychiatry. The amalgamation of behavioral, sexological, sociological, forensic, psychological, psychiatric, and erotic categories into a single unifying idea is a hallmark of the modern concept of sexuality.[19] That all these things are not in fact equivalent is something I learned on the very first day of the very first course in lesbian and gay studies that I ever taught, more than a dozen years ago now. One of the lesbian members of our group declared, in what was obviously intended to be a programmatic rebuke to the implicit assumptions on which the course seemed to be proceeding, "I am not interested in the history of women who *fucked* other women. I'm interested in the history of women who *loved* other women." To which another lesbian in the group mildly rejoined, "Actually, I couldn't care less about the history of women who loved other women, but what I'd really like to find out more about is the history of women who fucked other women." Those differences in stated interest and emphasis effectively point the researcher in two very different directions, toward two very different chronologies, literary traditions, social and political contexts, sets of archival material—in short, toward two very different histories of "lesbianism."[20] Brooten's way of formulating her project neatly elides all such distinctions: by organizing her material, implicitly at least, around the modern concept of homosexuality, she manages to impose a questionable unity and homogeneity upon it, to redescribe the ancient phenomena in terms of the modern concept, and to insinuate that sexuality and sexual orientation are more or less objective phenomena, independent of human perception, rooted in some transhistorical reality.

Brooten here more or less explicitly follows in the tracks of the late John Boswell, recapitulating his realist approach to the history of sexuality, his emphasis on seeing through the screen of discourse to the reality of sexual contacts and desire, and his insistence on the objective facts of same-sex sexual attraction.[21] For Brooten, like Boswell, same-sex sexual attraction qualifies as a fact, and thus lends factuality to homosexuality, which means that no historical falsification occurs when one redescribes the ancient phenomena in terms of the modern concept. The implication appears to be that the modern concept refers to an objective phenomenon that exists apart from us, outside of history and culture—namely, the erotic attraction and conjunction of female bodies. Brooten hastens to concede, like Boswell, that things have changed over time (though only to the extent that "ancient lesbians" did not necessarily think or live like "contemporary lesbians": "For example, I find no evidence of political organizations in antiquity created to promote lesbian rights," she remarks [17]), and she makes it very clear that she sees her task as analyzing "the specific gender constructions and social-sexual arrangements of the Roman and early Byzantine worlds" (18). Nonetheless, without denying that there have been discontinuities in the history of sexuality, she argues that "the historical discontinuities are . . . no greater than with such other terms as 'slavery,' 'marriage,' or 'family,' and yet we have no qualms about applying these terms to historical and cross-cultural phenomena" (18), despite the great variety of institutions to which such terms are applied.

Of course, some of us do have qualms about applying those terms indifferently across historical and cultural boundaries, even if we sometimes fail to be as rigorously historicist in our scholarly practices as we would like or as our historiographical principles might require.[22] Here, for example, are some qualms that the historian Henry Abelove once expressed to me and that I invoked many years ago in a book of my own.[23] In response to Boswell's concession that homosexuality was different in the ancient world, but no more different than marriage and family and work, which historians continue to call by those names,[24] Abelove had pointed out that just because feudal peasants work with their hands and factory laborers work with their hands, it doesn't follow that feudal peasantry should be described as the form that proletarianism took before the rise of industrial capitalism, because such a description would efface the specificity of proletarianism, its social and definitional dependence on a particular, historical system of economic organization. And yet working with one's hands can certainly be taken to be an objective fact, and as such it would seem to ground the factuality of "proletarianism" in history, just as same-sex sexual attraction or contact can be taken to be an objective fact that would guarantee the transhistorical reality of "homosexuality." And if you really *want* to describe feudal peasantry as a medieval version of factory labor, well, you can, and the claim will even make a kind of sense: after all, both peasants and factory workers are low on the social and economic ladder; both constitute oppressed and exploited social classes whose labor produces surplus value that enriches the property owners to whom they sell their labor. And both work with their hands. To say that peasants are the proletarians of the feudal system, then, *is not exactly wrong*. It gets at something, something important. But such an approach won't take you very far if what you want to acquire is a historical understanding of the specific, and systematic, economic and social organization of feudalism and capitalism, or an understanding of the differences between them. Nor will it yield a concept of "work" that is likely to be of much use as an all-purpose tool for historical analysis.

It is always tempting to highlight correspondences between distant historical periods and more recent ones, to describe the worlds we continually discover in terms of the world we have come to know, and to integrate unfamiliar objects into an existing knowledge of the already familiar. I sympathize with that approach, but I have also learned to be wary of it. On the first day of my first visit to Australia, a country where I was later to live for six years, I kept pointing out to my friend Susan, an American long since transplanted to Australia whom I had come to visit, all the features of the place that I thought I recognized: "Oh, that looks so English," I would say, or "that looks so Californian." To which Susan patiently replied, with a forbearance that I would later come to admire as subsequent visitors to Australia repeatedly tested my own by behaving exactly as I did then, "No, it looks *Australian.*" And Susan was right — *not because I was wrong*, not because there were no points of resemblance between Australian architecture or landscape and its English or American analogues, but because, in my haste to bring my initial impressions into focus by assimilating individual elements of the Australian scene to what I already knew, I had overlooked the distinctive cultural system that combined those elements in peculiar ways and that enabled them to cohere according to a unique social and aesthetic logic. While eagerly drinking in all the Australian sights, what I had somehow failed to see was, quite simply, Australia itself. Those historians of sexuality who redescribe in modern conceptual terms the culturally specific phenomena they observe in the distant historical record behave, in effect, like tourists in the archives: they misrecognize the sexual features of the period they study as exotic versions of the already familiar.

⟡

The real threat posed to the history of sexuality by this understandable if overhasty tendency to collapse concrete, local human activities upward into some abstracted, generalized, homogenized, decontextualized, and transhistorical concept — of "work," for example, or "homosexuality" — can be dramatized most vividly by documenting the specific interpretative damage that results from it. For once historians succumb to the lure of the false universals that they themselves have devised or absorbed, the next thing they typically do is take one highly particularized *instance* — of "work" or "homosexuality," such as factory labor or cocksucking — and proceed to despecify it, generalize it, broaden it, and ultimately make it serve as a placeholder for the concept — of "work" or "homosexuality" — as a whole. The social or cultural values that were originally attached to the particular instance are then transposed to the general concept. The dubious outcome that is produced by such a procedure appears plainly enough from the embarrassing record of gaffes committed by otherwise reputable historians of sexual life in classical antiquity who have repeatedly translated what the ancient sources have to say about particular homosexual acts into erroneously totalizing statements of disapproval (or, less often, approval) of "homosexuality" per se.[25] Thus, behind modern scholarly claims about the Romans' supposed condemnation of "homosexuality," as Craig Williams has shown, lies a set of ancient texts that express a much more specific abhorrence of particular practices: for example, receptive anal intercourse on the part of males, or the ostentatious, public, adult male courtship of free, citizen youths.[26] It is interesting, though not altogether surprising, that the same strategy is never used to establish the ancient "disapproval" of "heterosexuality," although since many of the sexual acts which ancient moralists singled out for strong condemnation—from adultery to "luxury," from rape to cunnilingus—involve sexual contact between men and women, it would be no less logical to mine the ancient sources for evidence that ancient Greek and Roman civilization abhorred "heterosexuality." In the case of "heterosexuality," however, scholars seem more reluctant to identify the whole of the sexual phenomenon with highly specific instances of it. No matter how many "heterosexual" practices or desires are frowned upon, after all, it remains impossible for modern scholars to imagine that any society could possibly have disapproved of "heterosexuality" itself.

So let's see what would happen if we were to extrapolate "particular, and discursively contingent, instances of disorderly male-female sexuality into the norm or truth of a monolithic system of 'heterosexuality,'"[27] as classical scholars continue to do with instances of same-sex sexual conduct and "homosexuality." A highly instructive exercise of this sort has in fact been undertaken by a scholar of early modern England, working with a documentary record that similarly contains both celebrations and condemnations of specific instances of both same-sex and different-sex erotic desire and confronting a tradition of scholarly commentary that similarly manifests a lopsided tendency to extract totalizing generalities from the available evidence about "homosexuality" but not "heterosexuality." Whence the following attempt to redress the balance:

> In early modern England, heterosexuality was considered a shameful and dangerous practice; it was therefore socially and legally proscribed. Laws and local customs punished those people who engaged in premarital sex, had illegitimate children, or committed adultery. Insults like "whore," "cuckold," and "bastard" reveal the opprobrium attached

to heterosexual acts. In sonnet sequences and tragedies, heterosexual relations are often represented as anguished, violent, or politically disastrous affairs, structured around male misogyny and possessiveness, female rebelliousness and duplicity, and an overall impasse of communication between the sexes. The prevalence of cuckoldry jokes in comedies suggests that husbands were unable to satisfy or control their sexually promiscuous wives. Indeed, a variety of discourses held that women were problematic sexual partners for men, and that men were compromised, diminished, or endangered by their passion for women. In the aggregate, these sources indicate that heterosexual relations were highly stigmatized, often led to deviant behavior (including "unnatural," nonprocreative, and nonmarital sexual acts, destructive jealousy, and even murder), and hence had to be carefully monitored and circumscribed.[28]

This account is, in its own way, scrupulously accurate and exact. It reproduces, with the very minor shift of register from homosexual to heterosexual, the procedures of much current work on same-sex erotic practices and identities in classical antiquity. As such, it dramatizes vividly the consequences of an approach to the history of sexuality that plays down discontinuities between premodern and modern sexual formations and that insists on salvaging from the corrosive effects of historical critique such allegedly transhistorical and transcultural categories of social life as "slavery," "marriage," "the family," "work," "homosexuality," "heterosexuality," and "sexuality."

As this example implies, the theoretical and methodological issues confronting the historian of sexuality cannot be neatly captured by the problematics of reference: they cannot be innocently reformulated in terms of the relation between words and things. It is not simply a matter of determining whether or not we can apply our word or concept of (homo/hetero)sexuality to the ancients—whether or not we can discover in the historical record of classical antiquity evidence of behaviors or psychologies that will fit, without too much forcing, the concepts and categories we are accustomed to using nowadays. Nor is it a matter of documenting whether or not the ancients were able to express within the terms provided by their own conceptual schemes an experience of something approximating our notions of (homo/hetero)sexuality. As my story about visiting Australia illustrates, and as Henry Abelove's cautionary lesson about the historical category of "working with one's hands" dramatizes, *just because it is possible to construct a nonfalsifiable relation of identity or resemblance between two distinct cultural forms does not necessarily mean that it is heuristically or cognitively ad-vantageous to do so.* We should be wary of the seductive objectivism of any method that consists in stripping cultural phenomena of their cultural spec-ificity and then imputing factuality and objectivity to whatever stripped-down transcultural category or concept may emerge from that strategically despecified redescription. The real question confronting the historian of sex-uality is how to recover the terms in which the erotic experiences of individ-uals belonging to past societies were actually constituted, how to measure and assess the differences between those terms and the ones we currently employ, and how to deal with the conceptual, methodological, political, and emotional consequences of the conclusions we draw from the evidence — the consequences for ourselves, for others, and for the history of sexual-ity that we hope to create (and, by creating, to be changed by).[29] Ultimately, the hardest issue we face as scholars and activists is how to make a livable world for ourselves out of the tension between identity and identification that structures both our relations with the objects of our historical study and the discursive and institutional practices by which we engage those objects.

That being the case, the last thing I would object to is Brooten's decision to frame her inquiry into the history of sexuality around lesbianism as a concept and a category. In fact, that is precisely what gives her book its com-pelling interest. Nor is there anything problematic about Brooten's claim to have contributed to lesbian history; indeed, her book is a major event in the growth and consolidation of that burgeoning field. It is surely both in-evitable and admirable that an inquiry into the history of the construction of female same-sex love and desire should frame itself in terms of contem-porary preoccupations and should address itself to the discursive and po-litical situation from which it emerges. All the recent classical scholarship on the history of male homosexuality (including my own) is entirely framed — some of it quite explicitly, some of it less so — by its engagement with con-temporary sexual ideology.

Brooten's work demonstrates the great promise — often denied by tradi-tional classical scholarship and the objectivist hermeneutic theory of which it is both an inheritor and a transmitter — of a situated knowledge, a per-spective on the ancient world that emerges from a specific cultural and po-litical location rather than from (supposedly) nowhere at all. At the same time, her work also makes it imperative to draw a distinction that is crucial for the historiography of homosexuality as well as for any historical research that is powered by the force of identification, by the researcher's sense of personal or political engagement with the object of study. And that is the distinction (which, I am well aware, it would be child's play to deconstruct, but perhaps that is not the most interesting thing to do with it) between the present-day concerns which frame all contemporary historical analysis and the historical material framed by them. I believe I can dramatize the usefulness of this distinction by showing that Brooten's work is vulnerable not because it is framed by a modern conception of lesbianism but because that conception tends to break through the frame, to permeate the interior space of the analysis, and to determine the treatment of individual details in it. In order to illustrate this claim, I will need to examine closely a number of Brooten's arguments about individual discourses, authors, and texts.

I begin with the following example. Brooten contends that "astrologers in the Roman world knew of what we might call *sexual orientation*" (140, my italics). What is the evidence for this already defensively qualified and tentative claim? Well, Ptolemy and Firmicus Maternus, among others, identify certain configurations of stars which cause women who are conceived or born under them to become "tribades" or "viragos," words that generally (although not always) refer to masculine, phallic women who desire and sexually penetrate other women and even boys (see, e.g., Seneca *Epistle* 95.21; Martial 1.90, 7.67, 7.70). Now that fantasized image of gender inversion, that phobic male construction of a hypermasculine woman, does not exactly correspond to any "sexual orientation" I know—nor does it correspond to Brooten's notion of lesbianism, as she makes perfectly clear (7)—but never mind all that for the moment. Brooten concludes that "the stars [according to these ancient astrologers] determined a woman's erotic inclinations for the duration of her life" (140), and hence that there was "a category of persons viewed in antiquity as having a long-term or even life-long homoerotic orientation" (8–9). Of course, the astrologers' sexual system was rather more complicated, as Brooten hastens to point out: "they saw a plethora of orientations" (3), not just two or three. "Ptolemy, for example, distinguished between active and passive orientations, and he also took account of such factors as age, wealth, and whether the person to whom one is attracted is a foreigner" (140; also 242).

As a persistent if promiscuous expatriate myself, I am hardly in a position to object to the notion of a sexual orientation defined by the love of foreigners. Still, from the perspective of modern sexual categories, such a notion seems bizarre. And the more Brooten explicates it, the curiouser Ptolemy's sexual system becomes. Its startling proliferation of "sexual orientations," and its weird focus on tribades to the exclusion of their female or male partners, which Brooten bravely acknowledges (128: "The question of the *tribas*'s partner remains open; Ptolemy devotes no attention to her"), awaken no doubts in Brooten and certainly do not deter her from sticking by her basic conclusion, which is that the ancients — contrary to what Michel Foucault, Arnold Davidson, John J. Winkler, Craig Williams, and I, among many others, have argued — had a concept of sexual orientation and of homosexuality that lesbians and gay men today might recognize as our own.[30]

All this is cause enough for some disquiet on the part of a historian of sexuality. But the problems with Brooten's attempt to translate the ancient astrological categories into modern sexological ones do not end here. For the astral configurations that, according to Firmicus Maternus and others, produced tribades also produced, with only slight astrological variations, female prostitutes — an unexpected contiguity in the ancient sexual spectrum whose logic Brooten spends some time puzzling over (140–41), although the association is a very common one in antiquity. What Brooten does not notice, though, is that, whatever sort of identity is implied by the terms "tribade" and "virago," a *meretrix* or "prostitute" is not the name of a life-long erotic orientation. Rather, it describes a particular and particularly disgraceful kind of social actor, a deviant from the norms of female social and sexual propriety, a recognizable figure on the fringes of ancient Mediterranean societies. In that sense, *meretrix* may well have designated "a category of persons," as Brooten says. But such a category would not be a category of *erotic subjectivity* of the sort that would *orient* a person's *sexual desires* for the duration of her life, which is what "a lifelong erotic orientation" implies. On the contrary, to invoke the astral signs under which certain women were conceived or born in order to explain why they become prostitutes in later life is to account for the fact that some women turn out to disgrace themselves and their families, not to impute to these women a peculiar sort of sexual interiority, a pathological condition, or distinctive configuration of sexual desire. No doubt, such women, in the eyes of the male astrologers, were bad women and had a whorish disposition. In that sense, they might have been seen as having a sexual identity. But what the term *meretrix* registers is less a subjectivity than a career choice.[31] The astrologers are accounting for the origin of certain *social types*. Prostitutes, like tribades, are recognizable and disgraceful exemplars of female sexual impropriety. To trace their origins to the influence of the stars is not to ascribe to such women an innate, fixed, lifelong sexual or erotic orientation — except insofar as social disgrace typically implies some congenital moral depravity. At the very least, it makes no more sense to see in the astrological account of tribades evidence for the ancient notion of a lifelong erotic orientation than it does to see evidence for it in the astrological account of prostitutes, and we would not be likely to infer from reading the astrological texts that the principal meaning of "meretrix" had to do with what Brooten, speaking of the astrological construction of tribades, calls "a woman's erotic inclinations" (140). So in my view the ancient evidence does not support the thesis that Brooten bases on it—namely, that "astrologers in the Roman world knew of what we might call sexual orientation."

My view has lately received some support from scholarship on prostitution in the Middle Ages, especially the evolving work of Ruth Mazo Karras on medieval *meretrices*.[32] In medieval Europe, according to Karras, to be a prostitute was not merely to engage in an activity but to be a recognizable "type of person."[33] Although Karras goes further, and claims (misleadingly, in my view) that medieval prostitutes were defined by their "sexuality,"[34] she does not of course mean that prostitutes were seen as being distinguished from decent women by a deep, inner orientation of their erotic desires. Rather, she argues that a *meretrix* was a woman with a particular sort of sinful, sexually transgressive character, and that "prostitute" was therefore an identity category. As Carla Freccero, in the course of a subtle and helpful discussion of Karras's most recent study, points out,

> Karras marshals considerable legal and religious or moral evidence to
> demonstrate that *meretrices* in the Middle Ages were constituted as an
> identity by their characterization as "lustful" women, an identitarian
> category unlike the modern occupational category accorded to the
> prostitute. "To summarize, medieval people were aware that *meretrices*
> commonly engaged in sex for money, but this did not identify or define
> them. Although canonists recognized that *meretrices* operated commer-
> cially, they did not consider the acceptance of money to make them
> *meretrices;* rather, it was the public nature of their sexual activity, the
> fact that they did not refuse any partner, or the number of partners
> they had that placed them in that category." Later in her discussion, she
> notes that rather than "prostitute," the modern term "whore" might be
> a more useful translation of *meretrix,* which ostensibly characterizes a
> certain type of woman rather than a woman who engages in particular
> activities.[35]

In other words, the label *meretrix* may well have tagged the person to whom that label was attached with something like a social identity, or even a sexual identity, and it certainly branded her as a specific type of person. Karras even goes so far to say—at the risk of engaging in what I would consider tendentious cultural and historical despecification—that a *meretrix* was "permanently marked" by her "essential sinfulness" and in that sense needed to change her "orientation" in order to shed her "identity." Still, even on this account, to be a whore is not to reveal the lifelong configuration of one's erotic desires but to display a sexually depraved character attached to a disreputable social identity. "Whore" is thus a category of persons but not the name of a psychosexual orientation of erotic desire. That medieval understanding of *meretrix* would make the word even more closely comparable to *tribade* or *virago*, as I understand the functioning of those terms in the ancient astrological discourses.

The theoretical issues underlying these questions of historical interpretation have been very well articulated by the lesbian literary historian Valerie Traub, in her own review of Brooten. Observing that Brooten conflates "erotic orientation" with "category of person," Traub doubts that the two should be treated as synonymous. Although as an early modernist she is not able to document or confirm her doubts by means of an independent analysis of the ancient sources, she registers what turns out to be a very canny suspicion, to the effect "that the existence of certain nouns that indicate a 'category of persons' does not indicate necessarily 'a belief in long-term or even lifelong homoerotic orientation'" (quoting Brooten, 9). Traub goes on to wonder "whether the presence of nouns in the lexicon is adequate to mark such women [*tribades* and *frictrices*] as possessing a stable or self-evident erotic orientation."[36] It is precisely my argument here that the astrologers' usage of both *tribades* and *meretrices* indicates that they conceived the personages designated by those terms as social types but *not* as the possessors of a lifelong erotic orientation. My argument thus bears out Traub's prescient doubts about the noncoincidence of a category of person (or, as I would prefer, a category of social actor) with a category of erotic orientation. Premodern societies may well have had a number of categories of social actor to which sexual characteristics were attached without those categories necessarily approximating sexual orientations—in the sense of particular configurations of erotic desire—let alone modern homo- and heterosexual ones. Not every *identity* expresses an *orientation*.

⚓

I turn now to Brooten's account of Aristophanes' famous speech in Plato's *Symposium*, where I find a similarly tendentious (mis)reading of the ancient source. Aristophanes, it will be remembered, defines *erōs* as "the desire and pursuit of the whole" and he offers a myth to support his definition. The human race, according to the myth, was once composed of two-faced, eight-limbed creatures who came in three sexes: male, female, and androgyne.

Human beings as we know them were created when Zeus cut our ancestors in two. Each of us is descended from the half of an original whole, and erotic desire is the longing to restore an earlier state of wholeness through union with another individual. Every person we desire is in fact a symbolic substitute for an originary object once loved and subsequently lost in an archaic trauma, and our sexual preferences are determined by the sex of the missing half of our amputated ancestor. Aristophanes mentions a number of contemporary social types whose odd predilections and flagrant behaviors are explained by reference to their genetic origin. Thus, males whose ancestors were double males are eager for adult male lovers when they are boys and become lovers of boys in turn when they become men—and it is they who go into politics: this is the standard Aristophanic joke about the leaders of Athens having all been buggered in their youth. The portion of Plato's text that deals with females whose ancestors were double females is the only Greek text from the classical period that explicitly and unambiguously testifies to the existence of erotic desire among contemporary Greek women (though Plato at least alludes to the possibility again in the *Laws* [636c]);[37] as such, its testimony is unique and precious. But what does Plato's Aristophanes actually say?

According to Brooten, "Aristophanes . . . speaks of *hetairistriai*, women who are attracted to women, as having their origin in primeval beings consisting of two women joined together" (41); when she comes to discuss the use of the same word by the Greek satirist Lucian, some five hundred years later, she writes that "Lucian also presupposes that his readers know the meaning of *hetairistria*. . . . In fact, Lucian's dialogue assumes a familiarity with the phenomenon of sexual love between women" (53). Now since what Lucian's characters relate is the story of the seduction of one Leaena, your average girl, by a wealthy, shaven-headed, hypermasculine woman named Megilla, who claims to be "all man" (as Brooten, 52, notes), what Lucian's readers would seem to be familiar with is nothing so blandly nonspecific as "the phenomenon of sexual love between women" but, rather, the stereotype of gender inversion, of sexual role reversal—the phenomenon of "tribadism," that is, *not* homoeroticism *as such*—which is the only sort of female same-sex sexual behavior that regularly evokes skeptical or disapproving comment from the ancient pagans. In fact, Arethas, the early-tenth-century bishop of Caesarea mentioned earlier, glossed *hetairistria* in this passage of Lucian as "tribade," and in a note on yet another late antique text, the pseudo-Lucianic *Erōtes*, he repeated the conflation of *hetairistria* with "tribade" (although his testimony provides little evidence for the original meanings of these words).[38] In this context, Brooten's assertion that ancient readers were familiar with sexual love between women *in a categorical sense* depends on the exact meaning of *hetairistria* in Plato and Lucian.[39]

Unfortunately for Brooten, no one knows exactly what *hetairistria* means. Its etymology points in two directions, companionship and prostitution—the best we can do to convey a sense of what the word implies is to invoke some rough etymological approximations, such as "companionizer" (from *hetairos*, "companion") and "courtesanizer" (from *hetaira*, "courtesan")—but its actual meaning is anybody's guess. For the word occurs once and only once in all of extant Greek literature before Lucian, and that one occurrence is in the tantalizing passage from Plato's *Symposium* under discussion. The word evidently refers to *some* social type who represented a case of female same-sex sexual attraction—thus far, Brooten's interpretation of its meaning is indisputable—but the larger context in Aristophanes' speech prohibits any secure inferences as to its precise meaning.

For when Aristophanes mentions the men and women descended from original androgynes, he says that the majority of *moikhoi* and *moikheutriai* come from this race (191D–E). Now, if the meanings of those words had been as utterly lost as the meaning of *hetairistria*, and if we felt justified— as Brooten does—in construing all these words to be categorical designations for forms of erotic attraction defined by sexual object-choice, then we would certainly and confidently take *moikhoi* and *moikheutriai* to signify "male heterosexuals" and "female heterosexuals," or, at least, to borrow Brooten's cautious periphrases, "men who are attracted to women" and "women who are attracted to men." And we would believe that, whatever the words actually meant, our interpretation had to be correct, at least in a general sense. As it happens, however, we *do* know what those words meant, and it was something altogether different and quite specific. A *moikhos* is a male who has consenting but unauthorized sex with a female under the guardianship of an Athenian citizen ("adulterer" is the standard if misleading translation; "seducer" better captures some of the other dimensions of the word's meaning); a *moikheutria* is the women he seduces or who seduces him. Both represent instances of "attraction" between women and men, to be sure. But no student of classical Greek would ever think of translating *moikhos* as "heterosexual."

Aristophanes, once again, is making a joke about certain extreme social types who owe their sexual dispositions and their disreputable behavior to the passionate erotic longings they have inherited from their distant ancestors—much as the astrologers traced the origin of certain disreputable types of people to the influence of the stars. Presumably, the reference to *hetairistriai* makes a similar sort of joke, but it is now lost on us. And whatever the point of the joke was, taking *hetairistriai* to mean "women who are attracted to women," or even "lesbians," doesn't produce a terribly witty punchline. The most attractive and ingenious solution to the conundrum has been proposed by T. Corey Brennan, who notes in a review of Brooten's book that, according to the intriguing testimony of the ancient grammarian Moeris (s.v. "hetairistria"), the word "tribade" was avoided in the Attic dialect. The word *hetairistria* was the Attic term, for which the (Koine) Greek language in general employed "tribade."[40] Similarly, as Alan Cameron helpfully points out, in his own critique of Brooten, Timaeus's lexicon to Plato glosses *hetairistriai* as "the so-called tribades."[41] This testimony clearly implies that Attic writers, such as Plato, would have used the term *hetairistria* instead of "tribade." If *hetairistria* was in fact the Attic word used to refer to the same thing that was referred to elsewhere in the Greek world by "tribade," the point of the otherwise baffling joke about *hetairistriai* in the speech of Plato's Aristophanes would be evident: just as the shameless sexual behavior of the rulers of Athens points to their all-male ancestry, and just as seducers and seductresses owe their uncontrollable desires and disgraceful conduct to their genetic makeup, so their descent from a powerful double female accounts for the nature of those aggressive, commanding women who can make a normal girl forget herself in their arms. Such a hypothesis about the meaning of the word *hetairistria* would also explain why the Atticizing writer Lucian chose it to describe Leaena's hypermasculine lover.

Of course, it is also possible that Moeris's conclusion about the avoidance of "tribade" in Attic merely reflects a conjecture on his part about the meaning of *hetairistria*, based on nothing more than the suggestive textual evidence under discussion here, and it is similarly possible that Lucian didn't understand the point of Aristophanes' joke any better than we do and simply wanted to show off his erudition by putting a five-hundred-year-old word from a classic text into the mouth of contemporary reprobate for humorous effect in a plausible approximation of its original meaning. No doubt it was the very enigmatic and mysterious quality of the term *hetairistria* that grabbed his attention, just as it still grabs ours. Even the Alexandrian lexicographer Hesychius's definition of *dihetairistriai* merely echoes the language of Plato's Aristophanes, plainly revealing that Hesychius, far from possessing independent knowledge of the word's meaning, relied exclusively for his understanding on the Platonic text. Still, even a modest effort to suspend our modern sexual categories when reading the ancient texts opens up their meanings to the possibility of interesting and unforeseen interpretations and makes of the history of sexuality something rather more startling and adventurous than is suggested by the version of *hetairi-striai* that emerges from Brooten's reading of Plato. That alone, it seems to me, illustrates the heuristic value of a historicist reading practice.

～

The more conventional advantages of a historicizing approach to the study of the ancient sexual vocabulary, such as scholarly precision and historical accuracy, appear plainly enough in the light of Brooten's tendentious (mis)-construal of other ancient terms. For example, she says that "we can define a *kinaidos/cinaedus* as a male who passively receives a male phallus [*sic*] into his body" (24). But in fact we cannot define the term in that way without obliterating the entire basis for the ancient distinction between honorable and dishonorable conduct on the part of a subordinate male partner. Not only is Brooten's definition inaccurate (a victim of male sexual assault would not normally have been described as a *cinaedus*),[42] but it would have been deeply shocking and offensive to the ancients, especially to the classical Greeks (even though they did place great significance on a male's maintenance of his bodily integrity, his physical impenetrability, the question of whether or not he received "a male"—or indeed a female [?]—"phallus into his body"). To be sure, it was always at least potentially shaming for a Greek male of any age to be sexually penetrated by anyone. Nonetheless, and perhaps for that very reason, the Greeks made a big deal of distinguishing, in the case of men's male love objects, between a willing but respectable and virile boy and his debased, sluttish, effeminate opposite.[43]

To characterize *any* boy who allowed his lover to penetrate him as a *kinaidos* would have indicated that such a boy "submitted" to his lover for the sake of pleasure, that he had pathic desires and enjoyed being fucked—for that is what the insulting word *kinaidos* implied. It was in order to *avoid* that very implication that the ancients sharply differentiated in the case of men between the mere *fact* of being penetrated and the *desire* to be penetrated. As K. J. Dover and Michel Foucault pointed out long ago, the protocols governing paederasty, especially in classical Athens, were elaborately crafted in such a way as to protect boys from any suggestion that they were motivated in their sexual relations with adult men by sexual desire or sexual pleasure, let alone that they took any pleasure in being sexually penetrated. A boy might well choose to "gratify" (*kharizesthai*), as the Greeks delicately and euphemistically put it, the desire of his older lovers for a variety of motives—ranging from esteem, gratitude, and love (at the respectable end of the scale) to gold digging (at the other end)—so long as he did not act for the sake of sexual pleasure. In this fashion a boy upheld his honor, displayed his sense of decency, demonstrated his masculinity, and helped to preserve his reputation.

A *cinaedus*, by contrast, was a gender-deviant male, an effeminate and lascivious man possessed of a supposedly feminine love of being sexually penetrated or dominated. This was the most disgraceful, the most stigmatized identity a free male could acquire, and it carried with it a number of devastating social disqualifications.[44] As Craig Williams explains, "a *cinaedus* is a man who fails to live up to traditional standards of masculine comportment. . . . Indeed, the word's etymology suggests no direct connection to any sexual practice. Rather, borrowed from Greek *kinaidos* (which may itself have been a borrowing from a language of Asia Minor), it primarily signifies an effeminate dancer who entertained his audiences with a *tympanum* or tambourine in his hand, and adopted a lascivious style, often suggestively wiggling his buttocks in such a way as to suggest anal intercourse." And Williams adds, "the primary meaning of *cinaedus* never died out; the term never became a dead metaphor."[45] Brooten seems to have imported her understanding of the word directly from cultural feminist critiques of "intercourse" that foreground the politics of giving and/or receiving the phallus and that treat homophobia as a by-product of sexism; for once, she seems oblivious to two decades of classical scholarship and social history. Her definition of paederasty as "the male sexual use of children" (56), which conflates it with paedophilia, is equally misleading, tendentious, and inaccurate, and it gratuitously supports the vicious sexual stereotyping of gay male eroticism that has been one of the uglier by-products of historical tensions and misunderstandings between lesbian feminists and gay men.[46]

Among the contributions that Brooten claims her book makes to the history of sexuality is its establishment of the fact "that nineteenth-century medical writers were not the first to classify homoerotic behavior as diseased" (3). If, on the one hand, Brooten includes within her category of "homoerotic behavior" *any and all* sexual acts that take place among two or more persons of the same sex, as she clearly does, and if she means that *some* of those acts were classified by the ancients as diseased, then this contribution is hardly news: it has long been known that at least some "homoerotic behavior"—that is, some quite specific same-sex sexual acts—incurred the disapproval of the ancients, and that sometimes the ancients attributed the propensity to commit such stigmatized sexual acts to a disease-like condition (see, for example, the much-remarked passage in Aristotle's *Nicomachean Ethics* 7.5.3–4 [1148b26–35]).[47] Indeed, a number of Brooten's claims to originality are inflated.[48] If, on the other hand, Brooten means that ancient medical writers occasionally classified as diseased *all homoerotic behavior as such,* as she also does, her claim is highly misleading. Here, once again, we see how interpretative problems are produced by the historian's practice of taking quite specific same-sex sexual acts or relations and generalizing them in such a way that they come to stand in for the totalizing, undifferentiated category of "homoerotic behavior" as a whole. Let us have a closer look at the hermeneutic procedure by which Brooten arrives at this questionable result.

First of all, Brooten tends to neglect the historical specificities that distinguish ancient medical discourses and the attitudes to sexual behavior manifested in them. For example, a study of the applications of the word "disease" (Latin *morbus*) by Roman writers reveals that it did not imply the same kind of disqualification that a modern diagnosis of pathology does. Instead, it could be used to refer generally to the character traits responsible for an individual's immoral or disreputable habits — to depravity, in other words, not necessarily to a morbid or unhealthy condition. As Craig Williams shows, "a predilection for various kinds of excessive or disgraceful behavior was capable of being called a disease" by the Romans and therefore *"cinaedi* were not said to be *morbosi* in the way that twentieth-century homosexuals have been pitied or scorned as 'sick.'"[49] Medicalizing language, in other words, does not operate in the two cultures in the same way, nor does it mean quite the same thing. The point is an important one: the ancient usage is disapproving, but it is not wholly pathologizing; indeed, it could hardly be, in the absence of modern technical understandings of the "normal" and the "pathological."

Next, in her analysis of one particularly revealing medical text — a chapter of the obscure treatise *On Chronic Diseases* by Caelius Aurelianus, a fifth-century-A.D. translator of the Greek physician Soranus — Brooten quite explicitly refuses to distinguish between the author's disapproval of certain stigmatized homoerotic behaviors and all "homoerotic behavior" as such: she insists on treating his comments on *some* homoerotic behavior as if they referred to *all* homoerotic behavior. She begins by claiming categorically that "same-sex desire and behavior did fall within the realm of medical theory" in antiquity (144) and she criticizes me in particular for maintaining in *One Hundred Years of Homosexuality* that Caelius Aurelianus is "unconcerned about same-sex love per se" (162).[50] Yet she admits that Caelius is interested "only in sexually passive men (and not in the active male partners in anal intercourse)" and that he presumes "penetrating males to be healthy" (148). In short, Caelius implies that "while adult men's desire for boys may be seen as healthy, boys' passive sexual behavior is not" (162). But if that is indeed the position that Caelius takes, if he does in fact apply different standards of judgment to different same-sex sexual acts, considering some of them to be healthy and others not, what else does that indicate, if not precisely that, in the case of males at least, Caelius is "unconcerned about same-sex love per se"?

Brooten goes on to say that Caelius "explicitly defines the passivity of boys as diseased" (162). But of course it is not the fact of a boy's sexual penetration by a man that Caelius regards as a symptom of a mental or moral disease but rather a boy's desire (*passio*) to be penetrated (*On Chronic Diseases* 4.9.137), a desire which is by no means characteristic of all boys who are sexually penetrated by men. Moreover, it is only the boy's temporary lack of sufficient virility to play an "active" sexual role that, when viewed by Caelius according to the standards of adult manhood, is problematic, because this transient lack of virility, entirely normal and natural in a boy, will, if not remedied by the onset of maturity, become incapacitating in an adult male and will afflict him with *mollitia*, the unnatural, inverted condition of "softness" or effeminacy. Brooten's conclusion, that "according to the system of *On Chronic Diseases*, there exists no same-sex encounter in which both partners are disease-free" (162), is not only wrong in the case of men and boys (since both "active" men and boys who do not desire to be penetrated are in fact disease free, according to Caelius),[51] but beside the point. After all, the ancients did not consider *both* partners in a sexual encounter to share or participate in the same "sexuality"; rather, they regarded sex as an intrinsically nonrelational act, a miniature drama of polarization in which the participants expressed and acted out the relevant hierarchical distinctions between them in social status and sexual role.[52]

When it comes to Caelius's treatment of tribades, moreover, Brooten notes, as I do, that Caelius "emphasizes their bisexuality over their same-sex preference" (151n) and she agrees with me that "the text is concerned with reversing proper sex roles or with alternating between behaviors and characteristics proper to women and to men respectively" (161–62). She objects to my reading of the text on the grounds that Caelius sees no way "for women to have sexual contact with other women other than to take on male sex roles or to alternate between characteristics and practices proper to women and those proper to men," which means that, on Brooten's reading, Caelius ends up condemning *all* forms of homoeroticism *in the case of women*, if not in the case of men. A lesbian-oriented interpretation of Caelius, then — one that treats his account of female same-sex relations as central, primary, and defining, instead of treating it as a mere afterthought, a supplement to his account of men and boys — has the potential to disclose dimensions of his text that a gay male reading may overlook, according to

Brooten (that is a point with which I would, in principle at least, register strong agreement). But, in the present instance, even this modified objection to my reading of Caelius — namely, that Caelius does indeed pathologize all same-sex love in the case of women (insofar as women, unlike men, cannot both play their socially assigned roles and engage in same-sex sexual acts, and insofar as women "cannot both respect phallocentric protocols and obtain sexual pleasure from contact with other females" [161])—fails on obvious grounds. In fact, it is neatly disposed of by Brooten herself. For Brooten also emphasizes that "the women whom the *tribades* pursue are of no interest to the text"; in other words, the female partners of tribades are not regarded as diseased (151). So, despite what Brooten claims, women *can* have sexual contact with other women while respecting all the phallocentric protocols: all they have to do is to get themselves seduced by a tribade.[53]

The woman whom a tribade seduces will obtain sexual pleasure from contact with another woman while conforming to her proper (passive, receptive, feminine) role in the phallocentric system. Indeed, the pagan sources Brooten examines do not contain a single instance in which a conventionally feminine female partner of a tribade is unambiguously and categorically treated as deviant or diseased.[54] That does not mean that women who had nontribadic sex with each other were necessarily beyond reproach. The Hellenistic poet Asclepiades, in his seventh epigram, which Brooten discusses briefly (42), voices disapproval of two women who prefer women to men. A sixteenth-century Cretan humanist scholar by the name of Marcus Musurus, in a gloss on this poem, called the two women "tribades," which would certainly help to explain the poet's hostility to them and bring it into line with the dominant patterns of ancient sexual discourse.[55] But this remark is not of much use in establishing what Asclepiades intended nearly two thousand years earlier. Brooten appears to take this comment to imply that the two women were having a sexual relationship *with each other,* which may well be what the humanist thought, but nothing in the poem or in the accusation that they were both tribades implies this: they might both have been imagined as separately pursuing other women, which seems indeed to be the likely reading of the epigram. *If* the two women in Asclepiades' poem are imagined as having a sexual relationship *with each other,* and are also imagined *not to be tribades themselves,* then this text would indeed constitute a counterexample to the usual discursive pattern: an instance of pagan sources morally problematizing nontribadic participants in female same-sex eroticism. Such a reading, however, seems far-fetched. In any case, whether Asclepiades' poem is an exception to the general pattern or not, the basic point remains: to be fucked by a tribade was not necessarily to assume a deviant identity.

In short, Brooten seems to have forgotten all about the femme.[56] Like Amy Richlin, who makes similar errors in her reading of ancient texts and who seems to believe that, in the case of men, there is something *more homosexual* about getting fucked by one than fucking one,[57] Brooten seems to believe that there is something *more lesbian* about being butch than being femme.[58]

So what about that femme? Brooten herself appears to be of several minds about how the female partners of tribades were viewed. Caelius himself says nothing about them. Certainly, being seduced by a tribade does not necessarily make you a tribade yourself. Some texts do refer to the partner of a tribade as a tribade,[59] but they are highly exceptional (cf. 6–7, 18, 128). Brooten argues, rather theoretically, that "women who derive sexual pleasure from contact with women . . . have to be medically problematic" (161). Here Brooten quite uncharacteristically steps into the realm of pure speculation, into a hypothetical world quite beyond the limits of the evidence. Why do the female partners of tribades *have to be* medically problematic? So that sexual asymmetries can be banished from the ancient record and the undifferentiated category of "female homoeroticism" can be upheld as an ancient concept? *Even at the cost of pathologizing some "ancient lesbians"?* Brooten asserts that there is "no positive evidence that passive sexual behavior by adult women in relations with other adult women was societally acceptable" (161n), but she presents no positive evidence from pre- or non-Christian sources to show that it was considered sexually abnormal in and of itself. Lucian's portrayal of Leaena as an ordinary girl testifies eloquently to the contrary, but Brooten does not seem to notice. In sum, Brooten's argument that Roman-period medical writers considered women who responded to the erotic advances of a tribade to be "medically problematic" is based on nothing but the silence of our sources, on the absence of statements explicitly endorsing the behavior of such women. But such endorsements are hardly to be expected from ancient Greek and Roman writers.

Brooten's recurrent imprecision in interpreting the ancient texts is regrettable especially because it could so easily have been avoided without affecting her basic claims about the existence and knowledge of love between women in classical antiquity: earlier research had already indicated the traps into which unwary modern students of ancient sexual discourses were likely to fall. Although these mistakes mar Brooten's interpretation of the ancient texts, they do not invalidate her general descriptive survey of the pagan Greek and Latin sources (Brooten's interpretations are in general much more sound and reliable than Boswell's, for example). Nonetheless, since Brooten bases large-scale conclusions about the history of sexuality on matters of semantics, claiming about "tribade," "virago," *hetairistria*, and other such words that "all of these nouns demonstrate that people in the ancient Mediterranean had the concept of an erotic orientation with respect to women" (5), her tendency to reformulate the meanings of the ancient terms to conform with modern sexual concepts has the effect of begging the very questions she sets out to answer, and it thereby undermines the larger project of her book.[60]

The consistent anachronisms in Brooten's approach to the ancient evidence are all the more bizarre because almost all the evidence with which she has to deal reflects, as she points out (16), not the experiences of ancient women but the fantasies, jokes, abuse, or moral judgements of hostile male authors. "This study contributes to the history of male ideas about lesbians far more than to women's history," she writes; "the sources bear witness to male constructions of female homoeroticism, rather than to lesbians' perceptions of themselves" (25). We might have expected Brooten to bring out the ideological and cultural specificity of these male constructions, their oddity and remoteness from commonly accepted modern notions. We might have expected her to foreground the opacity of the ancient sexual discourses and, instead of trying to see through them to the "real women" who are so bizarrely represented in them and whose own experiences of same-sex desire and same-sex eroticism have left only exiguous traces in the surviving record of classical antiquity, to make those discourses reflect on the men who produced and maintained them. Brooten however, would rather highlight the continuity of male incomprehension, prejudice, and hostility to lesbians than historicize its discursive and institutional manifestations.

In adopting this approach, Brooten makes one extremely important point about the history of homosexuality with which I vigorously agree (in fact, it may have come to her, indirectly, from me). She suggests that there may be fewer turning points in the history of lesbianism than in the history of male homosexuality (21–25). This has got to be right. As Gayle Rubin brilliantly argued more than twenty-five years ago, the subordination of women to men in society — in all its "endless variety and monotonous similarity, cross-culturally and throughout history"—and the asymmetrical sex/gender systems that it produces entail radically different social experiences of sex for women and for men.[61] The massive, universal or nearly universal fact of male dominance, the corresponding kinship structures, the sexual division of labor, and the traffic in marriageable women that results from it mean, in particular, that women must submit to a system of compulsory heterosociality, in which they are not permitted to have a social existence apart from men, whereas men are permitted various forms of homosociality so long as they have occasional sex with women. The dominating feature of women's sexual lives is not so much heterosexual desire as the inescapability of sexual relations with men, the inability to deny men sexual access to themselves, whereas the dominating feature of men's sexual lives is merely the requirement to desire women some of the time, which leaves a good deal of men's erotic life available for various other sorts of social and sexual uses. The effects of this asymmetrical system are various and complex: sexual relations among women represent a perennial threat to male dominance, especially whenever such relations become exclusive and thereby take women out of circulation among men, but they also represent a perennial option for women, so long as women otherwise submit to the requirements of the kinship system, do not attempt to deny men access to themselves, and do not resist male control. As Valerie Traub says (she is speaking specifically about early modern England, but her words may have a more general application), "Only when women's erotic relations with one another threaten to become exclusive and thus endanger the fulfillment of their marital and reproductive duties, or when they symbolically usurp male sexual prerogatives, are cultural injunctions levied against them."[62] Sexual relations among men remain open to many more specific sorts of social elaboration and construction.

The conclusion we should derive from this model is not that the social construction of sexuality applies only to men and not to women. On the contrary, one of the great virtues of Rubin's model is that it accounts for the nearly universal fact of male dominance in constructionist terms — that is, without essentializing it, naturalizing it, or treating it as necessary, uniform, or inevitable. (That is why Rubin's approach is superior to Catharine MacKinnon's, which also tries to account for structural, transhistorical continuities in the oppression of women, but which — despite MacKinnon's intentions — lends itself more readily to an essentializing interpretation: it is highly indicative, therefore, that Brooten invokes MacKinnon's model, instead of Rubin's, to highlight "the long-term structures of male dominance and female subordination" [23–24].)[63] Nonetheless, a social-constructionist approach to sexuality that is derived from the study of men will not succeed in bringing into precise focus the history and diversity of sexual relations among women.[64] To see the historical dimensions of the social construction of same-sex relations among women, we need a new optic that will reveal specific historical variations in a phenomenon that necessarily exists in a constant and inescapable relation to the institutionalized structures of male dominance. It is this constant and inescapable relation to a social structure that varies relatively little, both historically and culturally, which endows female same-sex relations with a greater degree of continuity, of thematic consistency, over time and space, making each historical instance both different and the same, both old and new. It is also the threat that love between women can pose to monopolies of male authority that lends plausibility to the hypothesis that a notion of female-female eroticism may have been consolidated relatively early in Europe, even before similar notions emerged that could apply to all forms of male homoeroticism. Perhaps lesbianism was the first homoeroticism to be conceptualized categorically as such. Perhaps, in that sense, lesbianism should be seen, historically, as the first homosexuality. That is a hypothesis that will require considerably more knowledge than we presently possess in order to confirm or disprove. In the meantime, lesbian history certainly deserves to be studied in all its specificity, by means of an independent set of conceptual and historiographic tools, according to a different periodization. Whatever else the current and ongoing explorations of lesbian history have to offer us, one of their most startling benefits may well be a much-enhanced understanding of the different historicities of female and male homosexuality.[65]

Notes

Previous versions or sections of this argument have appeared, in somewhat more specialized form, as "Response: Halperin on Brennan on Brooten," *Bryn Mawr Classical Review* (bmcr-l@brynmawr.edu), 97.12.3 (5 December 1997), "Lesbian Historiography before the Name? Commentary," *GLQ: A Journal of Lesbian and Gay Studies* 4, no. 4 (1998): 559–78, and "Sex, Sexuality, and Sexual Classification," in *Critical Terms for Gender Studies*, ed. Gilbert Herdt and Catharine R. Stimpson (Chicago: University of Chicago Press, forthcoming).

1. For recent examples of contrasting approaches to the problem of how to balance continuities and discontinuities in feminist and gay male historiography, see Judith M. Bennett, "Confronting Continuity," *Journal of Women's History*, 9, no. 3 (autumn 1997): 73–94; and David M. Halperin, "How to Do the History of Male Homosexuality," *GLQ: A Journal of Lesbian and Gay Studies* 6, no. 1 (2000): 87–124.

2. See D. Graham J. Shipley's entry on Lesbos in *The Oxford Classical Dictionary*, 3d ed. (Oxford: Oxford University Press, 1996), 845.

3. Chapter 21 of Aldous Huxley's *Antic Hay* (London: Flamingo, 1994), 226.

4. For a detailed survey of the evidence, on which my summary is based, see Peter F. Dorcey, *Before Lesbianism* (unpublished manuscript, in the possession of Professor John Rundin of the University of Texas at San Antonio).

5. Bernadette J. Brooten translates, more literally but less idiomatically, "who are unwilling to suffer 'it' from men": see her "Lesbian Historiography before the Name? Response," *GLQ: A Journal of Lesbian and Gay Studies* 4, no. 4 (1998): 606–30 (quotation on 619).

6. Alan Cameron, "Love (and Marriage) between Women," *Greek, Roman, and Byzantine Studies* 39 (1998): 137–56 (quotation on 149 n. 36; my italics).

7. This is even clearer in Lucian's Greek, where "women like that" (which is a translation of the single word *toiautas*) refers back to the noun *hetairistria*: "I don't know what you mean, unless she's a *hetairistria*—they say there are women like that [or "such women"] in Lesbos," etc. In other words, "they say there are *hetairistriai* in Lesbos," etc. Since there is considerable evidence (discussed in my text, below) that *hetairistria* is a synonym of "tribade," the reference to "women like that in Lesbos" is, in context, mostly likely an allusion specifically to tribadism.

8. On this text, see Bernadette J. Brooten, *Love between Women: Early Christian Responses to Female Homoeroticism* (Chicago: University of Chicago Press, 1996), 5, and the detailed, convincing critique of her interpretation of Arethas's usage by Cameron, "Love (and Marriage) between Women," 144–49.

9. Two authoritative French dictionaries, Frédéric Godefroy's ten-volume *Dictionnaire de l'ancienne langue française* (1880) and *Le Grand Robert de la langue française*, agree in dating the earliest occurrence of "tribade" in French to bk. 1, chap. 13, of Henri Estienne's treatise, *Introduction au traité de la conformité des merveilles anciennes avec les modernes ou Traité préparatif à l'apologie pour Hérodote*, published in Geneva in 1566: see Elizabeth Susan Wahl, *Invisible Relations: Representations of Female Intimacy in the Age of Enlightenment* (Stanford, Calif.: Stanford University Press, 1999), 23, 258 n. 3.

10. Cf. Valerie Traub, "The Renaissance of Lesbianism in Early Modern England," *GLQ: A Journal of Lesbian and Gay Studies* 7, no. 2 (2001): 245–63, esp. 249: "representations of female-female desire during this period depend heavily on classical antecedents for their modes of comprehension. It is through, quite literally, a rebirth of classical idioms, rhetorics, tropes, and illustrative examples that female homoeroticism gained intelligibility in early modern England. By renovating the discourses of the ancients, writers in the sixteenth and seventeenth centuries attempted to legitimize their own formulations, drawing on authoritative precedents . . . for risqué or troubling ideas."

11. See Brantôme, *Recueil des dames, poésies et tombeaux*, ed. Etienne Vaucheret, Bibliothèque de la Pléiade (Paris: Gallimard, 1991), 361–71 (quotation on 367).

12. Brantôme, *Recueil des dames*, 364, 365.

13. I owe this formulation, as well as the information in the following sentence, to Elizabeth S. Wahl, personal communication, 1999, and her book *Invisible Relations*, 61, 277–78n.

14. Emma Donoghue, *Passions between Women: British Lesbian Culture 1668–1801* (New York: HarperCollins, 1995 [originally published 1993]), 3, 258–59.

15. All further pages references to *Love between Women* will be included in the text. The study of lesbianism in classical antiquity has accelerated since the publication of Brooten's book. I confess that I have not seen Juan Francisco Martos Montiel, *Desde Lesbos con amor: Homosexualidad femenina en la Antigüedad* (Madrid: Ediciones Clásicas, 1996) or the new collection of papers edited by Nancy Rabinowitz and Lisa Avanger, *From the Homosocial to the Homoerotic: Women's Relations to Women in Antiquity* (Austin: University of Texas Press, 2001).

16. A number of sources omitted by Brooten are helpfully assembled by T. Corey Brennan in a dazzling review of *Love between Women* in the *Bryn Mawr Classical Review* (bmcr-l@brynmawr.edu), 97.5.7: 15 May 1997.

17. See my entry "Homosexuality" in *The Oxford Classical Dictionary*, 720–23, and my earlier remarks in *One Hundred Years of Homosexuality and Other Essays on Greek Love* (New York: Routledge, 1990), 33–35.

18. In "Lesbian Historiography before the Name? Response," 623–25, Brooten passionately declares her "skepticism about contemporary genetic and neuroscientific research on sexual orientation," asserts that "the current dimorphic model" of sexual orientation is "culturally limited," and concludes that the "ancient etiological attempts to make sense of erotic inclination . . . do not resemble twentieth-century conceptualizations."

19. See Halperin, "How to Do the History of Male Homosexuality," 110.

20. A similar point is convincingly made about the history of male homosexuality by George Haggerty, *Men in Love: Masculinity and Sexuality in the Eighteenth Century* (New York: Columbia University Press, 1999).

21. In the course of a very favorable assessment of Brooten's book, Natalie Boymel Kampen, "Lesbian Historiography before the Name? Commentary," *GLQ: A Journal of Lesbian and Gay Studies* 4, no. 4 (1998): 595–601, cites Mark Jordan's apt comments about Boswell's "commitment to the ideal of historiography of sex as a positive science," his presumption that "human sexuality . . . is just another hard-edged object in an external world, there to be observed and subsumed under generalizations" (596; see Mark D. Jordan, "A Romance of the Gay Couple," *GLQ: A Journal of Lesbian and Gay Studies* 3, nos. 2–3 [1996]: 301–310 [quotation on 302]). This characterization captures better than I can do the principles implicitly guiding Brooten's own approach to the history of sexuality.

22. In a commentary on my critique of her work, Brooten claims that I, too, employ the terms *slavery, marriage,* and *family* without historical qualification in *One Hundred Years of Homosexuality:* see Brooten, "Lesbian Historiography before the Name? Response," 619–20. And perhaps I do: it is hard to suspend all modern categories all the time in the course of historical analysis. But my lapses, however serious or regrettable, do not justify Brooten's. Nor does my failure to apply consistently my own historicist principles provide other historians of sexuality with a license to be anachronistic. Brooten's riposte may score a point against me, personally or intellectually, but it hardly invalidates the point of my own critique of *her* methods.

23. See Halperin, *One Hundred Years of Homosexuality,* 46.

24. See John Boswell, "Categories, Experience and Sexuality," in *Forms of Desire: Sexual Orientation and the Social Constructionist Controversy,* ed. Edward Stein, Garland Gay and Lesbian Studies, no. 1 (New York: Garland, 1990), 133–73.

25. See, for example, Ramsay MacMullen, "Roman Attitudes to Greek Love," *Historia* 31 (1982): 484–502; more recently, Amy Richlin, "Not before Homosexuality: The Materiality of the *Cinaedus* and the Roman Law against Love between Men," *Journal of the History of Sexuality* 3 (1992/93): 523–73, and Thomas K. Hubbard, "Popular Perceptions of Elite Homosexuality in Classical Athens," *Arion* 6, no. 1 (1998): 48–78. In a much more unusual move, Giulia Sissa attempts to rehabilitate "homosexuality," "homophobia," and even "gay" as authentically classical Greek categories of thought and experience while carefully avoiding the mistake of confusing acts with identities; instead, she substitutes a highly tendentious and misleading paraphrase of Aeschines' *Against Timarchus* for a close reading of it and then advances her argument on the basis of her own paraphrase: see Sissa, "Sexual Bodybuilding: Aeschines against Timarchus," in *Constructions of the Classical Body*, ed. James I. Porter (Ann Arbor: University of Michigan Press, 1999), 147–68.

26. Craig A. Williams, "Greek Love at Rome," *Classical Quarterly* 45 (1995): 517–39, revised and expanded in Williams, *Roman Homosexuality: Ideologies of Masculinity in Classical Antiquity* (New York: Oxford University Press, 1999), esp. 62–72.

27. Mario DiGangi, *The Homoerotics of Early Modern Drama* (Cambridge: Cambridge University Press, 1997), 16.

28. DiGangi, *The Homoerotics of Early Modern Drama*, 16. (The entire passage is quoted by Valerie Traub, "The Rewards of Lesbian History," *Feminist Studies* 25, no. 2 [summer 1999]: 363–94 [quotation on 376]. Traub's magisterial review essay also includes an appreciation and critique of Brooten's book.) Cf. Williams, *Roman Homosexuality*, 217: "To describe ancient bias against *cinaedi* as 'homophobic' or as constituting a problematization of male homosexuality is, I suggest, comparable to suggesting that Roman biases against female prostitutes or adulteresses were 'heterophobic' or in some way problematized heterosexuality."

29. Cf. Halperin, *One Hundred Years of Homosexuality*, 28–29, 40.

30. See Michel Foucault, *The Use of Pleasure*, trans. Robert Hurley, vol. 2 of *The History of Sexuality* (New York: Random House, 1985); Arnold I. Davidson, "Sex and the Emergence of Sexuality," *Critical Inquiry* 14 (1987/88): 16–48, and "Closing Up the Corpses: Diseases of Sexuality and the Emergence of the Psychiatric Style of Reasoning," in *Meaning and Method: Essays in Honor of Hilary Putnam*, ed. George Boolos (Cambridge: Cambridge University Press, 1990), 295–325; John J. Winkler, *The Constraints of Desire: The Anthropology of Sex and Gender in Ancient Greece* (New York: Routledge, 1990); Halperin, *One Hundred Years of Homosexuality*; and Williams, *Roman Homosexuality*.

31. In "Lesbian Historiography before the Name? Response," 620, Brooten expresses a certain indignation that I should characterize female prostitution in the Roman world as a "career choice," as if it were merely one profession among many open to socially empowered "career women," when in fact, as she observes, many ancient prostitutes were slaves. To the extent that this objection is anything more than pure grandstanding (after all, I had intended the turn of phrase to be heard as a deliberate anachronism), Brooten's objection is of course entirely just—though its effect in this context is to undermine still further her interpretation of the astrological texts. For if *meretrix* describes the unwilling fate to which an unfree person was consigned by her master or mistress, then it is even less plausibly conceptualized as a lifelong erotic

orientation, and "prostitute" becomes even more disanalogous with "tribade" and "virago," if the meaning of those terms in the writings of the ancient astrologers is understood the way Brooten seems to understand it, as a personal, erotic identity rather than as a public, socially stigmatized behavior (Brooten, "Lesbian Historiography before the Name? Response," 624–25, denies, however, that she intends any such opposition between public and personal identity). So that consideration does more, not less, damage to the logic of Brooten's overall argument.

32. See, for example, the following works: Ruth Mazo Karras, "Holy Harlots: Prostitute Saints in Medieval Legend," *Journal of the History of Sexuality* 1, no. 1 (1990): 3–32; David Lorenzo Boyd and Ruth Mazo Karras, "The Interrogation of a Male Transvestite Prostitute in Fourteenth-Century London," *GLQ: A Journal of Lesbian and Gay Studies* 1, no. 4 (1994): 459–65; Ruth Mazo Karras and David Lorenzo Boyd, "*Ut cum muliere:* A Male Transvestite Prostitute in Fourteenth-Century London," in *Premodern Sexualities,* ed. Louise Fradenburg and Carla Freccero (New York: Routledge, 1996), 101–16; Ruth Mazo Karras, *Common Women: Prostitution and Sexuality in Medieval England* (New York: Oxford University Press, 1996); "Prostitution and the Question of Sexual Identity in Medieval Europe," *Journal of Women's History* 11, no. 2 (1999), 159–77; and "Response: Identity, Sexuality, and History," *Journal of Women's History* 11, no. 2 (1999), 193–98.

33. Karras, "Prostitution and the Question of Sexual Identity in Medieval Europe," 171; more generally, 161–63.

34. Karras fully anticipates this objection: "I expect Halperin would disagree with much of what I have said here," she remarks in "Response: Identity, Sexuality, and History," 198 n. 19.

35. Carla Freccero, "Acts, Identities, and Sexuality's (Pre)Modern Regimes," *Journal of Women's History* 11, no. 2 (1999): 186–92 (quotation on 188), citing Karras, "Prostitution and the Question of Sexual Identity in Medieval Europe," 173 n. 14.

36. Traub, "The Rewards of Lesbian History," 369.

37. Nathalie Ernoult, "L'homosexualité féminine chez Platon," *Revue française de psychanalyse,* 58, no. 1 (1994): 207–18.

38. See the learned discussion by Cameron, "Love (and Marriage) between Women," 145–49. Brooten is well aware of these two scholia (see *Love between Women,* 5, 55 n. 119).

39. In her objection to this critique ("Lesbian Historiography before the Name? Response," 619), Brooten correctly observes that both Megilla and her girlfriend Demonassa are involved in the seduction of Leaena. It might also be possible to argue that the role played by Demonassa in the whole affair does not conform to a strict division between conventionally defined masculine and feminine sex roles, since she is the "wife" of Megilla but an aggressor in lovemaking with Leaena.

40. Moeris (p. 196.24 Bekker): "hetairistriai Attikoi, tribades Hellēnes." See Brennan, review of *Love between Women.* See also Cameron, "Love (and Marriage) between Women," 148–49, who provides the citation from Moeris quoted here (149 n. 34).

41. Cameron, "Love (and Marriage) between Women," 149, noting that Timaeus glosses *hetairistriai* as *hai kaloumenai tribades.*

42. Williams, *Roman Homosexuality,* 178.

43. The difference seems to have been a matter of reputation and social standing rather than one of actual conduct. As Williams points out, "[respectable] boys could get away with things that *cinaedi* could not" (*Roman Homosexuality*, 183).

44. See my entry "Homosexuality" in the *Oxford Classical Dictionary*, as well as my subsequent clarification of these points in "Questions of Evidence: Commentary on Koehl, DeVries, and Williams," in *Queer Representations: Reading Lives, Reading Cultures*, ed. Martin Duberman (New York: New York University Press, 1997), 39–54.

45. Williams, *Roman Homosexuality*, 175–76. Williams recapitulates his definition on 178 as follows: "In sum, the word *cinaedus* originally referred to men who were professional dancers of a type associated with the East, dancing with a *tympanum* and seductively wiggling their buttocks in such a way as to suggest anal intercourse. In a transferred sense it came to describe a man who was not a dancer but who displayed the salient characteristics of a *cinaedus* in the strict sense: he was a gender-deviant, a 'nonman' who broke the rules of masculine comportment and whose effeminate disorder might be embodied in the particular symptom of seeking to be penetrated."

46. See also Brooten, *Love between Women*, 7, on "the existence of 'man-boy love' sections in gay bookstores." Traces of these polemics can be discerned (to cite two distinguished examples) in Adrienne Rich's opprobrious remarks about "the patterns of anonymous sex among male homosexuals, and the pronounced ageism in male homosexual standards of sexual attractiveness" ("Compulsory Heterosexuality and Lesbian Existence" [1980], reprinted in *The Lesbian and Gay Studies Reader*, ed. Henry Abelove, Michèle Aina Barale, and David M. Halperin [New York: Routledge, 1993], 227–54 [quotation on 239]) and in Marilyn Frye's treatment of male homosexuality as an expression of male supremacism and the worship of phallic power (*The Politics of Reality: Essays in Feminist Theory* [Trumansburg N.Y.: Crossing Press, 1983]). For a balanced and insightful critique of this strand in lesbian feminism, see Earl Jackson, Jr., *Strategies of Deviance: Studies in Gay Male Representation* (Bloomington: Indiana University Press, 1995), 7–13, 267 n. 1. Brooten's own tendency to represent my disagreements with her about the correct interpretation of the ancient sources as symptoms of my supposed resistance to feminism continues this regrettable tradition. And she doesn't help matters when she insists that I look at female homoeroticism "through the phallocentric lens of male pederasty," that I employ "a male model," that I am every bit as much "steeped in the Greek pederastic model" as the Roman authors I study (see Brooten, "Lesbian Historiography before the Name? Response," 616). These characterizations of my approach to the history of sexuality, which read like personal slurs, are beside the point: my account of the hierarchical model used to represent female same-sex sexual relations in antiquity is not a blind projection of my own phallocentric obsessions onto the ancient texts, as Brooten seems to suggest, but a scrupulous description of the salient features of the male-authored ancient sexual discourses themselves. My aim in interpreting such discourses is to reconstruct their terms as accurately as possible and to reproduce their characteristic point of view, whether or not it happens to coincide with my own: after all, being "steeped" in such ancient discourses is what classical scholars are ideally supposed to be. It says much about the modern social and political context of Brooten's critique that this scholarly immersion in the ancient literature can itself be made to constitute, in the case of an openly gay male scholar, a personal and intellectual disqualification.

47. By this I do not mean to imply, of course, that Aristotle in this passage pathologizes *all* same-sex sexual behavior without distinction, as some have concluded: for a convincing argument that Aristotle's disapproval is limited to certain stigmatized instances of homosexual behavior and does not extend to homosexuality as such, see K. J. Dover, *Greek Homosexuality* (London: Duckworth, 1978), 168–69.

48. For example, Brooten is not, as she claims (*Love between Women*, 3), the first scholar to examine astrological texts in order to document the existence of sexual categories in antiquity: cf. Maud W. Gleason, "The Semiotics of Gender: Physiognomy and Self-Fashioning in the Second Century C.E.," in *Before Sexuality: The Construction of Erotic Experience in the Ancient Greek World*, ed. David M. Halperin, John J. Winkler, and Froma I. Zeitlin (Princeton, N.J.: Princeton University Press, 1990), 389–415 (cited favorably by Brooten, *Love between Women*, 56n, 158n, but not in connection with astrology), and *Making Men: Sophists and Self-Presentation in Ancient Rome* (Princeton, N.J.: Princeton University Press, 1995).

49. Williams, *Roman Homosexuality*, 181.

50. See Halperin, *One Hundred Years of Homosexuality*, 22–24.

51. Brennan, review of *Love between Women*, makes a number of additional and quite cogent criticisms of Brooten's reading of Caelius Aurelianus. See also Williams, *Roman Homosexuality*, 353–54 n. 298, whose refutation of Brooten's interpretation of Caelius I have largely followed here. Williams concludes, "In fact, by Caelius' standards, a situation in which a master penetrated his male slave who derived no pleasure from the act but who was merely doing what he was told would be entirely 'disease-free.'"

52. See Halperin, *One Hundred Years of Homosexuality*, 29–33.

53. Brooten herself now prefers a more cautious formulation: "We do not know if the *tribas*'s partner counted as disease-free; we can only say that the text does not focus on her" ("Lesbian Historiography before the Name? Response," 630 n. 29). This seems to me grudging but unobjectionable.

54. In "Lesbian Historiography before the Name? Response," 616, 621, Brooten wonders why in my critique of her work I restrict myself to pagan texts. She objects to my division of the ancient sources into pagan and Christian categories, protests against the "artificiality" of the distinction, and wonders about its motivation. Such rebukes are bizarre, coming from her, since that very distinction structures her entire book, separating it into its two major "Parts," divided according to this very opposition between the Roman context of Christianity (27–186) and early Christian attitudes (187–357). And for good reason: as Brooten shows (and this is one of the important achievements of her book as a work of history), there are significant differences between pagan and Christian perspectives on same-sex sexual relations: it is only in Christian sources, for example, that male homoeroticism and female homoeroticism are routinely categorized together and treated analogously. Thus, as she remarks, "early Christians, who generally classified both female and male homoerotic activity as sinful, probably played a crucial role in the development of the concept of homosexuality" (9). All the more reason, then, to treat the Christian sources separately.

55. See Cameron, "Love (and Marriage) between Women," 149 n. 37.

56. Brooten herself, of course, strenuously repudiates the categories of "butch" and "femme" as they apply to "ancient lesbians" and accuses me in turn of imposing

modern categories on the ancient evidence ("Lesbian Historiography before the Name? Response," 620). She cites a number of excellent historical considerations as reasons against applying, "even tongue in cheek," these modern subcultural terms to the ancient material. But of course my own usage is meant, among other things, not to convey accurately the ancient categories but rather the modern mindset that seems to inform, no doubt inadvertently, Brooten's own approach to the ancient evidence—in particular, her tendency to imply that she is speaking about all women, or all forms of homoeroticism among women, when she is in fact speaking about only one female sexual or social role. It is, I believe, her unreflective adherence to this modern habit of according more lesbian specificity to the butch than to the femme which explains her otherwise uncharacteristic practice of reproducing the prejudices of the ancient sources by problematizing only the active, aggressive, gender-deviant, or sexually deviant partner in female homoerotic relations.

57. See Richlin, "Not before Homosexuality," whose entire argument that sexual relations in the ancient Roman world were "not before homosexuality" rests on the unshakable (if unvoiced and unexamined) presumption that passive males were *the real homosexuals* of antiquity and that ancient discourses of male passivity were therefore *really* discourses of homosexuality. The sexually insertive male partners of Richlin's *cinaedi*, who are not comparably vilified by our sources, somehow do not seem to enter into her thinking on the subject or to qualify for inclusion in her concept of homosexuality.

58. For a brilliant critique of such presumptions, see Biddy Martin, "Sexualities without Genders and Other Queer Utopias," *Diacritics* 24, nos. 2–3 (summer/fall 1994): 104–21, reprinted in Biddy Martin, *Femininity Played Straight: The Significance of Being Lesbian* (New York: Routledge, 1996), 71–94; more generally, Teresa de Lauretis, "Sexual Indifference and Lesbian Representation," *Theatre Journal* 40 (1988): 155–77, reprinted in Abelove, Barale, and. Halperin, eds., *The Lesbian and Gay Studies Reader*, 141–58 (cited approvingly by Brooten, *Love between Women*, 6n).

59. See, for example, Seneca the Elder *Controversiae* 1.2.23 (discussed by Brooten, *Love between Women*, 43–44, 45). For further discussion, see Brooten, "Lesbian Historiography before the Name? Response," 616–21.

60. Brennan, too (review of *Love between Women*), makes a similar complaint on philological grounds about Brooten's despecification of the term "tribade" and her tendency to understand it as if it were a generic designation for a woman possessed of a lifelong homoerotic orientation.

61. Gayle Rubin, "The Traffic in Women: Notes on the 'Political Economy' of Sex," in *Toward an Anthropology of Women*, ed. Rayna R. Reiter (New York: Monthly Review Press, 1975), 157–210 (quotation on 160).

62. Traub, "The Renaissance of Lesbianism in Early Modern England," 258. For her earlier, classic formulation of this point, see Valerie Traub, "The (In)Significance of 'Lesbian' Desire in Early Modern England," in *Erotic Politics: Desire on the Renaissance Stage*, ed. Susan Zimmerman (New York: Routledge, 1992), 150–69.

63. See Catharine A. MacKinnon, 'Does Sexuality Have a History?' in *Discourses of Sexuality: From Aristotle to AIDS*, ed. Domna C. Stanton (Ann Arbor: University of Michigan Press, 1992), 117–27; see also Catharine A. MacKinnon, *Toward a Feminist Theory of the State* (Cambridge Mass.: Harvard University Press, 1989), esp. 126–54.

See Pierre Bourdieu, *La domination masculine* (Paris: Seuil, 1998), who aligns himself in a general way with MacKinnon, without, however, taking proper account of her work, or Rubin's, or the theoretical differences between them. For a similar critique of MacKinnon's neglect of cultural difference in her account of large-scale social structures of male dominance, see Lori L. Heise, "Violence, Sexuality, and Women's Lives," in *The Gender/Sexuality Reader: Culture, History, Political Economy*, ed. Roger N. Lancaster and Micaela di Leonardo (New York: Routledge, 1997), 411–33.

64. See the polemical but important arguments of Terry Castle, *The Apparitional Lesbian: Female Homosexuality and Modern Culture* (New York: Columbia University Press, 1993).

65. See, for example, Susan S. Lanser, "Befriending the Body: Female Intimacies as Class Acts," *Eighteenth-Century Studies* 32, no. 2 (1998–99): 179–98; and Traub, "The Renaissance of Lesbianism in Early Modern England," and her forthcoming book of the same title.

Chapter Ten

MARRIAGE AND SEXUALITY IN REPUBLICAN ROME:
A ROMAN CONJUGAL LOVE STORY

➳❧

Eva Cantarella

$\mathcal{T}$he story I will discuss is the story of a Roman marriage—namely, the marriage between Cato the Younger and Martia. The reason it deserves to be discussed is related to the presence and the role of a third man, the rhetorician Hortensius, whose relationship both with Cato and Martia was in antiquity, and still is, controversial.

The story, very well known, is described by Appianus in a few words: "Cato had married Martia the daughter of Philippus as a girl; he was extremely fond of her, and she had borne him children. Nevertheless, he gave her to Hortensius, one of his friends, who desired to have children, but was married to a childless wife, until she bore a child to him also, after which Cato took her back to his own house as though he had merely lent her" (App. *BCiv.* 2.14.99).[1]

The aim of this chapter is to show that if we analyze the story in light of the idea of marriage and of conjugal sexuality of that period, it does not appear as strange as it may appear today and as modern scholarship has generally considered it. In that time (the late republican era) to hand over one's own wife to a friend, so that she could give him children, was far from being considered eccentric or unbecoming, at least among the elite families (and maybe, as we shall see, not only among them). It was considered to have a civic function, which I will illustrate. In order to demonstrate this hypothesis, the chapter will be divided into three parts. The first part will be devoted to reviewing the details of the story, the commentaries of the Romans, and the interpretations of modern scholars. The second part will try to contextualize the story, analyzing Roman ideas concerning marriage and procreation through the recognition both of laws and of social attitudes. The third part will try to explain Cato, Martia, and Hortensius's story in light of these rules and attitudes.

PART 1: THE DETAILS OF CATO AND MARTIA'S STORY

The longest and most detailed description of Cato, Martia, and Hortensius's story is in Plutarch. Hortensius, writes Plutarch, was a friend and a great admirer of Cato. Therefore, desiring to be more than a mere companion, and to bring his whole family and line into community of kinship with him, he asked Cato for the hand of his daughter Portia (Plut. *Cat. Min.* 25.3–9).[2] But at the time Portia was married to Bibulus (consul in 59 B.C.E.), and Cato did not accept his friend's request. He replied that he loved Hortensius and thought highly of a community of relationship with him but considered it absurd for him to propose to marry a daughter who had been given to another. Then Hortensius changed his request and asked for Cato's own wife, "since she was still young enough to bear children, and Cato had heirs enough."[3] This time Cato did not refuse. He told Hortensius that he wished to consult Philippus, his father-in-law, who in turn declared himself in favor. We are not told what Martia thought of the situation. As far as we know, her opinion was not even asked. We are told only that she married Hortensius and bore him two children. When Hortensius died (he was already in his fifties at the time of the marriage), Cato remarried Martia.

What was the reaction of the Romans to this story? As Cato and Hortensius were two important public characters, the affair did cause something of a stir. It is said that rhetoricians used to train in the schools by discussing "an Cato recte Marciam Hortensio tradiderit" (whether Cato did well to give Martia to Hortensius) or "conveniatne res talis bono viro" (whether such behavior befits a decent man) (Quint. *Inst.* 3.5.11, 10.5.13). From Plutarch we also know that Caesar criticized Cato: "Hortensius, on his death, had left Martia his heir. It was with reference to this that Caesar charged him with avarice and with trafficking in marriage. 'For why,' said Caesar, 'should Cato give up his wife if he wanted her, or why, if he did not want her, should he take her back again? Unless it was true that the woman was at first set as a bait for Hortensius, and lent by Cato when she was young in order to take her back when she was rich.'" But first, Caesar was a political enemy of Cato. Second, he did not criticize Cato for giving Martia to Hortensius. He criticized him for taking her back out of sheer greed for money after Hortensius's death and with Hortensius's inheritance. Furthermore, it does not seem that his criticism was widely shared. Plutarch, for example, writes that to charge Cato with a sordid love of gain was like reproaching Herakles with cowardice (52.4), and that Cato took back Martia "since his household and his daughters needed someone to look after them" (52.3). Immediately after the remarriage, in fact, Cato left Rome to fight Pompey. And Strabo invoked ethnological precedents to justify Cato's action (Strab. 11.9.1). As far as we can see, Cato's behavior was discussed, and sometimes criticized with specific reference to the reasons that moved him, but not for the fact, per se, of having given his wife to a friend.

But even if the Romans were not, modern scholarship has often been embarrassed by the story. Cato and Martia's relationship is so inconsistent with modern occidental sexual morality that modern authors have often tried to explain it as a peculiarity, an oddity tied to the personal attitudes of the protagonists. The first explanation from this perspective was proposed years ago by an American scholar.[4] Cato's and Martia's behavior, as well as Hortensius's, could be explained by the age and personalities of the protagonists: all three were adults, and having gone beyond juvenile romanticism, they considered marriage an institution whose aim was the reproduction of citizens. But I strongly doubt this explanation: the idea that the aim of marriage was the reproduction of citizens was a general belief of the Romans, whether they were old or young. Furthermore, to believe that the aim of marriage was the reproduction of citizens did not imply that one should hand over one's own wife to a friend. A second and different interpretation explains Cato's behavior as the result of his philosophical beliefs: as a Stoic, he would have applied the precept that as women were intended to procreate, they were to be common to all.[5] But I am not going to discuss this hypothesis. We do not need to take Cato's philosophical beliefs into account to understand his conjugal story. In my opinion his behavior may be understood in light of general rules concerning marriage and procreation, both legal and social.

PART 2: CONTEXTUALIZING CATO AND MARTIA'S STORY: ROMAN ATTITUDES TOWARD MARRIAGE AND PROCREATION

In recent years, social historians of Rome, mainly in the United States, have often advanced a new interpretation of the Roman family and of Roman marriage in the last century of the republic and the beginning of the empire.[6] Richard Saller, one of the first scholars to propose this interpretation, criticized the theory which represents the Roman family as a unit under the strong, authoritarian power of a paterfamilias (as, for example, represented by Paul Veyne). In his opinion the Roman family tended to be very similar to the modern companionate and affectionate nuclear Western family.[7] This hypothesis was soon widely accepted. Though disputed by some scholars,[8] it has strongly influenced later studies, as demonstrated by Susan Treggiari's *Roman Marriage*, where the relationship between husband and wife (at least from an ideological point of view) is presented as a strong and affectionate personal relation, and it is stated that the decision to arrange a marriage was very frequently made by the persons who were going to marry, even if they still were under their fathers' power.[9]

But I am skeptical about this view of the Roman family. In my opinion, in order to understand Roman marriage we must forget our modern ideas of marriage, love, and the relationship between a couple. In Rome, both legal and social rules were such as to exclude the existence of similar ideas, and the Roman conception and legal structure of marriage were indeed always very different from the modern Western ones.

The first kind of marriage practiced in Rome involved the passage of the wife from her father's family into her husband's family, where she was subjected to a personal power called *manus*, very similar to the *patria potestas*. The possessor of this power was her husband, if he was independent (*sui iuris*), that is to say, if he had no more living male ascendents; if he was not independent, but still in power, she was subjected to her father-in-law's power (as the jurist Gaius says, in the second century C.E., the wife *in manu* was *loco filiae* in her relation to the head of her new family).

But starting in the third century B.C.E. the rules of marriage changed. This kind of marriage, the so-called *manus* marriage, was replaced by a new marriage which did not have the consequence of transferring the wife into the new family. That did not mean that the women were free: though they were not under the authority of their husbands, they remained in the *potestas* of their own fathers, whose *potestas* included the right to interrupt their marriages.[10] The new marriage, in fact, was based on consent. But Roman consent was very different from the type on which the modern Western marriage is based. Modern marriage starts at the moment when the consent to marriage is given. Once given, this consent is supposed to be in force until death or divorce (of course, in the countries where divorce exists, which must not be taken for granted, even in the modern Western world: in Italy, for example, divorce did not exist until 1968). In Rome, instead, the new marriage was based on a "permanent" consent. This meant that the consent given at the wedding had to continue to exist every single day of the conjugal life. The wedding ceremonies had only a social function, not a legal one (as modern ones have). Cohabitation was a marriage when accompanied by the so-called *maritalis affectio,* that is to say, the intention to consider the cohabitation a marriage. If the *maritalis affectio* ceased to exist, the marriage ended.[11]

But even in the classical period (until the beginning of the third century C.E.), the texts tell of the necessity of both the couple's and the fathers' consent. As the jurist Paulus writes: "Marriage does not exist unless everyone consents, that is, those who come together and those under whose power they are" [Nuptias consistere non possunt nisi consentiant omnes id est qui coeunt quorumque in potestate sunt] (Justinian *Dig.* 23.2.2). A later source confirms: "A marriage is valid if . . . both parties consent, if they are independent; or also if their parents consent, if they are in power" [iustum matrimonium est si . . . utrique consentiant, si sui iuris sunt, aut etiam parentes eorum, si in potestate sunt] (Tituli Ulpiani, 5.2). Therefore, if the father changed his mind, he had the right to interrupt his son's or daughter's marriage (*abducere filium* or *filiam*).[12]

These were the laws, and we also know that fathers exercised their rights at least until the second century C.E. Some papyri from Roman Egypt, in fact, offer clear evidence of the fact that around the second century C.E. some daughters started to oppose their father's will, and that some of them won out. In 186 C.E., at Oxyrincus, a woman called Dionisia asked the local magistrate to prevent her father from interrupting her happy marriage and taking her away from her husband (*POxy.* 237). In support of her request the woman recalled that in two cases, some thirty years before, the magistrates had denied fathers the right to take their daughters away from their husbands.[13]

Precedents in Roman law were very important but not binding. The principle that a son had the right to make his own decisions concerning his private life was difficult to affirm. In the third century C.E. a legal instrument was still in use that aimed at enforcing the paternal power to interrupt a marriage. This instrument (introduced by the *praetor*) was the *interdictum de liberis ducendis,* an enforceable order given to the reluctant spouse to allow the father to take his daughter away from the conjugal house.[14] In 312 C.E., we read in an Egyptian papyrus (*Papiri greco-egizii,* vol. 1, *Papiri fiorentini* [Milan: Hoepli, 1905], 36) that a father had compelled his daughter to leave her conjugal house possibly against her will and certainly against her husband's will. In this case, when the husband, to get her back, appealed to the local magistrates, their decision was that the problem had to be solved in accordance with the woman's desire, but we are already in 312 C.E.

Roman marriage was not a matter of personal choice, but a family matter, involving the economic interests and the social expectations and ambitions of the two families arranging the marriage. And this affected the relations between husband and wife. Even in a happy marriage there was no need for the couple to share a romantic love. This does not mean, of course, that love marriages never occurred. But conjugal love had nothing to do with passion; it should not be disturbing (as passion is). In fact, it was after the marriage that affection was supposed to develop, not before, as suggested by the lawyers' phrase *bene concordantia matrimonia*.

The Romans did not marry for love. Marriage was a practice often dictated by necessity, whose main function was the creation of children. But children were not desired by the couples only for their own sake. Even before Augustus, marriage laws (namely the *lex Iulia et Papia*) designed to counter the population decrease obliged Roman citizens (men and women) of reproductive age to be married.[15] Reproduction was a civic duty: Romans married and had children not only in order to have legitimate offspring to continue their estate. The main reason for marrying was the necessity of reproducing citizens.

PART 3: BACK TO CATO AND MARTIA

This is the context in which Cato and Martia's story took place, and this context helps us to see their behavior from the right perspective. Let us start with the legal problems. The paternal power to interrupt a daughter's marriage allows us to understand how it could happen that Hortensius asked for Portia's hand. Probably, although married, Portia was still in Cato's power. Even if *manus* marriage still existed at that time, she had probably been given to Bibulus in a marriage that did not involve her passage into Bibulus's *manus*. Therefore, Cato still having control of her, could have broken her marriage if he chose. Whether Cato refused the request for political reasons or out of paternal love we do not know, nor are we interested in knowing. What is interesting, for us, is the fact that we can understand Hortensius's request for a married woman. And we can also understand why, when Hortensius asked for Martia's hand, Cato asked for his father-in-law's consent: Martia and Cato's marriage was probably a *sine manu* marriage. This meant that Martia's father was the person who had the right to give her as a wife to Hortensius—of course, after her divorce from Cato.

Let us now turn to the psychological aspects of the story. The conception of marriage and procreation seen above helps us to understand how it could happen that Cato agreed to divorce Martia in order to let her marry Hortensius. In the context of this conception, it is no wonder, although adoption existed and was widely practiced, that the Romans sometimes passed women around when a child was needed. As we shall see, it happened not only when they were Stoics, like Cato. The practice of passing women around had several advantages: first, it gave the families an opportunity to establish social and political alliances through a "community of children," as explicitly stated by Hortensius in the speech he gave in order to convince Cato to give him Portia. Second, it helped to rationalize the population growth. The city needed the maximum exploitation of the procreative abilities of fertile women, but too high a number of offspring in a single family jeopardized its well-being. Again, this is clearly stated by Hortensius, in the speech quoted above. As Plutarch described it, Hortensius said to Cato that "according to the law of nature it was honorable and good for the state that a woman in the prime of youth and beauty should neither quench her reproductive power and lie idle nor yet, by bearing more than enough offspring, burden and impoverish a husband who does not want them."

To pass a wife to a new husband when she had given enough offspring to the old one gave good results from both the familial and the civic perspectives. The only disadvantage of such a practice compared to adoption was that adoption granted a descendant immediately and certainly. To marry a fertile woman instead, although offering a strong possibility, did not give certain results. But the Romans had found a way to achieve this result: they passed around women who were already pregnant. And Cato did so. In fact, the most interesting feature of the story, which is generally untold, is that when Martia was given to Hortensius, she was already pregnant by Cato. As Plutarch writes: "It cannot be said that he [Hortensius] did this [asked for Martia's hand] because he knew that Cato neglected Martia, for she was at that time *kuousa* [pregnant], as we are told " (Plut. *Cat. Min.* 25.5). And there are other examples. In 81 B.C.E. Aemilia was pregnant when she was forced to divorce her husband and marry Gnaeus Pompeius by Sulla, whose fourth marriage was to Aemilia's mother Metella and who had always acted as Aemilia's father.

Of course the most famous case is that of Augustus's wife, Livia. When given to Octavian, in 38 B.C.E., Livia was married to Tiberius Claudius Nero and, having already given birth to Tiberius, was pregnant with Drusus. And yet she was given to Octavian (Suet. *Tib.* 4). In fact, this was another case which was much talked about. A brief quote from Tacitus actually suggests that Augustus had violently imposed his will on the situation (Tac. *Ann.*, 1.10.5). Suetonius, in his life of Augustus, writes that Augustus *abduxit Liviam* (*Aug.*, 62.2). But in his life of Tiberius the same Suetonius writes that Nero *concessit* his wife *tunc gravidam* (Suet. *Tib.* 4.2). The idea of Livia's abduction is a clear attempt, by Tacitus, to portray Octavian as a dictator, in contrast with all the other sources.[16] In fact, Nero and Octavianus made an agreement concerning Livia's future. Was this an agreement against the Roman mentality or against Roman law? As far as the law is concerned, no rule existed that prohibited marriages with pregnant women. According to Augusto Fraschetti such marriages were prohibited by Roman *mores* until the woman had delivered the baby.[17] This could be deduced from the fact that Octavian, before marrying Livia, asked the opinion of the *pontefices*. But according to Tacitus the answer of the *pontefices* was that the marriage was allowed if it was possible to know who was the father. And Tacitus adds that this was allowed by an ancient *mos*. Fraschetti disposes of Tacitus's comment by stating that this *mos* had disappeared in classical times. But a few years before Livia, Martia had remarried while pregnant.[18] It does not seem to me that Livia's and Octavian's marriage was against the Roman *mores*. Besides any other consideration, it was celebrated with the consent of Nero, to whom the sources even attribute an active role in the celebration. In the words of Velleius Paterculus, Livia was *desponsa* (betrothed) by him to Augustus (Vell. Pat. 79.2.2), and Dio Cassius writes that Nero gave Livia as a wife to Augustus, as if he were her father (Dio Cass. 48.44.3). Cato did the same thing. In fact, Cato, too, was present at the wedding of Martia and Hortensius. (Plut. *Cat. Min.* 25.5). Of course, legally the woman was not given by her husband, but by her father. The presence of the former husband, when the bride was pregnant by him, was the sign of his agreement and the consecration of an alliance that tied not just two, but three families.

One could certainly observe, at this point, that the examples quoted involve the members of elite families. And it is very likely that the passing around of women occurred mainly among such people. But we can find in the sources some indications that it was accepted also by the less wealthy and powerful. In a very interesting and controversial passage of the lives of Lycurgus and Numa Plutarch writes: "With regard to community in marriage and parentage, though both [Lycurgus and Numa], by a sound policy, inculcated in husbands a freedom from selfish jealousy, still, their methods were not entirely alike. The Roman husband, if he had a sufficient number of children to rear and another, who lacked children, could persuade him to the step, relinquished his wife to him, having the power of surrendering her entirely, or only for a season; but the Spartan, while his wife remained in his house and the marriage retained its original rights and obligations, might allow any one who gained his consent to share his wife for the purpose of getting children by her" (Plut. *Lyc.-Numa*, 3.1).[19]

Some interesting information comes from the juridical sources. Unlike the historical and other literary sources, the juridical sources do not register the lives only of the wealthy and powerful, but also of hoi polloi, whose mentality concerning marriage and reproduction appears in wills preserved in Justinian's *Corpus Iuris Civilis*. These wills show that unknown husbands, concerned with the future of their future widows, wanted to help (or perhaps allow) them to express their reproductive abilities after their own death.

Let us start with an example: a husband (in the era of Hadrian) left part of his assets to his wife on the condition that she remarry and bear children to her new husband. However, in this case, it turned out that after this husband had written this will, he divorced his wife, who remarried and bore her new husband children. She then divorced the second husband and remarried the first. When this one died, a problem arose: did the conditions laid down in his legacy apply to her or not? The case was submitted to Julian, whose opinion is preserved in *Digesta* 35.1.25, and who decided as follows: the conditions laid down by the husband in the legacy had not been fulfilled, since his wife was supposed to give birth to the children after his death and not while he was still alive. Of course, we are not interested, now, in the juridical solution of the case. We are interested in seeing that in Rome there existed ordinary (common) husbands, who were neither powerful nor eccentric intellectuals but did not want their still fertile wives, when widows, to waste their ability to reproduce. Echoes of this preoccupation filter through a passage of the jurist Pomponius when he writes that "It is in the public interest to preserve women's dowries. Indeed, it is necessary that women continue to have a dowry in order to procreate and fill the city with children" (*Dig.* 24.3.1). Obviously, Pomponius is referring to widows and divorced women, who, without a dowry, would have greater difficulty in remarrying and continuing their civic duty to procreate. And in *Dig.* 22.1.48 the jurist Scaevola (in the first century B.C.E.) recalls the will of a husband who left the usufruct of one-third of his assets to his widow, establishing that she would get the property of this third if she had children. Of course, these cases were not identical to Cato's. These husbands did not pass around their wives during their lifetimes. But the basic attitude was the same: for the sake of the city, no reproductive ability should be wasted. It was almost as if women able to have children were an endangered species and the law had taken it upon itself to help them (or sometimes to oblige them) to do their childbearing duties.

Again we must recall some laws. When pregnant, a Roman wife was called by the jurists a *venter* (an abdomen), a technical term that indicated both the fetus and the woman who contained it. And the husband had such power over the contents of the woman-abdomen that, if he divorced a pregnant wife, he had the right to ask for the nomination of a person, called a *curator* (or *custos*) *ventris*, charged with ensuring that she would not induce an abortion (*Dig.* 25.4.1; Ulpian, *Ad edictum*). But what is more striking is that the *custodia ventris* was not only in the interest of the husband. It was in his interest, in his family's interest, and in the interest of the city, as shown by the rules imposed on pregnant widows by the *praetor urbanus* in his edict. As we read in *Dig.* 25.4.1.7 (Ulpianus), the control of the *venter* (in both senses of the word) was not entrusted only to the relatives of the divorced husband. The *praetor urbanus*, instead, was in charge of appointing a *custos* to the *venter* (par. 1) and of controlling the *venter* during the pregnancy, at the moment of the birth, and after the baby was born. After the birth, if the father failed to do it, he designated the person to whom the baby was to be entrusted and imposed on this person the duty of exhibiting it a certain number of times each month (perhaps to the mother, perhaps to the *praetor*). Pregnancy was not only a private and not even only a family matter. It was a state matter. From such a perspective, it is no wonder that the practice of passing around one's own pregnant wife was far from being perturbing for the Romans. It was in the husband's interest, in the interest of the two families involved, and in the interest of the state. And it would also appear that the Roman women accepted it, to the point that they considered it normal to be given by their husband to an another man, or—in a specular situation—to be replaced by an another woman, whenever they were unable to carry on their duty.

Let me recall a famous story showing this attitude. Sometime between 12 and 8 B.C.E. a *matrona* called Turia died, and her husband quoted her virtues in her funeral eulogy: "We longed for children, which an envious fate denied us. Had Fortune smiled on us in this, what had been lacking to complete our happiness? But an adverse destiny put an end to our hopes. . . . Disconsolate to see me without children, you wished to put an end to my chagrin by proposing to me a divorce, offering to yield the place to another spouse more fertile, with the only intention of searching for and providing for me a spouse worthy of our mutual affection, whose children you assured me you would have treated as your own. Nothing would have been changed, only you would have rendered to me henceforth the services of a devoted sister or mother-in-law" (*Corpus Inscriptionum latinarum* 6.1527 = Dessau, *ILS* 8393).[20] The story is difficult to understand in its details: what did Turia mean when she said that "nothing would change" and that she would treat the new wife's children as her own? Did she mean that she would continue to be devoted to him, even if she was no longer his wife? Or was she offering to let him have a new wife only until he had an heir and then to remarry her, assuring him that she would consider the child hers? This we do not know, but one thing is clear and certain: thinking that she was not fertile, she offered her husband the possibility of having children with an another wife. In this case, it is interesting to notice that the husband refused the offer: as he says in the eulogy, he did not want to exchange *certa dubiis*, that is to say, a good wife, such as Turia had been for years, for an unknown woman, maybe not as perfect as she had proven to be. But this makes the story even more interesting. There were wives who went even beyond their husbands' desires. Finally, it is very interesting to observe that the husband, far from being embarrassed at Turia's offer, praised her for it. She had given further evidence of her perfection. Turia's situation was different from Martia's, yet it was comparable, insofar as they both, Martia and Turia, in different ways, accepted their role as childbearers.

In recalling the events of Hortensius's death, Lucan writes: "Meanwhile the sun was dispelling a chilly night, when a loud knocking was heard at the door, and in rushed the matron, Martia, mourning for Hortensius, whose pyre she just had left. And thus she spoke, sorrowing: 'While there was warm blood in these veins and I had the power to be a mother, I did your bidding, Cato. I took two husbands and bore them children. Now I return wearied and worn out with childbearing and must not again be surrendered to any other husband. Grant me to renew the faithful compact of my first marriage; grant me only the name of wife; suffer men to write on my tomb: Martia, wife of Cato'" (Luc. *Pharsalia* 2.326–44).[21] Of course, this is Lucanus's imagination, and the events are obviously dramatized. Nevertheless, it is evident that Lucanus's account of the story had to seem plausible to his readers. Martia's attachment to Cato was plausible; he had not offended her. It was plausible that she still wished to be his wife.

Analyzing Martia's story and the practice of passing around fertile women, a French scholar, Yan Thomas, wrote that Romans invented a form of prenatal adoption.[22] I would go further and suggest that they invented surrogate motherhood. Of course, they did it in their own way, which may seem strange to us. But we must always remember, as L. P. Hartley writes (*The Go-Between,* incipit), that "the past is a foreign country: they do things differently there."

Notes

Drafts of this chapter have been discussed at the "Colloquium at the University of Virginia by the Classics Graduate Association" (Charlottesville, March 1997), at the faculty of classics at the University of Texas at Austin (March, 1997), and at the faculty of classics at Brown University (October 1999). I am very grateful for all the comments and criticisms, which helped me to better understand many points and to take into account different points of view.

1. Translation from Appian, *Roman History,* trans. Horace White, Loeb Classical Library (Cambridge, Mass.: Harvard University Press, 1969).

2. Portia was celebrated after her death as the most noble of widows. Having taken as her second husband Brutus, one of Caesar's killers, when Brutus was killed at Philippi, Portia decided to commit suicide. Her relatives, in order to prevent it, hid all the weapons existing in the house, including knives. But Portia did not give up, and she ended her life by eating hot coal.

3. Translations from Plut. *Cat. Min.* are from Plutarch, *Cato the Younger,* in *The Parallel Lives,* trans. Bernadotte Perrin (1919; reprint, Cambridge, Mass.: Harvard University Press, 1949), vol. 8.

4. H. Gordon, "The Eternal Triangle," *Classical Journal* 28 (1933): 574.

5. E. Malcovati, *Donne di Roma antica,* Quaderni di storia romana (Rome: Reale Istituto di Studi romani, 1945), fasc. 8, 1.

6. This interpretation is also based on the comparison of the Roman family with occidental family models. See R. Wall, G. Robin, and P. Laslett, eds., *Family Forms in Historic Europe* (Cambridge: Cambridge University Press, 1983).

7. Adult men under *patria potestas,* in his opinion, were too few to be a real problem. In addition, although according to the law fathers had the same power over their sons that they had over their slaves, in reality the relationship between father and son was characterized by bilateral *pietas,* and the fathers respected their sons' dignity and individuality. Among Richard Saller's many specialized articles, see "Men's Age at Marriage and Its Consequences for the Roman Family," *Classical Philology* 82 (1987): 21–34. See also R. Saller and P. Garnsey, *The Roman Empire: Economy, Society, and Culture* (Berkeley: University of California Press, 1987).

8. K. Bradley, *Discovering the Roman Family: Studies in Roman Social History* (New York: Oxford University Press, 1991).

9. S. Treggiari, *Roman Marriage: Iusti Coniuges from the Time of Cicero to the Time of Ulpian* (Oxford: Clarendon Press, 1991).

10. Roman girls married in their teens, when their fathers were usually still living. Furthermore, we must recall that a Roman woman was not really free even upon her

father's death. Roman law required that an independent woman have a guardian (*tutor*) for her lifetime. As a consequence of wars and the absence of men from Rome, however, women's guardianship weakened through the centuries, until it almost disappeared in imperial times. In other words, Roman imperialism also had domestic consequences, but Roman ideology continued to praise the model of the obedient and dependent wife and to criticize the "emancipated" woman.

11. In such cases, the divorce was considered to have taken place by itself, automatically. In fact, the sources record a phrase that usually accompanied divorce. The phrase is "take your stuff with you" (*tuas res tibi habeto*), usually pronounced by a Roman husband. But this was not a legal formula; it was only a way to let others know that the divorce had taken place.

12. Evidence of the actual use of this paternal power can be found also in the literary sources. In *Rhetorica ad Herennium* 2.38 a daughter asks her father why he wants her to divorce her husband: "si improbum esse Chresiphontem existimas, cur me huic locabas nuptiis? Si est probus / cur talem invitam invitum cogis linquere?" Here is the father's answer: "nulla te indigna, nata, afficio iniuria. / Si probus est, te locavi; si est improbus divortio te liberabo incommodis." On this paternal privilege in Plautus, see M. McDonnell, "Divorce Initiated by Women in Rome," *AJAH* (*American Journal of Ancient History*) 8 (1983): 56.

13. In two similar cases, in fact, both the *praefectus Aegypti* Flavius Titianus (in 128–29 C.E.) and the officer (*epistrategos*) Paconius Felix (in 133–34 C.E.) had asked the interested woman's opinion and decided the case according to it.

14. That this instrument was still used in the third century C.E. is proved by a passage of the jurist Ulpian. Cf. *Dig.* 43.30.1.5.

15. The law punished with economic sanctions so-called *orbi* (i.e., people who did not have children). These people were not allowed to receive *hereditates* and *legati*. See R. Astolfi, *La lex Iulia et Papia*, 3d. ed. (Padua: CEDAM, 1995).

16. M. Flory, "Abducta Neroni uxor: The Historiographical Tradition on the Marriage of Octavian and Livia," *Transactions and Proceedings of the American Philological Association* 118 (1988): 343ff.

17. A. Fraschetti, "Livia, la politica," in *Roma al femminile*, ed. A. Fraschetti (Bari: Laterza, 1994), 123ff.

18. Fraschetti quotes Tacitus's opinion that the fact was *ludibrium* (Tac. *Ann.* 1.10.5), but, again, Tacitus was a political enemy of Augustus. In his opinion, furthermore, Dio Cassius (48.44.2) seems to imply that the *pontifices* were bound to give a favorable answer to Augustus's question.

The fact that Augustus sent Drusus to Nero, after his birth, and that he went back to Augustus's house only after Nero's death, seems to show that Nero was the legal father. But when Drusus was born, in Augustus's house, it was Augustus who raised him from the hearth, where the baby had been laid at the paternal feet, as usual. In fact, in this case the situation is very complicated. I think that this is tied to Augustus's political role, and that the case does not represent the normal relationship.

19. Translation from Plutarch *Lycurgus-Numa*, in *The Parallel Lives*, trans. Bernadotte Perrin, Loeb Classical Library (1914; reprint, Cambridge, Mass.: Harvard University Press, 1967), vol. 1.

20. Abridged translation by D. C. Munro in *Women's Life in Greece and Rome,* ed. M. Lefkowitz and M. Fant (London: Duckworth, 1992).

21. Translation from Lucan, *The Civil War,* trans. J. D. Duff, Loeb Classical Library (Cambridge, Mass.: Harvard University Press, 1969).

22. Y. Thomas, "Le ventre: *Corps maternel, droit paternel,*" *Le genre humain* 14 (1986): 211ff. See also, by the same author, "A Rome, pères citoyens et cité des pères (II siècle avant JC–III siècle après J.C.)," in *Histoire de la famille,* vol. 1, ed. André Burguière (Paris: A. Colin, 1986), 216ff.

Chapter Eleven

THE INCOMPLETE FEMINISM OF MUSONIUS RUFUS, PLATONIST, STOIC, AND ROMAN

⋙⋘

Martha C. Nussbaum

I

One of the most remarkable figures in Roman Stoicism, the Roman *eques* Musonius Rufus has suffered from an odd combination of neglect and unsubstantiated praise.[1] Philosophical scholars have more or less totally neglected this Roman Stoic philosopher (c. C.E. 30–100), who taught Epictetus, who was exiled by Nero to the island of Gyaros for his alleged participation in the conspiracy of Piso, and who is known to posterity from a group of short works, apparently public speeches, on ethical and practical topics (including the need for rulers to learn philosophy!).[2] In late antiquity, Musonius was regarded as a major figure, both as teacher and as moral exemplar. Origen, for example, names Musonius and Socrates as the two exemplars of the highest type of life in the pagan world; the pairing was apparently widespread.[3] But our philosophical contemporaries have little time for the "Roman Socrates." The comprehensive collection of texts by A. A. Long and David Sedley, *The Hellenistic Philosophers*, includes neither any text from Musonius nor any mention of him, even in the section dealing with Stoic views on the political equality of women.[4] The burgeoning recent scholarly literature on Hellenistic ethics has not yet, to my knowledge, devoted any extensive attention to the analysis of his arguments. Although his works were well translated by Cora Lutz in a 1947 article in *Yale Classical Studies*,[5] no anthology available to students includes selections from his work. And Lutz's own introductory essay, though valuable, focuses on historical matters and does not present any detailed analysis of Musonius's arguments.

On the other hand, Musonius has some avid fans who have praised him warmly for his views on women, but they have done little to indicate what in the text merits such praise. Most striking of these is the distinguished Marxist historian, the late G. E. M. de Ste. Croix, who included a treatment of the subordination of women in his remarkable magnum opus, *The Class Struggle in the Ancient Greek World*.[6] De Ste. Croix argues that women are an oppressed class in the technical Marxian sense, and that a work on class struggle in the ancient world ought therefore to include some discussion of efforts to free women from this class oppression. Musonius, he argues, was the ancient writer who made the most valuable proposals for women's equal treatment, proposals that were unfortunately eclipsed by the more repressive views of his Christian successors, who in general taught the subordination of women to men.[7] If only the world had listened to Musonius rather than to Saint Paul, our world would have been a lot happier, and more just. This claim had, and has, a certain plausibility, despite the rhetorical excess with which it was expressed.[8] But it does not take us far as analysis. De Ste. Croix made no effort to trace Musonius's debt to earlier Stoicism (about which he showed little curiosity), to Plato (a philosopher whom he despised), or to Roman culture generally. Animus against the Christians so engrossed him that he had little interest in investigating ideas about women and marriage in other areas of the culture surrounding Musonius. His praise thus serves more to pique the reader's interest than to provide any helpful analysis of Musonius's views.

By far the most valuable analytical contribution so far has been the useful treatment of Musonius's views on marriage and sexuality by Michel Foucault in volume 3 of his *History of Sexuality*.[9] Foucault linked Musonius's views helpfully with those of some related authors such as Epictetus and Plutarch and argued persuasively that Musonius forms part of a philosophical and also a more general culture that was trying out new views about marital companionship and women's equality. But again, Foucault provides no precise account of the origins of different elements in Musonius's work, something that we badly need if we are to assess his originality and the precise nature of his proposals. Indeed, he tended to treat Musonius as an example of emerging popular thought, rather than as a thinker in a definite philosophical tradition. Furthermore, he confined his analysis to the writings on sexuality, in keeping with his theme, and therefore did not discuss the texts relating to women's education, where Musonius actually presents arguments for women's equal treatment designed to convince interlocutors who disagree (something he does more rarely in the works on sexuality).

Finally, in her fascinating book *Roman Marriage*, Susan Treggiari includes much material from Musonius in the course of assembling her picture of the evolution of companionate marriage at Rome.[10] Through her valuable study of the ways in which husbands and wives referred to their mutual love in funerary inscriptions, combined with a scrutiny of legal texts and a variety of sources for popular thought, Treggiari has given the philosophical interpreter of Musonius invaluable assistance in situating him within his culture, assistance of which I shall gladly avail myself. But again, her work does not carry us far as a study of Musonius, since she is not concerned to pursue his philosophical antecedents, or to analyze his arguments.[11]

My aim in this chapter will be to begin to address this lack by providing close analyses of the arguments of two works of Musonius: *Should Daughters and Sons Get the Same Education?* and *That Women Too Should Do Philosophy.* (I shall also discuss pertinent passages of several others works, which I have therefore translated along with the primary works in the appendix.) It is evident that Musonius is a Stoic. He speaks as a Stoic philosopher, and his writings are saturated with the ideas of the Stoic tradition. It is also evident that he owes a large debt to Plato's *Republic* (and other Platonic works):[12] like many Stoics he views Plato as an important philosophical source, and he is prepared to borrow Plato's arguments liberally in constructing his own. Finally, it is also evident that Musonius is a Roman gentleman. He addresses an audience of well-born Roman males in households with many slaves and servants, and he makes it clear that he is one of them. (Once he contrasts the Cynic philosopher Crates, who had no property and slept in the public stoas of Athens, with "[us] who set out from a household, and some of us have servants to wait on us."[13] Throughout, he assumes a prosperous household with a staff of slaves.) Even his preference for the simple life of agricultural labor[14] corresponds to a common Roman fantasy, and there is no reason to suppose that Musonius ever lived out that fantasy. It is men such as himself, above all, whom he wishes to persuade about some matters concerning their daughters and wives. This gives his Stoicism strict practical limits and shapes the way in which he presents characteristic Stoic ideas. I shall ask exactly how these arguments work, how each of Musonius's three identities figures in their structure, and what tensions we may discern among the claims of the different identities. Once this has been done, we can at least begin to ask what sort of feminist Musonius was, and how helpful his proposals actually are.

One caveat before we begin. We are able to trace Musonius's debt to

Plato, and to general features of Stoic ethics. But we know all too little about Zeno's *Republic,* the major work of Stoic political thought.[15] And we know that we totally lack a number of Stoic works in which women were discussed: Cleanthes' *On the Fact that the Same Excellence [aretē] Belongs to a Man and a Woman* (D.L.7.175); a work of Chrysippus in which he defended that same thesis (see Philodemus *de Fato* col v.8–11); Seneca's *De Matrimonio,* scanty fragments of which are preserved in Jerome; and, no doubt, other works that simply are lost to us.[16] An additional complication is that some of these works may themselves have used Plato—so we cannot be sure that Musonius is going straight back to the source. So we must proceed as best we can, bearing in mind that not all our inferences will be good ones.

II

Should Daughters and Sons addresses an interlocutor who asks whether the same *paideia* should be given to both. Musonius begins his reply (A) with a famous Platonic example: male and female dogs have the same training, because they have the same functions (*Republic* 451B 4ff.). To Plato's example Musonius adds that of horses. But he omits an important part of the Platonic argument, namely, the observation that dogs are not assigned different functions "on the grounds that bearing and rearing the puppies incapacitates them" (451D6–7). This was one of Plato's most striking points: the fact of a difference in pregnancy and lactation does not entail a lifelong division of functions.[17] As we shall later see, the omission fits well with Musonius's reluctance to challenge traditional spheres of activity and his interest in perpetuating a female form of life shaped around household management and child care.

In the case of humans, however, Musonius continues, we somehow think that males should have a superior education. Musonius now argues (B) that differential education could be justified only in two ways: we need to show either that it is not essential that men and women have the same excellences,[18] or that it is possible to arrive at the same excellences through different types of education. He strongly suggests that neither ground will prove plausible (*hōsper ouchi deon*).

The first task, then, is (C) to establish that the same functions and excellences belong to both men and women. Here Musonius departs from Plato and conceives of the question in a thoroughly Stoic way. Plato, of course, considers people fitted by birth for a wide range of different functions. The education he proposes in *mousikē* and gymnastics is to be given only to the children of guardians, and a notorious problem is that this makes it virtually impossible for the ideal city to be the meritocracy it purports to be.[19] But even among these guardian children, some will ultimately prove unsuitable for guardianship and migrate downward in the class hierarchy; on the other end, only a select few will ascend, through an arduous winnowing process, to the status of philosopher-ruler. These will have an education in mathematics and dialectic that will not be given to anyone else. So when Plato speaks of similar excellences, he means that the highly diverse excellences that characterize different classes in the city are distributed across the two sexes, and that wherever talents are the same, the training should be the same. He does not mean that all people have the same talents and should therefore have the same education.

Not so Musonius. In Stoic fashion, he conceives of the excellences of a good human life as the same for all humans alike: they are the ethical excellences, which Musonius standardly takes to be the usual four, courage, moderation, justice, and wisdom. He construes wisdom consistently, in Stoic fashion, as practical wisdom (*phronein*) and takes it to be concerned, above all, with moral choice. In this work Musonius does not discuss the innate equipment for these excellences; he assumes, in standard Stoic fashion, that it is innate in all human beings. Thus, he does not even consider the possibility that women have a different goal because they have different innate equipment. Elsewhere, however, he asserts that all human beings have the basic equipment for these excellences: "We are all by nature equipped to live blamelessly and well."[20] He supports this claim by pointing to the fact that lawgivers prescribe behavior for everyone, not just for certain special people.

His argument confronts, instead, the question whether the same menu of moral excellences befits both women and men.[21] Practical understanding (*phronein*) he treats as obvious: "What after all would be the use of a foolish man or woman?" Justice requires a little more attention, but Musonius argues that just as a man requires justice to be a good citizen, so a woman requires it to be a good household manager. He adds a point designed to persuade the reluctant male interlocutor: he does not, after all, want a wife who would behave unjustly like the murderous Eriphyle! Self-control (*sōphrosunē*) Musonius takes to be an obvious desideratum for females, but, interestingly, less obvious for males. He points out, supporting his claim that it is important for males, that "the law decrees the same penalty for *moicheuein* as for *moicheuesthai*," for male as for female adultery. As we shall see later, this is literally true but involves a big equivocation, since any intercourse outside marriage for a woman is defined as adulterous, but this is not true for a male. Musonius conceals the distance that separates his own view of proper male self-control (see section V) from legal reality. He adds the point that gluttony and drunkenness are vices in both sexes.

But the biggest problem (D) is clearly courage, *andreia*, which is always closely linked, as its name implies, to the idea of manliness. Interestingly, Musonius's text shows us that this etymological link is still in force, for he shifts to the verb *andrizesthai* in the next sentence, as if the word is still heard as a part of its word family.[22] So the question must be: what is it for a woman to behave "like a real man," and why should we think this good for a woman? Musonius gives three answers, all of them interesting. First, a woman had better have the capacity not to "bend under either hardship or fear," or she will not even have self-control, for she will not stand up to men who assail her virtue by threats. Second, she had better know how to fight defensively, if she is going to be able to defend her children from a possible attack: he points out that hens and many birds have this ability. Third, he points out that there is no reason to think that even armed fighting is off limits for women, since we all know about the victories of the Amazons. If "other women lack something of their ability, it is due to lack of practice, rather than because they lack some innate equipment."

This fascinating paragraph offers something for everyone, drawing on a variety of traditions as it does so. The idea that courage can be displayed in resisting shameful things outside of the military context is common in Stoic authors and in Cicero: indeed, Cicero's *De Officiis*, to take just one example, pries courage more or less completely loose from its military roots and makes it a general attitude of despising fortune and withstanding its blows. This argument about the connection between courage and wifely virtue is surely the one most pertinent to the concerns of the interlocutor. But just in case the interlocutor should object that courage is essentially a virtue concerned with fighting, Musonius is ready for him. The argument about defensive fighting on behalf of one's young is highly practical—and indeed Roman history of the first century offers many examples of parents who either do or do not protect their children against attack. (Seneca reproves one such father as "a slave in soul more than in circumstance"; *De Ira* 3.14.) It is significant, and characteristic, that Musonius chooses to illustrate his claim from the world of hens and birds, rather than from the Neronian court, where such examples of courage on behalf of others (and of its absence) would not have been difficult to find.

But it might be objected that so far we have not been shown that women have the *same* courage, since the paradigm case of courage in the tradition involved armed combat. Here Musonius does find it necessary to address the question of equal capacities for the first time — since the interlocutor is likely to doubt whether women are capable of military excellence. His final argument therefore takes us straight into the world of Plato's *Republic*, where women develop the same gymnastic and military skills as men. The idea is not foreign to the Stoic tradition: it seems plausible that Zeno's *Republic* similarly integrated women into the military and defensive functions of the city.[23] Citing the victories of the Amazons (an example that he apparently derives from Plato's *Laws* 806B, where Plato uses it to support a fully equal physical education),[24] Musonius says that this example shows that women can do extremely well in war; the fact that today's women do not fight in the army shows only that they lack practice.

Musonius's interest in armed fighting is more theoretical than practical: he is not proposing to reform the Roman army, and his example of the mythical Amazons lies further from reality than others he might have used. (He writes close to the time of Boudicca's troublesome rebellion in Britain.) But he keeps things safely abstract, establishing only that there are no grounds for thinking that women differ in any respect, either with regard to the goal or with regard to their equipment for reaching it.

Throughout this passage, there is a conspicuous absence of metaphysical and psychological analysis. Earlier philosophical discussions of female virtue were sometimes built on an analysis of the soul and its parts. Thus, Aristotle's denial that women have the same virtues uses his analysis of the soul into ruling and ruled parts (*Politics* 1.13). The Greek Stoics' assertion of similarity in virtue presumably made use of the Stoic one-part model of the soul. Musonius's account draws the Roman interlocutor into no such contested waters. By separating the ethical argument from its metaphysical basis, Musonius presumably hopes to address a wider group of readers; he also follows a common Roman tendency to portray ethical arguments as self-sufficient.

Musonius now turns (E) to the other premise he needs to establish: if the functions are the same, the education should be the same. He does not think this very controversial; indeed, he assumes that the interlocutor will agree quickly that "in the case of every animal and plant, one must produce the excellence appropriate to it by applying the correct sort of concern." He now gives two musical examples: if what we wanted to teach was *aulos* playing, surely we would not teach it differently to men and to women; it is the same with *kithara* playing. So too with the virtues: "if both need to become good, possessing the excellence that is appropriate to human beings, . . .

won't we then educate them both similarly, and teach the skill from which one becomes a good human being to both on an equal basis? Surely we are obliged to do it this way, and no other way."

Musonius fails to consider a possible objection. For there are some cases where we do think it right to use different educational strategies to reach a single result. These are cases where we think that different starting points (whether biological or cultural) influence learning. Some children seem to grasp mathematical concepts quickly through visual strategies, others through abstract numerical and conceptual strategies. Good teachers approach children in ways that suit their learning style, which may have biological dimensions. Sometimes, these differences are sex linked: to teach girls any athletic skill, a good teacher will need to know the differences between female and male anatomy and how these influence functioning. (When Little League baseball authorities required a female catcher to wear an athletic supporter, claiming in Musonian fashion that what is good for one must be good for both, she came to practice wearing the protective cup on her arm, just to show how silly the rule was.) Again, a voice teacher who trained young male and female singers similarly would ruin many voices: careful attention to different developmental patterns and different periods of fragility is essential for good training. Finally, there are differences created by differential social placement: many educators now think special programs important to encourage girls to go into math and science, because they believe that only such programs will overcome the cultural portrayal of these fields as male, giving girls a fully equal chance to see what they can do. In all these ways, education "on an equal basis" need not mean the *same* education. True equality can sometimes require differential treatment.

Why does Musonius ignore these possibilities? In the case of innate differences, it is because he holds that there are no significant innate differences with respect to the basic aptitude for learning morality. (He assumes that here, but argues for it in *That Women Too* and in the short work cited above.) As for different learning styles, distributed along general lines, we should bear in mind that all Stoic moral education is supposed to be responsive to the particularity of each pupil; it is therefore plausible to suppose that any differences that individuals have along these lines will be picked up in that way, far more accurately than through any generalizations about gender groups.

But what of different cultural impediments to virtue? Isn't it plausible to suppose that, while males brought up at Rome have to struggle especially hard against anger and the desire to lord it over others, women may need to struggle against excessive timidity, or lack of self-esteem? But here again,

Stoic education is one step ahead of the objector. If there is one thing that is the persistent focus of Stoic moral education, it is the need to counteract bad stereotypes of male and female excellence, especially as these are presented in normative pictures of "proper" emotion. Men have to be taught that anger is not the mark of the real manly man; women have to be taught that erotic passion is not the mark of the real woman (witness Epictetus's sermon to Medea); all have to be taught to avoid excessive attachments to worldly externals, such as honor, political position, money, and family, especially as those are presented in normative paradigms tought by culture. The general Stoic position is that wherever culture has damaged the pupil, that is where education should focus; wherever there is disease, there medical treatment should be applied. So any gendered differences in moral impediment will already be taken account of in the very idea of a Stoic moral education; and Musonius plausibly thinks that this does not amount to a *different* education for the two sexes. That is simply what it is to "teach the skill from which one becomes a good human being to both on an equal basis." Stoicism, with its reliance on the medical analogy, has already internalized the fact that sometimes truly equal treatment requires different concrete strategies.

The interlocutor now objects (F) that it is implausible to imagine that all physical exercise will be the same. We might expect Musonius to return to the Amazons and the need for female practice in the martial arts. At this point in Plato's argument in the *Laws*, the Athenian Stranger takes a very strong stand, insisting on vigorous lifelong bodily training and contrasting his own proposal with Spartan custom, which strikes him as half-hearted, since women learn physical skills of war in youth and never use them in adulthood (806BC). Musonius, however, takes a more pragmatic Roman tack. "No," he says, "I would not require this." The stronger bodies should do the heavier and outdoor work, the weaker bodies the lighter and indoor work. In general, these differences are distributed along lines of sex, but that will not always be the case. The capacities of the individual should be the touchstone. Some men may prove more suited for light work, some women for heavier "male" work. Musonius concludes by strongly reproving the idea that there is any task that is by nature only for men, or only for women. "For all human tasks . . . belong to us in common, and are common to both men and women."

Why does Musonius pull up short here, rather than following Plato (and probably Zeno) in assigning outdoor physical tasks to women on a regular basis? The answer is obvious: he is making practical proposals for Roman daily life in upper-middle-class households. In theory he remains a strict Platonist, insisting that there is no task that is not by nature suited for both sexes. But since, with Plato, he grants that physical strength is generally distributed somewhat unequally, he can grant consistently with Platonism that the heavier tasks will generally be more suited to males. And if this is so, why not accept, for the most part, the traditional division of indoor and outdoor activities, rather than making women go outside for physical exercise? Plato would say: because otherwise we shall never know what the capacities of each individual are. (Our own century's experience with female athletics gives him strong support.) And in the *Laws* he adds, because if they ever really need to fight for their city they will otherwise be unable to do so (806AB). Musonius, less adventurous — and able to rely on the rather considerable skills of the Roman army at its zenith — rests content with a bold theoretical assertion and a conservative practical proposal.

Having made this sizable concession to custom, however, Musonius immediately returns to his central, and strictly egalitarian, theme (G): where teaching related to ethical excellence is concerned, everything is exactly the same for both, "inasmuch as we agree that the excellences are in no way more appropriate to one rather than the other." Physical exercise can be different, apparently, only because it is not seen by Musonius as having a bearing on the real goal. He therefore elaborates his central theme, emphasizing once again (H) the uniformity of moral education that should belong to boys and girls, "straight from infancy," asserting that there are no group differences in the basic mode of moral learning. He runs through the four excellences again, giving a sense of the sort of thing one must learn to acquire them. (Clearly, he is speaking of the education of young children, not the more sophisticated education in arguments discussed in *That Women Too*.)

Once again, Musonius concedes that there may be small differences of expertise (I): a man may know some specialized piece of "technical" knowledge that a woman does not know, and vice versa. About "the really important things," however, they must know exactly the same. The art that supervises this education? It is, of course, philosophy (J), and both men and women need to learn it. Musonius hastens to add that this does not mean women must learn a professional competence in logic and so forth, but men do not need to either. The important thing is that both should acquire "excellence of character and nobility of life," and philosophy provides this.

In short, Musonius takes a radical Platonic (and perhaps Zenonian) idea of equal education and adapts it to Roman reality. His view is Platonic in that it looks to the capacities of the individual, rather than to customary gender divisions, as the touchstone for what education can be. It is Stoic in that it looks to the ethical excellences, and their basis in a capacity shared by all humans, as the touchstone for what education should be. (Logic and "sophistical cleverness" are dismissed as unnecessary for either sex, and mathematics does not even figure in the account.) It is Roman, finally, in its determination to integrate this education of character, without omitting anything truly essential, into a Roman way of life, to challenge contemporary norms of superior male education without producing the laughter and hostility that Plato's Socrates imagined greeting his proposals for the ideal city.

III

That Women Too begins, in a sense, where *Should Daughters and Sons* left off, with the topic of female philosophizing. But it tackles an issue that *Should Daughters and Sons* left for the most part unargued: the question of innate female capacities. Musonius begins (A) with an elaborate enumeration of the capacities that are distributed by the gods to male and female alike. First, the rational faculty (*logos*). Musonius imagines this not as a specialized Platonic capacity for theoretical contemplation, but as a basic practical faculty "that we use to communicate with one another and to reason about each thing, whether it is a good thing or not, and whether it is noble or shameful." Why does he expect the interlocutor to accept the premise that women have "the same rational faculty as men"? We learn later that the interlocutor is a male, probably a husband, who wants a wife who is a good partner and companion; the suggestion is that such a man will recognize that his daily dealings with his wife presuppose her possession of such a communicative and choice-making capacity. To this similarity, Musonius adds similarity in faculties of sensing, and similarity in bodily parts. (In keeping with ancient tendencies to treat female and male genitals as functional equivalents, he asserts that there is no part that one has that the other does not have.)[25] Finally, Musonius finds in both sexes the desire for ethical excellence and a natural orientation toward it (*oikeiōsis phusei*). He supports this claim by pointing to the fact that women "no less than men are pleased by noble and just actions, and reject the opposite." The interlocutor is expected to accept this—logically enough, since he is depicted as someone who has high ethical expectations for his wife's conduct.

This account of human faculties is clearly Stoic, rather than Platonic or derivative from popular Roman thought. It focuses on the faculties of the person Stoics consider most important for ethical development, and it uses the characteristic Stoic terms *logos* and *oikeiōsis* to make these origins clear.

Special theoretical talents, such as those discussed in Plato's account of the natural equipment of his philosopher rulers, are altogether ignored.[26]

Now Musonius abruptly concludes, (B) "Since this is the way things are, why on earth would it be appropriate for men to inquire and examine how one should live well—which is what it is to do philosophy—and women not?" Strictly speaking, the conclusion here is only that *if* it is appropriate for men to do philosophy, *then* it is appropriate for women to do so. But since Musonius plainly thinks that it *is* appropriate for men to do philosophy, the rhetoric of his question strongly suggests that it is appropriate for women as well. How does this argument work?

Apparently, Musonius assumes that the characteristics just discussed are all relevant to doing philosophy, and that they are the only characteristics relevant to doing philosophy. Beginning from these assumptions, he appears to be reasoning as follows. Suppose (as has already been argued) (1) A and B are similarly situated with reference to the basic skills to be developed in a pursuit P. Then (2) if P is appropriate to A it is also appropriate to B. But in fact (3) a philosophical development of these skills is appropriate for men. And so, by *modus ponens* we get, as our conclusion, (4) that it is appropriate to women also.

The conditional premise 2 is the controversial one. The problem is that the basic equipment named by Musonius is basic equipment for hundreds of pursuits, not all of which can be cultivated simultaneously. So both men and women have to opt for some of the pursuits for which they are basically qualified, and to reject others. The fact that they have the basic equipment thus does not settle what they will do. We may wonder why Musonius is so confident about what men should do. But even if we grant him that premise, and grant him, as well, the very general idea that similar cases should be treated similarly, we may yet wonder whether there is not some as yet undisclosed dissimilarity between men and women that would dictate a different choice among the available activities in their case. For example, it might be the case that one cannot pursue both philosophy and household management (as the irate interlocutor will later object). In that case, given that women have the basic equipment for both, we will simply have to decide which is more important for them to pursue. In short, before Musonius can really earn his conclusion, he will have to say a good deal more about how philosophy fits in with the other pursuits of life. In particular, it would be helpful for him to establish two points: (a) that philosophy is extremely important for all human beings, so that there is a strong prima facie case for pursuing it if one can, and (b) that philosophy is not at odds with the other important uses a woman should make of her basic equipment.

This Musonius now undertakes to do. In the next section of the work, he argues for the central importance of philosophy in producing all the excellences that are most important for a woman's life as well as a man's.

He begins (C) with a rhetorical question: "Is it because it is appropriate for men to be good, and women not?" He thus suggests an argument of the following form: (1) Human beings cannot be good without philosophy. (2) It is appropriate for all human beings to be good, both male and female. (3) So, it is appropriate for all human beings, both male and female, to pursue philosophy.

The rest of this section of the work (D) is taken up with establishing the first premise with regard to women, since 2 in some form is taken for granted. But establishing 1 turns out to require a fuller account of what it is for a woman to be good, and therefore a detour through the subject matter of *Should Daughters and Sons*. Musonius is concerned to ward off the possible objection that a different menu of excellences belongs to women, and therefore, possibly, a different training. So he goes, one by one, through each of the four ethical excellences, arguing in each case (a) that it is an appropriate excellence for a female, and (b) that philosophy is the art that will secure to her its possession.

Like the first section of the work, this section is thoroughly Stoic. Philosophy is not abstract speculation or theoretical contemplation. It is understood in a Stoic practical way (and in a way that, even among Stoic conceptions, downplays the importance of logic and study of nature): it is the systematic art of life (*epistēmē peri biōn*); its subject matter is arguments about what is worth enduring for the sake of what, what is to be despised and what chosen, and so forth. In familiar Stoic fashion, Musonius invokes the example of Socrates to back his idea. He argues that a systematic understanding of ethical arguments gives a firmness and consistency in ethical conduct that one can get in no other way. One reason for this is that philosophy, so imagined, leads to a modification of the passions: the philosophically trained woman will not be quarrelsome, or fearful, or "wiped out by pain," or prone to unfair grasping.

Since this discussion closely parallels the discussion in *Should Daughters and Sons*, it is not necessary to analyze it at length, but the discussion of courage requires comment. In *Should Daughters and Sons*, Musonius had oscillated between a Platonic idea of warlike women and a more conservative Roman idea of women who use courage to stand up to the travails of a typical woman's life. In *That Women Too*, the former conception is completely absent, and the latter holds the scene alone. The motif of standing up to the threats of the powerful is repeated, and given great rhetorical emphasis, especially in the phrase "or, by Zeus, because he is a tyrant." (Here one might see a reference to contemporary events in the Neronian court, were Musonius's whole style of presentation not so remote and abstract.) The woman who resists the tyrant is now characterized in Stoic fashion as having self-esteem (*mega phronein*) and being an autonomous agent (*autourkigēn*). But lest the reader start thinking about fearsome Amazons who might upset the balance of power in the household, Musonius hastens to add that all this autonomy and self-esteem are put to work in the courageous acts of "nursing her children from her own breast and serving her husband with her own hands"—not to mention doing a slave's work without shrinking! The reluctant husband is cajoled with the question, "Would such a woman not be a great help to the man who married her, an adornment to her relatives, a good example to all those who know her?"

Why is *That Women Too* even less bold than *Should Daughters and Sons* in pursuing the Platonic (and perhaps Zenonian) vision of women's strength? One obvious point is that it speaks to husbands about their wives, rather than to fathers about their daughters. Roman women would be married at around sixteen, and philosophy is standardly not pursued until that age or later: so we have shifted to a new form of life and a new interlocutor. It is a truth of experience that fathers can frequently countenance in their daughters a strength and independence that would strike them as deeply threatening were it to be found in the wives by their sides. The idea that marriage rests on subordination and obedience frequently coexists, in our own time, with a strong interest in nurturing the talents of daughters. Was this at all the case at Rome? One might suppose not, since the asymmetry of power between father and child is far more marked legally than the asymmetry between husband and wife—even, in some respects, after the woman's marriage. And yet marriage is exogamous, so a strong daughter is ultimately someone else's problem. And it is striking that in the case of daughters Musonius is not afraid to mention warlike exercises (if only to reassure the reader that he is not actually going to require them); in the case of wives, at every point he is at pains to emphasize the function of philosophy in reinforcing the status quo and producing wifely good behavior.

Some people (husbands?) now object: philosophizing women will become "stubborn and bold. They will abandon their housework and come into the company of men and busy themselves with arguments and fine logical distinctions and the dissection of inferences, when they should be at home doing the spinning" (E). (Perhaps these objectors are thinking of stories told about Hipparchia, who went around with her husband Crates to dinner parties and had fun jousting with visiting sophists, including one

Theodorus the Atheist, who was so angry at his own inability to detect the fallacy in her argument that he ripped off her cloak.)[27]

Musonius's answer (F) is interesting. In one way he reassures the interlocutors: he himself does not approve of women who leave their practical tasks to focus on arguments. But at the same time it involves a stern symmetry: men should not leave their practical tasks either for the sake of arguments. A good Stoic, Musonius reminds the interlocutors that philosophical argument should be understood as a contribution to life.[28] In classic Stoic fashion, he deploys a medical analogy: "Just as a medical argument is no use, unless it contributes to the healing of a human body, so if a philosopher has or teaches an argument, it is no use, unless it contributes to the excellence of the human soul."[29] In other words, you must hold yourself to the same standard to which you hold a wife: each in his or her own sphere must pursue appointed practical duties, viewing philosophical argument as a way of leading a better practical life, not as a way of showing off intellectually.

After that rather challenging paragraph, however, Musonius returns to reassurance: how can philosophy possibly produce bold, heedless, and wanton behavior, when its content is that proper shame is the greatest good, that prudence is great, that wantonness is the greatest evil? The work, apparently incomplete, breaks off at this point.

Like *Should Daughters and Sons*, this work is a strange combination of boldness and reticence. In its context, it has real force: for so far as we can see, women at Rome generally did not go to study with the philosophers, and Musonius means to encourage real intellectual study in the philosophical schools (albeit at Rome, not by going away to Athens). His reference to women who "go to study with the philosophers" means more than just learning some phrases.[30] (Cicero's mediocre son Marcus went off to Athens, but the estimable Tullia would appear not to have had such formal training.)[31] So one plausible way of looking at the text is that it is urging a quite radical educational step and sugarcoating it with reassurances to the husband. On the other hand, the strong egalitarianism of *Should Daughters and Sons* — watered down with respect to sports, but not with respect to virtue — seems to have become a bit more loose jointed in this work, where we do hear of a single set of basic capacities and a single set of excellences, but where examples of conduct are always chosen to depict a woman who will fulfill traditional norms of the good wife and mother.

One further point should be observed about both works: they are considerably more optimistic than are most Stoic works about the likelihood that virtue will actually be produced by training. Seneca and Cicero are far more guarded, and it was typical, after the first generations of the school, to deny that any fully virtuous person had existed since the original founders. Musonius's optimism is functional for his feminism, for the husband is reassured that if he allows the wife to study philosophy, she actually will have the excellences mentioned, and will not just be flopping around in a lawless condition. But it also seems to be sincere: throughout his works Musonius proceeds as if there were a reliable method one can select to produce excellence, and as if there really were many excellent people in the world.

IV

I have suggested that Musonius is more cautious in dealing with husbands than with fathers. Elsewhere, however, he shows us that his conception of marriage is not a simply traditional one. By his time in Rome there is a well-developed ideal of companionate marriage.[32] As Treggiari argues, basing her argument on funerary inscriptions as well as on texts, the idea that marriage is based on male domination had become very much muted by the time of Cicero, and ideals of partnership and lifelong friendship and affection were increasingly the norm. Nonetheless, even in this cultural climate, Musonius's conception of marriage is striking. He asserts that the goal of marriage is a partnership, and he illustrates the structure of this partnership with the image of two oxen pulling behind a yoke, and with the even more intimate image of "breathing together" *sumpnein*. These images suggest a much greater symmetry and equality than the word *koinōnia* by itself implies. Furthermore, this partnership is not simply for the sake of reproduction: that, Musonius observes, one could achieve without marriage, as we see in the case of animal mating. The goal is a complete sharing of life, "whether in health or in sickness and in every circumstance." The partners are to compete with one another, to see who can offer this care more completely—an idea that looks far more symmetrical than the idea in *That Women Too*, where the wife is waiting on her husband in a somewhat unilateral way. The observation that marriage will fall apart if one partner "looks elsewhere in his mind," pursuing his own interests to the neglect of the partnership, is in one way an accurate observation about Roman divorce; but it also contains a high expectation of mutual concern in marriage that seems to go even beyond the Roman norm.

The extent to which Musonius does go beyond norms of his time becomes clear from *On Sexual Intercourse*. Not only is he prepared to criticize all forms of intercourse undertaken for pleasure alone—even when nobody is wronged—he is especially eager to attack the sexual double standard, which was still dominant in Roman culture and law (see below).[33] It is generally thought blameless for a man, married or unmarried, to have intercourse with a hetaira; and it is thought especially unremarkable, and an instance of a master's clear entitlement, that he should be able to have intercourse with his own slave. Musonius assails both of these common practices, pointing out that it would be regarded as intolerable if a woman (whether married or unmarried) were to have sex with her own male slave. Men, he says, have sex with their slaves only out of appetitive lack of control (*akrasia*). Nobody will deny this. (In other words, nobody will say that it is love or overwhelming passion). But then there is a contradiction that needs sorting out. On the one hand, men claim to be suitable to have authority over women—so they claim to be more capable of control. On the other hand, they claim latitude for *akrasia* that they do not allow to women, by representing themselves as in the grip of strong appetites. Well, if they are really creatures who cannot control their own powerful appetites, then they will have to forfeit their claim to control. If, on the other hand, they are capable of controlling their appetites, they had better do so.

Finally, in *Whether Marriage Is an Impediment*, Musonius gives us an account of the function of the biological difference between the sexes. It is a thoroughly symmetrical account. Musonius spurns traditions (for example, the Aristotelian tradition) that associate biological dimorphism with the distinction of ruling and being ruled. Nor does he portray the female as in any sense biologically lacking (in keeping with the thesis of *That Women Too*, that each sex has all the parts that the other has). He says, instead, that the goal of dimorphism is simply difference itself, and that difference itself exists in order to create a basis for longing, and that longing in turn exists for the sake of creating association and partnership. In other words, the function of sexual dimorphism is to create lasting couples who will be held together for life, both for the sake of one another and for the sake of children. The role of these observations in the argument is to underline the conclusion of *That Women Too*: the right way to pursue philosophy is in the context of this kind of partnership.

These three works in many ways depart from Greek Stoic traditions regarding marriage and sexuality, as we shall see. They are less clearly Stoic than their fellows, as is signaled by the fact that Pythagoras comes in for praise alongside Socrates and Crates. Nonetheless, the basic spirit of symmetry and equal dignity that animates them is Stoic, as well as the strong emphasis on control over desire and pleasure. There are traces of Plato to be seen in *Whether Marriage Is an Impediment*: the reference to the *dēmiourgos* who made our species is probably a reference to the *Timaeus,* and the idea of cutting our kind into two, making two types of genitals, harks back to Aristophanes' myth in the *Symposium*—although it is used for a notably different purpose, in which homosexual relations, much disliked by Musonius, do not figure at all. Instead of three original "wholes," whose cut pieces produce male-male, female-female, and male-female couples, we now have a single original whole, and an account of sexual attraction that is based on genital difference. This is another departure from original Greek Stoicism in the direction of Roman norms and values, for Zeno's preferred couples were male-male, and his account of sexual attraction, steeped in the traditions of Greek pederasty, focused on youthful bloom rather than genital difference.[34]

These works are, then, both Stoic and Roman. They employ Stoic ideas of universal capacity for excellence, gender symmetry, and self-mastery to develop further the contemporary ideal of companionate marriage as a partnership in reproduction, practical affairs, excellence, and affection.

V

How shall we assess the feminism of Musonius? In some respects, clearly, he is in advance of Roman customs of the day, a pioneer, even in an era of companionate marriage, in his insistence that males and females should be treated on an equal basis with respect to education and cultivation of the innate capacities central to humanity. His conception of education, Platonic in its thoroughgoing dedication to the development of the faculties of the individual, is Stoic in its nonelitism about the capacities that suit the person for the pursuit of philosophy and the highest good. This makes it more hospitable than Plato's actual view to the development of intellectual and moral capacities in women as a class. And he puts these ideas to work in developing a conception of marriage that involves a thoroughgoing partnership and sharing (the image of the two oxen pulling equally in the yoke), and a thoroughgoing symmetry of moral duties, even with regard to sexual monogamy. In these respects Musonius draws on views already current in his culture, but moves considerably beyond them.

These achievements should not be belittled. And yet there are aspects of Musonius's feminism that should be questioned by anyone with an interest in women's complete equality.

1. Separate spheres. Musonius does indeed advocate equal education for males and females, including philosophical education. And yet he imagines this education being used by each in the traditionally separate spheres of Roman male and female life. The husband is imagined as a "good citizen"; the wife as a "good household manager." He uses justice in political life, she in managing the servants. He uses courage in fighting, or standing up to tyrants, she in nursing her children from her own breast—and, in an extraordinary example, in serving her husband with her own two hands! Musonius does mention that she had better be prepared to stand up to tyrants if they make a shameful sexual proposition. And she should even know skills of defensive fighting, in order to defend herself and her children from assault. Further, Musonius does cite the Amazons as proof that women can excel in traditionally male warfare if they get enough practice. But for the most part his wife is indoors arranging the household, and he makes no attempt to move her into the larger world of political and military affairs. He makes it clear that males and females have all the same ethical excellences, so presumably he thinks there is no natural barrier to full citizenship for women; but he does not criticize the conventions that confine them to the domestic sphere. Doesn't this show that Musonius's feminism is only skin deep? Surely he seems to lack in the commitment to radical social change that animated the Greek Stoics, whose women were fully equal citizens in their unisex clothing, and Plato, whose Socrates criticizes Glaucon's sexist language in order to remind him that women are expected to be among the very rulers of the city?[35]

Yes and no. We must point out, first of all, that Musonius, unlike Greek Stoics, is talking about real-life women and making practical suggestions for actual lives, rather than doing ideal political theory. His chance of achieving large-scale political change in Nero's Rome is zero, and so he should not be unduly penalized for proposing only what seems feasible. He emphasizes women's fitness for all the virtues frequently enough that we can conclude that he thinks them in principle fit for citizenship; if he does not defend the proposals of the Greek Stoics, it is likely to be on pragmatic grounds.

Still, the very point of doing ideal political theory is to describe a goal clearly for those who would like to pursue social justice. Isn't it a failure in Musonius that he does not even indicate clearly that full citizenship would in principle be appropriate for women?

Here we arrive at an interesting feature of Musonius's ethical theory. It is that he apparently believes that the all-important thing is having and exercising the virtues; the sphere of life in which one does this is relatively unimportant. In *That Women Too*, he treats the women's household duties as parallel to the man's worldly duties—both are "deeds" for the sake of which arguments should be undertaken, alternative spheres in which virtues can be cultivated, the same virtues for both alike. In this way of thinking, we have not really set up separate spheres for men and for women. With respect to "the really important things," they have the same and do the same. It is only in the rather trivial matter of location and context that their lives differ.

In putting things this way, Musonius is refusing a route to social differentiation that the Stoicism of Panaetius and Cicero made available, for he does not allude to the well-known account of the four *personae*, according to which individual temperament, social role, and circumstance can all influence what choice is right for someone to make. This theory was used by Roman Stoics such as Cicero and Epictetus to argue that a different deportment is appropriate for men and for women.[36] Musonius conspicuously does not say this. He says that the really important things are to be the same, only they will take place inside a different social context—which, strictly speaking, should, being external to virtue, be indifferent so far as virtue is concerned. To alter one of his examples, it is as if we thought musical functioning the main thing in life, and we had two groups that our society has traditionally treated differently, teaching one group to play the *kithara* and the other the *aulos*. If the really important thing is musicality, and the context for the exercise of musicality is secondary, why would it be important to upset this traditional assignment of functions?

To this a modern feminist will reply that the male and female spheres are simply not like playing the *kithara* and playing the *aulos*. Those two instruments are social equals; neither is hierarchically ranked above the other.[37] Not so with citizenship and domestic life. As Musonius himself says, one is the sphere of the "rulers"; the other the sphere of the "ruled." One sphere is valued as that of wisdom and power; the other devalued as subordinate and obedient to power. Musonius may think differently, emphasizing the symmetry of the spheres, but that does not change social reality. And when one occupies, not by choice, a sphere that is socially marked as subordinate, surely that has an adverse impact on the very sense of dignity and self-esteem that Musonius himself values as a part of virtue.

Here we encounter a limitation that Musonius shares with many other Stoics: the failure to understand the extent to which human dignity and self-respect require support from the social world. When Seneca speaks about slavery, he enjoins masters to recognize and respect the equal human dignity of their slaves, acknowledging that virtue is the one important thing, and that this is available to human beings in any walk of life (*Ep. Mor.* 47). Does he, however, call for the abolition of the institution of slavery, as an insult to human dignity? By no means. He only asks masters to treat their slaves decently, not to use them as unwilling sexual tools, not to beat them, and so on. His Stoic sense of the irrelevance of externals for virtue, together with his unwillingness to challenge entrenched structures of power, pulls him away from any more radical proposal. Musonius is in some matters more radical, closer to the Cynic strand in original Greek Stoicism. And yet here he too fails to acknowledge the extent to which female virtue may be undermined by the very fact of social hierarchy. In this sense, Musonius's Stoicism and his Romanness go all too well together, insulating him from the thought of profound social upheaval.

2. Continued male domination. Worse still, Musonius at times seems actively to collude in the hierarchy between male and female. In some areas, of course, he does ask men to give up traditional prerogatives and to adopt a symmetrical moral role: his repudiation of the sexual double standard is a salient example. Nonetheless, symmetry is not complete. The entire structure of his text implies male control over women. Musonius addresses his proposals on the education of daughters to fathers, it appears, not mothers; and the interlocutor in *That Women Too* is also male, a husband who needs to be talked into letting his wife do some studying. Musonius never questions the fact of male authority over women, and he tacitly supports it when he gives these characters gentle persuasion, rather than telling them they have no right to give orders to the woman one way or another. Many of his appeals further reinforce the idea of male authority: for example, he argues that one great advantage of education in courage is that the wife will serve her husband with her very own hands, and that education in other virtues will make them less threatening to men — more prudent, less extravagant, less tempted by sexual transgression. Of course, Musonius demands many of these same virtues of men also, but it is no small part of his rhetoric to appeal to a male's sense of power and to urge that philosophy reinforces, rather than threatens, that power.

In *On Sexual Intercourse* he goes one step further and appears to justify the overall superiority of men to women (*proestanai*), calling men "the stronger in judgment" and women "weaker in judgment," men "the rulers," women "the ruled." It seems likely that Musonius has put this language in the mouth of the interlocutor — the idea being that *if he thinks* men are superior to women, *he* surely should not concede that men are less able to control their sexual appetites. But the bottom line is that men will forfeit their claim to control if they concede they cannot control themselves, and Musonius is at least silent about the warrant behind this claim. It would have been good of him to have said, "This whole idea that men are superior and control women is a bad idea, quite apart from the fact that men do not appear to be very good at controlling their own sexual appetites. For remember, we are conceiving of marriage as a partnership of equals, like two oxen pulling together behind a yoke. And we have also argued that women, far from being 'inferior in judgment,' are fully capable of all the virtues." But he does not say this. To the extent that he does not, he at least colludes in the maintenance of hierarchies of power whose moral basis his own arguments call into question.

3. *Laws and institutions.* Musonius rarely mentions laws and institutions governing the sexes, and never in order to suggest that they ought to be changed. And yet laws of property, inheritance, personal autonomy, and marital autonomy were not exactly equal in first-century-c.e. Rome. Let us review a few of these inequalities, focusing on marriage law.

Women appear to have gained the right of marital consent by Musonius's time, and this shift marks a distinct erosion of paternal authority. She may make her own engagement, and Augustan law forbids the father to prevent such a marriage; indeed, he may be forced to give her a dowry.[38] Nonetheless, the elaborate customs of matchmaking and chaperonage, and the restrictions on female mobility, distinctly limit the extent to which choice is really choice.[39] Clearly, sexual freedom enjoyed by women prior to marriage remains highly asymmetrical. Sexual intercourse by an unmarried girl is always a crime, while young men enjoy considerable sexual freedom, provided they select slaves or prostitutes.

Within marriage, asymmetry continues. A husband who takes his wife in adultery, prior to the first century c.e., may or may not have been legally entitled to kill wife and lover; this is unclear. But he can be expected to be acquitted of murder if he does.[40] Under the new first-century law, the *Lex Iulia De Adulteriis* (introduced by Augustus, ostensibly to stem the tide of moral decline), he apparently could kill the lover with complete impunity only if the lover belonged to certain lower classes, including prostitutes, gladiators, and those who fight wild animals in the arena.[41] And he could not kill the wife, although the crime was still likely to be treated with relative leniency.[42] The father's rights are more explicitly established: prior to the first century the power of life and death that a paterfamilias holds over his family extends to the killing of an adulterous daughter. This right is explicitly reasserted in the *Lex Iulia*.[43] Although killings appear to have been uncommon, there are many references in comedy to violence against the male adulterer and some, at least, to violence against women.[44]

Even if the wronged husband does not have resort to violence, he and his wife still have unequal legal privileges. Adultery on the part of the wife is always automatic grounds for divorce.[45] Indeed, a man who takes his wife in the act of adultery and does *not* divorce her is liable to a harsh criminal penalty for "pandering" [*lenocinium*], although he can try to defend himself by saying that he did not know, or did not believe it, or did not really take them in the act.[46] Once a woman has been condemned for adultery, it is a crime "as if adultery" [*pro adulterio*] for any other man to marry her; and a condemned adulteress may not give evidence in court.[47]

For males, by contrast, the big worry is the reaction of other males if his partner in adultery is another man's wife or unmarried daughter. A married man who visits a prostitute, or who has sex with a woman of slave status, is not called *adulter* and is not considered to be committing any offense. Even the repressive *Lex Iulia* defines adultery in a way that exempts such husbands.[48] Obviously a wife is not entitled to kill husband or lover in cases of adultery. More striking, under the *Lex Iulia* she may not even bring a legal prosecution for adultery.[49] Although penalties for males convicted of adultery appear symmetrical to those for females — involving on both sides confiscation of property and relegation to an island — the definition of adultery is itself highly asymmetrical, so these penalties also are asymmetrical.

My account so far suggests that Augustus simply codified and extended earlier laws and customs. But reality is more complex, since the earlier customs were not strictly enforced and allowed much latitude for personal negotiation and gradual social change. The Augustan laws, with their elaborate codification of private morality and the severe enforcement that went with it, dramatically expanded the domain of state interference with private life. Although under the republic there had been some public control of sexual morality, Cicero is speaking for general sentiment when he prescribes the norm that the state should keep out of the homes of its citizens.[50] Treggiari argues with much plausibility that it was this attitude of public restraint that created the climate within which marriage was gradually redefined as a symmetrical partnership no longer resting on women's subordination. It was this very freedom of the female that inspired the reaction that led to Augustan repression. Augustus's claim that he was simply reintroducing ancient customs, while in some details accurate, was simply false, a construction of an imaginary past in order to justify an expanded role for government.[51]

As Treggiari notes, these Augustan laws were much admired and emulated during the 1920s and 1930s by a rather unsavory group of modern students of antiquity, including Mussolini and Hitler. Admirers included, as well, some conservative British scholars who similarly favored more state regulation of private life. Hugh Last praises the *Lex Iulia* as "an outstanding piece of legislation, . . . a notable advance in the conception of the proper functions of the State;" P. E. Corbett asserts that the law "would . . . provide a very necessary check up on the growing independence and recklessness of women."[52] Such views have not disappeared; indeed, it would not be surprising to hear the *Lex Iulia* praised in the United States as a model for the public crusade against adultery, in a time of moral decline.

Here, then, is a place where we would expect any philosopher truly interested in the dignity and equality of women to go to work. Musonius might have taken two distinct positions on the *Lex Iulia*, compatibly with his interest in women's dignity. He might have insisted, with Cicero, that the state should as a rule stay out of the private affairs of citizens, defending this claim both on grounds of liberty and on grounds of usefulness, as the best way to promote the evolution toward full female equality that he favors. Or he might have approved of public interference with private morality but argued that laws should be far more symmetrical and more protective of women's equality and dignity. To some extent, even a Ciceronian Musonius would have had to concern himself with legal reform, since on some matters, such as the nature of the marriage contract, the grounds for divorce, and homicide law, the public sphere would plausibly remain involved even in the more liberal regime envisaged by Cicero.

Musonius, of course, makes neither type of argument. He avoids the issue of law completely. This is understandable, since another trip to the island of Gyaros was no doubt not an appetizing prospect. And indeed, one might say that, if he really did participate in the conspiracy against Nero for which he was exiled, he approached the issues in the only possible way, and at great personal risk, by seeking to overthrow Nero in favor of a more acceptable ruler. So Musonius should not be blamed for these gaps in his argument. But for anyone interested in him as a feminist, they remain gaps nonetheless. Especially in an era in which we see increasing support for increased state action to stem the tide of private sexual lawlessness, and a similar nostalgia for a semifictional past in which marriage was a blameless partnership till death, we should note that increased state interference at Rome did indeed have the effect of providing "a check up on the growing independence . . . of women"—and was, in large measure, inspired by this very purpose. Feminists may forgive Musonius for his silence, but they should not emulate his example.

4. Dignity and rights. Musonius argues that women *should* do philosophy, that daughters *should* have the same education as sons. But what is the force of this *should?* Throughout the two works on education, the primary emphasis is on the teleology of ethical excellence: women *should* have this because we all agree that it is a good thing for women to have the excellences, and this education is necessary for excellence. Women's ethical excellence is presented as a good for her, as well as a good thing for men (though for rhetorical purposes the accent is frequently on the latter issue). One problem with Musonius's arguments is that he focuses so intently on what is good *for men*, but we can regard this as necessitated by his rhetorical purpose. What I now want to argue is that there is an ethical problem, too, in his focus (less emphatic, but still clear) on what is good *for women*.

It is clear that without the necessary equipment for the excellences women lack something that is valuable for them, something that is necessary and appropriate for their full development as human beings. To withhold equal education is in that sense to wrong women. But the idea that never comes through quite clearly in the text is that of women's dignity, and their potential for virtue, as aspects of humanity that exert a claim against the male-dominated world that they should be respected. We get the sense that women are worse off by not being educated, but not that they have a right to be treated well. Musonius elaborately shows that the world will be better with equal treatment of women; he never quite says, look, they just *are* equals in fundamental respects and have the right, therefore, to be treated as equals.

I am not making, here, the old familiar argument that there is no notion of rights in ancient Greek thought. That was always an oversimple idea, true of some concrete notions of rights (as immunity from government interference, for example), but by and large untrue. There are many ways in which Greek philosophy contains the notion of an urgent claim grounded not in contingent social relations, but in the nature of the person, that gives rise to corresponding moral duties. In Stoic philosophy especially, we often encounter arguments based on an idea of the dignity of humanity, the idea that just because someone is human and a sharer in reason, a person has a right not to be treated in certain ways. This mode of argument, for example, underlies Cicero's theory of war in the *De Officiis*, giving substance to his arguments about proper treatment even of the enemy; it also underlies his extremely strict prohibitions against force and fraud, arguments that directly influenced Kant's notion of the universal obligation to treat humanity as an end.[53] What I am saying is that there is no such argument in Musonius, no sense that we violate the humanity of women, or fail to treat them as their dignity requires, when we fail to give them an equal education.

Indeed, we notice this absence throughout Musonius's writing. Why is it bad for a man to visit a hetaira, granting that he is not wronging any other man by depriving him of his hope of legitimate children (the only sort of wrong the interlocutor can envisage)? Musonius might have replied: because he shows disrespect to his wife, who has a claim to fidelity. Instead he answers: because he harms himself. The case is a little unclear, since the man's marital status has not been established. But the very fact that the question of a possible wife is not raised is extremely striking (especially in light of the fact that it is always salient whether the woman in question has a husband to be insulted). Again, why is it bad for a man to sleep with his household slaves? Because he is carrying on like a pig and indulging himself—not because the female slave has a claim not to be used as a sexual tool. Seneca, in letter 47, inspires indignation at the thought of a (male) slave who is made to serve at table dressed like a woman with his beard plucked out, and thus to spend his life "divided between serving his master's drunkenness and his lust." The rhetoric of the argument clearly implies that the slave, who has been repeatedly called a human being, has a claim not to be treated in a way that violates his human dignity. Again, physical cruelty to slaves is ruled out on the grounds that such behavior "abuses them, treating them not even as human beings, but as beasts of burden" [*ne tamquam hominibus quidem sed tamquam iumentis*].[54] It is this type of appeal to the dignity of the person that I find lacking in Musonius, whose appeals for continence are always justified by reference to the virtue of the powerful.

5. Sex and marriage. Musonius's boldest feminist claim is also, in the detail of its justification, his most questionable. The idea that the sexual double standard should end is, of course, in some ways enormously appealing, and it is perhaps the most original aspect of his view. It cannot be found in Plato or the Greek Stoics, since they did away with the whole institution of marriage as conventionally understood. And it cannot really be found in his surrounding society either, given its great tolerance of relations between males and prostitutes or slaves. But the grounds Musonius gives for his conclusion need scrutiny. As I have said, he does not rest his case on the idea that sexual relations outside marriage are a wrong to the offended wife as much as to the offended husband. Instead, he rests it on the far more sweeping claim that sexual relations undertaken only for pleasure harm the self. This claim is to be carefully distinguished from the Christian claim that sexual relations are inherently sinful and are only to some degree redeemed by marriage. As de Ste. Croix, Foucault, and Treggiari all argue, this attitude is absent from first-century Roman culture, just as it is from the Greek culture that preceded it.[55] Musonius's operative category is the familiar Greek category of *akrasia:* the fault of the person who has sex outside marriage is a lack of proper self-control over his bodily pleasures. But the area in which pleasure is considered nonakratic has shrunk dramatically. Musonius does not clearly state the view that sexual relations are legitimate only for reproductive purposes. The crucial text is ambiguous: he says that appropriate sexual relations those that are "in marriage and aimed at the the reproduction of children" [*ta en gamōi kai epi genesei paidōn sunteloumena*], leaving it somewhat unclear whether a sexual act has to satisfy both of those conditions in order to be appropriate.[56] He clearly states that relations undertaken for the sake of "bare pleasure" [*psilēn hēdonēn*] are inappropriate, even inside marriage; but this leaves sexual acts undertaken to express the other aspects of marriage, such as friendship and partnership. And we do know that Musonius thinks reproduction an insufficient goal for marriage, if it is pursued without those other ends (*On the Goal*). We have no clear basis, then, for a firm conclusion about his attitude toward loving and friendly sexual acts that are not potentially reproductive, but the standing Roman conception of marriage as a partnership until death would have made it peculiar to deny the legitimacy of sexual relations between aging spouses, or even spouses one of whom has proven to be infertile. Even where abortion and contraception are concerned, Musonius's central concern is for population growth and the good of the city; and his main worry in the area of infanticide is that older children will encourage it in order to augment their inheritance.[57] So it seems plausible that Musonius's view is not precisely that sex should be limited to the reproductive; nonetheless, it is clear that sexual pleasure should never be pursued as an end in itself, and that the occasions for legitimate sexual activity are confined to marriage.

In some ways, in its actual historical context, this appears to be a remarkably feminist position, since it is in this way that Musonius argues against the sexual double standard. But it has the effect of maintaining in place a set of prohibitions against sexual expression that, in the real Roman world, were above all applied against women and used to confine them. The close linking of sex to reproduction, moreover, tends to perpetuate the confinement of women to a primarily domestic and maternal function, something that Musonius finds unproblematic but that we might not.

Not so his illustrious predecessors. Plato clearly believes that freeing women for guardianship and rule requires taking the burden of child rearing out of their hands. Guardian women will have numerous pregnancies, but the children will be taken away almost immediately to be reared by wet nurses and brought up in the public child care program. As for sexual relations, the eugenic purposes of the ideal city[58] impose tight limits on nonreproductive heterosexual sex for both sexes. But in book 7 we encounter reference to permissible indulgence of all the appetites "up to the point of health and well-being" (558D–559C, mentioning sexual intercourse after eating and drinking). This makes it plausible to suppose that some form of nonpassionate sexual release, perhaps with prostitutes, would be permitted, presumably to male and female on an equal basis so long as reproduction could be carefully controlled; and no restrictions on female same-sex relations are mentioned in the work, despite their presence in the roughly contemporaneous *Symposium*.

The Greek Cynics, like Plato, connected the equality of women with an overthrowing of sexual conventions. Diogenes' view that intercourse should be free, based only on persuasion and consent,[59] created an equality of sexual initiative and pleasure between male and female, separating sexuality from child rearing in the sense that the sexual couple would not have special responsibility for rearing any resulting children. Crates and Hipparchia did, of course, marry, but Musonius carefully omits the more scandalous aspects of their union when he cites Crates as an example of the married philosopher. In the full story, the fact of marriage is probably a result of Hipparchia's good birth and her need to get out of her parents' control somehow, but the marriage itself had a very unconventional character. In Musonius we hear nothing of the unisex clothing (D.L. 6.97), nothing of the infamous public lovemaking, nothing of how Hipparchia was not embarrassed when an angry sophist who had just lost an argument with her ripped off her cloak (D.L. 6.97). And Musonius carefully fails to comment on the fact that, despite all the famous lovemaking, and the longevity of the pair, there is no clear evidence of children.[60]

The Greek Stoics appear to have followed the Cynics' lead, at least in accounts of the ideal city, recommending that women be in common (D.L. 7.33), and "that men and women wear the same clothing and keep no part of the body entirely covered" (7.33). This last proposal presumably echoes the choice of Hipparchia and Crates, but it also goes straight back to the *Republic*, where Socrates made the injunction that women should exercise stripped[61] an extremely important part of the educational program of the ideal city—one that would inspire laughter when first presented, but one whose rationale would become clear over time. That rationale (inspired, in turn, by actual Spartan customs regarding women)[62] would seem to be to dispel the sense of distance and shame that men typically have before women's bodies, getting men used to seeing them as useful vehicles for civic and warlike action. Sexual relations in the ideal city seem to have followed the Cynic program: intercourse by decision, parental affection for all children, and by this radical strategy the removal of jealousy arising from adultery.[63] Zeno was certainly more interested in male-male sexual relations than in women; and Stoic definitions of *erōs* focus on that relationship.[64] But the best guess is that his *Republic* offered women freedom to pursue sexual relations without a focus on marriage or reproduction; apparently the "removal of jealousy" was seen as an essential prop for women's equality, the plausible thought being that the seclusion of women and other impediments to women's mobility and political functioning are inspired by anxiety about paternity, and that women cannot enjoy equality unless their sexuality ceases to inspire that type of anxious scrutiny. Furthermore, Zeno offered all women full military and civic equality, supporting that by a common scheme of child care. Even today, traditional marriage and child rearing make it difficult for women to enjoy full equality, even when they are wealthy and certainly if they are not so wealthy. At that time, even for wealthy women, the absence of reliable contraception and the early age of marriage would have made equality within traditional marriage yet more difficult.

In this line of illustrious feminists, Musonius is a sexual reactionary. He does not attempt to do away with the anxious scrutiny of female sexuality: indeed, he encourages it, telling his husbands that philosophy will contribute to female chastity. Nor does he at all attempt to do away with the traditional division of labor in child care: again, he encourages it, telling his husbands that philosophy will make women better at doing their own breast-feeding. Unisex clothing is nowhere to be seen: Musonius's frugal and shame-motivated wives will hardly disport themselves in the manner of Hipparchia. The end to the sexual double standard in this context seems less like a radical challenge to male prerogative than like a bandage over the wound caused to women by Musonius's profound assault on the Cynic and Stoic tradition of real equality and sexual freedom. No doubt there are some good things that such a solution brings with it: Musonius's conception of mutual loyalty and genuine partnership in marriage is a highly attractive one. But even someone who is sympathetic to Musonius's defense of monogamous partnerships has reason to be bothered by his defense of the institution of marriage as traditionally practiced. Crates and Hipparchia got to marital loyalty by mutual persuasion in a context of (philosophically constructed) social freedom. Musonius gets to loyalty by leaving repressive conventions largely unchallenged.

6. The voices of women. When one reads Musonius, one reads a lot *about* women. But after a while, the reader begins to notice that women themselves are more or less totally absent. The interlocutors in Musonius's works are always male: husbands who need to be persuaded to educate their wives, patresfamilias who need to hear that their daughters deserve the same education as sons. We get no sense that Musonius is teaching women, or addressing any of his arguments directly to them.

Women figure in the text, too, in a highly abstract and remote fashion.

In *Should Daughters and Sons*, the only women named are the Amazons and the murderous Eriphyle—despite the fact that Roman life provided a rich range of cases of female excellence, from the noble matronae of legend to more recent examples—Agrippina accompanying the remains of her husband Germanicus, the wife of Stoic Thrasea Paetus, joining him in death on behalf of republican liberty, even that remarkable other Agrippina, who resourcefully eluded her son Nero's murder plots again and again, once by a long swim in inhospitable waters. Tacitus and Livy tell us far more about female excellence than Musonius does, since they put real women on the page.[65]

In *That Women Too*, it is even more damaging that no concrete woman is named. One excellent way of arguing that women can do philosophy would have been to point out that they have done so, and a wealth of examples lay ready to hand: Aspasia the learned hetaira; the two hetairai who apparently studied in Plato's Academy;[66] the famous Hipparchia, who even gets her own chapter in Diogenes Laertius; the five daughters of Diodorus Cronus, all of whom are said to have studied dialectic;[67] women recorded in the evidence about Epicurus's school;[68] neo-Pythagorean women of Musonius's own day;[69] female pupils of the Greek and Roman Stoics. Musonius, unlike Seneca, is not a philosopher who uses concrete examples much; but his omissions here are nonetheless striking. Particularly glaring is the absence of Hipparchia, since Musonius discusses Crates and his marriage extensively, along with those of Socrates and Pythagoras, in arguing that marriage is no impediment to the philosopher. Why didn't he even name the famous philosopher-bride, or mention that marriage was no impediment to her either? This issue seems to be connected to the issue about interests and rights, for women are always treated as beings who have a good that we are trying to promote, not as active subjects who have claims, and voices, and demands.

For this absence of female images and voices, we must hold Musonius himself to blame—or at least the tradition that reports his work. It is not a characteristic of Roman authors to omit female agency; indeed, Roman women emerge from historical, rhetorical, poetic, and philosophical texts as an extraordinary group. We know that the Greek Stoics were often rather abstract: Cicero criticizes them for just this, finding it a philosophical defect. But still, Chrysippus is said to have copied the whole of Euripides' *Medea* in one of his works, and Epictetus, another relatively abstract philosopher, speaks about Medea's heroic strength in a very interesting way. Plato is abstract about women only because he is so absorbed in giving vivid descrip-

tions of male-male love and so relatively uninterested in and contemptuous of marriage; this certainly is not Musonius's excuse, since he exalts marriage and criticizes male-male relations. And even Plato gives us Diotima,
and Aspasia, and the example of Alcestis's devotion. Musonius has no excuse, then, for his lack of curiosity about women, real and mythical. All we
can say on his behalf is that this remoteness from the surrounding social
context is a common characteristic of writers of the Second Sophistic,
within which group we might plausibly place him, and for these writers the
difficulty of addressing the actual political context is surely among the dis-
incentives to concrete engagement with the Rome of their time or recent
times. Even this, however, by no means excuses his silence about historical
and mythical exempla.

⟋⟍

Musonius Rufus remains a remarkable character. Viewed in the most generous light, he combines the radical Stoic commitment to sex equality with
an appreciation of the possibilities of marriage that he derives from a Roman culture in which mutually loving companionate unions had become
an accepted goal, and to a large extent a reality. Viewed in the least generous light, he compromises the original Stoic dedication to sex equality by
his acceptance of Roman traditions of patriarchy and female purity. Both
assessments say something true about Musonius, and about the goals of
feminism. If one plausible feminist goal is to make it possible for men and
women to be fully equal in education and in self-command, to enjoy full
civic and legal equality, and to love each other on terms of autonomous
choice and full equality, Musonius has indeed mapped out a part of the
route to that goal—but only a part. And in giving us that part he has rejected Platonic, Cynic, and Stoic ideas that seem in their own way essential
for the full articulation of the goal.

Perhaps this just shows us what we should have known already: how
hard it is to combine full equality of the sexes with companionate marriage
and the rearing of children in nuclear families. It is not too surprising that
none of these philosophers thinks it can be done. Most modern feminists remain skeptical about the combination too, whether they choose the
path of Musonius or the path of Hipparchia. But if the combination can be
worked out, Musonius's ideas about equal education, the equal development of practical reason, and the equal sharing of marital love and responsibility are some of the ideas that will help us do it—so long as we are
careful not to forget just how incomplete they are.

313

Appendix

Texts by MUSONIUS RUFUS

Translations by MARTHA C. NUSSBAUM

Should Daughters Get the Same Education as Sons? (Complete Text)

Once when the question was put to him, whether sons and daughters should get the same education [*paideian*], he said: (A) Trainers of horses and dogs make no distinction in their training between the male and the female. For female dogs are taught to hunt just as males are, and one can see no difference in the training of female horses, if what is wanted is for them to do a horse's work well, and the training of male horses. In the case of humans, however, it seems to be thought necessary to provide males with something superior in their education and upbringing by comparison to females, as if (B) it were not essential that the same excellences should belong to both men and women alike, or as if it were possible to arrive at the same excellences not through the same, but through different, education.

(C) And yet that there is not one set of excellences for a woman and another for a man is easy to grasp. In the first place, a man must have understanding [*phronein*], and so too must a woman. What after all would be the use of a foolish man or woman? Then it is essential no less for the one than for the other to live justly. For the man who is unjust would not be a good citizen, and the woman who is unjust would not be a good manager of the household. If she is unjust she will do wrong to her husband, as they say Eriphyle did. Again, it is a good thing for a woman to be self-controlled [*sōphronein*], but it is good as well for a man. For the law decrees the same penalty for male as for female adultery [*to moicheuein tōi moicheuesthai*]. Gluttony, drunkenness, and other related vices, which are vices of excess and bring disgrace in a big way upon those are in their grip, show that self-control is most necessary for every human being, female and male alike. For the only escape from wantonness is through self-control; there is no other. (D) Perhaps someone may say that courage [*andreian*] is an excellence appropriate to men only. That is not so. For the best woman must also be courageous [*andrizesthai*] and free from cowardice, so that she will not bend under either hardship or fear. If not, how will she even have self-control, if someone can force her to put up with some shameful act by terrifying her or making her endure hardships? But furthermore, it is necessary for women to be able to fight defensively [*amuntikōs echein*], unless indeed, by Zeus, they are to appear more cowardly than hens and other female birds, which fight with creatures much larger than themselves in defense of their chicks. How then should women not need courage? That women partake in the skill of armed fighting the race of the Amazons proved, when they defeated many other tribes in war. If, therefore, other women lack something of their ability, it is due to lack of practice, rather than because they lack some innate equipment.

(E) If, then, the same excellences befit men and women, the same upbringing and education must be appropriate for both. For in the case of every animal and plant, one must produce the excellence appropriate to it by applying the correct sort of concern. Surely if men and women needed in a similar way to be able to play the *aulos,* and this was necessary for the life of both of them, then we would teach both the skill of *aulos* playing on an equal basis, and if both had to learn to play the *kithara* [lacuna]. And if both need to become good, possessing the excellence that is appropriate to human beings, and to be similarly capable of practical reasoning [*phronein*] and self-control and of sharing in courage and justice, one no less than the other, won't we then educate them both similarly, and teach the skill from which one becomes a good human being to both on an equal basis [*ep'ison*]? Surely we are obliged to do it this way, and no other way.

(F) "Come now," I suppose someone will say, "Do you expect that men should learn spinning the same as women, and that women should pursue physical exercise the same as men?" No, I would not require this. But I do say that, since in the human species the male body is stronger and the female body weaker, tasks should be assigned that are suited to the capacities of each—the heavier tasks to the physically stronger and the lighter to the weaker. Thus, spinning and indoor work would generally be more fitting for women than for men, while exercise and outdoor work would be suited to men. Sometimes, however, some men might plausibly undertake the lighter jobs and what is considered women's work, and again women might perform heavier jobs that seem more to be suited for men, whenever conditions of body or need or circumstance warrant. For all human tasks, I think, belong to us in common, and are common to both men and women, and none is necessarily appointed for one rather than the other, but some are more convenient for the capacities of one, some for the other, and for this reason some are called men's work and some women's work.

(G) But whatever things have reference to excellence, these one would correctly say are equally appropriate to the capacities of both, inasmuch as we agree that the excellences are in no way more appropriate to one rather than the other. (H) Hence, I think it is plausible that whatever has reference to excellence should be taught to male and female alike; and furthermore that straight from infancy they should be taught that this is good and that bad, and that it is the same for both alike; and that this is helpful, this harmful, that one must do this and must not do that. From this education practical wisdom [*phronēsis*] develops in those who learn, in boys and girls [*korais kai korois*] alike, and one group is no different from the other. Then again, we must produce proper shame toward everything disgraceful [*aischron*]. When this is present, it is necessary that both men and women will be self-controlled. And indeed, the person who is correctly educated, whoever it is, whether male or female, must become accustomed to endure hardship, and not to fear death, and not to be brought low by any misfortune. Through such training a person will be courageous. A little while ago it was demonstrated that women too should partake in courage. Then again, to avoid unfair grasping, to honor equality of condition [*isotēta*], and to want to do good and not to do harm to human beings, being a human being oneself, this is an especially fine teaching and makes those who learn it just. Why should a male be especially suited to learn this? If, by Zeus, it is fitting that women should be just, then they both need to learn these things, inasmuch as they are the most pertinent and the most important.

(I) If it happens that a man will know some detail about some particular technical matter that a woman doesn't know, or, again, that she will knows something that he does not know, this does not yet suggest any difference in the education of the two. But about the really important things let one not know something and the other not, but let them both know the same things. (J) If you ask me what knowledge supervises this education, I shall reply that just as without philosophy no man would be properly educated, so too no woman would be. I don't mean that women should possess professional competence in logic and sophistical cleverness of a high degree if they are going to pursue philosophy as women. I do not admire this sort of thing much in men either. But they should acquire excellence of character and nobility of life; and philosophy, and nothing else, is training in nobility.

That Women Too Should Do Philosophy (Complete Text)

When someone asked him whether women too should do philosophy, this is how he began to argue that they should. He said: (A) Women have received from the gods the same rational faculty [*logon*] as men, the faculty that we use to communicate with one another and to reason about each thing, whether it is a good thing or not, and whether it is noble or shameful. Similarly, the female has the same faculties of sense perception as the male: sight, hearing, smelling, and the rest. Similarly, each has the same bodily parts, and neither has any part that the other doesn't have. Furthermore, a desire [orexis] for ethical excellence and a natural orientation toward it [oikeiōsis phusei] belong not only to men, but also to women. For women no less than men are pleased by noble and just actions, and reject the opposite. (B) Since this is the way things are, why on earth would it be appropriate [prosēkoi] for men to inquire and examine how one should live well—which is what it is to do philosophy—and women not?

(C) Is it because it is appropriate for men to be good, and women not? (D) Let us now examine one by one each of the qualities that befit [prosēkontōn] a woman who is going to be good. For it emerges that each of these accrues to her especially through the practice of philosophy. In the first place, a woman must be a good household manager and a careful accountant of what is advantageous to the household, and a director of the household staff. I claim that these qualities are especially likely to belong to a woman who pursues philosophy. For, as is obvious, each of these is a part of life, and philosophy is nothing other than systematic understanding of how to conduct one's life, and the philosopher, as Socrates used to say, spends his whole life investigating "What is bad and good in the dwelling places." But a woman should certainly also be self-controlled [sōphrona]: she must not have illicit sexual relations, and must be free of all uncontrol [akrasias] with respect to other pleasures, not being a slave to appetites, or a lover of quarreling, or extravagant, or vain. Those are the acts of a self-controlled person, and in addition I would add: to control one's temper, not to be wiped out by pain, to be stronger than any suffering. But philosophical argument provides all this. For someone who studies those teachings and practices them will, I think, become most orderly [kosmiōtatos], whether male or female. Well then, so much for that issue. As for justice, would not the woman who pursues philosophy be just, and a blameless partner in life, a good fellow agent of agreements, a concerned nurturer of her husband and children, and entirely free of greed [philokerdeias] and unfair grasping [pleonexias]? And who would be like this more than the woman trained in philosophy? For she of necessity, if she has really pursued philosophy, would consider doing wrong worse than being wronged, insofar as it is more shameful, and being cheated better than unfair grasping, and would also love her children more than her life. What woman would be more just than one like this? And indeed, as for courage, certainly it is to be expected that the educated woman will be more courageous than the uneducated, and one who has studied philosophy more than one who has not; and she will not submit to anything shameful out of fear of death or unwillingness to endure suffering, and she will not be intimidated by anyone because he is well born or powerful or rich or, by Zeus, because he is a tyrant. For in fact she has schooled herself to have self-esteem [*mega phronein*] and to think that death is not an evil, and life not a good, and similarly not to shun hardship or to pursue freedom from hardship at all costs. So it is plausible that such a woman would be autonomous [*autourgikēn*] and capable of enduring difficulty, for example, nursing her children from her own breast and serving her husband with her own hands, and to do, without shrinking, things that many think suited to slaves. Would such a woman not be a great help to the man who married her, an adornment to her relatives, a good example to all those who know her?

(E) Yes, but by Zeus, some people will say, it is inevitable that women who study with the philosophers will be, for the most part, stubborn and bold. They will abandon their housework and come into the company of men and busy themselves with arguments and fine logical distinctions and the dissection of inferences, when they should be at home doing the spinning. (F) For my part, however, I would not think it right that either philosophizing women or philosophizing men should leave their appointed practical duties to deal only in arguments. But whatever arguments [*logous*] they undertake, I say that these should be undertaken for the sake of deeds [*erga*]. For just as a medical argument is no use, unless it contributes to the healing of a human body, so if a philosopher has or teaches an argument, it is no use, unless it contributes to the excellence of the human soul. (G) Above all, one should consider whether the argument that we think philosophizing women should follow can possibly make them bold when it teaches that proper shame [*aidō*] is the greatest good, whether the argument teaching the greatest prudence produces heedless living, whether the argument showing that wantonness is the greatest evil doesn't teach self-control [*sōphronein*], whether the argument that says household management is an excellence doesn't spur them on to manage the household. Philosophical argument also calls women to love and [lacuna] to act for herself [*autourgein*].

What Is the Goal of Marriage? (Complete Text)

The goal of marriage is a partnership [*koinōnian*] of living and having children. Husband and wife, he used to say, should come together in order to live together with one another, and also to reproduce, and also to regard all things in common between them, and nothing private [*idion*] to one or to the other, not even the body itself. The birth of a human being that results from such a yoking is a great thing. But this is not yet enough for marriage, inasmuch as quite apart from marriage it could result from any other sexual mating, just as when animals mate with one another. But in marriage there must be in every respect a merger of life and a mutual caring between husband and wife, whether in health or in sickness and in every circumstance. It was aiming at this, as well as at begetting children, that each of them entered marriage. Where this mutual care is complete, and both partners provide it to one another completely, competing with one another for victory in this achievement, the marriage is appropriate and one to be emulated. For this sort of partnership is a fine thing. But where each looks only to his own interest neglecting the other, or, by Zeus, when one is like this, and lives in the same house with the other, but looks elsewhere in his mind, and is not willing to pull together with his yoke-mate and to breathe together, then their partnership will be bound to fall apart, and though they are living together, things will go badly with them. Eventually they separate entirely or they stay together in a state worse than loneliness.

On Sexual Intercourse (Extract)

[Musonius criticizes all forms of intercourse undertaken for pleasure alone, even when no issue of marriage is concerned] "By Zeus," someone says, "it's not like when an adulterer wrongs [adikei] the husband of the ruined [diephtharmenēs] woman, it's not like that when someone has intercourse with a hetaira: he doesn't wrong anyone or deprive anyone of a hope of children." [Musonius replies that, nonetheless, the person makes himself worse, being overtaken by pleasure and delighting in sex the way pigs do.] And such a person, not least of all, is the man who is intimate with his own female slave, which some people think is especially blameless, given that every master has full authority to use his slave in any way he wants. To this, my reply is simple. If someone thinks it is not shameful or out of place for a master to be intimate with his own slave, especially if she happens to be a widow, then let him consider what he would think if the mistress of the house were to be intimate with a male slave. For wouldn't he think this unbearable, not only if a woman who has a lawful husband had relations with a slave, but also if an unmarried woman did this? And yet surely he will not judge that men are inferior to women, or less capable of disciplining their own appetites—the stronger in judgment inferior to the weaker, and the rulers to the ruled. For it is fitting that men should be much stronger than women, if indeed they deem it right that they should have superiority over [*prosestanai*] women. If, however, they are revealed to be less self-controlled [lacuna] and worse. Why do we even need to argue that it is a case of *akrasia* and nothing else, when a master is intimate with a female slave? Everyone knows this.

Whether Marriage Is an Impediment to Doing Philosophy (Extract)

When someone said to him that marriage and life with a wife seemed to be an impediment to doing philosophy, Musonius said that it wasn't an impediment to Pythagoras, or to Socrates, or to Crates, each of whom lived with a wife. And yet one could not find better philosophers than these. Indeed, Crates married despite the fact that he was utterly without an estate or goods or property. Then, since he didn't have a residence of his own, he spent his days and nights with his wife in the public stoas of Athens. And do we, who set out from a household, and some of us have servants to wait on us, nonetheless dare to assert that marriage is an impediment to philosophy? In fact, the philosopher is surely a teacher and leader of all human beings with regard to what is fitting for a human being by nature. And if there is anything that is in accordance with nature, marriage clearly is. For what purpose, after all, did the craftsman of the human species in the beginning cut our kind into two, and then make two types of genitals, the one female and the other male, and then make in each a strong desire [*epithumian ischuran*] for the other, for association [*homilias*] and partnership [*koinōnias*], and mix into both a strong longing [*pothon ischuron*] for one another, in the male for the female and in the female for the male? Isn't it clear that he wanted them to be together [*suneinai*] and to live together and to devise together [*summēchanasthai*] things for one another's livelihood, and to engage together in the reproduction and rearing of children, so that our species will be eternal?

Notes

I would like to thank Simon Goldhill, Miriam Griffin, Stephen Halliwell, David Halperin, Christopher Jones, Robert Kaster, Richard Saller, Malcolm Schofield, and David Sedley for their helpful comments on a previous draft. I am also grateful to Gretchen Reydam-Schils for showing me a draft of an unpublished work on marriage. I wish to dedicate this chapter to the memory of G. E. M. de Ste. Croix, a great scholar whose work was animated equally by a love of the truth and a passion for justice, prominently including justice for women. When I was a young scholar in Oxford in 1973, he warmly encouraged my work. He died in 2000 at the age of ninety.

1. Musonius's surviving texts and fragments (largely preserved through citation in Stobaeus) are edited by O. Hense, *Musonius Rufus, Reliquiae* (Leipzig: Teubner, 1905).

2. It is likely, though not certain, that Musonius taught in Greek, and we simply do not know whether he wrote treatises. As to the date of his lectures, we hear most about Musonius during the reign of Nero, but there is little in the text itself to help us. The only indication is a reference to "kings in Syria" (Hense 32.5–6). If that means the Commagenian dynasty, it should refer to a time before 72 or 73 (*Prosopographia Imperii Romani*, 2d ed., 1.149). The end of the kingdom of Emesa is less securely dated; Fergus Millar (*The Roman Near East, 31 B.C.– A.D. 37* [Cambridge, Mass.: Harvard University Press, 1993], 84) puts it tentatively in the 70s. On the other hand, Dio of Prusa and Pliny (see *Ep.* 3.11.5) could not have heard him before about 80. So it is possible that the surviving lectures represent work developed over a period of time.

3. See Cora Lutz, "Musonius Rufus: The Roman Socrates," *Yale Classical Studies* 10 (1947): 3–147, at 3–4, discussing evidence from Philostratus and Julian as well. The phrase "the Roman Socrates" was used of Musonius by R. Hirzel, *Der Dialog* (Leipzig: Teubner, 1895) 2:239.

4. A. A. Long and D. N. Sedley, *The Hellenistic Philosophers* (Cambridge: Cambridge University Press, 1984).

5. All the translations from Musonius in this chapter are my own — not because I do not admire the Lutz translation, but because I want to draw attention to certain philosophical terms and therefore to provide an extremely literal and inelegant version. Also useful is the French translation by A. J. Festugière, *Deux Prédicateurs de l'antiquité: Télès et Musonius* (Paris: J. Vrin, 1978), with some introductory remarks and notes.

6. G. E. M. de Ste. Croix, *The Class Struggle in the Ancient Greek World* (London: Duckworth, 1981). Women are discussed on pp. 98–111; Musonius on p.110.

7. As readers of de Ste. Croix know, his animus toward the upper classes is exceeded only by his animus toward Christianity. He used to remark frequently that the three most evil influences on our civilization were Plato, Saint Paul, and Augustine — Saint Paul being the worst.

8. De Ste. Croix focuses in particular on the law of marriage at Rome and the rights it allowed to women, showing that Christians repeatedly sought the abolition of divorce by consent, a tendency that he calls "disastrous, . . . productive of much unnecessary suffering" (*The Class Struggle*, 108). Musonius is held to be in advance even of Roman culture, Rome in general in advance of Christian proposals.

9. Michel Foucault, *Le Souci de Soi*, vol. 3 of *Histoire de la sexualité* (Paris: Gallimard, 1984); English translation by R. Hurley as *The Care of the Self*, vol. 3 of *The History of Sexuality* (New York: Pantheon, 1985), chap. 5, pp. 173–216. The only rival is A. C. Van Geytenbeek, *Musonius Rufus and Greek Diatribe*, original 1948, rev. ed., trans. B. L. Hijmans, Jr. (Assen: Van Gorcum, 1962), a rather detailed treatment that certainly devotes much more attention than does Foucault to Musonius's links with Platonism and earlier Stoicism and that makes a valuable contribution by comparing the works on women to later neo-Pythagorean works by Phintys and Periktione. But Van Geytenbeek does not have very many *ideas* about what is going on, and his treatment of earlier Stoic views on sex equality is highly idiosyncratic: relying on the premise that women as a class have a "rich emotional life," he concludes quickly that any school that urges the extirpation of passion cannot possibly believe in the equality of the sexes (57). But

of course the Stoics hold that the passions are socially taught false judgments, for women as much as for men. Nor does the monograph attempt in any way to link Musonius to his Roman social context. Far more interesting and provocative is Simon Goldhill's treatment of Musonius in *Foucault's Virginity: Ancient Erotic Fiction and the History of Sexuality* (Cambridge: Cambridge University Press, 1995), 133–43; but Goldhill's focus is primarily on Musonius's relationship to contemporary nonphilosophical texts on sex and love, and he says little either about the structure of Musonius's arguments or about their philosophical antecedents.

10. Susan Treggiari, *Roman Marriage: Iusti Coniuges from the Time of Cicero to the Time of Ulpian* (Oxford: Clarendon Press, 1991). Discussion of Musonius is found primarily on pp. 221–23.

11. Other recent works that make some contribution to issues surrounding Musonius include C. E. Manning, "Seneca and the Stoics on the Equality of the Sexes," *Mnemosyne*, 4th ser., 26 (1973): 170–77; Daniel Babut, "Les Stoïciens et l'amour," *Revue des études grecques* 76 (1963): 55–63; and Marcel Benabou, "Pratique matrimoniale et représentation philosophique: Le Crépuscule des stratégies," *Annales ESC*, November–December. 1987, pp. 1255–66.

12. An important source for the subsequent tradition is *Meno* 72A, apparently the referent of Aristotle's critique of Socrates when he argues, in *Politics* 1.13, that Socrates was wrong to hold that male and female have the same excellence (1260a20–24).

13. "Whether Marriage Is an Impediment to Doing Philosophy"; see the appendix.

14. See "What Is the Appropriate Livelihood for a Philosopher?" in Hense 57–63.

15. For an excellent attempt to recover what we do know, see M. Schofield, *The Stoic Idea of the City* (Cambridge: Cambridge University Press, 1992).

16. The Socratic Antisthenes is also said to have held the view that male and female have the same *aretē* (D.L. 6.12). Diodorus Cronus was said to have had five daughters who all learned dialectic (see discussion in n. 67 below).

17. The most thorough and convincing treatment of Plato's arguments on women in *Republic 5* is in Stephen Halliwell, *Plato: Republic 5* (Warminster: Aris and Phillips, 1993), 9–16.

18. Both in my discussion and in my translation, I use "excellence" for *aretē*, in light of the fact that Musonius, like Plato, uses it to designate outstanding characteristics generally (e.g., of plants and animals), not only ethical qualities; occasionally I add the word "ethical" before "excellence," where it is clear that Musonius is speaking of the canonical human virtues, and where failure to spell that out might be misleading.

19. See G. F. Hourani, "The Education of the Third Class in Plato's *Republic*," *Classical Quarterly* 43 (1949): 58–60; see also T. H. Irwin, *Plato's Moral Theory* (Oxford: Clarendon Press, 1977), 329–31.

20. Hense, 6, a work called simply "By Musonius."

21. On Musonius's account of the moral excellences, Van Geytenbeek's discussion in *Musonius Rufus and Greek Diatribe*, 26ff., is helpful: he observes that in general Musonius places less stress on the intellectual aspects of the excellences than did Chrysippus. My own sense is that this is a difference of emphasis only: Musonius still insists that philosophy is the only art that will deliver the right result, so he is clearly thinking of excellence as requiring knowledge of what is to be chosen.

22. Compare Cicero, *Tusculan Disputations* 2, which treats the courage to surmount physical pain as a male trait, associated with war, athletics, and the public life in general; 2.43 reminds us that *virtus* derives from *vir*. He offers only two examples of female courage: the ability of old women to go without food (40), and the military fortitude of Spartan women (36). (An exception to the generally negative portrayal of women in *Tusculan Disputations* is 1.27–28, where Cicero includes women among the heroes who have gone to heaven.) The failure to treat female courage more fully is especially striking in light of the death of Tullia, apparently from complications of childbirth, only several months before the composition of the work. Given his evident love for her and grief at her death, might Cicero not have seen in her endurance of pain a distinguished example of courage? (For discussion of Cicero's views, I am grateful to Gretchen Reydams-Schils.)

Goldhill, *Foucault's Virginity*, has a valuable discussion of this passage, pp. 137–42. He emphasizes the boldness of the choice of *andrizesthai*, noting that in texts of the period it can even denote playing the male role in sexual intercourse. The "virile woman" is a figure of fear, he shows, in much of Greek literature; in Xenophon's *Oeconomicus* Socrates' remark on the manly (*andrikē*) quality of Ischomachus's wife is sometimes read as approving. but Goldhill argues against this reading with reference to the scandalous career of the real-life original. Goldhill concludes that "Musonius' bold expression that a 'woman should be manly,' then, goes beyond other Greek writings." (He offers no more than a passing glance at Plato and says nothing about the Greek Stoa, however.)

23. See Schofield's general argument (in *The Stoic Idea*) that all functions were open to both sexes, and that the society was organized along military and erotic lines in a way reminiscent of Spartan norms.

24. Goldhill, *Foucault's Virginity*, pointing to the standard negative evaluation of the Amazons (but apparently not aware of their appearance in the *Laws*), calls Musonius's claim culturally "counterintuitive," and says that "Musonius strains against the boundaries of convention and tradition." This he does indeed, but with Plato on his side.

25. See Thomas Laqueur, *Making Sex: Body and Gender from the Greeks to Freud* (Cambridge, Mass.: Harvard University Press, 1990).

26. One might wonder about "gods"in the plural, but Stoic texts often use the plural, despite the official focus on Zeus.

27. D.L. 6.97. Hipparchia's sophism: "Any action that would not be called wrong if done by Theodorus, would not be called wrong if done by Hipparchia. Theodorus does no wrong when he strikes himself. So: Hipparchia does no wrong if she strikes Theodorus."

28. For Stoic attitudes toward logical distinctions, see Jonathan Barnes's *Logic and the Imperial Stoa* (Leiden: Brill, 1997); see also my *Therapy of Desire* (Princeton, N.J.: Princeton University Press, 1994), chap. 9.

29. For Stoic and other uses of this analogy, see Nussbaum, *Therapy*, chap. 9. The analogy is so common in Stoicism that Cicero protests that he is "tired" of the Stoics' excessive use of such analogies (*Tusc.* 4.23).

30. See *tas prosiousas tois philosophois gunaikas*, in *That Women Too*, sec. E. This is the standard way of talking about enrolling oneself as a pupil of someone.

31. Tullia was married by age sixteen, and her father took little interest in her further education. As Ernst Badian nicely puts the matter in his article in the new *Oxford Classical Dictionary*, "Cicero, though sincerely attached to her, had taken little account of her happiness, but was overwhelmed by her death. He proposed to build a shrine for her, ultimately had to abandon the project, and turned to philosophy for consolation."

32. See Treggiari, *Roman Marriage*, passim, and see also the subtle treatment in Reydams-Schils (ms.), who correctly argues that Musonius makes the affectional aspect of marriage to some extent independent of the reproductive.

33. For a history of the marital double standard in this period, see Benabou, "Pratique matrimoniale."

34. See Schofield, *The Stoic Idea*; and Nussbaum, "*Erōs* and the Wise: The Stoic Response to a Cultural Dilemma," *Oxford Studies in Ancient Philosophy* 13 (1995): 231–67.

35. *Republic* 540C: Glaucon has referred to the rulers using the masculine (also the unmarked) form of the accusative present participle, *archontas*. *Kai archousas ge*, replies Socrates, apparently convinced that the failure to use the feminine form may give rise to the false impression that only males are to be included.

36. See Manning, "Seneca and the Stoics," citing Cicero *De Officiis* 1.130 and Epictetus *Disc.* 1.16.11–14.

37. There are complexities here too, given the complex associations of the *aulos* with extreme emotionality; but let us assume for the sake of argument that they are equal.

38. Treggiari, *Roman Marriage*, 146–47.

39. See ibid., chap. 4, passim. See chap. 2 for extensive discussion of the elaborate rules of marriage-eligibility, and the procedures for signifying "marital intent."

40. See the review of the evidence in Treggiari, *Roman Marriage*, 264–75. Caesar praises the strict customs of the Gauls, whose men have power of life and death over their wives as well as their children, implying that husbands at Rome have no such official power (*BGall.* 1.58.4).

41. Treggiari, *Roman Marriage*, 284.

42. Ibid., 284.

43. See ibid., 282–83. The father has to catch the daughter in the act, and to kill daughter and lover in one "immediate and uninterrupted act." If he kills only one of them, or kills one and merely wounds the other, he can be tried for murder; and he must kill with his own hand.

44. Ibid., 275.

45. If the marriage continues, however, the wife apparently cannot be prosecuted for adultery by a third party—Treggiari, *Roman Marriage*, 286; continuation of the marriage is taken as a sign that the marriage ought not to be disturbed.

46. Ibid., 288–89.

47. Ibid., 289–90.

48. See ibid., 277ff.

49. Ibid., 285.

50. See ibid., 293.

51. Ibid., passim, but on Augustus 292–93; Treggiari approvingly cites Leo Raditsa's judgment that "the whole conception of the Roman past upon which he sought to erect the moral and spiritual basis of the New State was in a large measure imaginary or spurious."

52. H. Last, *Cambridge Ancient History* (Cambridge: Cambridge University Press) 10.447; P. E. Corbett, *The Roman Law of Marriage* (Oxford: Clarendon Press, 1930), quoted by Treggiari, *Roman Marriage*, p. 291.

53. For further discussion of this parallel, see my "Kant and Stoic Cosmopolitanism," *Journal of Political Philosophy* 5 (1997): 1–25.

54. One should not deny that Seneca adds other less dignity-based considerations. Part of his argument, like Musonius's, appeals to the moral damage done to the slave owner by overindulgence; and part appeals to considerations of safety, claiming that well-treated slaves are less likely to rebel and kill their owners.

55. Foucault, *History of Sexuality*, vols. 2 and 3, passim; Treggiari, *Roman Marriage*, esp. 316; de Ste. Croix, *The Class Struggle*, 103–10.

56. Van Geytenbeek, *Musonius Rufus*, 71, without argument, takes it that it *is* clear that all nonreproductive acts are inappropriate and remarks on the unparalleled stringency of that position.

57. *Should One Raise All the Children Who Are Born?* Hense 77–81.

58. The best treatment of these schemes, and the problems understanding them presents, is in Halliwell, *Plato: Republic 5*.

59. D.L. 6.72: "He [Diogenes the Cynic] said that women should be in common, and he recognized no institution of marriage, believing that a man who persuades should have intercourse with [*suneinai*] a woman who is persuaded. And he thought that in this way children too should be in common."

60. Diogenes cites a verse of Menander's *Twin Sisters* that alludes to a daughter of Crates, and a month-long trial marriage that he allegedly arranged for her. But this can easily be interpreted as scandal and hyperbole, since allowing such a breach of conventions regarding virginity, as a father, would be about the most shocking thing a Cynic could have done.

61. Halliwell, *Plato: Republic 5*, argues plausibly that *gumnos* need not mean completely nude, but would be compatible with a loincloth and perhaps also a breastband.

62. See ibid.

63. D.L. 7.131. Note that Diogenes Laertius presents the Stoics as holding that "a man who meets a woman can have intercourse with the woman he meets" [*ton entuchonta tēi entuchousēi chrēsthai*], removing the Cynic emphasis on persuasion. Whether this has any significance is unclear. Another text relating to Zeno and Chrysippus holds that the sage will marry and have children (7.121); the conflict between the two texts has generated a large scholarly literature, well summarized in Schofield, *The Stoic Idea*, appendix D. With Schofield, I think that the grounds for ascribing this view to Zeno's *Republic* are weak; either it is a later view only loosely connected with Zeno, or it may possibly reflect a view of the way a Stoic will live under nonideal conditions.

64. See Nussbaum, "Erōs and the Wise," discussing evidence from Sextus and other sources.

65. See also the wide-ranging discussions of Roman portrayals of women in Eva Cantarella, *Passato Prossimo: Donne romane da Tacita a Sulpicia* (Milan: Feltrinelli, 1996).

66. See D.L. 3.46: Axiothea (who dressed like a man) and Lastheneia are named. A recent papyrus discovery has confirmed Diogenes' report: see discussion in Mary Lefkowitz, *Women in Greek Myth* (Baltimore: Johns Hopkins University Press, 1986).

67. See *Socraticorum Reliquiae*, ed. Gabriele Giannantoni (Naples: Bibliopolis, 1983), 1:76. Clement of Alexandria (*Strom.* 4.19.121,5) says, "The daughters of Diodorus Cronus were all trained in dialectic, as Philo the dialectician says in his *Menexenus*. Their names were Menexena, Argeia, Theognis, Artemisia, and Pantakleia." Hieronymus (*Adv. Iovinian.* 1.42) adds that the five were "renowned for their chastity" [*insignis pudicitiae*], and that Philo wrote a full history about them.

68. See my *Therapy*, chap. 4, for this evidence.

69. Fragments are attributed to Theano (*On Piety*), Phintys (*On Moderation of Women*), Perictione (*On Harmony of Women* and *On Wisdom*), and, possibly, Aesara (*On Human Nature*). See Holger Thesleff, ed., *The Pythagorean Texts of the Hellenistic Period* (Åbo: Åbo Akademi, 1965); and for a good comprehensive summary, ranging over all the schools, see Victoria Lynn Harper, "Women in Philosophy," *Oxford Classical Dictionary*, 3d ed. (1996), pp. 1625–26.

Chapter Twelve

EROS AND *APHRODISIA*
IN THE WORKS OF DIO CHRYSOSTOM

✖

J. Samuel Houser

𝒟uring the early years of this decade John Winkler and David Halperin turned their attention to Dio Chrysostom's condemnation of prostitution at the end of his *Euboean Discourse* (7.133–52). There, Dio insists that prostitution has no place in the ideal city and explores the consequences of allowing prostitution to flourish. Indeed, he indicates that those who visit prostitutes will whet their desire for sexual pleasure, and that these *akolastoi*, as he calls them, will turn from prostitutes to the women of noble households and finally to the corruption of the youths therein, youths who will be the future leaders of the city.[1] This last step exceeds "the limit of nature" (ὅρον τὸν τῆς φύσεως) and constitutes a form of *hybris* "greater and more lawless" (μείζω καὶ παρανομωτέραν ὕβριν) than the seduction of women and will bring shame upon (καταισχύνειν) the youths seduced.

Both Winkler and Halperin have used this passage as evidence for their arguments on different aspects of sexual behavior and its representation in Greece. Winkler studies rhetorical appeals to "nature" in ancient discussions about sexual behavior. Examining a variety of sources, he concludes that, from a scholar's detached perspective, the precise meaning and significance of "nature" shifts from culture to culture, and indeed from context to context. In general, Winkler finds that participants in a culture regard behavior that is conventional as "natural," while the unconventional is marked out as "unnatural." He accordingly observes that "natural" in Greek texts usually means "conventional and proper."[2] As for Dio's use of "nature" in the *Euboean Discourse*, Winkler observes Dio's praise for the virtuous simplicity of his impoverished Euboean hosts and his criticism of the self-indulgence of city life, which includes the availability of prostitutes. He points to several passages where Dio praises the simple life of the poor rural dweller as "natural." His treatment of the seduction of youths then must be interpreted in the context of the discourse's "thematic of expenditure and loss," where "unnatural" refers to "behavior that is self-indulgent, luxurious, and exceedingly appealing," rather than that which "contravenes the necessary order of the world." According to this point of view, sex not aimed at procreation is not natural. Above all, it is a crime against nature to treat the future leaders of the city as prostitutes.[3]

David Halperin too discusses this passage, though in a different context. He argues that sexual behavior in Greece was an expression of political and social relations, a "generalized ethos of penetration and domination" which made penetration of a social and political inferior, whether male or female, one criterion for virility, and penetration of a social or political peer unacceptable. According to Halperin, the biological sex of the insertee was of no consequence for evaluating the virility of the active performer.[4] To support this position, Halperin cites our passage above, where Dio simply assumes that one who is interested in penetrating females will also be interested in penetrating males — in and of itself apparently not surprising to the orator. Halperin likens the agent's progress from women to boys to an addict's progress "from wine to hard drugs."[5] Neither Winkler nor Halperin argues away Dio's discomfort with the idea that his *akolastoi* will attempt sexual relations with noble youth; however, both implicitly make the point that Dio does not condemn sexual contact between males simply because it occurs between males. Rather, Winkler indicates that Dio's revulsion springs from concerns that extend beyond the biological sex of the object of desire, specifically from an ethics obvious in a great many of his orations, which recommends against self-indulgence and elevates principles of simplicity, self-restraint, and stability.[6]

During the middle of the 1990s, scholars discussing Dio's views on sexual behavior, as he alludes to them in a variety of discourses, concluded that Dio is hostile to all sexual relations that occur between males. Both D. A. Russell and Simon Swain fastened upon Dio's treatment of prostitution in the *Euboean Discourse* and used this text as evidence for Dio's sweeping condemnation of male-male relations.[7] Swain, following an early suggestion of Gilbert Highet, also found evidence for Dio's condemnation of male-male relations in the orator's earnest attack on ῥέγχειν in the *First Tarsian* oration.[8]

328

This term of uncertain meaning is often translated by "snort" or "snore." Swain for his part suggests the sound is that of men having intercourse. Nevertheless, Swain is aware that Dio praises Epaminondas, founder of the Sacred Band, the famed Theban force of male lovers fighting side by side. Still, he dismisses this instance as a special case—an exception to Dio's otherwise thorough disgust at male-male relations.[9]

Given the diversity of scholarly opinion about Dio's views on male-male sexual relations, it will be salutary to examine this question afresh, bearing in mind that Dio Chrysostom treats this subject in a variety of discourses delivered under a variety of circumstances and with a variety of rhetorical approaches. The purpose of this study, then, is to consider texts informative about Dio's views on male-male relations. Ultimately, I contend that Dio's ethical framework does accommodate a positive view of male-male and male-female sexual relations, so long as the agent initiating sexual contact pursues certain specific goals. On the other hand, I argue that Dio's discomfort with male-male sexual contact, so evident in the *Euboean Discourse*, is a product of his rejection of self-indulgence and of hedonism, thus supporting Winkler's conclusions. In addition, I suggest that some of his discussions of male-male sexual relations reflect Dio's acquaintance with Stoic philosophy and with the rhetoric of popular moralizing, which itself seems to have seen wide application among later Stoics. To these ends, the first section following discusses a passage from the third *Discourse on Kingship*, where Dio bestows measured praise on male-male and male-female relations alike in a way that suggests he has been influenced by Stoic thought on the subject. Second, I examine Dio's condemnation of male-male relations in the *Euboean Discourse*. I agree with Winkler that Dio's attack on prostitution and his treatment of sexual relations in that passage reflects his wider concern to stigmatize behavior that is self-indulgent and excessively pleasant, and that this passage should not be read as a comprehensive account of Dio's preferred system of sexual ethics. I also suggest that his discussion shows Dio's awareness of later Stoic teachings against self-indulgence, such as those evident in the so-called Cynic-Stoic diatribe. Third, I consider Dio's remarks in the *First Tarsian* oration; in that section, I contend that the oration demonstrates Dio's hostility to the sexual passivity of adult males, though Dio stops short of condemning all sexual relations between males. Fourth, I discuss briefly a passage from the *Borystheniticus*, which Russell suggests is evidence for Dio's condemnation of male-male sexual contact. I suggest instead that Dio's remarks arise from an anxiety about the capacity of non-Greeks to engage in male-male relations in a manner of which he approves—that is, in the manner of morally commendable agents. At any rate, this passage is not evidence for a condemnation of all sexual relations between men.

1. Dio Chrysostom and Stoic *Eros:* The Third *Discourse on Kingship*

The third *Discourse on Kingship* is usually thought to have been delivered before Trajan at Rome, perhaps on the occasion of the emperor's birthday in C.E. 103 or 104.[10] Of the four *Discourses on Kingship,* the first and the third are addressed to the emperor, while the second and fourth are dialogues between historical figures. Dio begins the third *Discourse* with lavish praise for the emperor (3.1–11); then at similar length he defends himself against suspicion of flattery (3.12–24) and devotes the rest of the speech to a discussion of the ideal king who, as C. P. Jones notes, is quite similar to Trajan (3.25–138).[11] Such a ruler is extraordinarily attentive to his subjects (3.55–85) and relies on his friends and associates, to whom he is devoted (3.86–122). Dio concludes with a description of the ideal king's goodness and recommends hunting as a suitable source of diversion (3.123–38). The third *Discourse on Kingship* is one of several which, taken together, allow us to form a rough estimation of Dio's ideas about monarchy, and indeed about the nature of the cosmos. He endorses the notion of a kinship between human and divine and insists that the good king on earth must strive to imitate the divine king of the universe, which is itself divine.[12] As Swain has observed, Dio's interpretation of the universe suggests that he is heavily influenced by Stoic thinking in such matters.[13]

Just before Dio embarks upon his discussion of *philia* and its importance to the ideal king, he distinguishes between those things which are profitable, but not pleasant, and those things which are pleasant, but not necessarily profitable. By contrast, he subsequently argues, *philia* is both profitable and pleasant. During the discussion, Dio alludes twice to sexual relations which the ideal king might have. Both passages show that, as Halperin observes with respect to the *Euboean Discourse,* Dio imagines that a man, and here an ideal man, may sexually desire either a woman or a boy. In addition, the second passage suggests that Dio feels some anxiety about sexual relations. Moreover, Dio's description of *eros* here reflects his broader debt to Stoic teachings on the subject and suggests that male-male sexual contact may, under some conditions, meet with the moralist's approval.

According to Dio, the ideal king must acknowledge the importance of *philia* to his success as a monarch. Indeed, *philia* will be the most beautiful and sacred of his possessions (3.86). Next, he suggests that a king's need for friends and their goodwill (*eunoia*) increases as his own responsibilities are multiplied (3.87–88). The king must be able to distinguish between things that are useful but not necessarily pleasant, and their opposites, things that are pleasant but not necessarily useful.[14] The latter category includes beautiful groves, expensive homes and their adornments, purple dye, amber, ivory, and "young women and young boys"— γυναῖκες ὡραῖαι καὶ παιδικὰ ὡραῖα (3.93).[15] Dio's use of παιδικά to describe one object of sexual desire and his application of ὡραῖαι and ὡραῖα to all the objects of desire recall the terminology of pederasty and sexual attractiveness, confirming that Dio's phrase here is intended to suggest sexual activity or desire.[16] This phrase, offered nonchalantly as part of a series, indicates Dio finds it unremarkable that the ideal king would have a sexual interest in a person of either biological sex. It also indicates that Dio may freely associate sexual interest with the agent's desire for pleasure over and above more noble ends, excessive devotion to which, he has already stated in the same discourse, may render one an unfit ruler.[17]

Dio now argues that all things bringing pleasure are still more pleasant when shared with friends (3.96), thus supporting his position that the good king should act out of *philia*. He offers examples, including a drinking party and a sacrificial festival. He continues:

> οὐ γὰρ καὶ τὰ ἀφροδίσια ταῦτα ἥδιστα καὶ ἀνυβριστότατα ὅσα γίγνεται μετὰ φιλίας τῶν συνόντων καὶ ὅσα μαστεύουσιν εὔνοιαν ἀνθρώποις ἐπῆλθε παρὰ παιδικῶν ἢ παρὰ γυναικῶν; πολλαὶ μὲν γὰρ ἐπωνυμίαι τῆς φιλίας ὥσπερ ἀμέλει καὶ χρεῖαι· ἡ δὲ μετὰ κάλλους καὶ ὥρας γιγνομένη φιλία δικαίως ἔρως ὠνόμασται καὶ δοκεῖ κάλλιστος τῶν θεῶν.

[Are not also those sexual relations most pleasant and least expressive of *hybris* which are accompanied by affection on the part of those coming together, and which come about for men seeking goodwill from boys and women? For many are the titles of affection just as are, doubtless, its uses, but the affection that is associated with beauty and youth is justly named *eros* and seems the most beautiful of the gods.] (3.98–99)

Here, as before, we find Dio assuming that a man may be sexually interested in a male or a female. More interesting is his tepid endorsement of sexual relations with male or female, where apparently the best he can say is that sexual relations pursued under certain conditions are least suggestive of *hybris*. (I shall return to this threat of *hybris* below.) The conditions to be met are apparently the agent's *philia*, or his search for *eunoia*, implying consent, which Dio elsewhere indicates is a necessary condition for *philia*.[18] This in turn implies that the object of desire, the passive partner in the sexual encounter, is not merely an instrument in the agent's search for pleasure, but is being used (in Dio's opinion) for more noble ends. Certainly, according to Dio's classification of objects and activities, these sexual relations will be pleasant. It appears, however, that this pleasure is a result of the agent's disposition and his goals in initiating sexual activity and at any rate is certainly not itself the primary goal.

Dio's parting comment in 3.99 (ἡ μετὰ κάλλους καὶ ὥρας γιγνομένη φιλία δικαίως ἔρως ὠνόμασται καὶ δοκεῖ κάλλιστος τῶν θεῶν) suggests that his analysis of sexual relations in this passage owes a debt to Stoic teachings on *eros* and *aphrodisia*.[19] Eros, then, is a form of *philia* accompanied by youth and beauty. It may be cultivated, according to this definition, with either a female or a male, as these qualities are available in either. That this form of *philia*, this *eros*, allows for sexual relations is clear from Dio's prior comments.

That *philia* and *eros* are related is not new to Dio, nor for that matter to the Stoics. One need only recall, for example, Plato's *Lysis*.[20] Nevertheless, Dio's expression of the relationship does echo Stoic discussions of how and where *philia* and *eros* overlap. Take, for example, the school definition preserved by Arius Didymus:[21] τὸν δὲ ἔρωτά φασιν ἐπιβολὴν εἶναι φιλοποιίας διὰ κάλλος ἐμφαινόμενον νέων ὡραίων [They say that *eros* is an attempt to create *philia* because of the apparent beauty of young persons] (Stob. *Ecl.* 2.115.1–2 = SVF 3.164.1–2).[22] According to Diogenes Laertius (7.130), this definition belongs to Zeno and Chrysippus. Diogenes, for his part, adds a bit of interpretation: εἶναι δὲ τὸν ἔρωτα ἐπιβολὴν φιλοποιίας, διὰ κάλλος ἐμφαινόμενον καὶ μὴ εἶναι συνουσίας, ἀλλὰ φιλίας [that *eros* is an attempt to create *philia*, because of apparent beauty, and that it is not [an attempt at] intercourse, but [an attempt at] *philia*] (D.L. 7.130 = SVF 3.180.17–19). The Stoics then associate *eros* with *philia* and with beauty. Unlike Zeno and Chrysippus, Dio does not explicitly mark out *philia* as the goal of *eros*, though he does indicate that the agent will pursue *eunoia*, or will act out of *philia*. His way of expressing himself does not disallow the possibility that he shares the Stoic point of view here, though we are unable to confirm this. Certainly, the Stoics indicate that the young person's beauty will be one impetus for the emergence of *eros*. Dio on the other hand maintains that beauty does accompany *eros*, although he does not assign it a precise role in the formation of *eros*.

We also notice that Dio, like the Stoics, does not specify a preference that the object of sexual interest be a male or a female. The Stoics themselves seem to have considered this a matter of moral indifference, as citations of Chrysippus's *On the Republic* suggest.[23] However, the Stoics do routinely limit the definition to pederastic relationships, according to the definition Arius Didymus reports. According to the Stoics, these relationships came about for educative purposes, where the beauty of the young person indicated a capacity for virtue.[24] Dio never gives a full account of the pederastic relationship or its educative purpose, though his discussion of *eros* does accommodate both.

Before leaving this topic, we should remind ourselves that the Stoics' and Dio's characterizations of *eros* were not conventional. Plutarch points out that the Stoic notion of a relationship between *philia* and *eros* was not widely accepted: οὐδεὶς γὰρ ἦν ὁ κωλύων τὴν περὶ τοὺς νέους τῶν σοφῶν σπουδήν, εἰ πάθος αὐτῇ μὴ πρόσεστι, θήραν ἢ φιλοποιίαν προσαγορευομένην, ἔρωτα δὲ καλεῖν [For there was no one who objected to the eagerness of the wise for young men, if there was no passion in it, being called a hunt or creation of *philia*, but they objected to its being called *eros*] (Plut. *De communibus notitiis* 1073C). Plutarch's comment here suggests that *eros* was commonly linked to passion (*pathos*), something that the Stoics apparently denied.

In their discussions of Dio's attitudes to sexual relations, both Russell and Swain overlook the passages above from the third *Discourse*. Indeed, consideration of Dio's remarks therein suggests that he is not prepared to condemn male-male sexual contact wholesale, as something inherently and uniquely wrong. Instead, these passages demonstrate that Dio can give a certain amount of endorsement to sexual relations between a male agent and either a male or female, so long as the agent's disposition is healthy. Dio's understanding of *eros* in this context is similar to, if less precisely expressed than, that of the Stoics. On the other hand, Dio also explicitly associates sexual relations with *hybris*, which Zeno and Chrysippus do not seem to have done. In this section, I examine the *Euboicus*, where Dio's reservations about sexual relations are most forcefully expressed.

2. The *Euboean Discourse: Eros* and Self-Indulgence

If the third *Discourse on Kingship* suggests that Dio's views on male-male sexual contact are more tolerant than Russell and Swain argue, the *Euboean Discourse* is well known for its condemnation of sexual relations between debauched men and citizen youths. Indeed, Dio apparently considers this the worst possible effect of permitting prostitution to flourish in urban settings. Yet, as Winkler has noticed, this condemnation is a function of Dio's ethical stance, which militates against excessive self-indulgence and hedonism. In this section, I examine Dio's argument in greater detail than Winkler or Halperin, in order to lend additional support to Winkler's conclusions about the discourse and to call still further into question the views of Russell and Swain about Dio's stance on male-male relations. First, I argue that Dio's analysis of sexual immorality at the end of the *Euboean Discourse* is characteristic of his arguments against sexual self-indulgence and other forms of hedonism, which he condemns in similar terms elsewhere. Then I show that Dio's rhetorical approach to sexual behavior in this passage resembles that of the Cynic-Stoic diatribe, the most famous pagan practitioner of which, Musonius Rufus, was Dio's Stoic mentor. I close with the suggestion that Dio's treatment here may owe a direct debt to Musonius, noted for his recommendation of a strict sexual ethics not typical of earlier Stoics. Thus, this passage, like the one analyzed from the third *Discourse,* may reflect Stoic influence, despite the obvious difference in Dio's handling of sexual relations.

Dio's treatment of sexual relations in the final chapters of the *Euboean Discourse* comes at the end of a considerably longer discussion, and condemnation, of prostitution.[25] Dio is absolutely opposed to permitting prostitution, since it enhances the appetites of those who solicit prostitutes. Bored with sex so easy to have, these men will next prey on the women and boys of noble households (7.139). The remainder of the discourse plays on this idea, with Dio imagining a kind of slippery slope down which men slide as they focus their sexual attention on first the women and then the boys of these households. The discourse ends abruptly while Dio compares these agents to those who have had their fill of wine but who induce sweating and eat salted foods and condiments to heighten their thirst, so that they may continue to drink (7.152). As Winkler observes, this lengthy attack comes at the end of a discourse encouraging the audience to reject self-indulgence induced by wealth and to embrace simplicity and frugality, after the example of Euboea's poor country folk.[26] Immediately one notices that the tone and approach Dio takes here differ dramatically from those of the third *Discourse.* It will be worthwhile to highlight several of the differences.

First, throughout his attack on prostitution and its effects, Dio refers to the agents in question as *akolastoi* and repeatedly refers to their activities in derogatory terms including *hybris, akolasia,* and *phthora.* For example, at the beginning of his discussion, Dio enjoins his audience to forbid brothel keepers from collecting a fee for *hybris* and *akolasia*, that is, for prostitution.[27] Again, Dio considers the brothel keeper's work so revolting because it amounts to linking humans possessing a sense of shame to undisciplined men who are themselves stung to madness—οἰστρῶντας καὶ ἀκολάστους ἀνθρώπους (7.134). When asserting that these agents will desire the women and boys of noble households, Dio refers to their attempts at seduction as "subtle and stealthy acts of *hybris*"—τῶν ἀδήλων καὶ ἀφανῶν . . . ὕβρεων (7.139). After exploring in detail the plights of females, both married women and unmarried girls, in a city where prostitution flourishes, Dio imagines with horror what will be the plight of boys at the hands of the *akolastoi*, who are tired of sex with easy women and desire a more difficult path to sexual gratification: ἔσθ' ὅπως ἂν ἀπόσχοιτο τῆς τῶν ἀρρένων λώβης καὶ φθορᾶς τό γε ἀκόλαστον γένος, τοῦτον ἱκανὸν καὶ σαφῆ ποιησάμενον ὅρον τὸν τῆς φύσεως, ἀλλ' οὐκ ἂν ἐμπιμπλάμενον πάντα τρόπον τῆς περὶ γυναῖκας ἀκρασίας διακορὲς γενόμενον τῆς ἡδονῆς ταύτης ζητοίη ἑτέραν μείζω καὶ παρανομωτέραν ὕβριν; [Is there a way that this undisciplined class would keep away from the ruin and destruction of the males, having considered the limit of nature clear and sufficient, but not satisfy itself in every respect with lack of restraint in women, become tired of this pleasure, and seek another worse and more lawless form of *hybris*?] (7.149). This passage, which Winkler and Halperin have noted, refers to the agents' sexual desire for the youths. Dio is obviously uncomfortable with this coupling of male with male, apparently more so than with the agents' sexual relations with women.[28] Here at the bottom of the slippery slope, we find the *akolastos*: τοὺς ἄρξοντας αὐτίκα μάλα καὶ δικάσοντας καὶ στρατηγήσοντας ἐπιθυμῶν καταισχύνειν, ὡς ἐνθάδε που τὸ χαλεπὸν καὶ δυσπόριστον εὑρήσων τῶν ἡδονῶν εἶδος [desiring to put to shame those who will be magistrates, judges, and generals, intending as he does to find a kind of pleasure difficult and tough to get] (7.152). In a place where nature dictates he should not be, the *akolastos* continues to search for pleasure, preying on the future leaders of the city.[29]

If the use of nature in this discourse denotes the boundary the self-restrained agent must observe, *hybris* apparently is foremost among the offenses of one who steps across this line. The term has a broad range of applications, but here, in a specifically sexual context, *hybris* may refer to the agent's use of another for his own pleasure, without regard for the status or the well-being of the "used" person.[30] That this aspect of *akolasia* concerns Dio here is suggested by his specification of the threatened households as "high born" or "noble," and by the care he takes to mention that the young men to whom the *akolastoi* pose a danger are future leaders in the city.[31]

Thus, he is apparently concerned with traditional differentiations of status, which place citizen males in the top stratum among the residents of a city, over noncitizen residents, women, and young children, for example. Moreover, Dio condemns prostitution because it requires the customers in brothels to mistreat their fellow human beings, even the slaves and disfranchised, because, like all human beings, they enjoy divine honor, share in reason, and have experience with the noble and base (7.138).[32] In other words, prostitution is an offense against one's equal, where the criteria for judging equality are one's capacities for reasoning and the distinction between right and wrong. Indeed, as Winkler concludes, the offense that transgresses the boundary of nature at the end of the *Euboean Discourse* is treating the city's future rulers as common prostitutes in the service of hedonism.[33] We can also see that the prostitutes themselves do not deserve this treatment. Thus, misusing noble youths for one's sexual gratification constitutes a double offense—against their humanity and against their citizenship.

Dio's handling of *akolasia* and the dangers it poses to others is not unique to the *Euboean Discourse*. A review of Dio's treatment of the issue in other works shows that the criticisms of prostitution we find in the *Euboean Discourse* are typical of Dio's reservations about a life devoted to pleasure. We can see that Dio associates *akolasia* with the pursuit of pleasure, including sexual pleasure, and we also observe that the life of *akolasia* may pose a threat to others, a threat which Dio expresses at times in terms of *hybris*.

Comparison of the *Euboean Discourse* to a passage from the fourth *Discourse on Kingship* suggests that the *Euboean Discourse* refers to only a single aspect of *akolasia*. In the fourth *Discourse*, Dio adopts the persona of Diogenes the Cynic, who lays out for Alexander the Great various sorts of *daimones* and describes the man each controls. This forms one part of a longer argument supporting the thesis that the true king must master his own impulses before ruling other people.[34] Second in the series of *daimones* are the *daimon* and man who exalt the rites of pleasure (4.101–15).[35] The man whom this *daimon* governs is devoted to, among other things, warm baths, anointings, and soft robes. He is especially devoted to τὴν τῶν ἀφροδισίων ὀξεῖαν καὶ διάπυρον μανίαν θηλυκῶν τε καὶ ἀρρενικῶν μίξεων καὶ ἔτι πλειόνων ἀρρήτων καὶ ἀνωνύμων αἰσχρουργιῶν. ἐπὶ πάντα ὁμοίως τὰ τοιαῦτα φερόμενος καὶ ἄγων, οὐδὲν ἀπώμοτον οὐδὲ ἄπρακτον ποιούμενος. [the sharp and fiery madness of sexual relations, of intercourse with females and males, and of yet more unspeakable and unmentionable shameful deeds. He rushes headlong after all things of this sort and also leads, esteeming nothing as to be forsworn or left undone][36] (4.102). This *daimon* governing such a man, Dio asserts, is "undisciplined and enslaved by pleasure"—ἀκόλαστον καὶ δεδουλωμένον ὑφ' ἡδονῆς (4.103). The hedonist will require a great deal of money to live luxuriously, and may end his life bankrupt (4.104), a violation of the ethical framework elevating simplicity that is most clearly exemplified in the *Euboean Discourse.* Dio also expresses his contempt for the hedonist by suggesting that he will be incapable of effective service as a general or an orator. Dio reproaches him with effeminacy and dissimulation, supposing that he will shed his feminine attire, actor that he is, only so long as he has a public role to fulfill (4.108).[37] As Dio, in the *Euboean Discourse,* inveighs against a life given over to self-indulgent pleasure seeking, so in the fourth *Discourse* he is critical of the life enslaved to pleasure. The brief passage above also suggests that the hedonist may corrupt others. The critical point rests with how one construes ἄγων. Dio specifies no object. I have here translated the term as "leads," which would imply that the hedonist carries others towards the same shameful behavior in which he engages.[38] His immorality thus may be contagious.

Dio's *Discourse on Envy* also suggests that he considers hedonism and *akolasia* threats to others, though here he imagines a harsher, physical peril. In this discourse, as in the *Euboean Discourse,* Dio associates *akolasia* with the agent's use of a male for sexual gratification. The passage occurs during a bizarre comparison of cultivating flatterers with castrating the object of one's desire.[39] Cultivation of flatterers for oneself is, he says: ὅμοιον . . . ἑτέρῳ ἐπιχειρήματι τῶν σφόδρα ἀκολάστων, οἳ γυναικῶν ἀφθόνων οὐσῶν δι' ὕβριν καὶ παρανομίαν ἐπιθυμοῦσιν ἐκ τῶν ἀνδρῶν γυναῖκας σφίσι γενέσθαι καὶ λάβοντες παῖδας ἐξέτεμον. ὅθεν πολὺ κάκιον καὶ δυστυχέστερον γένος ἐγένετο, ἀσθενέστερον τοῦ γυναικείου καὶ θηλύτερον [like another undertaking of those who are very undisciplined, who, although there are women in abundance, desire in arrogance and lawlessness to make out of men women for themselves, and take boys and castrate them. So a worse and more unfortunate race is created, weaker than the female and more feminine] (77–78.36). Here, Dio describes mutilation of another human being to satisfy one's own desire for pleasure in the same terms he uses in the *Euboean Discourse.* In both speeches, Dio links *akolasia* to *hybris* and *paranomia.*

In brief, on the basis of these comparisons, we can see that Dio's handling of sexual relations at the end of the *Euboicus* is consonant with his treatments of *akolasia* and hedonism elsewhere. The terms in which Dio describes the hedonist and his actions are similar in the *Euboean* and other discourses. The *akolastos* risks committing *hybris* against others, including young men who may fall under his control. This *hybris* may also be characterized as *paranomia.* Dio's attacks against male-male sexual relations occur within such contexts and taken alone should not suggest that Dio is hostile to male-male or male-female relations, defined as such.

Dio's attack on prostitution is potent and memorable. Some of its power derives from Dio's pointed opposition of hedonistic intercourse, which we have seen he considers unlawful, unnatural, and destructive, to the forms of intercourse of which he approves. Dio's rhetorical technique is broadly to contrast sex initiated for pleasure with conjugal sex undertaken for pro-creation. He suggests that the latter is sanctioned by the gods and is natural. Near the opening of his tirade, as we have seen, Dio attacks brothel keep-ers for introducing prostitutes with a sense of shame to the *akolastoi*, who are "stung to madness"—οἰστρῶντας (7.134). He asserts that the brothel keepers feel no shame before men or gods, and then offers a list of those gods before whom they feel no shame: οὔτε Δία γενέθλιον οὔτε ῞Ηραν γα-μήλιον οὔτε Μοίρας τελεσφόρους ἢ λοχίαν ῎Αρτεμιν ἢ μητέρα ῾Ρέαν, οὐδὲ τὰς προεστώσας ἀνθρωπίνης γενέσεως Εἰλειθυίας οὐδὲ Ἀφροδίτην ἐπώνυ-μον τῆς κατὰ φύσιν πρὸς τὸ θῆλυ τοῦ ἄρρενος συνόδου τε καὶ ὁμιλίας [not Zeus of the family, nor Hera of marriage, nor the Fates, who oversee fulfill-ment, nor Artemis of childbirth, nor mother Rhea, nor the Eileithyiai, who oversee human birth, nor even Aphrodite, whose name signifies the natu-ral intercourse and union of male with female] (7.135). With this list Dio stakes out his rhetorical position.[40] Prostitution and its consequences, all the products of *akolasia*, in other words, are to be understood as the oppo-sites of conjugal, procreative intercourse, which is natural and sanctioned by the gods. Dio at no point in the *Euboean Discourse* countenances the pos-sibility that agents might desire and seek sexual intimates for reasons other than self-indulgence or procreation (and that within marriage).

This opposition of hedonistic intercourse to conjugal sex is typical of the so-called Cynic-Stoic "diatribe," or popular philosophical discourse. The precise definition of "diatribe," and indeed its proper application to philosophical essays and teachings, continues to excite scholarly debate.[41] For the sake of clarity, I use the term here to refer to popular philosophical teachings from the Cynic and Stoic teachers, such as the essays outlining the teachings of Teles the Cynic, and the Stoic philosophers Musonius Ru-fus and Epictetus.[42] Musonius Rufus in particular is often considered an ex-emplary practitioner of the diatribe on the basis of the essays recording his teachings, written by a student known to us only as "Lucius."[43] Dio Chry-sostom too is reported to have been a student of Musonius, though by no means all of his works should be classified as diatribes.[44] It is perhaps not surprising then to find that Dio's handling of sexual ethics in the *Euboean Discourse* bears some resemblance to that of Musonius Rufus.

All of the essays by Lucius are incomplete, excerpted from larger works by Stobaeus. Despite their condition, one may gain some impression of Musonius's teachings on sexual ethics and note the similarity of Dio's own approach, as well as some of the important differences. Stobaeus's excerpt from Lucius's most important essay on this topic, "On Intercourse," begins in medias res, with Musonius asserting that part of the life of luxury (*tryphe*) is indulging oneself in *aphrodisia*. He condemns intercourse sought for pleasure as "unlawful," whether it occurs between the agent and a male or a female:

Μέρος μέντοι τρυφῆς οὐ μικρότατον κἂν τοῖς ἀφροδισίοις ἐστίν, ὅτι ποικίλων δέονται παιδικῶν οἱ τρυφῶντες οὐ νομίμων μόνον ἀλλὰ καὶ παρανόμων, οὐδὲ θηλειῶν μόνον ἀλλὰ καὶ ἀρρένων, ἄλλοτε ἄλλους θηρῶντες ἐρωμένους, καὶ τοῖς μὲν ἐν ἑτοίμῳ οὖσιν οὐκ ἀρκούμενοι, τῶν δὲ σπανίων ἐφιέμενοι, συμπλοκὰς δ' ἀσχήμονας ζητοῦντες, ἅπερ ἅπαντα μεγάλα ἐγκλήματα ἀνθρώπου ἐστίν.

[But not the smallest share of the life of luxury is in *aphrodisia*, because those who live the luxurious life need various young loves, not only lawful ones, but also unlawful, nor even only female, but also male. At one time they hunt one beloved, at another time another, and not being satisfied with those easily available, but aiming at the rare, they seek indecent unions, all of which are great indictments against a person]. (Hense 63)

Here, Musonius appeals to many of the same stereotypes we have seen in the *Euboicus* and in the fourth *Discourse on Kingship*. One expression of *tryphe* is sexual relations. The persons living the pleasurable life are searching for what is ever rarer.[45] The objects of their desire are both male and female.[46] Musonius continues by arguing that agents who are not hedonistic or evil (τοὺς μὴ τρυφῶντας ἢ μὴ κακούς) must consider only those *aphrodisia* just (δίκαια) which occur in marriage and which aim at procreation, because they are lawful (νόμιμα). All *aphrodisia*, he continues, which aim at raw pleasure (ἡδονὴν ψιλήν) are unjust and unlawful, even in marriage. He now catalogues the various combinations of sexual relations which he rejects, and labels them shameful, the products of *akolasia*.[47] Before the essay breaks off, Musonius also asserts that *akolasia* is present in the agent who has been overcome by base pleasure (αἰσχρᾶς ἡδονῆς).[48]

In this essay, we see Musonius drawing a clear connection between *akolasia* and the search for pleasure, and in turn rejecting all sexual relations which grow out of such a search. Dio also rejects this pursuit in favor of conjugal relations aimed at procreation. He describes sex undertaken for pleasure and for production of legitimate offspring in opposing terms, thereby underscoring their differences. He apparently allows no middle ground. Dio approaches sexual relations from the same perspective in the *Euboicus*. While he only hints at the conditions under which sexual relations will meet with his (and the gods') approval, he lavishes his attention on the search for sexual pleasure undertaken by the hedonist. This he expressly rejects.

And, what of the gods' approval? Dio, the reader will recall, lists the divinities who oversee marriage, the family, childbirth, and "natural" (κατὰ φύσιν) sexual relations, between a male and a female. Lucius reports that Musonius produced a similar list for one who asked whether marriage impedes philosophy. Musonius replied in the negative, among other reasons because great divinities watch over marriage—Hera, Eros, and Aphrodite:

πρώτη μὲν Ἥρα, καὶ διὰ τοῦτο ζυγίαν αὐτὴν προσαγορεύομεν· εἶτα Ἔρως, εἶτα Ἀφροδίτη· πάντας γὰρ τούτους ὑπολαμβάνομεν ἔργον πεποιῆσθαι τοῦτο, συνάγειν ἀλλήλοις πρὸς παιδοποιίαν ἄνδρα καὶ γυναῖκα. ποῦ μὲν γὰρ Ἔρως παραγένοιτ' ἂν δικαιότερον ἢ ἐπὶ νόμιμον ἀνδρὸς καὶ γυναικὸς ὁμιλίαν; ποῦ δὲ Ἥρα; ποῦ δὲ Ἀφροδίτη; πότε δ' ἂν εὐκαιρότερον εὔξαιτό τις τοῖς θεοῖς τούτοις ἢ πρὸς γάμον ἰών;

[First Hera, and for this reason we address her as Hera "of the yoke"; then Eros, and next Aphrodite. For we understand that they all have done this—bring man and woman together to procreate. Where would Eros more justly attend than lawful intercourse of man and woman? Where would Hera? Where Aphrodite? And when would one more appropriately pray to these gods than when going to his marriage?]. (Hense 75)

The questions continue, but his point is clear. Musonius, apparently following Stoic practice, links these gods to conjugal and procreative intercourse.[49] Dio's list of gods points in the same direction. Where Musonius refers to the preferred mode of intercourse as "lawful," Dio calls it "natural."[50]

A comparison of Dio's treatment of hedonistic sexual activity in the *Euboean Discourse* with Musonius's teachings on sexual ethics suggests that Dio's handling of the topic is influenced by Cynic-Stoic rhetoric on the subject, and that Dio could be indebted to Musonius for his treatment. Thus, Dio's harsh condemnation of male-male sexual relations, itself part of a greater argument against prostitution, must be read as a condemnation of all sexual relations aimed at giving pleasure. This rhetorical approach excludes from consideration all possible motivations for sexual intercourse except procreation and self-indulgence. Cultivation of goodwill, pursuit of friendship, and a host of other motivations simply do not arise. The closest Dio comes to condemning male-male sexual relations, defined as such, is his reckoning that male-female relations are natural. Such a position does not preclude the naturalness of male-male relations that spring from a source *other than self-indulgence*, nor does it preclude condoning male-male relations on grounds other than their naturalness. Dio never approaches these questions in the *Euboicus*, and we should not, I would argue, assume that this speech is meant to be a comprehensive account of Dio's positions on sexual ethics, or even on sexual relations between males.

To illustrate this important point, let us return to Musonius's treatment of *aphrodisia*. I would argue that Musonius's treatment is no more complete than Dio's.[51] Indeed, given the fragmentary state of the essay "On Intercourse," I think that it is less comprehensive. As the passage quoted from the beginning of "On Intercourse" above shows, the part of Musonius's discussion Stobaeus preserves is concerned with *tryphe*. To judge from his catalogue of disallowed sexual acts, it seems that Musonius very probably condemns all male-male sexual relations. Indeed, he would condone only conjugal intercourse between a man and a woman, and then only for procreation. All other intercourse, as an expression of the agent's self-indulgence, is condemned. When he takes up the possibility that self-indulgence will prompt the male agent to pursue another male, Musonius delivers the following paraphrase from Plato's *Laws:*[52] συμπλοκαὶ δ' ἄλλαι αἱ μὲν κατὰ μοιχείαν παρανομώταται, καὶ μετριώτεραι τούτων οὐδὲν αἱ πρὸς ἄρρενας τοῖς ἄρρεσιν, ὅτι παρὰ φύσιν τὸ τόλμημα [And other unions in adultery are most unlawful, and no less serious than these are unions between males, which are an outrage against nature] (Hense 64). This is just the sort of condemnation that we do not find in Dio — a rejection of male-male relations, so defined.

Before moving on to the *First Tarsian Oration*, I would suggest that Dio's teachings on *eros* and *aphrodisia* in the third *Discourse on Kingship* and the *Euboean Discourse* may be reconciled along the lines I have indicated above. Dio can countenance sexual relations between male agents and either male or female partners so long as the agents have the proper dispositions and are pursuing sexual relations for purposes of which Dio approves. Sexual relations initiated in a pursuit of pleasure are condemned as unlawful, unnatural, and acts of *hybris*. On *hybris* a final word: we recall that in the third *Discourse*, Dio implies that even sex motivated by noble ambitions is not altogether divorced from *hybris*. I tentatively offer that this implication arises from Dio's awareness that sex is pleasant and may reflect his anxiety that those exposed to sexual pleasure are in danger of desiring pleasure for its own sake, and that they might draw near the slippery slope of *akolasia,* whose danger he assumes in the *Euboean Discourse.*

3. The First *Tarsian Oration:* Condemning Male-Male Sexual Relations?

Dio's *First Tarsian Oration* condemns an activity denoted by the term ῥέγ-κειν, which had apparently become popular at Tarsus. The precise definition of this term is uncertain, though it is usually thought to refer to nasal snorting or to snoring.[53] Dio's denunciation follows a long prelude in which he warns his audience that they should expect him to offer reproach, rather than praise (33.1–16). He then offers the opinion that the dissolute city will lose the advantage of its natural resources (33.17–30). Only now does Dio introduce his subject, for which he offers no definition but which he expects his Tarsian audience to recognize (33.33). This behavior, according to Dio, brings shame on the city and does the greatest *hybris* to it (33.34). Such behavior is a sign of shamelessness (ἀναισχυντίας) and the utmost licentiousness (ἀσελγείας τῆς ἐσχάτης). Unlike funeral dirges, which are the sounds of those in grief, this is the sound of *akolastoi* (33.35). The sound is typical, Dio asserts, of effeminates (ἀνδρογύνων) and of eunuchs (33.39).[54] After imagining a city in which all residents snort in the Tarsian manner and suggesting that its moral character would be obviously lacking, Dio returns to the subject of who emits this sound. He emits the voice of neither man nor woman, nor of any other creature. It is the sound he would make if engaged in the most shameful deed (τοῦ αἰσχίστου ἔργου) and most wanton activity (τῆς ἀσελγεστάτης πράξεως) (33.60). Dio concludes by outlining the progress of the condition that leads to the affliction. One begins by trimming the beard, then shaves the cheeks to look handsome and boyish. He next shaves chest and legs, then arms, and finally genitals. In Dio's view shaving in this manner violates the art of nature (ἡ τῆς φύσεως τέχνη) (33.63).

Most scholars fall into two camps as they evaluate Dio's argument. On the one hand, some think that Dio's attack on *rhengkein* is an allegory. According to this idea, "snorting" denotes some fault in popular morality or education. Jones, for example, suggests that Dio may target generally the moral condition of the Tarsians and their lack of concern for their reputation. By contrast, C. B. Welles takes the position that Dio's target is the

Tarsians' disregard for philosophy.[55] Other scholars think that Dio does actually condemn snorting, and sometimes link it to other activities of which it is symptomatic.[56] Maud Gleason, for example, sees Dio's invective as typical of a physiognomic approach to the assessment of an individual's morality. Like other physiognomists, Dio considers the voice an important indicator of one's masculinity or femininity and regards snorting as an unacceptable sign of their conflation.[57]

Yet other scholars from the second group have suggested a connection between the sound and Dio's rejection of some type of sexual behavior.[58] Indeed, two scholars of note have suggested that Dio is here specifically condemning sexual activity between males. Gilbert Highet asserts that *rhengkein* refers to the heavy breathing of males during sex. Following a claim advanced without any evidence, Swain takes this passage as typical of Dio's strong opposition to sex between males.[59] Such interpretations must assume that the word ἀνδρογύνων (33.39) refers to males who have sex with other males, and may assume that the phrases "most shameful deed" and "most wanton activity" (33.60) refer to sexual activity between men, both of which are plausible though not certainly correct assumptions. In what follows, though I accept both assumptions, I argue that the discourse offers evidence to support a significant modification in the views of Highet and Swain.

Like the *Euboicus*, the *First Tarsian Oration* lacks an explicit rejection of male-male sexual relations. Indeed, Dio here as in the *Euboicus* is explicitly concerned about the behavior of people he calls *akolastoi*, and he assumes their behaviors are indicative of both *hybris* and a disregard for nature. Yet his use of *androgynoi* to describe them and his extensive account of their self-depilation suggest that he is concerned with adult men who submit themselves sexually to other men. As Gleason has noted, *androgynos* "in its most literal sense describes an appearance of gender-indeterminacy," whereas *kinaidos* "describes sexual *deviance*, in its most specific sense referring to males who prefer to play a 'feminine' (receptive) role in intercourse with other men." But, she continues, "the two terms become virtually indistinguishable when used to describe men of effeminate appearance and behavior."[60] Dio here seems to use *androgynos* in a broad sense that incorporates a range of behaviors considered unacceptable for a male, from depilation to sexually submitting himself to another male.[61]

This interpretation differs from that of Highet and Swain partly because neither of these critics draws any distinction between passivity and activity in sexual relations, an important distinction in ancient Mediterranean cultures, as Winkler and Halperin among others have pointed out. In fact, because Greek culture construes sexual activity and passivity so differently, I would argue that condemnation of an adult male's passivity does not automatically entail rejection of a man's taking the active role in sexual relations. According to Swain, who offers the fuller interpretation of Dio, the orator is hostile to sex between men.[62] Yet the first *Tarsian Oration* does not ever discuss the man taking the active role in male-male sexual relations. Instead, Dio apparently is concerned only with the adult male taking the passive role and the "snorting" in which he engages. Thus, like the *Euboean Discourse*, the first *Tarsian Oration* is a treatment of only one aspect of *aphrodisia* and must not be considered a comprehensive account of Dio's views on sex and desire.[63]

4. EXCURSUS: SEX AND *HYBRIS* IN THE *BORYSTHENITICUS*

Dio's *Borystheniticus* was reportedly delivered before his fellow citizens at Prusa.[64] In it, he describes to his audience his reception at Borysthenes, an Ionian outpost in Olbia and follows with an account of the conversations he had there, first about the nature of the earthly city and then about the nature of the divine city and the cosmos. He concludes with an account of the kingship of Zeus, derived he says from the Magi. Dio's debt to the Stoa for his account of the city of the gods and the nature of the cosmos is well recognized.[65] However, the Stoic material will not occupy us here. Instead, Dio's reception in the city and his description of a young man, which in turn gives way to a comment on Olbian sexual practices, demand attention.

Shortly after the beginning of the discourse, Dio recounts his meeting with a young man of Greek descent, dressed in the garb of his Scythian neighbors. This young man, Callistratus, rides out of the city on horseback to meet Dio. He cuts an impressive figure—he is comely, tall, and reputed to be brave in war.[66] Moreover, he is so eager for philosophy and argument that he is ready to sail away with Dio. Because of his beauty, Callistratus has many lovers, and Dio adds that "the loves of males" (τοὺς ἔρωτας τοὺς τῶν ἀρρένων) are a custom inherited from the Ionian metropolis by its outpost. Dio then offers a word of caution about male-male sexual relations. Of the Borysthenites and their Ionian custom, Dio says: κινδυνεύουσιν ἀναπείθειν καὶ τῶν βαρβάρων ἐνίους οὐκ ἐπ' ἀγαθῷ σχεδόν, ἀλλ' ὡς ἂν ἐκεῖνοι τὸ τοιοῦτον ἀποδέξαιντο, βαρβαρικῶς καὶ οὐκ ἄνευ ὕβρεως [they run the risk of persuading even some of the non-Greeks, not for anything good at all, but as those men would receive a thing of that kind, in a non-Greek way, and not without *hybris*] (36.8). Russell counts this passage as evidence for Dio's hostility to male-male relations, and Swain sees it as a piece of "strong criticism" of sexual activity between men.[67] Nevertheless, this passage comfortably accommodates another interpretation, one which harmonizes with Dio's stance on *eros* and *aphrodisia*, as I have described it above.

First, we must observe that Dio does not condemn all sexual relations between males, nor does he treat the topic of sexual relations in any detail. His criticism is reserved here only for sexual relations as the non-Greek neighbors of the Olbians would practice them. That they would occur with *hybris* suggests that the agents initiating sexual contact will pay no heed to their partners, or indeed may even foist themselves on unwilling partners, as Russell suggests.[68] However this may be, it says nothing at all about the sexual attitudes or behaviors of the Olbians, nor for that matter of anyone other than non-Greeks.[69] Thus, it is only through a gross generalization of these remarks that one can claim this passage as valid evidence for Dio's ideas about sex and desire.

5. CONCLUSION

At the beginning of this chapter, I reminded the reader that Winkler and Halperin have found Dio's *Euboean Discourse* illustrative of typical Greek views about sexual desire and sexual behavior. According to this view, male-male sexual relations are not in and of themselves worthy of condemnation or considered against nature, though self-indulgence and willing passivity do typically meet with reproof. Despite the results of Winkler and Halperin's research, there persists a view of Dio which presents him as outraged at sexual relations between males. In response to this position, I have argued that Dio in no single work gives a comprehensive account of his views on *eros* or *aphrodisia*, but that careful study of individual discourses shows that Dio's views are more complex than some scholars have realized. I have indicated that the third *Discourse on Kingship* and the *Euboicus* bear the imprints of Dio's Stoic training, albeit from different sources. On the other hand, I have argued that the *First Tarsian Oration* not only is not a comprehensive account of Dio's position on sexual activity between males, but actually treats sexual relations in the broader context of gender indeterminacy. Finally, we have seen that the *Borystheniticus* does not provide sound evidence for Dio's ideas about sexual relations as practiced in Greece, and I have suggested that his views in the *Borystheniticus* may be the product of a fear that non-Greeks will behave violently when engaged in male-male relations. On the basis of the foregoing discussions, I am now prepared to offer some general conclusions about Dio's views.

First, it should be clear that Russell and Swain reach their conclusion that Dio is unyielding in his hostility to male-male relations by failing to consider evidence to the contrary from the third *Discourse*. The *Euboean Discourse* is indeed a hostile treatment, not of all sexual relations, but of all sexual relations aimed at producing pleasure. I have attempted to show that the *First Tarsian Oration*, to the extent that it is concerned with sex at all, denounces adult male sexual passivity. Its silence on men who take the active role in sexual relations indicates that Dio's account here is not a blanket denunciation of male-male sexual activity.

Second, one might reconstruct an account of Dio's ideas about *aphrodisia*, based upon the orations discussed. Dio has no use for sexual relations pursued out of hedonism, a reflection of his disdain for pleasure seeking in general. Such relations, whether pursued with boys or women, grow out of *akolasia* and put the object of desire at risk of being treated with *hybris*. Sexual relations pursued for pleasure are condemned as unlawful and unnatural. When these relations are sought with youths from noble households, Dio becomes especially nervous. Of relations for pleasure, these are the worst of all because they allow the hedonist to treat future citizens and leaders like common prostitutes. As the *First Tarsian Oration* points out, Dio is also unnerved at the thought of adult males submitting themselves to sexual penetration.

The third *Discourse* raises the possibility that Dio warily associates all sexual relations with *hybris*, whether the agent pursues them with males or females, and regardless of the agent's motives. This said, the third *Discourse* also indicates that Dio can countenance sexual relations between a male agent and a youth or a woman. The important condition is that the agent pursues *eunoia* or acts out of *philia* for his sexual partner. The biological sex of the partner is not a source of concern. The *Euboean Discourse* suggests in addition that Dio favors conjugal, procreative intercourse over hedonistic sex.

Finally, we have seen that Dio's views are influenced by Stoic teachings.[70] Indeed, I think that Dio's position outlined here actually replicates some aspects of Stoic teachings on *eros* and *aphrodisia*. His failure to condemn male-male sexual relations wholesale in the third *Discourse* and his acceptance of it as a reflection of *philia* are similar to the older Stoic position. Moreover, his recommendation of *aphrodisia* with male or female in the third *Discourse* reflects the older Stoic position that the biological sex of one's sexual partner is a matter of moral indifference—a constituent of the Stoic *adiaphora*. The *Euboicus* also seems to reflect Dio's philosophical training, though his rhetorical approach to demonizing prostitution means he treats *aphrodisia* in a way very different from his approach in the third *Discourse*. In his argument against prostitution, Dio attacks sex for pleasure, and his general approach and scope indicate that he has been influenced by the Cynic-Stoic diatribe, best exemplified by his teacher Musonius Rufus. Unlike Musonius, however, Dio does not condemn male-male relations per se, although he does condemn the hedonist's attempts to gain sexual access to the youths from noble households. His concern here reflects his broader interest in recommending a life of frugality and simple living over one characterized by self-indulgence and wasteful expenditure. This interest, I would argue, frames all of Dio's moralizing and is responsible for the condemnations and recommendations about sexual behavior which Dio makes. Anyone failing to recognize this runs the risk of undermining his or her proper appreciation both of Dio's work and of his place in the history of moralizing discourse.

Notes

I gratefully acknowledge many helpful suggestions by two anonymous readers and especially by the chair of the editorial board of *Classical Antiquity*, Ralph Hexter. I read a preliminary version of this essay at Brown University in December 1997. The current chapter has benefited greatly from the incisive comments of David Konstan, Stanley Stowers, and other members of the audience who attended that presentation.

1. At 7.151, Dio refers to these youths as those who will hold office, be judges, and act as generals — τοὺς ἄρξοντας καὶ δικάσοντας καὶ στρατηγήσοντας.

2. See John J. Winkler, *The Constraints of Desire* (New York, 1990), 17–44. Winkler concerns himself with usages which attest widely accepted points of view. Philosophers arguably had little "cultural authority" in the Greek world in general, and their works do not figure prominently in his discussions. Plato *Laws* 636C, for example, condemns male-male relations as contraventions of nature, in the sense of a "universal and necessary order," as opposed to convention.

3. See Winkler, *Constraints of Desire*, 21–22, for the argument and for the quotations in this paragraph.

4. See David Halperin, *One Hundred Years of Homosexuality* (New York, 1990), 15–40, esp. 29ff.

5. See ibid., 34–35.

6. The *Euboicus* is by no means the only place where this point of view is obvious. See, e.g., *Or.* 3, 13, 33.

7. See D. A. Russell, ed., *Dio Chrysostom: Orations VII, XII and XXVI* (Cambridge, 1992), esp. 150, 157, 216. Russell finds evidence for this point of view in *Or.* 4, 7, 36, and 77/78. See too Simon Swain, *Hellenism and Empire: Language, Classicism, and Power in the Greek World*, A.D. *50–250* (Oxford, 1996), 84, 125–26, 214–16. Both of these

scholars hold that Dio consistently condemns "homosexuality," itself a problematic term that I have chosen to avoid in this chapter. For the term's inappropriateness in discussions of ancient attitudes towards sexual behavior and desire, see M. Foucault, *The History of Sexuality*, vol. 2, *The Use of Pleasure*, trans. Robert Hurley (New York, 1985), 187–203. John Boswell, *Christianity, Social Tolerance, and Homosexuality* (Chicago, 1980), writes a chapter on the history of "gay people," a phrase Boswell uses throughout his introduction (3–39). The approach from the perspective of "gay history" relies on an anachronism whose shortcomings are discussed by Halperin, *One Hundred Years*, 15–40. Halperin considers sexuality from a constructionist point of view and includes a helpful discussion of the evolution of the concept of "homosexuality" and its difference from Greek analysis of sexual behavior and desire. For discussion of Halperin and Winkler, *Constraints of Desire*, and their critical approaches and discussion of the possibility that a class of men at Rome practiced "homosexuality" more or less as it is today understood, see Amy Richlin, "Not before Homosexuality: The Materiality of the *Cinaedus* and the Roman Law against Love between Men," *Journal of the History of Sexuality* 3 (1993): 523–73. Additional bibliography is available in Amy Richlin, *The Garden of Priapus: Sexuality and Aggression in Roman Humor*, rev. ed. (Oxford, 1992), xiii–xxx.

8. See Swain, *Hellenism and Empire*, 214–15. For Highet's suggestion, see G. A. Highet, "Mutilations in the Text of Dio Chrysostom," in *The Classical Papers of Gilbert Highet*, ed. R. J. Ball (New York, 1983), 95.

9. For Dio's praise of the Sacred Band, see *Or*. 22.2. See also Swain, *Hellenism and Empire*, 215.

10. No emperor is named, though the hypothesis that the third *Discourse* was delivered before the emperor is widely accepted. See Swain, *Hellenism and Empire*, 192, and C. P. Jones, *The Roman World of Dio Chrysostom* (Cambridge, Mass., 1978), 115–20. Scholars are less willing to argue for a particular year or date, though Hans von Arnim, *Leben und Werke des Dio von Prusa* (Berlin, 1898), 405, argues that this speech was delivered on Trajan's birthday, September 18, in either c.e. 103 or 104. Jones (119) suggests that the third *Discourse* was delivered after the first, but he is unwilling to offer a specific date.

11. See Jones, *The Roman World of Dio Chrysostom*, 120.

12. See *Or*. 36.29–37.

13. See Swain, *Hellenism and Empire*, 195–200, for a discussion of Dio's ideas about kingship and their resemblance to Stoic teachings. Swain lays particular importance on the first and third *Discourses on Kingship*. On the nature of the divine, an account which also owes a debt to the Stoa, see the *Olympic Discourse* (*Oration* 5).

14. As examples of what are profitable but not necessarily pleasant, Dio mentions weapons, seige engines, and soldiers (3.92).

15. The adjective ὡραῖαι/ὡραῖα means literally "blooming" or "blossoming" and signifies the beauty of youth.

16. For Stoic philosophical discussions and their references to the "bloom of youth," see Malcolm Schofield, *The Stoic Idea of the City* (Cambridge, 1991), 113–14, 117.

17. At 3.84, Dio has already suggested that excessive self-indulgence will make one weak in the face of toil and insensate to pleasure.

18. On the relationship between *eunoia* and *philia*, see *Or.* 12.12, 44.1–2, and 65.10.

19. Daniel Babut, "Les Stoiciens et l'amour," *Revue des études grecques* 76 (1963): 56, long ago noticed that Dio bears some similarity to the Stoics in matters of love and sexual relations. See too Russell, *Dio Chrysostom*, 150. P. A. Brunt, "Aspects of the Social Thought of Dio Chrysostom and the Stoics," *Proceedings of the Cambridge Philological Society* 19 (1973): 9–34, argues that Dio owes a debt to the Stoa in matters of practical morality in general.

20. For a discussion of these concepts and their operation in the *Lysis*, see A. W. Price, *Love and Friendship in Plato and Aristotle* (Oxford, 1989), 1–14. More interesting is Dio's apparent allowance of a bond of *philia* between a man and a woman. The term *philos* was routinely applied to the relationship between a man and a courtesan, but apparently seldom to free men and women. On the other hand, women could apparently enjoy the *philia* of one another. For a discussion of these topics with analysis of relevant passages, see David Konstan, *Friendship in the Classical World* (Cambridge, 1997), 91.

21. Schofield, *The Stoic Idea of the City*, 29–30, considers this definition sufficiently authoritative for Stoic teachings to use it as the basis of his analysis of Stoic *eros*.

22. The νέων here may refer to either males or females.

23. For the Stoic indifference to the biological sex of an *eromenos/e*, see Sext. Emp. *Pyr.* 1.160, 3.200, 3.245 and Stob. *Ecl.* 2.9–11. We should also notice that Zeno's *Republic* provided for common access to women, and J. M. Rist has suggested that nothing in the evidence for Zeno's work precludes common access to youths. Zeno's *Republic* is reported by Plutarch to have discussed intercrural intercourse, an indication of homosexual relations in that work. See Plut. *Quaest. conv.* 653E. See Rist's suggestion in Andrew Erskine, *The Helenistic Stoa* (Ithaca, N.Y., 1990), 23. For a discussion of the role of females in the Stoics' ideal city, see Schofield, *The Stoic Idea of the City*, 43–46.

24. That the Stoics imagined an educative purpose for these relationships has been amply demonstrated by a variety of scholars. For one succinct discussion, see Schofield, *The Stoic Idea of the City*, 32–34. They also held that youthful beauty would attract the wise man. See, e.g., D.L. 7.130 and Plut. *De communibus notitiis* 1073B, where *eros* is also characterized as a "hunt" for the youth.

25. Dio first brings up prostitution at 7.133, and the discussion continues to the abrupt end of the discourse, twenty-nine chapters later.

26. See Winkler, *Constraints of Desire*, 22.

27. μισθὸν ὕβρεως καὶ ἀκολασίας (7.133). Historically, prostitutes might have been male or female, and male prostitution seems to have been relatively common in the empire. See Epictetus *Dissertationes* 4.1.35 and Plutarch *Moralia* 759f–760c. For references to male prostitutes in other authors, see D. F. Wright, "Homosexuals or Prostitutes? The Meaning of ARSENOKOITAI (I Cor. 6:9, I Tim. 1:10)," *Vigiliae Christianae* 38 (1984): 125–53. For a discussion of male prostitution in fifth-century Athens, see Halperin, *One Hundred Years*, 88–112.

28. As Winkler, *Constraints of Desire*, 21–22, notices, Dio situates sexual relations with these noble males at the very bottom of the slippery slope at whose top sits solicitation of prostitutes. Moreover, Dio here enlists the authority of nature to forbid sexual activity with the city's future leaders.

29. In their search for sexual pleasures increasingly difficult to experience, the *akolastoi* seem to display symptoms of a "hyperbolic" desire, which intensifies as the agent attempts to satisfy it. For a discussion of the hyperbolic potential of sexual appetite, see Foucault *History of Sexuality*, 2:49–50. Their attempts to create increasingly difficult opportunities for sexual intercourse also suggest what Foucault has called "immoderation of artifice." See Foucault, 57, who refers this immoderation to efforts directed at experience of "unnatural" pleasures for their own sake, and not for the sake of "fullness" or satiation. In the *Euboicus*, Dio does not explicitly distinguish sexual desire from sexual action, but refers to *aphrodisia* in general.

30. For this meaning of *hybris*, see K. J. Dover, *Greek Homosexuality* (Cambridge, Mass., 1978), 34–39. The broad range of applications for the term *hybris* is studied by D. M. MacDowell, "*Hybris* in Athens," *Greece and Rome* 23 (1976): 14–31; and by N. R. E. Fisher, *Hybris: A Study in the Values of Honour and Shame in Ancient Greece* (Warminster, 1992). For an exploration of the differences between their views, see Douglas L. Cairns, "*Hybris*, Dishonour, and Thinking Big," *Journal of the History of Sexuality* 116 (1996): 1–32.

31. He calls the women and boys of these households ἐντίμους (7.139). While the *akolastoi* do not belong to any particular social or political class, Dio's indication that the households at risk are among the political elite makes it likely that his *akolastoi* would be victimizing their political or social equals or superiors, which classical Athenian sexual mores, at any rate, would militate against. See Halperin, *One Hundred Years*, 32ff.

32. ἐμπειρίαν καλῶν τε καὶ αἰσχρῶν. This entire passage has a strong Stoic ring to it. See, e.g., Musonius Rufus's argument that women should study philosophy, on the grounds that women and men equally have reason and moral judgment (Hense 9).

33. See Winkler, *Constraints of Desire*, 22.

34. Like the third *Discourse on Kingship*, the piece may have been delivered before Trajan at Rome. See Jones, *The Roman World of Dio Chrysostom*, 121. If both the *Fourth Discourse* and the *Euboean* were delivered at Rome, they may be particularly suitable for comparison. There are three *daimones* and corresponding classes of men—the greedy (φιλοχρήματος), the hedonistic described here, and the ambitious (φιλότιμος).

35. τὰ ἡδονῆς . . . ὄργια.

36. Dio does not indicate precisely what "unspeakable and unmentionable shameful deeds" he has in mind. The context suggests he means something other than sex between male and female.

37. Of course, being a general or an orator requires one to appear masculine and self-restrained. Femininity was considered a sign of inability to serve effectively the state or the people. At Rome, accusations of effeminacy and softness (*mollitia*) could be used to challenge the authority of a powerful figure, or even to disqualify one from public service. For a study of the rhetoric of *mollitia* in Rome, see C. Edwards, *The Politics of Immorality in Ancient Rome* (Cambridge, 1993), chap. 2. Dio's description of the hedonist at 4.109–15 paints this figure as a *kinaidos*, a type whose traits are well discussed by M. Gleason, *Making Men: Sophists and Self-Presentation in Ancient Rome* (Princeton, N.J., 1995), 55–81. Edwards also discusses Roman anxiety about pleasure seeking as a possible precursor to bankruptcy (*Politics*, chap. 5).

38. In his Loeb edition of the speech, Cohoon renders φερόμενος καὶ ἄγων "he rushes and also leads others." François translates the same phrase as "il est toujours porté et où il entraîne les autres." See Louis François, trans., *Dion Chrysostome, Deux Diogéniques (IVe de regno et fabula Lybica) en Grec et en Français* (Paris, 1922), 72–73.

39. The point may be that a potential competitor is rendered harmless, or even defenseless, through both operations.

40. Dio's position is at odds with the positions of the interlocutors in Plato's *Symposium*, most notably that of Diotima, as Socrates relates it.

41. For an excellent account of the diatribe question, see Stanley Stowers, *The Diatribe and Paul's Letter to the Romans* (Chico, Calif., 1981), 7–75. Other important studies of the diatribe include André Oltramare, *Les origines de la diatribe romaine* (Lausanne, 1926); A. C. van Geytenbeek, *Musonius Rufus and Greek Diatribe* (Assen, 1963), 13–14; J. F. Kindstrand, *Bion of Borysthenes* (Uppsala, 1976); and Barbara P. Wallach, "A History of the Diatribe from Its Origin up to the First Century B.C. and a Study of the Influence of the Genre upon Lucretius" (Ph.D. diss., University of Illinois, 1974; Ann Arbor, Mich.: UMI, 1976).

42. The texts of these philosophers' teachings are readily available in both Greek and in English translations. For Teles, see E. N. O'Neil, *Teles the Cynic Teacher* (Missoula, 1976), for a Greek text and translation. For Greek texts with translations of Musonius's work, with a useful historical introduction, see Cora Lutz, "Musonius Rufus: The Roman Socrates," *Yale Classical Studies* 10 (1947): 3–147. For a more detailed discussion of these essays and their place in the tradition of the diatribe, see Geytenbeek, *Musonius Rufus*. Greek texts of Epictetus are available in the Teubner and Loeb collections. The most widely available translations of Arrian's discourses of Epictetus are those in the Loeb collection.

43. The precise identity of this "Lucius" is not known. For an account of various attempts to identify him, see Lutz, "Musonius Rufus," 7–8. Musonius himself apparently wrote nothing, though scholars sometimes write as if he did. Most of our information on his teachings derives from the essays by Lucius, whose reliability as a source for his mentor's teachings is nearly impossible to determine with certainty.

44. For Dio's relationship to Musonius Rufus, see Fronto *Ep. ad Verum* 1.1.4 (Haines). For another discussion of their relationship, touching on matters of sexual ethics, see Geytenbeek, *Musonius Rufus*, 51–77. Stowers, *The Diatribe*, 206 n. 332, gives a list of those works by Dio that he considers diatribes. The *Euboean Discourse* is not among these, though as he remarks "many other orations which are not diatribes, may still contain certain elements of diatribe style." I include the *Euboean Discourse* in this later category.

45. Compare Musonius here with Dio, who uses *poikilos* to describe the hedonist in the fourth *Discourse on Kingship* (4.101)

46. Note that Musonius's use of *paidika* here must refer to male and female. Indeed, the word is neuter and presumably can refer to either males or females in other instances, though I know of no other passage where the word *must* refer to both. K. J. Dover remarks that the word *paidika* was most often used as a synonym for *eromenos*, though he does find two instances in Old Comedy where it refers, facetiously perhaps, to a female. See Dover, *Greek Homosexuality*, 16–17. Commentators and translators of

Musonius Rufus have passed over this remarkable usage apparently without noticing its oddity. Cora Lutz, for example, translates ποιχίλων παιδιχῶν "variety of loves" and offers no note on this. See Lutz, "Musonius Rufus," 84, 87. Jagu calls the *paidika* "mignons." See Amand Jagu, *Musonius Rufus: Entretiens et fragments: Introduction, traduction et commentaire* (Hildesheim, 1979), 62.

47. For the full passage, which I paraphrase here, see Hense 63–64.

48. See Hense 65–66.

49. Seneca, for example, ridicules Chrysippus for saying that the wise man's failure to marry offends "*Iovem Gamelium et Genethlium.*" See Jerome *Adv. Iovinian.* 2.48.

50. Dio does call "natural" the intercourse between "male and female," which is different from "man and woman" and may suggest that he is thinking about the natural world as his paradigm for intercourse, rather than exclusively human beings. Nevertheless, the context (a discussion of marriage and family life set against prostitution) suggests of course that he is thinking especially of human beings.

51. On the question of the completeness of Musonius's account, see Geytenbeek, *Musonius Rufus,* 72–77.

52. Cf. *Laws* 636c.

53. See, for example, Swain, *Hellenism and Empire,* 214. Also see Gleason, *Making Men,* 82–83, who thinks that the precise definition of the term may not be recoverable. She also cites a description of snorting speech associated with antisocial behavior found in Polemo's *Physiognomy* (52, 1.266–68F). Also see Jones, *The Roman World of Dio Chrysostom,* 73–74.

54. Dio reasserts his point about *androgynoi* at the end of the discourse (33.64).

55. See Jones, *The Roman World of Dio Chrysostom,* 73–74. For the generally discredited position of Welles, see "Hellenistic Tarsus," *Mélanges de l'Université Saint-Joseph* (Beirut) 28 (1962): 43–75.

56. There is ample evidence that snorting was considered offensive in the ancient world. See, in addition to the comments by Polemo, *Physiognomy,* the article by C. Bonner, "A Tarsian Peculiarity," *Harvard Theological Review* 35 (1942): 1–11.

57. See Gleason, *Making Men,* 82–83.

58. Bonner, "A Tarsian Peculiarity," thus thinks *rhengkein* accompanies sexual activity, though he stops short of specifying exactly what kind.

59. See Highet, "Mutilations in the Text of Dio Chrysostom," 95. Highet does not argue for his idea, but simply states it. See Swain, *Hellenism and Empire,* 214–15.

60. These quotations are from Gleason, *Making Men,* 64.

61. For the importance of hair to the identity of the male, see Gleason, *Making Men,* 67–70. It is well understood that Dio, like Musonius Rufus, had disdain for depilation. See Swain, *Hellenism and Empire,* 215–16.

62. Swain refers to "male homosexual sex." See Swain, *Hellenism and Empire,* 215.

63. It might of course be argued that Dio's rejection of passive sexual behavior on the part of adult males automatically implies condemnation of their active male partners. The possibility cannot be excluded. Nevertheless, this discourse does not condemn, for example, sexual relations with youths who have not reached the age of majority, nor does it discuss sexual relations initiated by agents other than the *akolastoi.*

64. See Russell, *Dio Chrysostom*, 19–20, for a discussion of the possible origin of this information.

65. See ibid., 21. See Jones, *The Roman World of Dio Chrysostom*, 62–63, for a discussion of how Dio's account of the city compares with evidence from the site itself.

66. Russell, *Dio Chrysostom*, 216, suggests that Callistratus has a "somewhat effeminate . . . appearance" signified by his Ionian looks. But Dio elsewhere describes masculine beauty in terms similar to those in his account of Callistratus. At 21.15, Dio links size and bravery, and at 28.2 he describes the boxer Melancomas as πάνυ μέγας καὶ καλός. Compare this to his characterization of Callistratus as πάνυ καλὸς καὶ μέγας (36.8). At 29.18, Dio again links bravery and beauty, calling Theseus and Achilles the only two men distinguished for both of these qualities.

67. See Russell, *Dio Chrysostom*, 216; and Swain, *Hellenism and Empire*, 83.

68. See Russell, *Dio Chrysostom*, 216; and Dover, *Greek Homosexuality*, 34–39.

69. Compare Herodotus 1.135, where it is suggested that the Persians learned pederasty from the Greeks. Dio's assumption that one culture can "pick up" male-male sexual relations from another is certainly not new with him. See also 21.4, where Dio criticizes the violence that accompanies the Persians' male-male sexual practices, which involve castration of youths.

70. Jones, *The Roman World of Dio Chrysostom*, 45–55, has reviewed evidence for Dio's life, including his supposed "conversion" to philosophy. Jones also argues that Dio's life, including his involvement in public affairs, appears to have harmonized with a Stoic inclination.

Chapter Thirteen

ENACTING *EROS*

David Konstan

I. ROMAN GREECE

*A*mong the *Dialogues of the Gods* composed by Lucian is a brief skit between Zeus and Eros (number 6 in the Oxford Classical Texts edition). Zeus is on the point of shackling Eros for his sins. When Eros protests that he is but a boy (*paidion*), Zeus retorts: "You, Eros, a boy? You're older than Iapetus, by far." [1] The joke, which Lucian enjoyed enough to tell more than once, depends of course on Hesiod's account of Eros as one of the primal deities in the universe, a point that Plato too exploited in the *Symposium*. "Just because you haven't sprouted a beard or gray hairs," Zeus continues, "you think you should be treated as a baby, though you're a dirty old man?" Old man or not, says Eros, "what's the big harm I've done you?" To which Zeus replies: "Look here, you rascal: is it small stuff, when you make so much fun of me that there's nothing you haven't made of me: satyr, bull, gold, swan, eagle? What you haven't made is any woman to fall in love [*erasthēnai*] with me. I've never become pleasing to a woman thanks to you, so far as I'm aware; no, I always have to play tricks on them and disguise myself. What they love [*philousin*] is the swan or bull; if they catch sight of me, they die of fear."

Eros answers that it is only natural that mortal women cannot endure the sight of him. When Zeus remarks that Branchus and Hyacinthus love (*philousin*) Apollo, Eros answers that Daphne, at all events, fled from him, despite his long hair and beardlessness. "If you want to be loved [*eperastos einai*], stop brandishing the aegis and carrying the thunderbolt and make yourself really pleasing and soft to look at; let your curls grow and tie them in a ribbon, wear a purple gown, strap on gold sandals, walk to the beat of a flute and tambourines, and you'll see, more of them will tail you than Dionysus's maenads." Zeus, however, indignantly rejects the idea: "Get out of here! I don't want to be loved [*eperastos einai*] by becoming that sort." "Okay, Zeus, then stop falling in love [*mēde eran thele*]. It's easier that way." "No," Zeus shoots back, "I want to love [*eran*], but catch them with less trouble [*apragmonesteron*]. On these terms I release you."

Let us begin with the conclusion. Clearly, Zeus has altered the terms of his original complaint. He began by protesting that his love was not reciprocated. Though he succeeds, in his various metamorphoses, in having his way with mortal women, their affection ends up being directed to his outer form as bull or swan, and not to himself—or not, at all events, to himself in his own, proper shape. Zeus wants to be loved for what he is. In the end, however, he frees Eros on the condition that he obtain what he wants with less effort, as though the problem with assuming the guise of a satyr or an eagle were merely the discomfort it involves.

Zeus shifts his goal because Eros has convinced him that he is, in fact, unlovable in his own shape. The reason is not, as Eros hints, that the undissimulated glory of a god, or at all events a thunder and lightning god like Zeus, annihilates human beings: the allusion is manifestly to the incineration of Semele, who, at Hera's suggestion, demanded to see the true shape of Zeus. It is rather that tough-guy looks, complete with fierce weaponry, do not arouse passionate love in others. If Zeus wants reciprocal enamorment, he must adopt an effeminate manner like that of Dionysus, whom the maenads pursue, it is implied, because he is attractive to them. Such an alteration in Zeus's appearance, moreover, is more than a disguise, like the swan or gold he turns into to gain his amorous ends. If he dresses and struts as Eros advises, women will fall in love with the real Zeus. But looking soft and sweet is too high a price to pay for requited passion, and Zeus elects instead to keep his traditional image and content himself with further conquests, provided only that they are a little easier to achieve.

The story is cleverly constructed to suggest that for real he-men, erotic love is necessarily asymmetrical: they pursue the objects of their desire, but there is no possibility of being loved in return. Yet the dialogue acknowledges that men do want to be desired. What is more, it is open to them to be so, provided they sacrifice the macho style for a gentle and decorous manner. Zeus, as the very model of the aggressive lover, cannot make the switch, but then he is something of a boor. Apollo, with his boyish looks, has more success, especially with youths like Branchus and Hyacinth, as opposed to girls, while Dionysus, who is even more dandified, has loads of women in train. True, Apollo is still young; being loved, however, does not depend on age, but on style. This is the reason for the byplay concerning Eros's antiquity at the beginning of the dialogue: he appears to be a boy, and we may assume that he is sexually attractive, but in fact he is more ancient than the Titans. Gods, after all, are ageless. The question is, How do they choose to present themselves?

Nor is the issue one of sexual identity. The costume that Eros proposes is not so much effeminate as effete. Zeus refuses to play the pretty boy. The choice is between two ways of being masculine: macho versus mild. With the one, you overpower women or boys (Zeus's guise as eagle alludes to the rape of Ganymede); with the other, you gain their love—and not just the affection suggested by the word *philein*, such as Leda and Europa may have experienced for the swan and bull (unless *philein* here means simply "kiss"), and Branchus and Hyacinth feel for Apollo, but the active passion connoted by *eran*. The latter, Lucian implies, is the more civilized way. In his desire to be desired, and his simultaneous fear of seeming soft, Zeus is rather a pathetic figure, though he remains intimidating. He is like a bully who suffers because he does not know how to play with others.[2]

Lucian's comic dialogue seems subtly to subvert the prevailing structure of erotic relations in the classical Greek city-state. David Halperin, for example, who has contributed brilliantly to elucidating the pattern, offers the following summary (Halperin 1993, 418): "In classical Athens a relatively small group made up of the adult male citizens held a virtual monopoly of social power and constituted a clearly defined élite within the political and social life of the city-state. The predominant feature of the social landscape of classical Athens was the great divide in status between this superordinate group, composed of citizens, and a subordinate group, composed of women, children, foreigners, and slaves. . . . Sexual relations not only respected that divide but were strictly polarized in conformity with it." Halperin adds: "sexual penetration was thematized as domination: the relation between the insertive and the receptive sexual partner was taken to be the same kind of relation as that obtaining between social superior and social inferior."

The desire characteristic of women and boys was correspondingly imagined to be different in kind from that of adult males. Women were typically represented as yielding to sex rather than commanding it, and feminine desire, like that of boys, was expressed as a willingness to be penetrated rather than as an urge to penetrate. This polarity did not necessarily coincide with the distinction between genders, but depended rather on differences of power. Adult citizen males were the subjects of erotic passion, while women, boys, and others of inferior status were its objects. Free men might assume the role of *erastēs*, never of *erōmenos;* it was demeaning to be perceived as an object of sexual desire.[3]

Lucian's Zeus, then, in seeking to be loved in turn, has implicitly compromised his masculinity and his status as all-powerful god. In recommending that he dress in the effeminate style of Dionysus, Eros is simply drawing the logical conclusion from Zeus's request, given the traditional code of sexual relations. At the same time, Eros also suggests that another style of erotic interaction is possible and no less proper to divinities. In this regard, Lucian seems to reflect the ethos of the Greek novels, which bear witness to a valorization of reciprocal *erōs* between men and women. Here too, symmetrical love entails an equivalence of sexual roles. The novelistic hero, like the heroine, is young and physically desirable to adult males. In Xenophon of Ephesus's *Ephesiaka*, both Habrocomes and Anthia are wooed by the pirates who capture them. Daphnis, in Longus's *Daphnis and Chloe*, is pursued by Gnatho, a parasite attached to the household of Daphnis's true father. In Chariton's *Callirhoe*, the rejected suitors for Callirhoe's hand seek to disrupt the marriage between the protagonists by leaving wreaths and other signs of a *kōmos* at the couple's door, thereby rousing the young groom's suspicions concerning the fidelity of his bride. Callirhoe, however, parries the charge: "There has been no riotous party at my father's house! Perhaps *your* house is used to parties, and your lovers are upset at your marriage!" (1.3, trans. Reardon in Reardon 1989). Commentators have remarked that this suggestion of homoerotic behavior on the part of the protagonist is exceptional in the Greek novels, but I am inclined to think that it is of a piece with the parallel representation of both the hero and heroine in the novels as objects of erotic attraction.

We may appreciate better the quality of Eros's advice in Lucian's dialogue by comparing (and contrasting) it with a passage in the orations of Dio of Prusa, to which David Halperin (1990, 34) has called attention. Writing a half-century or so prior to Lucian, Dio castigates the loose morals of cities where adultery is common practice. He concludes his speech:

> Well then, among those people for whom affairs with girls are so
> simple, what can we expect concerning boys . . . ? Is there any way that
> a licentious people will refrain from the violation and corruption of

males, and establish this as the sufficient and clear boundary of nature? Will they not rather, having fulfilled in every way their intemperance in the case of women, and having now become satiated with this kind of pleasure, pursue another outrage, greater and more illicit? For the business with women, and those for the most part free and virgins, proved easy, and there was no great effort for those who engaged in this kind of hunt with the help of money. . . . But the rest is pretty obvious, since it happens to many: the one who is unsatiated with this kind of passion, when he finds nothing scarce or resisting in that sex, comes then to despise what is easy and feels contempt for Aphrodite among women, as being an available thing and in truth utterly feminine; and he will switch over to the male type, passionate to dishonor those who someday will be magistrates and judges and generals, in order to find there some difficult and unavailable form of pleasure. (*Orations* 7.148–52)

The lawless citizens of Dio's vicious city act in accord with the schema that David Halperin has educed. They are imagined as well-to-do adult males, and they seek to corrupt first women, then upper-class boys. The difference in roles is thus grounded in a distinction in station, whether in respect to gender or age. True, the boys will grow up to be "magistrates and judges and generals," but while they are still young, they are assimilated to women as the receptive partner in sex, whereas the active role of pursuit and penetration is reserved for men.

Dio disapproves of this behavior, which he takes as exploitative of feminine weakness and degrading to citizen youths. Though he represents the desire for boys as the inevitable consequence of an excessive passion for women, he nevertheless, and somewhat contradictorily, portrays pederastic sex as contrary to nature. In well-ordered communities, *erōs* is subject to strict control, and citizens are taught to exercise restraint. But this is not to say that Dio rejects the asymmetrical and hierarchical construction of erotic relations that Halperin has described for classical Athens. On the contrary, it is just because he takes it for granted that he is concerned to regulate erotic behavior. Men are by nature hunters, women and boys their prey. Dio does not imagine that these roles might be reversed or collapsed; his view of sexual morality is predicated on temperance, not equality.

The tension that animates Lucian's dialogue, on the contrary, does not depend, like Dio's, on an opposition between licentiousness and self-control. Correspondingly, Lucian's Eros is not concerned with the status or reputations of Zeus's victims. Lucian's theme is reciprocity, not moderation. What Eros proposes is, accordingly, a kind of unisex comportment which,

however much it may repel Zeus, the crude heavy, is, on Eros's view, necessary to mutual love. Lucian thus pokes fun at manliness, and seems to ad-
umbrate a style in which sexual roles are less polarized and desire is evenly
distributed between the erotic partners.

II. GREECE

Like Dio's ideal of masculine self-control, Lucian's evocation of bilateral
passion and the collapse of gender differences also has roots in the sexual
discourse of classical Athens. Taking our example from Eros in Lucian's dialogue, we may instance the representation of Dionysus in the late fifth century B.C.E. When Pentheus comes on stage in Euripides' *Bacchae*, his first
words reveal his suspicion that the women who have left their homes to
perform Bacchus's rites have in fact been drinking wine and "slinking off . . .
to lonely places to serve the lust of males" (222–23, trans. Dodds 1960,
ad loc.). He then turns to the stranger who has incited the women, "with
sweet-smelling hair in blond ringlets" (235), who has the charms of Aphrodite and "who day and night keeps company with young girls, dangling
before them his mysteries of joy" (237–38, trans. Dodds 1960, ad loc.).
Later, Pentheus addresses the god directly: "Well, stranger, you're not physically ugly, as to women, which is why you're here in Thebes; for you have
long locks, no thanks to wrestling, that trickle down your cheeks, laden
with longing [*pothos*], and you've pale skin on purpose, from shade instead
of the sun's rays, as you chase Aphrodite with your loveliness" (453–59).
Dionysus, then, is both lewd and attractive to women, a subject of erotic desire and the sort who rouses it in others. Both these qualities, moreover, are
associated with his effeminate appearance: the white skin and girlish curls
which mark him as unathletic and are suited to the pursuit of sex rather
than real hunting. The qualities in Dionyus that disgust Pentheus include
both his supposed lustfulness and his sex appeal.

Dionysus, then, poses a challenge to the rigid distinction between erotic
roles inscribed in the prevailing phallic model of sex that Halperin has de-
lineated. Any binary opposition, of course, is vulnerable to deconstruction
by the assimilation of its extremes, but the image of an effeminate but erotically threatening figure like Dionysus derives in this case, I believe, from
an inconsistency internal to the Athenian sexual ideology. As Foucault has
explained, the hierarchical relation between the sexes was both projected
outward onto the domain of politics, in which only free adult males had
the right to participate in governing the community, and inward onto the

construction of the individual psyche. For Foucault, the central principle of the moral life in the classical epoch was self-mastery (*enkrateia*), which was achieved by practices of self-discipline (*askēsis*). Self-mastery was conceived as a masculine virtue: "Just as, within the house, it is the man who commands, and just as, within the city, it falls neither to slaves nor children nor women to exercise power, but to men and men only, so too must each one make his manly qualities prevail over himself" (Foucault 1984, 96). That women constitute the more libidinous sex follows directly from Foucault's model, since they are by nature less capable of controlling themselves. We thus have the paradox that men are lovers, women and boys beloveds, or *erōmenoi*, but it is the erotic passion of women that is the more ungovernable: hence the obsessive jokes in Aristophanic comedy, for example, on women's irrepressible desire for sex.

But if women, rather than men, are less capable of temperance and more susceptible to lust, then the same should hold true of effeminate men, to the degree that they lack masculine *enkrateia*. The ideological move of analogizing men's domination over women with their control over their own appetites has the paradoxical consequence that less manly males are perceived as erotically more active. Simultaneously, however, by virtue of their assimilation to women, effeminate males are naturally constituted as objects of sexual desire in the eyes of men, or at least of those men who are sexually overcharged or indiscriminate, and also in the eyes of women, inasmuch as they succumb the more readily to sexual cravings. Hence the representation of Dionysus as simultaneously wanton and sexually appealing.[4]

Visual images of Dionysus as effeminate are characteristic of the latter part of the fifth century, as opposed to the fully bearded and masculine type that regularly appears on black-figured vases (Dodds 1960, 133–34, ad vv. 453–59). This development is coordinate with a change in the representation of men in pederastic scenes from bearded to beardless; in addition, a new predilection for soft physiques among *erōmenoi* seems to have emerged in the fourth century B.C.E. (Dover 1978, 71–73, 76–81).[5] If, however, an ideology of phallic domination, together with a high valuation on self-control as a masculine ideal, generated a paradox that was, perhaps, especially characteristic of the classical city-state, the combination of an unruly sexual drive and sex appeal was already associated with an effete style in the Homeric epics, most conspicuously in the figure of Paris. Having brashly challenged the Achaean chieftains to a duel, Paris slinks away when Menelaus, the least of the Achaean warriors, confronts him. Perceiving Paris's faint-heartedness, Hector rebukes him:

Evil Paris, beautiful, woman-crazy, cajoling,
Better had you never been born, or killed unwedded. . . .
Surely now the flowing-haired Achaians laugh at us,
thinking you are our bravest champion, only because your
looks are handsome, but there is no strength in your heart, no
    courage. . . .
And now you would not stand up against warlike Menelaos?
Thus you would learn of the man whose blossoming wife you have
    taken.
The lyre would not help you then, nor the favours of Aphrodite,
nor your locks, when you rolled in the dust, nor all your beauty.
(3.39–40, 43–45, 52–55, trans. Lattimore 1951)

Hector is contemptuous of Paris's sexual attractiveness, which may give him the look of a fighter but is in fact a sign of softness. But this in no way compromises Paris's erotic energy. Having been wafted by Aphrodite from the battlefield to his chamber, he bids Helen:

Come, then, rather let us go to bed and turn to love-making.
Never before as now has passion enmeshed my senses.
(3.441–42, trans. Lattimore 1951)

Paris loves and inspires love, just as Lucian's Zeus had hoped to do until Eros advised him of what it required.[6]

In early Greek culture, then, men who fell short of the macho ideal, which was represented by figures like Hector, were perceived as both more given to erotic behavior and more liable to stimulate erotic desire in others, even though the role of lover was normally conceived of as dominant or active, and thus characteristic of the free adult male. The sexual bivalence of a Paris or a Dionysus, in which the contrast between masculine and feminine identities is subdued, suggests the coexistence of active and passive roles and the possibility of reciprocal desire, in which each partner is simultaneously *erastēs* and *erōmenos* or *erōmenē*. In the complexly determined ideology of *erōs*, women were capable of erotic desire, but it was directed not so much at brawny heroes like Heracles as at the softer sort of male whom other men might also experience as desirable. As lovers, women's erotic role was assimilated to that of men.[7]

Euripides' *Hippolytus* represents a manifestly virile youth who is passionate about hunting (109–10) but at the same time betrays an odd prudish-

361

ness in respect to the pleasures of Aphrodite (106). Hippolytus resembles Pentheus in this respect, and, like Pentheus, he too will be destroyed by a normally mild deity whom he recklessly offends. Euripides does not indicate why Phaedra falls in love with Hippolytus, and the question may be irrelevant: the tension in the play requires her quasi-incestuous passion, and that is reason enough for its existence.[8] Nevertheless, Hippolytus's commitment to virginity serves, I think, to feminize him, as does his identification with the goddess Artemis, and thus renders him a natural object of sexual desire. When Phaedra, in her lovesickness, expresses her passion (*eramai*) to call to the hounds, let down her hair, and brandish javelin and spear (219–22), her wish is, of course, to share the activities of Hippolytus, but by taking on an identity as a hunter she may also be assuming the masculine role of pursuer, thereby implicitly casting Hippolytus in the role of *erōmenos*.

After Phaedra's death, Theseus, having been persuaded by her suicide note that she had been raped by Hippolytus (885–86), accuses his son of parading his vegetarianism as well as Orphic and Dionysian doctrines, although he in fact hunts his prey with a show of fine words (952–57). As Barrett plausibly argues (1964, 342–45), the charge of Orphism is merely a jibe and is inconsistent, among other things, with the representation of Hippolytus as a hunter. But why this jibe? Hippolytus's sexual abstinence has put Theseus in mind of ascetic practices generally (cf. the coexistence of continence and vegetarianism in the cult promoted by Empedocles), which he sees as a cover for licentiousness. Hippies are presumed to lack self-control.

While Phaedra seems to become enamored of Hippolytus for his virginal forbearance, Theseus sees in his youthful eccentricity evidence of his libidinousness. Thus, in forestalling Hippolytus's defense, he asks rhetorically: "Such foolishness is not in men but innate in women? But I know that young men are no safer than women when Aphrodite excites their adolescent hearts: their own masculinity assists them" (966–70). Young men, like women, are especially subject to *erōs*, as well as being potential objects of sexual desire in others. The tragedy plays on the equal plausibility of two scenarios: in the one, which constitutes the plot of the drama, a mature woman is passionate for a chaste youth; in the other, which is initiated by Phaedra's letter and finds a willing believer in Theseus, a youth, by virtue of his immaturity, is presumed to be subject to an excessive desire for a woman. Taken together, the two versions position the woman and the young man as both lover and beloved.[9]

Even if it is the case that Greek men might wish to be desired actively by the women they loved, it does not automatically follow that a similar

pattern of reciprocal erotic attraction was acknowledged in regard to homoerotic relations, in which, as Dover (1978, 16) puts it, "the distinction
between the bodily activity of the one who has fallen in love and the bodily
passivity of the one with whom he has fallen in love is of the highest importance." Although the analogy with women's position in erotic relations
suggests that boys too could in theory be seen as playing a sexually active
role, they might nevertheless be differentiated from women as being too
young to be subjects of erotic desire.[10] Furthermore, an adult male lover
would have a stake in maintaining control of erotic subjectivity in order to
avoid the stigma attaching to the passive role in a relationship with a man;
Greek pederastic poetry is scrupulous in not ascribing *erōs* to the *paidika*.
But, as scholars have observed, the lover's own subjection to *erōs*, expressed
by verbs such as "dominated" or "mastered" (e.g., *dameis;* Theognis 1344),
signifies a loss of masculine control, and the *erastēs* is further feminized by
being at the mercy of his beloved. Though it is the lover's voice that is heard
in pederastic literature, the beloved is implicitly empowered, and the lover
is in danger of being relocated as the dependent partner. Since the *erōmenos*
is typically portrayed as inveterately fickle, his behavior may seem to be entirely determined by the will of competing lovers, but the choice nevertheless remains his, and it is not altogether reducible to a passive gesture of ac-
quiescence. Much depends on how the beloved plays his part.

III. Greek Rome

Though Catullus is in many ways a special case, his poetry interestingly illustrates the dynamics of the pederastic relationship.[11] When it comes to
marriage, Catullus is content to represent the bride as the object of a transaction between males. Thus, in his antiphonal epithalamium (62), the girls
recite:

> Hesperus, what crueller star than you rides in the sky?
> For you can tear a daughter from her mother's embrace,
> from her mother's embrace tear clinging daughter
> and give the chaste girl to an ardent youth.
> What crueller deed does the foe commit when a city falls?
>
> (62.20–24, trans. Goold 1983)

Later, the boys respond:

And you, maiden, fight not with such a husband.
You must not fight with him your father gave you to himself,
your father himself with your mother, whom you have to obey.

(62.59–61, trans. Goold 1983)

When it comes to Lesbia, however, Catullus resorts to various strategies to indicate the reciprocity of their relationship. For example, he exploits the terminology of familial affection to express their mutual love, as in poem 72: "I was fond of you then not so much the way common folk feel for a girlfriend, but as a father is fond of his sons and sons-in-law." The verb is *diligere*, which is equivalent to the Greek *philein* and the term of art for the sentiment experienced by an *erōmenos* (cf. 81.2); elsewhere (76.23) he says he used to wish that Lesbia could like him back in this way. In poem 109, Catullus invokes the language of *amicitia* to express his ideal of erotic reciprocity:

You promise me, my life, a pleasant love [*amor*]—
    that ours will be so and be forever, too.
Great gods, make her able to promise honestly,
    and say it sincerely and from the heart,
so that we may continue our whole life through
    this eternal pact of holy friendship.[12]

Catullus may also make *amare* a bilateral expression, as in poem 92:

Lesbia always disparages me and never shuts up
    about me; I'm damned if she doesn't love me.
My proof? It's ditto for me: I constantly
    insult her, but I'm damned if I don't love her.

Though *amare* has a wider range than the Greek *eran*, and often corresponds to *philein*, the context here suggests an erotic attachment, as it does in *"vivamus, mea Lesbia, atque amemus"* [Let us live, my Lesbia, and let us love] (5.1), where Catullus bids Lesbia to kiss him (*da mi basia*), and speaks of their exchange of kisses (*fecerimus* [*basia*]; 10). It is no surprise that the sixteenth-century French poetess Louise Labé should have found in Catullus's poem inspiration for her racy sonnet:

Baise m'encor, rebaise-moi et baise;
Donne m'en un de tes plus savoreux,

Donne m'en un de tes plus amoureux:
Je t'en rendrai quatre plus chaud que braise.

Kiss me again, kiss me and kiss me more;
Give me one of your juiciest,
Give me one of your sexiest:
Hotter than coals, I'll give you back four.

By contrast, in the cycle of six poems that Catullus addresses to Juventius (the name suggests *iuvenis*), the boy is never represented as the subject of *amare*, and the kissing is all on Catullus's part (c. 48):

If anyone would let me kiss those honeyed
  eyes of yours thoroughly, Juventius,
I'd kiss you three hundred thousand kisses
  nor do I think I'd ever be satisfied,
not if the crop of our kissing were
  thicker than dry ears of grain.

Catullus is insatiable, while Juventius is portrayed as desirable rather than desiring.

In poem 99, Catullus describes an occasion on which he was punished for stealing a kiss from Juventius:

I stole a kiss from you at play, honey-sweet Juventius,
  a teeny kiss sweeter than sweet ambrosia:
but not with impunity, since for more than an hour,
  I remember, I was impaled at the top of a cross,
trying to excuse myself to you and unable for all my tears
  to wash away the least little bit of your anger.
For the moment it was done, you washed your lips with plenty
  of water and wiped them clean with your dainty fingers,
in case any contagion from my mouth remained
  as though it were some filthy whore's foul spit.
Then you hastened to hand me over, poor wretch,
  to angry Love and torture me in every way,
so that from being ambrosia that teeny kiss
  became nastier than nasty gall.

365

If that's the penalty you set on my unhappy love,
I shan't steal kisses from you any more.

(Trans. Goold 1983)

Catullus represents himself as the aggressor and Juventius as a pouting boy who refuses him: it is not that Juventius fails to reciprocate Catullus's passion but that he does not yield to it. But the division between active and passive roles in the poem is nevertheless unstable. The image of Catullus "impaled at the top of a cross" [*suffixum in summa . . . cruce*] suggests that penetration is reversible, and from his tears it is clear that he deems himself to be the injured party, as though he, and not Juventius, had been assaulted. Although Juventius's only mode of resistance is an expression of distaste—there is no suggestion, for example, that he tried to fend Catullus off—the gesture is construed as a punishment, and Catullus is the victim. Indeed, Catullus even appropriates Juventius's disgust, as the kiss he himself planted turns bitter for him, and his refusal to bestow more—despite the bravado of the word "steal" [*surripiam*]—is in fact a gesture of noncompliance, like Juventius's own, designed to sting the boy into seeking Catullus's favor. The poem's argument thus implicitly recasts Juventius as pursuer, Catullus as pursued, and intimates that Catullus, perhaps, will cease to requite the boy's feeling for him.

Catullus turns the tables on Juventius and casts his refusal to be kissed as a hostile act by representing his sentiment for the boy not as a possessive and domineering passion but as a helpless submission to love. What he professes to suffer, accordingly, is not just resistance but rejection, the psychological wound resulting from the want of caring. In the whining finale, Catullus sounds like an injured child: by depicting Juventius as guilty of denying him love, Catullus has assumed the position of his juvenile *erōmenos*—has colonized, we may say, the space of the love object.[13]

Catullus's poem conveys the impression that Juventius's behavior is unexpected: at an earlier time he presumably welcomed Catullus's kisses. Perhaps Juventius is being coy, and what looks like flightiness is in fact a ploy further to inflame Catullus's passion. There is the possibility, then, of self-conscious role playing on Juventius's part, and a measure of experience and calculation that belie the apparent innocence or naïveté of the boy. Then again, perhaps Catullus is deliberately representing him as a sophisticated tease in order to coerce his compliance by publicly shaming him in his verses. Or is Juventius simply a sulky brat?

The difficulty in interpreting Juventius's behavior may be due not only to the rhetorical purpose of the poem, but also to the fact that both Catullus and Juventius are acting out positions in an amatory duet. The poem, which is quite remarkable in the corpus of Roman pederastic literature, makes the reader aware of the extent to which such scenes of seduction depend on a particular construction of roles and performances.[14] In wiping away the kiss, and in accepting rather than giving kisses in the first place, Juventius appears both as a spoiled but callow child and as an actor who assumes mastery in the situation by a canny manipulation of his part.

It is through dramatic strategies of this sort that the complex game of sexual roles is normally negotiated in practice. As Judith Butler (1993, 315) has argued: "To claim that there is no performer prior to the performed, that the performance is performative, that the performance constitutes the appearance of a 'subject' as its effect is difficult to accept. This difficulty is the result of a predisposition to think of sexuality and gender as 'expressing' in some indirect or direct way a psychic reality that precedes it."[15] It is conceivable that what we today interpret as a matter of essence or identity was, for the Roman poet and his audience, at least in part a function of rhetoric and playacting.[16]

Among the poems of the Juventius cycle (15, 21, 24, 81) that deal with Catullus's rivals for the boy, the performative nature of sexual roles is especially evident in 21, where Catullus accuses Aurelius of attempting to seduce Juventius:[17]

> Aurelius, father of famines,
> not just of these, but of all that were
> or are or will be in years to come,
> you wish to bugger my boy. And not on the quiet:
> for you're always with him, always laughing with him,
> and fussing over him you leave nothing untried.
> It's no good: for though you plot against me,
> I'll get in first and stuff you.
> If you did it on a full stomach, I'd keep quiet:
> as it is, I'm vexed that the boy is going
> to learn from you to starve and thirst.
> So stop it, while you decently can,
> or else you'll finish by getting stuffed.
>
> (Trans. Goold 1983)

Aurelius's hunger is on the one hand a sign of poverty, which renders him an unfit lover for a youth who is "the flower of the Juventii" (24.1), an ancient aristocratic family. But Aurelius's hunger also signifies his sexual appetite, manifested in his desire to penetrate Juventius. The sexual and class hierarchies are thus crossed (cf. c. 24). Catullus's threat to bugger Aurelius realigns the axes of wealth and desire by forcing Aurelius into the passive position. Simultaneously, it assimilates him to Juventius's role as receptive partner. However, the cravings that Juventius is likely to acquire in the company of Aurelius derive not from Aurelius's indigence but from his lust; Juventius will thus become, thanks to Aurelius, an active subject of desire. By these means, too, the vectors of status and erotic dominance are synchronized. Once again, moreover, the roles of Juventius and Aurelius are rendered parallel, allowing, indeed, for the possibility that they will hunger mutually for one another. The poem thus intimates that Aurelius and Juventius are each potentially both passive and active, their roles shifting according to act and opportunity.

In their research on sexuality and the spread of AIDS in Mexico, Ana Maria Alonso and Maria Teresa Koreck record that men who play only the active or "inserter" role are not conceived of as homosexual, while those who play the passive role in anal intercourse "are demarcated as a particular category of beings—*jotos* or *putos*." [18] Alonso and Koreck observe: "There is no distinct linguistic term to designate *machos* who have sex with *jotos*, nor are they socially or culturally set off in any way" (117). Alonso and Koreck note that in the rural areas of Mexico that they investigated, all males occupy either the active or the passive role, but in urban areas "men playing both roles are called 'internationals,' a term which indexes the 'foreignness' of practices which are much more like those of American gays." [19]

In the Greco-Roman world, young men like Juventius are not classified as a distinct type; on the contrary, their role is fluid and is understood to vary both with age and with such factors as class, wealth, and the company they keep.[20] But these roles are nevertheless contained by an ideology of phallic sexuality that inhibits the simple, stable parity of relations among "internationals." In this situation, performance is particularly salient in the representation of pederastic relations.

In his last book, John Boswell sought to demonstrate that same-sex unions based on reciprocal love were valorized in classical antiquity as well as in the Middle Ages. Unfortunately, Boswell made free with the evidence; his claim, for example, that friendship might designate a romantic relationship (Boswell 1994, 75–77) is simply false. Boswell himself recognized the difficulty: "Since most ancient concepts of male sexuality presupposed that the 'active' or insertive party somehow dominated the 'passive' or receptive partner, sex would appear to introduce an element of subordination or inequality into a friendship, and thus complicate it" (79). This account is consistent with, indeed derived from, David Halperin's characterization, but Boswell seeks to evade the manifest consequences for his argument by asserting that it "should not be confused with a description of reality" (ibid.). Despite the public conflict, as he calls it, between friendship and sexuality, Boswell concludes that "there is no reason to believe that a sexual friendship was any rarer or more (or less) difficult then than now" (79–80). The business of philology, however, is not to intuit the true feelings of the ancients but to understand how they were realized and constrained within the context of the prevailing social codes. The argument of this chapter has been that contradictions in the sexual ideology of the classical world opened up a space for a conception of mutual *erōs*, as indicated in Lucian's witty dialogue, and that pederastic literature was, or could be, in the hands of a poet like Catullus, a dynamic site in which conventional erotic roles were both enacted and subverted. The result was not a valorization of sexual reciprocity as such but rather the recognition of a possibility that surfaced as inexorably as it was repressed.

Notes

1. Unless otherwise indicated, translations are my own.

2. For the distinction between erotic passion (*erōs*) and affectionate love (*philia*), see Faraone 1999, 29–30, 96–97, 146–51, who shows that married women use magic spells to induce *philia*, while men and courtesans are more likely to employ charms to instill erotic desire. On the attractiveness of effeminate-looking men, see Edwards 1993, 81–84; Edwards cites (pp. 82–83) Arrian *Discourses* 3.1.27–33, where Epictetus is said to have "chastised a young man, alleging that he cultivated an effeminate appearance in order to appeal to women."

3. Recently, Nicole Loraux has sought to trace "another tradition that is equally Greek, a tradition that, from Homeric epic to heroic legend, postulates that a man worthy of the name is all the more virile precisely because he harbors within himself something of the feminine" (1995, 4). To the extent that such an alternative tradition exists, however, it is largely an unconscious one and its manifestations are characteristically symbolic; Loraux's arguments do not, in my view, vitiate the model of sexuality educed by Halperin.

4. Hubbard 1998, 55–59, illustrates "the fluidity and interchangeability of sex roles" (p. 57) in Athenian Old Comedy, and remarks: "The concept behind this curious mixture of roles is, as Foucault has emphasized, that any form of sexual excess, whether adultery or, as here, pederasty, is a state of moral passivity toward physical appetites, a weakness of character like that of women" (p. 56). Hubbard rejects, however, the model of domination and subordination developed by Dover and Halperin and argues rather that ordinary people in classical Athens were suspicious of homoerotic behavior,

whether active or passive, and associated both roles particularly with upper-class attitudes. Hubbard summarizes his view as follows (p. 69): "it has been my argument that the active/passive dichotomy was of far less salience to ancient Greek judgments of homosexuality than the class-dynamics associated with its practice. Inasmuch as pederasty was perceived as an upper-class phenomenon, any practitioner, whether man or boy, was suspect in the eyes of the masses." In my view, the evidence for the polarization of sex roles in both Greece and Rome is overwhelming; I prefer, therefore, to interpret the fluidity of the active and passive positions as symptomatic of a contradiction in the classical ideology of sex.

5. During and after the French Revolution, French painting exhibits an analogous fascination with the epicene male figure; see Solomon-Godeau 1997, with the review by Warner (1997, 19), who compares the figure of Cupid in Apuleius's *Metamorphoses*.

6. Cf. Monsacré 1984, 41–50, who contrasts the beauty and weakness of Paris with the virile image of Hector, and notes that epic warriors are feminized in defeat (64–65).

7. Cf. also Aristophanes *Lysistrata* 414–15, where an Athenian official complains that husbands contribute to corrupting their wives by having craftsmen visit them at home: "Another says to the shoemaker, who is a youth [*neanian*] and has a penis that is not a child's [*peos ekhont' ou paidikon*]"; the implication is that the wife will be attracted by the boy's youthful appearance, although in the event it will be he who plays the active role of *erastēs* rather than the passive role of *paidika*. This and related passages are discussed in Konstan forthcoming.

8. Seneca, in his *Phaedra*, is more explicit about the causes of Phaedra's infatuation (646–58); she is seduced by the image of the young Theseus that Hippolytus's features reproduce, at the age when his beard first sprouted, "golden modesty tinged his tender cheeks, and strong muscles lay beneath his delicate arms" (652–53). The emphasis on Hippolytus's youth elaborates a suggestion in Ovid's *Heroides* 4.71–72, where Phaedra writes to Hippolytus: "your hair was bound up on flowers, and a modest blush tinged you golden cheeks" (cf. Boyle 1987, ad loc.), though Ovid's Phaedra is rather more interested in Hippolytus's rugged good looks (4.73–86). Hippolytus's resemblance to Theseus in Seneca's version was perhaps inspired by Virgil *Aeneid* 4.84–85, where Dido seeks to ease her passion for Aeneas by holding Ascanius in her lap, "captivated by the resemblance to his father" [*genitoris imagine capta*].

9. Various sources report that Phaedra's sister, Ariadne, fell in love with Theseus when he came to Crete to challenge the Minotaur and provided Theseus with the thread by which he escaped from the labyrinth (after she eloped with him, Theseus abandoned Ariadne on the island of Naxos). What explains Theseus's attractiveness? Apart from the fact that he was then a youth, we may note his condition of weakness and dependence; compare Odysseus's appeal to Nausicaa's pity (*Odyssey* 6), or Jason's to Medea's (Apollonius of Rhodes *Argonautica* 3). Dido's passion for Aeneas is inspired by a similar compassion; in his dalliance with Dido, moreover, Aeneas is feminized as a Phrygian with a taste for finery. It is also worth noting that Cupid ignites Dido's desire by assuming the form of Aeneas's young son, Ascanius; Dido's love is thus initially directed at the father's likeness in the boy. For further discussion of the objects of women's passion, see Konstan forthcoming.

10. Adolescent boys, making the transition from passive children to active adults, had an ambiguous sexual identity. Cf. the quip, already old in Terence's time, comparing an erotically active youth to a hare (considered a delicacy as well as prey) feasting on meat (Terence *Eunuch* 426). The saying was proverbial in Greek as well; see Barsby 1999, ad loc., and cf. Konstan forthcoming.

11. For an excellent overview of Roman attitudes toward homosexuality, see Williams 1999.

12. For the translation of the first couplet, see Konstan 1972–73.

13. See Skinner 1993, 120: "Although their helplessness is gendered as 'feminine', men are expected to engage with it vicariously—to identify with their sense of powerless yearning and capitulate, as they do, to tumultuous passion. . . . Ostensibly the assumption of such a passive feminized posture might seem acutely degrading. Paradoxically, however, it may also have been a channel for imaginative escape."

14. There is a growing body of scholarship on the instability of sexual identities in Roman literature, and specifically in the poetry of Catullus; see especially Skinner 1993; Miller 1998.

15. On performance, cf. also Friedman 1996, 21–22; Lindheim 1998, 63, who remarks of the episode of Hercules' cross-dressing in Propertius 4.9 that "the split predicated upon anatomy . . . dissolves before the reader's eyes as a fixed and ascertainable dichotomy and emerges as no more than an alternative performance or construction."

16. We may thus, perhaps, reorient the quarrel between constructionist views of sexuality and the essentialism defended, for example, by Richlin 1993 and Boswell 1990 (discussion in Skinner 1996): not even the asymmetries of status and power were wholly reified in antiquity. Cf. Clark 1993, 195: "some theorists argue that any unified conception of gay/lesbian identity is reductive and ahistorical"; on essentialism and constructionism, see also Fuss 1989, 3.

17. That the boy in this poem, though not named, is to be identified with Juventius is plausibly argued by Wiseman 1969, 7, and others.

18. Alonso and Koreck 1993, 115, following Carrier 1985; cf. also Lancaster 1988.

19. Alonso and Koreck 1993, 119, following Carrier 1989; cf. Almaguer 1993, reporting on Carrier's research in Guadalajara: "Only a segment of the homosexually active youth . . . develop a preference for the anal receptive, *pasivo* sexual role, and thus come to define their individual sense of gender in a decidedly feminine direction" (261).

20. Cf. Skinner 1993, 111: "Ancient gender identities seem to have been more fluid, at least in the case of men"; also Gleason 1990, 391.

References

Abelove, Henry, Michèle Aina Barale, and David M. Halperin, eds. 1993. *The Lesbian and Gay Studies Reader*. New York: Routledge.

Almaguer, Tomás. 1993. "Chicano Men: A Cartography of Homosexual Identity and Behavior." In *The Lesbian and Gay Studies Reader*, ed. Henry Abelove, Michèle Aina Barale, and David M. Halperin, 255–73. New York: Routledge.

Alonso, Ana Maria, and Maria Teresa Koreck. 1993. "Silences: 'Hispanics,' AIDS, and Sexual Practices." In *The Lesbian and Gay Studies Reader*, ed. Henry Abelove, Michèle Aina Barale, and David M. Halperin, 110–26. New York: Routledge.

Barrett, W. S., ed. 1964. *Euripides: Hippolytus*. Oxford: Clarendon Press.

Barsby, John, ed. 1999. *Terence: Eunuchus*. Cambridge: Cambridge University Press.

Boswell, John. 1990. "Concepts, Experience, and Sexuality." *differences* 2, no. 1: 67–78.

———. 1994. *Same-Sex Unions in Premodern Europe*. New York: Villard Books.

Boyle, A. J., ed. 1987. *Seneca's Phaedra*. Liverpool: Francis Cairns Publications.

Butler, Judith. 1993. "Imitation and Gender Insubordination." In *The Lesbian and Gay Studies Reader*, ed. Henry Abelove, Michèle Aina Barale, and David M. Halperin, 307–20. New York: Routledge.

Carrier, J. M. 1985. "Mexican Male Bisexuality." In *Bisexualities: Theory and Research*, ed. Fritz Klein, M.D., and Thomas J. Wolf, 75–85. New York: Haworth.

———. 1989. "Sexual Behavior and the Spread of AIDS in Mexico." *Medical Anthropology* 10:129–42.

Clark, Danae. 1993. "Commodity Lesbianism." In *The Lesbian and Gay Studies Reader*, ed. Henry Abelove, Michèle Aina Barale, and David M. Halperin, 186–201. New York: Routledge.

Dodds, E. R., ed. 1960. *Euripides: Bacchae*. 2d ed. Oxford: Clarendon Press.

Dover, K. J. 1978. *Greek Homosexuality*. London: Duckworth.

Edwards, Catharine. 1993. *The Politics of Immorality in Ancient Rome*. Cambridge: Cambridge University Press.

Faraone, Christopher A. 1999. *Ancient Greek Love Magic*. Cambridge, Mass.: Harvard University Press.

Foucault, Michel. 1984. *Histoire de la sexualité*. Vol. 2, *L'usage des plaisirs*. Paris: Gallimard.

Friedman, Susan Stanford. 1996. "'Beyond' Gynocriticism and Gynesis: The Geographics of Identity and the Future of Feminist Criticism." *Tulsa Studies in Women's Literature* 15, no. 1: 13–40.

Fuss, Diana. 1989. *Essentially Speaking: Feminism, Nature and Difference*. New York: Routledge.

Gleason, Maud W. 1990. "The Semiotics of Gender: Physiognomy and Self-Fashioning in the Second Century C.E." In *Before Sexuality: The Construction of Erotic Experience in the Ancient Greek World*, ed. David M. Halperin, John J. Winkler, and Froma I. Zeitlin, 389–415. Princeton, N.J.: Princeton University Press.

Goold, G. P., ed. and trans. 1983. *Catullus*. London: Duckworth.

Halperin, David M. 1990. *One Hundred Years of Homosexuality and Other Essays on Greek Love*. New York: Routledge.

———. 1993. "Is There a History of Sexuality?" In *The Lesbian and Gay Studies Reader*, ed. Henry Abelove, Michèle Aina Barale, and David M. Halperin, 416–31. New York: Routledge.

Hubbard, T. K. 1998. "Popular Perceptions of Elite Homosexuality in Classical Athens." *Arion* 6:48–78.

Konstan, David. 1972–73. "Two Kinds of Love in Catullus." *Classical Journal* 68:102–06.

———. Forthcoming. "El amante adolescente." In *Actas del Primer Simposio Internacional de Filología Griega: El amor in la literatura griega 1998,* ed. Juan Antonio López Férez. Madrid: Universidad Nacional de Educación a Distancia. English version available on "Diotima" at uky.edu/AS/Classics/gender.html.

Lancaster, Roger N. 1988. "Subject Honor and Object Shame: The Construction of Male Homosexuality and Stigma in Nicaragua." *Ethnology* 28, no. 2: 111–26.

Lattimore, Richmond, trans. 1951. *Homer: The Iliad.* Chicago: University of Chicago Press.

Lindheim, Sara. 1998. "Hercules Cross-Dressed, Hercules Undressed: Unmasking the Construction of the Propertian *Amator* in Elegy 4.9." *American Journal of Philology* 119: 43–66.

Loraux, Nicole. 1995. *The Experiences of Tiresias: The Feminine and the Greek Man.* Trans. Paula Wissing. Princeton, N.J.: Princeton University Press.

Miller, Paul Allen. 1998. "Catullan Consciousness, the 'Care of the Self,' and the Force of the Negative in History." In *Rethinking Sexuality: Foucault and Classical Antiquity,* ed. David H. J. Larmour, Paul Allen Miller, and Charles Platter, 171–203. Princeton, N.J.: Princeton University Press.

Monsacré, Hélène. 1984. *Les larmes d'Achille.* Paris: Albin Michel.

Reardon, Bryan P., trans. 1989. "Chariton: Chaereas and Callirhoe." In *Collected Ancient Greek Novels,* ed. B. P. Reardon, 17–124. Berkeley: University of California Press.

Richlin, Amy. 1993. "Not before Homosexuality: The Materiality of the *Cinaedus* and the Roman Law against Love between Men." *Journal of the History of Sexuality* 3: 523–73.

Skinner, Marilyn B. 1993. "*Ego mulier:* The Construction of Male Sexuality in Catullus." *Helios* 20: 107–30.

———. 1996. "Zeus and Leda: The Sexuality Wars in Contemporary Classical Scholarship." *Thamyris* 3: 103–23.

Solomon-Godeau, Abigail. 1997. *Male Trouble: A Crisis in Representation.* London: Thames on Hudson.

Warner, Marina. 1997. "A Revolution in Classical Drag: Thermidor *Déshabillé:* Effeminate Heroes and the Return of the Repressed." Review of *Male Trouble: A Crisis in Representation,* by Solomon-Godeau. *Times Literary Supplement* 4928 (12 September): 18–19.

Williams, Craig A. 1999. *Roman Homosexuality: Ideologies of Masculinity in Classical Antiquity.* New York: Oxford University Press.

Wiseman, T. P. 1969. *Catullan Questions.* Leicester: Leicester University Press.

Chapter Fourteen

The Erotic Experience of Looking:
Cultural Conflict and the Gaze
in Empire Culture

⚜

Simon Goldhill

Sex and sex and sex and sex and LOOK AT ME.

Mick Jagger

$\mathcal{T}$he erotics of the gaze is a hot subject. "The look" has become a privileged site for articulating the tensions and ambiguities of how "erotic experience" is conceptualized in contemporary society. In particular, the extensively discussed and theorized notion of the "objectifying male gaze" has made "looking" a highly contested battleground for issues of gender and power, the social regulation of media, the very construction of a desiring subject.[1] On the one hand, debates around pornography—both its understanding and its legal control—depend in part at least on models of how the act of looking relates to desire and to consequent behavior.[2] Thus, between feminist attempts to outlaw pornographic representation—taken to one point of extreme conclusion by Susanne Kappeler, who declares "all art must go"[3]—and highly public right-wing attempts to ban the works, say, of Robert Mapplethorpe,[4] the corrupting power which certain images are supposed to embody requires a particular, ideologically charged understanding of the erotic experience of viewing. On the other hand, in psychoanalytic theory, "the gaze," "the look," "the glance" have made visual perception central to self-formation as a desiring subject, at the same time as sociological theory has begun to explore the changing dominance of visual media in modern Western society and its impact on contemporary "erotic experience."[5] "Knowing how to look"—both in the sense of looking at art, film, people, and in the sense of knowing how one should appear—is a sign of being in culture—of being cultivated and of being acculturated. If one powerful, historically specific, modern image is of the male viewer objectifying the female body by his eyeing, and corrupted by his voyeuristic pleasures (and thus socially dangerous),[6] another equally powerful conceptualization is of the person who is defined as socially acceptable by a proper engagement with the regime of the visual. Looking right is fitting in. In discussing "erotic experience and sexual ethics," the eye has a fundamental place.

There is a long, but, as so often, scarcely appreciated history to this contemporary issue, a history which has a profound effect on the construction of modern understandings.[7] In particular, many of the conflicting idea(l)s of how vision and erotic experience interrelate find an important crisis of development in the second century C.E., as Christianity is being formulated as a social and theological movement within the Roman Empire. My interest in this chapter (thus) is in the process of erotic looking and its constitution in and through cultural and epistemological models, and I shall be focusing primarily on the last fifty years of the second century C.E. I am particularly interested in this period because it offers such a fascinating view of cultural clash, and the writings I will consider in most detail have been chosen in part precisely for the way that they highlight issues of cultural conflict. Each of the works I will be discussing comes from the Roman Empire, but not one of the writers is simply Roman, not one is centrally placed in the dominant political culture of empire which remains centered on Rome and the emperor. "Looking right and fitting in" becomes such a charged issue because of the dynamic interplay between the centers and margins of cultural power in the empire. I shall begin by discussing a Greek novelist, said to be from Alexandria, whose novel begins in Sidon and ends with a sailing to Byzantium. He will be juxtaposed to a Christian from Alexandria, writing for an educated Greek audience in that polyglot metropolis. From further down the coast, there will be a stern African Christian writing extremely fierce Latin. Earlier writers will include a Jew from Alexandria and a Greek priest from Delphi; later writers will include a novelist who claims he is a Phoenician from Emesa, whose novel starts from the center of the Greek world, Delphi, but finds its home in Ethiopia, Homer's "end of the world," the most marginal of places. In each case, we will find that the dominant intellectual discourse—produced in part by the education system, which links the elite of the empire[8]—is manipulated for different purposes, articulates a range of strategies, and explores different perspectives on the centers and margins of power. Postcolonial discourse is a bandwagon that is not always aware of the length of its history, and this writing from the mother of empires has a sophistication and complexity that will provide a remarkable and instructive set of models for what has often been a rather simplistic contemporary take on the problems of writing the imperial margins. The discussions of how to look that I will be tracing necessarily become engaged in the dynamics of social authority and cultural display, and with questions of how the boundaries of social and cultural inclusion and exclusion are negotiated within the empire. It is here, too, with this imbrication of the erotic with the structures of education and power, that I hope this discussion will prove exemplary.

I

I want to begin with two benchmark texts that I hope will help set an agenda. My first author is Achilles Tatius, whose great novel *Leukippe and Cleitophon* is impossible to date with certainty, although there is a least a measure of critical consensus for the last quarter of the second century. His birthplace is given by later writers as Alexandria (though some have reasonably supposed that this might be an assumption based on the extended and honorific description of that city which opens book 5). It is a reasonable suggestion that this highly articulate, sophisticated, and literary novel was written for an audience of privileged educated readers (such as existed in Alexandria and throughout the empire). Nothing more than these tenuous presuppositions is known of Achilles Tatius. His novel contains a most wonderful bricolage of strange sights, high theory, and lovers' melting glances, in the course of a baroque narrative which travels around the Mediterranean taking in and reflecting on the spectacles of empire. Throughout the novel, the knowing sophistication of the intellectual narrator and author explores the variety of the world with extraordinary narratological and visual panache. (The first person narrative of the hero Cleitophon allows for disjunctions and plays between the knowingness of the narrator and the knowingness of the author.) From the lovers' first glances at each other to the famous scenes of the forced observation of the beloved's apparent disembowelling, the erotic narrative traces a particular engagement with the look, but the novel also contains extended passages of "art history" with the description and interpretation of paintings, of "tourism" with its outsiders' views of the different sites and sights of the Mediterranean, of "paradoxography" with its ornate descriptions of natural wonders such as the crocodile, and of rhetorical display with its extended portrayal of the effect of seeing Alexandria for the first time. Together—and in ironic tension with one another—these different discourses of looking construct what can be called in Helen Morales's fine phrase a "scopophiliac paradise."[9] Shadi Bartsch has written on the relation between the descriptions of paintings and the narrative's strategies of interpretation, and I have discussed elsewhere at length how Achilles' characteristic blend of (pseudo)science, rhetorical formulation, and self-conscious slyness (always with his narratological twisting of readers' expectations) depends on and distorts a specific discourse of τὸ εἶχος—the probable, natural, likely—that is, how his text mobilizes and manipulates a reader's knowledge and his/her knowingness—his/her implication in dominant narratives of how things are.[10]

For the purposes of this chapter, I want to look first at one brief passage from the opening of the book which focuses on the physiology of the desiring eye. Cleitophon, the hero, who has fallen in love with Leucippe, has gone to see Cleinias, his cousin and confidant, for advice. The hero expounds his situation and explodes that he cannot shut his eyes to sleep: because of desire, "Impressions of Leukippe face me all the time" [πάντοτε Λευχίππην φαντάζομαι]. Now φαντάζομαι and the noun φαντασία, normally translated "impression," are central terms in Stoic (and other materialist) theories of vision—which I have discussed with regard to Hellenistic culture of art and perception in *Art and Text in Ancient Greek Culture*. In Hellenistic society a new caste of expert viewer—sophisticated, educated, cultivated—grew up. The viewing subject as articulate, witty uncoverer of sedimented and learned images found its most fully developed epistemological and physiological model for viewing in Stoic theory—which, unlike Platonic paradigms of mimesis, privileges viewing as a mode of access to knowledge of the world. *Phantasia* is the central term for the impact the external world makes on the viewing subject and the articulate reaction it produces. So when Cleitophon, the hero, exclaims πάντοτε Λευχίππην φαντάζομαι [an impression of Leukippe is constantly being impressed on me], he is not just uttering the well-known lover's complaint of "I see her everywhere," but is expressing it in a term which, while certainly not requiring a full Stoic (or other systematic) epistemology, evokes a theoretical perspective on the eye's work. In a similar mixture of generalization and physiological expression, the reprobate Callisthenes is said to exemplify how words can have the same effect as that which "wounded eyes minister to the soul": he falls in

SIMON GOLDHILL

love without even seeing the woman whose praises he has heard, ἀναπλάτ-
των γὰρ ἑαυτῷ τῆς παιδὸς τὸ κάλλος καὶ φανταζόμενος τὰ ἀόρατα [imaging
the girl's beauty for himself and forming an impression of the unseen]—a
phrase perhaps more paradoxical than its common translation, "imagining
what he could not see," suggests.[11] Cleitophon's technical-sounding expression prompts Cleinias's response—"You have no idea," he argues, "how
marvelous a thing it is to look at one's beloved"—and he proceeds to offer
in the typical style of this novel a ludic theoretical exposition of his generalization: "Some lovers have to be content with a mere flashing glance
[βλέμμα—which seems always to imply a special look in the eye, of pleasure, say, or of disdain] [12] at a carefully watched over maiden, and if a lover
has good luck with even such eyeing [καὶ μέχρι τῶν ὀμμάτων], he thinks it
is the greatest good." So sharing a house with Leucippe is an excellent advantage. Indeed, as a teacher of desire, he proceeds to remove his pupil's
ignorance (1.9.4):

> οὐκ οἶδας οἷόν ἐστιν ἐρωμένη βλεπομένη· μείζονα τῶν ἔργων ἔχει τὴν
> ἡδονήν· ὀφθαλμοὶ γὰρ ἀλλήλοις ἀντανακλώμενοι ἀπομάττουσιν ὡς
> ἐν κατόπτρῳ τῶν σωμάτων τὰ εἴδωλα· ἡ δὲ τοῦ κάλλους ἀπορροή, δι'
> αὐτῶν εἰς τὴν ψυχὴν καταρρέουσα, ἔχει τινὰ μίξιν ἐν ἀποστάσει. καὶ
> ὀλίγον ἐστὶ τῆς τῶν σωμάτων μίξεως· καινὴ γάρ ἐστι σωμάτων συμ-
> πλοκή. [You do not know what a thing it is when a lover is looked at.
> It has a greater pleasure than the Business. For the eyes receive each oth-
> ers' reflections and impress from there little images as in mirrors. Such
> an emanation of beauty, flowing down through them into the soul, is a
> kind of copulation at a distance. This is not far from the intercourse of
> bodies. For it is a novel kind of embrace of bodies.]

If theory proposes a materialist account of vision, Achilles Tatius, with
sly wit and brilliant manipulation of the possibilities of the technical language of vision and desire, rewrites the penetrating and longing gaze as a
kind of copulation. Thus, the pleasure of looking is greater than *ta erga*,
"the Business," "the deed." The verbs ἀντανακλύω, "reflect," and ἀπομάττω,
"impress," are technical terms from optics—I will return to ἀπομάττω in
particular later—and the vocabulary of flowing and mixing is familiar from
science—the theory of "emanation"[13]—and from Plato's highly ornate description of the desiring soul (which talks also of the "emanation," or "out-
flowing" [*aporroe*] "of beauty through the eyes" [*Phaedrus* 251b9ff.] and
which itself is paralleled in technical physiological discussions back to the

fifth century). But this vocabulary is here eroticized as an oozy step on the path to sex. Indeed, looking is called "almost a *mixis*," "intercourse," and also a συμπλοκή, "embrace," which is the usual term in general intellectual discourse for a sexual position. Finally, the eye is called a πρόξενος φιλίας, "an ambassador of love," a rather grand go-between or pimp — as the discourse moves through its science, with a nod to ethical philosophy, toward a more familiar "ars amatoria." The theory of the eye here becomes part of a knowingly eroticized discourse, as Achilles Tatius playfully explores the space between the consolations of theory and the performance of erotics. A theory of perception is mobilized as part of the boys' wise talk about how to get the girl. The Hellenistic theory of the expert viewing subject as cultured and articulate commentator on the world of impressions becomes intertwined with and erotically stained by the lovers' play. Not only is looking the height of erotic stimulation, but even (the) theory itself is pretty sexy stuff.

Using a theoretical exposition of the physiology of the eye as part of a sly and self-conscious erotic discourse is a strategy used to amusing effect by Heliodorus some hundred and fifty years later in his novel the *Aethiopika*. Calasiris, the tricky Egyptian priest and prime mover of the plot, is called on to explain why the heroine, Charicleia, has an undiagnosed sickness. (We the readers know that she has seen Theagenes, the hero, parading in a spectacular procession at Delphi and fallen in love, despite her commitment to virginity.) Calasiris, who is also in the know, explains to Charicles, the father, that she may be the victim of the "evil eye." When Charicles laughs and expresses surprise that the sophisticated Calasiris believes in such folk theories, the priest responds with a finely nuanced scientific account (3.7.3): "We are completely enveloped in air, which permeates our bodies by way of our eyes, nostrils, respiratory tract, and other channels, bringing with it, as it enters, various properties from outside, thus engendering in those who take it in an effect corresponding to the properties it introduces." The *poroi* (channels) of the body as a route for infection and circulation are standard in medical theory; this materialist model of sight draws on a long tradition of philosophical and physiological writing. This leads from the example of plague which is passed on without bodies touching (3.7.4) to the "conclusive proof" (3.7.5.):

> the genesis of love, which originates from visually perceived objects,
> which, if you will excuse the metaphor, shoot arrows of passion, swifter
> than the wind, into the soul by way of the eyes. This is perfectly logical,

because, of all our channels of perception, sight is the least static
and contains the most heat, and so is more receptive of such emana-
tions, for the spirit which animates it is akin to fire, and so is well
suited to absorb the transient and unstable impressions of love.

The language of heat and desire passed through the eyes to the soul recalls not merely Plato's *Phaedrus* (which I have already cited and which is
so often a dominant presence in later Greek writing on erotics and vision)
but also, and more surprisingly, Plutarch, writing earlier than Achilles, in
the first century, at the center of the Greek mainland, Delphi. For in his
Tabletalk (680cff.), he too offers an explanation of the "evil eye" which is remarkably similar to Heliodorus's account, and indeed has identical phras-
ing in places. As Matthew Dickie has nicely analyzed,[14] although scholars
have argued whether Heliodorus and Plutarch share a common source or
whether Heliodorus is quoting Plutarch, in either case Heliodorus is utiliz-
ing a parodic, veiled, and tricky discourse of science for rhetorical and
comic effect. Indeed, the layers of quotation, together with the technical
language of materialist optics, as well as the standard metaphorical language of desire (marked as metaphorical by the speaker with disingenuous
coyness),[15] signal this passage as a rhetorical tour de force, and one whose
design is evident. For Calasiris is here misleading the girl's father prior to
her elopement. The parodic quotation—blinding the father with science—
plays with the ideas of clear sight and malice (as with the example of the
erotic gaze itself), as it is uttered to be misinterpreted. Making visuality visible here is a blind, a device to stop the father's seeing what is happening
with his daughter, displayed for the reader's knowing pleasure. As the girl
falls in love "at first sight," the desiring eye is given a physiological account
that on the one hand grounds this novel's language of art history and tourism (as the *Aethiopika* traces the lovers' journey to the exotic Ethiopia), and
that, on the other hand, plays a role in the narrative of the novel as a lure,
a distraction of the father's attention in order to aid the young lovers' elopement. The reader enjoys the trick, but as Calasiris becomes a central figure
for the model of reading and interpretation in the novel (as Winkler and
Morgan have shown),[16] the reader (also) becomes set up as the dupe of Heliodorus's scientific and storytelling panache. In Heliodorus, seeing is not
merely theory laden but laden with the history of theory, as the narrative's
scenes of viewing, and commentary on viewing, and manipulation of the
language of viewing, interrelate. As in Achilles Tatius, the scientific knowledge of how the eye works is fully integral to the ludic and collusive de-
ceptions of erotic narrative.

II

We will return to Achilles' lascivious theorizing gaze later, but first I want to look at my second benchmark, a there-or-thereabouts contemporary text, probably from the same city. This is Clement of Alexandria's *Protrepticus*, a homiletic text which adopts and adapts Greek philosophy, via Philo's Jewish allegorizing, toward a Christian normative message. Little is known of Clement's life and background, but there is little reason to doubt that he had a conventional and extensive Greek education before converting to Christianity.[17] He worked and taught in Alexandria in the last quarter of the second century, where the Christian community, although not large, was beginning to become significant. The *Protrepticus* is ostensibly and primarily aimed at the educated Greek community of polyglot Alexandria, and it passionately argues against the *muthoi* and religious practice of the Greek tradition in favor of a Christianity that absorbs and redirects Greek philosophy toward a Christian belief and practice. Although the visual is explicitly theorized only quite briefly in his voluminous output, Clement's discussion is paradigmatic of a Christian engagement with the spectacular world of empire culture— on Christianity's highly convoluted and violent journey toward iconoclasm.

Chapter 4 of the *Protrepticus*, with which I will be concerned here, is an extended critique of the practice of idol worship, and it will lead up to an extraordinary attack on the pagan practices of looking at sexy images. Surprisingly, the obvious point that the Hebrew Bible explicitly bans idolatry is not made until the very end of his case— only after Clement has formulated an argument in terms that speak more closely to the dominant Greek intellectual tradition— and, indeed, Exodus 20 emerges only as a final confirmation rather than as a starting point for his argument. (This contrasts with several later treatises written within church polemics leading up to iconoclasm which take Exodus as a starting point.)[18] The chapter opens with a history of art which apothegmatically makes art the source of sin: ἐπειδὴ ἤνθησεν ἡ τέχνη, ηὔξησεν ἡ πλάνη [When art flourished, error grew]. This leads into a dismissive account of the human construction of cults and cultic objects, which culminates in an outraged attack on Hadrian's deification of Antinous, whose very beauty is sullied by such treatment: "I will recognize beauty, when you have guarded the image in purity; I will reverence beauty when it is a true archetype of the beautiful." The technical, philosophical language of "archetype of the beautiful" is conjoined here with a moral outrage at an image which is impure because it is designed "to celebrate fornication": the very act of recognizing beauty itself is made subject to Clement's moral positioning. (It is, of course, also significant that the object which thus arouses Clement's ire is an image circulated by the emperor himself through the empire as part of his own expression of cultural and political power.) [19] This is followed by a lengthier attack on the lifelessness of statues, their materiality. They are senseless and soulless — eyes they have but see not — and yet are honored by people. Even worms and caterpillars, he declares, the lowest of animals, who do not possess all five senses, are better than statues, which are perfectly deaf and dumb and have not a single sense. The implications of this — that statues can be stolen, destroyed, and made to look like particular people — are drawn out at length (without engaging in the simple point that Lucian makes — and Dio expounds at length — that no sensible person would confuse a real god and a statue). [20] Thus, ringingly, he concludes his attack on materiality with "my practice is to tread on earth, not worship it. For it is not right to entrust to soulless objects the hopes of the soul."

At this point, the treatise takes a new turn, as he aims to prove that the lure or attraction of statues is an integral element which raises special problems for a Christian in pagan culture: "we must approach the statues very closely to prove from their very appearance how error is integral. For the statues are quite clearly impressed [ἐναπομέμαχται] with the attitudes of demons." Statues of gods are recognizable as such by their form, and men have fallen in love with statues of Aphrodite. So Pygmalion fell in love with his Aphrodite, and Clement continues with academic references to the story of the statue of Aphrodite of Knidos, which was so beautiful that it led a besotted man to have sexual intercourse with its cold marble. (You can still see the stain of his semen on her thigh, adds Lucian, in his fuller and more eroticized version.) Thus, concludes Clement, "Such is the strength of art to deceive and to seduce men of desire toward the pit." The vocabulary of Greek intellectual discourse, framing the Christian theology, is marked here, not just in the Platonic tone of the deceptiveness of *techne* or the seductions of *mimesis* (even to the point of copulating with a statue), but also in the verb ἐναπομάττω, "impress." So, indeed, the threat of idolatry is located precisely in the corruption of the visual. For although powerful art could not beguile those who live according to *logos*, in the case of such passion for statues "the faculty of sight of the spectators was deceived" [ἦσαν τῶν θεατῶν οἱ ὄψεις ἠπατημέναι ὑπὸ τῆς τέχνης]. Wrong looking is wrong living. Even if you do not desire statues, honoring them betokens the same error. Worshiping statues is but a weaker form of copulating with them. Art may be praised, he concedes, but only if it does not pass for the truth, does not aim to deceive. For what is at stake in looking is your very soul, the truth of things. How you look is part of your relation to God.

Even this bare allowance of some praise for art's skill, however, will turn out to be a foil for a further damning attack on the content of art's imagery. For both painters and poets in representing the sexual transgressions and corrupt behavior of the divinities of paganism encourage such behavior in humans. Poetry is the theory; adultery is the practice. So, in words to warm Plato's heart, he quotes the first four lines of Homer's account of Aphrodite's adulterous relationship with Ares, and exclaims: "Stop your singing, Homer! It teaches adultery. We have refused to lend our ears to fornication!" Because man is a "living and moving statue" which carries in it the "image of god," he must not be sullied by such unholy influences. (Note how the language of statues and images here is turned, via its echo of Genesis, to construct a holy materiality for man, to juxtapose to his earlier rejection of the mere materiality of cult statues.) The threat that is in poetry is integral to images too:

> They throw aside shame and fear, and have their homes decorated with the unnatural lusts of gods. Committed to lewdness, they have decorated their bedrooms with painted tablets, hung up like offerings, since they think licentiousness is piety. As they lie on the bed, while still in a sexual embrace, they fix their gaze on that naked Aphrodite, bound too in a sexual embrace. Accepting the image of femininity, they engrave on their rings the bird, the lover, flapping around Leda, using as a seal the representation of Zeus's licentiousness.

Men look at pictures of naked Aphrodites, bound in a sexual embrace (as she was caught by Hephaistus's nets in the act of adultery), as they themselves are in the very embrace of the sexual act. (Thus, a remarkable first-century mirror cover — itself a significant object both for the dynamics of mimesis and for its associations with desire and decoration — represents a couple making love on a bed, and on the wall of the room there is a picture of a couple making love: the mirror with a scene mirrored by a picture creates a fine *mise-en-abîme* of the interplay of the image and the act in sex, or the role of imaging in sexuality.)²¹ So these images become "archetypes of voluptuousness." The archetype, the seal, the imprint — Clement's language recalls Greek theories of perception as he attacks pagan cultures of display and practices of looking. Indeed, as the following catalog of corrupt images reaches a climax, he declares that not merely the use of such pictures, but even looking at them is forbidden: τούτων οὐ μόνον τῆς χρήσεως, πρὸς δὲ καὶ τῆς ὄψεως καὶ τῆς ἀκοῆς αὐτῆς ἀμνηστίαν καταγγέλλομεν. ἡταίρηκε ὑμῖν τὰ ὦτα, πεπορνεύκασιν οἱ ὀφθαλμοὶ καὶ τὸ καινότερον πρὸ τῆς συμπλοκῆς αἱ ὄψεις ὑμῖν μεμοιχεύκασιν [We declare that not only the use, but also the sight and the very hearing of these things is to be forgotten. Your ears have fornicated; your eyes have whored; your sight has committed adultery before you have embraced].

For Clement, just as for Achilles Tatius, looking is a kind of copulation, a sexual embrace before the act of fornication, a corruption akin to adultery or prostitution. The attraction of art is a seduction toward loss of control: imaginary stimulation is the threat. So don't look now. Beyond "use"— either religious[22] or sexual—even to look at images of naked bodies is to be dragged toward the pit. Idolatry and sexual error are linked through the error of the eye. Indeed, the conclusion of the argument significantly is that by allowing such images in society you become a mere "spectator [*theates*] of virtue, but an athlete in sin." Clement's rhetoric seems to suggest that the presence of such images makes the citizen into a passive observer, whose only activity is the pursuit of the sins so represented. The spectacular arena of the games becomes a charged metaphor for the failure of self-control in the regime of the visual.

Clement's commitment to Greek philosophy as a means of engaging with the educated of Alexandria has been frequently discussed by scholars.[23] This passage is a perfect example of how elements of Greek theorizing on sight are appropriated and adapted toward his Christian moralism for persuasive effect. I want to take one word to show in further detail precisely how such a rhetoric works. I marked ἀπομάττω, "impress," as a significant choice of vocabulary in my first passage of Achilles Tatius; ἐναπομάττω, "impress on," opens Clement's description of statues. *Apomatto* and *ekmatto* quite often occur in technical discussions of *mimesis*,[24] but the rarer *enapomatto* is particularly marked because it is one of the central terms in Zeno the Stoic's definition of *phantasia kataleptike*.[25] Zeno the Stoic was one of the founding fathers of Stoicism, and thus an authority for the philosophy which is the lingua franca of the Greek and Roman intellectual world of the empire. Only fragments of Zeno now survive, and it is always hard to pin down exact wording through the doxographic tradition, but both Diogenes Laertius and Sextus Empiricus offer definitions of *phantasia kataleptike*:

κaταληπτικὴν μέν, ἣν κριτήριον εἶναι τῶν πραγμάτων φασί, τὴν γινομένην ἀπὸ ὑπάρχοντος κατ' αὐτὸ τὸ ὑπάρχον ἐναπεσφραγισμένην καὶ ἐναπομεμαγμένην. [The cognitive, which the Stoics say is the criterion of things, is that which arises from what is and is *stamped and impressed* exactly in accordance with what is.] (Diogenes Laertius 7.46)

καταληπτικὴ δέ ἐστιν ἡ ἀπὸ ὑπάρχοντος κατ' αὐτὸ τὸ ὑπάρχον ἐναπεσφραγισμένη καὶ ἐναπομεμαγμένη. [A cognitive impression is one which arises from what is and is *stamped and impressed* exactly in accordance with what is.] (Sextus Empiricus 7.247)

οὐ μὴν ἀλλὰ καὶ ἐναπεσφραγισμένην καὶ ἐναπομεμαγμένην τυγχάνειν, ἵνα πάντα τεχνικῶς τὰ ἰδιώματα τῶν φανταστῶν ἀναμάττηται . . . καὶ ὅν τρόπον αἱ διὰ τῶν δακτυλίων σφραγῖδες ἀεὶ πάντας ἐπ' ἀκριβὲς τοὺς χαρακτῆρας ἐναπομάττονται τῷ κηρῷ . . . [Furthermore, its being *stamped and impressed*, so that all its impressors' peculiarities are *stamped* on it in a craftsmanlike way . . . just as the seals on rings always *stamp* their markings precisely on the wax . . .] (Sextus Empiricus 7.252)

Phantasia kataleptike is a fundamental element in the Stoic account of perception that explains the process whereby images of the physical world enter the mind of the subject. You will note that *enapomatto* is conjoined with ἐναποσφραγίζω, "to emboss as with a signet ring"—an image which may perhaps lie behind Clement's odd choice of signet rings as a particular example of corrupting representation.[26] Clement's choice of a word particularly associated with Stoic theory is designed to bolster his purchase on an educated audience—to be a hook. It appropriates the privileged language of Greek education against Greek culture and its visual regime.

Now Clement is not the only writer to appropriate this model of perception to a moral argument. Philo, the Jewish writer also from Alexandria, more than a century earlier, offered extensive allegorical readings of the Hebrew Bible and was so carefully read by Clement that one scholar comments that Clement writes as if he had Philo constantly open "on his desk."[27] Philo repeatedly uses the language of Stoic impressions to explore how meaning is constructed: "the souls of the young are impressed [ἐναποματτόμεναι] with the first indelible imprints [τύπους] of *phantasiai*," he writes in typical vein.[28] Particularly relevant, however, is the following passage from his discussion of why pleasure uses its wiles on women to snare men — part of his reading of the Adam and Eve narrative of Genesis (*On the Account of the World's Creation According to Moses* 166):

οἷα ἑταιρὶς καὶ μαλχὰς οὖσα, ἡδονὴ γλίχεται τυχεῖν ἐραστοῦ καὶ μαστροποὺς ἀναζητεῖ, δι' ὧν τοῦτον ἀγκιστρεύσεται· μαστροπεύουσι δ' αὐτῇ καὶ προξενοῦσι τὸν ἐρῶντα αἰσθήσεις. ἃς δελεάσασα ῥαδίως ὑπηγάγετο τὸν νοῦν, ᾧ τὰ φανέντα ἐκτὸς εἴσω κομίζουσαι διαγγέλλουσι καὶ ἐπιδείκνυνται, τοὺς τύπους ἑκάστων ἐνσφραγιζόμεναι, καὶ τὸ ὅμοιον ἐνεργαζόμεναι πάθος· κηρῷ γὰρ ἐοικὼς δέχεται τὰς διὰ τῶν αἰσθήσεων φαντασίας, αἷς τὰ σώματα καταλαμβάνει δι' αὐτοῦ μὴ δυνάμενος. [Pleasure is like a whore and a degenerate, and lusts for a lover and searches for pimps through which she will hook one. The senses are the pimps and ambassadors for her. Pleasure ensnares the senses, and she easily leads on the mind. The senses carry, announce, and display what appears outside us inside, impressing the imprints of each thing and producing the corresponding affect. For like wax, it receives the impressions of the senses, by which it apprehends material substance].

The eye was the "ambassador of love" in Achilles Tatius; here the senses in general are "the ambassadors of pleasure" for the desiring man. In his attack on pleasure itself as a whore and degenerate, Philo manipulates the same terms that Achilles uses to anticipate and flirt with the pleasures of consummation. The senses receive *phantasiai*, "impressions," like wax, they impress like a seal the imprint of objects on the soul: they "grasp" them *katalambanein*—the very process of *phantasia kataleptike*. Philo's passionate distrust of the whore pleasure leads easily to Clement's rejection of visual stimulation, and both assimilate Stoic accounts of perception to construct a philosophical and physiological base for their ethical normativity. As Jewish and Christian apologists, writing in Greek in Egypt, attempting to reread the culture of visual display central to classical and Hellenistic societies, they adapt the normative language of philosophical schooling to negotiate a space of engagement with dominant cultural modes. The turn to theory is part of a rhetoric of self-positioning.

Achilles Tatius himself gives an even fuller picture of the philosophizing sexy look. By book 5 of *Leukippe and Cleitophon,* our hero Cleitophon thinks he has lost his heroine, beheaded by a pirate. He is being pursued by a wealthy widow who fancies him (although her husband, presumed dead, will also reappear). Cleitophon describes how at dinner she could not keep her eyes off him (V.13):

πάντα δὲ ἔβλεπεν ἐμέ. οὐδὲν γὰρ ἡδὺ τοῖς ἐρῶσι πλὴν τὸ ἐρώμενον·
τὴν γὰρ ψυχὴν πᾶσαν ὁ ἔρως καταλαβών, οὐδὲ αὐτῇ χώραν δίδωσι τῇ
τροφῇ. ἡ δὲ τῆς θέας ἡδονὴ διὰ τῶν ὀμμάτων εἰσρέουσα τοῖς στέρνοις
ἐγκάθηται· ἕλκουσα δὲ τοῦ ἐρωμένου τὸ εἴδωλον ἀεί, ἐναπομάττεται
τῷ τῆς ψυχῆς κατόπτρῳ, καὶ ἀναπλάττει τὴν μορφήν· ἡ δὲ τοῦ κάλλους ἀπορροὴ δι' ἀφανῶν ἀκτίνων ἐπὶ τὴν ἐρωτικὴν ἑλκομένη καρδίαν

ἐναποσφραγίζει κάτω τὴν σκίαν. [She did nothing but gaze at me. To a lover, nothing is as sweet as the beloved. For desire seizes the whole soul and gives no space for eating. Pleasure from the gaze flows through the eyes into the chest and sits there. Drawing up the little image of the beloved constantly, it impresses it in the mirror of the soul, and forms a picture of the shape. The emanation of beauty through invisible rays is drawn into the desiring heart and seals down a shadow image inside it.]

Desire "seizes" (*katalambanein* again) "the whole soul." Pleasure from the gaze flows (*eisreousa*) through the eyes into the chest and sits there. Drawing up the little image (*eidolon*) it "impresses it" (*enapomattei*) in the mirror of the soul and moulds its shape. The "emanation" (*aporroe*) of beauty is drawn into the desiring heart and "seals down" (*enaposphragizein*) the shadow image. The hero's reflection on why he likes being doted on by a beautiful woman runs through the full gamut of Stoic materialist vocabulary, as the first-person narrative knowingly plays with the lover's response to his objectification in the gaze of the woman.[29] The same phraseology of Zeno — "impressing on and sealing down" — is conjoined with other more standard and common terms of materialist physiology — emanation, flowing, molding, the little image (all familar from Plato, especially in earlier writing, but also, indeed, from contemporary Epicurean theory).[30] Theory here becomes on the one hand part of the narrator's observing distance from the passion of the desiring woman — a neat twist on a Stoic's imperviousness to emotional disturbance. But on the other hand, and more paradoxically, it also becomes part of his flirtatious engagement with her. For his refusal to consummate his relationship leads through heavy petting, to a *mariage blanc*, and finally to her pleas for willful adultery in a prison cell. The repeated narrative joke of the narrator's highly theorized response to erotics will find its culminating twist when she finds the correct arguments successfully to persuade him to commit adultery, a persuasiveness he duly notes is highly philosophical . . . as he gives in. The first passage of Achilles Tatius used its theory of vision to reflect on the delays and relays of consummation; this second passage uses its theory to formulate and enforce the delay of consummation. The theory of the look for Achilles Tatius plays a dynamic role in the narrative of deferred bliss and blissful deferral which is the novel's erotic agenda.

⟋⟋

My two benchmark texts — with a few digressive glosses — have led to four general points with which to conclude the first part of my chapter.

First, there is in the second century a considerable production of discourse about the visual specifically with regard to the culture of display and the erotic work of the eye. It is a nexus of theoretical expositions which draws on different materialist models, and which utilizes terms from the history of the theory of vision from Plato onward (and Plato, despite his well-known distrust of visual perception, is especially often recalled), but which repeatedly reuses Epicurean and especially a highly developed and specifically Stoic vocabulary and paradigm, not least because Stoicism is throughout the period the lingua franca of the philosophical schools in which educated Greeks and Romans study. (Even when there are four chairs of philosophy in Athens and the different schools claim different professional adherents, it is Stoic vocabulary and "coloring" which dominate the general intellectual, philosophizing discourse.) Whereas terms such as *apomatto* or the language of sealing per se may invoke a rather general sense of "materialist theory," the combination and clustering of rarer technical vocabulary also suggests a more specific and pointed allusivity. Thus, Clement and Achilles—and earlier, Philo—from their very different viewpoints each quote Zeno the Stoic. Jew, Greek, Christian—all in turn cite the same words from the most mainstream philosopher in their different versions of erotic viewing.

This leads to my second point. Because it draws on the lingua franca of theory, this model of the eye is manipulated by Christian and Jewish apologists to engage the cultured Greek in a new normative program—but adapted by the novelist to a quite different erotic agenda. It is not merely that Clement inveighs against the threat of erotic stimulation through the visual and Achilles revels in it, but rather that each fully incorporates the theory of the eye into a narrative argument and makes it fully integral to a self-positioning, an account of the engagement of the desiring subject with the world. Looking in the right way—and thinking about it—for both of these writers matters. How you look, for both Clement and Achilles, is integral to who you are and to the narrating of that self.

Third, it is fundamental that both Achilles and Clement are in different ways negotiating a space in and against what might be called the dominant culture of Rome and its empire. Clement, for all that he is a central figure in the church hierarchy in Alexandria, speaks for a marginal and aggressive religion that is fighting for monotheistic space in polytheistic multicultural Alexandria (as well as for his Hellenized version of Christianity within the church). Clement is necessarily engaged in cultural (as well as theological) polemic. As Clement's proselytizing straddles the boundaries of communities, so his prose interweaves different discourses to claim a powerful speaking position. Clement is fighting through his writing about "looking right and fitting in." Achilles Tatius, whose name appears to combine Greek and Latin genealogies (but about whose background there is only speculation), revels in the polyphonic possibilities of the bastard and unrecognized genre of the novel. But he does not even recognize the Roman Empire, for all that he beats the bounds of the civilized world. There is no mention of the empire (although the novel is not set, as other Greek novels are, in the distant past). This studious silence, I suggest, toward the politics of local-ism as much as the politics of empire is typical of a certain cultural politics in Second Sophistic Greek writing—a paradigmatic reaction to the impos-sibility of writing Thucydidean history now.[31] The reader of Achilles, unlike the reader of the Latin novel, or Lucian or Tertullian or Philo or Clement, is allowed the pleasures of a topography without Rome, a system of power and experience without the control or threat of empire. The amused, intel-lectualized response to the erotic experience of looking is in part to be com-prehended within the enforced disengagement of Greek political and mil-itary life.[32] From an outside looking in, the theory of the eye is used to aid speculative admission to or negotiate space against dominant discur-sive strategies.

Fourth, the very juxtaposition of these two writers from (probably) the same city and date is itself a convenient sign and symptom of the clash of cultures in this period and helps focus the question of who has control over the dominant intellectual discourse. Clement and Achilles should be viewed not only in relation to the empire's power centers but also in relation to each other. While Greek education links elites across the empire—at the very least in the eyes of Greek writers—in such a mixed culture as the ma-jor metropolis of Alexandria, or, say, in the further outposts of empire, the very distance (in all senses) from the centers of power at Rome allows for "local knowledge" to have a certain autonomy (such as within the church at Alexandria), in the same way as local elites construct a power base in social terms. It would be too simple to locate dominant discourse (or in-deed power) wholly and solely in the Imperial Palace or in the Senate. What the juxtaposition of Clement and Achilles Tatius may show is how contests around cultural dominance take place not merely within a matrix of dominance and resistance (the imperial gaze and the subaltern text), but with a more complex dynamic of local and central knowledge, practices of displacement and marginalization, imagined forces and unrecognized collusiveness. There are many interlocking strategies by which the empire writes back . . . [33]

III

For the next section of this chapter, I want to develop these four points through a very different set of textual strategies and a very different author. It would be possible here to trace further a Greek intellectualizing response to erotic looking (through the cultural satire of Lucian or the art history of Philostratus and Callistratus); it would also be possible to broaden the frame of viewing to include Pausanias's tourism, or the politics of display involved with, say, Dio's discussion of statues. But I wish rather for my final text to travel briefly round the coast of Africa from Alexandria and Clement's Hellenizing to Carthage and a Christian writing in Latin, namely, Tertullian, who raged and wrote at the very end of the second century, shortly after Clement, and was eventually excommunicated for his commitment to the Montanist heresy. His Christianity is forged in passionate opposition to the culture of the Roman Empire and shows a powerful antagonism to its displays and spectacle. Tertullian is often treated as something of an embarrassment: his fierce argumentation, lumpen wit, and vile Latin—not to mention his heresy—have left him with rather an uneasy status amid the fathers of the church.[34] But his treatise *De Spectaculis—On Games*, or *On Spectacles*—is a fundamental text for my project, not least for its passionate attempt to redefine the dominant ethos of bread and circuses within the Christian world of the bread of Christ's body and the athletes of chastity.

Tertullian attacks the games under the general heading of idolatry, but it is pleasure as much as anything that is the perceived threat. As he says at the beginning of the piece, "the danger of pleasure more than the danger to life turns people from Christianity." Tertullian begins by running through the origins, names, and religious elements of both gladiatorial games and stage plays, seeing in all of them both idolatry and an unholy commitment to useless and corrupt pleasure. By chapter 14, he claims he has established the charge of idolatry adequately and moves on to other criticisms. The first is the psychological disturbance that comes from being a spectator. To look at the spectacles is to lose one's cool: "omne enim spectaculum sine concussione spiritus non est" [there is no spectacle without violence to the spirit]. Pleasure requires eagerness, which requires rivalry, from which flows madness, bile, anger—everything which is incompatible with moral discipline. For no one—not even a good man—can escape the lures of pleasure at a spectacle: "for even if a man enjoys the spectacles in modest and upright manner, in accordance with his dignity, age or nature, still he cannot with a mind unstirred and without some unspoken disturbance of spirit." The problem is integral not merely to spectacles, however, but to pleasure itself: "Nemo ad voluptatem venit sine affectu, nemo affectum sine casibus suis patitur" [No-one has pleasure without affect; no-one experiences affect without its own slippage], its own sense of falling, *casibus suis*. Indeed, that sense of the fall is integral to the affect, a stimulation to feeling that leads to pleasure. Without that affect there would indeed be no pleasure. For Tertullian, then, it is not the mechanics of the eye so much as the stimulation to pleasure that makes the spectacular so worrying. Looking is "mined at the center with a fall . . . "

This sense of the fall from control and order is further linked to the nature of representation itself later in the treatise (23): "iam vero ipsum opus personarum quaero an deo placeat, qui omnem similitudinem vetat fieri, quanto magis imaginis suae? Non amat falsum auctor veritatis; adulterium est apud illum omne quod fingitur" [then this business of masks, I ask if God can be pleased with it, when he forbids the likeness of anything to be made, how much more so his own image. The author of truth does not like the false: everything which is made up is adultery in his sight]. All forms of representation—and he goes on to list not merely actors and pantomimes, but even, and far more bizarrely, the scars of a boxer and the performance of a gladiator—by virtue of their fictive quality (fingitur) are a form of adultery in the eyes of god. God is the *author* of truth, and consequently the Devil is the *interpellator*—he who makes up and inserts false stories and words in the book of truth. The slides of emotion in being a spectator, and the performative as fictive in the spectacle, together show that, as Tertullian concludes, "nothing to do with spectacles pleases God."

Up to this point the argument is clear enough. Both the performance and the watching itself make spectacles dangerous. Deceptive mimesis and pleasure are both lures away from the truth. As he writes in the treatise *On Veiling Virgins* (2.15), "Seeing and being seen belong to the same lust." Looking at the games is paradigmatic of the dangerously erotic or pleasurable business of looking and being looked at, which veiling helps reduce. It is a rhetoric aimed at turning the reader from the secular games to the contemplation of Christ's struggles. Accordingly, Tertullian begins to appropriate the language of the games, as he invites and hectors and cajoles the reader to celebrate a different spectacular contest: "You want fightings and wrestling. Here they are: see impurity thrown down by chastity, perfidy slain by faith, cruelty crushed by pity, impudence shaded by modesty: such are our contests, our crowns of victory. You desire blood: you have the blood of Christ." But the conclusion of Tertullian's treatise throws the previous twenty-nine chapters into turmoil. For he fully instantiates this idea of "another spectacle" with a startling and bloodthirsty image of the judgment day. With a set of emotive exclamations, he imagines himself watching the torment of the magistrates who have tormented Christians, now liquefying in hellfire, and the trembling poets who never expected to stand before Christ instead of Minos: "And the magistrates who persecuted the name of the lord, liquefying in fiercer flames than they kindled in their rage against the Christians?! . . . And the poets, trembling before the judgment seat not of Rhadamanthus nor Minos but, to their surprise, of Christ?!" Indeed, he positively revels in and savors the power of his role as spectator: "tunc xystici contemplandi, non in gymnasiis, sed in igne iaculati, nisi quod ne tunc quidem illos velim visos, ut qui malim ad eos potius conspectum insatiabilem conferre, qui in dominum desaevierunt" [Then the athletes have to be watched, tossed not in the gym but in the flames, unless I would not wish to look even then at them, in my desire rather to turn an insatiable gaze instead on those who vented their rage and mockery on the Lord]. The gym is a privileged arena of the erotic gaze and of the culture of display, but now there is another show and another form of impassioned viewing. Tertullian is so thrilled with the prospect of the violent suffering of his opponents that he cannot decide whether his insatiable gaze at the mockers of God would keep him from the delight of this new way of looking at athletes' physical sufferings. Not for Tertullian Augustine's careful discrimination of hating the sin and not the sinner . . . Tertullian is as wildly excited a spectator of the judgment day as the baying and gambling crowd in his own portrayal of the games. Indeed, he introduces his image with "Quae tunc spectaculi latitudo! Quid admirer? Quid rideam? Ubi gaudeam, ubi exultem tot spectans reges" [What an immensity of spectacle then! What shall I gaze on in wonder? What laugh at? Where shall I rejoice, where exult, when I see so many kings] and sums it all up with "ut talia spectes, ut talibus exultes" [to see such sights, to feel such *exultation!*]." The man who had attacked "spectacula" because of the dangers of stimulating pleasure, and because of the dangers of spectating itself, here revels in and exults in his own spectating of the violent dismemberment of his enemies. He revels both in the punishment and in his ability to watch and calculate the pleasures of his insatiable gaze. Is not the stern moralist completely undermined by his own attack on the pleasures of the look? Unless it could be argued that Tertullian's extremism *performs* the dangers of stimulation it inveighs against, as an enacted warning to others — a highly ironic strategy difficult to find in Tertullian's writing elsewhere, and wholly at odds with his express views on acting—it must seem that Tertullian's visual politics lapses into violent self-contradiction.

Perhaps the final sentences of the treatise are an attempt to salvage something from what might seem the wreckage of his self-positioning. These visions of hell are "represented through faith in the spirit's imagining" [spiritu imaginante repraesentata]. They are "things which an eye has not seen, nor ear heard, nor heart felt. But they bring more joy, more pleasure than stadium or theatre" [ceterum qualia illa sunt, quae nec oculus vidit nec auris audivit nec in cor hominis ascenderunt? Credo, circo et utraque cavea et omni stadio gratiora]. The imagination or vision of hell trumps the mere physical sights of the spectacular and brings a greater joy. The imagination, internal viewing, here is set against the physics of the eye in an attempt to privilege the Christian's unflinching moral gaze and acceptable pleasure. But this from the man who had said, "everything that is made up is adultery in the eyes of God." It seems as if Tertullian's attempt to construct a philosophically loaded account of why there is an integral danger in the pleasure of looking means that his own pleasure in imagining a different looking can only appear as a paradoxical and contradictory self-positioning. Tertullian's desire to police the regime of the visual in the spectacular world of Carthage leads only to a failure to regulate his own images and imagining.

Tertullian has little time for philosophy. "What has Athens to do with Jerusalem?" he explodes famously, "Away with all efforts to produce a mottled Stoic-Platonic-Dialectic Christianity." "Where is there any likeness between the Christian and the philosopher?"[35] This violent dismissal of Greek culture could not be further from Clement's sly negotiations with cultivated Hellenism. What interests me is not so much the mess that Tertullian gets into when he does slip into philosophically led models of pleasure, nor Tertullian's obvious debt to his pagan training in rhetoric, but rather the way in which both Clement and Tertullian, these two outsiders to dominant culture, find their concerns overlapping around the erotics of the gaze, and its comprehension in models of pleasure and the body. Tertullian, for all his differences from Clement, cannot finally keep his Christianity free of a mottling of the Stoic-Platonic-Dialectic. His strong sense of the conflict between himself as Christian and Roman and Greek culture nonetheless develops surprising nodes of implication. It is here perhaps that we find a most telling indication of the complex dialectic of conflict and appropriation in such writing against the empire.

Tertullian is more extreme than Clement. Where Clement worries about images of naked bodies, and how looking at such images is a form of corrupt copulation, Tertullian wishes to criticize any look which leads toward or stimulates desire or pleasure. Hence the requirement of veiling for virgins in particular, and the need to make the pleasure of the look a central problem in his attack on games. The social impact — or at least the social implications — of such theorizing about vision are strikingly evident here. Indeed, his arguments continue to fuel the long debates toward iconoclasm in the Christian church and its institutional control of the empire — and the violent conflicts that result from such ideological differences. And there is a strong echo of this passion about stimulation to be heard in modern debate, especially when it is taken for granted that erotic stimulation or pleasure in looking at art is proof that either the artwork or the viewer is to be thought of as improper, corrupt, or corrupting. "The scandal of pleasure," in Wendy Steiner's phrase, is overdetermined by its long and violent history.

IV

The analysis of the second-century texts I have focused on could well be extended, as could the roll call of significant writers for this project, and its chronological scope. My aim has been to trace a particular line of argument about the connection between erotic viewing, culture, and power, through a selection of paradigmatic works, in a period of particular interest. But enough has been shown, I hope, of how writing about the "stimulated eye" engages a range of Second Sophistic writers in the personal politics of the empire — and how exploring the twists and turns of this writing about seeing gives a particular and telling perspective on the cultural conflicts of this period — and on modern cultural theory's construction of the gaze, so often formulated without taking the history of visuality seriously.[36]

In Roman culture, spectacular display is a central dynamic of the performance and politics of power. The Greek or African or Syrian intellectual outsiders — whether ironically assimilating like Lucian or violently opposed like Tertullian — engage in this politics of visuality through their writing. This is, in Jane Gallop's terminology,[37] *writing through the visual*. Whether screaming defiance at the Roman magistrate, or writing a novel without Rome, or composing Christian apologetics for Greeks in a Roman province, an engagement with visual erotics becomes also an engagement with the politics of dominance and the politics of culture. In the Second Sophistic, the construction of the subject in the regime of the visual is a central dynamic in the construction of cultural identity.

Notes

This chapter is a much shortened and refocused version of "The Erotic Eye: Visual Stimulation and Cultural Conflict" in *Being Greek under Rome: Cultural Identity, the Second Sophistic and the Development of Empire*, ed. S. Goldhill (Cambridge, 2001).

1. Mulvey's famous essay (reprinted most conveniently in Mulvey 1989) is followed and qualified by (among many others) de Lauretis 1984; Doane 1987; Parker and Pollock 1987; Gallop 1988; Copjec 1994; Leppert 1996; Ullmann 1997. See also the works cited in n. 2.

2. For a representative sample of these debates, see Steiner 1995; MacKinnon 1992; Kappeler 1986; Rose 1986; Pointon 1990; Itzin 1992; Nead 1992; Hunter, Saunders, and Williamson 1993; Hunt 1996; Gibson and Gibson 1993; Melville and Readings 1995; Brennan and Jay 1996; Bal 1996; Bryson, Holly, and Moxey 1996. In classics, see now Kampen 1996; Richlin 1992; and Keuls 1985.

3. Kappeler 1986.

4. The story of this case is told most insightfully by Steiner 1995, 7–59; and Dubin 1992, esp. 170–96.

5. Psychoanalytic discussion follows Lacan 1977a on "the gaze" and also Lacan 1977b on the "mirror stage." See also Gallop 1985; Copjec 1994; and Silverman 1994. On the sociological, see, e.g., Berger 1972; Fiske and Hartley 1976; Hodge and Kress 1988; Bal 1996; and the burgeoning work in "media and communication studies."

6. On the cultural specificity of this image, see Kendrick 1987.

7. For one fine art historical account, see Freedberg 1987.

8. See in particular Morgan 1998; and Too 1998.

9. Morales 1997.

10. Bartsch 1989; Goldhill 1995, 70–111.

11. For an extended version of the "seeing the absent lover" motif, but *without* any such technical language, see Chariton *Chaereas and Callirhoe* 6.4.5–7.

12. See, e.g., Aristophanes *Plutus* 1022, Demosthenes 21.72, and Philostratus *VS* 491 of the orator.

13. The best general introduction to this area is Simon 1988.

14. Dickie 1991.

15. The implications of οἷον are brought out well by Morgan's translation, which I have used here.

16. Winkler 1982; Morgan 1982, 1989.

17. See Chadwick 1966; Lilla 1971; Timothy 1973; Dawson 1992, 183–240; and Ridings 1995.

18. For this long history, see, e.g., Belting 1994; Barasch 1992; Clerk 1915; and Finney 1994.

19. I have learned in particular from the forthcoming work of Caroline Vout on the circulation of images of Antinous.

20. See Lucian *Hyper ton eikonon*, and Dio Chrysostom 12.46, where he says that "more inexperienced viewers" (*apeiroteroi theatai*) take ideas of gods from statues.

21. From Rome's Capitoline Museum: it is nicely illustrated in Johns 1982, color pl. 35. See also Jacobelli (1995, pl. 32), who puts it in the context of recently discovered erotic wall decorations in Pompeii. Suetonius's *Life of Horace* 10 complains that the poet had mirrors in his bedroom for lascivious purposes. Seneca *QNat.* 1.16 records the case of Hostius Quadra and his enlarging mirrors used for outrageous sexual pleasures.

22. On religious use of images see Elsner 1996.

23. Particularly useful are Chadwick 1966 and the more detailed studies of Timothy 1973; Ridings 1995 (with further bibliography); and Lilla 1971.

24. See, e.g., the well-known discussions of Philostratus *VA* 6.19 and Dionysus of Halicarnassus *De Imit.* fr. 3. So too the imagery of wax molding for artistic construction is familiar, without any necessary Stoic implications or vocabulary, in Latin works: see, e.g., Ovid *Met.* 10.282–86; and Statius *Achil.* 1.332–34.

25. On *phantasia kataleptike*, see Goldhill 1994 for discussion; also Long 1971; Sandbach 1971; Imbert 1980; Burnyeat 1983; Watson 1988; and Frede 1983. Rispoli 1985 has the most useful historical overview. On Roman art, see Elsner 1995.

26. Although the language of "sealing" is seen as early as Aristotle (*Mem.* 450a32) and remains important in Mnemotechnics, the combination with *enapomatto* and its place in Zeno's definition give it new weight in this period. Clement also writes about signet rings at *Paedegogus* 3.59.2–60.1.

27. Runia 1993, 132. See van den Hoek 1988; and Osborn 1987.

28. *Quod omnis probus* 15.5. See also *De Post.* 165; *De Mutatione* 212; *De Vita Mos.* 2.76; *De Special.* 1.47; 2.228; 4.163. He also uses *ensphragizesthai*: see, e.g., *de ebr.* 90.

29. The references to Stoic theory in these passages have been missed by commentators (and by historians of philosophy, although they give interesting evidence for the diffusion of Stoic ideas in "nonphilosophical" texts).

30. See Bychkov 1999, which appeared after this chapter was finished. Although Bychkov is right to see echoes also of Epicurean epistemology here—Stoic and Epicurean theories of perception have many similarities—it is important to stress both the eclectic nature of Achilles' engagements and the specificity of the Stoicism of the echo of Zeno's definition here. Achilles combines a general philosophical patina with some more precisely technical terminology (if scarcely developed in a "philosophical" manner).

31. For local histories' often increasingly bizarre historical claims, see Millar 1993; Gruen 1996 for a particularly interesting early example; and Gruen 1997. For the politics of this writing see Henderson 2001 and Elsner 2001, which are far more attuned to the issues than Swain 1996.

32. This is further discussed in the various essays collected in Goldhill 2001.

33. See the exemplary studies of Alcock 1993; Woolf 1994; and Millar 1993.

34. See, e.g., Barnes 1971; and Sider 1971. I have learned in this section throughout from Piers Aitman.

35. *De praescr. haeret.* 7.9–12; *Apol.* 46.18.

36. Exemplary, however, are Summers 1987; and Crary 1990, 1994.

37. Gallop 1988.

References

Alcock, S. 1993. *Graecia Capta: The Landscapes of Roman Greece.* Cambridge.

Bal, M. 1996. *Double Exposures: The Subject of Cultural Analysis.* London.

Barasch, M. 1992. *Icon.* New York.

Barnes, T. 1971. *Tertullian: A Historical and Literary Study.* Oxford.

Bartsch, S. 1989. *Decoding the Ancient Novel.* Princeton.

Belting, H. 1994. *Likeness and Presence.* Chicago.

Berger, J. 1972. *Ways of Seeing.* Harmondsworth.

Brennan, T., and M. Jay, eds. 1996. *Vision in Context.* London.

Bryson, N., M. Holly, and K. Moxey, eds. 1996. *Visual Culture: Images and Interpretations.* Hanover, N.H.

Burnyeat, M. 1983. "Can the Sceptic Live His Scepticism?" In *The Skeptical Tradition,* ed. M. Burnyeat. Berkeley.

Bychkov, O. 1999. "ἡ τοῦ κάλλους ἀπορροή: A Note on Achilles Tatius 1.9.4, 5.13.4." *Classical Quarterly* 49:339–341.

Chadwick, H. 1966. *Early Christian Thought and the Classical Tradition.* New York.

Clerk, C. 1915. *Les Théories relatives au cultes des images.* Paris.

Copjec, J. 1994. *Read My Desire: Lacan against the Historicists.* Cambridge, Mass.

Crary, J. 1990. *Techniques of the Observer: On Vision and Modernity in the Nineteenth Century.* Cambridge, Mass.

———. 1994. "Unbinding Vision." *October* 68:21–44.

Dawson, D. 1992. *Allegorical Readers and Cultural Relativism in Ancient Alexandria.* Berkeley.

de Lauretis, T. 1984. *Alice Doesn't: Feminism, Semiotics, Cinema.* London.

Dickie, M. 1991. "Heliodorus and Plutarch on the Evil Eye." *Classical Philology* 86: 17–29.

Doane, M. 1987. *The Desire to Desire: The Woman's Film of the 1940s.* Bloomington, Ind.

Dubin, S. 1992. *Arresting Images: Impolitic Art and Uncivil Actions.* London.

Elsner, J. 1995. *Art and the Roman Viewer.* Cambridge.

———. 1996. "Image and Ritual: Reflection on the Religious Appreciation of Classical Art." *Classical Quarterly* 46:515–31.

———. 2001. "Describing Self in Language of the Other: Pseudo(?) Lucian at the Temple of Hire." In *Being Greek under Rome: Cultural Identity, the Second Sophistic and the Development of Empire,* ed. S. Goldhill. Cambridge.

Finney, P. C. 1994. *The Invisible God: The Earliest Christians in Art.* Oxford.

Fiske, J., and J. Hartley. 1976. *Reading Television.* London.

Frede, M. 1983. "Stoics and Skeptics on Clear and Distinct Impressions." In *The Skeptical Tradition,* ed. M. Burnyeat. Berkeley.

Freedberg, D. 1987. *The Power of Images: Studies in the History and Theory of Response.* Chicago.

Gallop, J. 1985. *Reading Lacan.* Ithaca, N.Y.

———. 1988. *Thinking Through the Body.* New York.

Gibson, P. C., and R. Gibson, eds. 1993. *Dirty Looks: Women, Pornography and Power.* London.

Goldhill, S. 1994. "The Naive and Knowing Eye: Ecphrasis and the Culture of Viewing in the Hellenistic World." In *Art and Text in Ancient Greek Culture,* ed. S. D. Goldhill and R. G. Osborne. Cambridge.

———. 1995. *Foucault's Virginity.* Cambridge.

———. ed. 2001. *Being Greek under Rome: Cultural Identity, the Second Sophistic and the Development of Empire.* Cambridge.

Gruen, E. 1996. "The Purported Jewish-Spartan Affiliation." In *Transitions to Empire: Essays on Greco-Roman History, 360–146 B.C.,* ed. R. Wallace and E. Harris. Norman, Okla.

———. 1997. "Fact and Fiction: Jewish Legends in a Hellenistic Context." In *Hellenistic Constructs,* ed. P. Cartledge, P. Garnsey, and E. Gruen. Berkeley.

Henderson, J. 2001. "From Megapolis to Cosmopolis: Polybius or There and Back Again." In *Being Greek under Rome: Cultural Identity, the Second Sophistic and the Development of Empire,* ed. S. Goldhill. Cambridge.

Hodge, R., and G. Kress. 1988. *Social Semiotics.* Cambridge.

Hunt, L., ed. 1996. *The Invention of Pornography.* New York.

Hunter, I., D. Saunders, and D. Williamson, eds. 1993. *On Pornography: Literature, Sexuality and the Obscenity Law.* Basingstoke.

Imbert, C. 1980. "Stoic Logic and Alexandrian Poetics." In *Doubt and Dogmatism: Studies in Hellenistic Epistemology,* ed. M. Schofield, M. Burnyeat, and J. Barnes. Oxford.

Itzin, C., ed. 1992. *Pornography: Women, Violence and Civil Liberties.* Oxford.

Jacobelli, L. 1995. *Le pitture erotiche delle terme suburbane di Pompei.* Rome.

Johns, C. 1982. *Sex or Symbol? Erotic Images of Greece and Rome.* London.

Kampen, N., ed. 1996. *Sexuality in Ancient Art.* Cambridge.

Kappeler, S. 1986. *The Pornography of Representation.* Cambridge.

Kendrick, W. 1987. *The Secret Museum: Pornography in Modern Culture.* New York.

Keuls, E. 1985. *The Reign of the Phallus.* Berkeley.

Lacan, J. 1977a. *The Four Fundamental Concepts of Psychoanalysis.* Translated by A. Sheridan. Harmondsworth.

———. 1977b. *Écrits: A Selection.* Translated by A. Sheridan. London.

Leppert, R. 1996. *Art and the Committed Eye: The Cultural Functions of Imagery.* Boulder, Colo.

Lilla, S. 1971. *Clement of Alexandria: A Study in Christian Platonism and Gnosticism.* Oxford.

Long, A. A. 1971. "Language and Thought in Stoicism." In *Problems in Stoicism.* ed. A. A. Long. London.

MacKinnon, C. 1992. "Pornography, Civil Rights and Speech." In *Pornography: Women, Violence and Civil Liberties*, ed. C. Itzin. Oxford.

Melville, S., and B. Readings, eds. 1995. *Vision and Textuality*. Basingstoke.

Millar, F. 1993. *The Roman Near East: 318 BC–AD 337*. Cambridge, Mass.

Morales, H. 1997. "A Scopophiliac Paradise." Ph.D. diss., University of Cambridge..

Morgan, J. 1982. "History, Romance and Realism in the *Aethiopika* of Heliodorus." *Classical Antiquity* 1:221–65.

———. 1989. "A Sense of the Ending: The Conclusion of Heliodorus' *Aethiopika*." *Transactions of the American Philological Association* 119:221–65.

Morgan, T. 1998. *Literate Education in the Hellenistic and Roman World*. Cambridge.

Mulvey, L. 1989. *Visual and Other Pleasures*. Basingstoke.

Nead, L. 1992. *The Female Nude: Art, Obscenity and Sexuality*. London.

Osborn, E. 1987. "Philo and Clement." *Prudentia* 19:35–49.

Parker, R., and G. Pollock. 1987. *Framing Feminism*. London.

Pointon, M. 1990. *Naked Authority*. Cambridge.

Richlin, A., ed. 1992. *Pornography and Representation in Greece and Rome*. Oxford.

Ridings, D. 1995. *The Attic Moses*. Gothenberg.

Rispoli, G. 1985. *L'artiste sapiente: Per una storia della fantasia*. Naples.

Rose, J. 1986. *Sexuality in the Field of Vision*. London.

Runia, D. T. 1993. *Philo in Early Christian Literature*. Assen.

Sandbach, H. 1971. "*Phantasia kataleptike*." In *Problems in Stoicism*. ed. A. Long. London.

Sider, R. D. 1971. *Ancient Rhetoric and Tertullian*. Oxford.

Silverman, K. 1994. "Fassbinder and Lacan: A Reconsideration of Gaze, Look and Image." In *Visual Culture: Images and Interpretations*, ed. N. Bryson, M. Holly, and K. Moxey. Hanover, N.H.

Simon, G. 1988. *Le Regard, l'être, et l'apparence dans l'optique de l'antiquité*. Paris.

Steiner, W. 1995. *The Scandal of Pleasure*. Chicago.

Summers, D. 1987. *The Judgement of Sense: Renaissance Naturalism and the Rise of Aesthetics*. Cambridge.

Swain, S. 1996. *Hellenism and Empire: Language, Classicism and Power in the Greek World, AD 50–250*. Oxford.

Timothy, H. 1973. *The Early Christian Apologists and Greek Philosophy*. Assen.

Too, Yun Lee, ed. 1998. *Pedagogy and Power: Rhetorics of Ancient Learning*. Cambridge.

Ullmann, S. 1997. *Sex Seen: The Emergence of Sexuality in Modern America*. Berkeley.

van den Hoek, A. 1988. *Clement of Alexandria and His Use of Philo in the Stromateis*. Leiden.

Watson, G. 1988. *Phantasia in Classical Thought*. Galway.

Winkler, J. J. 1982. "The Mendacity of Kalasiris and the Narrative Strategy of Heliodorus." *Yale Classical Studies* 27:93–158.

Woolf, G. 1994. "Becoming Roman, Staying Greek: Culture, Identity and the Civilizing Process in the Roman East." *Proceedings of the Cambridge Philological Society* 40:116–43.

Chapter Fifteen

AGENTS AND VICTIMS:
CONSTRUCTIONS OF GENDER AND
DESIRE IN ANCIENT GREEK LOVE MAGIC

⋙⋘

Christopher A. Faraone

*C*lassical literature, from the "deception of Zeus" episode in the *Iliad* to the scenes of witchcraft in Apuleius's *Golden Ass*, is replete with allusions to and parodies and detailed descriptions of love magic, and in recent years, beginning with a pathbreaking essay by Jack Winkler, scholars have shown how the veracity of these literary accounts can be affirmed by the growing archaeological, epigraphical, and papyrological evidence for the actual use of love spells in the Greco-Roman world.[1] Given the celebrated polarization of male and female in Greek thought and social practices, it will come as no surprise that these popular love spells generally fall into two very distinct categories: those rituals used mainly by men to instill *erōs* (erotic passion) in women and those used mainly by women to maintain or increase *philia* (affection or friendship) in men.[2] We shall see, however, how this taxonomy forces us to think about the small number of exceptions where the general pattern is violated: for example, when socially inferior men seem to use the same types of facial ointments, amulets, and love potions that women use to ensure the affection of a male superior—a parallelism that confirms traditional feminist and Foucauldian readings of the ancient Greek construction of the female as a weak or otherwise inferior male. On the other hand, the fact that courtesans, prostitutes, and other autonomous women occasionally seem to co-opt traditional male spells for producing *erōs* suggests that these women were understood to be anomalous "males," a reading that confronts traditional interpretations of courtesans as an abused and despised group and suggests that they could in fact be admired (somewhat like Spartan women) for their "masculine" vigor and independence. My first goal, then, is to show in detail what the evidence for ancient Greek love spells can tell us about the social construction of gender of those who performed such spells in classical antiquity.

Second, I will discuss how the expected effects of the two types of love magic on males and females allow us to delve a little deeper into the Greek understanding of men and women as different kinds of desiring subjects. My conclusions here will call into question the existence of a monolithic "misogynist" model according to which ancient Greek males saw female sexuality as a source of great fear and imagined that women were a weak link in patriarchal schemes for the orderly transference of property down through the generations by means of betrothal marriage and property exchange. According to this view, if left to their own devices (Greek men feared) their women would mate indiscriminately with whatever males might cross their paths. In my conclusion I shall argue to the contrary that the evidence for Greek love magic suggests the existence of another, competing set of cultural assumptions that I follow Winkler in dubbing the "misandrist" model, according to which autonomous men are the "naturally" lascivious, passionate, and hypersexed gender, while women — on the other hand — are "naturally" resistant to sexual adventures and more inclined to be loyal to their fathers and husbands. My second goal, then, is to see how the intended male or female victims of a love charm are constructed as desiring subjects.

Before I begin, however, it will be helpful to offer a very brief survey of ancient Greek love magic and a taxonomy that separates the field of "love magic" into two distinct categories: those rituals used *generally* by men to instill erotic passion in women and those used *generally* by women to maintain or increase affection in men. I summarize these categories of use in table 1. The first column shows the types of spells that women traditionally use to induce *philia* and similar affections in men, while the second column shows those magic rituals that men usually employ to throw *erōs* into women.[3] Note how each group of rituals is deployed in a very different social context. The former were generally used within a household or at least within an existing relationship to increase a man's affection and esteem for his partner or associates. The Greeks generally describe such feelings with words connected etymologically with the nouns *philia* and *agapē*,[4] both of which in their root meaning refer to "affection" and "love" in a wide range of relationships, including but not limited to family members, friends, and spouses. In the last case (marriage), these terms can be used to signal bodily

Table 1: A Taxonomy of Ancient Greek Love Spells

	Spells for Inducing *Philia*	Spells for Inducing *Erōs*
TYPE OF SPELL OR DEVICE	Amulets, rings, love potions, or ointments	Apple-spells or spells that lead the victim to the agent
EXPECTED ACTION	Binds, enervates, or mollifies its victims, thereby reducing their anger and making them esteem their companions	Burns, tortures, or maddens its victims, thereby emboldening them to leave their homes and come to the practitioner
EXPECTED EFFECT	Love or affection (*philia, agapē, storgē*)	Uncontrollable lust (*erōs, pothos, himerōs, oistros*)
SOCIAL CONTEXT	Used by an insider within a marriage or an existing relationship to repair or heal it	Used by an outsider in courtship or seduction to destroy existing loyalties to natal family, spouse, or community
TYPICAL USERS	Wives or social inferiors	Men, courtesans, or whores
TYPICAL VICTIMS	Husbands, kings, and other male "heads of households"	Young women and men, usually living in their natal home
MYTHIC EXEMPLA	Hera against Zeus; Deianeira against Heracles	Hippomenes against Atalanta; Hades against Persephone; Jason against Medea

passions as well, which is precisely what we see in the *Iliad*, where Hera clearly uses an amulet to arouse sexual desire in Zeus. The charms that arouse *erōs*, on the other hand, are almost always used to begin a new relationship by forcing the victims (usually but not always women) from their homes and into the arms of the people who perform the spell. In this case the spell is designed explicitly to arouse the victim's sexual desire for the practitioner, as is abundantly clear from the repeated use of the Greek nouns *erōs* and *pothos* and related verbs and adjectives.

I should pause for a moment to make the linguistic distinctions between the categories "*erōs* magic" (= "spells that induce passion") and "*philia* magic" (= "spells that induce affection") as clear as possible, since modern notions of the meanings of "erotic" may cause problems here. In archaic and classical Greek discourse there is a clear difference between the invasive and dangerous onset of *erōs* and the more benign feelings of *philia*, a term which generally describes a reciprocal relationship based on mutual affection.[5] Thus, from the earliest periods Greeks either describe the onset of *erōs* as an invasive, demonic attack or use a ballistic model whereby Aphrodite is said to throw at or hit someone with *erōs* or *pothos*.[6] On the other hand, Greeks never personify or demonize *philia* or *agapē*, nor do they ever picture a deity hurling *philia* or *agapē* at mortals in a hostile way. This distinction should not, as I have noted, be overdrawn in a way that denies a sexual component to "*philia* magic." Indeed, here I am careful to avoid the polar opposition of "erotic magic" to "nonerotic magic" and insist that the real emphasis lies on the term *erōs*, which for the Greeks was clearly and narrowly defined as a dangerous, unwelcome, and irresistible lust that aims squarely and explicitly at sexual intercourse.

Finally, note that these two types of love spells accord well with the two larger categories of Greek magical technology: beneficial charms (i.e., "white magic") which usually aim at warding off or curing an illness, and harmful "black magic," which generally seeks to harm or destroy its victim. Thus, although some of the *philia* charms traditionally deployed by women against men — ointments and amulets — dovetail in obvious ways with the adornment of Greek women, who use jewelry and ointments to increase their personal attractiveness, such devices — especially when we include love potions in the group — are also part of the Greek corpus of healing and prophylactic lore, a fact which suggests that this whole branch of *philia* magic may aim (at least conceptually) at protecting an existing relationship or curing a sick one.[7] The various types of *erōs* spells, on the other hand, are clearly related to the large arsenal of rituals used in the more masculine world of curses and other invasive techniques: for example, the binding, burning, melting, and torture of effigies of the victim.[8] These commonalties suggest that the general category of "love magic" — which appears in the title of this article — may not, in fact, have been recognizable to the Greeks themselves, who may have seen *erōs* magic as a specialized extension of cursing rituals and *philia* spells as a subcategory of healing and protective rites.

THE SOCIALLY CONSTRUCTED GENDER OF THE AGENT

In the fourteenth book of the *Iliad*, Hera asks Aphrodite to lend her the magical *kestos himas*, mendaciously asserting that she wishes to stop the bickering of her parents, Oceanus and Tethys (14.197–210): "since now for a long time they have stayed apart from each other and from their marriage bed, since bitter anger has fallen upon their hearts." Hera, however, goes on to use the *kestos himas* against her own husband, and parallels from contemporary Mesopotamian magic and later Greek love spells suggest that there existed in the Near East and the Mediterranean basin a long tradition of wives using knotted cords and other amulets to calm angry husbands and to make them more affectionate, in part by increasing their own attractiveness.[9] And although we are accustomed to think of an amulet as self-induced "protective" magic and an aphrodisiac as invasive magic aimed at another, passages from Theophrastus, Pliny the Elder, the *Cyranides,* and the Greek magical papyri reveal a continuous tradition of belief that some amulets could be used to affect the way other people perceive and interact with the person who wears or carries the amulet. Thus, instead of simply asking that some evil be turned away, the invocations inscribed on these amulets often request that some abstract benefit be granted. For instance, a second- or third-century-C.E. silver amulet from Oxyrhynchus reads: "Grant charm, friendship, success, and sexiness to the man wearing this amulet [*phylacterion*]."[10] Here the charm in a self-referential manner uses the Greek word *phylacterion* (literally "a thing that protects") to describe a device that is primarily concerned with increasing the beauty of the owner and affection of others. It is also significant that amulets designed to increase a man's affection and those that work as general "good luck charms" are often combined and blurred with still another genre, the "charm to restrain anger." A good example is the following recipe from a Greek magical handbook:[11] "A charm to restrain anger and a charm to secure favor and the best charm for gaining victory in the law courts—it even works against kings; no charm is greater! Take a silver tablet and inscribe with a bronze stylus the following . . . and wear it under your garment and you will be victorious." The prayer to be inscribed on the tablet reads: "Give to me, Mr. So-and-So, whom Ms. So-and-So bore, victory, charm, reputation, advantage over all men and women, especially over Mr. So-and-So, whom Ms. So-and-So bore, forever and all time." This is a recipe for a general charm that will bring success over *all* men and women, but the mention in the advertisement of kings and law courts and the place to insert the name of a single man as the primary target ("especially over Mr. So-and-So") suggests that we have a spell aimed originally at a king, a judge, or some other male at the apex of some social group. A second-century-C.E. gold amulet from Thessalonika includes a similar stipulation: "Grant favor, success with all men and women, but especially with him, whomever she herself wishes."[12] Indeed, these spells are often designed for political situations such as an appearance in a royal audience or a court of law, where the petitioner finds himself in "the presence of a king or magnate."[13] An elaborately inscribed Greek amulet from Arabia gives us some sense of how such charms worked in the practical world of a Roman provincial capital: "Give charm, glory, and victory to Proclus, whom Salvina bore, before Diogenianus, the military governor of Bostra in Arabia and before Pelagius the assessor, and before all men small and great . . . in order that he might win, justly or unjustly, every law suit before every judge and adjudicator."[14]

There is, then, good evidence for the use of a special kind of amulet that people might place upon their own bodies in hopes of increasing their own personal charm and beauty in the eyes of a husband or a male superior. We see a similar pattern in the abundant testimony that wives regularly prepared love potions and ointments for their husbands.[15] The evidence ranges from the myth about Deianeira's gift to Heracles of a garment smeared with a putative love potion and a complicated legal trial in classical Athens of two women accused of killing their husbands with love potions to the repeated anecdotes about Greek tyrants and Roman emperors similarly attacked by their spouses or concubines. Plutarch tells us, for example, the story of Aretaphila, who was accused of poisoning her husband, the hated tyrant of Cyrene during the first century c.e. (*Mor.* 256c): "But when she was apprehended by the proofs, and saw that her preparations for the poisoning admitted no denial, she confessed but said that she had prepared no fatal poisoning: 'No, my dear' she said 'my striving is for very important things: your goodwill [*eunoia*] for me, and the repute and influence which I enjoy because of you. . . . It was foolish and feminine, perhaps, but not deserving of death, unless you as judge decide to put to death because of love spells and sorcery a woman who yearns for more affection [*pleon . . . phileisthai*] than you are willing to grant her.'" Plutarch, Juvenal, and Greco-Roman marriage contracts attest, moreover, to a persistent male fear that their wives might ply them with *pharmaka* as a means of controlling them. This broad background of wifely love potions, however, considerably raises our interest in the case of the Roman general Lucullus, whose demise was reported by the first-century-b.c.e. Roman biographer Nepos:[16] "Cornelius Nepos says that Lucullus was affected neither by old age or sickness, but rather that he was crippled by drugs [*pharmaka*] given to him by Callisthenes, his freedman. The drugs were given in order that Callisthenes might be loved more [*hōs agapōito mallon*] by him — they were supposed to have that sort of power — but they diverted and overwhelmed Lucullus's mind to such a degree that while he was still alive his brother took charge of his affairs." One might in this case assume that Lucullus's Greek freedman was motivated by jealousy arising out of an erotic relationship; this may be true, although the verb used here (*agapasthai*) is an impediment to such an argument, as it almost never connotes sexual love.[17] It is perhaps more important to note that there is here a clearly discernible political dimension to the act: like the wife of a tyrant or king, Callisthenes, a socially inferior freedman, may have feared for his powerful position in the general's retinue — in other words, he had a concern about his personal prestige much like those which underlie many other narratives about wives who attack their spouses with love potions.[18] Thus, although the great preponderance of evidence from Sophocles to Plutarch suggests that wives were the traditional users of love potions and husbands were invariably their victims, we can see how Callisthenes, Lucullus's Greek freedman, apparently used the same kind of "wifely" magic when he found himself in a similar social situation. This exception to the rule that love potions and ointments are usually given by women to their husbands dovetails neatly with the crossovers discussed earlier between amulets used by women to control their husbands and those worn by men to gain the esteem, friendship, and goodwill of other men in positions of authority, such as kings or Roman governors. In the case of *philia*-producing magic, then, it is fairly obvious that the female gender of the user is constructed in such a way as to include socially inferior males as well, a common feature of ancient Greek culture that feminist scholars and others have noted for some time now.[19]

We find a similar set of anomalies when we turn to the gender of those who deploy *erōs*-producing spells, the great majority of which are aimed by men at women. These spells are notorious for their focus on the torture of the female victim with fire and pain until she comes to the male practitioner, as, for example, in this Roman-era spell: "attract, inflame, destroy, burn, cause her to swoon from love as she is being burnt . . . goad the tortured *psyche*, the heart of Karosa, whom Thelo bore, until she leaps forth and comes to Apalos, whom Theonilla bore, out of passion and love, in this very hour, immediately, immediately; quickly, quickly." These spells are at least as old as the classical period,[20] and the great majority of them are deployed by men against women in the hopes of driving them out of their homes and into the arms of the man who uses the spell. Thus, of the eighty or more extant *erōs* spells, only seven are used by women to attract men.[21] We are unable to say, of course, precisely who these women were, but literary evidence beginning in the classical period suggests that one special group of females regularly co-opted these traditionally male forms of magic: courtesans and prostitutes. Socrates' banter with the famous courtesan Theodote, for example, hints quite openly that courtesans learned and used such spells on their clients, and the speech of Just Argument in Aristophanes' *Clouds* likewise informs us that another type of *erōs* spell used traditionally by men against women—the charmed apple—was also deployed by prostitutes in hopes of gaining new customers.[22]

In fact, courtesans and prostitutes appear regularly in our literary evidence as users of *erōs* spells. Lucian, for example, depicts two Athenian courtesans, Melitta and Bacchis, swapping tales and recipes. He begins with Melitta's plea for some help in retrieving a lost boyfriend (*Dialogues of the Courtesans* 4.1): "Do you know of any old women of the kind called 'Thessalians'? . . . They sing incantations and they make women desirable [*erasmious*] even if they are entirely despised." Contrast Melitta's goal here of being sexually desirable (*erasmios*) with that of the Greek wives and queens, who give their husbands love potions so that they will be more loved or esteemed.[23] It turns out that Bacchis does not know any "Thessalians," but she recalls how a Syrian sorceress living near the Ceramicus once performed a ritual for her that (she claims) successfully led back Phanias, a boyfriend who had apparently gone off to live with another woman: "She hangs these [i.e., the clothes or hairs of the man] from a peg and heats them up with burning sulfur, sprinkling salt over the fire, and says in addition the names of both people, his and yours. Then she brings out from her bosom a *rhombos* and whirls it round while speaking with a rapid tongue some incantation of barbaric and frightening names. . . . And not long afterwards . . . he came to me led by the incantation, despite the fact that his buddies had told him off and Phoebis, the girl with whom he was living, kept pleading with him." Lucian clearly depicts the typically destructive *erōs* spell: it uses fire and the whirling device known as a *rhombos*, similar to many of the later spells in which a man tortures a woman and forces her to come to him.[24] Here, however, there is an inversion of the usual gender of the participants: a woman uses an *erōs* spell to penetrate the "house" of her boyfriend and force him to return to her.

The logistical problem faced by Bacchis—"leading" or "drawing" a lover out of the house of a rival—is, in fact, precisely the one faced in Theocritus's second *Idyll* by Simaetha, who performs an elaborate erotic spell designed to get her boyfriend Delphis away from *his* new lover. Here, too, the ritual has all the hallmarks of a violent *erōs* spell. Simaetha and her servant use a *rhombos*, like the one employed by Lucian's Syrian sorceress, and they burn various household items such as barley, bay leaves, and wax in hopes of similarly burning the victim. The following lines illustrate the technique:[25]

Delphis brought me trouble, and I for Delphis burn this bay. And as these bay leaves crackle loud in the fire . . . so too may the flesh of Delphis waste in the flame!

Iunx, draw [*helke*] to my house the man I love!

As with the goddess's aid I melt this wax, so straightway may Delphis of Myndus waste with love. And as by Aphrodite's power turns this brazen *rhombos*, so may he turn about my door.

Iunx, draw to my house the man I love.

Commentators have long noted that nearly all of these magical actions find direct parallels in the Greek magical papyri,[26] but they have often failed to realize that the forms of magic used by Simaetha are those traditionally used by *males* to get females out of their homes.

As it turns out, Simaetha's apparent appropriation of traditionally male forms of erotic magic fits in very well with recent analyses of the poem which stress her aggressive, masculine role throughout the poem, especially in the detailed description of her first encounter with Delphis, where she puts herself in the role of the male viewer and makes Delphis the object of her own erotic gaze—a startling co-optation of the traditional male role in homosexual courtship.[27] This equation of Simaetha with an *erastēs* is helpful in showing how in her behavior Simaetha inverts traditional Greek expectations of the female as the passive partner in an erotic encounter. In the past, this peculiar independence of Simaetha has also been interpreted as a sign of the increased mobility and power of all women in Hellenistic cities like Alexandria,[28] but I would argue that the character of Simaetha in the second *Idyll*, is—like the whore in Aristophanes' *Clouds* or Lucian's Athenian courtesans—most probably drawn from a traditional literary stereotype of the courtesan, who could often be especially forthright in her pursuit of men and thus was liable to perform the sort of aggressive erotic magic that was otherwise typical of men. In short, Theocritus seems to present Simaetha in a situation that would have been instantly recognizable to his ancient audience as typical of a courtesan who was trying to get a former lover to return to her.[29]

The suspicion that prostitutes and mistresses used aggressive types of *erōs* magic is, moreover, a very popular one in later Mediterranean history. The church father John Chrysostom warns married men to stay away from such women because they use magic to alienate men from their wives,[30] an accusation that recurs in Byzantine and medieval sources,[31] in Renaissance Florence and Venice,[32] in sixteenth-century Modena,[33] and in modern Algeria.[34] Such accusations, however, are undoubtedly exaggerated and sometimes even manufactured by the understandable desire to save face: how else might a family explain such unseemly behavior by an errant husband or son? The prosecution of such women for erotic magic is further complicated by issues of social class; there is evidence from premodern Italy and Spain, for example, that lower-class prostitutes who captivated upper-class youths were much more frequently and more severely punished by the authorities than upper-class courtesans who used the same devices.[35] The detailed testimony and court records of the Italian Inquisition show, however, that these accusations were not simply invented out of whole cloth, but were in fact based on a core of historically documented practices. In short: most courtesans and prostitutes seem to know and use erotic magic, although not all of them were prosecuted or (if they were prosecuted) punished.[36]

In fact, it makes good sense that courtesans in the ancient Greek world would also use these types of aggressive "male" magic, once we realize that as a group they were in many ways quite similar to autonomous Greek men, especially in their economic independence and their education. The successful ones, at least, lived in their own houses, provided for their own income, fell in love at first sight, aggressively hunted out their lovers,[37] and employed other types of public stances and gestures that were traditionally limited to males. Even the notorious fact that they were mentioned by name in Athenian oratory and comedy—usually interpreted as contempt for their low status[38]—can be taken as a backhanded compliment, for such treatment was usually reserved for the notable men of the city. Indeed, they were enormously popular on the comic stage. Athenaeus cites dozens of lost fifth- and fourth-century Attic comedies which reveal how well educated these women were and how they excelled in the games and wit of the symposium, another exclusively male domain.[39] This peculiar "maleness" of prostitutes and courtesans has, in fact, been noted by ethnographers working on circum-Mediterranean cultures. Prostitutes in Morocco and Algeria, for instance, regularly co-opt aspects of male dress and behavior, as well as certain types of body language that are culturally defined as male—for instance, sitting or standing with legs spread apart or leaning on doorposts.[40]

This regular equation of courtesan and autonomous male has obvious parallels in the popular suspicions that powerful queens like Cleopatra used love magic to attract and then control men; such accusations, of course, have great explanatory value, for how else might a Roman understand why a soldier's soldier like Mark Antony would flee ignominiously at the battle of

Actium?[41] Aristophanes slyly alludes to this exchange of "natural" roles when the chorus praises Lysistrata for her skillful use of erotic magic:[42] "Hail, O most manly (*andreiotatē*) of all women, since the most powerful of the Greeks have been seized by your *iunx* spell and have come to you en masse." This is figurative language, of course, but quite appropriate for a stage full of Greek men with painful erections. I am, however, most interested in the fact that Lysistrata, in her putative role as expert handler of a *iunx* spell, is called "most manly." This odd understanding of the maleness of women who use *erōs* magic also shows up in the stereotypical representations of witches in later Roman literature. Horace alludes to the "masculine passion" of Canidia—perhaps a prostitute herself—who performs an erotic spell that employs one dominant female effigy abusing and threatening a smaller male doll.[43] In Apuleius's *Metamorphoses*, the protagonist Lucius is warned about a sexually ravenous woman named Pamphile, who like a typical male *erastēs* falls in love at first sight and uses erotic magic to have her way:[44] "No sooner does she catch sight of some young man of attractive appearance than she is consumed by his charm and immediately directs both her gaze and her desire at him. She . . . [i.e., using magic] attacks his soul and binds him with everlasting shackles of passionate love . . . . I advise you to beware of her, for she is always burning and you are young and handsome enough to suit her." Widows, especially in the Roman period, when they seem to have an autonomy similar to that of a courtesan, were also prone to erastic behavior, as in the scandalous case of Ismenodora, a young widow who "though previously blameless" was influenced by "the divine force of Erōs" and began to pursue a younger man of lower social status, eventually kidnapping and marrying him. In doing so she, too, appropriated a traditionally male act of aggression, bridal theft,[45] which is similar in important ways to the genre of *erōs* spells, which also aim at "kidnapping" their victims by violent means.[46] Ismenodora, it would seem, accomplished with her own hands and slaves what other independent women of means attempted with erotic spells.

It would seem, then, that the notions of gender that emerge from this material are social constructions based either on Greek hierarchical notions of the "effeminacy" of subordinates or the "masculinity" of the socially autonomous. Thus, in the case of *philia*-inducing magic the female gender of the user is constructed vertically according to Greek ideas of social rank and therefore includes males in subservient positions like the freedman Callisthenes and those men who use amulets to charm kings, judges, governors, and other males in positions of authority. In the *erōs*-charms, however, the male gender of the user is constructed according to the relative positions of a protected, ideally chaste victim on the inside and an independent agent on the outside, who tries to force his or her victims from their homes. As such, *erōs* spells are useful both to males—who try to force the daughters and wives of other men out of their homes—and to courtesans and prostitutes, who face similar problems when they need to flush rich young men out of the houses of their parents or girlfriends.

THE CONSTRUCTION OF THE DESIRING VICTIM

In addition to giving us special insights into how the ancient Greeks constructed gender, the forms of ancient Greek love magic and the context of their use also give us some interesting new vantage points for seeing how males and females were constructed as desiring subjects. For instance, the burning, madness, and bodily torture demanded for the (usually) female victim in the *erōs* spells finds parallels in Hippocratic and hagiographic descriptions of female adolescent hysteria and mythographic accounts of the daughters of Proetus, raising the distinct possibility that perhaps these are consistent features of a Greek understanding of female erotic desire.[47] In fact, we find a very similar description of this kind of female desire—also incited by an erotic spell—in a most unlikely source and pertaining to a most unlikely population. Aelian, an early-third-century-c.e. natural historian, reports that a species of land tortoise employs a special herb to facilitate sexual intercourse, an act which—according to the source he cites, a Roman senator named Demostratus—was normally a difficult one, for although the male was by nature a "most lustful creature," the female was coy and fearful of mating (*NA* 15.19):

This then is what the females dread . . . and since they are chaste [*sophronousai*] and prefer personal safety to pleasure, the males are unable to coax them to the act. And so by some mysterious instinct the males hold out to them an erotic *iunx* spell and a "banisher of all fear."[48] But it turns out that the *iunx* spells of an amorous male tortoise are not songs, by Zeus, such as those which Theocritus, the composer of playful herding songs, sings, but a strange herb of which Demostratus admits that neither he nor anyone else knows the name. Apparently the males adorn themselves with this herb [corruption in the text]. At any rate, if they hold this herb in their mouths, there ensues the exact opposite to what I have described above, for the male becomes enervated, while the female, who hitherto was fleeing, now is burning [*phlego-menē*]; she is made wild with frenzy [*exoistratai*] and desires intercourse.

I suspect that this passage tells us far more about the popular understanding of the expected effects of contemporary love spells on humans than it does about the actual habits of tortoises, but since both Aristotle and Theophrastus tell us quite explicitly that people learn about the healing properties of herbs by watching the behavior of wild animals,[49] we should perhaps keep an open mind on the subject.

In any event, the usually moderate character of the female tortoise (*sophronousa*: "chaste" or "self-controlled"), who is then "burning" and made "wild with frenzy," accords well with anticipated effects of the *erōs* spells discussed earlier. The famous orator Polemo, writing about a century earlier than Aelian, reflects a similar understanding about the changes that erotic magic brings about in the female victim. In a thinly veiled diatribe, he accuses his rival Favorinus of fraudulently claiming knowledge of magic:[50] "On top of this, he was a charlatan in the magic arts. . . . He made men believe that he could compel women to pursue men the way men pursue women." Here we have one side of the equation given by Aelian: erotic magic forces women to pursue the male practitioner in the same manner as men are (i.e., "naturally") predisposed to pursue women. This idea of "turning tables" or "trading places" is, of course, implicit in other instances of love magic, most famously in Sappho's *Hymn to Aphrodite* ("for if she flees, quickly she will pursue"), and reminds us that the images of "pursuing" and "fleeing" that we find in both Aelian and Polemo are indeed more commonly applied to homoerotic relationships.[51] In fact, Aelian's tortoises provide a very suggestive model for understanding the wider ramifications of the use of love magic in ancient Greek society, for it seems—broadly speaking—that the technologies of *erōs* magic and *philia* magic do aim in similar ways at reversing the "natural" roles of men and women as desiring subjects. Indeed, it would appear from the evidence for love spells that Greek women were thought to be moderate and self-controlled "by nature" like Aelian's female tortoises and that erotic magic somehow manages to reverse their traditional antipathy or coolness to sexual intercourse, whereas conversely it was thought that although men were "naturally" passionate and sexually aggressive, they could be cooled and calmed by the *philia* spells of women, who seek more permanent and satisfying relations with them. As we shall see below, both of these assumptions are potentially controversial, since they fly in the face of much scholarly work which sees male fear of the "natural" wildness and promiscuity of women as a primary cause of ancient Greek misogyny.[52] In other words, the construction of the victims in ancient Greek love magic as desiring subjects seems to presuppose an inverted model, according to which it is rampant *male* sexuality that needs to be controlled by chaste and thoughtful women.

This construct of the "naturally" chaste female is by no means limited to the arcana of ancient Greek magical practices or to the later beliefs of Roman authors such as Polemo or Aelian. Indeed, the image of aggressive male pursuit of a reluctant young woman is a staple of Greek myth and is often depicted on vase paintings.[53] Hesiod and Alcaeus, however, give us the first evidence that this normative female chastity can in fact be altered by noxious environmental effects—in this case the rising of the Dog Star (Sirius):[54]

> then . . . women are most lustful and men most weak, since Sirius dries out their head and knees and their skin is withered by the heat. (Hesiod *Op.* 585–88)

> Soak your lungs in wine, for the star is on the rise and the season is harsh and all things are thirsty in the heat . . . and now women are most polluted and men are weak, since the Dog Star dries out their head and knees. (Alcaeus fr. 347a)

The textual relation between these two passages is controversial but need not detain us, as they are both obviously drawn from the same stratum of folk belief.[55] Indeed, it can hardly be a coincidence that the Adonia—a festival of Aphrodite devoted to female sexuality and a traditional lightning rod for male suspicions about female licentiousness—was also held at the rising of the Dog Star.[56] Later authors certainly understand that both passages refer explicitly to the Dog Star's effect on the sexual desire of females and males. Thus, Pliny the Elder paraphrases: "They (sc. Hesiod and Alcaeus) have written that when the song of the cicada is most piercing, women are most keen for lust and men are most sluggish for sexual intercourse." The author of the Aristotelian *Problems* explains the rationale behind this belief:[57]

> QUESTION: "Why is it that in summer, men are less able to make love but women more able, just as the poet says of the time when the thistle blooms: 'Women are most wanton and men most weak'"?
> ANSWER: Because hot natures collapse in summer by excess of heat,

while cold ones flourish. Now a man is hot and dry but a woman is
cold and moist. So the power of a man is diminished at that time,
but a woman's power flourishes.

Although this discussion somewhat obscures the Hesiodic emphasis on female lust, it does point up the fact that this early understanding of the seasonal effects [58] of hot summer weather is closely related to traditional Greek
beliefs about the bodily humors, whereby males are generally believed to
be "naturally" dry and hot, and females cool and wet.[59] Thus, the Dog Star,
said to "dry out" and "wither" the heads and knees in a period when "all
things are thirsty," would logically have the effect of changing normally
moist and cool women into dry and hot men, that is, into "naturally" lascivious beings. This belief, moreover, fits well with the advice of animal
herders that one must artificially heat up and dry out the females of the
herd in order to encourage them to mate,[60] and may explain the great popularity of those *erōs* spells which aim mainly at burning the female victim.[61]

We should recall at this point that in Aelian's report on the effects of a
love charm on land tortoises and in the Hesiodic description of the effects
of the rising Dog Star on humans, *both* sexes were adversely affected, albeit
in very different ways: naturally chaste and cool females were made hot and
lustful, while normally passionate men were rendered cool and listless. In
my discussion above, I focused primarily on the female victim of *erōs* magic
as a desiring subject, but it is also true that *philia* magic was thought to fundamentally alter the naturally aggressive and passionate males who were its
typical victims.[62] This is most clearly spelled out by Plutarch in his advice to
young brides (*Mor.* 139a): "In the same way, women who use love potions
[*philtra*] and sorcery [*goēteia*] against their husbands, and who gain mastery
over them through pleasure, end up living with stunned, senseless, crippled
men. The men bewitched by Circe were of no service to her, nor did she
have any 'use' at all for them after they had become swine and asses. But
Odysseus, who kept his senses and behaved prudently, she loved in excess."
Plutarch claims here that by controlling your husband with spells or potions, you weaken his manliness. This is why he mentions the Circe episode
in the *Odyssey,* where the ship's crew (once they have been "domesticated"
by her magic potions) are no longer of any "use" to Circe, a veiled reference
to sexual intercourse.[63] The bottom line of the argument is that using drugs
or magic to increase your husband's affection is counterproductive, since it
leads paradoxically to a loss in his virility.

Although space does not allow a full discussion of the generally enervat-
ing and desire-dampening effect of love potions and other forms of *philia*

Table 2: Inversion of the "Natural" Genders in Ancient Greek Love Spells

Type of Spell	Construction of Agent	"Natural" State of Victim	Effect of Magic on Victim
ERŌS SPELLS	Autonomous male *erastēs*	Moderate and chaste female	Becomes a passionate *erastēs*
PHILIA SPELLS	Usually female social inferior	Angry, passionate male	Becomes moderate, calm, subordinate

magic, I summarize in table 2 how ancient Greek love spells construct the genders of both agent and victim (see the first two columns) and then in the third column I describe how the victim was thought to change as the result of the spell. This table gives us, I think, some valuable new insights into the theme of "table turning" that frequently turns up in love spells and confirms my suspicions that such spells are often thought like Aelian's unnamed herb to invert the "natural" gender of their victims. Thus, males and other *erastai*, such as courtesans and widows, use erotic magic to project the burning desires and mad behaviors typical of an *erastēs* onto their female (or feminized) victims, while in the case of *philia* charms, chaste women and other subordinates seek to calm and subordinate their angry and passionate male superiors.

This startling flexibility in the victim's constructed gender seems to presuppose a belief that men and women are essentially of the same species and have the same "nature" (*physis*), a belief associated with Aristotle and with later medical writers such as Hierophilus, Soranus, and Galen,[64] who with the help of human dissection in the Hellenistic period were able to contest the alternate and earlier Hippocratic theory that men and women were essentially two separate species, with different flesh, organs, and diseases.[65] Soranus, for example, noted that excessively active women, like professional acrobats and dancers — that is, those who most closely approximated living a physically demanding male lifestyle — often stopped menstruating, while men who adopted a sedentary lifestyle were thought to grow soft and effeminate.[66] Likewise, we can explain why the rising Dog Star or an erotic magic spell can, for a time at least, turn "naturally" chaste females into *erastai*, since according to this popular Aristotelian model, at least, environment played an important role in the gendering of an individual. In the light of this cultural background, it is not surprising that (as we saw above) Greek ideas about the effects of the environment and magic on human sexuality also presuppose Aristotelian, not Hippocratic, ideas about the bodily humors.

CONCLUSION

It would seem, then, that the evidence of ancient Greek love magic reflects both a flexible understanding of the gender of the agents of these spells and a model of the desiring subject, according to which females are "naturally" chaste and males "naturally" lascivious. This second model is equally flexible, however, in that it allows for seasonal and other environmental effects, which like love magic can change the "natural" desire in both males and females. This model of the desiring subject, however, runs counter to a large body of scholarship on a popular misogynist vein of Greek thought from Hesiod to Aristotle and beyond that sees woman as physically, intellectually, and morally inferior to men.[67] This negative view of women, moreover, is thought to be connected in various ways with a deep-felt male fear that females were "naturally" wild and promiscuous and that it was incumbent upon moderate and self-controlled males—in their roles as fathers, brothers, and husbands—to imprison their womenfolk in the house and control their sexuality so that it was deployed only in the context of a betrothal marriage.[68] The evidence for love magic surveyed in this essay argues, however, for the existence of an alternative to this misogynist model—we might call it a "misandrist model"[69]—according to which men must torture and burn women, because like Aelian's female tortoises women are by nature self-controlled and sedate, and reluctant to have intercourse. Conversely, women use soporific potions and knotted cords to control the anger and the passion of their "naturally" wild husbands, because like Aelian's male tortoises they are otherwise naturally wild, passionate, and difficult to control.

The idea that erotic magic attacks a woman's "natural" loyalty and chastity is, in fact, also manifest in earlier Greek texts that describe the erotic seizure of women. In Euripides' *Hippolytus* Phaedra appears as a paragon of female virtues and an embodiment of the ideals of shame (*aidōs*) and modesty (*sophrosyne*), whose "natural" state is completely perverted by the attacks of Aphrodite and Erōs.[70] Occasionally the extant erotic spells also mention the goal of attacking the woman's moral character, for instance, "Make her cease from her arrogance, her thoughtfulness [*logismou*], and her sense of shame [*aischunēs*]."[71] The attack on the female victim's "natural" sense of shame is, moreover, often accompanied by an attempt to alienate her from her community. Thus, Jason is said to deploy an *erōs* spell in order to strip Medea of the respect (*aidōs*) that she (i.e., "naturally") feels for her parents, and many of the extant *erōs* spells specifically aim at making the woman forget her parents, children, husband, siblings, friends, and neighbors, that is, all those people that make up her moral community.[72] In short, it appears that concerns about female infidelity and impurity were the purview of the women of the family and of the neighborhood themselves, who stress ideals of loyalty to family (both natal and marital) above all else.[73] This dependence on very local emotional ties and female fidelity shows up, in fact, in the *erōs* spells themselves, for although they do imagine success in terms of physically forcing the woman out of her house, these spells never aim to remove the physical barriers to the female victim's escape, such as one might expect in a culture that assumed the "natural" infidelity of its women. Thus, it is striking that with all of our evidence for the use of *erōs* magic against women, we have absolutely no hint that erotic charms were needed to unbar a locked door[74] or to cast sleep on the eyes of a vigilant father or husband—situations that we might expect in a culture that actively secluded its womenfolk.[75] In short, it would appear that the main obstacles to the users of these spells is not the locked door or the males who guard it, but rather the "natural" modesty of young women and the reverence and loyalty they feel towards their parents, their husbands, or their community.[76]

Finally, although I argue that this "misandrist" model of the chaste female and the wild, passionate male is widely reflected in the practices of ancient Greek love magic, I do not wish to imply that this model is more pervasive or important than the "misogynist," which is also widely attested in literary texts, albeit primarily in those that survive from Athens. I would argue instead for the existence of at least two competing constructions of and discourses about gender and desire among the Greeks, some which privilege the male and others which privilege the female. We might characterize these competing ideologies as "opposed" or "complementary" or suggest a hierarchy with the terms "dominant" and "muted,"[77] but such fixed and neat schemata run the risk of missing the fluidity in the conceptions of gender that we find regarding love magic. I have pointed out elsewhere, for example, how indications of what we might call "situational gender"[78] surface in those Greek myths in which "naturally" chaste and obedient girls are driven from their homes precisely because it is "*un*natural" for them to remain forever modest and devoted to their parents. Thus, in some sense it is correct to say that the misandrist model describes and prescribes a "natural" modest state for prepubescent girls and married women, while the misogynist model does the same for adolescent girls, whose brief period of "naturally" wild and lascivious behavior is sanctioned in myth and explained as the result of divine anger or human magic.

Confusion arises, then, when scholars wrongly argue for a misogynist model that sees *all* women as wild and lascivious all the time, when in fact such behavior seems to the ancient Greeks to be a kind of developmental pathology limited to the period of adolescence, when according to patriarchal expectations they must make the transition from their roles as daughters in their fathers' homes to their new roles as wives and then mothers in the homes of their husbands.[79] Such a flexible and situational model of desire allows Greek women to be chaste daughters and wives but also desirable and desiring brides, a split that appears elsewhere in our sources — for example, in the treatment of women in Aristophanes' *Lysistrata*, in which the older women are portrayed in very positive roles as self-disciplined soldiers of a comic sort, while the younger women appear as slaves to their desires for wine and sex who must to be locked in the Acropolis by Lysistrata.[80] This notion of rabid female passion as a transitional or developmental phase is implicit in the mythological pattern, in which female adolescent hysteria (often eroticized) is to be cured by marriage and childbirth, and explicit in the testimony of the cuckold in Lysias 1, who says that *after* his first child was born he relaxed his scrutiny of his young wife's behavior and gave her the keys to the house.[81] Many years ago Jack Winkler suggested that the imagined effects of erotic magic might in fact give us a faint and rare glimpse of ancient Greek women as desiring subjects.[82] I would in fact agree, but I suggest that the Greeks might limit the time period of such a snapshot, as it were, to the brief years of optimum marriageability or to a few weeks each year when the Dog Star rises and brings its own brief period of female lust.

Notes

1. Winkler 1991.

2. Faraone 1999, 27–30.

3. Kieckhefer 1991, 31–36, suggests a similar taxonomy of medieval European love spells, which he divides into three categories: (i) "sex-inducing magic," which was used "to induce a person to become a sexual partner" (= my *erōs* magic); (ii) "love magic," which was used "to encourage an intimate and lasting amorous relationship" (roughly = my *philia* magic); and (iii) "sex-enhancing magic," used "to enhance the sexual experience of partners who were already willing," a category that corresponds to "self-help" magic, which is irrelevant here; see Faraone 1999, 18–22.

4. Faraone 1999, 29–30.

5. The Greeks understood that *erōs* was basically incompatible with *philia*; see Konstan 1997, 38–39.

6. Faraone 1999, 43–55 (*erōs*) and 118–19 (*philia* and similar terms).

7. Kieckhefer (1991, 34–35) points out how in medieval formularies recipes for increasing marital affection are "often explicitly remedial" and aimed at healing angry rifts or recovering love lost. He also notes that women who use magic to improve their own marriage were much less likely to be persecuted for magic than those women (e.g., courtesans) who used magic to facilitate adultery.

8. Faraone 1999, 55–69.

9. Faraone 1999, 97–110.

10. *SM* 64 = *GMA* 60. (Abbreviations for magical corpora are given at the head of the reference list.)

11. *PGM* XXXVI.35–68. For similar combinations of these three types of spells, see *PGM* XX.270–273 (all three); XXXVI.161–177 (an anger-binding spell and a victory spell) and 211–30 (all three).

12. *GMA* 40.

13. *PGM* 13.250.

14. *GMA* 58.12–19; see Kotansky 1991 for an excellent discussion. For a more detailed inquiry into the text discussed in this paragraph, see Faraone 1999, 107–9.

15. For a much more detailed analysis of what follows, see Faraone 1999, 110–19.

16. Cornelius Nepos fr. 52 (Marshall) = Plutarch *Lucullus* 43.1–2.

17. See LSJ, s.v. *agapō*, I.1, where the basic meanings are "to hold in great affection", "to love" and "to be content with." Joly 1968, 36–41, surveys the various uses of this verb from the classical to the imperial period, stressing how it gradually ousts the verb *philein* as the most popular word for love.

18. Faraone 1999, 110–19.

19. See Richlin 1991 for a survey of the early feminist contributions of Keuls, Hallet, Skinner, and others. Dover 1978, 100–110; Foucault 1985, 1986; Winkler 1990, 17–44 passim; and Halperin 1990 passim, but esp. 266, have discussed in detail how such hierarchical notions play out in classical Athenian homoerotic love as the distinctions between the masculine *erastēs* (the "lover" who penetrates) and the "feminized" *erōmenos* (the "beloved" who is penetrated). Gleason 1990 profitably extends this type of analysis to the culture of the late antique orators, and Loizos 1994, 71–74, discusses similar modern Greek notions.

20. Pindar gave us a charter myth for their invention in his version of Jason's seduction of Medea (*Pythian* 4.213–19), and Aristophanes parodied this type of spell in his lost play *Amphiaraus*; see Faraone 1999, 55–69.

21. Four are used in a homoerotic context; see Faraone 1999, 147–49.

22. Xenophon *Memorabilia* 3.11.16 (they talk of love potions [*philtra*] and incantations [*epōidai*]) and Aristophanes *Clouds* 996–97. See Faraone 1999, 1–2 and 149–50, for discussion.

23. When apprehended in such situations, wives (as early as the law case to which Antiphon 1 belongs) repeatedly use *philia, agapē,* or related verbs (never *erōs*) to describe what they seek from their apparently disaffected husbands; see Faraone 1999, 114–19 for discussion.

24. The *rhombus* was a device that was apparently whirled about during the ritual; see Faraone 1999, 150–51.

25. *Idyll* 2.23–32, as translated by Gow (1952) with minor revisions.

26. E.g., Gow 1952, ad loc.; and Dover 1971, ad loc.

27. See, e.g., Griffiths 1981, 266–67, who notes perceptively: (i) how she pursues a fickle but beautiful object of desire, (ii) how she is attracted by Delphis' well oiled and athletic body, and (iii) how her lament in the second half of the poem is similar to those of the aging pederasts in *Idylls* 29 and 30. More recently Burton 1995, 43–44, stresses how Simaetha assumes the male initiative in courtship and how she falls in love at first sight, another topos of pederastic infatuation.

28. See, e.g., Gow 1952, 33; Burton 1995, 69–73; and Cameron 1996.

29. I am not, of course, the first to suggest that Simaetha is a courtesan: see Gow 1952, ad loc.; and Dover 1971, 95–96. Arnott 1996, 60, notes that Simaetha is associated by various details with the lifestyle of a courtesan.

30. Migne, *PG* 51.216. I thank M. Dickie for this reference.

31. Kazhdam 1995, 78; and Kieckhofer 1991, 31–35 and 44.

32. Brucker 1963, 9–10, discusses the case of a Florentine merchant who in 1375 accused a prostitute of using a doll stuck with iron pins to cause his brother to desert his wife, children, and business. Ruggiero 1993, 28–31, mentions other accusations in Florence. For Venice, see Ruggerio 1985, 35. Brucker 1963, 11 and 18, mentions a brother and sister accused of using magic to attract customers to their brothel.

33. O'Neil 1987, 99–102 and 111–12 n. 41.

34. Janson 1987, 188.

35. Ruggiero 1993, 28–31; 1985, 35; O'Neil 1987, 99, 111–12 n. 41, and 113 n. 61.

36. Ruggiero 1985 and 1993, passim.

37. Fantham 1986, 47–48, notes how the courtesans in New Comedy seem to exhibit the violent emotions and actions of the traditional male *erastēs*.

38. Schaps 1977.

39. *Deipnosophistae* book 13 passim. Cooper 1995, 317 n. 39, aptly describes how in these comic fragments "courtesans are characterized as witty, sophisticated, quick at repartee, and associating with philosophers, poets and politicians." Henry 1985; and Keuls 1985, 187–203, are generally skeptical of this image, the latter (pp. 199–200) pointing out that the dirty jokes they tell are not refined. Perhaps not, but such jokes only strengthen my argument that courtesans co-opted *male* practices and performance modes.

40. Janson 1987, 179–83.

41. Faraone 1999, 121.

42. *Lysistrata* 1108–11.

43. *Epistle* 5.41: *mascula libido.* See Faraone 1999, 158. Scholiasts at *Epode* 3.7–8 identify her as Gratidia, a Neapolitan perfume seller (*unguentaria*), and Dedo 1904, 42–44, suggests that the character is based on a real woman; such *unguentariae* apparently worked prostitutes as well; see Cameron 1981, 286–87.

44. *Metamorphoses* 2.5, in the Loeb translation of J. A. Hanson, with minor changes.

45. Ismenodora's story provides the dramatic frame for Plutarch's *Erotikos;* for an engaging recent discussion see Goldhill 1995, 146–61. On the financial power of

widows during the Roman period, see Fantham 1995. Pitt-Rivers 1977, 80–84, and Brandes 1981, 226–27, note the popular Andalusian belief that widows take on "the predatory male attitude toward sexual promiscuity," and they point out that their image is often blurred with that of the witch.

46. Faraone 1999, 78–95.

47. Faraone 1999, 84–95.

48. An allusion (quoting half of *Od.* 4.221) to the *pharmakon* of Helen that makes people forget their fear.

49. Preus 1988, 83–85.

50. Polemo, *De physiognomia* in *Scriptores physiognomonici Graeci* 1.160–64. See Gleason 1995, 7–8, for this translation and a detailed discussion.

51. See, e.g., Giacomelli 1980, for the general pattern.

52. For a good summary, see Cantarella 1987, 24–51 and 66–69, who mainly uses literary evidence.

53. Zeitlin 1986; and Sourvinou-Inwood 1987.

54. See Carson 1990, 139–41, for discussion. For the danger of the star's rising, see, especially the simile of the Dog Star rising at *Il.* 22.25–32 ("it brings great fever to mortals").

55. Traditionally philologists have argued that Alcaeus is copying Hesiod, but the important variants in vocabulary suggest that they reflect different versions the same folk tradition. See Nagy 1990, 462–63; and Petropoulos 1994, 17.

56. Winkler 1991, 188–209.

57. Pliny *NH* 22.86 and [Aristotle] 879 a26–28, both referring explicitly to this poetic tradition.

58. Carson 1990, 139–41, misses the point, I think, when she cites these passages as proof for beliefs in the *general* promiscuity of women.

59. There is some difference of opinion about the relative temperatures of males and females. The Hippocratics generally thought that women were moist and hot, whereas Aristotle and the Hippocratic author of *Regimen* 1 thought women were moist and cold, a theory that won out in the end. See Dean-Jones 1991, 134 n. 31.

60. Aristotle reports that "the warmer the weather," the more eagerly cows and mares desire to mate (*HA* 572a30–b4). Virgil notes that horse breeders deny mares water and food to increase their ardor for mating, since this makes them "thirsty for seed" (*Georgics* 2.130ff.). Pliny (*NH* 10.83.181) tells us that male horses, dogs, and swine prefer mating in the morning (i.e., when it is cooler and wetter), while the females prefer the afternoon (i.e., when it is hotter and drier). Similar beliefs may underlie Aelian's advice concerning the breeding of asses, goats, and horses: rub salt and sodium carbonate on the genitals of the females to produce a greater appetite for sexual intercourse (it makes the females "go mad for" for the males: *On Animals* 9.48).

61. Faraone 1999, 50–60 passim.

62. Faraone 1999, 119–31.

63. It is important to stress the fact that Circe turns the men into *domesticated* farm animals, not noble, wild animals. The expression Plutarch uses, "did not have any use

for them" (chrēsthai tini), is most probably a euphemism (like Latin uti familiariter) for sexual relations with a man.

64. Laqueur 1986, 2–5; and Gleason 1990, 380 n. 4.

65. Dean-Jones 1991, 115–17; and Gleason 1990, 390, summarize the differences.

66. Soranus Gynaeceia 1.22–23. See Gleason 1990, 390.

67. See, e.g., Keuls 1985, passim; Cantarella 1987, 24–51 and 66–69; and Carson 1990.

68. Apparently a common belief of Mediterranean males; see Brandes 1981 for discussion and earlier bibliography and Cohen 1991, 138–45, for ancient Athens.

69. See Winkler 1991, 139–40 and 205–7, for misandrist discourse as an alternate and subordinated—Ardener would call it "muted"—ideology that women use in patriarchal cultures to resist, complement, and (at times) even accommodate the dominant ideology. Cohen 1991, 137–41 (discussing the confused image of women in Greek literature) sees conflicting normative ideals about women, one of praise and another of contempt.

70. Zeitlin 1985, 52–53. We should remember, moreover, that this play won first prize at Athens, while his earlier attempt at this story, in his lost play Hippolytus Veiled, had been widely condemned precisely because the poet had portrayed Phaedra as a shameless, wildly enamored woman who propositioned her stepson directly. See Barrett 1964, 11–15, for discussion.

71. PGM 17a, discussed by Petropoulos 1993, 50 n. 46. See also PGM 4.1759–60, where the god Eros, in the midst of an elaborate hexametrical hymn used in an agōgē spell, is described as "you, who obscure self-controlled thoughts [sōphronas logismous] and instill dark frenzy [oistron]."

72. Faraone 1999, 55–58 (Jason) and 86–89 (forgetting parents).

73. Cohen 1991, 155, notes that the neighborhood is probably "one of the major mechanisms for social control" in ancient Athens and Mediterranean cultures generally.

74. See, e.g., PGM 12.160–78, a spell used to escape prison, which reads in part, ". . . let the doors be opened for him," or PGM 36.312–20, which is addressed to the door bolt. Note also that in his list of things magicians claim to do, Arnobius lists opening doors and inflaming women with passion separately and far apart as if they were two separate operations (Adversus Gentes 1.43): "that they send lethal decay to whomever they want, disrupt family relations, open locked doors without a key, reduce mouths to silence, speed or slow down horses in chariot races, send the flames of love and furious desires to housewives."

75. There is, however, some evidence that in classical Athens men did keep close surveillance over adolescent girls. When the cuckold in Lysias 1, for example, says that once his first child was born he relaxed his scrutiny of his young wife's behavior and gave her the keys to the house, he probably hopes the jury will see this as a traditional male response to the end of a period during which women were susceptible to erotic attacks.

76. This is not to say, of course, that there were not "easy" women in ancient Greek culture, but rather that there was no need to use erotic magic to get at them. Indeed, this is the point of the comic tale about a foolish rich youth who pays an enormous sum to a magician to perform an erotic spell against the wife of another man,

even though this woman (as Lucian tells us with a grin) was a "lusty and forward lady" who would have come to him for a fraction of the sum (Lucian *Philopseudes* 13–15); see Winkler 1991, 88, for discussion.

77. Winkler 1991, 139–40 and 205–7.

78. See Foxhall 1994, 134–35 for a general discussion, and Cornwall 1994 for the astonishing fluidity in the gender roles adopted by Brazilian sex workers.

79. Sourvinou-Inwood 1987, 136–39; and Seaford 1988.

80. Faraone 1997, 38–59. The division of female characters by generation and the generally more positive presentation of the older generation is a feature of Old Comedy; see Henderson 1987.

81. See note 75 above.

82. Winkler 1991, 233.

Abbreviations of Magical Corpora

GMA: R. Kotansky. *Greek Magical Amulets: The Inscribed Gold, Silver, Copper, and Bronze Lamellae.* Part 1, *Published Texts of Known Provenance.* Papyrologica Coloniensia 22, vol.1. Opladen, 1994.

PGM: K. Preisendanz [and A. Henrichs]. *Papyri Graecae Magicae: Die Griechischen Zauberpapyri* [2]. Stuttgart 1973–74.

SM: R. Daniel and F. Maltomini. *Supplementum Magicum.* 2 vols. Papyrologica Coloniensia 16, vols. 1 and 2. Opladen, 1990 and 1991.

References

Arnott, W. G. 1996. "The Preoccupations of Theocritus: Structure, Illusive Realism and Allusive Parody." In *Theocritus*, Hellenistica Groningana 2. ed. M. A. Harder, R. F. Regtuit, and G. C. Wakker, 55–70. Groningen.

Barrett, W. S. 1964. *Euripides: Hippolytus.* Oxford.

Brandes, S. 1981. "Like Wounded Stags: Male Sexual Ideology in an Andalusian Town." In *Sexual Meanings: The Cultural Construction of Gender and Sexuality,* ed. S. B. Ortner and H. Whitehead, 216–39. Cambridge.

Brucker, G. A. 1963. "Sorcery in Early Renaissance Florence." *Studies in the Renaissance* 10:7–24.

Burton, J. B. 1995. *Theocritus' Urban Mimes: Mobility, Gender and Patronage.* Berkeley.

Cameron, Alan. 1981. "Asclepiades' Girlfriends." In *Reflections of Women in Antiquity,* ed. H. Foley, 275–302. New York.

———. 1996. *Callimachus and His Critics.* Princeton, N.J.

Cantarella, E. 1987. *Pandora's Daughters: The Role and Status of Women in Greek and Roman Antiquity.* Translated by M. Fant. Baltimore.

Carson, A. 1990. "Putting Her in Her Place: Woman, Dirt, and Desire." In *Before Sexuality: The Construction of Erotic Experience in the Ancient Greek World,* ed. D. M. Halperin, J. J. Winkler, and F. I. Zeitlin, 135–69. Princeton, N.J.

Cohen, D. 1991. *Law, Sexuality, and Society: The Enforcement of Morals in Classical Athens*. Cambridge.

Cooper, C. 1995. "Hyperides and the Trial of Phryne." *Phoenix* 49:303–18.

Cornwall, A. 1994. "Gendered Identities and Gender Ambiguity among *Travestis* in Salvador." In *Dislocating Masculinity*, ed. A.Cornwall and N. Lindisfarne, 111–32. London.

Dean-Jones, L. 1991. "The Cultural Construct of the Female Body in Classical Greek Science." In *Women's History and Ancient History*, ed. S. B. Pomeroy, 111–37. Chapel Hill, N.C.

Dedo, R. 1904. *De antiquorum superstitione amatoria*. Gryphia.

Dover, K. J. 1971 *Theocritus: Select Poems*. Glasgow.

———. 1978. *Greek Homosexuality*. London.

Fantham, E. 1986. "ZHLOTUPIA: A Brief Excursion into Sex, Violence, and Literary History." *Phoenix* 40:45–57.

———. 1995. "Aemilia Pudentilla or a Wealthy Widow's Choice." In *Women in Antiquity: New Assessments*, ed. R. Hawley and B. Levick, 220–32. London.

Faraone, C. A. 1997. "Salvation and Female Heroics in the Parodos of Aristophanes' *Lysistrata*." *Journal of Hellenic Studies* 117:38–59.

———. 1999. *Ancient Greek Love Magic*. Cambridge, Mass.

Foucault, M. 1985. *The History of Sexuality*. Vol. 2, *The Uses of Pleasure*. Translated by R. Hurley. New York.

———. 1986. *The History of Sexuality*. Vol. 3, *The Care of Self*. Translated by R. Hurley. New York.

Foxhall, L. 1994. "Pandora Unbound: A Feminist Critique of Foucault's *History of Sexuality*." In *Dislocating Masculinity*, ed. A.Cornwall and N. Lindisfarne, 133–46. London.

Giacomelli, A. 1980. "The Justice of Aphrodite in Sappho Fr. 1." *Transactions of the American Philological Association* 110:135–42.

Gleason, M. W. 1990. "The Semiotics of Gender: Physiognomy and Self-Fashioning in the Second Century C.E." In *Before Sexuality: The Construction of Erotic Experience in the Ancient Greek World*, ed. D. M. Halperin, J. J. Winkler, and F. I. Zeitlin, 389–415. Princeton, N.J..

———. 1995. *Making Men: Sophists and Self-Presentation in Ancient Rome*. Princeton.

Goldhill, S. 1995. *Foucault's Virginity: Ancient Erotic Fiction and the History of Sexuality*. Cambridge.

Gow, A. S. F. 1952. *Theocritus*. 2 vols. Cambridge.

Griffiths, F. T. 1981. "Home before Lunch: The Emancipated Woman in Theocritus." In *Reflections of Women in Antiquity*, ed. H. Foley, 247–73. New York.

Halperin, D. M. 1990. "Why Is Diotima a Woman? Platonic *Eros* and the Figuration of Gender." In *Before Sexuality: The Construction of Erotic Experience in the Ancient Greek World*, ed. D. M. Halperin, J. J. Winkler, and F. I. Zeitlin, 257–308. Princeton, N.J.

Henderson, J. 1987. "Older Women in Attic Old Comedy." *Transactions of the American Philological Association* 107: 105–29.

Henry, M. M. 1985. *Menander's Courtesans and the Greek Comic Tradition*. Studien zur Klassichen Philologie 20. Frankfurt am Main.

Janson, W. 1987. *Women without Men: Gender and Marginality in an Algerian Town*. Leiden.

Joly, R. 1968. *Le vocabulaire chrétien de l'amour est-il original? Phileîn et agapan dans le grec antique*. Brussels.

Kazhdam, A. 1995. "Holy and Unholy Miracle Workers." In *Byzantine Magic*, ed. H. Maguire, 73–82. Washington D.C.

Keuls, E. 1985. *The Reign of the Phallus*. New York.

Kieckhefer, R. 1991. "Erotic Magic in Medieval Europe." In *Sex in the Middle Ages*, ed. J. E. Salisbury, 30–55. New York.

Konstan, D. 1997. *Friendship in the Classical World*. Cambridge.

Kotansky, R. 1991. "Magic in the Court of the Governor of Arabia." *Zeitschrift für Papyrologie und Epigraphik* 88:41–60.

Laqueur, T. W. 1996. *Making Sex: Body and Gender from the Greeks to Freud*. Cambridge, Mass.

Loizos, P. 1994. "A Broken Mirror: Masculine Sexuality in Greek Ethnography." In *Dislocating Masculinity*, ed. A. Cornwall and N. Lindisfarne, 66–81. London.

Nagy, G. 1990. *Pindar's Homer: The Lyric Possession of the Past*. Baltimore.

O'Neil, M. 1987. "Magical Healing, Love Magic and the Inquisition in Late-Sixteenth Century Modena." In *Inquisition and Society in Early Modern Europe*, ed. S. Halizer, 88–114. London.

Petropoulos, J. C. B. 1993. "Sappho Sorceress: Another Look at Frag. 1 (L–P)." *Zeitschrift für Papyrologie und Epigraphik* 97:43–56.

———. 1994. *Heat and Lust: Hesiod's Midsummer Festival Scene Revisited*. London.

Pitt-Rivers, J. 1977. *The Fate of Shechem*. Cambridge.

Preus, A. 1988. "Theophrastus' Psychopharmacology (*HP* IX)." In *Theophrastean Studies on Natural Sciences, Physics, Metaphysics, Ethics, Religion and Rhetoric*, Rutgers University Studies in Classical Humanities 3, ed. W. W. Fortenbaugh and W. Sharples, 76–99. New Brunswick, N.J.

Richlin, A. 1991. "Zeus and Metis: Foucault, Feminism, Classics." *Helios* 18:160–80.

Ruggiero, G. 1985. *The Boundaries of Eros: Sex Crime and Sexuality in Renaissance Venice*. New York.

———. 1993. *Binding Passions: Tales of Magic, Marriage, and Power at the End of the Renaissance*. New York.

Schaps, D. 1977. "The Woman Least Mentioned: Etiquette and Women's Names." *Classical Quarterly* 27:323–30.

Seaford, R. 1988. "The Eleventh Ode of Bacchylides: Hera, Artemis and the Absence of Dionysus." *Journal of Hellenic Studies* 108:118–36.

Sourvinou-Inwood, C. 1987. "A Series of Erotic Pursuits: Images and Meanings." *Journal of Hellenic Studies* 107:131–53.

Winkler, J. J. 1990. *The Constraints of Desire: The Anthropology of Sex and Gender in Ancient Greece*. New York.

————. 1991. "The Constraints of Eros." In *Magika Hiera: Ancient Greek Magic and Religion*, ed. C. A. Faraone and D. Obbink, 214–43. New York.

Zeitlin, F. I. 1985. "The Power of Aphrodite: Eros and the Boundaries of Self in the *Hippolytus*." In *Directions in Euripidean Criticism: A Collection of Essays*, ed. P. Burian, 52–111. Durham, N.C.

————. 1986. "Configurations of Rape in Greek Myth." In *Rape*, ed. S. Tomaselli and R. Porter, 122–51. Oxford.

Appendix

Major Historical Figures Discussed

Because the chapters are aimed at an interdisciplinary audience and because they treat many figures who are not well known, we offer a brief guide to the main dramatis personae, asking scholars' indulgence for including, as well, the obvious. No attempt is made to give full biographies, especially for well-known figures.

Achilles Tatius (active c. 150 C.E.). Greek novelist who lived at Alexandria, author of *Leucippe and Cleitophon.*

Aeschines (c. 397– c. 322 B.C.E.). Athenian orator, whose speech "Against Timarchus" provides important evidence for sexual norms and practices of the period.

Aeschylus (c. 525 – c. 456 B.C.E.). Athenian tragic poet.

Aristophanes (probably b. between 460 and 450, d. c. 386 B.C.E.). Athenian comic poet.

Aristotle (384/3 – 322 B.C.E.). Philosopher, born in Stagira, active both in Athens and in Asia Minor.

Catullus, Gaius Valerius (c. 84 – c. 54 B.C.E.). Roman lyric poet.

Chrysippus of Soli (c. 280 – 207 B.C.E.). Third head of the Stoa, after Zeno and Cleanthes; he succeeded Cleanthes in 232. Evidently one of the greatest philosophers of antiquity, he more or less invented propositional logic and the philosophy of language, and he made important contributions in every area of the subject. Only fragments of his works survive.

Cicero, Marcus Tullius (106–43 B.C.E.). Roman statesman, orator, philosopher, and poet (he would hardly have wanted even the briefest summary to omit the last of these occupations).

Cleanthes of Assos (c. 331–c. 230 B.C.E.). Second head of the Stoic school, beginning in 262/261. Formerly a boxer, he seems to have been less intellectually original than his predecessor, Zeno, and his successor, Chrysippus. We have a long fragment of his *Hymn to Zeus*.

Clement of Alexandria (Titus Flavius Clemens) (c. 150–211/16 C.E.). Convert to Christianity, bishop, leading Christian thinker and writer, strongly influenced by Greek philosophy and particularly by Stoicism.

Dio Chrysostom (also known as Dio Cocceianus and Dio of Prusa; Chrysostom, "gold-mouthed," is an epithet he won from his oratory) (c. 40/50–c. 110 C.E.). Orator and popular philosopher, born at Prusa in Bithynia, active in Rome, and then (after being banished by Domitian) in Greece, the Balkans, and Asia Minor. Influenced by Stoic (and Cynic) thought, and especially by Musonius Rufus, he addressed ethical and political as well as mythological and literary topics.

Diogenes Laertius (probably second to third centuries C.E.). Author of voluminous *Lives of the Philosophers*, summarizing the lives and doctrines of philosophers from Thales to the Greek Epicureans, Stoics, and Skeptics. Although Diogenes is a superficial writer, his work, faute de mieux, is a major source for our knowledge of many ancient thinkers, including the Cynics, Epicurus, and the three great Stoic founders, Zeno, Cleanthes, and Chrysippus. Particularly drawn to Epicurus, he quotes three entire letters of Epicurus in his *Life*, and that is how we have them.

Diogenes of Sinope (c. 412/403–c. 324/321 B.C.E.). Itinerant philosopher and practitioner of a type of public self-dramatization, he was nicknamed "the Dog" after his practice of eating in public, and became the founder of the "Cynic" tradition, which exercised considerable influence on both Greek and Roman culture, in part through its influence on Stoicism.

Epictetus (c. 55–c. 135 C.E.). Major Stoic philosopher at Rome, a former slave. His lectures (in Greek) were transcribed by his pupil Arrian and are among our major sources for Roman Stoic philosophy.

Epicurus (341–270 B.C.E.). Philosopher and founder of one of the leading schools of Hellenistic philosophy, he set up outside Athens in a school called the Garden. Three detailed letters on doctrinal topics and a large (and growing) number of other fragments of his work survive—as well as accounts in followers such as the Roman poet Lucretius. Although his thought was less influential at Rome than was Stoicism, it could claim some important followers, including Cicero's friend and correspondent Titus Pomponius Atticus (110–32 B.C.E.) and the tyrannicide Gaius

Longinus Cassius (d. 42 B.C.E.), killer (with Brutus and others) of Julius Caesar.

EURIPIDES (b. 480s B.C.E., d. c. 406 B.C.E.). Athenian tragic playwright; died in Macedon.

HELIODORUS (active 3d c. C.E.). Greek novelist, author of the *Aithiopica*.

LUCIAN of Samosata (b. c. 120 C.E.). Witty author and lecturer, strongly influenced by philosophy. His comic prose dialogues are a unique blend of popular philosophy and literary cleverness.

MUSONIUS RUFUS, GAIUS (c. 30–c. 101/2 C.E.). Roman *eques* and Stoic philosopher, teacher of Epictetus. Banished by Nero to the island of Gyaros for his alleged role in the conspiracy of Piso (in which Lucan and Seneca lost their lives), he returned after Nero's death and became a highly influential teacher. A number of his public discourses were recorded and survive.

PHILO of Alexandria, also known as Philo Judaeus (c. 20 B.C.E.–45 C.E.), Jewish philosopher who combined elements of the Greek philosophical tradition, particularly Platonism, with the Jewish tradition, believing that Plato's ideas ultimately derived from those of Moses and that they should be reclaimed for the Jewish tradition. Philo is also strongly influenced by Stoicism, especially in his practice of allegorical interpretation of Scripture.

PLATO (427–347 B.C.E.). Athenian philosopher, descendant of a prominent wealthy family and founder of one of the most influential schools of philosophy in antiquity.

PLUTARCH of Chaeronea (c. 45–125 C.E.). Platonist ethical philosopher and biographer, author of the parallel *Lives* of Greek and Roman figures, and of many essays on ethical topics, many with a polemical anti-Epicurean and/or anti-Stoic purpose.

SENECA, LUCIUS ANNAEUS (c. 1–65 C.E.). Major Roman Stoic philosopher and poet, writing in Latin. He was also active in politics, serving as tutor and adviser to the young emperor Nero, and as regent of the empire in the early days of Nero's reign. His philosophical works include a series of "dialogues" (in which the addressee, however, does not respond) and the fictive philosophical correspondence with Lucilius usually known as the *Moral Epistles*. He also wrote a series of highly influential tragedies and a satirical work, the *Apocolocyntosis*, ridiculing the recently dead emperor Claudius. He committed suicide, following the manner of Socrates' death, after being accused of participating in a plot to overthrow Nero.

SOPHOCLES (c. 496–406 B.C.E.). Athenian tragic playwright.

TERTULLIAN (Quintus Septimius Florens Tertullianus) (c. 160–c. 240 C.E.). Christian thinker, essayist, and polemicist, born near Carthage, highly influential in the intellectual life of the church.

Xenophon (c. 430 – c. 370 B.C.E.). Athenian politician, general, essayist, and follower of philosophy.

Zeno of Citium (335 – 263 B.C.E.). Founder of Stoicism. Although in general it is very difficult to separate the achievements of Zeno from those of his great successor Chrysippus, Zeno is credited with a strong interest in sexual ethics, and with the plan for an ideal republic in which erotic ties would constitute the bonds of civic unity.

Contributors

Eva Cantarella is professor of Roman law in the Law School of the University of Milan, Italy, where she also teaches ancient Greek law. Prior to coming to Milan she was professor of Roman and ancient Greek law at the Universities of Camerino, Parma, and Pavia, and she has been a visiting professor at the University of Texas at Austin and New York University. Among her books are *L' ambiguo malanno: Condizione e immagine della donna nell' antichità greca e romana* (Rome: Editori Riuniti, 1981), translated into English as *Pandora's Daughters. The Role and Status of Women in Greek and Roman Antiquity* (Baltimore: Johns Hopkins University Press, 1986); *Secondo natura: La bisessualità nel mondo antico* (3d ed., Milan: Rizzoli, 1995), translated into English as *Bisexuality in the Ancient Word* (New Haven, Conn.: Yale University Press, 1993); *I supplizi capitali in Grecia e a Roma* (Milan: Rizzoli, 1991); *Passato prossimo: Donne romane da Tacita a Sulpicia* (Milan: Feltrinelli, 1996); and *Pompei: I volti dell' amore* (Milan: Mondadori 1998).

Sir Kenneth Dover was professor of Greek at the University of St. Andrews from 1955 to 1976 and president of Corpus Christi College, Oxford, from 1976 to 1986. He has been a visiting professor at Harvard; the University of California, Berkeley; and Cornell.

Christopher A. Faraone is professor of classical languages and literatures at the University of Chicago. His most recent publications include (with

T. Carpenter) *Masks of Dionysus* (1993) and *Ancient Greek Love Magic* (1999). His main teaching and research interests are ancient Greek poetry, religion, and magic.

SIMON GOLDHILL is reader in Greek literature and culture at Cambridge University and a fellow of King's College, where he is also co-ordinator of research. He has published widely on Greek literature including *Reading Greek Tragedy, The Poet's Voice,* and *Foucault's Virginity* (all from Cambridge University Press). His forthcoming book is called *Who Needs Greek?* and will be published by Cambridge University Press in 2002.

STEPHEN HALLIWELL is professor of Greek at the University of St. Andrews, Scotland. His books include *Aristotle's Poetics* (1986), *The Poetics of Aristotle: Translation and Commentary* (1987), commentaries on *Plato Republic 10* (1988) and *Plato Republic 5* (1993), *Aristophanes: Birds and Other Plays* (1996), and *The Aesthetics of Mimesis: Ancient Texts and Modern Problems* (2002). He is currently writing a book entitled *The Laughter of Dionysos: Aristophanic Satire in Its Cultural Context.*

DAVID M. HALPERIN is W. H. Auden Collegiate Professor of English Language and Literature at the University of Michigan in Ann Arbor and visiting professor of sociology at the University of New South Wales in Sydney. His most recent book is *How to Do the History of Homosexuality* (Chicago: University of Chicago Press, 2002). He is currently working on a study of gay men's cultural identifications.

J. SAMUEL HOUSER is assistant professor of classics at Franklin and Marshall College. In addition to his work on Dio Chrysostom, his research includes a dissertation on Musonius Rufus and an ongoing research project addressing conceptions of the past and citations of historical precedent in Roman philosophy.

MAARIT KAIMIO is professor of Greek language and literature at the University of Helsinki. Her books include *The Chorus of Greek Drama in the Light of the Number Used* (Helsinki: Societas Scientiarum Fennica, 1970) and *Physical Contact in Greek Tragedy: A Study of Stage Conventions* (Helsinki: Academia Scientiarum Fennica, 1988). Recently she has published several articles about Greek drama, theater performance, and actors. She has also published editions of Greek documentary papyri and is currently working on the carbonized papyri found in Petra, Jordan.

DAVID KONSTAN is the John Rowe Workman Distinguished Professor of Classics and professor of comparative literature at Brown University. Among his books are *Some Aspects of Epicurean Psychology* (1973), *Catullus' Indictment of Rome* (1977), *Roman Comedy* (1983), *Sexual Symmetry: Love in the Ancient Novel and Related Genres* (1994), *Greek Comedy and Ideology* (1995), *Friendship in the Classical World* (1997), and *Pity Transformed* (2001). He has also translated two volumes of the ancient Greek commentators on Aristotle. In 1999, he was president of the American Philological Association. Currently, he is preparing a book on the emotions of the ancient Greeks.

DAVID LEITAO is an associate professor of classics at San Francisco State University. He has published numerous articles on adolescent transition rites in ancient Greece and on the history of gender and sexuality in the ancient world.

MARTHA C. NUSSBAUM is Ernst Freund Distinguished Service Professor of Law and Ethics at the University of Chicago, with appointments in the Law School, Philosophy Department, and Divinity School. She is an associate in the Classics Department, an affiliate of the Committee on Southern Asian Studies, and a board member of the Center for Gender Studies. Her most recent book is *Upheavals of Thought: The Intelligence of Emotions* (2001).

A. W. PRICE is reader in philosophy at Birkbeck College, University of London. He is the author of *Love and Friendship in Plato and Aristotle* (1989; expanded 1997), and *Mental Conflict* (1995).

JUHA SIHVOLA is professor of history at the University of Jyväskylä and also teaches ancient philosophy at the University of Helsinki. He is the author of *Decay, Progress, and the Good Life? Hesiod and Protagoras on the Development of Culture* (1989), has published articles on Aristotle and Hellenistic philosophy, and edited *The Emotions in Hellenistic Philosophy* (1990), together with Troels-Engberg-Pedersen, and *Ancient Scepticism and the Sceptical Tradition* (2000).

Index of Subjects

Index Locorum